NISSAN
SENTRA/PULSAR/NX
1982-96 REPAIR MANUAL

CHILTON'S

CEO	Rick Van Dalen
President	Dean F. Morgantini, S.A.E.
Vice President–Finance	Barry L. Beck
Vice President–Sales	Glenn D. Potere
Executive Editor	Kevin M. G. Maher, A.S.E.
Manager–Consumer Automotive	Richard Schwartz, A.S.E.
Manager–Professional Automotive	Richard J. Rivele
Manager–Marine/Recreation	James R. Marotta, A.S.E.
Production Specialist	Melinda Possinger
Project Managers	Tim Crain, A.S.E., Thomas A. Mellon, A.S.E., S.A.E., Eric Michael Mihalyi, A.S.E., S.T.S., S.A.E., Christine L. Sheeky, S.A.E., Richard T. Smith, Ron Webb
Schematics Editors	Christopher G. Ritchie, A.S.E., S.A.E., S.T.S., Stephanie A. Spunt
Editor	Joseph L. DeFrancesco, A.S.E., Richard Schwartz, A.S.E.

CHILTON Automotive Books

PUBLISHED BY **W. G. NICHOLS, INC.**

Manufactured in USA
© 1996 W. G. Nichols, Inc.
1025 Andrew Drive
West Chester, PA 19380
ISBN 0-8019-8816-0
Library of Congress Catalog Card No. 96-84541
9012345678 0987654321

Contents

Contents

DRIVE TRAIN 7

SUSPENSION AND STEERING 8

BRAKES 9

BODY AND TRIM 10

GLOSSARY

MASTER INDEX

See last page for information on additional titles

SAFETY NOTICE

Proper service and repair procedures are vital to the safe, reliable operation of all motor vehicles, as well as the personal safety of those performing repairs. This manual outlines procedures for servicing and repairing vehicles using safe, effective methods. The procedures contain many NOTES, CAUTIONS and WARNINGS which should be followed, along with standard procedures to eliminate the possibility of personal injury or improper service which could damage the vehicle or compromise its safety.

It is important to note that repair procedures and techniques, tools and parts for servicing motor vehicles, as well as the skill and experience of the individual performing the work vary widely. It is not possible to anticipate all of the conceivable ways or conditions under which vehicles may be serviced, or to provide cautions as to all possible hazards that may result. Standard and accepted safety precautions and equipment should be used when handling toxic or flammable fluids, and safety goggles or other protection should be used during cutting, grinding, chiseling, prying, or any other process that can cause material removal or projectiles.

Some procedures require the use of tools specially designed for a specific purpose. Before substituting another tool or procedure, you must be completely satisfied that neither your personal safety, nor the performance of the vehicle will be endangered.

Although information in this manual is based on industry sources and is complete as possible at the time of publication, the possibility exists that some car manufacturers made later changes which could not be included here. While striving for total accuracy, Nichols Publishing cannot assume responsibility for any errors, changes or omissions that may occur in the compilation of this data.

PART NUMBERS

Part numbers listed in this reference are not recommendations by Nichols Publishing for any product brand name. They are references that can be used with interchange manuals and aftermarket supplier catalogs to locate each brand supplier's discrete part number.

SPECIAL TOOLS

Special tools are recommended by the vehicle manufacturer to perform their specific job. Use has been kept to a minimum, but where absolutely necessary, they are referred to in the text by the part number of the tool manufacturer. These tools can be purchased, under the appropriate part number, from your local dealer or regional distributor, or an equivalent tool can be purchased locally from a tool supplier or parts outlet. Before substituting any tool for the one recommended, read the SAFETY NOTICE at the top of this page.

ACKNOWLEDGMENTS

Nichols Publishing expresses appreciation to Nissan Motor Company for their generous assistance.

Nichols Publishing would like to express thanks to all of the fine companies who participate in the production of our books:
- Hand tools supplied by Craftsman are used during all phases of our vehicle teardown and photography.
- Many of the fine specialty tools used in our procedures were provided courtesy of Lisle Corporation.
- Lincoln Automotive Products (1 Lincoln Way, St. Louis, MO 63120) has provided their industrial shop equipment, including jacks (engine, transmission and floor), engine stands, fluid and lubrication tools, as well as shop presses.
- Rotary Lifts (1-800-640-5438 or www.Rotary-Lift.com), the largest automobile lift manufacturer in the world, offering the biggest variety of surface and in-ground lifts available, has fulfilled our shop's lift needs.
- Much of our shop's electronic testing equipment was supplied by Universal Enterprises Inc. (UEI).
- Safety-Kleen Systems Inc. has provided parts cleaning stations and assistance with environmentally sound disposal of residual wastes.
- United Gilsonite Laboratories (UGL), manufacturer of Drylok® concrete floor paint, has provided materials and expertise for the coating and protection of our shop floor.

1

GENERAL INFORMATION AND MAINTENANCE

HOW TO USE THIS BOOK

This Chilton's Total Car Care manual is intended to help you learn more about the inner workings of your 1982–96 Datsun/Nissan Sentra or Pulsar while saving you money on its upkeep and operation.

The beginning of the book will likely be referred to the most, since that is where you will find information for maintenance and tune-up. The other sections deal with the more complex systems of your vehicle. Systems (from engine through brakes) are covered to the extent that the average do-it-yourselfer can attempt. This book will not explain such things as rebuilding a differential because the expertise required and the special tools necessary make this uneconomical. It will, however, give you detailed instructions to help you change your own brake pads and shoes, replace spark plugs, and perform many more jobs that can save you money and help avoid expensive problems.

A secondary purpose of this book is a reference for owners who want to understand their vehicle and/or their mechanics better.

Where to Begin

Before removing any bolts, read through the entire procedure. This will give you the overall view of what tools and supplies will be required. So read ahead and plan ahead. Each operation should be approached logically and all procedures thoroughly understood before attempting any work.

If repair of a component is not considered practical, we tell you how to remove the part and then how to install the new or rebuilt replacement. In this way, you at least save labor costs.

Avoiding Trouble

Many procedures in this book require you to "label and disconnect . . ." a group of lines, hoses or wires. Don't be think you can remember where everything goes—you won't. If you hook up vacuum or fuel lines incorrectly, the vehicle may run poorly, if at all. If you hook up electrical wiring incorrectly, you may instantly learn a very expensive lesson.

You don't need to know the proper name for each hose or line. A piece of masking tape on the hose and a piece on its fitting will allow you to assign your own label. As long as you remember your own code, the lines can be reconnected by matching your tags. Remember that tape will dissolve in gasoline or solvents; if a part is to be washed or cleaned, use another method of identification. A permanent felt-tipped marker or a metal scribe can be very handy for marking metal parts. Remove any tape or paper labels after assembly.

Maintenance or Repair?

Maintenance includes routine inspections, adjustments, and replacement of parts which show signs of normal wear. Maintenance compensates for wear or deterioration. Repair implies that something has broken or is not working. A need for a repair is often caused by lack of maintenance. for example: draining and refilling automatic transmission fluid is maintenance recommended at specific intervals. Failure to do this can shorten the life of the transmission/transaxle, requiring very expensive repairs. While no maintenance program can prevent items from eventually breaking or wearing out, a general rule is true: MAINTENANCE IS CHEAPER THAN REPAIR.

Two basic mechanic's rules should be mentioned here. First, whenever the left side of the vehicle or engine is referred to, it means the driver's side. Conversely, the right side of the vehicle means the passenger's side. Second, screws and bolts are removed by turning counterclockwise, and tightened by turning clockwise unless specifically noted.

Safety is always the most important rule. Constantly be aware of the dangers involved in working on an automobile and take the proper precautions. Please refer to the information in this section regarding SERVICING YOUR VEHICLE SAFELY and the SAFETY NOTICE on the acknowledgment page.

Avoiding the Most Common Mistakes

Pay attention to the instructions provided. There are 3 common mistakes in mechanical work:

1. Incorrect order of assembly, disassembly or adjustment. When taking something apart or putting it together, performing steps in the wrong order usually just costs you extra time; however, it CAN break something. Read the entire procedure before beginning. Perform everything in the order in which the instructions say you should, even if you can't see a reason for it. When you're taking apart something that is very intricate, you might want to draw a picture of how it looks when assembled in order to make sure you get everything back in its proper position. When making adjustments, perform them in the proper order. One adjustment possibly will affect another.

2. Overtorquing (or undertorquing). While it is more common for overtorquing to cause damage, undertorquing may allow a fastener to vibrate loose causing serious damage. Especially when dealing with aluminum parts, pay attention to torque specifications and utilize a torque wrench in assembly. If a torque figure is not available, remember that if you are using the right tool to perform the job, you will probably not have to strain yourself to get a fastener tight enough. The pitch of most threads is so slight that the tension you put on the wrench will be multiplied many times in actual force on what you are tightening.

There are many commercial products available for ensuring that fasteners won't come loose, even if they are not torqued just right (a very common brand is Loctite®). If you're worried about getting something together tight enough to hold, but loose enough to avoid mechanical damage during assembly, one of these products might offer substantial insurance. Before choosing a threadlocking compound, read the label on the package and make sure the product is compatible with the materials, fluids, etc. involved.

3. Crossthreading. This occurs when a part such as a bolt is screwed into a nut or casting at the wrong angle and forced. Crossthreading is more likely to occur if access is difficult. It helps to clean and lubricate fasteners, then to start threading the bolt, spark plug, etc. with your fingers. If you encounter resistance, unscrew the part and start over again at a different angle until it can be inserted and turned several times without much effort. Keep in mind that many parts have tapered threads, so that gentle turning will automatically bring the part you're threading to the proper angle. Don't put a wrench on the part until it's been tightened a couple of turns by hand. If you suddenly encounter resistance, and the part has not seated fully, don't force it. Pull it back out to make sure it's clean and threading properly.

Be sure to take your time and be patient, and always plan ahead. Allow yourself ample time to perform repairs and maintenance.

TOOLS AND EQUIPMENT

▶ **See Figures 1 thru 15**

Without the proper tools and equipment it is impossible to properly service your vehicle. It would be virtually impossible to catalog every tool that you would need to perform all of the operations in this book. It would be unwise for the amateur to rush out and buy an expensive set of tools on the theory that he/she may need one or more of them at some time.

The best approach is to proceed slowly, gathering a good quality set of those tools that are used most frequently. Don't be misled by the low cost of bargain tools. It is far better to spend a little more for better quality. Forged wrenches, 6 or 12-point sockets and fine tooth ratchets are by far preferable to their less expensive counterparts. As any good mechanic can tell you, there are few worse experiences than trying to work on a vehicle with bad tools. Your monetary savings will be far outweighed by frustration and mangled knuckles.

Begin accumulating those tools that are used most frequently: those associated with routine maintenance and tune-up. In addition to the normal assortment of screwdrivers and pliers, you should have the following tools:
- Wrenches/sockets and combination open end/box end wrenches in sizes ⅛–¾ in. and/or 3mm–19mm ¹³⁄₁₆ in. or ⅝ in. spark plug socket (depending on plug type).

➡**If possible, buy various length socket drive extensions. Universal-joint and wobble extensions can be extremely useful, but be careful when using them, as they can change the amount of torque applied to the socket.**

- Jackstands for support.
- Oil filter wrench.

- Spout or funnel for pouring fluids.
- Grease gun for chassis lubrication (unless your vehicle is not equipped with any grease fittings)
- Hydrometer for checking the battery (unless equipped with a sealed, maintenance-free battery).
- A container for draining oil and other fluids.
- Rags for wiping up the inevitable mess.

In addition to the above items there are several others that are not absolutely necessary, but handy to have around. These include an equivalent oil absorbent gravel, like cat litter, and the usual supply of lubricants, antifreeze and fluids. This is a basic list for routine maintenance, but only your personal needs and desire can accurately determine your list of tools.

After performing a few projects on the vehicle, you'll be amazed at the other tools and non-tools on your workbench. Some useful household items are: a large turkey baster or siphon, empty coffee cans and ice trays (to store parts), a ball of twine, electrical tape for wiring, small rolls of colored tape for tagging lines or hoses, markers and pens, a note pad, golf tees (for plugging vacuum lines), metal coat hangers or a roll of mechanic's wire (to hold things out of the way), dental pick or similar long, pointed probe, a strong magnet, and a small mirror (to see into recesses and under manifolds).

A more advanced set of tools, suitable for tune-up work, can be drawn up easily. While the tools are slightly more sophisticated, they need not be outrageously expensive. There are several inexpensive tach/dwell meters on the market that are every bit as good for the average mechanic as a professional model. Just be sure that it goes to a least 1200–1500 rpm on the tach scale and that it works on 4, 6 and 8-cylinder engines. The key to these purchases is to make them with an eye towards adaptability and wide range. A basic list of tune-up tools could include:

- Tach/dwell meter.
- Spark plug wrench and gapping tool.
- Feeler gauges for valve adjustment.
- Timing light.

The choice of a timing light should be made carefully. A light which works on the DC current supplied by the vehicle's battery is the best choice; it should

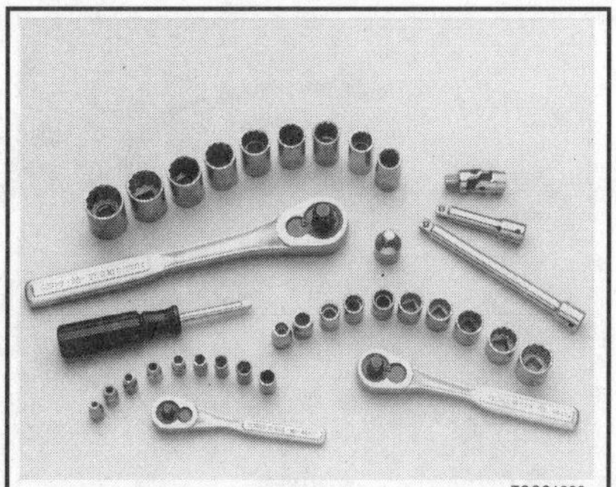

TCCS1200

Fig. 1 All but the most basic procedures will require an assortment of ratchets and sockets

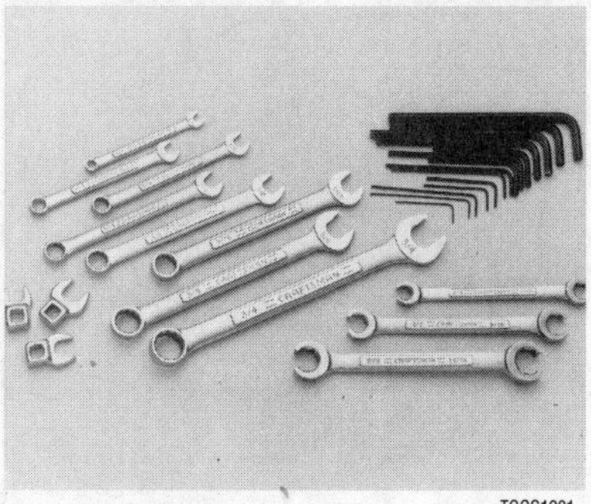

TCCS1201

Fig. 2 In addition to ratchets, a good set of wrenches and hex keys will be necessary

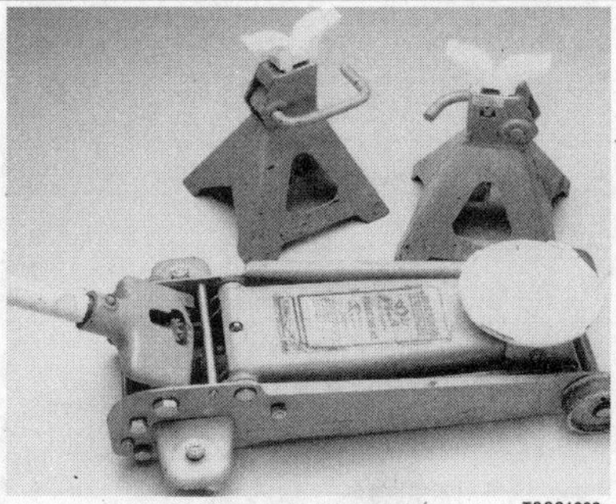

TCCS1202

Fig. 3 A hydraulic floor jack and a set of jackstands are essential for lifting and supporting the vehicle

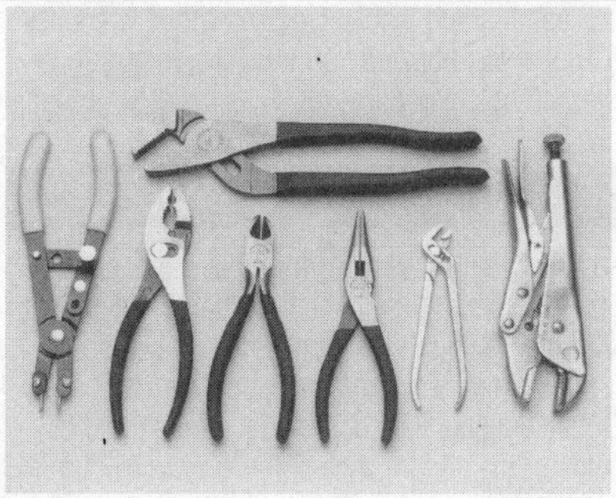

TCCS1203

Fig. 4 An assortment of pliers, grippers and cutters will be handy for old rusted parts and stripped bolt heads

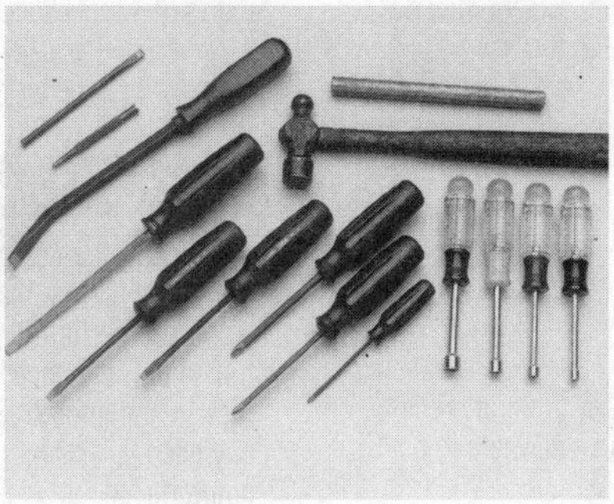

TCCS1204

Fig. 5 Various drivers, chisels and prybars are great tools to have in your toolbox

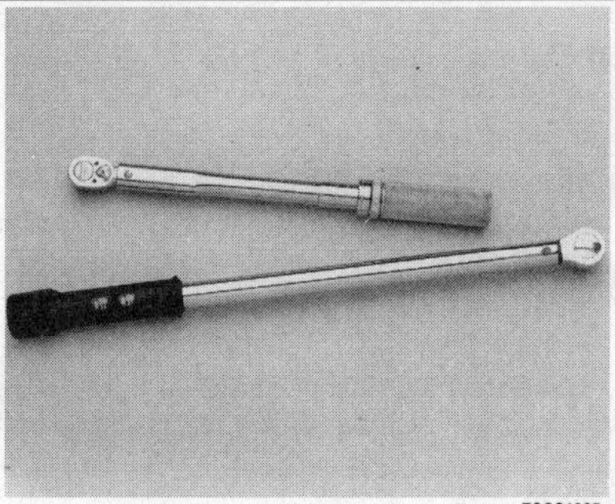

TCCS1205

Fig. 6 Many repairs will require the use of a torque wrench to assure the components are properly fastened

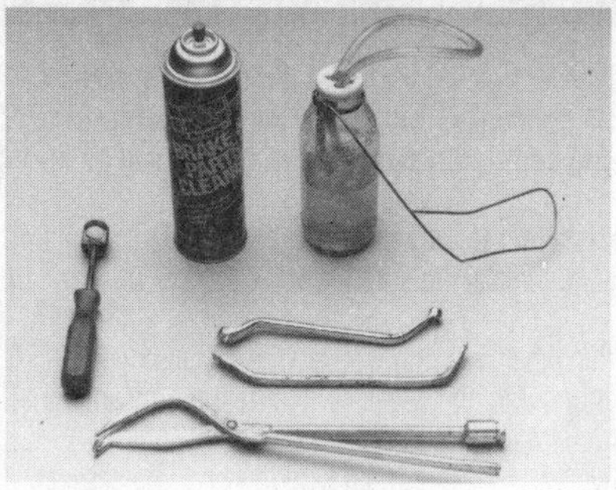

TCCS1209

Fig. 7 Although not always necessary, using specialized brake tools will save time

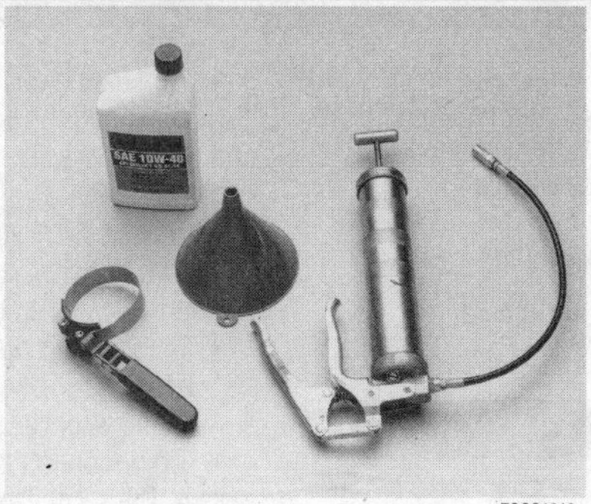

TCCS1210

Fig. 8 A few inexpensive lubrication tools will make maintenance easier

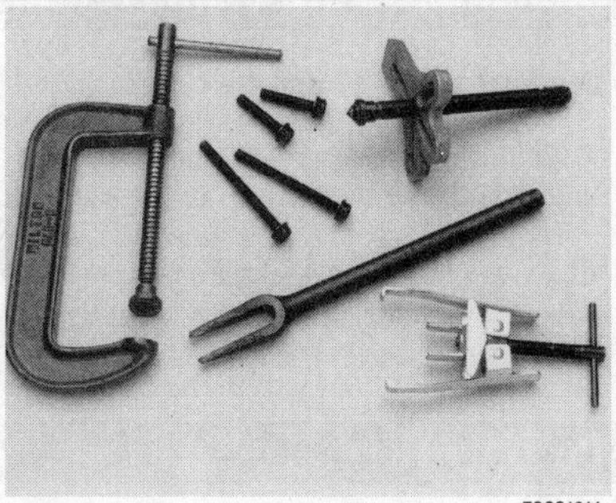

TCCS1211

Fig. 9 Various pullers, clamps and separator tools are needed for many larger, more complicated repairs

Fig. 10 A variety of tools and gauges should be used for spark plug gapping and installation

Fig. 11 Inductive type timing light

Fig. 12 A screw-in type compression gauge is recommended for compression testing

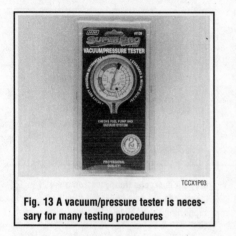

Fig. 13 A vacuum/pressure tester is necessary for many testing procedures

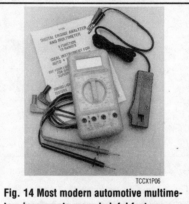

Fig. 14 Most modern automotive multimeters incorporate many helpful features

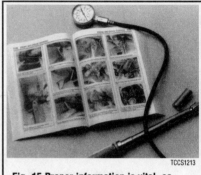

Fig. 15 Proper information is vital, so always have a Chilton Total Car Care manual handy

have a xenon tube for brightness. On any vehicle with an electronic ignition system, a timing light with an inductive pickup that clamps around the No. 1 spark plug cable is preferred.

In addition to these basic tools, there are several other tools and gauges you may find useful. These include:

• Compression gauge. The screw-in type is slower to use, but eliminates the possibility of a faulty reading due to escaping pressure.
• Manifold vacuum gauge.
• 12V test light.
• A combination volt/ohmmeter
• Induction Ammeter. This is used for determining whether or not there is current in a wire. These are handy for use if a wire is broken somewhere in a wiring harness.

As a final note, you will probably find a torque wrench necessary for all but the most basic work. The beam type models are perfectly adequate, although the newer click types (breakaway) are easier to use. The click type torque wrenches tend to be more expensive. Also keep in mind that all types of torque wrenches should be periodically checked and/or recalibrated. You will have to decide for yourself which better fits your pocketbook, and purpose.

Special Tools

Normally, the use of special factory tools is avoided for repair procedures, since these are not readily available for the do-it-yourself mechanic. When it is possible to perform the job with more commonly available tools, it will be pointed out, but occasionally, a special tool was designed to perform a specific function and should be used. Before substituting another tool, you should be convinced that neither your safety nor the performance of the vehicle will be compromised.

Special tools can usually be purchased from an automotive parts store or from your dealer. In some cases special tools may be available directly from the tool manufacturer.

SERVICING YOUR VEHICLE SAFELY

▶ **See Figures 16, 17 and 18**

It is virtually impossible to anticipate all of the hazards involved with automotive maintenance and service, but care and common sense will prevent most accidents.

The rules of safety for mechanics range from "don't smoke around gasoline," to "use the proper tool(s) for the job." The trick to avoiding injuries is to develop safe work habits and to take every possible precaution.

Do's

• Do keep a fire extinguisher and first aid kit handy.
• Do wear safety glasses or goggles when cutting, drilling, grinding or prying, even if you have 20–20 vision. If you wear glasses for the sake of vision, wear safety goggles over your regular glasses.

• Do shield your eyes whenever you work around the battery. Batteries contain sulfuric acid. In case of contact with, flush the area with water or a mixture of water and baking soda, then seek immediate medical attention.
• Do use safety stands (jackstands) for any undervehicle service. Jacks are for raising vehicles; jackstands are for making sure the vehicle stays raised until you want it to come down.
• Do use adequate ventilation when working with any chemicals or hazardous materials. Like carbon monoxide, the asbestos dust resulting from some brake lining wear can be hazardous in sufficient quantities.
• Do disconnect the negative battery cable when working on the electrical system. The secondary ignition system contains EXTREMELY HIGH VOLTAGE. In some cases it can even exceed 50,000 volts.
• Do follow manufacturer's directions whenever working with potentially hazardous materials. Most chemicals and fluids are poisonous.

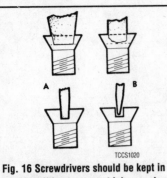

Fig. 16 Screwdrivers should be kept in good condition to prevent injury or damage which could result if the blade slips from the screw

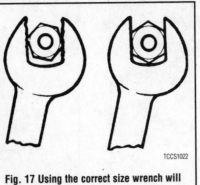

Fig. 17 Using the correct size wrench will help prevent the possibility of rounding off a nut

Fig. 18 NEVER work under a vehicle unless it is supported using safety stands (jackstands)

• Do properly maintain your tools. Loose hammerheads, mushroomed punches and chisels, frayed or poorly grounded electrical cords, excessively worn screwdrivers, spread wrenches (open end), cracked sockets, slipping ratchets, or faulty droplight sockets can cause accidents.

• Likewise, keep your tools clean; a greasy wrench can slip off a bolt head, ruining the bolt and often harming your knuckles in the process.

• Do use the proper size and type of tool for the job at hand. Do select a wrench or socket that fits the nut or bolt. The wrench or socket should sit straight, not cocked.

• Do, when possible, pull on a wrench handle rather than push on it, and adjust your stance to prevent a fall.

• Do be sure that adjustable wrenches are tightly closed on the nut or bolt and pulled so that the force is on the side of the fixed jaw.

• Do strike squarely with a hammer; avoid glancing blows.

• Do set the parking brake and block the drive wheels if the work requires a running engine.

Don'ts

• Don't run the engine in a garage or anywhere else without proper ventilation—EVER! Carbon monoxide is poisonous; it takes a long time to leave the human body and you can build up a deadly supply of it in your system by simply breathing in a little at a time. You may not realize you are slowly poisoning yourself. Always use power vents, windows, fans and/or open the garage door.

• Don't work around moving parts while wearing loose clothing. Short sleeves are much safer than long, loose sleeves. Hard-toed shoes with neoprene soles protect your toes and give a better grip on slippery surfaces. Watches and jewelry is not safe working around a vehicle. Long hair should be tied back under a hat or cap.

• Don't use pockets for toolboxes. A fall or bump can drive a screwdriver deep into your body. Even a rag hanging from your back pocket can wrap around a spinning shaft or fan.

• Don't smoke when working around gasoline, cleaning solvent or other flammable material.

• Don't smoke when working around the battery. When the battery is being charged, it gives off explosive hydrogen gas.

• Don't use gasoline to wash your hands; there are excellent soaps available. Gasoline contains dangerous additives which can enter the body through a cut or through your pores. Gasoline also removes all the natural oils from the skin so that bone dry hands will suck up oil and grease.

• Don't service the air conditioning system unless you are equipped with the necessary tools and training. When liquid or compressed gas refrigerant is released to atmospheric pressure it will absorb heat from whatever it contacts. This will chill or freeze anything it touches.

• Don't use screwdrivers for anything other than driving screws! A screwdriver used as a prying tool can snap when you least expect it, causing injuries. At the very least, you'll ruin a good screwdriver.

• Don't use an emergency jack (that little ratchet, scissors, or pantograph jack supplied with the vehicle) for anything other than changing a flat! These jacks are only intended for emergency use out on the road; they are NOT designed as a maintenance tool. If you are serious about maintaining your vehicle yourself, invest in a hydraulic floor jack of at least a 1½ ton capacity, and at least two sturdy jackstands.

FASTENERS, MEASUREMENTS AND CONVERSIONS

Bolts, Nuts and Other Threaded Retainers

▶ **See Figures 19 and 20**

Although there are a great variety of fasteners found in the modern car or truck, the most commonly used retainer is the threaded fastener (nuts, bolts, screws, studs, etc.). Most threaded retainers may be reused, provided that they are not damaged in use or during the repair. Some retainers (such as stretch bolts or torque prevailing nuts) are designed to deform when tightened or in use and should not be reinstalled.

Whenever possible, we will note any special retainers which should be replaced during a procedure. But you should always inspect the condition of a retainer when it is removed and replace any that show signs of damage. Check all threads for rust or corrosion which can increase the torque necessary to achieve the desired clamp load for which that fastener was originally selected. Additionally, be sure that the driver surface of the fastener has not been compromised by rounding or other damage. In some cases a driver surface may become only partially rounded, allowing the driver to catch in only one direction. In many of these occurrences, a fastener may be installed and tightened, but the driver would not be able to grip and loosen the fastener again.

If you must replace a fastener, whether due to design or damage, you must ALWAYS be sure to use the proper replacement. In all cases, a retainer of the

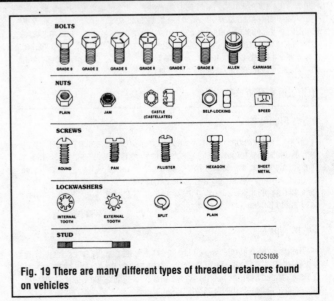

Fig. 19 There are many different types of threaded retainers found on vehicles

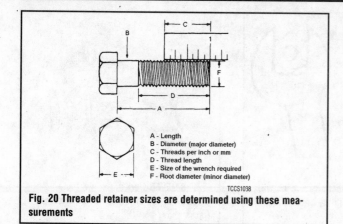

Fig. 20 Threaded retainer sizes are determined using these measurements

A - Length
B - Diameter (major diameter)
C - Threads per inch or mm
D - Thread length
E - Size of the wrench required
F - Root diameter (minor diameter)

TCCS1038

same design, material and strength should be used. Markings on the heads of most bolts will help determine the proper strength of the fastener. The same material, thread and pitch must be selected to assure proper installation and safe operation of the vehicle afterwards.

Thread gauges are available to help measure a bolt or stud's thread. Most automotive and hardware stores keep gauges available to help you select the proper size. In a pinch, you can use another nut or bolt for a thread gauge. If the bolt you are replacing is not too badly damaged, you can select a match by finding another bolt which will thread in its place. If you find a nut which threads properly onto the damaged bolt, then use that nut to help select the replacement bolt.

❉❉ WARNING

Be aware that when you find a bolt with damaged threads, you may also find the nut or drilled hole it was threaded into has also been damaged. If this is the case, you may have to drill and tap the hole, replace the nut or otherwise repair the threads. NEVER try to force a replacement bolt to fit into the damaged threads.

Torque

Torque is defined as the measurement of resistance to turning or rotating. It tends to twist a body about an axis of rotation. A common example of this would be tightening a threaded retainer such as a nut, bolt or screw. Measuring torque is one of the most common ways to help assure that a threaded retainer has been properly fastened.

When tightening a threaded fastener, torque is applied in three distinct areas, the head, the bearing surface and the clamp load. About 50 percent of the measured torque is used in overcoming bearing friction. This is the friction between the bearing surface of the bolt head, screw head or nut face and the base material or washer (the surface on which the fastener is rotating). Approximately 40 percent of the applied torque is used in overcoming thread friction. This leaves only about 10 percent of the applied torque to develop a useful clamp load (the force which holds a joint together). This means that friction can account for as much as 90 percent of the applied torque on a fastener.

TORQUE WRENCHES

♦ See Figure 21

In most applications, a torque wrench can be used to assure proper installation of a fastener. Torque wrenches come in various designs and most automotive supply stores will carry a variety to suit your needs. A torque wrench should be used any time we supply a specific torque value for a fastener. Again, the general rule of "if you are using the right tool for the job, you should not have to strain to tighten a fastener" applies here.

Beam Type

The beam type torque wrench is one of the most popular types. It consists of a pointer attached to the head that runs the length of the flexible beam (shaft) to a scale located near the handle. As the wrench is pulled, the beam bends and the pointer indicates the torque using the scale.

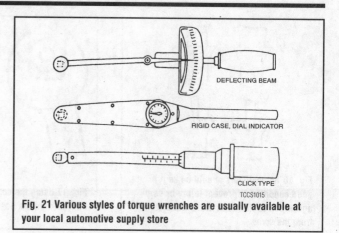

DEFLECTING BEAM

RIGID CASE, DIAL INDICATOR

CLICK TYPE

TCCS1015

Fig. 21 Various styles of torque wrenches are usually available at your local automotive supply store

Click (Breakaway) Type

Another popular design of torque wrench is the click type. To use the click type wrench you pre-adjust it to a torque setting. Once the torque is reached, the wrench has a reflex signaling feature that causes a momentary breakaway of the torque wrench body, sending an impulse to the operator's hand.

Pivot Head Type

♦ See Figure 22

Some torque wrenches (usually of the click type) may be equipped with a pivot head which can allow it to be used in areas of limited access. BUT, it must be used properly. To hold a pivot head wrench, grasp the handle lightly, and as you pull on the handle, it should be floated on the pivot point. If the handle comes in contact with the yoke extension during the process of pulling, there is a very good chance the torque readings will be inaccurate because this could alter the wrench loading point. The design of the handle is usually such as to make it inconvenient to deliberately misuse the wrench.

➡ It should be mentioned that the use of any U-joint, wobble or extension will have an effect on the torque readings, no matter what type of wrench you are using. For the most accurate readings, install the socket directly on the wrench driver. If necessary, straight extensions (which hold a socket directly under the wrench driver) will have the least effect on the torque reading. Avoid any extension that alters the length of the wrench from the handle to the head/driving point (such as a crow's foot). U-joint or wobble extensions can greatly affect the readings; avoid their use at all times.

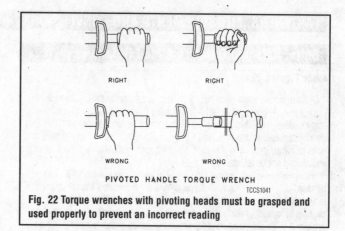

RIGHT   RIGHT

WRONG   WRONG

PIVOTED HANDLE TORQUE WRENCH

TCCS1041

Fig. 22 Torque wrenches with pivoting heads must be grasped and used properly to prevent an incorrect reading

Rigid Case (Direct Reading)

A rigid case or direct reading torque wrench is equipped with a dial indicator to show torque values. One advantage of these wrenches is that they can be held at any position on the wrench without affecting accuracy. These wrenches are often preferred because they tend to be compact, easy to read and have a great degree of accuracy.

TORQUE ANGLE METERS

Because the frictional characteristics of each fastener or threaded hole will vary, clamp loads which are based strictly on torque will vary as well. In most applications, this variance is not significant enough to cause worry. But, in certain applications, a manufacturer's engineers may determine that more precise clamp loads are necessary (such is the case with many aluminum cylinder heads). In these cases, a torque angle method of installation would be specified. When installing fasteners which are torque angle tightened, a predetermined seating torque and standard torque wrench are usually used first to remove any compliance from the joint. The fastener is then tightened the specified additional portion of a turn measured in degrees. A torque angle gauge (mechanical protractor) is used for these applications.

Standard and Metric Measurements

▶ See Figure 23

Throughout this manual, specifications are given to help you determine the condition of various components on your vehicle, or to assist you in their installation. Some of the most common measurements include length (in. or cm/mm), torque (ft. lbs., inch lbs. or Nm) and pressure (psi, in. Hg, kPa or mm Hg). In most cases, we strive to provide the proper measurement as determined by the manufacturer's engineers.

Though, in some cases, that value may not be conveniently measured with what is available in your toolbox. Luckily, many of the measuring devices which are available today will have two scales so the Standard or Metric measurements may easily be taken. If any of the various measuring tools which are available to you do not contain the same scale as listed in the specifications, use the accompanying conversion factors to determine the proper value.

The conversion factor chart is used by taking the given specification and multiplying it by the necessary conversion factor. For instance, looking at the first line, if you have a measurement in inches such as "free-play should be 2 in." but your ruler reads only in millimeters, multiply 2 in. by the conversion factor of 25.4 to get the metric equivalent of 50.8mm. Likewise, if the specification was given only in a Metric measurement, for example in Newton Meters (Nm), then look at the center column first. If the measurement is 100 Nm, multiply it by the conversion factor of 0.738 to get 73.8 ft. lbs.

CONVERSION FACTORS

LENGTH–DISTANCE

Inches (in.)	x 25.4	= Millimeters (mm)	x .0394	= Inches
Feet (ft.)	x .305	= Meters (m)	x 3.281	= Feet
Miles	x 1.609	= Kilometers (km)	x .0621	= Miles

VOLUME

Cubic Inches (in3)	x 16.387	= Cubic Centimeters	x .061	= in3
IMP Pints (IMP pt.)	x .568	= Liters (L)	x 1.76	= IMP pt.
IMP Quarts (IMP qt.)	x 1.137	= Liters (L)	x .88	= IMP qt.
IMP Gallons (IMP gal.)	x 4.546	= Liters (L)	x .22	= IMP gal.
IMP Quarts (IMP qt.)	x 1.201	= US Quarts (US qt.)	x .833	= IMP qt.
IMP Gallons (IMP gal.)	x 1.201	= US Gallons (US gal.)	x .833	= IMP gal.
Fl. Ounces	x 29.573	= Milliliters	x .034	= Ounces
US Pints (US pt.)	x .473	= Liters (L)	x 2.113	= Pints
US Quarts (US qt.)	x .946	= Liters (L)	x 1.057	= Quarts
US Gallons (US gal.)	x 3.785	= Liters (L)	x .264	= Gallons

MASS–WEIGHT

Ounces (oz.)	x 28.35	= Grams (g)	x .035	= Ounces
Pounds (lb.)	x .454	= Kilograms (kg)	x 2.205	= Pounds

PRESSURE

Pounds Per Sq. In. (psi)	x 6.895	= Kilopascals (kPa)	x .145	= psi
Inches of Mercury (Hg)	x .4912	= psi	x 2.036	= Hg
Inches of Mercury (Hg)	x 3.377	= Kilopascals (kPa)	x .2961	= Hg
Inches of Water (H₂O)	x .07355	= Inches of Mercury	x 13.783	= H₂O
Inches of Water (H₂O)	x .03613	= psi	x 27.684	= H₂O
Inches of Water (H₂O)	x .248	= Kilopascals (kPa)	x 4.026	= H₂O

TORQUE

Pounds–Force Inches (in-lb)	x .113	= Newton Meters (N·m)	x 8.85	= in–lb
Pounds–Force Feet (ft-lb)	x 1.356	= Newton Meters (N·m)	x .738	= ft–lb

VELOCITY

Miles Per Hour (MPH)	x 1.609	= Kilometers Per Hour (KPH)	x .621	= MPH

POWER

Horsepower (Hp)	x .745	= Kilowatts	x 1.34	= Horsepower

FUEL CONSUMPTION*

Miles Per Gallon IMP (MPG)	x .354	= Kilometers Per Liter (Km/L)		
Kilometers Per Liter (Km/L)	x 2.352	= IMP MPG		
Miles Per Gallon US (MPG)	x .425	= Kilometers Per Liter (Km/L)		
Kilometers Per Liter (Km/L)	x 2.352	= US MPG		

*It is common to covert from miles per gallon (mpg) to liters/100 kilometers (1/100 km), where mpg (IMP) x 1/100 km = 282 and mpg (US) x 1/100 km = 235.

TEMPERATURE

Degree Fahrenheit (°F)	= (°C x 1.8) + 32
Degree Celsius (°C)	= (°F – 32) x .56

TCCS1044

Fig. 23 Standard and metric conversion factors chart

SERIAL NUMBER IDENTIFICATION

Vehicle

▶ See Figures 24 thru 29

A vehicle identification plate is attached to the right side of the firewall. This plate gives the vehicle type, vehicle identification number (chassis number), model, body color code, trim color code, engine model and displacement, transaxle model and axle model. All vehicles also have a Vehicle Identification Number (VIN) on a plate attached to the top of the instrument panel on the driver's side, visible through the windshield. This number is also stamped into the firewall. Contained within the VIN is the chassis serial number, and other identifying codes.

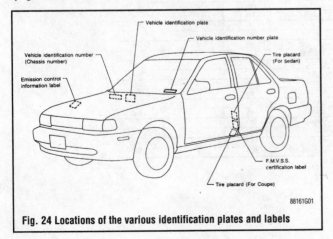

Fig. 24 Locations of the various identification plates and labels

88161G01

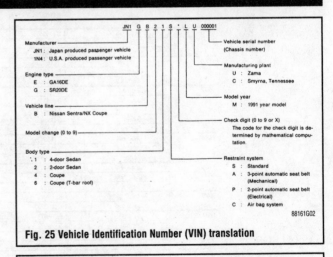

Fig. 25 Vehicle Identification Number (VIN) translation

88161G02

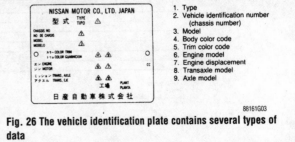

1. Type
2. Vehicle identification number (chassis number)
3. Model
4. Body color code
5. Trim color code
6. Engine model
7. Engine displacement
8. Transaxle model
9. Axle model

88161G03

Fig. 26 The vehicle identification plate contains several types of data

Fig. 27 The VIN is affixed to the top of the driver's side instrument panel

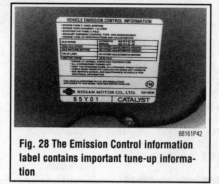

Fig. 28 The Emission Control information label contains important tune-up information

Fig. 29 The Federal Motor Vehicle Safety Standards certification label contains the VIN and other data

The vehicle identification number is broken down as follows:

- The first 3 digits are "JN1"—Nissan passenger vehicle; or "1N4"—USA produced passenger vehicle.
- The next letter refers to the type of engine in use. For example, "P" refers to the E16i gasoline engine and "S" refers to the CD17 diesel.
- The third letter refers to the model—for example, "B" refers to the Sentra.
- The fourth space is filled by a number referring to the model.
- The fifth space refers to the body type.
- Next comes the restraint system—"S" for Standard and "Y" for four wheel drive.
- The seventh space is occupied by a check digit (this keeps anyone from creating a fictitious serial number based on this basic information).
- Next comes the model year—for example, "J" for 1988.
- The ninth space contains a letter referring to the manufacturing plant.

- The final block contains the 6 digit sequential serial or "chassis" number for the actual vehicle.

All models also have an Emission Control information label on the firewall or on the underside of the hood, as well as a Federal Motor Vehicle Safety Standards (FMVSS) certification label and tire placard on the driver's door jamb.

Engine

The engine number is stamped on the right-side top edge of the cylinder block on all models. The engine serial number is preceded by the engine model code.

Transaxle

The transaxle number is stamped on the front upper face of the transaxle case for automatic or attached to the clutch withdrawal lever for manual transaxles.

ENGINE IDENTIFICATION

All measurements are given in inches.

Year	Model	Engine Displacement Liters (cc)	Engine Series (ID/VIN)	Fuel System	No. of Cylinders	Engine Type
1982	Sentra	1.5 (1488)	E15	2BC	4	SOHC
1983	Sentra	1.5 (1488)	E15	2BC	4	SOHC
	Sentra	1.6 (1597)	E16	2BC	4	SOHC
	Pulsar	1.6 (1597)	E16	2BC	4	SOHC
	Sentra	1.7 (1680)	CD17	Diesel	4	SOHC
1984	Pulsar	1.5 (1488)	E15ET	EFI-Turbo [1]	4	SOHC
	Sentra	1.6 (1597)	E16	2BC	4	SOHC
	Pulsar	1.6 (1597)	E16	2BC	4	SOHC
	Sentra	1.7 (1680)	CD17	DSL	4	SOHC
1985	Pulsar NX	1.6 (1597)	E16S	2BC	4	SOHC
	Sentra	1.6 (1597)	E16S	2BC	4	SOHC
	Sentra	1.7 (1680)	CD17	DSL	4	SOHC
1986	Pulsar NX	1.6 (1597)	E16S	2BC	4	SOHC
	Sentra	1.6 (1597)	E16S	2BC	4	SOHC
	Sentra	1.7 (1680)	CD17	DSL	4	SOHC
1987	Pulsar NX	1.6 (1598)	CA16DE	MFI	4	DOHC
	Pulsar NX	1.6 (1597)	E16i	TFI	4	SOHC
	Sentra	1.6 (1597)	E16i	TFI	4	SOHC
	Sentra	1.6 (1597)	E16S	2BC	4	SOHC
	Sentra	1.7 (1680)	CD17	DSL	4	SOHC
1988	Pulsar NX	1.6 (1597)	E16i	TFI	4	SOHC
	Pulsar NX	1.8 (1809)	CA18DE	MFI	4	DOHC
	Sentra	1.6 (1597)	E16i	TFI	4	SOHC
1989	Pulsar NX	1.6 (1597)	GA16i	TFI	4	SOHC
	Pulsar NX	1.8 (1809)	CA18DE	MFI	4	DOHC
	Sentra	1.6 (1597)	GA16i	TFI	4	SOHC
1990	Pulsar NX	1.6 (1597)	GA16i	TFI	4	SOHC
	Sentra	1.6 (1597)	GA16i	TFI	4	SOHC
1991	Sentra	1.6 (1597)	GA16DE	MFI	4	DOHC
	Sentra	2.0 (1998)	SR20DE	MFI	4	DOHC
1992	Sentra	1.6 (1597)	GA16DE	MFI	4	DOHC
	Sentra	2.0 (1998)	SR20DE	MFI	4	DOHC
1993	Sentra	1.6 (1597)	GA16DE	MFI	4	DOHC
	Sentra	2.0 (1998)	SR20DE	MFI	4	DOHC
1994	Sentra	1.6 (1597)	GA16DE	MFI	4	DOHC
	Sentra	2.0 (1998)	SR20DE	MFI	4	DOHC
1995	Sentra	1.6 (1597)	GA16DE	MFI	4	DOHC
	Sentra	2.0 (1998)	SR20DE	MFI	4	DOHC
1996	Sentra	1.6 (1597)	GA16DE	MFI	4	DOHC
	Sentra	2.0 (1998)	SR20DE	MFI	4	DOHC

BC - Barrel Carburetor
DSL - Diesel
EFI - Electronic Fuel Injection
TFI - Throttle body Fuel Injection
MFI - Multi-port Fuel Injection
SOHC - Single Overhead Camshaft
DOHC - Double Overhead Camshaft
1 - Twin Turbo

ROUTINE MAINTENANCE AND TUNE-UP

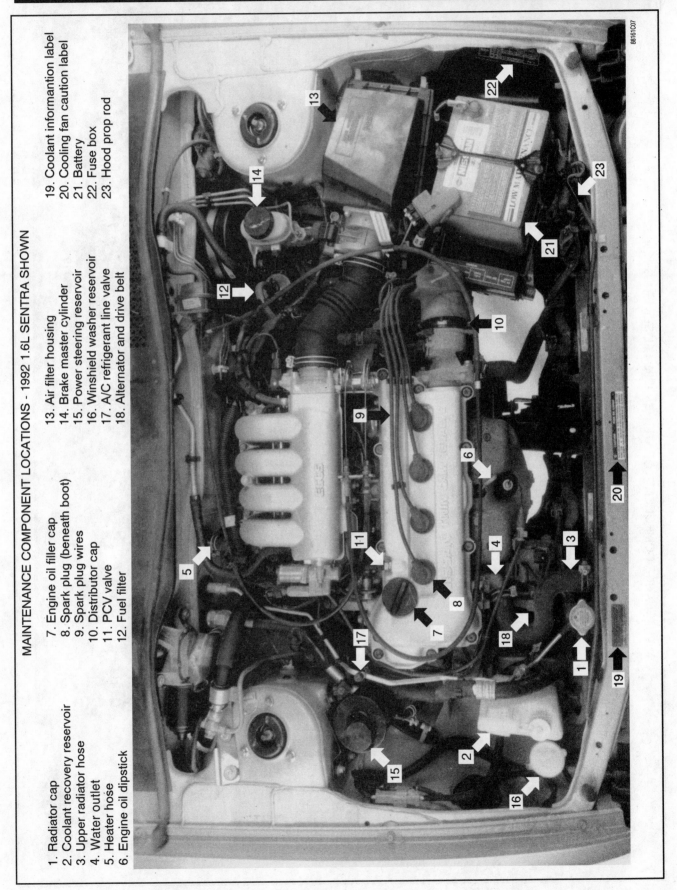

MAINTENANCE COMPONENT LOCATIONS - 1992 1.6L SENTRA SHOWN

1. Radiator cap
2. Coolant recovery reservoir
3. Upper radiator hose
4. Water outlet
5. Heater hose
6. Engine oil dipstick
7. Engine oil filler cap
8. Spark plug (beneath boot)
9. Spark plug wires
10. Distributor cap
11. PCV valve
12. Fuel filter
13. Air filter housing
14. Brake master cylinder
15. Power steering reservoir
16. Winshield washer reservoir
17. A/C refrigerant line valve
18. Alternator and drive belt
19. Coolant informantion label
20. Cooling fan caution label
21. Battery
22. Fuse box
23. Hood prop rod

88161C07

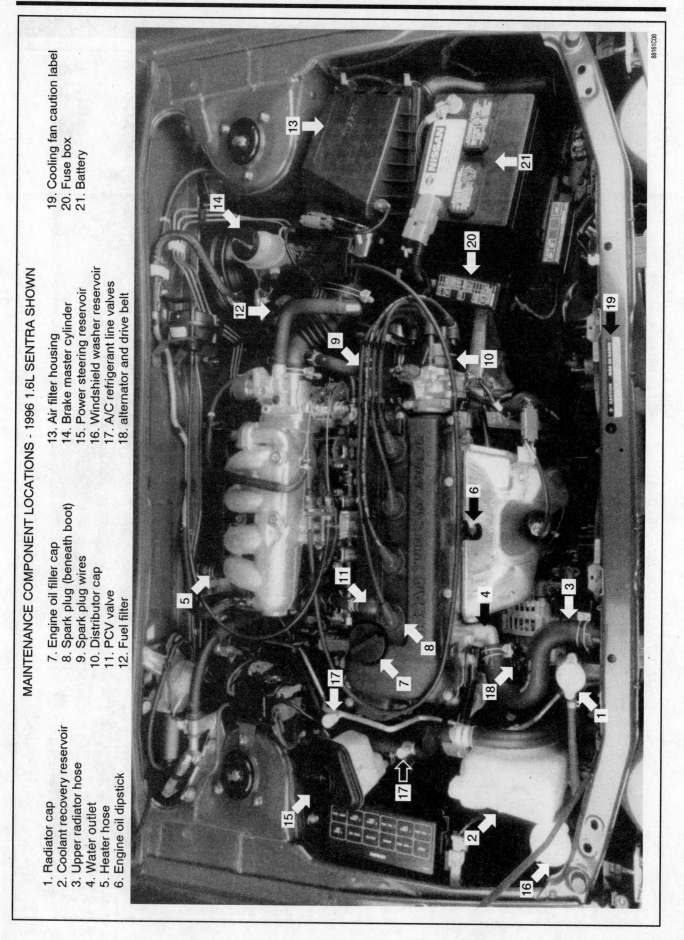

MAINTENANCE COMPONENT LOCATIONS - 1996 1.6L SENTRA SHOWN

1. Radiator cap
2. Coolant recovery reservoir
3. Upper radiator hose
4. Water outlet
5. Heater hose
6. Engine oil dipstick
7. Engine oil filler cap
8. Spark plug (beneath boot)
9. Spark plug wires
10. Distributor cap
11. PCV valve
12. Fuel filter
13. Air filter housing
14. Brake master cylinder
15. Power steering reservoir
16. Windshield washer reservoir
17. A/C refrigerant line valves
18. alternator and drive belt
19. Cooling fan caution label
20. Fuse box
21. Battery

Proper maintenance and tune-up is the key to long and trouble-free vehicle life. Studies have shown that a properly tuned and maintained vehicle can achieve better gas mileage than an out-of-tune vehicle. As a conscientious owner and driver, set aside a Saturday morning, say once a month, to check or replace items which could cause major problems later. Keep your own personal log to jot down which services you performed, how much the parts cost you, the date, and the exact odometer reading at the time. Keep all receipts for such items as engine oil and filters, so that they may be referred to in case of related problems or to determine operating expenses. As a do-it-yourselfer, these receipts are the only proof you have that the required maintenance was performed. In the event of a warranty problem, these receipts will be invaluable.

The literature provided with your vehicle when it was originally delivered includes the factory recommended maintenance schedule. If you no longer have this literature, replacement copies are usually available from the dealer.

Air Cleaner (Element)

REMOVAL & INSTALLATION

▶ **See Figures 30, 31, 32, 33 and 34**

➡**The filter should be replaced at least every 30,000 miles (48,309 km) or 24 months.**

All vehicles covered in this guide are equipped with a disposable paper cartridge air cleaner element. At every tune-up or sooner, if the car is operated in a dusty area, remove the housing cover and element. Inspect the element and replace if necessary.

1. On carbureted engines, unscrew the wingnut on top of the air cleaner housing and, if equipped, unsnap the spring clips around the edge of the housing. On fuel injected engines, unsnap the spring clips around the edge of the housing.

2. Lift off the housing cover and remove the air cleaner element.

3. Check the element by holding a drop light or equivalent up to the filter. If light can be seen through the filter, the filter is not clogged. Replace the filter, however, if it is extremely dirty. Loose dust can sometimes be removed by striking the filter against a hard surface several times or by blowing through it with compressed air from the inside out.

To install:

➡**Carbureted engines use a round element and fuel injected engines use a panel-type element. The panel (flat, rectangular) elements have the word UP printed on them; be sure the side with UP on it faces upward.**

4. Before installing either the original or a replacement filter, wipe out the inside of the air cleaner housing with a clean rag or paper towel.

5. Install the air cleaner element, then seat the top cover on the bottom housing and secure the cover with the spring clips, if so equipped. On carbureted models, fasten the wingnut.

Air Induction Valve Filter

REMOVAL & INSTALLATION

▶ **See Figure 35**

➡**Not all years and models use this filter.**

This filter is located in the air cleaner on both fuel injected and carburetor models. To replace it, remove the screws and the valve filter case. Install the new filter, paying attention to which direction the valve is facing, so that exhaust gases will not flow backwards through the system.

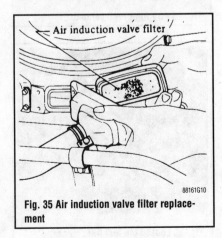

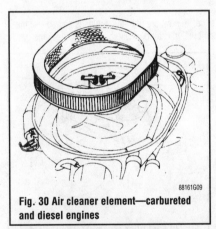

Fig. 30 Air cleaner element—carbureted and diesel engines

Fig. 31 Pull back the spring clips which secure the air cleaner cover

Fig. 32 Lift off the cover and . . .

Fig. 33 . . . remove the filter element

Fig. 34 A dirty filter, such as this, should be replaced

Fig. 35 Air induction valve filter replacement

PCV Filter

REMOVAL & INSTALLATION

♦ **See Figure 36**

➡ **The PCV filter is located in the air cleaner assembly.**

1. Remove the wingnut from the air cleaner lid, then remove the lid.
2. Gently lift out the filter which is mounted on the side of the air cleaner housing. This filter is usually about 4 in. (10.2cm) long.
3. Replace the filter if it is damaged or worn out. Otherwise, clean the filter in solvent, then thoroughly dry it and reinstall.
4. Install the air cleaner and tighten the wingnut.
5. Check the hoses and clamps for deterioration and leakage; replace if necessary.

Fuel Filter

REMOVAL & INSTALLATION

♦ **See Figures 37, 38, 39 and 40**

The fuel filter on all models is a disposable plastic unit, located at the rear of the engine compartment. The filter should be replaced at least every 24,000 miles (38,647 km). A dirty filter will starve the engine and cause poor running.

❊❊❊ CAUTION

If equipped with an Electronic Fuel Injected (EFI) engine, refer to the procedure for relieving fuel system pressure in Section 5 and release the pressure before removing the fuel filter.

1. Locate the fuel filter on the left (driver's) side of the engine compartment. Place a container under the filter to catch the excess fuel.

2. Loosen the hose clamps, then disconnect the inlet and outlet hoses from the fuel filter. Make certain that the inlet hose (bottom) doesn't fall below the fuel tank level or gasoline will drain out.
3. Pry the fuel filter from its clip and replace the assembly.
4. Position new hose clamps, if necessary, then connect the inlet and outlet lines. Make sure that the closest edge of each hose clamp is ⅛ in. (3mm) from the end of the hose before tightening.

➡ **Ensure that the screw does not contact adjacent parts.**

5. Start the engine and check for leaks.

Positive Crankcase Ventilation (PCV) Valve

REMOVAL & INSTALLATION

♦ **See Figures 41, 42 and 43**

This valve feeds crankcase blow-by gases into the intake manifold to be burned with the normal air/fuel mixture. The PCV valve should be replaced every 24,000 miles (38,647 km). Make sure that all PCV connections are tight. Check that the connecting hoses are clear and not clogged. Replace any brittle or broken hoses.
To replace the valve, which is located in the rocker arm cover:
1. Squeeze the hose clamp with pliers and remove the hose.
2. Using a wrench, unscrew the PCV valve and remove the valve.
3. Disconnect the ventilation hoses and flush with solvent.
4. Install the new PCV valve, then replace the hoses and clamp.

Evaporative Canister

SERVICING

♦ **See Figures 44 and 45**

A carbon filled canister stores fuel vapors until the engine is started and the vapors are drawn into the combustion chambers and burned. To check the oper-

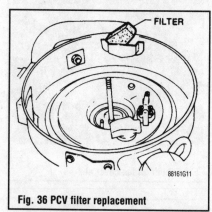

Fig. 36 PCV filter replacement

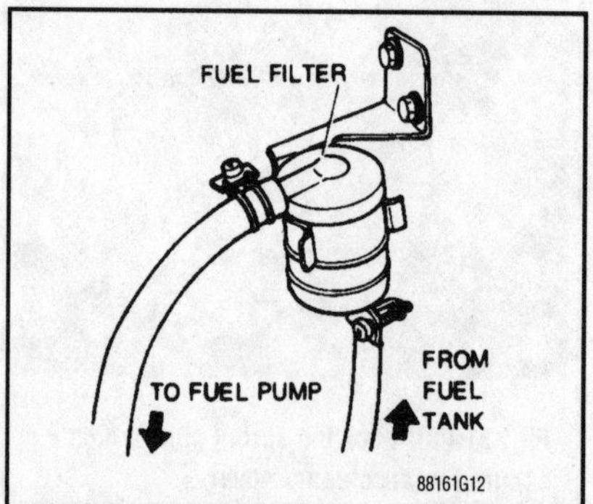

Fig. 37 Fuel filter assembly—carbureted engines

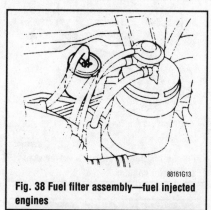

Fig. 38 Fuel filter assembly—fuel injected engines

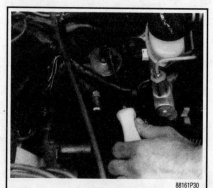

Fig. 39 Loosen the fuel filter's hose clamps before detaching the hoses

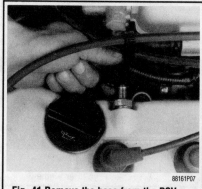

Fig. 40 The fuel filter is held by a metal clip

Fig. 41 Remove the hose from the PCV valve

Fig. 42 Use the proper size wrench to unscrew it . . .

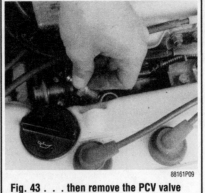

Fig. 43 . . . then remove the PCV valve from the rocker arm cover

Fig. 44 The evaporative canister is typically a black cylinder with 2 or 3 hoses attached to its top

1. Cover
2. Diaphragm
3. Retainer
4. Diaphragm spring

Fig. 45 Exploded view of evaporative canister components

ation of the carbon canister purge control valve, disconnect the rubber hose between the canister control valve and the T-fitting, at the T-fitting. Apply vacuum to the hose leading to the control valve. The vacuum condition should be maintained indefinitely. If the control valve leaks, remove the top cover of the valve and check for a dislocated or cracked diaphragm. If the diaphragm is damaged, a repair kit containing a new diaphragm, retainer and spring is available and should be installed.

The carbon canister has an air filter in the bottom of the canister. The filter element should be checked once a year or every 12,000 miles (19,323 km); more frequently if the car is operated in dusty areas. Replace the filter by pulling it out of the bottom of the canister and installing a new one.

Battery

PRECAUTIONS

Always use caution when working on or near the battery. Never allow a tool to bridge the gap between the negative and positive battery terminals. Also, be careful not to allow a tool to provide a ground between the positive cable/terminal and any metal component on the vehicle. Either of these conditions will cause a short circuit, leading to sparks and possible personal injury.

Do not smoke or all open flames/sparks near a battery; the gases contained in the battery are very explosive and, if ignited, could cause severe injury or death.

All batteries, regardless of type, should be carefully secured by a battery hold-down device. If not, the terminals or casing may crack from stress during vehicle operation. A battery which is not secured may allow acid to leak, making it discharge faster. The acid can also eat away at components under the hood.

Always inspect the battery case for cracks, leakage and corrosion. A white corrosive substance on the battery case or on nearby components would indicate a leaking or cracked battery. If the battery is cracked, it should be replaced immediately.

GENERAL MAINTENANCE

Always keep the battery cables and terminals free of corrosion. Check and clean these components about once a year.

Keep the top of the battery clean, as a film of dirt can help discharge a battery that is not used for long periods. A solution of baking soda and water may be used for cleaning, but be careful to flush this off with clear water. DO NOT let any of the solution into the filler holes. Baking soda neutralizes battery acid and will de-activate a battery cell.

Batteries in vehicles which are not operated on a regular basis can fall victim to parasitic loads (small current drains which are constantly drawing current from the battery). Normal parasitic loads may drain a battery on a vehicle that is in storage and not used for 6–8 weeks. Vehicles that have additional accessories such as a phone or an alarm system may discharge a battery sooner. If the vehicle is to be stored for longer periods in a secure area and the alarm system is not necessary, the negative battery cable should be disconnected to protect the battery.

Remember that constantly deep cycling a battery (completely discharging and recharging it) will shorten battery life.

BATTERY FLUID

♦ See Figure 46

Check the battery electrolyte level at least once a month, or more often in hot weather or during periods of extended vehicle operation. On non-sealed batteries, the level can be checked either through the case (if translucent) or by removing the cell caps. The electrolyte level in each cell should be kept filled to the split ring inside each cell, or the line marked on the outside of the case.

If the level is low, add only distilled water through the opening until the level is correct. Each cell must be checked and filled individually. Distilled water should be used, because the chemicals and minerals found in most drinking water are harmful to the battery and could significantly shorten its life.

If water is added in freezing weather, the vehicle should be driven several miles to allow the water to mix with the electrolyte. Otherwise, the battery could freeze.

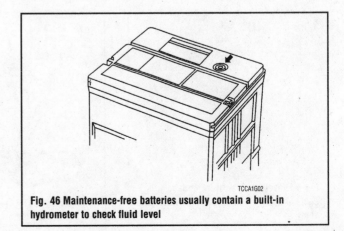

Fig. 46 Maintenance-free batteries usually contain a built-in hydrometer to check fluid level

Although some maintenance-free batteries have removable cell caps, the electrolyte condition and level on all sealed maintenance-free batteries must be checked using the built-in hydrometer "eye." The exact type of eye will vary. But, most battery manufacturers, apply a sticker to the battery itself explaining the readings.

➡Although the readings from built-in hydrometers will vary, a green eye usually indicates a properly charged battery with sufficient fluid level. A dark eye is normally an indicator of a battery with sufficient fluid, but which is low in charge. A light or yellow eye usually indicates that electrolyte has dropped below the necessary level. In this last case, sealed batteries with an insufficient electrolyte must usually be discarded.

Checking the Specific Gravity

♦ See Figures 47, 48 and 49

A hydrometer is required to check the specific gravity on all batteries that are not maintenance-free. On batteries that are maintenance-free, the specific gravity

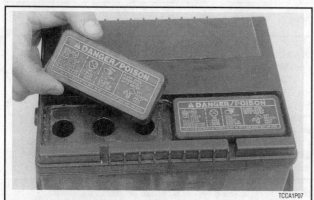

Fig. 47 On non-sealed batteries, the fluid level can be checked by removing the cell caps

TCCA1P07

is checked by observing the built-in hydrometer "eye" on the top of the battery case.

✳✳ CAUTION

Battery electrolyte contains sulfuric acid. If you should splash any on your skin or in your eyes, flush the affected area with plenty of clear water. If it lands in your eyes, get medical help immediately.

The fluid (sulfuric acid solution) contained in the battery cells will tell you many things about the condition of the battery. Because the cell plates must be kept submerged below the fluid level in order to operate, the fluid level is extremely important. And, because the specific gravity of the acid is an indication of electrical charge, testing the fluid can be an aid in determining if the battery must be replaced. A battery in a vehicle with a properly operating charging system should require little maintenance, but careful, periodic inspection should reveal problems before they leave you stranded.

At least once a year, check the specific gravity of the battery. It should be between 1.20 and 1.26 on the gravity scale. Most auto stores carry a variety of inexpensive battery hydrometers. These can be used on any non-sealed battery to test the specific gravity in each cell.

The battery testing hydrometer has a squeeze bulb at one end and a nozzle at the other. Battery electrolyte is sucked into the hydrometer until the float is lifted from its seat. The specific gravity is then read by noting the position of the float. If gravity is low in one or more cells, the battery should be slowly charged and checked again to see if the gravity has come up. Generally, if after charging, the specific gravity between any two cells varies more than 50 points (0.50), the battery should be replaced, as it can no longer produce sufficient voltage to guarantee proper operation.

CABLES

♦ See Figures 50, 51, 52 and 53

Fig. 48 If the fluid level is low, add only distilled water until the level is correct

TCCA1P08

Fig. 49 Check the specific gravity of the battery's electrolyte with a hydrometer

TCCA1P09

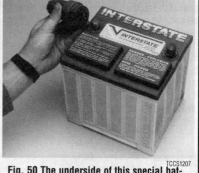

Fig. 50 The underside of this special battery tool has a wire brush to clean post terminals

TCCS1207

Fig. 51 Place the tool over the battery posts and twist to clean until the metal is shiny

TCCS1208

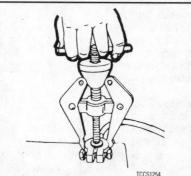

Fig. 52 A special tool is available to pull the clamp from the post

TCCS1254

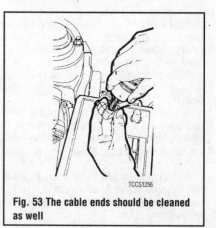

Fig. 53 The cable ends should be cleaned as well

TCCS1256

CHARGING

A battery should be charged at a slow rate to keep the plates inside from getting too hot. However, if some maintenance-free batteries are allowed to discharge until they are almost "dead," they may have to be charged at a high rate to bring them back to "life." Always follow the charger manufacturer's instructions on charging the battery.

REPLACEMENT

When it becomes necessary to replace the battery, select one with an amperage rating equal to or greater than the battery originally installed. Deterioration and just plain aging of the battery cables, starter motor, and associated wires makes the battery's job harder in successive years. This makes it prudent to install a new battery with a greater capacity than the old.

Belts

INSPECTION

▶ **See Figures 54, 55, 56, 57 and 58**

Check the drive belts for glazing, cracks, fraying, wear and tension every 6,000 miles (9,662 km). A glazed belt will be perfectly smooth from slippage, while a good belt will have a slight texture of fabric visible. Cracks will usually start at the inner edge of the belt and run outward. All worn or damaged drive belts should be replaced immediately. It is best to replace all drive belts at one time, as a preventive maintenance measure, during this service operation. It is recommended that the belts be replaced every 24 months or 24,000 miles (38,647 km). Belt deflection at the midpoint of the longest span between pulleys should not be more than $7/16$ in. (11mm) with 22 lbs. (10 kg) of pressure applied to the belt when engine is cold.

ADJUSTMENT

➡**An overly tight belt will wear out the pulley bearings on the assorted components.**

To adjust the tension on all components except the air conditioning compressor and power steering pump, loosen the pivot and mounting bolts of the component which the belt is driving, then, using a wooden lever or equivalent, pry the component toward or away from the engine until the proper tension is achieved. Tighten the component mounting bolts securely. If a new belt is installed, recheck the tension after driving about 1,000 miles (1,610 km).

Belt tension adjustments for the factory installed air conditioning compressor are made at the idler pulley. The idler pulley is the smallest of the 3 pulleys. At the top of the slotted bracket holding the idler pulley is a bolt which is used to either raise or lower the pulley. To free the bolt for adjustment, it is necessary to loosen the locknut in the face of the idler pulley. After adjusting the belt tension, tighten the locknut in the face of the idler pulley.

Belt tension adjustments for the power steering pump are made at the pump. Loosen the power steering pump's adjusting lockbolt and its mounting bolt. Turn the adjusting bolt until the belt deflection is correct. Tighten the adjusting bolt's lockbolt and the mounting bolt securely.

REMOVAL & INSTALLATION

▶ **See Figures 59 thru 65**

To replace a drive belt, loosen the pivot and mounting bolts of the component which the belt is driving, then, using a wooden lever or equivalent, pry the component inward to relieve the tension on the drive belt, always be careful where you locate the pry bar not to damage the component. Slip the belt off the component pulley, match up the new belt with the old belt for length and width, these measurement must be the same or problems will occur when you go to adjust the new belt. After new belt is installed correctly adjust the tension of the new belt.

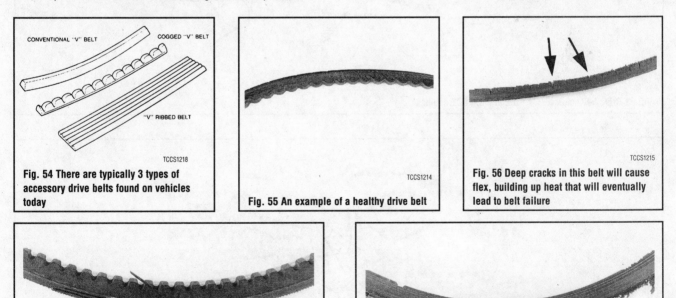

Fig. 54 There are typically 3 types of accessory drive belts found on vehicles today

Fig. 55 An example of a healthy drive belt

Fig. 56 Deep cracks in this belt will cause flex, building up heat that will eventually lead to belt failure

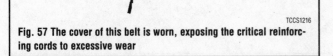

Fig. 57 The cover of this belt is worn, exposing the critical reinforcing cords to excessive wear

Fig. 58 Installing too wide a belt can result in serious belt wear and/or breakage

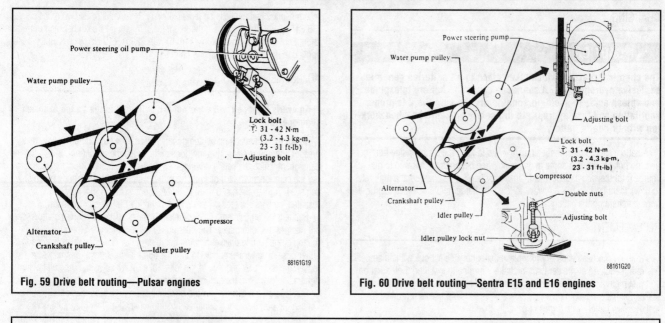

Fig. 59 Drive belt routing—Pulsar engines

Fig. 60 Drive belt routing—Sentra E15 and E16 engines

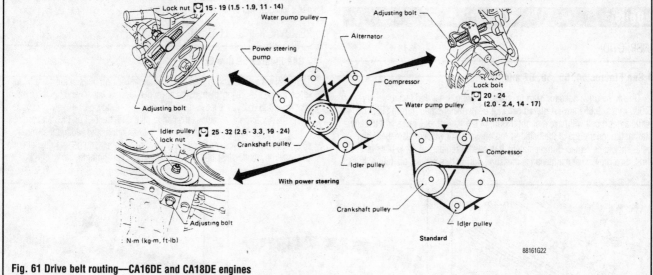

Fig. 61 Drive belt routing—CA16DE and CA18DE engines

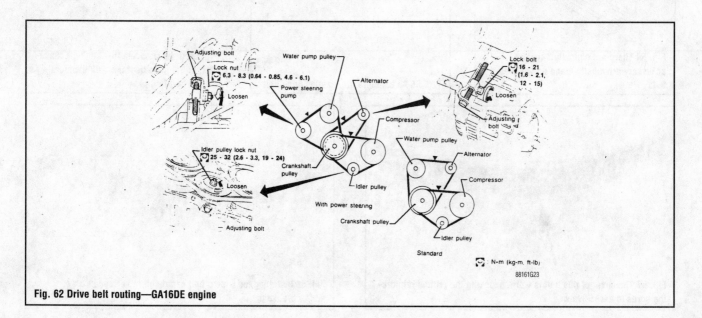

Fig. 62 Drive belt routing—GA16DE engine

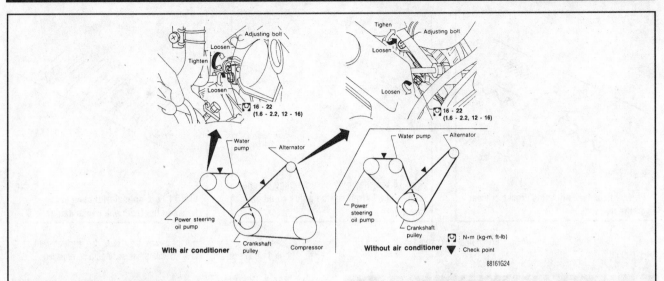

Fig. 63 Drive belt routing—SR20DE engine

Fig. 64 If so equipped, use a wrench to loosen the idler pulley lock-nut . . .

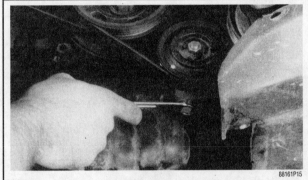

Fig. 65 . . . then turn the idler pulley's adjusting bolt to alter belt tension

➥When replacing more than one belt, it is a good idea to make note or mark what belt goes around what pulley. This will make installation fast and easy.

On air conditioning compressor and power steering pump belt replacements, loosen the lockbolt for the adjusting bolt on the idler pulley or power steering pump, then loosen the adjusting bolt. Pry the pulley or pump inward to relieve the tension on the drive belt, but always be careful where you locate the prybar so as not to damage the component or pulley.

Timing Belts

INSPECTION

▸ See Figures 66 thru 71

➥The engines covered in this manual are of an "interference" design. This means that should a timing belt break, there is the possibility of valve and piston damage. As a rule of thumb, it is recommended that the timing belt be replaced at least every 60,000 miles (96,618 km), in order to avoid potentially extensive and costly engine damage.

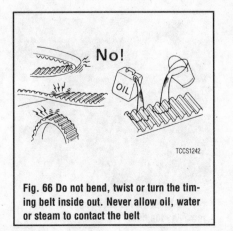

Fig. 66 Do not bend, twist or turn the timing belt inside out. Never allow oil, water or steam to contact the belt

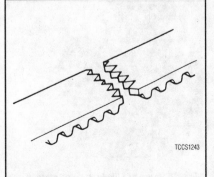

Fig. 67 Check for premature parting of the belt

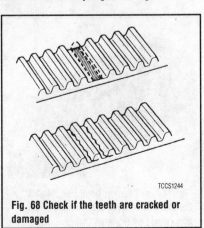

Fig. 68 Check if the teeth are cracked or damaged

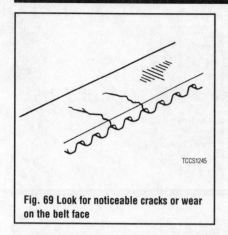

Fig. 69 Look for noticeable cracks or wear on the belt face

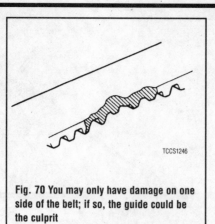

Fig. 70 You may only have damage on one side of the belt; if so, the guide could be the culprit

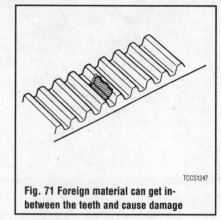

Fig. 71 Foreign material can get in-between the teeth and cause damage

Timing Belt removal and installation procedures are covered in Section 3 of this manual.

Hoses

INSPECTION

▶ **See Figures 72, 73, 74 and 75**

Upper and lower radiator hoses, along with the heater hoses, should be checked for deterioration, leaks and loose hose clamps at least every 15,000 miles (24,000 km). It is also wise to check the hoses periodically in early spring and at the beginning of the fall or winter when you are performing other maintenance. A quick visual inspection could discover a weakened hose which might have left you stranded if it had remained unrepaired.

Whenever you are checking the hoses, make sure the engine and cooling system are cold. Visually inspect for cracking, rotting or collapsed hoses, and replace as necessary. Run your hand along the length of the hose. If a weak or swollen spot is noted when squeezing the hose wall, the hose should be replaced.

REMOVAL & INSTALLATION

▶ **See Figure 76**

1. Remove the radiator pressure cap.

✳✳ CAUTION

Never remove the pressure cap while the engine is running, or personal injury from scalding hot coolant or steam may result. If possible, wait until the engine has cooled to remove the pressure cap. If this is not possible, wrap a thick cloth around the pressure cap and turn it slowly to the stop. Step back while the pressure is released from the cooling system. When you are sure all the pressure has been released, use the cloth to turn and remove the cap.

Fig. 72 The cracks developing along this hose are a result of age-related hardening

Fig. 73 A hose clamp that is too tight can cause older hoses to separate and tear on either side of the clamp

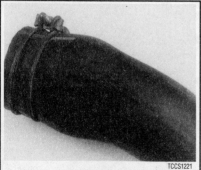

Fig. 74 A soft spongy hose (identifiable by the swollen section) will eventually burst and should be replaced

Fig. 75 Hoses are likely to deteriorate from the inside if the cooling system is not periodically flushed

Fig. 76 Unfasten the hose clamp before removing the hose

2. Position a clean container under the radiator and/or engine draincock or plug, then open the drain and allow the cooling system to drain to an appropriate level. For some upper hoses, only a little coolant must be drained. To remove hoses positioned lower on the engine, such as a lower radiator hose, the entire cooling system must be emptied.

> ### ✳✳ CAUTION
>
> **When draining coolant, keep in mind that cats and dogs are attracted by ethylene glycol antifreeze, and are quite likely to drink any that is left in an uncovered container or in puddles on the ground. This will prove fatal in sufficient quantity. Always drain coolant into a sealable container.**

3. Loosen the hose clamps at each end of the hose requiring replacement. Clamps are usually either of the spring tension type (which require pliers to squeeze the tabs and loosen) or of the screw tension type (which require screw or hex drivers to loosen). Pull the clamps back on the hose away from the connection.

4. Twist, pull and slide the hose off the fitting, taking care not to damage the neck of the component from which the hose is being removed.

➡ If the hose is stuck at the connection, do not try to insert a screwdriver or other sharp tool under the hose end in an effort to free it, as the connection and/or hose may become damaged. Heater connections especially may be easily damaged by such a procedure. If the hose is to be replaced, use a single-edged razor blade to make a slice along the portion of the hose which is stuck on the connection, perpendicular to the end of the hose. Do not cut too deep so as to prevent damaging the connection. The hose can then be peeled from the connection and discarded.

5. Clean both hose mounting connections. Inspect the condition of the hose clamps and replace them, if necessary.

To install:

6. Dip the ends of the new hose into clean engine coolant to ease installation.

7. Slide the clamps over the replacement hose, then slide the hose ends over the connections into position.

8. Position and secure the clamps at least ¼ in. (6.35mm) from the ends of the hose. Make sure they are located beyond the raised bead of the connector.

9. Close the radiator or engine drains and properly refill the cooling system with the clean drained engine coolant or a suitable mixture of coolant and water.

10. If available, install a pressure tester and check for leaks. If a pressure tester is not available, run the engine until normal operating temperature is reached (allowing the system to naturally pressurize), then check for leaks.

> ### ✳✳ CAUTION
>
> **If you are checking for leaks with the system at normal operating temperature, BE EXTREMELY CAREFUL not to touch any moving or hot engine parts. Once temperature has been reached, shut the engine OFF, and check for leaks around the hose fittings and connections which were removed earlier.**

CV-Boots

INSPECTION

▶ **See Figures 77 and 78**

The CV (Constant Velocity) boots should be checked for damage each time the oil is changed and any other time the vehicle is raised for service. These boots keep water, grime, dirt and other damaging matter from entering the CV-joints. Any of these could cause early CV-joint failure which can be expensive to repair. Heavy grease thrown around the inside of the front wheel(s) and on the brake caliper/drum can be an indication of a torn boot. Thoroughly check the boots for missing clamps and tears. If the boot is damaged, it should be replaced immediately. Please refer to Section 7 for procedures.

Fig. 77 CV-boots must be inspected periodically for damage

Fig. 78 A torn boot should be replaced immediately

Spark Plugs

▶ **See Figures 79 and 80**

A typical spark plug consists of a metal shell surrounding a ceramic insulator. A metal electrode extends downward through the center of the insulator and protrudes a small distance. Located at the end of the plug and attached to the side of the outer metal shell is the side electrode. The side electrode bends in at a 90° angle so that its tip is just past and parallel to the tip of the center electrode. The distance between these two electrodes (measured in thousandths of an inch or hundredths of a millimeter) is called the spark plug gap.

The spark plug does not produce a spark, but instead provides a gap across which the current can arc. The coil produces anywhere from 20,000 to 50,000 volts (depending on the type and application) which travels through the wires to the spark plugs. The current passes along the center electrode and jumps the gap to the side electrode, and in doing so, ignites the air/fuel mixture in the combustion chamber.

SPARK PLUG HEAT RANGE

▶ **See Figure 81**

Spark plug heat range is the ability of the plug to dissipate heat. The longer the insulator (or the farther it extends into the engine), the hotter the plug will operate; the shorter the insulator (the closer the electrode is to the block's cooling passages) the cooler it will operate. A plug that absorbs little heat and remains too cool will quickly accumulate deposits of oil and carbon since it is not hot enough to burn them off. This leads to plug fouling and consequently to misfiring. A plug that absorbs too much heat will have no deposits but, due to the excessive heat, the electrodes will burn away quickly and might possibly lead to preignition or other ignition problems. Preignition takes place when plug tips get so hot that they glow sufficiently to ignite the air/fuel mixture before the actual spark occurs. This early ignition will usually cause a pinging during low speeds and heavy loads.

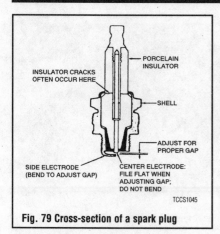

Fig. 79 Cross-section of a spark plug

Fig. 80 A variety of tools and gauges are needed for spark plug service

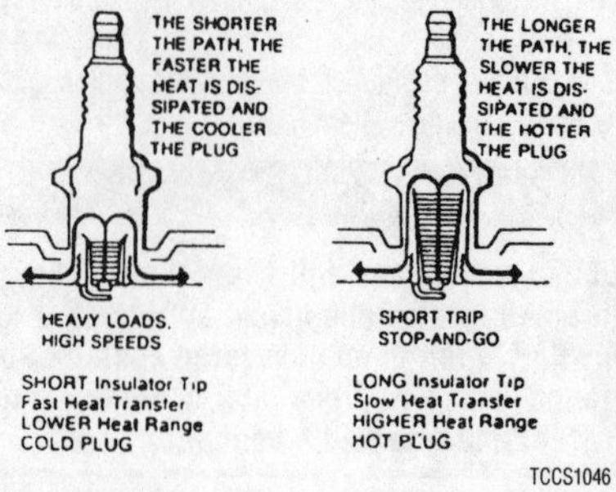

Fig. 81 Spark plug heat range

The general rule of thumb for choosing the correct heat range when picking a spark plug is: if most of your driving is long distance, high speed travel, use a colder plug; if most of your driving is stop and go, use a hotter plug. Original equipment plugs are generally a good compromise between the 2 styles and most people never have the need to change their plugs from the factory-recommended heat range.

REMOVAL & INSTALLATION

♦ See Figures 82 thru 87

A set of conventional spark plugs usually requires replacement after about 20,000–30,000 miles (32,000–48,000 km), depending on your style of driving. In normal operation, plug gap increases about 0.001 in. (0.025mm) for every 2,500 miles (4,000 km). As the gap increases, the plug's voltage requirement also increases. It requires a greater voltage to jump the wider gap and about two to three times as much voltage to fire the plug at high speeds than at idle. The improved air/fuel ratio control of modern fuel injection, combined with the

higher voltage output of modern ignition systems, will often allow an engine to run significantly longer on a set of standard spark plugs, but keep in mind that efficiency will drop as the gap widens (along with fuel economy and power).

➡Since they tend to resist wear better than conventional plugs, platinum-tipped spark plugs have longer maintenance intervals. Under normal operating conditions, they only need replacing every 60,000 miles (96,500 km) or 48 months, whichever comes first. Always refer to the spark plug manufacturer's recommendations.

When removing spark plugs, work on one at a time. Don't start by removing the plug wires all at once, because, unless you number them, they may become mixed up. Take a minute before you begin and number the wires with tape.

1. Disconnect the negative battery cable. If the vehicle has been run recently, allow the engine to thoroughly cool.

➡On CA16DE and CA18DE Pulsar engines, the ornament cover (and its 8 screws) must be removed to gain access to the spark plugs. These

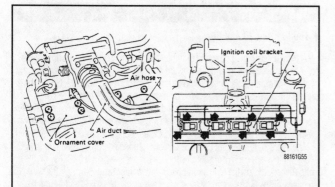

Fig. 82 On CA16DE and CA18DE engines, first remove the 8 screws which retain the ornament cover

Fig. 83 Twist and pull the spark plug boot from the spark plug

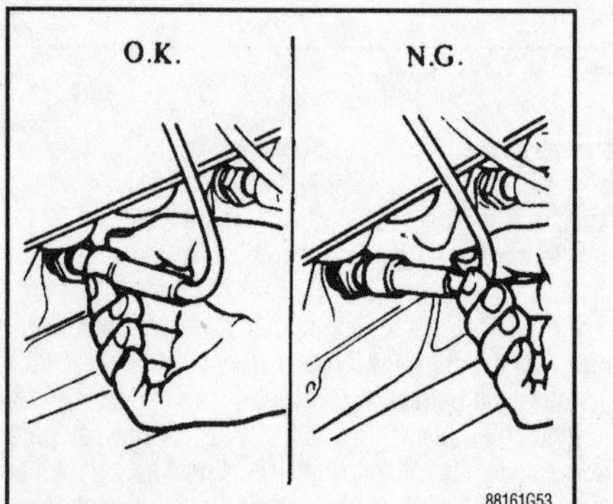

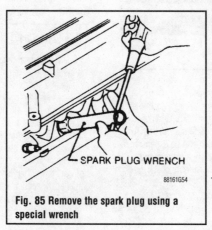

Fig. 84 Only pull on the boot, NEVER on the wire itself

Fig. 85 Remove the spark plug using a special wrench

Fig. 86 On some engines, such as this GA16DE, a socket extension is required

Fig. 87 Check the old spark plug for abnormal wear

engines have a Direct Ignition System, which does not use spark plug wires; instead, individual ignition coils are fitted directly to each spark plug.

2. Carefully twist the spark plug wire boot to loosen it, then pull upward and remove the boot from the plug. Be sure to pull on the boot and not on the wire, otherwise the connector located inside the boot may become separated.

3. Using compressed air, if available, blow any water or debris from the spark plug well to assure that no harmful contaminants are allowed to enter the combustion chamber when the spark plug is removed. If compressed air is not available, use a rag or a brush to clean the area.

➡Remove the spark plugs when the engine is cold, if possible, to prevent damage to the threads. If removal of the plugs is difficult, apply a few drops of penetrating oil or silicone spray to the area around the base of the plug, and allow it a few minutes to work.

4. Using a spark plug socket that is equipped with a rubber insert to properly hold the plug, turn the spark plug counterclockwise to loosen and remove the spark plug from the bore.

➡The cylinder head is aluminum, which is easily stripped. Remove the plugs ONLY when the engine is cold. If removal is difficult, loosen the plug only slightly and drip penetrating oil onto the threads. Allow the oil time enough to work and then unscrew the plug. If removal is still difficult, retighten and loosen until the plug comes free. Proceeding in this manner will prevent damaging the cylinder head threads. Be sure to keep the socket straight to avoid breaking the ceramic insulator. During installation, coat the plug threads with oil or anti-seize compound to ease future removal.

❊❊ WARNING

Be sure not to use a flexible extension on the socket. Use of a flexible extension may allow a shear force to be applied to the plug. A shear force could break the plug off in the cylinder head, leading to costly and frustrating repairs.

To install:

5. Inspect the spark plug boot for tears or damage. If a damaged boot is found, the spark plug wire must be replaced or repaired.

➡New spark plugs come pre-gapped, but double check the setting. The recommended spark plug gap is listed in the Tune-Up Specifications chart. Do not check or adjust the gap, however, on platinum-tipped plugs, since platinum is brittle and the electrode would break.

6. Using a wire feeler gauge, check and adjust the spark plug gap. When using a gauge, the proper size should pass between the electrodes with a slight drag. The next larger size should not be able to pass while the next smaller size should pass freely.

7. Using the electrode bending tool on the end of the gauge, bend the side electrode to adjust the gap, if necessary. Never attempt to adjust the center electrode.

8. Lightly lubricate the threads of the replacement plug and carefully thread it into the bore by hand. If resistance is felt before the plug is almost completely threaded, back the plug out and begin threading again. In small, hard to reach areas, an old spark plug wire and boot could be used as a threading tool. The boot will hold the plug while you twist the end of the wire, and the wire is supple enough to twist before it would allow the plug to crossthread.

❊❊ WARNING

Do not use the spark plug socket to thread the plugs. Always carefully thread the plug by hand or using an old plug wire to prevent the possibility of crossthreading and damaging the cylinder head bore.

9. Carefully tighten the spark plug. If the plug you are installing is equipped with a crush washer, seat the plug, then tighten about ¼ turn to crush the washer. If you are installing a tapered seat plug, tighten the plug to 14–22 ft. lbs. (19–30 Nm).

➡It is a good practice to use a torque wrench to tighten the spark plugs on any vehicle, especially the aluminum head type.

10. Apply a small amount of silicone dielectric compound to the end of the spark plug lead or inside the spark plug boot to prevent sticking, then install the boot to the spark plug and push until it clicks into place. The click may be felt or heard, then gently pull back on the boot to assure proper contact.

INSPECTION & GAPPING

▶ See Figures 88, 89, 90 and 91

Check the plugs for deposits and wear. If they are not going to be replaced, clean the plugs thoroughly. Remember that any kind of deposit will decrease the efficiency of the plug. Plugs can be cleaned on a spark plug cleaning machine, which can sometimes be found in service stations, or you can do an acceptable job of cleaning with a stiff brush. If the plugs are cleaned, the electrodes must be filed flat. Use an ignition points file, not an emery board or the like, which will leave deposits. The electrodes must be filed perfectly flat with sharp edges; rounded edges reduce the spark plug voltage by as much as 50%.

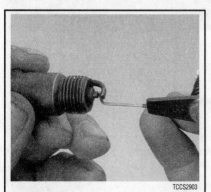

Fig. 88 Checking the spark plug gap with a feeler gauge

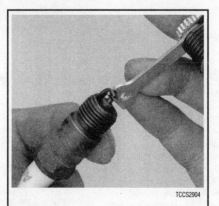

Fig. 89 Adjusting the spark plug gap

Fig. 90 If the standard plug is in good condition, the electrode may be filed flat— WARNING: do not file platinum plugs

A **normally worn** spark plug should have light tan or gray deposits on the firing tip.

A **carbon fouled** plug, identified by soft, sooty, black deposits, may indicate an improperly tuned vehicle. Check the air cleaner, ignition components and engine control system.

This spark plug has been **left in the engine too long,** as evidenced by the extreme gap- Plugs with such an extreme gap can cause misfiring and stumbling accompanied by a noticeable lack of power.

An **oil fouled** spark plug indicates an engine with worn poston rings and/or bad valve seals allowing excessive oil to enter the chamber.

A **physically damaged** spark plug may be evidence of severe detonation in that cylinder. Watch that cylinder carefully between services, as a continued detonation will not only damage the plug, but could also damage the engine.

A **bridged or almost bridged** spark plug, identified by a build-up between the electrodes caused by excessive carbon or oil build-up on the plug.

TCCA1P40

Fig. 91 Inspect the spark plug to determine engine running conditions

Check spark plug gap before installation. The ground electrode (the L-shaped one connected to the body of the plug) must be parallel to the center electrode and the specified size wire gauge (please refer to the Tune-Up Specifications chart for details) must pass between the electrodes with a slight drag.

➡**NEVER adjust the gap on a used platinum type spark plug.**

Always check the gap on new plugs as they are not always set correctly at the factory. Do not use a flat feeler gauge when measuring the gap on a used plug, because the reading may be inaccurate. A round-wire type gapping tool is the best way to check the gap. The correct gauge should pass through the electrode gap with a slight drag. If you're in doubt, try one size smaller and one larger. The smaller gauge should go through easily, while the larger one shouldn't go through at all. Wire gapping tools usually have a bending tool attached. Use that to adjust the side electrode until the proper distance is obtained. Absolutely never attempt to bend the center electrode. Also, be careful not to bend the side electrode too far or too often as it may weaken and break off within the engine, requiring removal of the cylinder head to retrieve it.

Spark Plug Wires

TESTING

▸ **See Figures 92 and 93**

At every tune-up/inspection, visually inspect the spark plug cables for burns, cuts or breaks in the insulation. Check the spark plug boots and the nipples on the distributor cap and coil. Replace any damaged wiring. If no physical damage is obvious, the wires can be checked with an ohmmeter for excessive resistance.

Every 50,000 miles (80,000 km) or 60 months, the resistance of the wires should be checked with an ohmmeter. Remove the distributor cap and leave the wires connected to the cap. Wires with excessive resistance will cause misfiring, and may make the engine difficult to start in damp weather. Connect one lead of the ohmmeter to the corresponding electrode inside the cap and the other lead to the spark plug terminal (remove it from the spark plug for the test). Replace

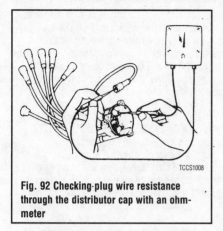

Fig. 92 Checking plug wire resistance through the distributor cap with an ohmmeter

Fig. 93 Checking individual plug wire resistance with a digital ohmmeter

Fig. 94 Grasp the spark plug wire by its boot, then gently twist and pull to remove

any wire which shows over 50,000 ohms. Generally speaking, however, resistance should run between 35,000–50,000 ohms.

Test the coil wire by connecting the ohmmeter between the center contact in the cap and either of the primary terminals at the coil. If the total resistance of the coil and the cable is more than 25,000 ohms, remove the cable from the coil and check the resistance of the cable. If the resistance is higher than 15,000 ohms, replace the cable. It should be remembered that wire resistance is a function of length and that the longer the cable, the greater the resistance. Thus, if the cables on your car are longer than the factory originals, resistance will be higher and quite possibly outside of these limits.

REMOVAL & INSTALLATION

▶ **See Figures 94 and 95**

When installing a new set of spark plug cables, replace the cables one at a time so that you can match up the length of each old plug wire with the new

ones and there will be no mix-up. Start by replacing the longest cable first. Install the boot firmly over the spark plug. Route the wire exactly the same as the original. Insert the nipple firmly into the tower on the distributor cap. Repeat the process for each cable.

➡ **On the CA16DE and CA18DE Pulsar engines, no spark plug wires are used.**

Distributor Cap and Rotor

REMOVAL & INSTALLATION

▶ **See Figures 96, 97, 98, 99 and 100**

➡ **The distributor cap may be concealed behind a protective flap or cover. If so, this cover must be unfastened in order to access the cap, rotor and spark plug wire boots.**

Fig. 95 This short wire runs from the distributor to the nearby ignition coil

Fig. 96 The distributor cap may be concealed behind a protective cover

Fig. 97 Unfasten the two clips or screws (shown) which retain the cap . . .

Fig. 98 . . . and remove the cap (with the spark plug wires attached)

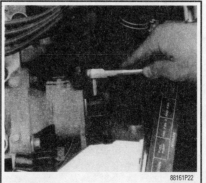

Fig. 99 If equipped, loosen the bolt which secures the rotor . . .

Fig. 100 . . . then pull the rotor straight off its shaft

1. Before disconnecting the spark plug wires, mark and label them along with their corresponding distributor cap towers to avoid confusion.

2. If so equipped, pry the two spring clips away from the distributor cap. Otherwise, loosen the two screws which retain the cap. Then, lift the cap away from the engine until it clears the rotor.

➡ **If a new cap and rotor are being installed, remove the old cap without disconnecting the spark plug wires. After replacing the rotor, hold the new cap next to the old one (so that they face the same direction) and transfer the wires to the corresponding terminals.**

3. If so equipped, loosen the bolt which retains the rotor, then pull the rotor straight off its shaft.

To install:

4. Line up the rotor with the end of the distributor shaft, then firmly push the rotor onto the shaft. If applicable, tighten the retaining bolt.

5. If installing a new cap, transfer the spark plug wires from the old cap.

6. Align the distributor cap properly over its base, then seat it securely. When properly positioned, the cap will not move.

7. If equipped with spring clips, snap them into position against the side of the cap. If equipped with screws, tighten them securely.

8. If so equipped, install the distributor cap's protective cover.

Ignition Timing

GENERAL INFORMATION

☀ CAUTION

When performing this or any other operation with the engine running, be very careful of the alternator belt and pulleys. Make sure that your timing light wires don't interfere with the belt. Also, avoid touching the spark plug wires while the engine is running. Failure to follow this caution may cause severe personal injury.

Ignition timing is an important part of the tune-up. The 3 basic types of timing lights are available, the neon, the DC and the AC powered. Of the 3 the DC light is the most frequently used by professional mechanics. The bright flash put out by the DC light makes the timing marks stand out on even the brightest of days. Another advantage of the DC light is that you don't need to be near an electrical outlet. Neon lights are available for a few dollars but their weak flash makes it necessary to use them in a fairly dark work area. The 1 neon light lead is attached to the spark plug and the other to the plug wire. The DC light attaches to the spark plug and the wire with an adapter and 2 clips attach to the battery posts for power. The AC unit is similar, except that the power cable is plugged into a house outlet.

Ignition timing is the measurement, in degrees of crankshaft rotation, of the point at which the spark plugs fire in each of the cylinders. It is measured in degrees before or after Top Dead Center (TDC) of the compression stroke. Basic Ignition timing is controlled by turning the distributor body in the engine. Electronic spark timing is controlled by the Electronic Control Unit (ECU).

Ideally, the air/fuel mixture in the cylinder will be ignited by the spark plug just as the piston passes TDC of the compression stroke. If this happens, the piston will be beginning its downward motion of the power stroke just as the compressed and ignited air/fuel mixture starts to expand. The expansion of the air/fuel mixture then forces the piston down on the power stroke and turns the crankshaft.

Because it takes a fraction of a second for the spark plug to ignite the mixture in the cylinder, the spark plug must fire a little before the piston reaches TDC. Otherwise, the mixture will not be completely ignited as the piston passes TDC and the full power of the explosion will not be used by the engine.

The timing measurement is given in degrees of crankshaft rotation before or after the piston reaches TDC (BTDC or ATDC). If the setting for the ignition timing is 5° BTDC, the spark plug must fire 5° before each piston reaches TDC. This only holds true, however, when the engine is at idle speed.

As the engine speed increases, the pistons go faster. The spark plugs have to ignite the fuel even sooner, if it is to be completely ignited when the piston reaches TDC. To do this, the distributor has a means to advance the timing of the spark as the engine speed increases. This is accomplished by centrifugal weights within the distributor and a vacuum diaphragm, mounted on the side of the distributor (vehicles without a crank angle sensor). It is necessary to disconnect the vacuum line from the diaphragm when the ignition timing is being set. 1987 and later vehicles are equipped with electronic spark timing to adjust timing as the engine rpm increases.

The timing is best checked with a timing light. This device is connected in series with the No. 1 spark plug. The current which fires the spark plug also causes the timing light to flash. The timing marks consist of a notch or cut out line on the crankshaft pulley and a numbered plate showing crankshaft rotation attached to the front cover. When the engine is running, the timing light is aimed at the marks on the crankshaft pulley and the pointer.

On 1987–88 models, the ECCS system controls the timing there is no mechanical or vacuum advance used in the distributor. Different sensors send signals to the ECU (ECCS control unit) which controls the timing.

On the CA16DE and CA18DE engines do not utilize a conventional distributor and spark plug wires. Instead, they use 4 small ignition coils fitted directly to each spark plug and a crank angle sensor mounted in the front timing belt.

INSPECTION & ADJUSTMENT

Except CA16DE, CA18DE, GA16DE and SR20DE Engines

▶ **See Figures 101 thru 107**

1. If equipped with an electronic ignition type distributor, check and/or adjust the reluctor air gap. For further information, refer to Section 2 of this manual.

2. Locate the timing marks on the crankshaft pulley and the front of the engine.

3. Clean off the timing marks so that you can see them.

4. Use chalk or white paint to color the mark on the crankshaft pulley and the mark on the scale which will indicate the correct timing when aligned with the notch on the crankshaft pulley.

5. Attach a tachometer and a timing light to the engine, according to the manufacturer's instructions.

6. Disconnect and plug the vacuum line at the distributor vacuum diaphragm, if so equipped. Distributors with a crank angle sensor or camshaft position sensor do not have a vacuum diaphragm. For distributors with a crank angle sensor or camshaft position sensor, proceed to Step 7.

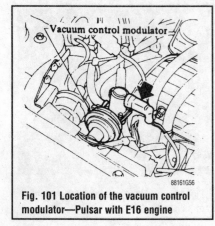

Fig. 101 Location of the vacuum control modulator—Pulsar with E16 engine

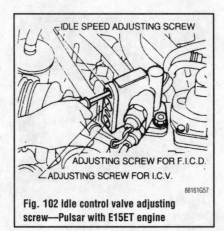

Fig. 102 Idle control valve adjusting screw—Pulsar with E15ET engine

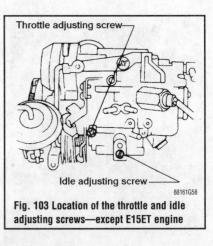

Fig. 103 Location of the throttle and idle adjusting screws—except E15ET engine

Fig. 104 Aim the timing light at the timing marks

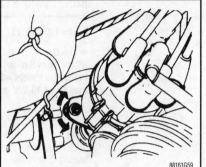

Fig. 105 Loosen the distributor lockbolt, then turn the distributor slightly to advance or retard the timing

Fig. 106 Watch for alignment of the timing marks as you rotate the distributor

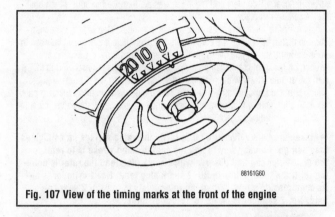

Fig. 107 View of the timing marks at the front of the engine

➡Vehicles which have a crank angle sensor (other than those models with CA16DE, CA18DE, GA16DE and SR20DE engines) include the turbocharged 1984 Pulsar, 1984–88 Pulsar with E16 engine (49 states), 1987–88 models with E16 engine (California and Canada), and 1989–90 Sentra/NX Coupe.

7. On the Pulsar E15ET engine (1984 Canadian Turbo), disconnect the Idle Control Valve (ICV) harness connector. On the Pulsar E16 engine (1984 and later, except California and Canada), disconnect the Vacuum Control Modulator (VCM) valve harness connector to adjust the idle speed, then reconnect the harness and make sure that the idle speed is within the proper range.

8. Check to make sure that all of the wires clear the fan and then start the engine. Allow the engine to reach normal operating temperature.

☀ CAUTION

Be sure to block the wheels and set the parking brake; if equipped with an automatic transaxle, place the shift selector in the DRIVE position.

9. Adjust the idle to the correct setting.

➡Before checking and/or adjusting the timing, make sure the electrical switches (such as those for the headlights, radiator cooling fan, heater blower and air conditioning) are turned OFF; if equipped with power steering, make sure that the wheels are faced straight ahead.

10. Aim the timing light at the timing marks at the front of the engine cover. If the timing marks are aligned when the light flashes, the timing is correct. Turn off the engine, then remove the tachometer and the timing light.

11. If the timing marks are not aligned, proceed with the following steps:
   a. Turn off the engine.
   b. Loosen the distributor lockbolt, just enough, so that the distributor can be turned with a little effort.
   c. Start the engine. Keep the wires of the timing light clear of the fan.
   d. With the timing light aimed at the crankshaft pulley and the timing plate on the engine, turn the distributor in the direction of rotor rotation to retard the spark and in the opposite direction to advance the spark. Align the marks on the pulley and the engine scale with the flashes of the timing light.
   e. Tighten the hold-down bolt. Remove the tachometer and the timing light.

CA16DE and CA18DE Engines

♦ See Figures 104, 108, 109 and 110

➡The CA16DE and CA18DE engines do not utilize a conventional distributor and high tension wires. Instead they use 4 small ignition coils fitted directly to each spark plug. The ECU controls the coils by means of a crank angle sensor. The crank angle sensor can be found attached to the upper front timing belt cover.

1. Run the engine until it reaches normal operating temperature.
2. Check that the idle speed is at specifications.
3. Disconnect the air duct and both air hoses at the throttle chamber.
4. Remove the ornament cover between the camshaft covers. It has 8 screws and says "Twin Cam".

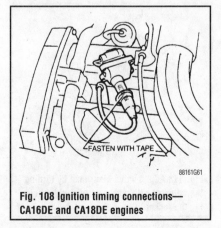

Fig. 108 Ignition timing connections—CA16DE and CA18DE engines

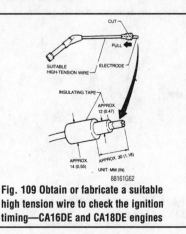

Fig. 109 Obtain or fabricate a suitable high tension wire to check the ignition timing—CA16DE and CA18DE engines

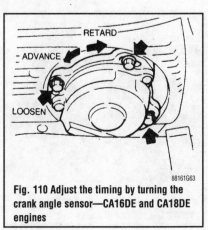

Fig. 110 Adjust the timing by turning the crank angle sensor—CA16DE and CA18DE engines

5. Remove the ignition coil at the No. 1 cylinder.
6. Connect the No. 1 ignition coil to the No. 1 spark plug with a suitable high tension wire.
7. Use an inductive pick-up type timing light and clamp it to the wire connected in Step 6.
8. Reconnect the air duct and hoses and then start the engine.
9. Check the ignition timing. If not to specifications, turn off the engine and loosen the crank angle sensor mounting bolts slightly.
10. Restart the engine and adjust the timing by turning the sensor body slightly until the timing comes into specifications.

GA16DE and SR20DE Engines

▶ **See Figures 104, 105 and 106**

1. Start the engine and allow it to reach normal operating temperature.
2. Run the engine at 2000 rpm for 2 minutes and return to idle.
3. Turn the engine **OFF** and disconnect the throttle position sensor harness connector.
4. Start the engine and race the engine to 2000 rpm, 3 times.
5. Connect a timing light to the No. 1 spark plug wire and battery.
6. Loosen the distributor hold-down bolt and adjust the ignition timing to 10 degrees BTDC for the GA16DE and 15 degrees for the SR20DE engines.
7. Turn the engine **OFF** and reconnect the throttle position sensor harness.

Valve Lash

Valve adjustment determines how far the valves enter the cylinder and how long they stay open and closed.

If the valve clearance is too large, part of the lift of the camshaft will be used in removing the excessive clearance. Consequently, the valve will not be opening as far as it should. This condition has 2 effects:
- The valve train components will emit a tapping sound as they take up the excessive clearance.
- The engine will perform poorly for the valves will not open fully and allow the proper amount of gases to flow through the cylinders.

If the valve clearance is too small, the valves will open too far and not fully seat in the cylinder head when they close. When a valve seats itself in the cylinder head, it does 2 things:
- It seals the combustion chamber so that none of the gases in the cylinder escape.
- It cools itself by transferring some of the heat it absorbs from the combustion process, through the cylinder head into the engine's cooling system.

If the valve clearance is too small, the engine will run poorly because of the gases escaping from the combustion chamber. The valves will also become overheated and warped, since they cannot transfer heat unless they are touching the valve seat in the cylinder head.

➡ **While all valve adjustments must be made as accurately as possible, it is better to have the valve adjustment slightly loose than slightly tight, as a burned valve may result from overly tight adjustments.**

EXCEPT GA16DE ENGINES

▶ **See Figures 111, 112 and 113**

➡ **The GA16i, CA16DE, CA18DE and SR20DE engines use hydraulic lifters. No valve adjustment is necessary or possible. Nissan recommends that valve adjustment on all other models be done every 12 months or 15,000 miles (24,000 km).**

1. Run the engine until it reaches normal operating temperature. Oil temperature, not water temperature, is critical to valve adjustment. With this in mind, make sure the engine is fully warmed up since this is the only way to make sure the parts have reached their full expansion. Generally speaking, this takes around 15 minutes. After the engine has reached normal operating temperature, shut it off.
2. Purchase a new valve cover gasket before removing the valve cover. The new silicone gasket sealers are just as good or better if you can't find a gasket.
3. Note the location of any hoses or wires which may interfere with valve cover removal, disconnect and move them aside. Remove the bolts which hold the valve cover in place.
4. After the valve cover has been removed, the next step is to get the number one piston at TDC on the compression stroke. There are at least two ways to do this: Bump the engine over with the starter or "turn it over" by using a wrench on the front crankshaft pulley bolt. The easiest way to find TDC is to turn the engine slowly with a wrench (after first removing No. 1 plug) until the piston is at the top of its stroke and the TDC timing mark on the crankshaft pulley is in alignment with the timing mark pointer. At this point, the valves for No. 1 cylinder should be closed.

➡ **Make sure both valves are closed with the valve springs up as high as they will go. An easy way to find the compression stroke is to remove the distributor cap and observe which spark plug lead the rotor is pointing to. If the rotor points to No. 1 spark plug lead, No. 1 cylinder is on its compression stroke. When the rotor points to the No. 2 spark plug lead, No. 2 cylinder is on its compression stroke.**

5. Set the No. 1 piston at TDC of the compression stroke, then check and/or adjust the valve clearance Nos. 1, 2, 3 and 6.
6. To adjust the clearance, loosen the locknut with a wrench and turn the adjuster with a screwdriver while holding the locknut. The correct size feeler gauge should pass with a slight drag between the rocker arm and the valve stem.
7. Turn the crankshaft one full revolution to position the No. 4 piston at TDC of the compression stroke. Check and/or adjust the valves (counting from the front to the rear) Nos. 4, 5, 7 and 8.
8. Replace the valve cover and torque the bolts on the valve cover down evenly.

GA16DE ENGINE

▶ **See Figures 114 thru 119**

1. Warm up the engine to normal operating temperature, then turn it **OFF**. Disconnect the negative battery cable.
2. Remove the valve cover and spark plugs.

Fig. 111 Set the No. 1 piston at TDC by turning the crankshaft pulley bolt

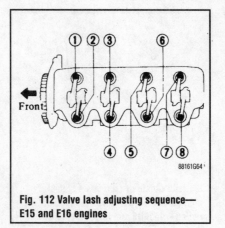

Fig. 112 Valve lash adjusting sequence—E15 and E16 engines

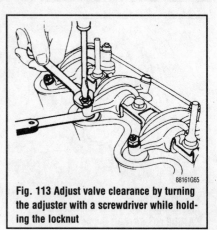

Fig. 113 Adjust valve clearance by turning the adjuster with a screwdriver while holding the locknut

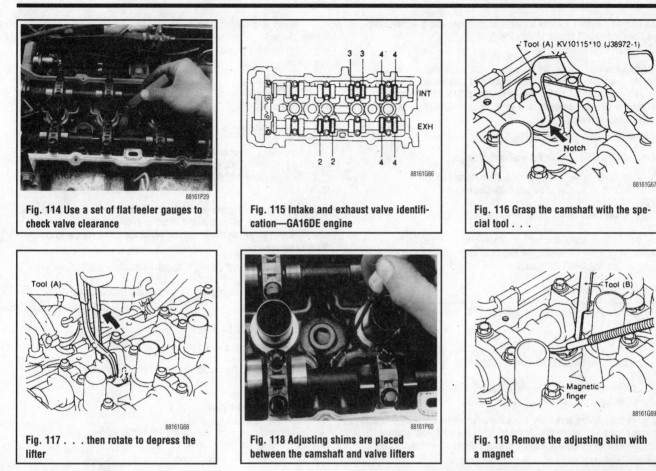

Fig. 114 Use a set of flat feeler gauges to check valve clearance

Fig. 115 Intake and exhaust valve identification—GA16DE engine

Fig. 116 Grasp the camshaft with the special tool . . .

Fig. 117 . . . then rotate to depress the lifter

Fig. 118 Adjusting shims are placed between the camshaft and valve lifters

Fig. 119 Remove the adjusting shim with a magnet

3. Set No. 1 cylinder to TDC of the compression stroke. Align the pointer with the TDC mark on the crankshaft pulley. Check that the valve lifters on No. 1 cylinder are loose and lifters for No. 4 cylinder are tight.

4. Check the valve clearance for intake valves of No. 1 and 2 cylinders. Check the clearance for exhaust valves of No. 1 and 3 cylinders.

5. Use a feeler gauge to measure the clearances:
- Intake valves (hot): 0.009–0.019 in. (0.23–0.48mm)
- Exhaust valves (hot): 0.012–0.023 in. (0.30–0.58mm)

6. Turn the crankshaft one revolution and align the TDC mark.

7. Check the valve clearance for intake valves of No. 3 and 4 cylinders. Check the clearance for exhaust valves of No. 2 and 4 cylinders.

8. To adjust the valves, turn the crankshaft so the camshaft lobe is in the upward position.

9. Place tool KVC10115110 or equivalent, under the camshaft. Rotate the tool so that the valve lifter is pushed down.

10. Place tool KV1011520 or equivalent, between the camshaft and the edge of the lifter. Remove tool KV10115110.

11. Remove the adjusting shim using a small prybar and a magnet.

12. Determine the replacement shim size using the following formula:
a. R = thickness of removed shim.
b. N = thickness of new shim.
c. M = measured valve clearance.
d. Intake valve N = R + (M—0.0146 in. (0.37mm)
e. Exhaust valve N = R + (M—0.0157 in. (0.40mm)

13. Shims are available in 50 sizes from 0.0787 in. (2.00mm) to 0.1173 in. (2.98mm).

14. Select a new shim with the thickness as close as possible to the calculated value.

15. Install the new shim using the tool.

16. Recheck all clearances after the new shims have been installed.

17. Install a new valve cover gasket and valve cover.

18. Install the remaining components, start the engine and check operation.

19. If the engine has an unusually rough idle, the valve clearance may be too tight. If this is the case, readjust the valve clearance before internal engine damage.

Idle Speed Adjustment

CARBURETED ENGINES

✷✷ CAUTION

When checking the idle speed, set the parking brake and block the drive wheels.

E15 and E16 Engines

▶ See Figure 120

1. Connect a tachometer to the engine according the manufacturer's instructions.

2. Start the engine and run it until it reaches normal operating temperatures.

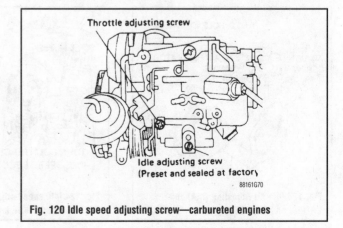

Fig. 120 Idle speed adjusting screw—carbureted engines

3. Operate it at idle for 2 minutes under no-load, then race to 2,000–3,000 a few times and allow it to return to idle speed.

4. Turn **OFF** the engine.

➡️**For USA models, disconnect the vacuum control modulator harness connector. For Canada models, disconnect and plug the air induction hose at the air filter; also, for Canada models (1984–86), disconnect and plug the throttle opener control valve vacuum hose at the throttle opener control valve side.**

5. Start the engine and check the idle speed.

➡️**If the cooling fan is operating, wait until it stops.**

6. If equipped with a manual transaxle, place the shift selector in **NEUTRAL**; if equipped with an automatic transaxle, place the shift selector in **DRIVE**.

7. If the idle speed is not correct, adjust the throttle adjusting screw at the carburetor.

8. When the idle speed is correct, stop the engine, reconnect the vacuum control modulator and the throttle opener control valve vacuum hose (if equipped), then disconnect the tachometer.

FUEL INJECTED ENGINES

E16i Engine

▶ **See Figure 121**

1. Connect a tachometer to the engine, according to the manufacturer's instructions.

2. Start and operate the engine until it reaches normal operating temperatures. Operate the engine for 5 minutes under no load.

➡️**Engage the parking brake and block the drive wheels. If equipped with a manual transaxle, place the shift selector in the NEUTRAL position. If equipped with an automatic transaxle, place the shift selector in the DRIVE position.**

3. Check and/or adjust the engine speed. If necessary to adjust, turn the idle speed adjusting screw on the Idle Air Adjusting (IAA) unit.

4. With the idle speed adjusted, stop the engine and disconnect the tachometer.

E15ET Engine

▶ **See Figure 122**

1. Connect a tachometer to the engine, according to the manufacturer's instructions.

2. Start and run the engine until it reaches normal operating temperatures. Operate the engine at 2,000 rpm, for 2 minutes under no-load.

3. Race the engine to 2,000–3,000 rpm a few times and allow it to go to idle speed.

➡️**Engage the parking brake and block the drive wheels. If equipped with a manual transaxle, place the shift selector in the NEUTRAL position. If equipped with an automatic transaxle, place the shift selector in the DRIVE position.**

4. Check and/or adjust the engine speed. If necessary to adjust, turn the throttle adjusting screw in the idle control valve.

5. With the idle speed adjusted, stop the engine and disconnect the tachometer.

CA16DE and CA18DE Engines

▶ **See Figures 123, 124 and 125**

1. Before adjusting the idle speed on these engines, visually check the following items:
- air cleaner for clogs
- hoses and ducts for leaks
- EGR valve for proper operation
- all electrical connectors, gaskets and the throttle valve
- throttle valve switch (CA16DE engine only)
- idle switch (CA18DE engine only)

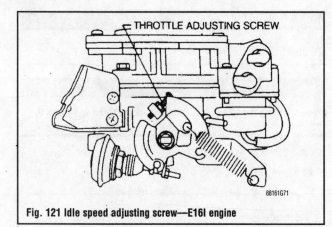
Fig. 121 Idle speed adjusting screw—E16I engine

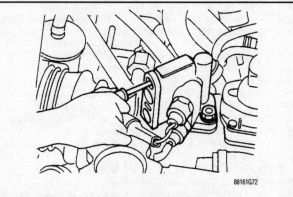
Fig. 122 Idle speed adjusting screw—E15ET engine

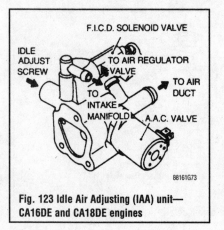
Fig. 123 Idle Air Adjusting (IAA) unit—CA16DE and CA18DE engines

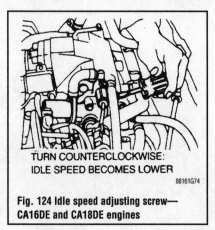
Fig. 124 Idle speed adjusting screw—CA16DE and CA18DE engines

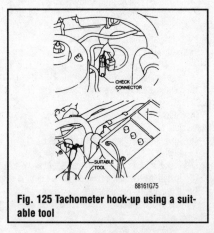
Fig. 125 Tachometer hook-up using a suitable tool

2. Start the engine and warm the engine so it reaches normal operating temperature. The water temperature indicator should be in the middle of the gauge.

3. Then race the engine to 2,000–3,000 rpm a few times under no load and then allow it to return to the idle speed.

4. Connect a voltage type tachometer to the engine by using a suitable type tool in the check connector for a lead outlet.

5. Check the idle speed on the manual transaxle model in **NEUTRAL** and on the automatic transaxle model check in **DRIVE**.

6. If the idle speed has to be adjusted you must disconnect the Auxiliary Air Control (AAC) valve harness connector.

7. Adjust the idle speed by turning the idle speed adjusting screw on the Idle Air Adjusting (IAA) unit.

8. Recheck the engine idle speed.

GA16i, GA16DE and SR20DE Engines

1. Before adjusting the idle speed on these engines you must visually check the following items first: air cleaner for being clogged, hoses and ducts for leaks, EGR valve for proper operation, all electrical connectors, gaskets and the throttle valve and throttle valve switch.

2. Start the engine and warm the engine so it reaches normal operating temperature. The water temperature indicator should be in the middle of the gauge.

3. Then race the engine to 2,000–3,000 rpm a few times under no load and then allow it to return to the idle speed.

4. Connect a voltage type tachometer to the engine by using a suitable type tool in the check connector for a lead outlet.

5. Check the idle speed with the transaxle in **NEUTRAL**.

6. Turn the engine **OFF** and disconnect the throttle valve switch at the throttle body assembly.

7. Start the engine and check idle speed. If not within specifications, turn the idle adjusting screw at the throttle body until idle is within specifications. Race the engine to 2,000–3,000 rpm and recheck the idle speed.

8. Turn the engine **OFF** and reconnect the throttle valve switch.

Idle Mixture Adjustment

CARBURETED ENGINES

♦ See Figures 126 and 127

➡**Idle mixture is adjusted on carbureted vehicles only, and then only by using a "CO meter", an expensive engine testing device used typically by well-equipped repair shops in the repair of emission system problems. Before attempting to adjust CO, make sure there are no vacuum system leaks, tuning problems (idle speed, ignition timing, spark plug condition or gap problems), or engine operating problems such as burned or misadjusted valves. It is possible that, if your car idles roughly in the absence of any of these problems, the cost of having the CO adjusted can be reduced by following the procedure given here.**

1. Remove the carburetor from the engine as described in Section 5.

2. Locate the seal plug to the right of and below the idle speed screw. Select a drill bit that is **considerably smaller** than the diameter of the orifice in the carburetor casting into which the plug is mounted.

3. Drill very cautiously and slowly. Feel for the point where the drill **just** penetrates the inner end of the plug. Don't drill farther, or the carburetor mixture screw will be damaged.

4. Once you have drilled through the plug, use a less brittle metal object that will fit through the hole in the plug to pry it out of the carburetor orifice. Carefully clean all metal shavings out of the bore so the mixture screw threads will not be damaged.

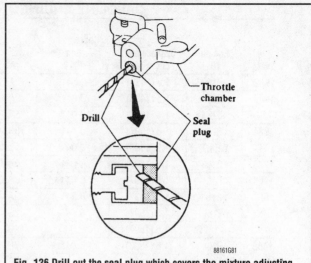

Fig. 126 Drill out the seal plug which covers the mixture adjusting screw

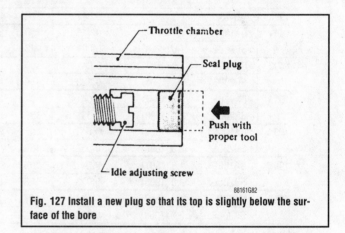

Fig. 127 Install a new plug so that its top is slightly below the surface of the bore

5. Reinstall the carburetor. Be sure to use a new gasket and make sure all vacuum lines are securely connected.

6. Have the person adjusting the CO with the required equipment follow these procedures:

   a. Run the engine until it is hot. Then, shut it off.

   b. Disconnect the air/fuel ratio solenoid harness connector. Disconnect the air induction hose from the air cleaner and plug or cap the hose.

   c. Start the engine and race it three times to 2,500 rpm. Then, allow it to idle.

   d. Insert the CO meter probe 16 in. (41cm) into the tailpipe. Read the CO level. If necessary, adjust the mixture screw to obtain 4–6% for California and Canadian cars, and 2–4% for 49 States cars.

7. Tap a new seal plug squarely into the carburetor bore with an object with a perfectly flat front. The object should be just slightly smaller than the bore.

8. Restore all disconnected hoses and electrical connectors. Then, repeat the idle speed adjustment procedure above.

FUEL INJECTED ENGINES

Fuel injected engines fuel mixture is controlled by the Electronic Control Unit (ECU). No fuel mixture adjustment is necessary or possible.

GASOLINE ENGINE TUNE-UP SPECIFICATIONS

Year	Engine ID	Engine Displacement Liters (cc)	Spark Plugs Gap (in.)	Ignition Timing (deg.)		Fuel Pump (psi)	Idle Speed (rpm)		Valve Clearance	
				MT	AT		MT	AT	In.	Ex.
1982	E15	1.5 (1488)	0.041	2A ①	6A	3.0–3.8	750	650	0.011	0.011
1983	E15	1.5 (1488)	0.041	2A	—	3.0–3.8	700	—	0.011	0.011
	E16	1.6 (1597)	0.041	5A	5A	3.0–3.8	750	650	0.011	0.011
1984	E16	1.6 (1597)	0.041	15B	15B	2.8–3.8	750	650	0.011	0.011
	E15ET	1.5 (1488)	0.041	15B②	8B②	30–37	800③	650	0.011	0.011
1985	E16	1.6 (1597)	0.041	15B②	8B②	2.8–3.8	800③	650	0.011	0.011
1986	E16	1.6 (1597)	0.041	10B②	10B②	2.8–3.8	800	650	0.011	0.011
1987	E16	1.6 (1597)	0.041	2A	2A	2.8–3.8	800	700	0.011	0.011
	E16i	1.6 (1597)	0.041	7B	7B	⑨	800	700	0.011	0.011
	CA16DE	1.6 (1597)	⑦	15B	—	36	800	—	Hyd.	Hyd.
1988	E16i	1.6 (1597)	0.041	7B	7B	⑨	800	700	0.011	0.011
	CA18DE	1.8 (1809)	⑦	15B	15B	36	800	700	Hyd.	Hyd.
1989	GA16i	1.6 (1597)	0.041	7B	7B	34	800	750	Hyd.	Hyd.
	CA18DE	1.8 (1809)	⑦	15B	15B	36	800	700	Hyd.	Hyd.
1990	GA16i	1.6 (1597)	0.041	7B	7B	34	800	900	Hyd.	Hyd.
1991	GA16DE	1.6 (1597)	0.041	10B	10B	36	650⑧	800	0.015	0.016
	SR20DE	2.0 (1998)	0.033	15B	15B	36	800	800	Hyd.	Hyd.
1992	GA16DE	1.6 (1597)	0.041	10B	10B	36	650⑧	800	0.015	0.016
	SR20DE	2.0 (1998)	0.033	15B	15B	36	800	800	Hyd.	Hyd.
1993	GA16DE	1.6 (1597)	0.041	10B	10B	36	650⑧	800	0.015	0.016
	SR20DE	2.0 (1998)	0.033	15B	15B	36	800	800	Hyd.	Hyd.
1994	GA16DE	1.6 (1597)	0.041	10B	10B	36	650⑧	800	0.015	0.016
	SR20DE	2.0 (1998)	0.033	15B	15B	36	800	800	Hyd.	Hyd.
1995	GA16DE	1.6 (1597)	0.041	10B	10B	36	650⑧	800	0.015	0.016
	SR20DE	2.0 (1998)	0.033	15B	15B	36	800	800	Hyd.	Hyd.
1996	GA16DE	1.6 (1597)	0.041	10B	10B	36	650⑧	800	0.015	0.016
	SR20DE	2.0 (1998)	0.033	15B	15B	36	800	800	Hyd.	Hyd.

NOTE: The lowest cylinder pressure should be within 75% of the highest cylinder pressure reading. For example, if the highest cylinder is 134 psi, the lowest should be 101. Engine should be at normal operating temperature with throttle valve in the wide open position.
The underhood specifications sticker often reflects tune-up specification changes in production. Sticker figures must be used if they disagree with those in this chart.

① Canada—4A
② California and Canada—5A
③ California and Canada—750
④ Turbo
⑤ EFI
⑥ DOHC
⑦ Do not adjust plug gap
⑧ Canada—750
⑨ 14 psi—2WD
37 psi—4WD

88161C03

Air Conditioning System

SYSTEM SERVICE & REPAIR

➡It is recommended that the A/C system be serviced by an EPA Section 609 certified automotive technician utilizing a refrigerant recovery/recycling machine.

The do-it-yourselfer should not service his/her own vehicle's A/C system for many reasons, including legal concerns, personal injury, environmental damage and cost.

According to the U.S. Clean Air Act, it is a federal crime to service or repair (involving the refrigerant) a Motor Vehicle Air Conditioning (MVAC) system for money without being EPA certified. It is also illegal to vent R-12 and R-134a refrigerants into the atmosphere. State and/or local laws may be more strict than the federal regulations, so be sure to check with your state and/or local authorities for further information.

➡Federal law dictates that a fine of up to $25,000 may be levied on people convicted of venting refrigerant into the atmosphere.

When servicing an A/C system you run the risk of handling or coming in contact with refrigerant, which may result in skin or eye irritation or frostbite. Although low in toxicity (due to chemical stability), inhalation of concentrated refrigerant fumes is dangerous and can result in death; cases of fatal cardiac arrhythmia have been reported in people accidentally subjected to high levels of refrigerant. Some early symptoms include loss of concentration and drowsiness.

➡Generally, the limit for exposure is lower for R-134a than it is for R-12. Exceptional care must be practiced when handling R-134a.

Also, some refrigerants can decompose at high temperatures (near gas heaters or open flame), which may result in hydrofluoric acid, hydrochloric acid and phosgene (a fatal nerve gas).

It is usually more economically feasible to have a certified MVAC automotive technician perform A/C system service on your vehicle.

R-12 Refrigerant Conversion

If your vehicle still uses R-12 refrigerant, one way to save A/C system costs down the road is to investigate the possibility of having your system converted to R-134a. The older R-12 systems can be easily converted to R-134a refrigerant by a certified automotive technician by installing a few new components and changing the system oil.

The cost of R-12 is steadily rising and will continue to increase, because it is no longer imported or manufactured in the United States. Therefore, it is often possible to have an R-12 system converted to R-134a and recharged for less than it would cost to just charge the system with R-12.

If you are interested in having your system converted, contact local automotive service stations for more details and information.

PREVENTIVE MAINTENANCE

Although the A/C system should not be serviced by the do-it-yourselfer, preventive maintenance should be practiced to help maintain the efficiency of the vehicle's A/C system. Be sure to perform the following:

• The easiest and most important preventive maintenance for your A/C system is to be sure that it is used on a regular basis. Running the system for five minutes each month (no matter what the season) will help ensure that the seals and all internal components remain lubricated.

➡**Some vehicles automatically operate the A/C system compressor whenever the windshield defroster is activated. Therefore, the A/C system would not need to be operated each month if the defroster was used.**

• In order to prevent heater core freeze-up during A/C operation, it is necessary to maintain proper antifreeze protection. Be sure to properly maintain the engine cooling system.

• Any obstruction of or damage to the condenser configuration will restrict air flow which is essential to its efficient operation. Keep this unit clean and in proper physical shape.

➡**Bug screens which are mounted in front of the condenser (unless they are original equipment) are regarded as obstructions.**

• The condensation drain tube expels any water which accumulates on the bottom of the evaporator housing into the engine compartment. If this tube is obstructed, the air conditioning performance can be restricted and condensation buildup can spill over onto the vehicle's floor.

SYSTEM INSPECTION

Although the A/C system should not be serviced by the do-it-yourselfer, system inspections should be performed to help maintain the efficiency of the vehicle's A/C system. Be sure to perform the following:

The easiest and often most important check for the air conditioning system consists of a visual inspection of the system components. Visually inspect the system for refrigerant leaks, damaged compressor clutch, abnormal compressor drive belt tension and/or condition, plugged evaporator drain tube, blocked condenser fins, disconnected or broken wires, blown fuses, corroded connections and poor insulation.

A refrigerant leak will usually appear as an oily residue at the leakage point in the system. The oily residue soon picks up dust or dirt particles from the surrounding air and appears greasy. Through time, this will build up and appear to be a heavy dirt impregnated grease.

For a thorough visual and operational inspection, check the following:
• Check the surface of the radiator and condenser for dirt, leaves or other material which might block air flow.
• Check for kinks in hoses and lines. Check the system for leaks.
• Make sure the drive belt is properly tensioned. During operation, make sure the belt is free of noise or slippage.
• Make sure the blower motor operates at all appropriate positions, then check for distribution of the air from all outlets.

➡**Remember that in high humidity, air discharged from the vents may not feel as cold as expected, even if the system is working properly. This is because moisture in humid air retains heat more effectively than dry air, thereby making humid air more difficult to cool.**

Windshield Wipers

ELEMENT (REFILL) CARE & REPLACEMENT

▶ **See Figures 128, 129 and 130**

For maximum effectiveness and longest element life, the windshield and wiper blades should be kept clean. Dirt, tree sap, road tar and so on will cause streaking, smearing and blade deterioration if left on the glass. It is advisable to wash the windshield carefully with a commercial glass cleaner at least once a month. Wipe off the rubber blades with the wet rag afterwards. Do not attempt to move wipers across the windshield by hand; damage to the motor and drive mechanism will result.

To inspect and/or replace the wiper blade elements, place the wiper switch in the **LOW** speed position and the ignition switch in the **ACC** position. When the wiper blades are approximately vertical on the windshield, turn the ignition switch to **OFF**.

Examine the wiper blade elements. If they are found to be cracked, broken or torn, they should be replaced immediately. Replacement intervals will vary with usage, although ozone deterioration usually limits element life to about one year. If the wiper pattern is smeared or streaked, or if the blade chatters across the glass, the elements should be replaced. It is easiest and most sensible to replace the elements in pairs.

If your vehicle is equipped with aftermarket blades, there are several different types of refills and your vehicle might have any kind. Aftermarket blades and arms rarely use the exact same type blade or refill as the original equipment.

Regardless of the type of refill used, be sure to follow the part manufacturer's instructions closely. Make sure that all of the frame jaws are engaged as the refill is pushed into place and locked. If the metal blade holder and frame are allowed to touch the glass during wiper operation, the glass will be scratched.

Tires and Wheels

Common sense and good driving habits will afford maximum tire life. Make sure that you don't overload the vehicle or run with incorrect pressure in the tires. Either of these will increase tread wear. Fast starts, sudden stops and sharp cornering are hard on tires and will shorten their useful life span.

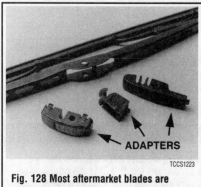

TCCS1223

Fig. 128 Most aftermarket blades are available with multiple adapters to fit different vehicles

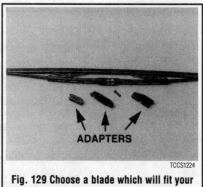

TCCS1224

Fig. 129 Choose a blade which will fit your vehicle, and that will be readily available next time you need blades

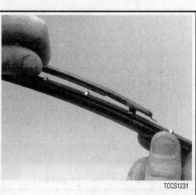

TCCS1231

Fig. 130 When installed, be certain the blade is fully inserted into the backing

➡**For optimum tire life, keep the tires properly inflated, rotate them often and have the wheel alignment checked periodically.**

Inspect your tires frequently. Be especially careful to watch for bubbles in the tread or sidewall, deep cuts or underinflation. Replace any tires with bubbles in the sidewall. If cuts are so deep that they penetrate to the cords, discard the tire. Any cut in the sidewall of a radial tire renders it unsafe. Also look for uneven tread wear patterns that may indicate the front end is out of alignment or that the tires are out of balance.

TIRE ROTATION

▶ **See Figure 131**

Tires must be rotated periodically to equalize wear patterns that vary with a tire's position on the vehicle. Tires will also wear in an uneven way as the front steering/suspension system wears to the point where the alignment should be reset.

Rotating the tires will ensure maximum life for the tires as a set, so you will not have to discard a tire early due to wear on only part of the tread. Regular rotation is required to equalize wear.

When rotating "unidirectional tires," make sure that they always roll in the same direction. This means that a tire used on the left side of the vehicle must not be switched to the right side and vice-versa. Such tires should only be rotated front-to-rear or rear-to-front, while always remaining on the same side of the vehicle. These tires are marked on the sidewall as to the direction of rotation; observe the marks when reinstalling the tire(s).

Some styled or "mag" wheels may have different offsets front to rear. In these cases, the rear wheels must not be used up front and vice-versa. Furthermore, if these wheels are equipped with unidirectional tires, they cannot be rotated unless the tire is remounted for the proper direction of rotation.

➡**The compact or space-saver spare is strictly for emergency use. It must never be included in the tire rotation or placed on the vehicle for everyday use.**

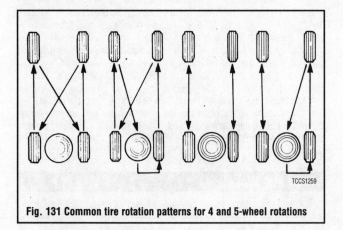

Fig. 131 Common tire rotation patterns for 4 and 5-wheel rotations

TCCS1259

TIRE DESIGN

▶ **See Figure 132**

For maximum satisfaction, tires should be used in sets of four. Mixing of different brands or types (radial, bias-belted, fiberglass belted) should be avoided. In most cases, the vehicle manufacturer has designated a type of tire on which the vehicle will perform best. Your first choice when replacing tires should be to use the same type of tire that the manufacturer recommends.

When radial tires are used, tire sizes and wheel diameters should be selected to maintain ground clearance and tire load capacity equivalent to the original specified tire. Radial tires should always be used in sets of four.

✳✳ CAUTION

Radial tires should never be used on only the front axle.

When selecting tires, pay attention to the original size as marked on the tire. Most tires are described using an industry size code sometimes referred to as

P-Metric. This allows the exact identification of the tire specifications, regardless of the manufacturer. If selecting a different tire size or brand, remember to check the installed tire for any sign of interference with the body or suspension while the vehicle is stopping, turning sharply or heavily loaded.

Snow Tires

Good radial tires can produce a big advantage in slippery weather, but in snow, a street radial tire does not have sufficient tread to provide traction and control. The small grooves of a street tire quickly pack with snow and the tire behaves like a billiard ball on a marble floor. The more open, chunky tread of a snow tire will self-clean as the tire turns, providing much better grip on snowy surfaces.

To satisfy municipalities requiring snow tires during weather emergencies, most snow tires carry either an M + S designation after the tire size stamped on the sidewall, or the designation "all-season." In general, no change in tire size is necessary when buying snow tires.

Most manufacturers strongly recommend the use of 4 snow tires on their vehicles for reasons of stability. If snow tires are fitted only to the drive wheels, the opposite end of the vehicle may become very unstable when braking or turning on slippery surfaces. This instability can lead to unpleasant endings if the driver can't counteract the slide in time.

Note that snow tires, whether 2 or 4, will affect vehicle handling in all non-snow situations. The stiffer, heavier snow tires will noticeably change the turning and braking characteristics of the vehicle. Once the snow tires are installed, you must re-learn the behavior of the vehicle and drive accordingly.

➡**Consider buying extra wheels on which to mount the snow tires. Once done, the "snow wheels" can be installed and removed as needed. This eliminates the potential damage to tires or wheels from seasonal removal and installation. Even if your vehicle has styled wheels, see if inexpensive steel wheels are available. Although the look of the vehicle will change, the expensive wheels will be protected from salt, curb hits and pothole damage.**

TIRE STORAGE

If they are mounted on wheels, store the tires at proper inflation pressure. All tires should be kept in a cool, dry place. If they are stored in the garage or basement, do not let them stand on a concrete floor; set them on strips of wood, a mat or a large stack of newspaper. Keeping them away from direct moisture is of paramount importance. Tires should not be stored upright, but in a flat position.

INFLATION & INSPECTION

▶ **See Figures 133 thru 139**

The importance of proper tire inflation cannot be overemphasized. A tire employs air as part of its structure. It is designed around the supporting strength of the air at a specified pressure. For this reason, improper inflation drastically reduces the tire's ability to perform as intended. A tire will lose some air in day-to-day use; having to add a few pounds of air periodically is not necessarily a sign of a leaking tire.

Two items should be a permanent fixture in every glove compartment: an accurate tire pressure gauge and a tread depth gauge. Check the tire pressure (including the spare) regularly with a pocket type gauge. Too often, the gauge on the end of the air hose at your corner garage is not accurate because it suffers too much abuse. Always check tire pressure when the tires are cold, as pressure increases with temperature. If you must move the vehicle to check the tire inflation, do not drive more than a mile before checking. A cold tire is generally one that has not been driven for more than three hours.

A plate or sticker is normally provided somewhere in the vehicle (door post, hood, tailgate or trunk lid) which shows the proper pressure for the tires. Never counteract excessive pressure build-up by bleeding off air pressure (letting some air out). This will cause the tire to run hotter and wear quicker.

✳✳ CAUTION

Never exceed the maximum tire pressure embossed on the tire! This is the pressure to be used when the tire is at maximum loading, but it is rarely the correct pressure for everyday driving. Consult the owner's manual or the tire pressure sticker for the correct tire pressure.

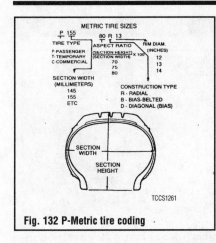

Fig. 132 P-Metric tire coding

Fig. 133 Tires with deep cuts, or cuts which bulge, should be replaced immediately

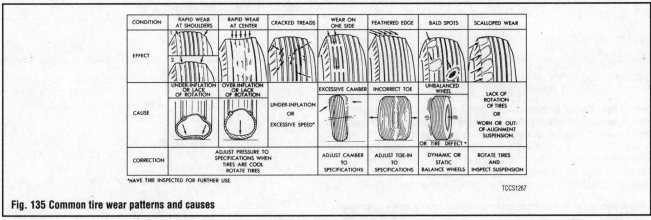

Fig. 134 Radial tires have a characteristic sidewall bulge; don't try to measure pressure by looking at the tire. Use a quality air pressure gauge

Fig. 135 Common tire wear patterns and causes

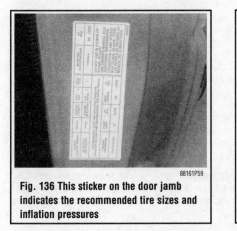

Fig. 136 This sticker on the door jamb indicates the recommended tire sizes and inflation pressures

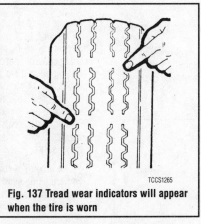

Fig. 137 Tread wear indicators will appear when the tire is worn

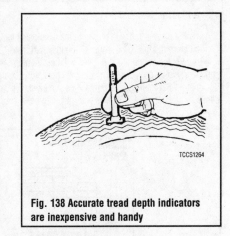

Fig. 138 Accurate tread depth indicators are inexpensive and handy

Once you've maintained the correct tire pressures for several weeks, you'll be familiar with the vehicle's braking and handling personality. Slight adjustments

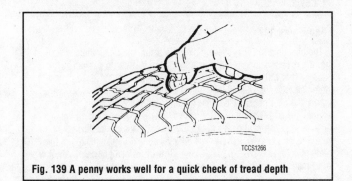

Fig. 139 A penny works well for a quick check of tread depth

in tire pressures can fine-tune these characteristics, but never change the cold pressure specification by more than 2 psi. A slightly softer tire pressure will give a softer ride but also yield lower fuel mileage. A slightly harder tire will give crisper dry road handling but can cause skidding on wet surfaces. Unless you're fully attuned to the vehicle, stick to the recommended inflation pressures.

All automotive tires have built-in tread wear indicator bars that show up as ½ in. (13mm) wide smooth bands across the tire when ¹⁄₁₆ in. (1.5mm) of tread remains. The appearance of tread wear indicators means that the tires should be replaced. In fact, many states have laws prohibiting the use of tires with less than this amount of tread.

You can check your own tread depth with an inexpensive gauge or by using a Lincoln head penny. Slip the Lincoln penny (with Lincoln's head upside-down) into several tread grooves. If you can see the top of Lincoln's head in 2 adjacent grooves, the tire has less than ¹⁄₁₆ in. (1.5mm) tread left and should be replaced. You can measure snow tires in the same manner by using the "tails" side of the Lincoln penny. If you can see the top of the Lincoln memorial, it's time to replace the snow tire(s).

FLUIDS AND LUBRICANTS

Fluid Disposal

Used fluids such as engine oil, transmission fluid, antifreeze and brake fluid are hazardous wastes and must be disposed of properly. Before draining any fluids, consult with your local authorities; in many areas, waste oil, antifreeze, etc. is being accepted as a part of recycling programs. A number of service stations and auto parts stores are also accepting waste fluids for recycling.

Be sure of the recycling center's policies before draining any fluids, as many will not accept different fluids that have been mixed together.

Fuel Recommendations

All engines covered in this book have been designed to run on unleaded fuel. The minimum octane requirement for non-turbo and high performance engines is 91 Research Octane Number (RON) or 87 Anti-Knock Index (AKI). Turbo and high performance engine require an octane of 93 RON. All unleaded fuels sold in the U.S. are required to meet minimum octane ratings.

The use of a fuel too low in octane (a measurement of anti-knock quality) will result in spark knock. Since many factors such as altitude, terrain, air temperature and humidity affect the operating efficiency, knocking may result even though the recommended fuel is being used. If persistent knocking occurs, it may be necessary to switch to a higher grade of fuel. Continuous or heavy knocking may result in engine damage.

➡**Your engine's fuel requirement can change with time, mainly due to carbon buildup, which will in turn change the compression ratio. If your engine pings, knocks or runs on, switch to a higher grade of fuel. Sometimes just changing brands will cure the problem. If it becomes necessary to retard the timing from the specifications, don't change it more than a few degrees. Retarded timing will reduce power output and fuel mileage, in addition to increasing the engine temperature.**

Engine Oil Recommendations

◆ **See Figures 140 and 141**

Oil must be selected with regard to the anticipated temperatures during the period before the next oil change. Using the chart, select the oil viscosity for the lowest expected temperature and you will be assured of easy cold starting and sufficient engine protection. The oil you pour into your engine should have the designation **SH** marked on the top of its container. Cheap engine oil is cheap engine protection. Is a few cents worth the engine in your vehicle?

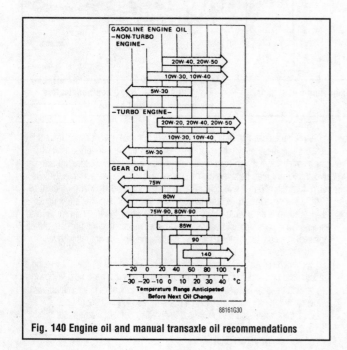

Fig. 140 Engine oil and manual transaxle oil recommendations

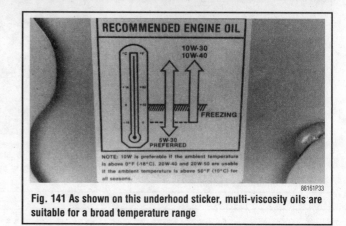

Fig. 141 As shown on this underhood sticker, multi-viscosity oils are suitable for a broad temperature range

SYNTHETIC OIL

There are many excellent synthetic and fuel-efficient oils currently available that can provide better gas mileage, longer service life, and in some cases better engine protection. These benefits do not come without a few hitches, however the main one being the price of synthetic oils, which is 3 or 4 times the price per quart of conventional oil.

Synthetic oil is not for every car and every type of driving, so you should consider your engine's condition and your type of driving. Also, check your car's warranty guidelines at the dealership that you purchased the car from, regarding the use of synthetic oils and your powertrain and or extended warranty.

Both brand new engines and older, high mileage engines are the wrong candidates for synthetic oil. The synthetic oils are so slippery that they can prevent the proper break-in of new engines; most manufacturers recommend that you wait until the engine is properly broken in (5,000 miles/8,051 km) until using synthetic oil. Older engines with wear have a different problem with synthetics: they use (consume during operation) more oil as they age. Slippery synthetic oils get past these worn parts easily. If your engine is using conventional oil, it will use synthetics much faster. Also, if your car is leaking oil past old seals you'll have a much greater leak problem with synthetics.

Cars used under harder circumstances, such as stop-and-go, city type driving, short trips, or extended idling, should be serviced more frequently. For the engines in these cars, the much greater cost of synthetic or fuel-efficient oils may not be worth the investment. Internal wear increases much quicker on these cars, causing greater oil consumption and leakage.

➡**The mixing of conventional and synthetic oils is not recommended. If you are using synthetic oil, it might be wise to carry 2 or 3 quarts with you no matter where you drive, as not all service stations carry this type of lubricant.**

Engine

OIL LEVEL CHECK

◆ **See Figure 142**

The best time to check the engine oil is before operating the engine or after it has been sitting for at least 10 minutes in order to gain an accurate reading. This will allow the oil to drain back in the crankcase. To check the engine oil level, make sure that the vehicle is resting on a level surface, remove the oil dipstick, wipe it clean and reinsert the stick firmly for an accurate reading. The oil dipstick has two marks to indicate high and low oil level. If the oil is at or below the **low level** mark on the dipstick, oil should be added as necessary. The oil level should be maintained in the safety margin, neither going above the **high level** mark or below the **low level** mark.

Fig. 142 To check the oil level, remove the dipstick from its tube

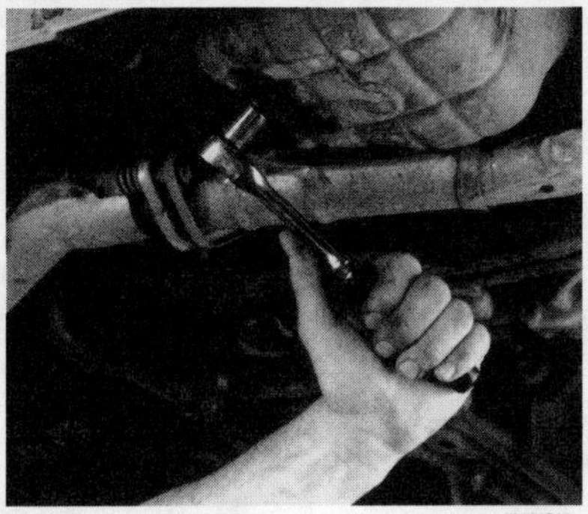

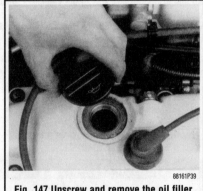

Fig. 143 Use the correct size wrench to loosen the drain plug

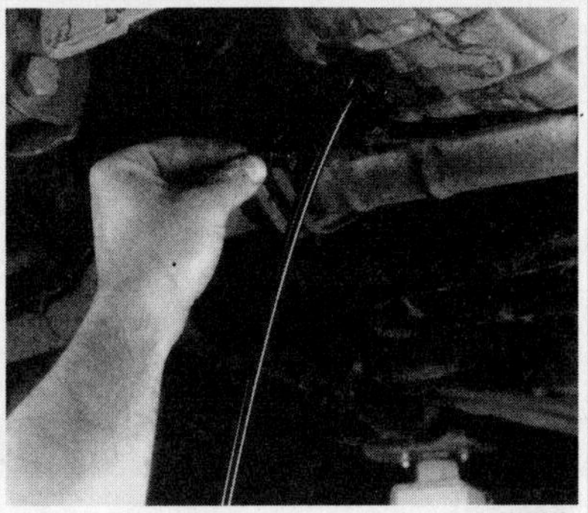

Fig. 144 Remove the plug, allowing the oil to drain into a suitable container

OIL AND FILTER CHANGE

▶ See Figures 143 thru 149

➡Nissan factory maintenance intervals (every 7500 miles or 12,077 km) specify changing the oil filter at every second oil change after the initial service. We recommend replacing the oil filter with every oil change. For the small price of an oil filter, it's cheap insurance to replace the filter at every oil change. One of the larger filter manufacturers points out in its advertisements that not changing the filter leaves about 1 quart (0.95L) of dirty oil in the engine. This claim is true and should be kept in mind when changing your oil.

1. Run the engine until it reaches normal operating temperature.
2. Jack up the front of the car and support it on safety stands if necessary to gain access to the filter.
3. Slide a drain pan of at least 6 quarts (5.7L) capacity under the oil pan.

4. Loosen the drain plug. Turn the plug out by hand. By keeping an inward pressure on the plug as you unscrew it, oil won't escape past the threads and you can remove it without being burned by hot oil.
5. Allow the oil to drain completely and then install the drain plug. Don't overtighten the plug or you'll be buying a new pan or a trick replacement plug for damaged threads.
6. Using a strap wrench (or other specialized oil filter removal tool, such as a cap wrench), remove the oil filter. Keep in mind that it's holding about 1 quart (0.95L) of dirty, hot oil.
7. Empty the old filter into the drain pan and dispose of the filter and old oil.

➡One ecologically desirable solution to the used oil disposal problem is to find a cooperative gas station owner who will allow you to dump your used oil into his tank or take the oil to a reclamation center (often at garages and gas stations.

8. Using a clean rag, wipe off the filter adapter on the engine block. Be sure that the rag doesn't leave any lint which could clog an oil passage.

Fig. 145 Unscrew the oil filter using a strap wrench (shown) or cap wrench

Fig. 146 Before installing a new oil filter, lightly coat the rubber gasket with clean oil

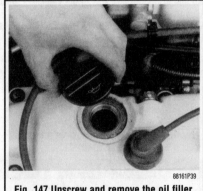

Fig. 147 Unscrew and remove the oil filler cap from the rocker arm cover

Fig. 148 A funnel will help avoid spillage when adding oil

Fig. 149 After refilling the oil, check the level on the dipstick; top off if necessary

9. Coat the rubber gasket on the filter with fresh oil. Spin it onto the engine by hand; when the gasket touches the adapter surface give it another ½–¾ turn. No more or you'll squash the gasket and it will leak.

10. Refill the engine with the correct amount of fresh oil. See the Capacities chart at the end of this section.

11. Crank the engine over several times and then start it. If the oil pressure indicator light doesn't go out or the pressure gauge shows zero, shut the engine down and find out what's wrong.

12. If the oil pressure is OK and there are no leaks, shut the engine off and lower the car.

Manual Transaxle

FLUID RECOMMENDATION

▶ **See Figure 140**

For manual transaxles, there are a variety of fluids available (depending upon the outside temperature); be sure to use fluid with an API GL-4 rating.

LEVEL CHECK

You should inspect the manual transaxle gear oil at 3,000 miles (4,831 km) or once a month at this point you should correct the level or replace the oil as necessary. The lubricant level should be even with the bottom of the filler hole. Hold in on the filler plug when unscrewing it. When you are sure that all of the threads of the plug are free of the transaxle case, move the plug away from the case slightly. If lubricant begins to flow out of the transaxle, then you know it is full. If not, add gear oil as necessary.

DRAIN AND REFILL

▶ **See Figures 150 and 151**

➡ **It is recommended that the manual transaxle fluid be changed every 30,000 miles (48,309 km). If the vehicle is normally used in severe service, the interval should be halved. You may also want to change it if you have bought your car used or if it has been driven in water deep enough to reach the transaxle case.**

1. Run the engine until it reaches normal operating temperature then turn key to the **OFF** position.

2. Jack up the front of the car and support it on safety stands if necessary to gain access.

3. Remove the filler plug from the left-side of the transaxle to provide a vent.

4. The drain plug is located on the bottom of the transaxle case. Place a pan under the drain plug and remove it.

❋❋ CAUTION

The oil will be HOT. Push up against the threads as you unscrew the plug to prevent leakage.

5. Allow the oil to drain completely. Clean off the plug and replace it. DO NOT OVERTIGHTEN PLUG!

6. Fill the transaxle with gear oil through the filler plug hole. Use API service GL-4 gear oil of the proper viscosity. This oil usually comes in a squeeze bottle with a long nozzle. If the bottle isn't, use a plastic squeeze bottle (the type used in the kitchen). Auto supply stores sell inexpensive hand pumps for gear oil and other fluids. The pump screws into the top of the fluid container for easy installation. Refer to the Capacities Chart for the amount of oil needed.

7. The oil level should come up to the edge of the filler hole. You can stick your finger in to verify this. Watch out for sharp threads.

8. Replace the filler plug. Lower the vehicle, dispose of the old oil in the same manner as old engine oil. Take a drive in the vehicle, stop and check for leaks.

Automatic Transaxle

FLUID RECOMMENDATION

All automatic transaxles use Dexron®II or equivalent Automatic Transmission Fluid (ATF).

LEVEL CHECK

▶ **See Figure 152**

You should inspect the automatic transaxle gear oil at 3,000 miles (4,831 km) or once a month, at this point you should correct the level or replace the oil as necessary. There is a dipstick at the right rear of the engine. It has a scale on each side, one for **COLD** and the other for **HOT**. The transmission is considered hot after 15 miles of highway driving. Park the car on a level surface with the engine running. If the transaxle is not hot, shift into Drive, Low, then Park. Set the handbrake and block the wheels.

➡ **The fluid level should be checked when the engine is at normal operating temperature and engine running. The COLD range is used for reference only.**

Remove the dipstick, wipe it clean, then reinsert it firmly. Remove the dipstick and check the fluid level on the appropriate scale. The level should be at the Full mark. If the level is below the Full mark, add Dexron®II Automatic Transmission Fluid (ATF) as necessary, with the engine running, through the dipstick tube. Do not overfill, as this may cause the transaxle to malfunction and damage itself.

DRAIN AND REFILL

▶ **See Figures 153, 154, 155 and 156**

➡ **It is recommended that the automatic transaxle fluid be changed every 30,000 miles (48,309 km). If the vehicle is normally used in severe service, the interval should be halved. You may also want to change it if you have bought your car used or if it has been driven in water deep enough to reach the transaxle case.**

1. Run the engine until it reaches normal operating temperature then turn the key to the **OFF** position.

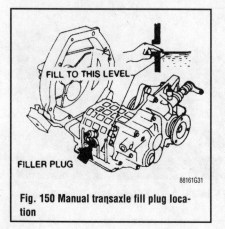

Fig. 150 Manual transaxle fill plug location

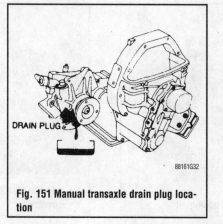

Fig. 151 Manual transaxle drain plug location

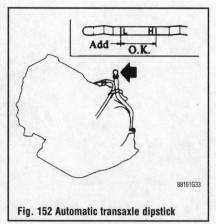

Fig. 152 Automatic transaxle dipstick

2. Jack up the front of the car and support it on safety stands if necessary to gain access.

➡️**If there is no drain plug, the fluid pan must be removed. On newer models, there is a hexagonal drain plug near the oil pan.**

3. If equipped with a drain plug, position a suitable container, then remove the plug and drain the transaxle.

4. If not equipped with a drain plug, partially remove the pan screws until the pan can be pulled down at one corner. Place a container under the transaxle, then lower a rear corner of the pan and allow the fluid to drain.

5. After draining, remove the pan screws completely, then the pan and gasket. On RL4F031A and RL4F01A transaxles, remove the drain plug in the side of the case or oil pan.

6. Clean the pan thoroughly and allow it to air dry. If you wipe it out with a rag, be sure there is no lint left behind to clog the oil passages.

➡️**It is very important to clean the old gasket from the oil pan, to prevent leaks upon installation. A razor blade does an excellent job.**

7. Install the pan using a new gasket and a small bead of RTV sealant; be sure to apply sealant around the outside of the pan bolt holes. Tighten the pan screws evenly in rotation from the center outwards, to 43–61 inch lbs. (5–7 Nm); then lower the vehicle.

8. It is a good idea to measure the amount of fluid drained to determine how much fresh fluid to add. This is because some part of the transaxle, such as the torque converter, will not drain completely and using the dry refill amount specified in the Capacities chart may lead to overfilling. Fluid is added through the dipstick tube. Make sure that the funnel, hose or whatever your are using is completely clean and dry before pouring transaxle fluid through it. Use Dexron®II automatic transmission fluid.

9. Replace the dipstick after filling. Start the engine and allow it to idle. DO NOT race the engine.

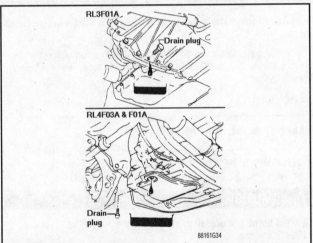

Fig. 153 Automatic transaxle drain plug—some early models do not have these plugs

10. After the engine has idled for a few minutes, shift the transaxle slowly through the gears, then return the lever to **PARK**. With the engine idling, check the fluid level on the dip stick. It should be between the **H** and **L** marks. If below **L**, add sufficient fluid to raise the level to between the marks.

11. Drive the car until the transaxle is at operating temperature. The fluid should be at the **H** mark. If not, add sufficient fluid until this is the case. Be careful not to overfill; overfilling causes slippage, overheating and seal damage.

➡️**If the drained fluid is discolored (brown or black), thick or smells burnt, serious transaxle problems due to overheating should be suspected. Your car's transaxle should be inspected by a transaxle specialist to determine the cause.**

PAN AND FILTER SERVICE

◆ **See Figures 153, 154, 155 and 156**

1. Raise and safely support the vehicle on jackstands.
2. Place a container under the transaxle to catch the oil when the pan is removed.
3. If equipped with a drain plug, remove the plug and drain the transaxle.
4. Remove the transaxle pan bolts and lower the pan.

➡️**If the pan sticks, bump it with a soft hammer to break it loose.**

5. Remove the control valve body, oil strainer plate bolts and the plate.

➡️**If the separator plate shows signs of scratches or damage, replace it.**

6. Using a putty knife, clean the gasket mounting surfaces.
To install:
7. Clean the pan with soap and water. Dry the pan, but be careful not to get any lint in it. Be sure to keep the pan magnet(s) in place.
8. Attach the oil strainer plate and control valve body.
9. Position a new gasket and sealant on the pan. After allowing the sealant to cure for a few minutes, raise the pan into position. Torque the oil pan bolts to 43–61 inch lbs. (5–7 Nm).
10. Remove the jackstands and lower the vehicle.
11. Refill the transaxle with DEXRON®II automatic transmission fluid.

4WD Transfer Case

FLUID RECOMMENDATIONS

The transfer case oil should be checked very 15,000 miles (24,155 km) for normal conditions and 7,500 miles (12,077 km) for severe conditions. Use GL-4 gear oil for adding or refilling the transfer case.

LEVEL CHECK

Never start the engine while check the oil level. Raise the vehicle and support safely. Remove the filler plug in the passenger side of the case. Fill with fluid until it reaches the bottom of the fill hole. Install the plug and torque to 13–18 ft. lbs. (18–25 Nm).

Fig. 154 Removing the pan to drain the automatic transaxle on models with no drain plug, and/or to service the filter

Fig. 155 Installing a new pan gasket

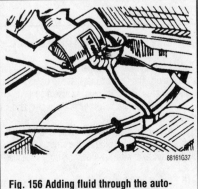

Fig. 156 Adding fluid through the automatic transaxle dipstick tube

DRAIN AND REFILL

▶ **See Figure 157**

1. Warm up the engine to normal operating temperature, then turn it **OFF**. Raise the vehicle and support safely.
2. Place a drain pan under the transfer case drain plug.
3. Remove the drain plug under the transfer case and allow to drain completely.
4. Install the drain plug and torque to 13–18 ft. lbs. (18–25 Nm).
5. Remove the fill plug on the side of the case. Using an approved pump, fill the transfer case with GL-4 gear oil until it reaches the bottom of the fill plug.
6. Install the fill plug and torque to 13–18 ft. lbs. (18–25 Nm).
7. Lower the vehicle and road test. Check for leaks after road test.

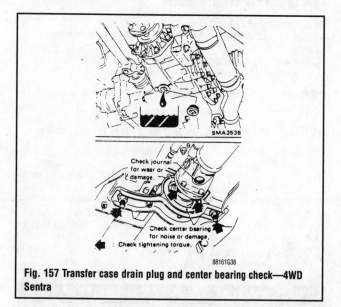

Fig. 157 Transfer case drain plug and center bearing check—4WD Sentra

4WD Drive Axle

FLUID RECOMMENDATIONS

The rear drive axle oil should be checked very 15,000 miles (24,155 km) for normal conditions and 7,500 miles (12,077 km) for severe conditions. Use GL-4 gear oil for adding or refilling the transfer case.

LEVEL CHECK

Never start the engine while check the oil level. Raise the vehicle and support safely. Remove the plug in the rear housing. Fill with fluid until it reaches the bottom of the fill hole. Install the plug and torque to 13–18 ft. lbs. (18–25 Nm).

DRAIN AND REFILL

1. Drive the vehicle to warm up the drive axle to temperature. Raise the vehicle and support safely.
2. Place a drain pan under the drive axle drain plug. The case may not have a drain plug. The gear oil may have to be sucked out of the fill hole in the rear of the housing. If this is the case, use a suction pump to remove the gear oil.
3. If so equipped, remove the drain plug under the drive axle housing and allow to drain completely.
4. Install the drain plug and torque to 13–18 ft. lbs. (18–25 Nm).
5. Remove the fill plug on the side of the case. Using an approved pump, fill the drive axle with GL-4 gear oil until it reaches the bottom of the fill plug hole.
6. Install the fill plug and torque to 13–18 ft. lbs. (18–25 Nm).
7. Lower the vehicle and road test. Check for leaks after road test.

Cooling System

FLUID RECOMMENDATION

The cooling fluid or antifreeze, should be changed every 30,000 miles (48,309 km) or 24 months. When replacing the fluid, use a mixture of 50% water and 50% ethylene glycol or other compatible antifreeze.

LEVEL CHECK

▶ **See Figure 158**

Check the coolant level every 3,000 miles (4,831 km) or once a month. In hot weather operation, it may be a good idea to check the level once a week. Check for loose connections and signs of deterioration of the coolant hoses. Maintain the coolant level ¾–1¼ in. (19–32mm) below the level of the filler neck when the engine is cold. If the engine is equipped with a coolant recovery bottle, check the coolant level in the bottle when the engine is cold; the level should be up to the **MAX** mark. If the bottle is empty, check the level in the radiator and refill as necessary, then fill the bottle up to the MAX level.

❊❊ CAUTION

Never remove the radiator cap when the vehicle is hot or over-heated. Wait until it has cooled. Place a thick cloth over the radiator cap to shield yourself from the heat and turn the radiator cap, SLIGHTLY, until the sound of escaping pressure can be heard. DO NOT turn any more; allow the pressure to release gradually. When no more pressure can be heard escaping, remove the cap with the heavy cloth, CAUTIOUSLY!

➡**Never add cold water to an overheated engine while the engine is not running.**

After filling the radiator, run the engine until it reaches normal operating temperature, to make sure that the thermostat has opened and all the air is bled from the system.

DRAIN AND REFILL

▶ **See Figures 158, 159, 160, 161 and 162**

To drain the cooling system, allow the engine to cool down **BEFORE ATTEMPTING TO REMOVE THE RADIATOR CAP**. Then turn the cap until it hisses. Wait until all pressure is off the cap before removing it completely.

❊❊ CAUTION

To avoid burns and scalding, always handle a warm radiator cap with a heavy rag.

1. At the dash, set the heater TEMP control lever to the fully HOT position.
2. With the radiator cap removed, drain the radiator by loosening the petcock at the bottom of the radiator.

➡**On the Sentra models, remove the heater inlet hose from the connector pipe at the left rear of the cylinder block to drain completely. After draining, reconnect the hose to the pipe.**

3. Close the petcock, then refill the system with a 50/50 mix of ethylene glycol or other compatible antifreeze; fill the system to ¾–1¼ in. (19–32mm) from the bottom of the filler neck. Reinstall the radiator cap.

➡**If equipped with a fluid reservoir tank, fill it up to the MAX level.**

4. Operate the engine at 2,000 rpm for a few minutes and check the system for signs of leaks.

❊❊ WARNING

If the cooling system is not bled, air can be trapped in the cylinder head and cause engine damage when the engine heats up. Always

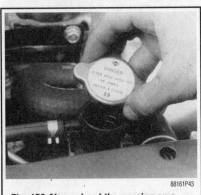
Fig. 158 Always heed the warning on a radiator cap

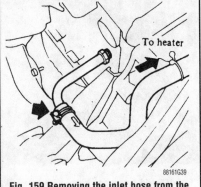
Fig. 159 Removing the inlet hose from the connector pipe

Fig. 160 After filling the radiator, also fill the coolant reservoir

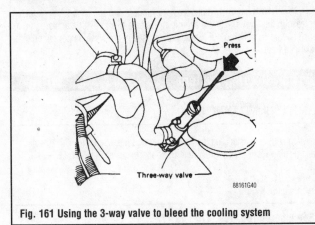
Fig. 161 Using the 3-way valve to bleed the cooling system

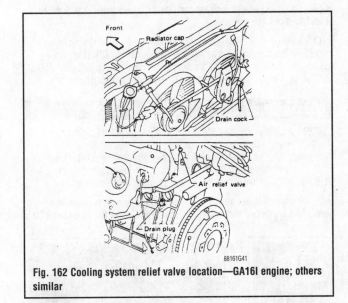
Fig. 162 Cooling system relief valve location—GA16I engine; others similar

bleed the cooling system after draining. The air has to escape from the highest point in the cooling system.

If you have replaced or repaired any cooling system component, the system must be bled. Insert a 3mm pin into the 3-way valve, located at the firewall, and push it in as far as it will go for early model vehicles. While pushing in on the pin, fill the radiator up to the filler opening. Replace the radiator cap and fill the reservoir. Loosen the plug in the upper part of the cylinder head for later model vehicles. If no plug or valve can be accessed, remove a cooling sender switch at the uppermost part of the cooling system. Fill the engine with coolant until it spills out of the removed sender. Install the sender and torque to 15 ft. lbs. (25 Nm).

FLUSHING AND CLEANING THE SYSTEM

To flush the system you must first, drain the cooling system but do not close the petcock valve on the bottom of the radiator. You can insert a garden hose, in the filler neck, turn the water pressure on moderately then start the engine. After about 10 minutes or less the water coming out of the bottom of the radiator should be clear. Shut off the engine and water supply, allow the radiator to drain then refill and bleed the system as necessary.

➡**DO NOT allow the engine to overheat. The supply of water going in the top must be equal in amount to the water draining from the bottom, this way the radiator will always be full when the engine us running.**

Usually flushing the radiator using water is all that is necessary to maintain the proper condition in the cooling system.

Radiator flush is the only cleaning agent that can be used to clean the internal portion of the radiator. Radiator flush can be purchased at virtually any auto supply store. Follow the directions on the label.

Brake and Clutch Master Cylinders

FLUID RECOMMENDATION

When adding or changing the fluid in the systems, use a quality brake fluid meeting DOT 3 specifications.

➡**Never reuse old brake fluid.**

LEVEL CHECK

▶ **See Figures 163, 164, 165, 166 and 167**

Check the levels of brake fluid in the brake and, if applicable, clutch master cylinder reservoirs every 3,000 miles (4,831 km) or once a month. The fluid should be maintained at a level between the bottom and top lines on the reser-

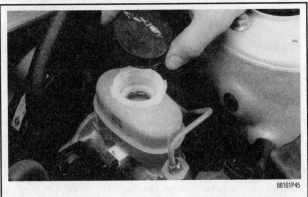
Fig. 163 Unscrew the cap from the top of the brake master cylinder

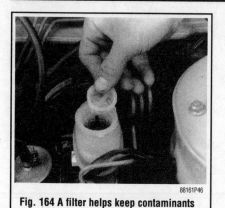

Fig. 164 A filter helps keep contaminants from entering the brake hydraulic system

Fig. 165 Add only clean brake fluid from a sealed container

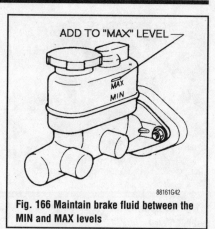

Fig. 166 Maintain brake fluid between the MIN and MAX levels

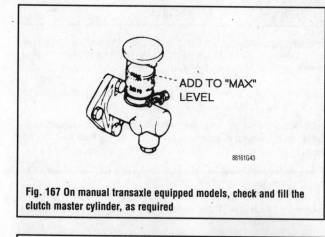

Fig. 167 On manual transaxle equipped models, check and fill the clutch master cylinder, as required

Fig. 168 Unscrew the cap, which has a built-in dipstick

voirs. (Note that some early brake master cylinders had two caps.) Any sudden decrease in the level in either reservoir indicates a leak in that particular system, which should be checked out. Gradual decreases in fluid level is normal due to brake pad wear.

Power Steering System

FLUID RECOMMENDATION

When adding or changing the power steering fluid, use Dexron®II Automatic Transmission Fluid (ATF); the system uses approximately 1⅛ qts. (1.06L) of fluid.

LEVEL CHECK

♦ **See Figures 168, 169, 170 and 171**

➥**Like all other general maintenance items, check every 3,000 miles (4,831 km) or once a month.**

Check the oil level in the reservoir by checking the side of the dipstick marked **HOT** after running the vehicle, or the side marked **COLD** when the car has not been used. In each case, the fluid should reach the appropriate full line. See Section 8 of this manual for system bleeding procedures if necessary.

Chassis Greasing

The manufacturer doesn't install lubrication fittings in lube points on the steering linkage or suspension. You can buy metric threaded fittings to grease these points or use a pointed, rubber tip end on your grease gun. Lubricate all joints equipped with a plug, every 15,000 miles (24,155 km) or once a year with NLGI No. 2 (lithium base) grease. Replace the plugs after lubrication.

➥**Do not over pack the steering components. The rubber boots will burst. This will allow dirt and contamination to enter the component. If**

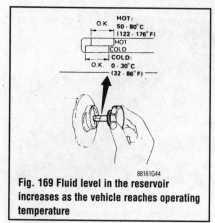

Fig. 169 Fluid level in the reservoir increases as the vehicle reaches operating temperature

Fig. 170 Slowly add the power steering fluid; be careful not to overfill

Fig. 171 Instead of a dipstick, some reservoirs have level markings on the side

this occurs, the component should be replaced or the component will have to greased frequently.

Body Lubrication

Lubricate all body hinges, latches and moving parts with high quality white lithium grease. Lubricate key locks with penetrating oil or motor oil. Do not use an excess amount because the key will be oily every time it is inserted into the lock. Lubricate rubber door seals with silicone spray. For best results, spray into a rag and wipe the seal with the rag.

Rear Wheel Bearings

For front wheel bearings and 1987–96 rear wheel bearings, refer to the procedures in Section 8.

REMOVAL, REPACKING AND INSTALLATION

▶ See Figures 172, 173, 174, 175 and 176

Before handling the bearings, there are a few things that you should remember to do and not to do:

Remember to DO the following:
- Remove all outside dirt from the housing before exposing the bearing.
- Treat a used bearing as gently as you would a new one.
- Work with clean tools in clean surroundings.
- Use clean, dry canvas gloves, or at least clean, dry hands.
- Clean solvents and flushing fluids are a must.
- Use clean paper when laying out the bearings to dry.
- Protect disassembled bearings from rust and dirt. Cover them up.
- Use clean rags to wipe bearings.
- Keep the bearings in oil-proof paper when they are to be stored or are not in use.

- Clean the inside of the housing before replacing the bearing.

Do NOT do the following:
- Don't work in dirty surroundings.
- Don't use dirty, chipped or damaged tools.
- Try not to work on wooden work benches or use wooden mallets.
- Don't handle bearings with dirty or moist hands.
- Do not use gasoline for cleaning; use a safe solvent.
- Do not spin-dry bearings with compressed air; they will be damaged.
- Do not spin dirty bearings.
- Avoid using cotton waste or dirty cloths to wipe bearings.
- Try not to scratch or nick bearing surfaces.
- Do not allow the bearing to come in contact with dirt or rust at any time.

➡The following procedure pertains to 1982–86 2WD vehicles only. These vehicles have serviceable rear wheel bearings. 1987–96 and 4WD vehicles have pressed-in wheel bearings, which are covered in Section 8.

1. Raise the rear of the vehicle and safely support it on jackstands.
2. Remove the rear wheels.
3. Work off the center (dust) cap by using a thin tool. If necessary, tap around it with a soft hammer while removing.
4. Use a pair of pliers to straighten, then pull out the cotter pin. Take off the adjusting cap and unfasten the wheel bearing locknut.

➡During removal, be careful to avoid damaging the O-ring in the dust cap.

5. Remove the drum with the bearing inside. To remove the wheel bearing races, knock them out of the brake drum using a suitable brass punch.

Fig. 173 Straighten the cotter pin with a pair of needlenose pliers

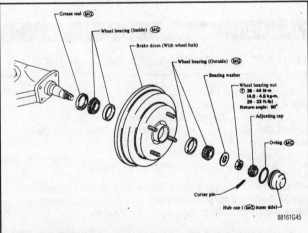

Fig. 172 Exploded view of rear wheel bearing installation

Fig. 174 Pull the cotter pin from the axle shaft

Fig. 175 Remove the adjusting cap from the locknut

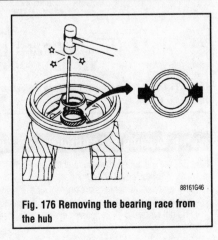

Fig. 176 Removing the bearing race from the hub

→On Pulsar models, a circular clip holds the inner wheel bearing in the brake hub.

6. Remove the bearing from the drum using a long brass drift pin or equivalent.

7. Remove the old grease from the bearing. Thoroughly clean the bearing before applying new grease.

To install:

8. Use a cone shaped bearing packer to thoroughly grease the wheel bearing. If such a bearing packer is not available, fill the palm of your hand with fresh grease and, using your other hand, move the bearing through the grease. Be sure to coat the entire circumference with grease, and thoroughly work it between the rollers.

9. Install the inner bearing assembly in the brake drum, then install the drum on the vehicle.

→The rear wheel bearings must be adjusted after installation; if a one-piece bearing is used, torque the wheel bearing locknut.

10. Install the outer bearing assembly, wheel bearing locknut, adjusting cap and a new cotter pin.

11. Install the center cap and the wheel assembly.

12. Remove the jackstands, then lower the vehicle.

ADJUSTMENT

◆ **See Figures 172, 173, 174 and 175**

1. Raise the rear of the vehicle and safely support it on jackstands.

2. Remove the wheel/tire assembly.

3. Remove the bearing dust cap with a pair of channel locks pliers.

4. Remove the cotter pin and retaining nut cap (if equipped); dispose of the cotter pin.

5. Tighten the wheel bearing nut to 29–33 ft. lbs. (39–45 Nm).

6. Rotate the drum back and forth a few revolutions to snug down the bearing.

7. After turning the wheel, recheck the torque of the nut, then loosen it 90° from its position.

8. Install the retaining nut cap (if equipped). Align the cotter pin holes in the nut or nut cap with the hole in the spindle by turning the nut clockwise. Do not loosen it. Tighten the nut no more than 15° to align the holes.

9. Install the cotter pin and bend up its ends, then install the dust cap.

10. Install the wheel/tire assembly.

11. Remove the jackstands, then lower the vehicle.

TOWING

Both types of transaxles may be towed for short distances and at speeds of no more than 20 mph (32 km/h) for automatics, or 50 mph (81 km/h) for manuals. If the car must be towed a great distance, it should be done with the drive wheels off the ground.

JUMP STARTING A DEAD BATTERY

◆ **See Figure 177**

Whenever a vehicle is jump started, precautions must be followed in order to prevent the possibility of personal injury. Remember that batteries contain a small amount of explosive hydrogen gas which is a by-product of battery charging. Sparks should always be avoided when working around batteries, especially when attaching jumper cables. To minimize the possibility of accidental sparks, follow the procedure carefully.

※ CAUTION

NEVER hook the batteries up in a series circuit or the entire electrical system will go up in smoke, including the starter!

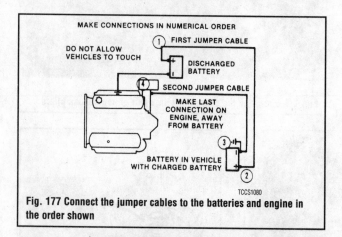

Fig. 177 Connect the jumper cables to the batteries and engine in the order shown

Jump Starting Precautions

- Be sure that both batteries are of the same polarity (have the same terminal, in most cases NEGATIVE grounded).
- Be sure that the vehicles are not touching or a short could occur.
- On non-sealed batteries, be sure the vent cap holes are not obstructed.
- Do not smoke or allow sparks anywhere near the batteries.

- In cold weather, make sure the battery electrolyte is not frozen. This can occur more readily in a battery that has been in a state of discharge.
- Do not allow electrolyte to contact your skin or clothing.

Jump Starting Procedure

SINGLE BATTERY GASOLINE AND DIESEL ENGINE MODELS

1. Make sure that the voltages of the 2 batteries are the same. Most batteries and charging systems are of the 12 volt variety.

2. Pull the jumping vehicle (with the good battery) into a position so the jumper cables can reach the dead battery and that vehicle's engine. Make sure that the vehicles do NOT touch.

3. Place the transmissions/transaxles of both vehicles in **Neutral** (MT) or **P** (AT), as applicable, then firmly set their parking brakes.

→If necessary for safety reasons, the hazard lights on both vehicles may be operated throughout the entire procedure without significantly increasing the difficulty of jumping the dead battery.

4. Turn all lights and accessories OFF on both vehicles. Make sure the ignition switches on both vehicles are turned to the **OFF** position.

5. Cover the battery cell caps with a rag, but do not cover the terminals.

6. Make sure the terminals on both batteries are clean and free of corrosion for good electrical contact.

7. Identify the positive (+) and negative (−) terminals on both batteries.

8. Connect the first jumper cable to the positive (+) terminal of the dead battery, then connect the other end of that cable to the positive (+) terminal of the booster (good) battery.

9. Connect one end of the other jumper cable to the negative (−) terminal on the booster battery and the final cable clamp to an engine bolt head, alternator bracket or other solid, metallic point on the engine with the dead battery. Try to pick a ground on the engine that is positioned away from the battery in order to minimize the possibility of the 2 clamps touching should one loosen during the procedure. DO NOT connect this clamp to the negative (−) terminal of the bad battery.

※ CAUTION

Be very careful to keep the jumper cables away from moving parts (cooling fan, belts, etc.) on both engines.

10. Check to make sure that the cables are routed away from any moving parts, then start the donor vehicle's engine. Run the engine at moderate speed for several minutes to allow the dead battery a chance to receive some initial charge.

11. With the donor vehicle's engine still running slightly above idle, try to start the vehicle with the dead battery. Crank the engine for no more than 10 seconds at a time and let the starter cool for at least 20 seconds between tries. If the vehicle does not start in 3 tries, it is likely that something else is also wrong or that the battery needs additional time to charge.

12. Once the vehicle is started, allow it to run at idle for a few seconds to make sure that it is operating properly.

13. Turn ON the headlights, heater blower and, if equipped, the rear defroster of both vehicles in order to reduce the severity of voltage spikes and subsequent risk of damage to the vehicles' electrical systems when the cables are disconnected. This step is especially important to any vehicle equipped with computer control modules.

14. Carefully disconnect the cables in the reverse order of connection. Start with the negative cable that is attached to the engine ground, then the negative cable on the donor battery. Disconnect the positive cable from the donor battery and finally, disconnect the positive cable from the formerly dead battery. Be careful when disconnecting the cables from the positive terminals not to allow the alligator clips to touch any metal on either vehicle or a short and sparks will occur.

DUAL BATTERY DIESEL MODELS

▸ **See Figure 178**

Some diesel model vehicles utilize two 12 volt batteries, one on either side of the engine compartment. The batteries are connected in a parallel circuit (positive terminal to positive terminal and negative terminal to negative terminal). Hooking the batteries up in a parallel circuit increases battery cranking power without increasing total battery voltage output. The output will remain at 12 volts. On the other hand, hooking two 12 volt batteries in a series circuit (positive terminal to negative terminal and negative terminal to positive terminal) increases the total battery output to 24 volts (12 volts plus 12 volts).

✳✳ WARNING

Never hook the batteries up in a series circuit or the entire electrical system will be damaged, including the starter motor.

In the event that a dual battery vehicle needs to be jump started, use the following procedure:

1. Turn the heater blower motor **ON** to help protect the electrical system from voltage surges when the jumper cables are connected and disconnected.

2. Turn all lights and other switches **OFF**.

➡**The battery cables connected to one of the diesel vehicle's batteries may be thicker than those connected to its other battery. (The passen-**

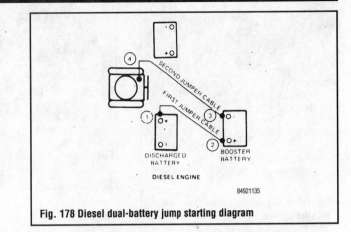

Fig. 178 Diesel dual-battery jump starting diagram

ger side battery often has thicker cables.) This set-up allows relatively high jump starting current to pass without damage. If so, be sure to connect the positive jumper cable to the appropriate battery in the disabled vehicle. If there is no difference in cable thickness, connect the jumper cable to either battery's positive terminal. Similarly, if the donor vehicle also utilizes two batteries, the jumper cable connections should be made to the battery with the thicker cables; if there is no difference in thickness, the connections can be made to either donor battery.**

3. Connect the end of a jumper cable to one of the disabled diesel's positive (+) battery terminals, then connect the clamp at the other end of the same cable to the positive terminal (+) on the jumper battery.

4. Connect one end of the other jumper cable to the negative battery terminal (-) on the jumper battery, then connect the other cable clamp to an engine bolt head, alternator bracket or other solid, metallic point on the disabled vehicle's engine. DO NOT connect this clamp to the negative terminal (-) of the disabled vehicle's battery.

✳✳ CAUTION

Be careful to keep the jumper cables away from moving parts (cooling fan, belts, etc.) on both engines.

5. Start the engine on the vehicle with the good battery and run it at a moderate speed.

6. Start the engine of the vehicle with the discharged battery.

7. When the engine starts on the vehicle with the discharged battery, remove the cable from the engine block before disconnecting the cable from the positive terminal.

JACKING

▸ **See Figures 179 thru 184**

Your vehicle was supplied with a jack for emergency road repairs. This jack is fine for changing a flat tire or other short term procedures not requiring you to go beneath the vehicle. If it is used in an emergency situation, carefully follow the instructions provided either with the jack or in your owner's manual. Do not attempt to use the jack on any portions of the vehicle other than specified by the vehicle manufacturer. Always block the diagonally opposite wheel when using a jack.

A more convenient way of jacking is the use of a garage or floor jack. You may use the floor jack to raise the vehicle at the points indicated in the jacking points illustration in this section.

Never place the jack under the radiator, engine or transmission components. Severe and expensive damage will result when the jack is raised. Additionally, never jack under the floorpan or bodywork; the metal will deform.

Whenever you plan to work under the vehicle, you must support it on jackstands or ramps. Never use cinder blocks or stacks of wood to support the vehicle, even if you're only going to be under it for a few minutes. Never crawl under the vehicle when it is supported only by the tire-changing jack or other floor jack.

➡**Always position a block of wood or small rubber pad on top of the jack or jackstand to protect the lifting point's finish when lifting or supporting the vehicle.**

Small hydraulic, screw, or scissors jacks are satisfactory for raising the vehicle. Drive-on trestles or ramps are also a handy and safe way to both raise and support the vehicle. Be careful though, some ramps may be too steep to drive your vehicle onto without scraping the front bottom panels. Never support the vehicle on any suspension member (unless specifically instructed to do so by a repair manual) or by an underbody panel.

Jacking Precautions

The following safety points cannot be overemphasized:
• Always block the opposite wheel or wheels to keep the vehicle from rolling off the jack.
• When raising the front of the vehicle, firmly apply the parking brake.
• When the drive wheels are to remain on the ground, leave the vehicle in gear to help prevent it from rolling.
• Always use jackstands to support the vehicle when you are working underneath. Place the stands beneath the vehicle's jacking brackets. Before climbing underneath, rock the vehicle a bit to make sure it is firmly supported.

Fig. 179 A scissors jack is often supplied with the vehicle

Fig. 180 Front jacking point for a floor jack

Fig. 181 Rear jacking point for a floor jack

Fig. 182 Front lifting point for a jackstand

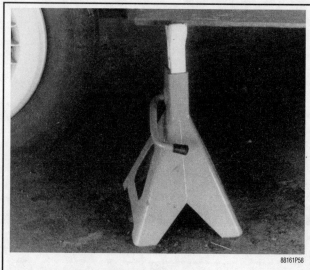

Fig. 183 Rear lifting point for a jackstand

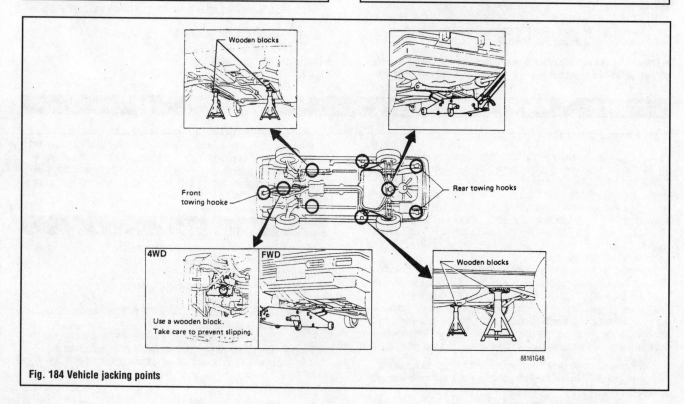

Fig. 184 Vehicle jacking points

MAINTENANCE INTERVALS CHARTS

▶ **See Figures 185 and 186**

Abbreviations R – Replace I = Inspect. Correct or replace if necessary.

MAINTENANCE OPERATION								MAINTENANCE INTERVAL									
Perform at number of miles, kilometers or months, whichever comes first.	Miles x 1,000	3.75	7.5	11.25	15	18.75	22.5	26.25	30	33.75	37.5	41.25	45	48.75	52.5	56.25	60
	(km x 1,000)	(6)	(12)	(18)	(24)	(30)	(36)	(42)	(48)	(54)	(60)	(66)	(72)	(78)	(84)	(90)	(96)
	Months	3	6	9	12	15	18	21	24	27	30	33	36	39	42	45	48
Emission control system maintenance																	
Drive belts	See NOTE (1).																I*
Air cleaner filter	See NOTE (2).								[R]								[R]
Vapor lines									I*								I*
Fuel lines									I*								I*
Fuel filter	See NOTE (3)*																
Engine coolant	See NOTE (4)																R*
Engine oil		R	R	R	R	R	R	R	R	R	R	R	R	R	R	R	R
Engine oil filter (Use Nissan PREMIUM type or equivalent for GA16DE engine.)		R	R	R	R	R	R	R	R	R	R	R	R	R	R	R	R
Spark plugs GA16DE engine									[R]								[R]
SR20DE engine (Use PLATINUM-TIPPED type.) See NOTE (5)																	[R]
Idle rpm (GA16DE engine)									I*								I*
Intake & exhaust valve clearance (GA16DE engine)	See NOTE (6)*																
Chassis and body maintenance																	
Brake lines & cables					I				I			I					I
Brake pads, discs, drums & linings			I		I		I		I		I		I		I		I
Manual & automatic transaxle oil	See NOTE (7)																
Steering gear & linkage, axle & suspension parts			I		I		I		I		I		I		I		I
Steering linkage ball joints & front suspension ball joints			I		I		I		I		I		I		I		I
Exhaust system					I				I				I				I
Drive shaft boots			I		I		I		I		I		I		I		I
Air bag system (Coupe models)	See NOTE (8)																

NOTE: (1) After 60,000 miles (96,000 km) or 48 months, inspect every 15,000 miles (24,000 km) or 12 months.
(2) If operating mainly in dusty conditions, more frequent maintenance may be required.
(3) If vehicle is operated under extremely adverse weather conditions or in areas where ambient temperatures are either extremely low or extremely high, the filters might become clogged. In such an event, replace them immediately.
(4) After 60,000 miles (96,000 km) or 48 months, replace every 30,000 miles (48,000 km) or 24 months.
(5) Original equipment platinum-tipped plugs should be replaced at 60,000 miles (96,000 km). Conventional spark plugs can be used but should be replaced at 30,000 mile (48,000 km) intervals.
(6) If valve noise increases, inspect valve clearance.
(7) If towing a trailer, using a camper or a car-top carrier, or driving on rough or muddy roads, change (not just inspect) oil at every 30,000 miles (48,000 km) or 24 months.
(8) Inspect the air bag system 10 years after the date of manufacture as noted on the F.M.V.S.S. certification label.
(9) Maintenance items and intervals with "*" are recommended by NISSAN for reliable vehicle operation. The owner need not perform such maintenance in order to maintain the emission warranty or manufacturer recall liability. Other maintenance items and intervals are required.

88161G49

Fig. 185 Gasoline engine vehicle maintenance schedule—normal conditions

MAINTENANCE OPERATION					MAINTENANCE INTERVAL				
Perform at number of miles, kilometers or months, whichever comes first.	Miles x 1,000	7.5	15	22.5	30	37.5	45	52.5	60
	(km x 1,000)	(12)	(24)	(36)	(48)	(60)	(72)	(84)	(96)
	Months	6	12	18	24	30	36	42	48
Emission control system maintenance									
Drive belts	See NOTE (1).								I*
Air cleaner filter					[R]				[R]
Vapor lines					I*				I*
Fuel lines					I*				I*
Fuel filter	See NOTE (2)*.								
Engine coolant	See NOTE (3).								R*
Engine oil		R	R	R	R	R	R	R	R
Engine oil filter (Use Nissan PREMIUM type or equivalent for GA16DE engine.)		R		R		R		R	
Spark plugs GA16DE engine					[R]				[R]
SR20DE engine (Use PLATINUM-TIPPED type.) See NOTE (4).									[R]
Idle rpm (GA16DE engine)					I*				I*
Intake & exhaust valve clearance (GA16DE engine)	See NOTE (5)*.								
Chassis and body maintenance									
Brake lines & cables			I		I		I		I
Brake pads, discs, drums & linings			I		I		I		I
Manual & automatic transaxle oil			I		I		I		I
Steering gear linkage, axle & suspension parts					I				I
Exhaust system			I		I		I		I
Drive shaft boots			I		I		I		I
Air bag system (Coupe models)	See NOTE (6).								

NOTE: (1) After 60,000 miles (96,000 km) or 48 months, inspect every 15,000 miles (24,000 km) or 12 months.
(2) If vehicle is operated under extremely adverse weather conditions or in areas where ambient temperatures are either extremely low or extremely high, the filters might become clogged. In such an event, replace them immediately.
(3) After 60,000 miles (96,000 km) or 48 months, replace every 30,000 miles (48,000 km) or 24 months.
(4) Original equipment platinum-tipped plugs should be replaced at 60,000 miles (96,000 km). Conventional spark plugs can be used but should be replaced at 30,000 mile (48,000 km) intervals.
(5) If valve noise increases, inspect valve clearance.
(6) Inspect the air bag system 10 years after the date of manufacture as noted on the F.M.V.S.S. certification label.
(7) Maintenance items and intervals with "*" are recommended by NISSAN for reliable vehicle operation. The owner need not perform such maintenance in order to maintain the emission warranty or manufacturer recall liability. Other maintenance items and intervals are required.

88161G50

Fig. 186 Gasoline engine vehicle maintenance schedule—severe conditions

CAPACITIES

Year	Model	Engine ID/VIN	Engine Displacement Liters (cc)	Engine Crankcase with Filter	Transmission (pts.)			Drive Axle Rear (pts.)	Fuel Tank (gal.)	Cooling System (qts.)
					4-Spd	5-Spd	Auto.			
1982	Sentra	E15	1.5 (1488)	4.1	4.9	5.8	13.0	—	13.3	5.5
1983	Sentra	E15	1.5 (1488)	4.1	4.9	5.8	13.0	—	13.3	5.5
	Sentra	E16	1.6 (1597)	3.5	4.9	5.8	13.0	—	13.3	5.5
	Pulsar	E16	1.6 (1597)	3.9	—	5.8	13.0	—	13.3	5.5
	Sentra	CD17	1.7 (1680)	4.3	4.9	5.8	13.0	—	13.3	7.5
198	Pulsar	E15ET	1.5 (1488)	4.8	—	5.8	13.0	—	13.3	5.5
	Sentra	E16	1.6 (1597)	3.5	4.9	5.8	13.0	—	13.3	5.5
	Pulsar	E16	1.6 (1597)	3.9	—	5.8	13.0	—	13.3	5.5
	Sentra	CD17	1.7 (1680)	4.3	4.9	5.8	13.0	—	10.8	7.5
1985	Sentra, Pulsar	E16	1.6 (1597)	3.5	4.9	5.8	13.0	—	13.3	5.5
	Sentra	CD17	1.7 (1680)	4.3	4.9	5.8	13.0	—	10.8	7.5
1986	Sentra, Pulsar	E16	1.6 (1597)	3.5	4.9	5.8	13.0	—	13.3	5.5
	Sentra	CD17	1.7 (1680)	4.3	4.9	5.8	13.0	—	10.8	7.5
1987	Sentra, Pulsar	E16	1.6 (1597)	3.5	—	5.8	13.0	2.1	13.3④	⑥
	Pulsar	CA16DE	1.6 (1598)	3.8	—	5.8	—	—	13.3	5.9
	Sentra	CD17	1.7 (1680)	4.3	—	5.8	13.0	2.1	13.8	6.9
1988	Sentra, Pulsar	E16	1.6 (1597)	3.4	5.7	5.9	13.2	2.1	13.3⑤	⑥
	Pulsar	CA18DE	1.8 (1809)	3.7	—	10.0	14.4	—	13.3	⑦
1989	Sentra, Pulsar	GA16i	1.6 (1597)	3.4	5.8	5.9	13.2	2.1	13.3	5.6
	Pulsar	CA18DE	1.8 (1809)	3.7	—	10.0	14.5	—	13.3	5.9
1990	Sentra	GA16i	1.6 (1597)	3.5	5.8	5.9	13.3	1.2	13.3⑤	5.8⑧
	Pulsar	GA16i	1.6 (1597)	3.4	—	5.9	13.3	—	13.3	5.8⑧
1991	Sentra	GA16DE	1.6 (1597)	3.4	5.9	⑨	13.3	—	13.3	⑩
	Sentra	SR20DE	2.0 (1998)	3.6	5.9	⑨	14.8	—	13.3	⑦
1992	Sentra	GA16DE	1.6 (1597)	3.4	5.9	⑨	12.8	—	13.3	⑩
	Sentra	SR20DE	2.0 (1998)	3.6	5.9	⑨	14.8	—	13.3	⑦
1993	Sentra	GA16DE	1.6 (1597)	3.4	5.9	⑨	12.8	—	13.3	⑩
	Sentra	SR20DE	2.0 (1998)	3.6	5.9	⑨	14.8	—	13.3	⑦
1994	Sentra	GA16DE	1.6 (1597)	3.4	5.9	⑨	14.8	—	13.3	⑩
	Sentra	SR20DE	2.0 (1998)	3.6	5.9	⑨	14.8	—	13.3	⑦
1995	Sentra	GA16DE	1.6 (1597)	3.4	5.9	⑨	14.8	—	13.3	⑩
	Sentra	SR20DE	2.0 (1998)	3.6	5.9	⑨	14.8	—	13.3	⑦
1996	Sentra	GA16DE	1.6 (1597)	3.4	5.9	⑨	14.8	—	13.3	⑩
	Sentra	SR20DE	2.0 (1998)	3.6	5.9	⑨	14.8	—	13.3	⑦

① Pulsar
② Turbo
③ DOHC
④ 4WD—13.8 gal.
⑤ 4WD—12.4 gal.
⑥ MT—4.9, AT—5.5
⑦ MT—5.9, AT—6.1
⑧ 4WD and AT—6.3 qts.
⑨ RN4F31A—5.9 pts.
RS5F21A—6.2 pts.
RS5F32V—7.8 pts.
⑩ MT—5.4, AT—5.7 qts.

88161C05

ENGLISH TO METRIC CONVERSION: MASS (WEIGHT)

Current mass measurement is expressed in pounds and ounces (lbs. & ozs.). The metric unit of mass (or weight) is the kilogram (kg). Even although this table does not show conversion of masses (weights) larger than 15 lbs, it is easy to calculate larger units by following the data immediately below.

To convert ounces (oz.) to grams (g): multiply th number of ozs. by 28
To convert grams (g) to ounces (oz.): multiply the number of grams by .035

To convert pounds (lbs.) to kilograms (kg): multiply the number of lbs. by .45
To convert kilograms (kg) to pounds (lbs.): multiply the number of kilograms by 2.2

lbs	kg	lbs	kg	oz	kg	oz	kg
0.1	0.04	0.9	0.41	0.1	0.003	0.9	0.024
0.2	0.09	1	0.4	0.2	0.005	1	0.03
0.3	0.14	2	0.9	0.3	0.008	2	0.06
0.4	0.18	3	1.4	0.4	0.011	3	0.08
0.5	0.23	4	1.8	0.5	0.014	4	0.11
0.6	0.27	5	2.3	0.6	0.017	5	0.14
0.7	0.32	10	4.5	0.7	0.020	10	0.28
0.8	0.36	15	6.8	0.8	0.023	15	0.42

ENGLISH TO METRIC CONVERSION: TEMPERATURE

To convert Fahrenheit (°F) to Celsius (°C): take number of °F and subtract 32; multiply result by 5; divide result by 9

To convert Celsius (°C) to Fahrenheit (°F): take number of °C and multiply by 9; divide result by 5; add 32 to total

Fahrenheit (F)		Celsius (C)		Fahrenheit (F)		Celsius (C)		Fahrenheit (F)		Celsius (C)	
°F	°C	°C	°F	°F	°C	°C	°F	°F	°C	°C	°F
−40	−40	−38	−36.4	80	26.7	18	64.4	215	101.7	80	176
−35	−37.2	−36	−32.8	85	29.4	20	68	220	104.4	85	185
−30	−34.4	−34	−29.2	90	32.2	22	71.6	225	107.2	90	194
−25	−31.7	−32	−25.6	95	35.0	24	75.2	230	110.0	95	202
−20	−28.9	−30	−22	100	37.8	26	78.8	235	112.8	100	212
−15	−26.1	−28	−18.4	105	40.6	28	82.4	240	115.6	105	221
−10	−23.3	−26	−14.8	110	43.3	30	86	245	118.3	110	230
−5	−20.6	−24	−11.2	115	46.1	32	89.6	250	121.1	115	239
0	−17.8	−22	−7.6	120	48.9	34	93.2	255	123.9	120	248
1	−17.2	−20	−4	125	51.7	36	96.8	260	126.6	125	257
2	−16.7	−18	−0.4	130	54.4	38	100.4	265	129.4	130	266
3	−16.1	−16	3.2	135	57.2	40	104	270	132.2	135	275
4	−15.6	−14	6.8	140	60.0	42	107.6	275	135.0	140	284
5	−15.0	−12	10.4	145	62.8	44	112.2	280	137.8	145	293
10	−12.2	−10	14	150	65.6	46	114.8	285	140.6	150	302
15	−9.4	−8	17.6	155	68.3	48	118.4	290	143.3	155	311
20	−6.7	−6	21.2	160	71.1	50	122	295	146.1	160	320
25	−3.9	−4	24.8	165	73.9	52	125.6	300	148.9	165	329
30	−1.1	−2	28.4	170	76.7	54	129.2	305	151.7	170	338
35	1.7	0	32	175	79.4	56	132.8	310	154.4	175	347
40	4.4	2	35.6	180	82.2	58	136.4	315	157.2	180	356
45	7.2	4	39.2	185	85.0	60	140	320	160.0	185	365
50	10.0	6	42.8	190	87.8	62	143.6	325	162.8	190	374
55	12.8	8	46.4	195	90.6	64	147.2	330	165.6	195	383
60	15.6	10	50	200	93.3	66	150.8	335	168.3	200	392
65	18.3	12	53.6	205	96.1	68	154.4	340	171.1	205	401
70	21.1	14	57.2	210	98.9	70	158	345	173.9	210	410
75	23.9	16	60.8	212	100.0	75	167	350	176.7	215	414

TCCS1C01

ENGLISH TO METRIC CONVERSION: LENGTH

To convert inches (ins.) to millimeters (mm): multiply number of inches by 25.4

To convert millimeters (mm) to inches (ins.): multiply number of millimeters by .04

Inches	Decimals	Milli-meters	Inches to millimeters (inches)	Inches to millimeters (mm)	Inches	Decimals	Milli-meters	Inches to millimeters (inches)	Inches to millimeters (mm)
1/64	0.051625	0.3969	0.0001	0.00254	33/64	0.515625	13.0969	0.6	15.24
1/32	0.03125	0.7937	0.0002	0.00508	17/32	0.53125	13.4937	0.7	17.78
3/64	0.046875	1.1906	0.0003	0.00762	35/64	0.546875	13.8906	0.8	20.32
1/16	0.0625	1.5875	0.0004	0.01016	9/16	0.5625	14.2875	0.9	22.86
5/64	0.078125	1.9844	0.0005	0.01270	37/64	0.578125	14.6844	1	25.4
3/32	0.09375	2.3812	0.0006	0.01524	19/32	0.59375	15.0812	2	50.8
7/64	0.109375	2.7781	0.0007	0.01778	39/64	0.609375	15.4781	3	76.2
1/8	0.125	3.1750	0.0008	0.02032	5/8	0.625	15.8750	4	101.6
9/64	0.140625	3.5719	0.0009	0.02286	41/64	0.640625	16.2719	5	127.0
5/32	0.15625	3.9687	0.001	0.0254	21/32	0.65625	16.6687	6	152.4
11/64	0.171875	4.3656	0.002	0.0508	43/64	0.671875	17.0656	7	177.8
3/16	0.1875	4.7625	0.003	0.0762	11/16	0.6875	17.4625	8	203.2
13/64	0.203125	5.1594	0.004	0.1016	45/64	0.703125	17.8594	9	228.6
7/32	0.21875	5.5562	0.005	0.1270	23/32	0.71875	18.2562	10	254.0
15/64	0.234375	5.9531	0.006	0.1524	47/64	0.734375	18.6531	11	279.4
1/4	0.25	6.3500	0.007	0.1778	3/4	0.75	19.0500	12	304.8
17/64	0.265625	6.7469	0.008	0.2032	49/64	0.765625	19.4469	13	330.2
9/32	0.28125	7.1437	0.009	0.2286	25/32	0.78125	19.8437	14	355.6
19/64	0.296875	7.5406	0.01	0.254	51/64	0.796875	20.2406	15	381.0
5/16	0.3125	7.9375	0.02	0.508	13/16	0.8125	20.6375	16	406.4
21/64	0.328125	8.3344	0.03	0.762	53/64	0.828125	21.0344	17	431.8
11/32	0.34375	8.7312	0.04	1.016	27/32	0.84375	21.4312	18	457.2
23/64	0.359375	9.1281	0.05	1.270	55/64	0.859375	21.8281	19	482.6
3/8	0.375	9.5250	0.06	1.524	7/8	0.875	22.2250	20	508.0
25/64	0.390625	9.9219	0.07	1.778	57/64	0.890625	22.6219	21	533.4
13/32	0.40625	10.3187	0.08	2.032	29/32	0.90625	23.0187	22	558.8
27/64	0.421875	10.7156	0.09	2.286	59/64	0.921875	23.4156	23	584.2
7/16	0.4375	11.1125	0.1	2.54	15/16	0.9375	23.8125	24	609.6
29/64	0.453125	11.5094	0.2	5.08	61/64	0.953125	24.2094	25	635.0
15/32	0.46875	11.9062	0.3	7.62	31/32	0.96875	24.6062	26	660.4
31/64	0.484375	12.3031	0.4	10.16	63/64	0.984375	25.0031	27	690.6
1/2	0.5	12.7000	0.5	12.70					

ENGLISH TO METRIC CONVERSION: TORQUE

To convert foot-pounds (ft. lbs.) to Newton-meters: multiply the number of ft. lbs. by 1.3

To convert inch-pounds (in. lbs.) to Newton-meters: multiply the number of in. lbs. by .11

in lbs	N-m	in lbs	N-m	in lbs	N-m	in lbs	N-m	in lbs	N-m
0.1	0.01	1	0.11	10	1.13	19	2.15	28	3.16
0.2	0.02	2	0.23	11	1.24	20	2.26	29	3.28
0.3	0.03	3	0.34	12	1.36	21	2.37	30	3.39
0.4	0.04	4	0.45	13	1.47	22	2.49	31	3.50
0.5	0.06	5	0.56	14	1.58	23	2.60	32	3.62
0.6	0.07	6	0.68	15	1.70	24	2.71	33	3.73
0.7	0.08	7	0.78	16	1.81	25	2.82	34	3.84
0.8	0.09	8	0.90	17	1.92	26	2.94	35	3.95
0.9	0.10	9	1.02	18	2.03	27	3.05	36	4.0

TCCS1C02

ENGLISH TO METRIC CONVERSION: TORQUE

Torque is now expressed as either foot-pounds (ft./lbs.) or inch-pounds (in./lbs.). The metric measurement unit for torque is the Newton-meter (Nm). This unit—the Nm—will be used for all SI metric torque references, both the present ft./lbs. and in./lbs.

ft lbs	N-m	ft lbs	N-m	ft lbs	N-m	ft lbs	N-m
0.1	0.1	33	44.7	74	100.3	115	155.9
0.2	0.3	34	46.1	75	101.7	116	157.3
0.3	0.4	35	47.4	76	103.0	117	158.6
0.4	0.5	36	48.8	77	104.4	118	160.0
0.5	0.7	37	50.7	78	105.8	119	161.3
0.6	0.8	38	51.5	79	107.1	120	162.7
0.7	1.0	39	52.9	80	108.5	121	164.0
0.8	1.1	40	54.2	81	109.8	122	165.4
0.9	1.2	41	55.6	82	111.2	123	166.8
1	1.3	42	56.9	83	112.5	124	168.1
2	2.7	43	58.3	84	113.9	125	169.5
3	4.1	44	59.7	85	115.2	126	170.8
4	5.4	45	61.0	86	116.6	127	172.2
5	6.8	46	62.4	87	118.0	128	173.5
6	8.1	47	63.7	88	119.3	129	174.9
7	9.5	48	65.1	89	120.7	130	176.2
8	10.8	49	66.4	90	122.0	131	177.6
9	12.2	50	67.8	91	123.4	132	179.0
10	13.6	51	69.2	92	124.7	133	180.3
11	14.9	52	70.5	93	126.1	134	181.7
12	16.3	53	71.9	94	127.4	135	183.0
13	17.6	54	73.2	95	128.8	136	184.4
14	18.9	55	74.6	96	130.2	137	185.7
15	20.3	56	75.9	97	131.5	138	187.1
16	21.7	57	77.3	98	132.9	139	188.5
17	23.0	58	78.6	99	134.2	140	189.8
18	24.4	59	80.0	100	135.6	141	191.2
19	25.8	60	81.4	101	136.9	142	192.5
20	27.1	61	82.7	102	138.3	143	193.9
21	28.5	62	84.1	103	139.6	144	195.2
22	29.8	63	85.4	104	141.0	145	196.6
23	31.2	64	86.8	105	142.4	146	198.0
24	32.5	65	88.1	106	143.7	147	199.3
25	33.9	66	89.5	107	145.1	148	200.7
26	35.2	67	90.8	108	146.4	149	202.0
27	36.6	68	92.2	109	147.8	150	203.4
28	38.0	69	93.6	110	149.1	151	204.7
29	39.3	70	94.9	111	150.5	152	206.1
30	40.7	71	96.3	112	151.8	153	207.4
31	42.0	72	97.6	113	153.2	154	208.8
32	43.4	73	99.0	114	154.6	155	210.2

TCCS1C03

ENGLISH TO METRIC CONVERSION: FORCE

Force is presently measured in pounds (lbs.). This type of measurement is used to measure spring pressure, specifically how many pounds it takes to compress a spring. Our present force unit (the pound) will be replaced in SI metric measurements by the Newton (N). This term will eventually see use in specifications for electric motor brush spring pressures, valve spring pressures, etc.

To convert pounds (lbs.) to Newton (N): multiply the number of lbs. by 4.45

lbs	N	lbs	N	lbs	N	oz	N
0.01	0.04	21	93.4	59	262.4	1	0.3
0.02	0.09	22	97.9	60	266.9	2	0.6
0.03	0.13	23	102.3	61	271.3	3	0.8
0.04	0.18	24	106.8	62	275.8	4	1.1
0.05	0.22	25	111.2	63	280.2	5	1.4
0.06	0.27	26	115.6	64	284.6	6	1.7
0.07	0.31	27	120.1	65	289.1	7	2.0
0.08	0.36	28	124.6	66	293.6	8	2.2
0.09	0.40	29	129.0	67	298.0	9	2.5
0.1	0.4	30	133.4	68	302.5	10	2.8
0.2	0.9	31	137.9	69	306.9	11	3.1
0.3	1.3	32	142.3	70	311.4	12	3.3
0.4	1.8	33	146.8	71	315.8	13	3.6
0.5	2.2	34	151.2	72	320.3	14	3.9
0.6	2.7	35	155.7	73	324.7	15	4.2
0.7	3.1	36	160.1	74	329.2	16	4.4
0.8	3.6	37	164.6	75	333.6	17	4.7
0.9	4.0	38	169.0	76	338.1	18	5.0
1	4.4	39	173.5	77	342.5	19	5.3
2	8.9	40	177.9	78	347.0	20	5.6
3	13.4	41	182.4	79	351.4	21	5.8
4	17.8	42	186.8	80	355.9	22	6.1
5	22.2	43	191.3	81	360.3	23	6.4
6	26.7	44	195.7	82	364.8	24	6.7
7	31.1	45	200.2	83	369.2	25	7.0
8	35.6	46	204.6	84	373.6	26	7.2
9	40.0	47	209.1	85	378.1	27	7.5
10	44.5	48	213.5	86	382.6	28	7.8
11	48.9	49	218.0	87	387.0	29	8.1
12	53.4	50	224.4	88	391.4	30	8.3
13	57.8	51	226.9	89	395.9	31	8.6
14	62.3	52	231.3	90	400.3	32	8.9
15	66.7	53	235.8	91	404.8	33	9.2
16	71.2	54	240.2	92	409.2	34	9.4
17	75.6	55	244.6	93	413.7	35	9.7
18	80.1	56	249.1	94	418.1	36	10.0
19	84.5	57	253.6	95	422.6	37	10.3
20	89.0	58	258.0	96	427.0	38	10.6

TCCS1C04

2

ENGINE ELECTRICAL

ELECTRONIC DISTRIBUTOR IGNITION SYSTEM

➡For information on understanding electricity and troubleshooting electrical circuits, please refer to Section 6 of this manual.

General Information

♦ See Figures 1, 2 and 3

The electronic ignition system differs from the conventional breaker points system in form only; its function is exactly the same: to supply a spark to the spark plugs at precisely the right moment to ignite the compressed gas in the cylinders and create mechanical movement.

Located in the distributor, in addition to the rotor cap, is a spoked reluctor which fits on the distributor shaft where the breaker points cam is found on non-electronic ignitions. The reluctor revolves with the rotor head, as it passes a pickup coil inside the distributor body it breaks a high flux field, which occurs in the space between the reluctor and the pickup coil. The breaking of the field allows current to flow to the pickup coil. Primary ignition current is then cut off by the electronic ignition unit, allowing the magnetic field in the ignition coil to collapse, creating the spark which the distributor passes on to the spark plug.

There are 4 different types of distributors used with electronic ignition systems. A single post pickup coil with a transistorized ignition unit, a ring-type pickup coil with an Integrated Circuit (IC) ignition unit, an IC ignition unit without a pickup coil, and a crank angle sensor are the main variations in the distributors used for these systems.

Because no points or condenser are used, and because dwell is determined by the electronic unit, no adjustments are necessary. Ignition timing is generally checked in the usual way (be careful to check for slight variations depending on model and engine), but unless the distributor is disturbed it is not likely to ever change very much.

Service consists of inspection of the distributor cap, rotor, and ignition wires, replacing when necessary. These parts can be expected to last at least 40,000

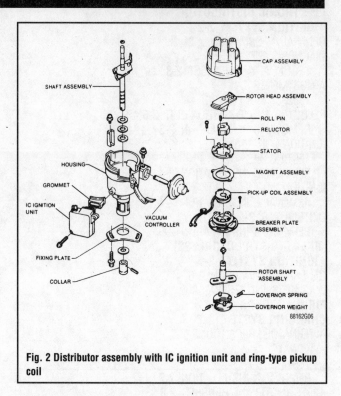

Fig. 2 Distributor assembly with IC ignition unit and ring-type pickup coil

miles (64,400 km). In addition, the reluctor air gap should be checked periodically.

The 1983 Pulsar for the 49 states, as well as the California and Canada models used no pickup coil for the electronic ignition system; on these models, the IC ignition unit is mounted on the inside of the distributor. The 1984–86 Pulsar for California and non-turbocharged Canadian models use no pickup coil for the electronic ignition system; on these models, the IC ignition unit is mounted on the inside of the distributor housing.

The 1984–88 (E16 engine only) for the 49 states, the 1987–88 California and Canada models (E16 engine only) and the turbocharged version of the Pulsar use a crank angle sensor. This sensor monitors engine speed and piston position and sends to the computer signals on which the controls of the fuel injection, ignition timing and other functions are based.

The Pulsar CA16DE and CA18DE engines do not utilize a conventional distributor and high tension wires. Instead they use 4 small ignition coils fitted directly to each spark plug, and a crank angle sensor is mounted in the front timing belt cover.

The 1982–86 IC ignition system uses a ring-type pickup coil which surrounds the reluctor instead of the single post type pickup coil on earlier models.

1987–96 Sentra models are equipped with a different means of generating the distributor signal. The reluctor and pickup coil are replaced by a rotor plate and crank angle sensor. The rotor plate is machined with slits that break and

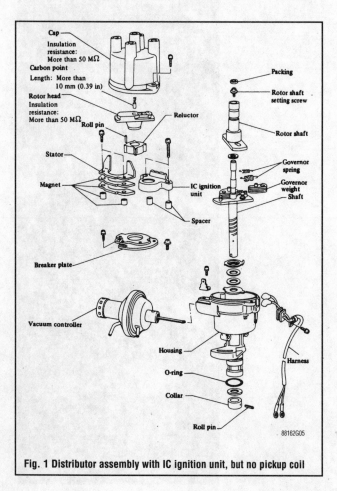

Fig. 1 Distributor assembly with IC ignition unit, but no pickup coil

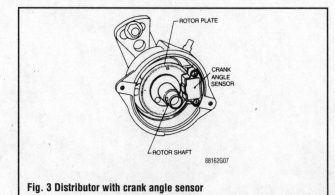

Fig. 3 Distributor with crank angle sensor

then restore a beam of light (a light emitting diode is situated above the plate and a photo-sensitive diode is located underneath). There are 360 slits in the plate to generate an engine speed signal and 4 slits to generate 180° crank angle signals.

When the slits in the rotor plate break and then restore the beam of light, the photo diode generates rough pulses. Then, a wave forming circuit located in the base of the distributor converts these pulses to clear on-off pulses. The Electronic Control Unit, a microcomputer, then utilizes these signals, in combination with others, to generate the actual on-off signal that controls the ignition coil and fires the ignition.

Service on electronic ignition systems consists of inspection of the distributor cap, rotor and ignition wires, and replacing them when necessary. Check the ignition wires for cracking of exterior insulation and for a proper fit on the distributor cap and spark plugs. These parts can be expected to last for at least 40,000 miles (64,400 km), but you should inspect these parts every 2 years or 30,000 miles (48,300 km). In addition, the reluctor air gap should be checked periodically if the system has no crank angle sensor.

Diagnosis and Testing

SECONDARY SPARK TEST

Using a spark tester, verify that spark is present at a plug wire. If a spark tester is unavailable, you can test for spark as follows:
1. Disconnect a spark plug wire from the spark plug.
2. Wrap a thick, dry cloth around the spark plug wire boot and hold the end of the wire approximately ¼ in. (6mm) from a good electrical ground.

✳ CAUTION

Be extremely careful holding the spark plug wire while cranking the engine. The secondary ignition circuit can generate as much as 50,000 volts.

3. Using a remote starter switch, or with the help of an assistant, crank the engine while observing the end of the spark plug wire. A strong blue spark should be observed jumping the gap between the wire and the ground. If a weak spark or no spark is present, the ignition coil may be faulty. Test the ignition coil, as described later in this section.
4. Reconnect the spark plug wire.

Adjustments

1982–86 MODELS

Air Gap
▶ See Figures 4 and 5

1. The distributor cap is held on by 2 spring clips. Release them with a screwdriver and lift the cap straight up and off, with the wires attached.

2. Pull the rotor head (not the spoked reluctor) straight up to remove it.
3. Check the reluctor air gap by using a non-magnetic feeler gauge. Rotate the engine until a reluctor spoke is aligned with the single post pickup coil or stator, depending on the type used on the vehicle. Bump the engine around with the starter or turn it with a wrench on the crankshaft pulley bolt. The gap should measure 0.012–0.020 in. (0.3–0.5mm). Adjustment, if necessary, is made by loosening the single post pickup coil mounting screws and shifting the coil either closer to or farther from the reluctor on early models. Measure the air gap between the reluctor and stator. If not within specifications, loosen the stator retaining screws and adjust.

Reluctor and IC Ignition Unit

REMOVAL & INSTALLATION

1982–86 Models
▶ See Figures 6, 7 and 8

➡**The engines of this period are equipped with a slightly different ignition system and do not utilize a pickup coil.**

1. Remove the distributor cap and pull the rotor from the distributor shaft.
2. Remove the wiring harness and the vacuum controller from the housing.
3. Using 2 flat bladed screwdrivers, place one on each side of the reluctor and pry it from the distributor shaft.

➡**When removing the reluctor, be careful not to damage or distort the teeth.**

4. Remove the roll pin from the reluctor.

➡**If it is necessary to remove the IC unit, mark and remove the breaker plate assembly and separate the IC unit from it. Be careful not to lose the spacers when you remove the IC unit.**

To install:
5. When installing the roll pin into the reluctor, position the cutout direction of the roll pin parallel to the notch in the reluctor. Make sure that the harness to the IC ignition unit is tightly secured.
6. Adjust the air gap between the reluctor and the stator. On Pulsar models, position the cutout of the rotor so it aligns with the keyway on the rotor shaft before installing the rotor.

Ignition Coil

TESTING

Primary Resistance Check
▶ See Figure 9

Turn the ignition key **OFF**, then remove the primary and ground wires from the coil. With the ohmmeter set on the X1 range, touch one lead to the primary

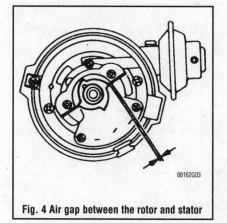

Fig. 4 Air gap between the rotor and stator

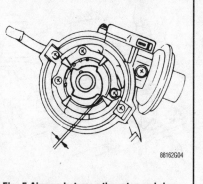

Fig. 5 Air gap between the rotor and ring-type pickup coil

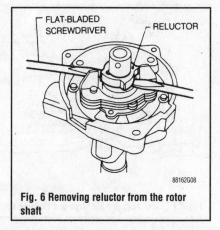

Fig. 6 Removing reluctor from the rotor shaft

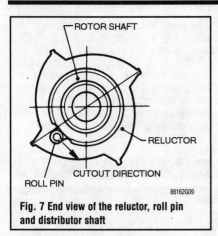

Fig. 7 End view of the reluctor, roll pin and distributor shaft

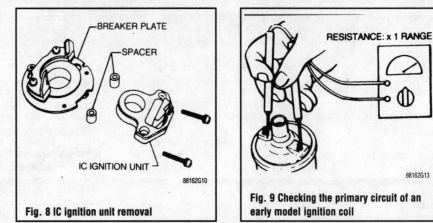

Fig. 8 IC ignition unit removal

Fig. 9 Checking the primary circuit of an early model ignition coil

terminal and the other lead to the ground terminal. The reading should be 1.04–1.27 ohms for 1982–86 models. For 1987–96 models, refer to the Ignition System diagnosis charts in Section 4. If the reading is more than specified, replace the ignition coil assembly.

Secondary Resistance Check

♦ See Figure 10

Turn the ignition key **OFF**, then remove the high tension wire (leading to the distributor) and the ground wire from the coil. Using an ohmmeter, set it on the X1000 scale, touch one lead to the ground terminal and the other lead to the center terminal. The resistance should be 7,300–11,000 ohms for 1982–86 vehicles. For 1987–96 models, refer to the Ignition System diagnosis charts in Section 4. If the reading is not correct, replace the ignition coil.

➡On the Pulsar E16 1984–86 (49 states models), Pulsar E16 1987–88 (all models), a power transistor is used with the ignition coil. The igni-

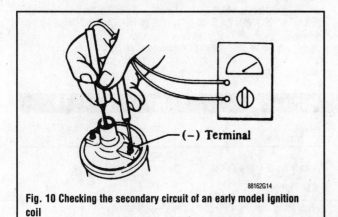

Fig. 10 Checking the secondary circuit of an early model ignition coil

tion signal from the ECU is amplified by the power transistor, which turns the ignition coil primary circuit on and off, inducing the proper high voltage in the secondary circuit. On these models, the ignition coil is a small molded type. Checking the ignition coils on the 1987–88 Pulsar (CA16DE and CA18DE) involves complicated diagnostic procedures. Refer to Ignition System diagnosis charts in Section 4.

REMOVAL & INSTALLATION

♦ See Figure 11

On all models, with the exception of the Pulsar CA16DE and CA18DE engines, the coil is either mounted to the wall of the engine compartment or the engine. To remove disconnect and mark all electrical connections then transfer coil mounting bracket if so equipped to the new coil. When installing the new coil make sure that the coil wire and all other electrical connections are properly installed.

On the Pulsar CA16DE and CA18DE engines, a small ignition coil fits directly onto each spark plug. The ECU controls the four coils by means of a crank angle sensor. To remove one (or more) of these coils, disconnect the air duct and the air hoses, then remove the ornament cover. Unfasten the hold-down screws and carefully remove the ignition coil(s) from the spark plug(s).

Ignition Module

REMOVAL & INSTALLATION

1982–86 Models

The ignition module will actually be an IC ignition unit, or crank angle sensor, depending on the type of distributor. In either case, the distributor cap must be removed.

➡To replace the crank angle sensor on non-reluctor type distributors, refer to Section 4.

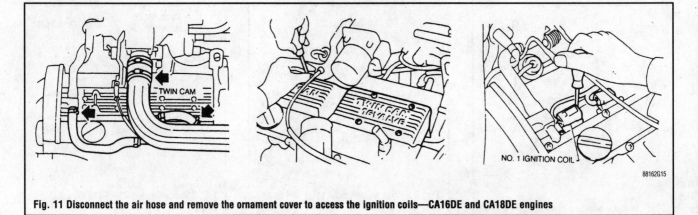

Fig. 11 Disconnect the air hose and remove the ornament cover to access the ignition coils—CA16DE and CA18DE engines

1. Remove the distributor cap, by releasing the two clips or unfastening the two screws with a screwdriver, then lift the cap straight up and off, with the wires attached.

2. Pull the ignition rotor (not the spoked reluctor, if so equipped) straight up to remove.

➡Performing this repair requires working with small parts in a confined space. Look the job over. It may be better to remove the distributor, as described just below, in order to make it easier to complete the work without losing any parts.

3. To replace the IC ignition unit on reluctor type distributors:

   a. First use two small, dull prying devices to work the reluctor off the distributor shaft. Pry evenly and simultaneously to do this. Make sure to catch the roll pin and save it with the reluctor.

   b. Note their routing and then unplug the two electrical connectors for the ignitor unit. Pull the grommet out of the side of the distributor for additional working space and to keep the wires out of the way.

   c. Remove the mounting screws, then remove the ignitor and two spacers.

4. Install in the reverse order. Make sure to install the reluctor roll pin so as to hold the reluctor in the proper position relative to the distributor shaft.

1987–96 Models

The 1987–93 ignition module (crank angle sensor) is an integral part of the distributor assembly. 1994–96 models utilize a camshaft position sensor to perform a similar function. These components are not serviceable separately. If a component is found defective, replace the entire distributor assembly.

Distributor

REMOVAL & INSTALLATION

▶ **See Figures 12 thru 19**

➡The Pulsar CA16DE and CA18DE engines do not utilize a conventional distributor. They have a crank angle sensor in place of the distributor. Except for the absence of wiring, removal and installation is essentially the same procedure.

1. Unfasten the retaining clips and lift the distributor cap straight up. It will be easier to install the distributor if the wiring is not disconnected from the cap. If the wires must be removed from the cap, mark their positions to aid in installation.

2. Disconnect the distributor wiring harness.

3. Disconnect the vacuum lines.

4. Note the position of the rotor in relation to the distributor base. Scribe or paint matchmarks on the rotor and the base of the distributor, as well as on the mating surface of the cylinder head, in order to facilitate reinstallation.

5. Remove the bolts which hold the distributor to the engine.

6. Pull the distributor assembly from the engine.

To install:

Engine Not Rotated

1. Insert the distributor shaft and assembly into the engine. Line up the mark on the distributor and the one on the engine with the metal tip of the rotor. Make sure that the vacuum advance diaphragm is pointed in the same direction as it was pointed originally. This will be done automatically if the marks on the engine and the distributor are lined up with the rotor.

2. Install the distributor hold-down bolt and clamp. Leave the screw loose so that you can move the distributor with heavy hand pressure.

3. Connect the primary wire to the coil. Install the distributor cap on the distributor housing. Secure the distributor cap with the spring clips.

4. Install the spark plug wires if removed. Make sure that the wires are pressed all the way into the top of the distributor cap and firmly onto the spark plug.

5. Set the ignition timing.

➡If the crankshaft has been turned or the engine disturbed in any manner (disassembled and/or rebuilt) while the distributor was removed or

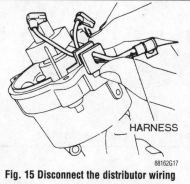

Fig. 12 Matchmark the cylinder head, distributor base and rotor

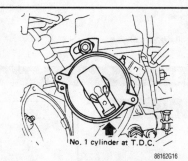

No. 1 cylinder at T.D.C.

88162G16

Fig. 13 On most 1987–96 engines, if the crankshaft is positioned at TDC, the rotor and marks on the distributor body will align

88162P02

Fig. 14 If equipped, slide the retaining clip from the wiring harness connector

HARNESS

88162G17

Fig. 15 Disconnect the distributor wiring harness on distributors equipped with a reluctor

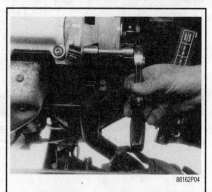

88162P03

Fig. 16 Separate the wiring harness connector from distributors equipped with a crank angle sensor

88162P04

Fig. 17 Unfasten the retaining bolts from the base . . .

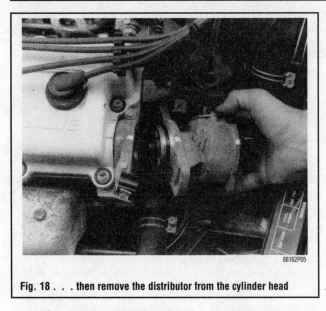

Fig. 18 . . . then remove the distributor from the cylinder head

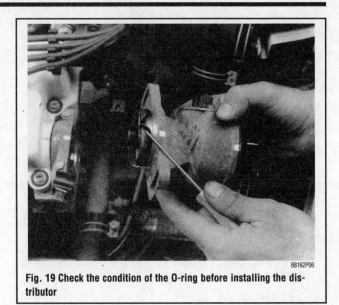

Fig. 19 Check the condition of the O-ring before installing the distributor

if the marks were not drawn, it will be necessary to initially time the engine. Follow the procedure given below.

Engine Rotated

1. It is necessary to place the No. 1 cylinder in the firing position to correctly install the distributor. To locate this position, the ignition timing marks on the crankshaft front pulley are used.
2. Remove the No. 1 cylinder spark plug. Turn the crankshaft until the piston in the No. 1 cylinder is moving up on the compression stroke. This can be determined by placing your thumb over the spark plug hole and feeling the air being forced out of the cylinder. Stop turning the crankshaft when the timing marks that are used to time the engine are aligned.
3. Oil the distributor housing lightly where the distributor bears on the cylinder head.
4. Install the distributor with the rotor, which is mounted on the shaft, pointing toward the No. 1 spark plug terminal on the distributor cap. Of course you won't be able to see the direction in which the rotor is pointing if the cap is on the distributor.

➡Lay the cap on top of the distributor and make a mark on the side of the distributor housing just below the No. 1 spark plug terminal. Make sure that the rotor points toward that mark when you install the distributor.

5. When the distributor shaft has reached the bottom of the hole, move the rotor back and forth slightly until the driving lug on the end of the shaft enters the slots cut in the end of the oil pump shaft or camshaft and the distributor assembly slides down into place.
6. Install the distributor hold-down bolt.
7. Install the spark plug.

DIRECT (DISTRIBUTORLESS) IGNITION SYSTEM

General Information

◆ See Figure 20

The CA16DE and CA18DE engines use a Direct Ignition System (DIS). This system has no conventional distributor or high tension wires. Instead, small efficient ignition coils are fitted directly to each spark plug.

The DIS system uses a crank angle sensor, as does the later model conventional distributor. The sensor monitors engine speed and piston position. It sends signals to the ECU for control of fuel injection, ignition timing and other functions. The crank angle sensor has a rotor plate and a wave forming circuit. The rotor plate has 360 slits for one degree and 4 slits for 180 degrees. A Light Emitting Diode (LED) and photo diode are built into the wave forming circuit.

When the rotor plate passes the space between the LED and photo diode, the slits of the rotor plate continually cut the light which is sent to the photo diode. This causes rough shaped pulses. They are converted into on-off pulses by the wave forming circuit and are then sent to the ECU.

Diagnosis and Testing

➡Diagnosis and testing of the DIS system are covered in Section 4, under "Electronic Engine Controls."

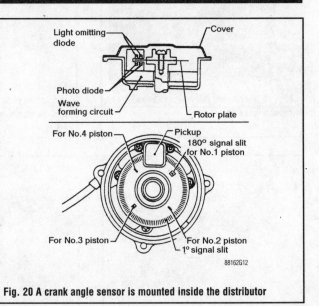

Fig. 20 A crank angle sensor is mounted inside the distributor

FIRING ORDERS

▶ **See Figures 21 and 22**

➡ **To avoid confusion, remove and tag the spark plug wires one at a time, for replacement.**

If a distributor is not keyed for installation with only one orientation, it could have been removed previously and rewired. The resultant wiring would hold the

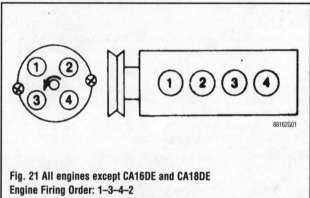

Fig. 21 All engines except CA16DE and CA18DE
Engine Firing Order: 1–3–4–2
Distributor Rotation: Counterclockwise

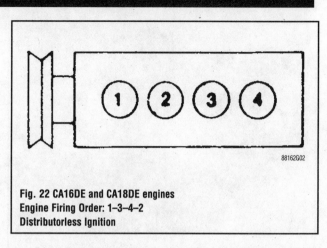

Fig. 22 CA16DE and CA18DE engines
Engine Firing Order: 1–3–4–2
Distributorless Ignition

correct firing order, but could change the relative placement of the plug towers in relation to the engine. For this reason it is imperative that you label all wires before disconnecting any of them. Also, before removal, compare the current wiring with the accompanying illustrations. If the current wiring does not match, make notes in your book to reflect how your engine is wired.

CHARGING SYSTEM

Alternator Precautions

To prevent damage to the alternator and regulator, the following precautionary measures must be taken when working with the electrical system.

1. Never reverse the battery connections.
2. Booster batteries for starting must be connected properly: positive-to-positive and negative-to-ground.
3. Disconnect the battery cables before using a fast charger; the charger has a tendency to force current through the diodes in the opposite direction for which they were designed. This burns out the diodes.
4. Never use a fast charger as a booster for starting the vehicle.
5. Never disconnect the voltage regulator while the engine is running.
6. Avoid long soldering times when replacing diodes or transistors. Prolonged heat is damaging to AC generators.
7. Do not use test lamps of more than 12 volts (V) for checking diode continuity.
8. Do not short across or ground any of the terminals on the AC generator.
9. The polarity of the battery, generator, and regulator must be matched and considered before making any electrical connections within the system.
10. Never operate the alternator on an open circuit. make sure that all connections within the circuit are clean and tight.
11. Disconnect the battery terminals when performing any service on the electrical system. This will eliminate the possibility of accidental reversal of polarity.
12. Disconnect the battery ground cable if arc welding is to be done on any part of the car.

Alternator

TESTING

The main reason for charging system problems is dirty, damaged or loose battery cables or alternator wiring. Always check these problems before going further. After eliminating these causes, a no charge condition usually is the fault of the IC regulator or worn brushes. The brushes have wear indicator lines. If the brush is near or at the indicator, the brush will not contact the rotor slip rings and cause a no charge condition.

REMOVAL & INSTALLATION

▶ **See Figures 23, 24 and 25**

➡ **The alternators for Pulsar and Sentra have not changed much over the years. However, the 1987–88 alternators for Pulsar and Sentra have a different internal diode assembly.**

1. Disconnect the negative battery terminal.
2. Disconnect the 2 lead wires and connector from the alternator.
3. Loosen the drive belt adjusting bolt and remove the belt.
4. Unscrew the alternator attaching bolts and remove the alternator from the vehicle.

To install:

5. Install the alternator and retaining bolts loosely.
6. Install the belt and connect the wiring.
7. Adjust the belt as outlined in Section 1. Torque the retaining bolts to 25 ft. lbs. (34 Nm).

Fig. 23 Unfasten the alternator mounting bolts

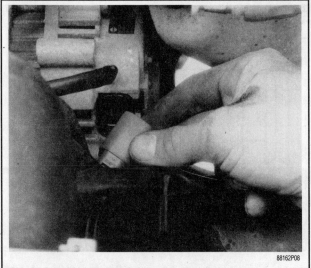

Fig. 24 Detach the electrical connector . . .

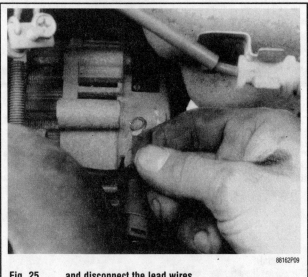

Fig. 25 . . . and disconnect the lead wires

IC Regulator And Brushes

REMOVAL & INSTALLATION

➡All models are equipped with internal voltage regulator. Since the regulator is part of the alternator, no adjustments are possible or necessary.

1. Disconnect the negative battery cable.
2. Remove the alternator from the vehicle.

STARTING SYSTEM

Starter

REMOVAL & INSTALLATION

♦ See Figures 26 and 27

In 1978, a gear reduction starter was introduced on some Canadian and United States models. The differences between the gear reduction and con-

3. Carefully remove the 3 or 4 long through bolts. Be careful not to damage the bolt head. Place a matchmark on the 2 case halves before disassembly.

4. Lightly tap on the rear housing and separate the 2 housings. If the halves will not come apart. Heat the rear housing bearing boss with a 200 watt soldering iron. Do not use heat gun, internal components may be damaged.

5. Remove the diode and brush holder assembly nuts from the rear case. Label all nuts and insulators before removal.

6. Remove the IC regulator from the housing.

7. Remove the brushes from the brush holder. Some units have soldered brush wires. Using a 200 watt soldering iron, remove the brush wire from the brush holder.

To install:

8. Install the brush into the holder so the wire is through the hole.

9. Solder the wire and make sure the brush moves freely inside the brush holder.

10. Install the brush holder, IC regulator and diode assembly into the rear case. Install the retaining nuts and insulators. Torque the nuts to 36 inch lbs. (4 Nm).

11. Push the brushes into the holder and insert a wire through the rear housing into the brush holder to retain the brushes during installation.

12. Carefully install the 2 case halves together, making sure the brushes are held in place.

13. After the halves are together, install the through bolts and torque to 48 inch lbs. (5.5 Nm).

14. Remove the brush retaining wire and install the alternator to the vehicle.

15. Adjust belt tension and reconnect all wiring.

16. Start the engine and check operation.

Battery

Refer to Section 1 for details on battery maintenance.

REMOVAL & INSTALLATION

1. Disconnect the negative (ground) cable from the terminal and then the positive cable. Special pullers are available to remove the cable clamps. To avoid sparks, always disconnect the ground cable first and connect it last.

2. Remove the battery hold-down clamp.

3. Remove the battery, being careful not to spill the acid.

➡Spilled acid can be neutralized with a baking soda/water solution. If you somehow get acid into your eyes, flush it out with lots of water and get to a doctor.

4. Clean the battery posts thoroughly before reinstalling or when installing a new battery.

5. Clean the cable clamps, using a wire brush, both inside and out.

6. Install the battery and the hold-down clamp or strap. Connect the positive, and then the negative cable. DO NOT hammer them in place.

➡The terminals should be coated lightly (externally) with petroleum jelly to prevent corrosion. Another corrosion inhibiting product is felt washers impregnated with an anti-corrosion substance; these washers, which are available in auto parts stores, are simply placed over the battery posts before installing the cables. Make absolutely certain that the battery is connected properly before you turn on the ignition switch. Reversed polarity can burn out your alternator and regulator within a matter of a split second.

ventional starters are: the gear reduction starter has a set of ratio reduction gears while the conventional starter does not. The extra gears on the gear reduction starter make the starter pinion gear turn at about half the speed of the starter, giving the starter twice the turning power of a conventional starter.

1. Disconnect the negative battery cable from the battery.

2. Tag and disconnect the wiring at the starter, taking note of the positions for correct reinstallation.

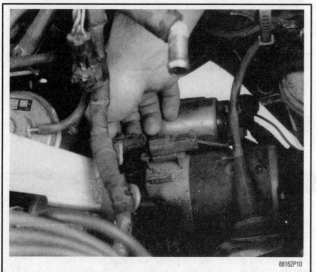

Fig. 26 Disconnect the wiring from the starter motor

88162P10

Fig. 27 After unbolting the starter, remove it from the vehicle

88162P11

3. Remove the bolts attaching the starter to the engine and remove the starter from the vehicle.

4. Install the starter in the reverse order of removal.

SOLENOID REPLACEMENT

All Models

➡**The starter solenoid is also know as the magnetic switch assembly.**

1. Disconnect the battery negative cable. Note routing and then disconnect all starter wiring.

2. Note the location of the solenoid on top of the starter motor itself. If there is plenty of room, you can remove the solenoid with the starter mounted on the engine. Otherwise, remove the starter from the engine as described above.

3. Remove the two through bolts from the starter front housing or gear case. Slide the solenoid to the rear slightly and grasp the shims which are mounted between the solenoid and front housing or gear case to keep them with the assembly. Then, pull the solenoid assembly upward and to the rear so as to disengage the front end of the solenoid plunger from the shift lever. Once the plunger is free, remove the solenoid assembly.

To install:

4. Position the shims against the front of the unit, carefully lining up the through-bolt holes in them with those in the front of the solenoid body. If nec-

essary, turn the plunger so the slot will fit over the vertical top of the shift lever, which is located in the front housing or gear case. Then, work the unit into position with the front end of the plunger near the top of the opening in the gear case or front housing.

5. Position the opening in the front of the plunger over the shift lever and then lower the assembly so as to engage the plunger with the lever. Then, position the shims and solenoid so all bolt holes will line up.

6. Install the through bolts and washers from in front of the gear case or front housing, if necessary turning the shims and solenoid assembly to line up the holes more perfectly. Torque the through bolts alternately and evenly to about 5 ft. lbs. (7 Nm).

7. If necessary, reinstall the starter. Then, install the main battery cable and the two ignition cables, each to its correct terminal. Make sure the terminals are clean, and install the nuts and washers securely. Connect the battery negative cable and test the starter.

BRUSH REPLACEMENT

Non-Reduction Gear Type

1. With the starter out of the vehicle, remove the bolts holding the solenoid to the top of the starter and remove the solenoid.

2. To remove the brushes, remove the 2 through-bolts, the 2 rear cover attaching screws (some models) and the rear cover.

➡**Remove the dust cover, E-ring and thrust washers from the armature shaft before the rear cover.**

3. Using a wire hook, lift the brush springs to separate the brushes from the commutator.

4. Install the brushes in the reverse order of removal and reassemble the rear cover to the starter.

Reduction Gear Type

1. Remove the starter, then the solenoid or magnetic switch.

2. Remove the dust cover, E-ring and thrust washers.

3. Remove the starter through-bolts and brush holder setscrews.

4. Remove the rear cover. The rear cover can be pried off with a screwdriver; be careful not to damage the O-ring or gasket, if so equipped.

5. Remove the starter housing, armature and brush holder from the center housing. They can be removed as an assembly.

6. Using a wire hook on the spring, lift the spring then remove the positive side brush from its holder. The positive brush is insulated from the brush holder and its lead wire is connected to the field coil.

7. Using a wire hook on the spring, lift the spring and remove the negative brush from the holder.

8. Replace all the brushes in the starter assembly.

To install:

9. Insert the new brushes in the brush holder.

10. Install the starter housing, armature and brush holder to the center housing.

11. Install the brush holder setscrews, rear cover and starter through-bolts.

12. Install the thrust washers, E-ring and dust cover.

13. Install the solenoid or magnetic switch.

STARTER DRIVE REPLACEMENT

Non-Reduction Gear Type

1. With the starter motor removed from the vehicle, remove the solenoid from the starter.

2. Remove the 2 through-bolts at the rear cover but do not disassemble the entire starter. Mark the front gear cover with relationship to the yoke housing.

3. Separate the front gear case from the yoke housing, then the shift lever from the armature, without removing the armature from starter assembly.

4. Push the pinion stopper toward the rear cover, then remove the pinion stopper clip and the pinion stopper.

5. Slide the starter drive from the armature shaft.

To install:

6. Install the starter drive on the armature shaft.

7. Install pinion stopper and stopper clip.

8. Reassemble the front gear case to the yoke and the shift lever to the armature.

9. Install the rear cover through-bolts.

10. Install the solenoid or the magnetic switch.

Reduction Gear Type

1. Remove the starter.

2. Remove the solenoid and the torsion spring. Mark the front housing with relationship to the center housing.

3. Remove the center housing-to-front housing bolts, then separate the front housing from the center housing. Do not disassemble the entire starter.

4. Remove the pinion/reduction gear assembly from the armature shaft. Try not to disassemble the entire starter when removing the pinion/reduction gear. Do not disturb the brush assembly in the rear cover.

➡It may be necessary to remove the shift lever pivot pin, to disconnect the pinion/reduction gear assembly from the armature shaft.

To install:

5. Install the pinion/reduction gear assembly onto the armature shaft.

6. Attach the front housing to the center housing, being careful to align the matchmarks, then fasten the retaining bolts.

7. Install the solenoid and torsion spring.

SENDING UNITS AND SENSORS

The following components are **not** electronic engine control related. Refer to Section 4 for electronic engine controls and related sensors.

All Engines

REMOVAL, INSTALLATION & LOCATION

❄ CAUTION

When draining the coolant, keep in mind that cats and dogs are attracted by ethylene glycol antifreeze, and are quite likely to drink any that is left in an uncovered container or in puddles on the ground. This will prove fatal in sufficient quantity. Always drain the coolant into a sealable container. Coolant should be reused unless it is contaminated or several years old.

1. Anti-dieseling solenoid. Is located on the side of the carburetor. Remove the wire and remove from the carburetor. Install and torque to 10 ft. lbs. (15 Nm).

2. Air Temperature control air cleaner temperature sensor. Is located inside the air cleaner housing. Remove the air cleaner cover, disconnect the vacuum hoses and remove the sensor (carbureted engine).

3. Coolant temperature sensor. Is located in water passage in intake manifold. Drain the engine coolant and remove the sensor from the manifold. Install and torque to 25 ft. lbs. (34 Nm).

4. Mixture heater. Is located under the carburetor. Remove the carburetor and remove the heater assembly. Install with new gaskets and torque the carburetor mounting nuts to 25 ft. lbs. (34 Nm).

5. Cooling fan sensor. Is located in bottom hose tee of radiator. Drain the coolant from the radiator. Remove the hose tee and place in a vise. Remove the sensor from the tee. Apply thread sealing tape to the threads and torque to 15 ft. lbs. (20 Nm). Some late model vehicles have the sensor threaded into the radiator tank. Be careful not to damage the radiator threads when removing.

6. Neutral safety switch. Is located at the transaxle.

7. Clutch switch. Is located at the clutch pedal.

3

ENGINE AND ENGINE OVERHAUL

ENGINE MECHANICAL

GENERAL ENGINE SPECIFICATIONS

Year	Engine ID/VIN	Engine Displacement Liters (cc)	Fuel System Type	Net Horsepower @ rpm	Net Torque @ rpm (ft. lbs.)	Bore x Stroke (in.)	Compression Ratio	Oil Pressure @ rpm
1982	E15	1.5 (1488)	2BC	67@5200	85@3200	2.92x3.23	9.0:1	43@1700
1983	E15	1.5 (1488)	2BC	67@5200	85@3200	2.92x3.23	9.0:1	43@1700
	E16	1.6 (1579)	2BC	69@5200	93@3200	2.99x3.46	9.4:1	43@1700
	CD17	1.7 (1680)	DSL	55@4800	104@2800	3.15x3.29	22.2:1	43@1700
1984	E15ET	1.5 (1488)	EFI-Turbo	100@5200	152@3200	2.92x3.23	7.8:1	43@1700
	E16S	1.6 (1579)	2BC	69@5200	93@3200	2.99x3.46	9.4:1	43@1700
	CD17	1.7 (1680)	DSL	55@4800	104@2800	3.15x3.29	22.2:1	43@1700
1985	E16S	1.6 (1579)	2BC	69@5200	93@3200	2.99x3.46	9.4:1	43@1700
	CD17	1.7 (1680)	DSL	55@4800	104@2800	3.15x3.29	22.2:1	43@1700
1986	E16S	1.6 (1579)	2BC	69@5200	93@3200	2.99x3.46	9.4:1	43@1700
	CD17	1.7 (1680)	DSL	55@4800	104@2800	3.15x3.29	22.2:1	67@700
1987	CA16DE	1.6 (1598)	MFI	113@6500	98@4800	3.07x3.29	10.0:1	67@700
	E16S	1.6 (1597)	2BC	69@5200	93@3200	2.99x3.46	9.4:1	43@1700
	E16i	1.6 (1597)	TFI	70@5000	92@2800	2.99x3.46	9.4:1	43@1700
	CD17	1.7 (1680)	DSL	55@4800	104@2800	3.15x3.29	22.2:1	50@2000
1988	E16i	1.6 (1597)	TFI	70@5000	92@2800	2.99x3.29	9.4:1	43@1700
	CA18DE	1.8 (1809)	MFI	125@6400	115@4800	3.27x3.29	10.0:1	67@700
1989	GA16i	1.6 (1597)	TFI	90@6000	96@2800	2.99x3.46	9.4:1	57@2000
	CA18DE	1.8 (1809)	MFI	125@6400	115@4800	3.27x3.29	10.0:1	67@2000
1990	GA16i	1.6 (1597)	TFI	90@6000	96@3200	2.99x3.46	9.4:1	57@3000
1991	GA16DE	1.6 (1597)	MFI	110@6000	108@4000	2.99x3.46	9.5:1	50@3000
	SR20DE	2.0 (1998)	MFI	140@6400	132@4800	3.39x3.39	9.5:1	46@3200
1992	GA16DE	1.6 (1597)	MFI	110@6000	108@4000	2.99x3.46	9.5:1	50@3000
	SR20DE	2.0 (1998)	MFI	140@6400	132@4800	3.39x3.39	9.5:1	46@3200
1993	GA16DE	1.6 (1597)	MFI	110@6000	108@4000	2.99x3.46	9.5:1	50@3000
	SR20DE	2.0 (1998)	MFI	140@6400	132@4800	3.39x3.39	9.5:1	50@3000
1994	GA16DE	1.6 (1597)	MFI	110@6000	108@4000	2.99x3.46	9.5:1	50@3000
	SR20DE	2.0 (1998)	MFI	140@6400	132@4800	3.39x3.46	9.5:1	46@3200
1995	GA16DE	1.6 (1597)	MFI	115@6000	108@4000	2.99x3.46	9.5:1	50@3000
	SR20DE	2.0 (1998)	MFI	140@6400	132@4800	3.39x3.39	9.5:1	46@3200
1996	GA16DE	1.6 (1597)	MFI	115@6000	108@4000	2.99x3.46	9.5:1	50@3000
	SR20DE	2.0 (1998)	MFI	140@6400	132@4800	3.39x3.39	9.5:1	46@3200

Note: Horsepower and torque are SAE net figures. These figures are representative, rather than exact, and vary when a given engine is installed in different models.
EFI - Electronic Fuel Injection
MFI - Multi-port Fuel Injection
DSL - Diesel
TFI - Throttle body Fuel Injection

88163C01

VALVE SPECIFICATIONS

Year	Engine ID/VIN	Engine Displacement Liters (cc)	Seat Angle (deg.)	Face Angle (deg.)	Spring Test Pressure (lbs. @ in.)	Spring Installed Height (in.)	Stem-to-Guide Clearance (in.) Intake	Exhaust	Stem Diameter (in.) Intake	Exhaust
1982	E15	1.5 (1488)	45	44.75-45.25	128@1.189	1.543	0.0008-0.0020	0.0018-0.0030	0.2744-0.2750	0.2734-0.2740
1983	E15	1.5 (1488)	45	44.75-45.25	128@1.189	1.543	0.0008-0.0020	0.0018-0.0030	0.2744-0.2750	0.2734-0.2740
	E16	1.6 (1597)	45	45.25	52@1.543	1.543	0.0008-0.0020	0.0018-0.0030	0.2744-0.2750	0.2734-0.2740
	CD17	1.7 (1680)	45	45.5	[1]	[2]	0.0008-0.0020	0.0016-0.0028	0.2748-0.2750	0.2734-0.2740
1984	E15ET	1.5 (1488)	45	45.5	NA	1.543	0.0020	0.0018-0.0030	0.2744-0.2750	0.2734-0.2740
	E16S	1.6 (1597)	45	44.75-45.25	52@1.543	1.543	0.0020	0.0018-0.0030	0.2744-0.2750	0.2734-0.2740
	CD17	1.7 (1680)	45	45.5	[1]	[2]	0.0020	0.0016-0.0028	0.2748-0.2750	0.2734-0.2740
1985	E16S	1.6 (1597)	45	44.75-45.25	52@1.543	1.543	0.0008-0.0020	0.0018-0.0030	0.2744-0.2750	0.2734-0.2740
	CD17	1.7 (1680)	45	45.5	[1]	[2]	0.0020	0.0016-0.0028	0.2742-0.2748	0.2734-0.2740
1986	E16S	1.6 (1597)	45	44.75-45.25	52@1.543	1.543	0.0008-0.0020	0.0018-0.0030	0.2744-0.2750	0.2734-0.2740
	CD17	1.7 (1680)	45	45.5	[1]	[2]	0.0020	0.0016-0.0028	0.2742-0.2748	0.2734-0.2740
1987	E16i	1.6 (1597)	45	44.75-45.25	52@1.543	1.543	0.0008-0.0020	0.0018-0.0030	0.2744-0.2750	0.2734-0.2740
	E16S	1.6 (1597)	45	44.75-45.25	52@1.543	1.543	0.0008-0.0020	0.0018-0.0030	0.2744-0.2750	0.2734-0.2740
	CA16DE	1.6 (1596)	45	45.5	121@0.065	NA	0.0020	0.0016-0.0030	0.2350-0.2354	0.2341-0.2346
	CD17	1.7 (1680)	45	45.5	[1]	[2]	0.0016-0.0021	0.0016-0.0029	0.2742-0.2748	0.2734-0.2740
1988	E16i	1.6 (1597)	45	44.75-45.25	52@1.543	1.543	0.0008-0.0020	0.0018-0.0030	0.2744-0.2750	0.2734-0.2740
	CA18DE	1.8 (1809)	45	45.5	121@0.065	NA	0.0020	0.0016-0.0029	0.2348-0.2354	0.2341-0.2346
1989	GA16i	1.6 (1597)	45	44.75-45.25	52@1.543	NA	0.0008-0.0020	0.0012-0.0022	0.2348-0.2354	0.2346
1990	CA18DE	1.8 (1809)	45	45.5	121@0.065	NA	0.0021	0.0016-0.0029	0.2152-0.2157	0.2144-0.2150
	GA16i	1.6 (1597)	45	44.75-45.25	[3]	NA	0.0021	0.0012-0.0022	0.2348-0.2354	0.2341-0.2346
1991	GA16DE	1.6 (1597)	45	45.5	76@0.9945	NA	0.0008-0.0020	0.0016-0.0028	0.2152-0.2157	0.2144-0.2150
	SR20DE	2.0 (1998)	45	45.5	134@1.181	NA	0.0008-0.0021	0.0016-0.0029	0.2348-0.2354	0.2341-0.2346

88163C02

CAMSHAFT SPECIFICATIONS

All measurements given in inches.

Year	Engine ID/VIN	Engine Displacement Liters (cc)	Journal Diameter 1	2	3	4	5	Elevation In.	Ex.	Bearing Clearance	Camshaft End-Play
1982	E15	1.5 (1488)	1.6515-1.6522	1.6498-1.6505	1.6515-1.6522	1.6498-1.6505	1.6515-1.6522	1.4170	1.4080	0.0014-0.0030	0.0059-0.0160
1983	E15	1.5 (1488)	1.6515-1.6522	1.6498-1.6505	1.6515-1.6522	1.6498-1.6505	1.6515-1.6522	1.4170	1.4080	0.0014-0.0030	0.0059-0.0160
	E16S	1.6 (1597)	1.6515-1.6522	1.6498-1.6505	1.6515-1.6522	1.6498-1.6505	1.6515-1.6522	1.4170	1.4080	0.0018-0.0035	0.0059-0.0160
	CD17	1.7 (1680)	1.1795-1.1803	1.1795-1.1803	1.1795-1.1803	1.1795-1.1803	1.1795-1.1803	1.7500-1.7520	1.7900	0.0008-0.0024	0.0024-0.0067
1984	E15ET	1.5 (1488)	1.6515-1.6522	1.6498-1.6505	1.6515-1.6522	1.6498-1.6505	1.6515-1.6522	1.4170	1.4080	0.0014-0.0030	0.0059-0.0160
	E16S	1.6 (1597)	1.6515-1.6522	1.6498-1.6505	1.6515-1.6522	1.6498-1.6505	1.6515-1.6522	1.4170	1.4080	0.0018-0.0035	0.0059-0.0160
1985	CD17	1.7 (1680)	1.1795-1.1803	1.1795-1.1803	1.1795-1.1803	1.1795-1.1803	1.1795-1.1803	1.7500-1.7520	1.7900	0.0008-0.0024	0.0024-0.0067
	E16S	1.6 (1597)	1.6515-1.6522	1.6498-1.6505	1.6515-1.6522	1.6498-1.6505	1.6515-1.6522	1.4170	1.4080	0.0018-0.0035	0.0059-0.0160
	CD17	1.7 (1680)	1.1795-1.1803	1.1795-1.1803	1.1795-1.1803	1.1795-1.1803	1.1795-1.1803	1.7500-1.7520	1.7900	0.0008-0.0024	0.0024-0.0067
1986	E16S	1.6 (1597)	1.6515-1.6522	1.6498-1.6505	1.6515-1.6522	1.6498-1.6505	1.6515-1.6522	1.4170	1.4080	0.0018-0.0035	0.0059-0.0160
	CD17	1.7 (1680)	1.1795-1.1803	1.1795-1.1803	1.1795-1.1803	1.1795-1.1803	1.1795-1.1803	1.7500-1.7520	1.7900	0.0008-0.0024	0.0067
1987	E16i	1.6 (1597)	1.6515-1.6522	1.6498-1.6505	1.6515-1.6522	1.6498-1.6505	1.6515-1.6522	1.4170	1.4080	0.0018-0.0035	0.0059-0.0160
	E16S	1.6 (1597)	1.6515-1.6522	1.6498-1.6505	1.6515-1.6522	1.6498-1.6505	1.6515-1.6522	1.4170	1.4080	0.0018-0.0035	0.0059-0.0160
	CA16DE	1.6 (1598)	1.0998-1.1006	1.0998-1.1006	1.0998-1.1006	1.0998-1.1006	1.0998-1.1006	1.5940	1.5940	0.0018-0.0035	0.0020-0.0060
	CD17	1.7 (1680)	1.1795-1.1803	1.1795-1.1803	1.1795-1.1803	1.1795-1.1803	1.1795-1.1803	1.7500-1.7520	1.7900	0.0008-0.0024	0.0067
1988	E16i	1.6 (1597)	1.6515-1.6522	1.6498-1.6505	1.6515-1.6522	1.6498-1.6505	1.6515-1.6522	1.4170	1.4080	0.0018-0.0035	0.0060-0.0067
	CA18DE	1.8 (1809)	1.0998-1.1006	1.0998-1.1006	1.0998-1.1006	1.0998-1.1006	1.0998-1.1006	1.5950	1.5950	0.0018-0.0035	0.0030-0.0060
1989	GA16i	1.6 (1597)	1.6510-1.6518	1.6510-1.6518	1.6510-1.6518	1.6510-1.6518	1.6510-1.6518	1.4150-1.4220	1.4070-1.4150	0.0018-0.0035	0.0010-0.0079
	CA18DE	1.8 (1809)	1.0998-1.1006	1.0998-1.1006	1.0998-1.1006	1.0998-1.1006	1.0998-1.1006	1.5940-1.5950	1.5940-1.5950	0.0018-0.0035	0.0030-0.0060
1990	GA16i	1.6 (1597)	1.6510-1.6518	1.6510-1.6518	1.6510-1.6518	1.6510-1.6518	1.6510-1.6518	1.4150-1.4220	1.4070-1.4150	0.0018-0.0035	0.0010-0.0079
	CD17	1.7 (1680)	1.1795-1.1803	1.1795-1.1803	1.1795-1.1803	1.1795-1.1803	1.1795-1.1803	1.7500-1.7520	1.7900	0.0008-0.0024	0.0060-0.0060
1991	GA16DE	1.6 (1597)	0.9423-0.9431	0.9423-0.9431	0.9423-0.9431	0.9423-0.9431	0.9423-0.9431	1.5980-1.6060	1.5710-1.5780	0.0018-0.0034	0.0040-0.0079
	SR20DE	2.0 (1998)	1.0998-1.1006	1.0998-1.1006	1.0998-1.1006	1.0998-1.1006	1.0998-1.1006	1.5120-1.5200	1.4930-1.5000	0.0018-0.0047	0.0022-0.0079
1992	GA16DE	1.6 (1597)	1.0998-1.1006	1.0998-1.1006	1.0998-1.1006	1.0998-1.1006	1.0998-1.1006	1.5980-1.6060	1.5710-1.5780	0.0018-0.0034	0.0040-0.0079
	SR20DE	2.0 (1998)	1.0998-1.1006	1.0998-1.1006	1.0998-1.1006	1.0998-1.1006	1.0998-1.1006	1.5120-1.5200	1.4930-1.5000	0.0018-0.0047	0.0022-0.0079

88163C04

VALVE SPECIFICATIONS

Year	Engine ID/VIN	Engine Displacement Liters (cc)	Seat Angle (deg.)	Face Angle (deg.)	Spring Test Pressure (lbs.@In.)	Spring Installed Height (In.)	Stem-to-Guide Clearance (In.) Intake	Exhaust	Stem Diameter (In.) Intake	Exhaust
1992	GA16DE	1.6 (1597)	45	45.5	76@0.9945	NA	0.0008-0.0020	0.0016-0.0028	0.2152-0.2157	0.2144-0.2150
	SR20DE	2.0 (1998)	45	45.5	134@1.181	NA	0.0008-0.0021	0.0016-0.0029	0.2348-0.2354	0.2341-0.2346
1993	GA16DE	1.6 (1597)	45	45.5	76@0.9945	NA	0.0008-0.0020	0.0016-0.0028	0.2152-0.2157	0.2144-0.2150
	SR20DE	2.0 (1998)	45	45.5	134@1.181	NA	0.0008-0.0021	0.0016-0.0029	0.2348-0.2354	0.2341-0.2346
1994	GA16DE	1.6 (1597)	45	45.5	76@0.9945	NA	0.0008-0.0020	0.0016-0.0028	0.2152-0.2157	0.2144-0.2150
	SR20DE	2.0 (1998)	45	45.5	134@1.181	NA	0.0008-0.0021	0.0016-0.0029	0.2348-0.2354	0.2341-0.2346
1995	GA16DE	1.6 (1597)	45	45.5	76@0.9945	NA	0.0008-0.0020	0.0016-0.0028	0.2152-0.2157	0.2144-0.2150
	SR20DE	2.0 (1998)	45	45.5	134@1.181	NA	0.0008-0.0021	0.0016-0.0029	0.2348-0.2354	0.2341-0.2346
1996	GA16DE	1.6 (1597)	45	45.5	76@0.9945	NA	0.0008-0.0020	0.0016-0.0028	0.2152-0.2157	0.2144-0.2150
	SR20DE	2.0 (1998)	45	45.5	134@1.181	NA	0.0008-0.0021	0.0016-0.0029	0.2348-0.2354	0.2341-0.2346

NA - Not Available

1 inner: 33@1.555
   outer: 19@1.1417
2 inner: 1.555
   outer: 1.1417
3 intake: 98-110@1.331
   exhaust: 109-122@1.346

88163C03

CRANKSHAFT AND CONNECTING ROD SPECIFICATIONS

All measurements are given in inches.

Year	Engine ID/VIN	Engine Displacement Liters (cc)	Crankshaft Main Brg. Journal Dia.	Main Brg. Oil Clearance	Shaft End-play	Thrust on No.	Connecting Rod Journal Diameter	Oil Clearance	Side Clearance
1982	E15	1.5 (1488)	1.9663-1.9671		0.002-0.007	3	1.5730-1.5738	0.0016-0.0024	0.002-0.007
1983	E15	1.5 (1488)	1.9663-1.9671	[1]	0.002-0.007	3	1.5730-1.5738	0.0016-0.0024	0.002-0.007
	E16S	1.6 (1597)	1.9663-1.9671	[3]	0.002-0.007	3	1.5730-1.5738	0.0016-0.0024	0.002-0.007
	CD17	1.7 (1680)	2.0847-2.0852	0.0016-0.0024	0.002-0.007	3	1.7701-1.7706	0.0013-0.0026	0.008-0.012
1984	E15ET	1.5 (1488)	1.9663-1.9671	[3]	0.002-0.007	3	1.5730-1.5738	0.0016-0.0024	0.002-0.007
	E16S	1.6 (1597)	1.9663-1.9671	[3]	0.002-0.007	3	1.5730-1.5738	0.0016-0.0024	0.002-0.007
	CD17	1.7 (1680)	2.0847-2.0852	0.0016-0.0024	0.002-0.007	3	1.7701-1.7706	0.0013-0.0026	0.008-0.012
1985	E16S	1.6 (1597)	1.9663-1.9671	[3]	0.002-0.007	3	1.5730-1.5738	0.0016-0.0024	0.002-0.007
	CD17	1.7 (1680)	2.0847-2.0852	0.0016-0.0024	0.002-0.007	3	1.7701-1.7706	0.0013-0.0026	0.008-0.012
1986	E16S	1.6 (1597)	1.9663-1.9671	[3]	0.002-0.007	3	1.5730-1.5738	0.0012-0.0024	0.002-0.007
	CD17	1.7 (1680)	2.0847-2.0852	0.0016-0.0024	0.002-0.007	3	1.7702-1.7706	0.0013-0.0026	0.008-0.012
1987	E16i	1.6 (1597)	1.9661-1.9671	[3]	0.002-0.007	3	1.5733-1.5738	0.0004-0.0017	0.004-0.015
	CA16DE	1.6 (1598)	1.0847-1.0856	0.0008-0.0019 [2]	0.002-0.007	3	1.7698-1.7706	0.0007-0.0018	0.008-0.014
	CD17	1.7 (1680)	[4]	0.0013-0.0026	0.002-0.007	3	1.7701-1.7706	0.0013-0.0026	0.008-0.012
1988	E16i	1.6 (1597)	1.9661-1.9671	[5]	0.002-0.007	3	1.5730-1.5738	0.0004-0.0017	0.004-0.015
	CA18DE	1.8 (1809)	1.0847-1.0856	0.0008-0.0019	0.002-0.007	3	1.7698-1.7706	0.0007-0.0018	0.008-0.014
	GA16i	1.6 (1597)	[2]	0.0008-0.0017	0.002-0.007	3	1.5738	0.0004-0.0014	0.008-0.018
1989	CA18DE	1.8 (1809)	1.0847-1.0856	0.0008-0.0019	0.002-0.007	3	1.7698-1.7706	0.0007-0.0018	0.008-0.016
	GA16i	1.6 (1597)	[2]	0.0008-0.0017	0.002-0.007	3	1.5731-1.5738	0.0004-0.0014	0.008-0.018
1990	GA16i	1.6 (1597)	[2]	0.0008-0.0017	0.002-0.007	3	1.5731-1.5738	0.0004-0.0014	0.008-0.018
1991	GA16DE	1.6 (1597)	[2]	0.0008-0.0017	0.002-0.007	3	[7]	0.0004-0.0014	0.008-0.018
	SR20DE	2.0 (1998)	[9]	0.0002-0.0009	0.0039-0.0102	3	[10]	0.0008-0.0018	0.008-0.014
1992	GA16DE	1.6 (1597)	[8]	0.0008-0.0017	0.002-0.007	3	[7]	0.0004-0.0014	0.008-0.018
	SR20DE	2.0 (1998)	[9]	0.0002-0.0009	0.0039-0.0102	3	[10]	0.0008-0.0018	0.008-0.014
1993	GA16DE	1.6 (1597)	[6]	0.0002-0.0017	0.002-0.007	3	[7]	0.0004-0.0014	0.008-0.018
	SR20DE	2.0 (1998)	[8]	0.0002-0.0009	0.0039-0.0102	3	[10]	0.0008-0.0018	0.008-0.014

88163C06

CAMSHAFT SPECIFICATIONS

All measurements given in inches.

Year	Engine ID/VIN	Engine Displacement Liters (cc)	Journal Diameter 1	2	3	4	5	Elevation In.	Ex.	Bearing Clearance	Camshaft End-Play
1993	GA16DE	1.6 (1597)	1.0998-1.1006	0.9423-0.9431	0.9423-0.9431	0.9423-0.9431	0.9423-0.9431	1.5980-1.6060	1.5700-1.5780	0.0018-0.0034	0.0040-0.0079
	SR20DE	2.0 (1998)	1.0998-1.1006	1.0998-1.1006	1.0998-1.1006	1.0998-1.1006	1.0998-1.1006	1.5120-1.5200	1.4930-1.5000	0.0018-0.0047	0.0022-0.0079
1994	GA16DE	1.6 (1597)	1.0998-1.1006	0.9423-0.9431	0.9423-0.9431	0.9423-0.9431	0.9423-0.9431	1.5980-1.6060	1.5700-1.5780	0.0018-0.0034	0.0040-0.0079
	SR20DE	2.0 (1998)	1.0998-1.1006	1.0998-1.1006	1.0998-1.1006	1.0998-1.1006	1.0998-1.1006	1.5120-1.5200	1.4930-1.5000	0.0018-0.0047	0.0022-0.0079
1995	GA16DE	1.6 (1597)	1.0998-1.1006	0.9423-0.9431	0.9423-0.9431	0.9423-0.9431	0.9423-0.9431	1.5980-1.6060	1.5700-1.5780	0.0018-0.0034	0.0030-0.0079
	SR20DE	2.0 (1998)	1.0998-1.1006	1.0998-1.1006	1.0998-1.1006	1.0998-1.1006	1.0998-1.1006	1.5120-1.5200	1.4930-1.5000	0.0018-0.0047	0.0022-0.0079
1996	GA16DE	1.6 (1597)	1.0998-1.1006	0.9423-0.9431	0.9423-0.9431	0.9423-0.9431	0.9423-0.9431	1.5980-1.6060	1.5700-1.5780	0.0018-0.0034	0.0030-0.0079
	SR20DE	2.0 (1998)	1.0998-1.1006	1.0998-1.1006	1.0998-1.1006	1.0998-1.1006	1.0998-1.1006	1.5120-1.5200	1.4930-1.5000	0.0018-0.0047	0.0022-0.0079

88163C05

PISTON AND RING SPECIFICATIONS
All measurements are given in inches.

Year	Engine ID/VIN	Engine Displacement Liters (cc)	Piston Clearance	Ring Gap			Ring Side Clearance		
				Top Compression	Bottom Compression	Oil Control	Top Compression	Bottom Compression	Oil Control
1982	E15	1.5 (1488)	0.0009-0.0017	0.0079-0.0138	0.0059-0.0118	0.0118-0.0354	0.0016-0.0029	0.0012-0.0025	0.0020-0.0049
1983	E15	1.5 (1488)	0.0009-0.0017	0.0079-0.0138	0.0059-0.0118	0.0118-0.0354	0.0016-0.0029	0.0012-0.0025	0.0020-0.0049
	E16S	1.6 (1597)	0.0009-0.0017	0.0079-0.0138	0.006-0.012	0.012-0.035	0.002-0.003	0.001-0.003	0.002-0.006
	CD17	1.7 (1680)	0.0020-0.0028	0.0079-0.0138	0.008-0.014	0.012-0.018	0.001-0.002	0.002-0.003	0.001-0.003
1984	E15ET	1.5 (1488)	0.0016-0.0024		0.0059-0.0098	0.0079-0.0236	0.0016-0.0029	0.0012-0.0025	0.0020-0.0049
	E16S	1.6 (1597)	0.0009-0.0017	0.0079-0.0138	0.006-0.012	0.012-0.035	0.002-0.003	0.001-0.003	0.002-0.006
	CD17	1.7 (1680)	0.0020-0.0028	0.0079-0.0138	0.008-0.014	0.012-0.018	0.001-0.002	0.002-0.003	0.001-0.003
1985	E16S	1.6 (1597)	0.0009-0.0017	0.0079-0.0138	0.006-0.012	0.012-0.035	0.002-0.003	0.001-0.003	0.002-0.006
	CD17	1.7 (1680)	0.0020-0.0028	0.0079-0.0138	0.008-0.014	0.012-0.018	0.001-0.002	0.002-0.003	0.001-0.003
1986	E16S	1.6 (1597)	0.0009-0.0017	0.0079-0.0138	0.006-0.012	0.012-0.035	0.002-0.003	0.001-0.002	0.002-0.006
	CD17	1.7 (1680)	0.0020-0.0028	0.0079-0.0138	0.008-0.014	0.012-0.018	0.001-0.002	0.002-0.003	0.001-0.003
1987	CA16DE	1.6 (1597)	0.0009-0.0017	0.009-0.016	0.007-0.018	0.008-0.030	0.002-0.003	0.001-0.003	0.001-0.003
	E16i	1.6 (1597)	0.0009-0.0017	0.0080-0.016	0.0060-0.018	0.0120-0.030	0.002-0.003	0.001-0.002	0.002-0.006
	CD17	1.7 (1680)	0.0010-0.0018 [3]	0.0140 [2]	0.0120	0.0350	0.001-0.002	0.002-0.003	0.001-0.003
1988	E16i	1.6 (1597)	0.0009-0.0017	0.0080-0.0140	0.0060-0.0120	0.0120-0.0350	0.002-0.003	0.001-0.002	0.002-0.006
	CA18DE	1.8 (1809)	0.0006-0.0014	0.009-0.015	0.007-0.018	0.008-0.030	0.002-0.003	0.001-0.003	0.001-0.003
1989	GA16i	1.6 (1597)	0.0009-0.0017	0.006-0.014	0.015-0.021	0.008-0.024	0.002-0.003	0.001-0.002	0.008-0.024
	CA18DE	1.8 (1809)	0.0006-0.0014	0.009-0.014	0.007-0.007	0.008-0.024	0.002-0.003	0.001-0.003	0.001-0.003
1990	GA16i	1.6 (1597)	0.0006-0.0014	0.008-0.015	0.014-0.018	0.008-0.030	0.002-0.003	0.001-0.003	0.008-0.024
1991	GA16DE	1.6 (1597)	0.0006-0.0014	0.008-0.014	0.015-0.020	0.008-0.024	0.002-0.003	0.001-0.003	0.008-0.024
	SR20DE	2.0 (1998)	0.0004-0.0012	0.008-0.014	0.014-0.020	0.008-0.024	0.002-0.003	0.001-0.003	NA
1992	GA16DE	1.6 (1597)	0.0006-0.0014	0.008-0.014	0.014-0.020	0.008-0.024	0.002-0.003	0.001-0.003	0.008-0.024
	SR20DE	2.0 (1998)	0.0004-0.0012	0.009-0.015	0.014-0.020	0.008-0.024	0.002-0.003	0.001-0.003	NA
1993	GA16DE	1.6 (1597)	0.0006-0.0014	0.008-0.014	0.015-0.020	0.008-0.024	0.002-0.003	0.001-0.003	0.008-0.024
	SR20DE	2.0 (1998)	0.0004-0.0012	0.008-0.012	0.014-0.020	0.008-0.024	0.002-0.003	0.001-0.003	NA

88163C08

CRANKSHAFT AND CONNECTING ROD SPECIFICATIONS
All measurements are given in inches.

Year	Engine ID/VIN	Engine Displacement Liters (cc)	Crankshaft				Connecting Rod		
			Main Brg. Journal Dia.	Main Brg. Oil Clearance	Shaft End-play	Thrust on No.	Journal Diameter	Oil Clearance	Side Clearance
1994	GA16DE	1.6 (1597)	6	0.0008-0.0017 [2]	0.002-0.0070	3	7	0.0004-0.0014 [2]	0.008-0.0180
	SR20DE	2.0 (1998)	8	0.0002-0.0009 [9]	0.0039-0.0102	3	10	0.0008-0.0018 [9]	0.008-0.014
1995	GA16DE	1.6 (1597)	6	0.0007-0.0017 [2]	0.002-0.007	3	7	0.0004-0.0014 [2]	0.008-0.018
	SR20DE	2.0 (1998)	8	0.0002-0.0009 [9]	0.0039-0.0102	3	10	0.0008-0.0018 [9]	0.008-0.014
1996	GA16DE	1.6 (1597)	6	0.0007-0.0017 [2]	0.002-0.007	3	7	0.0004-0.0014 [2]	0.008-0.018
	SR20DE	2.0 (1998)	8	0.0002-0.0009 [9]	0.0039-0.0102	3	10	0.0008-0.0018 [9]	0.008-0.014

1 Except MPG Model
  Bearings 1 and 5: 0.0012-0.0030; Wear limit: 0.004
  Bearings 2, 3 and 4: 0.0012-0.0036; Wear limit: 0.004
  MPG Model
  Bearings 1, 3 and 5: 0.0019-0.0030; Wear limit: 0.004
  Bearings 2, and 4: 0.0012-0.0036; Wear limit: 0.004
2 Wear Limit: 0.004
3 Bearings 1 and 5: 0.0012-0.0030; Wear limit: 0.004
  Bearings 2, 3 and 4: 0.0012-0.0036; Wear limit: 0.004
4 Grade 0: 1.2850-2.0853
  Grade 2: 2.0850-2.0850
5 Grade 1: 2.0850-2.0853
  Grade 2: 2.0847-2.0850
6 Bearings 1, 3 and 5: 0.0012-0.0022; Wear limit: 0.004
  Bearings 2 and 4: 0.0012-0.0036; Wear limit: 0.004
  Grade 0: 1.9668-9671
  Grade 1: 1.9665-9668
  Grade 2: 1.9661-9665
7 Grade 0: 1.5735-5738
  Grade 1: 1.5733-5735
  Grade 2: 1.5731-5733
8 Grade 0: 2.1643-1646
  Grade 1: 2.1641-1643
  Grade 2: 2.1639-1641
  Grade 3: 2.1636-1639
9 Wear limit: 0.0035
10 Grade 0: 1.8885-8887
   Grade 1: 1.8883-8885
   Grade 2: 1.8880-8883

88163C07

PISTON AND RING SPECIFICATIONS

All measurements are given in inches.

Year	Engine ID/VIN	Engine Displacement Liters (cc)	Piston Clearance	Ring Gap Top Compression	Ring Gap Bottom Compression	Ring Gap Oil Control	Ring Side Clearance Top Compression	Ring Side Clearance Bottom Compression	Oil Control
1994	GA16DE	1.6 (1597)	0.0006-0.0014	0.008-0.014	0.015-0.020	0.008-0.024	0.002-0.003	0.001-0.003	NA
	SR20DE	2.0 (1998)	0.0004-0.0012	0.008-0.012	0.014-0.020	0.008-0.024	0.002-0.003	0.001-0.003	NA
1995	GA16DE	1.6 (1597)	0.0006-0.0014	0.008-0.014	0.015-0.020	0.008-0.024	0.002-0.003	0.001-0.003	NA
	SR20DE	2.0 (1998)	0.0004-0.0012	0.008-0.012	0.014-0.020	0.008-0.024	0.002-0.003	0.001-0.003	NA
1996	GA16DE	1.6 (1597)	0.0006-0.0012	0.008-0.014	0.015-0.020	0.008-0.024	0.003	0.001-0.003	NA
	SR20DE	2.0 (1998)	0.0004-0.0012	0.008-0.012	0.014-0.020	0.008-0.024	0.002-0.003	0.001-0.003	NA

NA - Not Available

1 Piston grades 1 and 2
0.0079+0.102 (yellow)
Piston grades 3, 4 and 5
0.0055-0.0079

2 Grade 1: 0.008-0.009
Grade 2: 0.009-0.011
Grade 3: 0.011-0.012
Grade 4: 0.012-0.013
Grade 5: 0.013-0.015

3 Grade 1: 0.012-0.013
Grade 2: 0.013-0.014
Grade 3: 0.014-0.015
Grade 4: 0.015-0.016
Grade 5: 0.016-0.018

88163C09

TORQUE SPECIFICATIONS

All readings in ft. lbs.

Year	Engine ID/VIN	Engine Displacement Liters (cc)	Cylinder Head Bolts	Main Bearing Bolts	Rod Bearing Bolts	Crankshaft Damper Bolts	Flywheel Bolts	Manifold Intake	Manifold Exhaust	Spark Plugs	Lug Nuts
1982	E15	1.5 (1488)	51-54 [1]	36-43	23-27	108-120	58-65	14	14	14-22	70
1983	E15	1.5 (1488)	51-54 [1]	36-43	23-27	83-108	58-65	14	14	14-22	70
	E16S	1.6 (1597)	51-54 [1]	36-43	23-27	83-108	58-65	14	14	14-22	70
	CD17	1.7 (1680)	72-80 [2]	33-40	23-27	90-98	72-80	14	14	NA	70
1984	E15ET	1.5 (1488)	51-54 [1]	36-43	23-27	83-108	58-65	14	14	14-22	70
	E16S	1.6 (1597)	51-54 [1]	36-43	23-27	83-108	58-65	14	14	NA	70
	CD17	1.7 (1680)	72-80 [2]	33-40	23-27	90-98	72-80	14	14	NA	70
1985	E16S	1.6 (1597)	51-54 [1]	36-43	23-27	83-108	58-65	14	14	14-22	70
	CD17	1.7 (1680)	72-80 [2]	33-40	23-27	90-98	72-80	14	14	NA	70
1986	E16S	1.6 (1597)	51-54 [1]	36-43	23-27	80-94	58-65	14	14	14-22	70
	CD17	1.7 (1680)	72-80 [2]	33-40	23-27	90-98	72-80	14	14	NA	70
1987	E16S	1.6 (1597)	51-54 [1]	36-43	23-27	80-94	80-94	14	14	14-22	70
	E16i	1.6 (1597)	51-54 [1]	36-43	23-27	80-94	80-94 [3]	14	14	14-22	70
1988	CA16DE	1.6 (1597)	[6]	33-40	30-33	105-112	61-69	14	14	14-22	70
	CD17	1.7 (1680)	72-80 [2]	33-40	23-27	90-98	72-80	14	31	NA	70
1989	CA18DE	1.8 (1809)	[6]	33-40	30-33	105-112	61-69	17	31	14-22	70
	GA16i	1.6 (1597)	[7]	34-38	[10]	98-112	61-69	17	14	14-22	70
1990	CA18DE	1.8 (1809)	[6]	33-40	30-33	105-112	61-69	17	31	14-22	70
	GA16i	1.6 (1597)	[7]	34-38	[10]	98-112	61-69	14	14	14-22	70
1991	GA16DE	1.6 (1597)	[5]	34-38	[10]	98-112	61-69 [4]	14	14	14-22	75
	SR20DE	2.0 (1998)	[8]	34-38	[9]	105-112	61-69 [4]	14	30	14-22	75
1992	GA16DE	1.6 (1597)	[5]	34-38	[10]	98-112	61-69	14	14	14-22	75
	SR20DE	2.0 (1998)	[8]	34-38	[9]	105-112	61-69	14	30	14-22	75
1993	GA16DE	1.5 (1597)	[8]	34-38	[10]	98-112	61-69	14	14	14-22	75
	SR20DE	2.0 (1998)	[8]	34-38	[9]	105-112	61-69	14	30	14-22	75
1994	GA16DE	1.6 (1597)	[8]	34-38	[10]	105-112	61-69	14	14	14-22	75
	SR20DE	2.0 (1998)	[5]	34-38	[9]	105-112	61-69	14	30	14-22	79
1995	GA16DE	1.6 (1597)	[5]	34-38	[10]	98-112	61-69	14	19	14-22	75
	SR20DE	2.0 (1998)	[5]	34-38	[9]	105-112	61-69	14	30	14-22	75
1996	GA16DE	1.6 (1597)	[5]	34-38	[10]	98-112	61-69	14	14	14-22	79
	SR20DE	2.0 (1998)	[8]	34-38	[9]	105-112	61-69	14	30	14-22	75

1 Step 1: 10 ft. lbs.
Step 2: 22 ft. lbs.
Step 3: 51 ft. lbs.
Step 4: Loosen completely
Step 5: Repeat Steps 1-3 final torque 51-54 ft. lbs.

2 Step 1: 48 ft. lbs.
Step 2: 72-80 ft. lbs.

3 Manual transaxle: 58-65 ft. lbs.
Automatic transaxle: 69-76 ft. lbs.

4 Manual transaxle: 61-69 ft. lbs.
Automatic transaxle: 69-76 ft. lbs.

5 Step 1: 22 ft. lbs.
Step 2: 43 ft. lbs.
Step 3: Loosen completely and retorque to 22 ft. lbs.
Step 4: 43 ft. lbs. or an additional 50-55 degrees
Bolts 11-15: Torque last, to 72 inch lbs.

6 Step 1: 22 ft. lbs.
Step 2: 76 ft. lbs.
Step 3: Loosen completely then retorque to 22 ft. lbs.
Step 4: 76 ft. lbs. or an additional 90 degrees

7 Bolt Nos. 1-10:
Step 1: 22 ft. lbs.
Step 2: 47 ft. lbs.
Step 3: Loosen completely then retorque to 22 ft. lbs.
Step 4: 47 ft. lbs. or an additional 60-65 degrees
Bolt Nos. 11-15: Torque last, to 72 inch lbs.

8 Step 1: 29 ft. lbs.
Step 2: 58 ft. lbs.
Step 3: Loosen completely and retorque to 30 ft. lbs.
Step 4: Turn each bolt, in sequence, an additional 90-100 degrees
Step 5: Repeat Step 4

9 Step 1: 28 ft. lbs.
Step 2: 54-61 ft. lbs. or an additional 45-50 degrees
12 ft. lbs. plus an additional 60-65 degrees

10 Step 1: 10-12 ft. lbs.
Step 2: 35-40 degrees clockwise or 17-21 ft. lbs.

11 Step 1: 10-12 ft. lbs.
Step 2: 60-65 degrees clockwise or 28-33 ft. lbs.

88163C10

Engine

REMOVAL & INSTALLATION

1982–87 E15 and E16S Engines

The following procedures are for the 1987 and earlier models equipped with 1.5L and 1.6L engines that are not fuel injected. For EFI equipped models, follow the procedures later in this section.

➡The engine and transaxle must be removed as a single unit. The engine and transaxle is removed from the top of the vehicle. You must situate the vehicle on as flat and solid a surface as possible. Place chocks or equivalent at front and rear of rear wheels to keep the vehicle from rolling.

1. Mark the location of the hinges on the hood. Remove the hood by holding at both sides and unscrewing bolts.
2. Disconnect the battery cables and remove the battery.
3. Drain the coolant from the radiator, then remove the radiator and the heater hoses.

❊❊ CAUTION

When draining engine coolant, keep in mind that cats and dogs are attracted to ethylene glycol antifreeze and could drink any that is left in an uncovered container or in puddles on the ground. This will prove fatal in sufficient quantity. Always drain coolant into a sealable container. Coolant should be reused unless it is contaminated or is several years old.

4. Remove the air cleaner-to-rocker cover hose and the air cleaner cover, then place a clean rag in the carburetor or throttle body opening to keep out the dirt or any foreign object.

➡Disconnect and label all the necessary vacuum hoses and electrical connectors, for reinstallation purposes. A good rule of thumb when disconnecting the rather complex engine wiring of today's cars is to put a piece of masking tape on the wire and on the connection you removed the wire from, then mark both pieces of tape 1, 2, 3, etc. When replacing wiring, simply match the pieces of tape.

5. If equipped, disconnect the air pump cleaner and remove the carbon canister.
6. Remove the auxiliary fan, the washer tank and the radiator grille. Remove the radiator together with the fan motor assembly as a unit.
7. Remove the clutch control wire or cable from the transaxle. Remove the right and the left buffer rods but do not alter the length of these rods. Disconnect the speedometer cable from the transaxle and plug the hole with a clean rag.
8. If equipped with air conditioning, loosen the idler pulley nut and the adjusting bolt, then remove the compressor belt. Remove the compressor to one side and suspend on a wire. Do not disconnect the A/C hoses if at all possible. Remove the condenser and the receiver drier and place them on the right fender.

➡If equipped with AC, DO NOT ATTEMPT TO UNFASTEN ANY OF THE REFRIGERANT HOSES. See Section 1 for additional warnings. If equipped with power steering, loosen the idler pulley nut and adjusting bolt, then remove the drive belt and the power steering pulley.

9. If equipped with a manual transaxle, disconnect the transaxle shifting rods by removing the securing bolts. If equipped with an automatic transaxle, disconnect the mounting bracket and the control wire from the transaxle.
10. Attach the engine sling, tool 1000501M00 and 1000623M00 or equivalent at each end of the engine block. Connect a chain or cable to the engine slingers.
11. Unbolt the exhaust pipe from the exhaust manifold. There are 3 bolts which attach the pipe to the manifold and bolts which attach the pipe support to the engine.

➡Remove the tie rod ends and the lower ball joints. Disconnect the right and left side drive shafts from their side flanges and remove the bolt holding the radius link support. When drawing out the halfshafts, it is necessary to loosen the strut head bolts also be careful not to damage the grease seals.

12. Remove the axle shafts. You can refer to Section 7 for the axle shaft removal and installation procedures.
13. Remove the radius link support bolt, then lower the transaxle shift selector rods.
14. Unbolt the engine from the engine and the transaxle mounts.
15. Using an overhead lifting device, attach it to the engine lifting sling and slowly remove the engine and transaxle assembly from the vehicle.

➡When removing the engine, be careful not to knock it against the adjacent parts.

16. Separate the engine from the transaxle if necessary.
To install:
17. Installation is the reverse of removal but please note the following steps.
18. Attach the transaxle to the engine and torque the bolts to 35 ft. lbs. (48 Nm).
19. Install all the necessary parts on the engine before lowering it into the vehicle, such as, spark plugs, water pump etc.
20. Lower the engine and transaxle as an assembly into the car and onto the frame, make sure to keep it as level as possible.
21. Check the clearance between the frame and clutch housing and make sure that the engine mount bolts are seated in the groove of the mounting bracket.
22. Install the motor mounts, remove the engine sling and install the buffer rods, tighten the engine mount bolts first, then apply a load to the mounting insulators before tightening the buffer rod and sub-mounting bolts.
23. If the buffer rod length has not been altered, they should still be correct. Shims are placed under the engine mounts, be sure to replace the exact ones in the correct places.

1987–90 Fuel Injected Engines

◆ See Figures 1, 2 and 3

This procedure is for 1987–90 CA16DE, CA18DE, E16i and GA16i fuel injected models. Carbureted procedures for 1987 models can be found earlier in this section.

➡The GA16i engine cannot be removed separately from the transaxle. Even on the other models, it is recommended that the engine and transaxle be removed as a unit, then separated after removal. If equipped with 4WD, remove the engine, transaxle and transfer case together.

1. Mark the hood hinge relationship and remove the hood.
2. Release the fuel system pressure, disconnect the negative (-) battery cable and raise and support the vehicle safely.
3. Drain the cooling system and the engine oil.

❊❊ CAUTION

When draining engine coolant, keep in mind that cats and dogs are attracted to ethylene glycol antifreeze and could drink any that is left in an uncovered container or in puddles on the ground. This will prove fatal in sufficient quantity. Always drain coolant into a sealable container. Coolant should be reused unless it is contaminated or is several years old.

4. Remove the air cleaner and disconnect the throttle cable.
5. Disconnect or remove the following:
- Drive belts
- Ignition wire from the coil to the distributor
- Ignition coil ground wire and the engine ground cable
- Block connector from the distributor
- Fusible links
- Engine harness connectors
- Fuel and fuel return hoses
- Upper and lower radiator hoses
- Heater inlet and outlet hoses
- Engine vacuum hoses
- Carbon canister hoses and the air pump air cleaner hose
- Any interfering engine accessory: power steering pump, air conditioning compressor or alternator
- Driveshaft from transfer case.

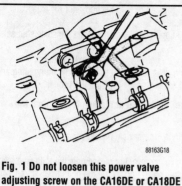

Fig. 1 Do not loosen this power valve adjusting screw on the CA16DE or CA18DE engine. This screw is adjusted at the factory

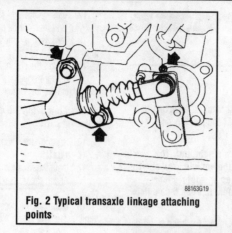

Fig. 2 Typical transaxle linkage attaching points

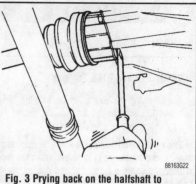

Fig. 3 Prying back on the halfshaft to remove it from the transaxle. Use care not to damage the seal

➡ Make sure to matchmark the driveshaft flanges.

6. Remove the air pump air cleaner.
7. Remove the carbon canister.
8. Remove the auxiliary fan, washer tank, grille and radiator (with fan assembly).
9. Remove the clutch cylinder from the clutch housing for manual transaxles.
10. Remove both buffer rods without altering the length of the rods. Disconnect the speedometer cable.
11. Remove the spring pins from the transaxle gear selector rods.
12. Install engine slingers to the block and connect a suitable lifting device to the slingers. Do not tension the lifting device at this point.
13. Disconnect the exhaust pipe at both the manifold connection and the clamp holding the pipe to the engine.
14. Remove the lower ball joint.
15. Drain the transaxle gear oil.
16. Disconnect the right and left side halfshafts from their side flanges and remove the bolt holding the radius link support.

➡ When drawing out the halfshafts, it is necessary to loosen the strut head bolts.

17. Lower the shifter and selector rods and remove the bolts from the engine mount brackets. Remove the nuts holding the front and rear engine mounts to the frame. Disconnect the clutch and accelerator wires and remove the speedometer cable with its pinion from the transaxle.
18. Lift the engine/transaxle assembly up and away from the vehicle.

To install:

19. Installation is the reverse of removal but please note the following steps.
20. Lower the engine transaxle assembly into the vehicle. When lowering the engine onto the frame, make sure to keep it as level as possible.
21. Check the clearance between the frame and clutch housing and make sure the engine mount bolts are seated in the groove of the mounting bracket.
22. After installing the engine mounts, adjust and install the buffer rods. On the 1988–92 Sentra 4WD: front should be 3.50–3.58 in. (89–91mm), and the rear, 3.90–3.98 in. (99–101mm).
23. Tighten the engine mount bolts first, then apply a load to the mounting insulators before tightening the buffer rod and sub-mounting bolts.
24. Make all the necessary engine adjustments. Charge the air conditioning system. Road test the vehicle for proper operation.

1991–94 1.6L and 1991–96 2.0L Engines

It is recommended that the engine and transaxle be removed as a unit. If necessary, they may be separated after removal.

➡ The 1.6L (GA16DE) engine cannot be removed separately from the transaxle. Remove the engine and the transaxle as a unit. If equipped with 4WD, remove the engine, transaxle and transfer case together.

1. Mark the hood hinge relationship and remove the hood.
2. Release the fuel system pressure, disconnect the negative (-) battery cable and raise and support the vehicle safely.
3. Drain the cooling system and the engine oil.

✷✷✷ CAUTION

When draining engine coolant, keep in mind that cats and dogs are attracted to ethylene glycol antifreeze and could drink any that is left in an uncovered container or in puddles on the ground. This will prove fatal in sufficient quantity. Always drain coolant into a sealable container. Coolant should be reused unless it is contaminated or is several years old.

4. Remove the air cleaner and disconnect the throttle cable.
5. Disconnect or remove the following:
   a. Drive belts.
   b. Ignition wire from the coil to the distributor
   c. Ignition coil ground wire and the engine ground cable
   d. Block connector from the distributor
   e. Fusible links
   f. Engine harness connectors
   g. Fuel and fuel return hoses
   h. Upper and lower radiator hoses
   i. Heater inlet and outlet hoses
   j. Engine vacuum hoses
   k. Carbon canister hoses and the air pump air cleaner hose
   l. Any interfering engine accessories: power steering pump, air conditioning compressor or alternator
   m. Driveshaft from transfer unit for 4WD vehicles.

➡ Make sure to matchmark the driveshaft flanges.

6. Remove the air pump air cleaner.
7. Remove the carbon canister.
8. Remove the auxiliary fan, washer tank, grille and radiator (with fan assembly).
9. Remove the clutch cylinder from the clutch housing for manual transaxles.
10. Remove both buffer rods without altering the length of the rods. Disconnect the speedometer cable.
11. Remove the spring pins from the transaxle gear selector rods.
12. Install engine slingers to the block and connect a suitable lifting device to the slingers. Do not tension the lifting device at this point.
13. Disconnect the exhaust pipe at both the manifold connection and the clamp holding the pipe to the engine.
14. Remove the lower ball joints.
15. Drain the transaxle gear oil.
16. Disconnect the right and left side halfshafts from their side flanges and remove the bolt holding the radius link support.

➡ When drawing out the halfshafts, it is necessary to loosen the strut head bolts.

17. Lower the shifter and selector rods, and remove the bolts from the engine mount brackets. Remove the nuts holding the front and rear engine mounts to the frame.
18. Disconnect the clutch and accelerator wires and remove the speedometer cable with its pinion from the transaxle.

19. Lift the engine/transaxle assembly up and away from the vehicle.

To install:

20. Installation is the reverse of removal but please pay close attention to the following important steps.

21. Lower the engine/transaxle assembly into the vehicle. When lowering the engine onto the frame, make sure to keep it as level as possible.

22. Check the clearance between the frame and clutch housing and make sure the engine mount bolts are seated in the groove of the mounting bracket.

23. After installing the engine mounts, adjust and install the buffer rods. The front should be 3.50–3.58 in. (89–91mm), and the rear 3.90–3.98 in. (99–101mm).

24. Tighten the engine mount bolts first, then apply a load to the mounting insulators before tightening the buffer rod and sub-mounting bolts.

25. Make all the necessary engine adjustments. Charge the air conditioning system. Road test the vehicle for proper operation.

1995–96 1.6L Engine

▶ **See Figure 4**

➡ **The engine and transaxle are removed as one unit from the underside of the vehicle.**

❋❋ CAUTION

Fuel injection systems remain under pressure after the engine has been turned OFF. Properly relieve fuel pressure before disconnecting any fuel lines. Failure to do so may result in fire or personal injury.

1. Relieve the fuel system pressure.
2. Disconnect the negative and positive battery cables.
3. Remove the battery and battery tray from the vehicle.
4. Raise and safely support the vehicle.
5. Remove both front wheels.
6. Remove the engine under covers and remove the engine side covers.
7. Drain the coolant from the radiator and the engine block.

❋❋ CAUTION

When draining engine coolant, keep in mind that cats and dogs are attracted to ethylene glycol antifreeze and could drink any that is left in an uncovered container or in puddles on the ground. This will prove fatal in sufficient quantity. Always drain coolant into a sealable container. Coolant should be reused unless it is contaminated or is several years old.

8. Drain the engine oil.
9. Remove the air cleaner assembly and remove air duct.
10. Note the locations and remove the vacuum hoses.
11. Disconnect the heater hoses from the engine.
12. If equipped, disconnect the A/T cooler hoses from the transaxle.
13. Disconnect the fuel hoses from the engine.
14. Note the locations and disconnect the harness and wiring connections.

15. Disconnect the throttle cable and the cruise control cable.
16. If equipped with automatic transaxle, disconnect the control cable.
17. Remove the cooling fans, radiator, and the recovery tank.
18. Remove the front driveshafts from the vehicle.
19. Remove the front exhaust pipe.
20. Disconnect the control rod and support rod from the transaxle.
21. Remove the starter motor and intake manifold support brackets.
22. Remove the engine drive belts.
23. Remove the alternator and adjusting brackets.
24. Remove the power steering pump and A/C compressor. It is not necessary to disconnect the lines.
25. Remove the cylinder head front mounting bracket.
26. Position a transmission jack under the transaxle and support the engine with engine slinger.
27. Remove the center crossmember.
28. On some models it may be necessary to remove the front stabilizer bar.
29. Remove the engine mounting bolts from both sides of the engine.
30. Slowly lower the jacking devices and remove the engine and transaxle from the vehicle.

To install:

31. Install the engine and transaxle assembly in the reverse order of removal but please note the following steps.

32. For vehicles with manual transaxles, adjust the height of the mounting bracket (buffer rod). The distance between the two through bolts should be 2.126–2.205 in. (54–56mm).

33. Tighten the control rod bolt to 10–13 ft. lbs. (14–18 Nm). Tighten the support rod bolt to 26–35 ft. lbs. (35–47 Nm).

34. Start the engine and check for leaks. Make all the necessary adjustments.

Rocker Arm (Valve) Cover

▶ **See Figures 5 thru 10**

REMOVAL & INSTALLATION

1. Remove or disconnect any electrical lines, hoses or tubes which may interfere with the removal procedures.

➡ **It may be necessary to remove the air cleaner (carburetor models) or the air duct (EFI and turbo models).**

2. Remove the rocker arm cover-to-cylinder head acorn nuts on E-Series engines or the mounting screws on others engines, then lift the cover from the cylinder head.

3. Use a gasket scraper or putty knife to clean the gasket mounting surfaces.

To install:

4. Apply a new gasket and/or RTV sealant, then position the rocker arm cover. Torque the cover-to-cylinder head bolts to 8.4–13.2 inch lbs. (1.0–1.5 Nm) or the acorn nuts to 35–70 inch lbs. (4–8 Nm). On the SR20DE engine, first tighten bolts 1, 10, 11, 13 and 8 to 35 inch lbs. (4 Nm). Then tighten all bolts in proper sequence to 72–84 inch lbs. (8–9 Nm).

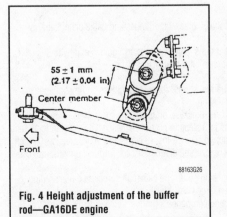

Fig. 4 Height adjustment of the buffer rod—GA16DE engine

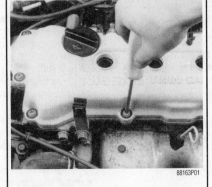

Fig. 5 Loosening the rocker cover screws

Fig. 6 Lifting the rocker cover clear of the camshaft assembly

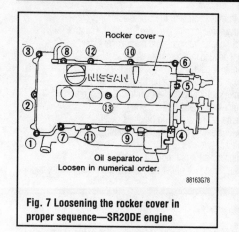

Fig. 7 Loosening the rocker cover in proper sequence—SR20DE engine

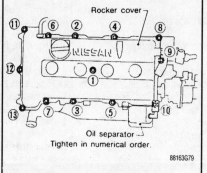

Fig. 8 Tightening the rocker cover in proper sequence—SR20DE engine

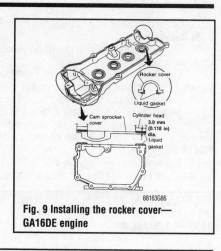

Fig. 9 Installing the rocker cover—GA16DE engine

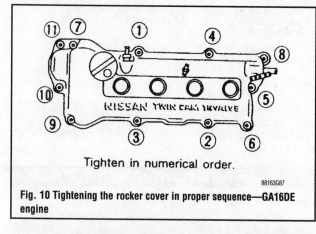

Fig. 10 Tightening the rocker cover in proper sequence—GA16DE engine

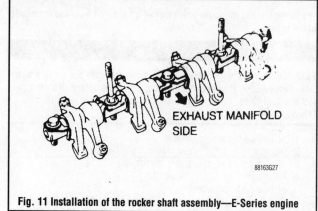

Fig. 11 Installation of the rocker shaft assembly—E-Series engine

➡ When using RTV sealant, make sure the surface you are working on is very clean before applying the sealant, then apply an even bead. The cover MUST be torqued before the RTV dries; a thin skin is OK.

Rocker Arm Shaft

REMOVAL & INSTALLATION

E-Series Engines

▶ See Figure 11

1. Refer the Rocker Arm Cover removal and installation procedure in this section and remove the cover.

➡ The CA16DE, GA16DE and CA18DE engines do not use rocker arm shafts.

2. Loosen the valve rocker adjusting nuts, then turn the adjusting screws to separate them from the push rods.

3. Evenly, loosen the rocker shaft bolts, then remove the bolts and lift the rocker shafts from the cylinder head.

➡ If it is necessary to remove the rocker arms from the shafts, perform the following procedures: remove the shaft bolts and the spring clips, then slide the rocker arms from the shaft. Be sure to keep the parts in order for reassembly purposes.

To install:

4. Position the rocker arm shaft and brackets in the correct place and hand-tighten the bolts. Torque the rocker arm shaft, from the center working to the end, bracket bolts to 12–15 ft. lbs. (16–20 Nm).

5. To adjust the valve clearance, refer to the Valve Adjustment procedure in Section 1.

6. Install the rocker arm cover.

SR20DE Engine

▶ See Figures 12, 13 and 14

1. Disconnect the negative (-) battery cable. Release the fuel pressure as described in Section 5.

2. Remove the rocker arm cover, gasket and oil separator.

3. Remove the intake manifold supports, oil filter bracket and power steering pump.

4. Set No. 1 cylinder at TDC on the compression stroke.

5. Remove the timing chain tensioner on the side of the head.

6. Matchmark and remove the distributor.

7. Remove the timing chain guide. Remove the camshaft sprockets while holding the camshaft stationary with a large wrench. Secure the timing chain with wire so the timing is not lost. The front cover will have to be removed if the chain timing is lost.

➡ When removing the camshafts, loosen the journal caps in the opposite sequence of tightening. Camshaft damage may result if this step is not followed.

8. Remove the camshafts, brackets, oil tubes and baffle plate. Label all components for proper installation.

9. Remove the rocker arms, shims, rocker arm guides and hydraulic lash adjusters. Label all components for proper installation.

To install:

10. Install the rocker arms, shims, rocker arm guides and hydraulic lash adjusters in the proper location.

11. Install the camshafts, brackets, oil tubes and baffle plate in the proper location. Torque the bolts in 3 steps in proper sequence. The 1st step to 17 inch lbs. (3.5 Nm), the 2nd step to 50 inch lbs. (9 Nm) and the 3rd step to 105 inch lbs. (11 Nm) for all caps, except the distributor cap. Torque the distributor cap to 230 inch lbs. (25 Nm).

12. Install the timing chain guide and camshaft sprockets while holding the camshaft stationary with a large wrench.

13. Install the remaining components in the reverse order of removal.

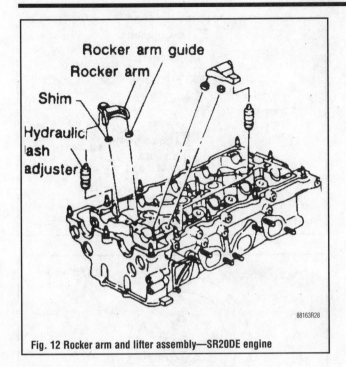

Fig. 12 Rocker arm and lifter assembly—SR20DE engine

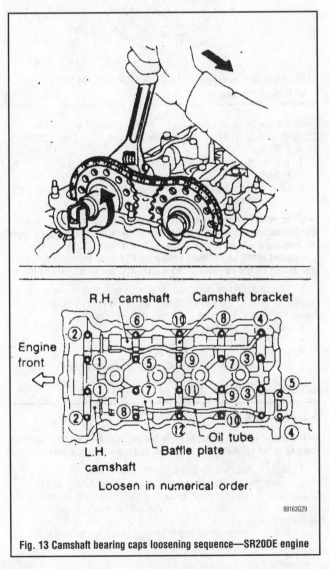

Fig. 13 Camshaft bearing caps loosening sequence—SR20DE engine

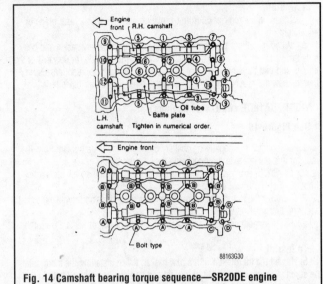

Fig. 14 Camshaft bearing torque sequence—SR20DE engine

14. Connect the negative (-) battery cable. Adjust the ignition timing as outlined in Section 1.

Thermostat

REMOVAL & INSTALLATION

✳✳ CAUTION

When draining the coolant, keep in mind that cats and dogs are attracted by ethylene glycol antifreeze, and are quite likely to drink any that is left in an uncovered container or in puddles on the ground. This will prove fatal in sufficient quantity. Always drain the coolant into a sealable container. Coolant should be reused unless it is contaminated or several years old.

E-Series Engines

▶ See Figure 15

➡ The engine thermostat is housed in the water outlet casting on the cylinder head.

1. Open the draincock on the radiator and drain the coolant into a suitable drain pan.
2. Remove the upper radiator hose from the water outlet side and remove the bolts securing the water outlet to the cylinder head.
3. On E16 models, remove the exhaust air induction tube clamp bolts, then the water outlet bolts.
4. Remove the water outlet and thermostat.

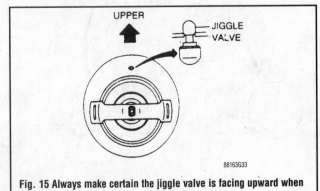

Fig. 15 Always make certain the jiggle valve is facing upward when installing the thermostat

To install:

5. Clean off the old gasket from the mating surfaces with a razor blade or equivalent.

6. When installing the thermostat, be sure to install a new gasket and be sure the air bleed hole in the thermostat is facing the left side (or upward) of the engine and that the spring is toward the inside of the engine. Also make sure that the new thermostat to be installed is equipped with an air bleed hole.

CA16DE, CA18DE and GA16i Engines

▶ See Figure 15

1. Disconnect the negative (-) battery cable and drain the coolant from the radiator and the left side draincocks on the cylinder block.

2. On GA16i engines, disconnect the water temperature switch connector from the thermostat housing.

3. Remove the radiator hose from the water outlet side and remove the bolts securing the water outlet to the cylinder head.

4. Remove the thermostat and clean off the old gasket or sealant from the mating surfaces.

To install:

5. Install the thermostat with a new gasket. When installing the thermostat, be sure to install a new gasket or sealant and be sure the air bleed hole in the thermostat is facing the left side or upward on the engine. The jiggle valve must always face up. Also make sure the new thermostat to be installed is equipped with an air bleed hole. Some thermostats have the word **TOP** stamped next to the jiggle valve. Again, the word **TOP** and the jiggle valve must be facing up.

➥When using RTV sealant instead of gaskets, make sure the surface you are working on is very clean before applying the sealant, then apply an even bead. Allow the RTV to dry slightly to form a thin skin. The component MUST be tightened before the RTV dries completely. The bolt torque should be checked again after RTV has completely dried.

6. Install the water outlet and upper radiator hose.

7. On GA16i engines, connect the water temperature switch connector to the thermostat housing.

8. Fill the cooling system and connect the negative (-) battery cable.

9. Bleed the cooling system as outlined in this section.

1.6L (GA16DE) and 2.0L (SR20DE) Engines

▶ See Figures 16, 17 and 18

➥The thermostat is housed in the water outlet casting on the cylinder head on most models. On the GA16DE engines, the thermostat is housed in the water outlet casting attached to the water pump.

1. Disconnect the negative (-) battery cable.

2. When cool, open the draincock on the radiator and drain the coolant into a suitable drain pan.

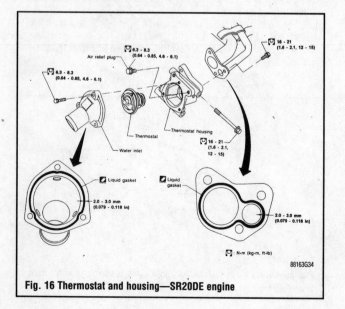

Fig. 16 Thermostat and housing—SR20DE engine

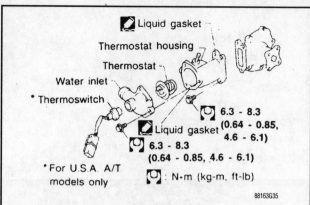

Fig. 17 Thermostat and housing—GA16DE engine

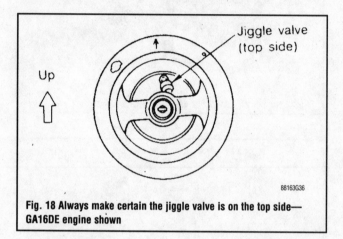

Fig. 18 Always make certain the jiggle valve is on the top side—GA16DE engine shown

3. Remove the upper radiator hose from the water outlet side and remove the bolts securing the water outlet to the cylinder head and any other components in the way.

4. Remove the water outlet and thermostat.

To install:

5. Clean off the old gasket from the mating surfaces of the thermostat housing and engine block.

➥When using RTV sealant instead of gaskets, make sure the surface you are working on is very clean before applying the sealant, then apply an even bead. Allow the RTV to dry slightly to form a thin skin. The component MUST be tightened before the RTV dries completely. The bolt torque should be checked again after RTV has completely dried.

6. When installing the thermostat, be sure to install a new gasket and be sure the air bleed hole in the thermostat is facing upward and that the spring is toward the inside of the engine.

7. Install the water outlet and tighten the bolts.
• GA16DE—13–16 ft. lbs. (18–22 Nm)
• SR20DE—60–72 inch lbs. (6–8 Nm)

8. Install the remaining components in the reverse order of removal.

COOLING SYSTEM BLEEDING

▶ See Figure 19

➥The engine may be damaged if the cooling system is not bled. Air gets trapped in the cylinder head, causing a buildup of heat and pressure.

1. Fill the radiator with the proper type of coolant.

2. Loosen the air relief valve in the cylinder head. Fill the engine with coolant until coolant spills out of the valve. If there is no valve, loosen a temperature sender that is nearest the top of the engine. Install the sender when coolant spills from the hole.

3. With the radiator cap off, start the engine and allow it to run and reach normal operating temperature.

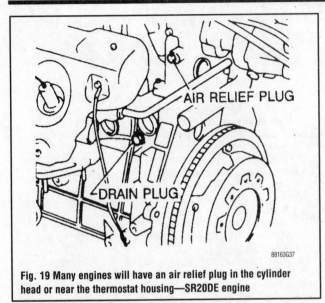

Fig. 19 Many engines will have an air relief plug in the cylinder head or near the thermostat housing—SR20DE engine

4. Run the heater at full force and with the temperature lever in the hot position. Be sure that the heater control valve is functioning.

5. Shut the engine off and recheck the coolant level, refill as necessary.

Intake Manifold

REMOVAL & INSTALLATION

✳✳ CAUTION

When draining the coolant, keep in mind that cats and dogs are attracted by ethylene glycol antifreeze, and are quite likely to drink any that is left in an uncovered container or in puddles on the ground. This will prove fatal in sufficient quantity. Always drain the coolant into a sealable container. Coolant should be reused unless it is contaminated or several years old.

Carbureted E-Series Engines

1. Remove the air cleaner assembly together with all of the hoses.

➡When unplugging wires and hoses, mark each hose and its connection with a piece of masking tape, then match code the 2 pieces of tape with the numbers 1, 2, 3, etc. When assembling, simply match up the pieces of tape.

2. Disconnect and label the throttle linkage, the fuel and the vacuum lines from the carburetor and the intake manifold components.

➡The carburetor can be removed from the manifold at this point or can be removed as an assembly with the intake manifold.

3. Remove the intake manifold bolts or nuts and the manifold from the engine.

4. Using a putty knife, clean the gasket mounting surfaces.

To install:

5. Install the intake manifold and gasket on the engine. Always use a new gasket. Tighten the mounting bolts from the, center working to the end, in two or three stages. Torque the intake manifold bolts to 12–15 ft. lbs. (15–18 Nm).

6. Install throttle linkage, fuel and vacuum lines and the air cleaner assembly.

7. Start engine and check for leaks.

1984 E15ET Turbocharged Engine

➡Refer to the Fuel Release Procedure in Section 5 and release the fuel pressure.

1. Disconnect the air intake duct between the air filter and the air pipe, then the air intake duct between the air pipe and the turbocharger. Remove the air inlet duct between the turbocharger and the throttle body. Remove the air pipe.

2. Disconnect and label all of the electrical connectors and the vacuum hoses to the throttle, the intake manifold assembly and the related components. Remove the high tension wires from the spark plugs.

3. Disconnect the EGR valve tube from the exhaust manifold and the fuel line(s) from the fuel injector assembly.

➡For clearance purposes, it may be necessary to remove the throttle body and the collector chamber from the intake manifold; if the fuel injector assembly is in the way, remove it.

4. Remove the intake manifold mounting nuts and the intake manifold.

To install:

5. Using a putty knife, clean the gasket mounting surfaces.

6. Install the intake manifold and gasket on the engine. Always use a new gasket. Tighten the mounting bolts from the, center working to the end, in two or three stages. Torque the intake manifold-to-cylinder head nuts to 12–15 ft.. lbs. (16–20 Nm), the intake manifold-to-collector chamber bolts to 35–52 inch lbs. (16–20 Nm) and the air pipe bolt(s) to 78–121 inch lbs. (9–14 Nm).

7. Install all remaining components in the reverse order of removal.

1987–90 CA16DE, CA18DE, E16i and GA16i Engines

▸ See Figures 20, 21 and 22

➡Refer to the Fuel Release Procedure in Section 5 and release the fuel pressure in the system.

1. Remove the air cleaner assembly together with all of the attending hoses.

2. Disconnect the throttle linkage and fuel and vacuum lines from the throttle body on the engines).

3. The throttle body can be removed from the manifold at this point or can be removed as an assembly with the intake manifold.

4. Remove the manifold support stay on the CA16DE and CA18DE.

5. Remove the EGR valve assembly, air regulator and F.I.C.D valve from the manifold on the CA16DE and CA18DE.

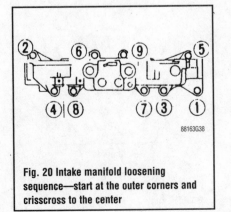

Fig. 20 Intake manifold loosening sequence—start at the outer corners and crisscross to the center

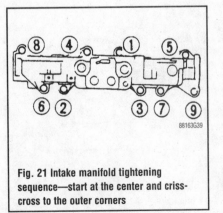

Fig. 21 Intake manifold tightening sequence—start at the center and crisscross to the outer corners

Fig. 22 Do not loosen this power valve adjusting screw on the CA16DE or CA18DE engine. This screw is adjusted on the production line at the factory

6. Loosen the intake manifold attaching nuts, working from the two ends toward the center, and then remove them.

➡**NEVER tighten or loosen the power valve adjusting screw on the CA16DE or CA18DE engines.**

7. Remove the intake manifold from the engine.

8. Install the intake manifold and gasket on the engine. Always use a new gasket. Tighten the intake manifold attaching nuts, working from the center toward the ends, in two or three stages. Torque the intake manifold to 12–15 ft. lbs. (15–18 Nm) on the E16i and GA16i engines and 27–35 ft. lbs. (34–48 Nm) on the CA16DE and CA18DE engines.

9. Install the EGR valve assembly, air regulator and F.I.C.D valve on the manifold on the CA16DE and CA18DE engine, if equipped.

10. Connect the manifold support stay on the CA16DE and CA18DE engines.

11. Install the throttle body if it was removed, then reconnect all fuel and vacuum lines and any related components.

12. Reconnect the throttle linkage and air cleaner assembly and all hoses.

➡**Don't forget to install the support stay on the CA16DE and CA18DE engines.**

13. Start engine and check for leaks.

GA16DE Engine

◆ **See Figures 23, 24, 25 and 26**

✸✸ CAUTION

Fuel injection systems remain under pressure after the engine has been turned OFF. Properly relieve fuel pressure before disconnecting any fuel lines. Failure to do so may result in fire or personal injury. Refer to Section 5 for fuel pressure relieving procedures.

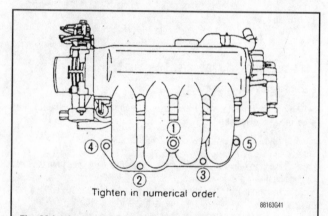

Tighten in numerical order.

88163G41

Fig. 23 Intake manifold collector bolts tightening sequence—GA16DE engine

1. Relieve the fuel system pressure, disconnect the negative (-) battery cable, and drain the cooling system.

2. Remove the air cleaner assembly.

3. Disconnect and tag the throttle linkage, electrical connections and vacuum lines from the throttle body.

4. Remove the intake manifold collector support brackets.

5. The throttle body can be removed from the manifold at this point or can be removed as an assembly with the intake manifold.

6. Remove the bolts holding the upper portion of the intake to the lower portion. Remove the bolts in reverse order of the tightening sequence.

7. Remove the upper portion of the intake.

8. Disconnect the fuel injector wiring harness connectors and the vacuum line from the fuel pressure regulator.

9. Disconnect the fuel hoses from the fuel rail assembly.

10. Remove the bolts that secure the fuel rail to the intake.

11. Remove the injectors with the fuel rail assembly.

12. Loosen the intake manifold retaining bolts in the proper sequence and separate the manifold from the cylinder head. Remove the bolts in reverse order of the tightening sequence

13. Remove the intake manifold gasket and clean all the gasket contact surfaces thoroughly with a gasket scraper and suitable solvent. All traces of old gasket material must be removed to ensure proper sealing. Inspect the intake manifold for cracks. Using a metal straightedge, check the surface of the intake manifold for warpage.

To install:

14. Lay the new intake manifold gasket onto the cylinder head and position the lower intake manifold over the mounting studs and onto the gasket. Install the mounting nuts and bolts; torque them to 13–15 ft. lbs. (18–21 Nm) in sequence.

15. Install the injectors with the fuel rail assembly. Be sure to install the fuel rail insulators.

16. Install the bolts that secure the fuel rail to the intake. Torque the bolts in two steps to 13–15 ft. lbs. (18–21 Nm).

17. Connect the fuel injector wiring harness connectors and the vacuum line from the fuel pressure regulator.

18. Using new hose clamps, connect the fuel hoses from the fuel rail assembly.

19. Using a new gasket, install the upper portion of the intake manifold and torque the bolts to 13–15 ft. lbs. (18–21 Nm) in sequence.

20. If removed, install the throttle body or throttle chamber and tighten the mounting bolts in a crisscross pattern. Torque the bolts in two progressive steps to 13–16 ft. lbs. (18–22 Nm).

➡**Be sure to properly position the throttle body gasket with the cutout facing down.**

21. Install the remaining components in the reverse order of removal.

2.0L (SR20DE) Engine

◆ **See Figures 27 thru 32**

1. Relieve the fuel system pressure, disconnect the negative (-) battery cable. Refer to Section 5 for procedure to relieve fuel pressure.

2. Drain the cooling system.

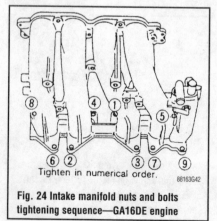

Tighten in numerical order.

88163G42

Fig. 24 Intake manifold nuts and bolts tightening sequence—GA16DE engine

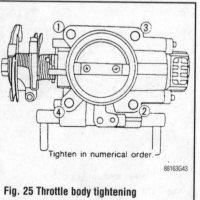

Tighten in numerical order.

88163G43

Fig. 25 Throttle body tightening sequence—GA16DE engine

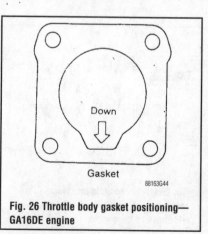

Down

Gasket

88163G44

Fig. 26 Throttle body gasket positioning—GA16DE engine

Fig. 27 Removing the intake manifold

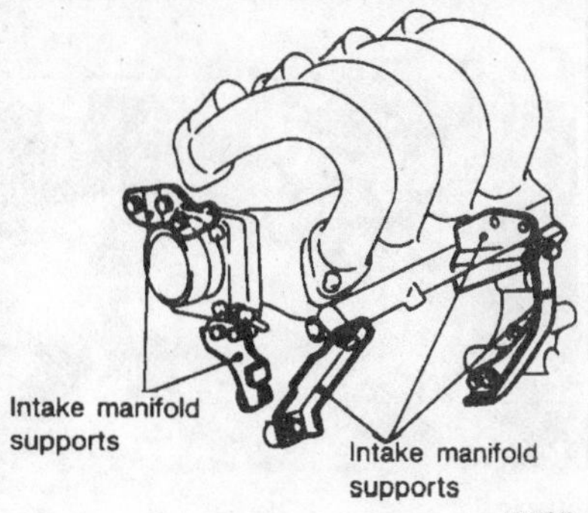

Fig. 28 Intake manifold supports—SR20DE engine

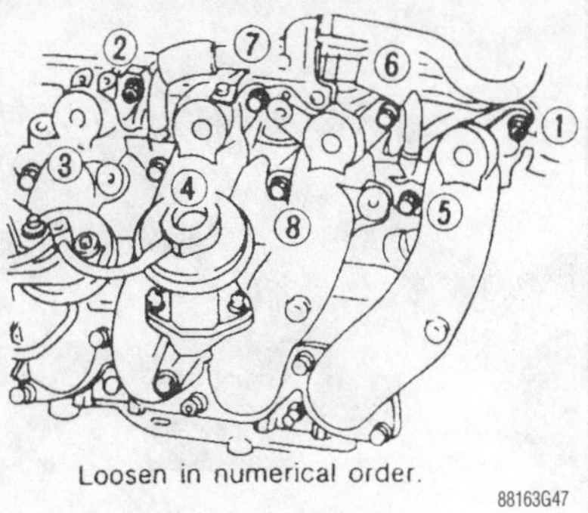

Fig. 29 Intake manifold loosening sequences—SR20DE engine

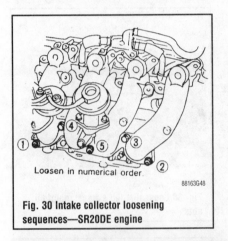

Fig. 30 Intake collector loosening sequences—SR20DE engine

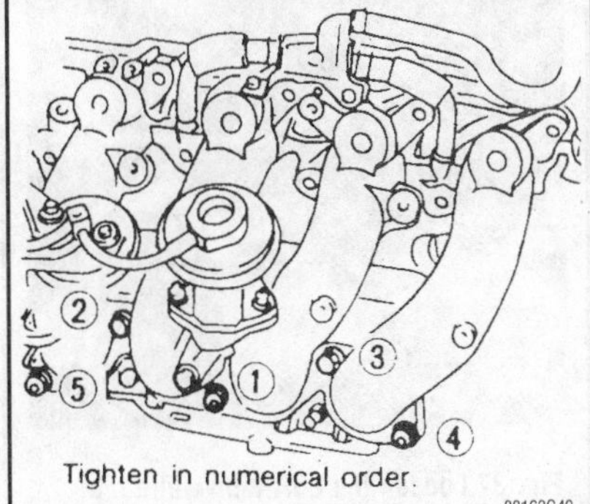

Fig. 31 Intake manifold tightening sequences—SR20DE engine

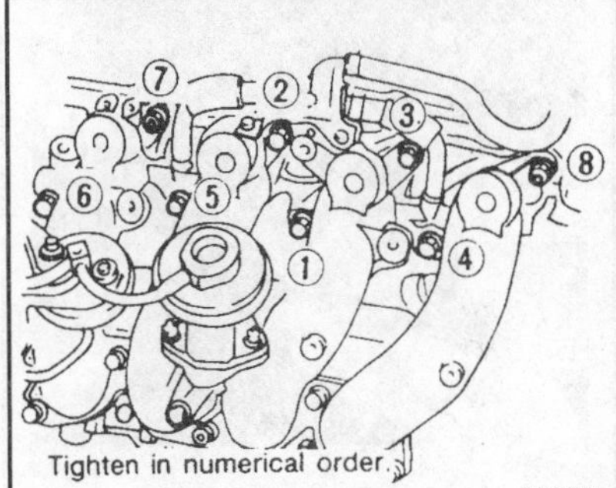

Fig. 32 Intake collector tightening sequences—SR20DE engine

✳✳ CAUTION

When draining engine coolant, keep in mind that cats and dogs are attracted to ethylene glycol antifreeze and could drink any that is left in an uncovered container or in puddles on the ground. This will prove fatal in sufficient quantity. Always drain coolant into a sealable container. Coolant should be reused unless it is contaminated or is several years old.

  3. Remove the air cleaner assembly.
  4. Disconnect the throttle linkage, electrical connections, fuel and vacuum lines from the throttle body.
  5. Remove the EGR tube from the manifold.
  6. Remove the drive belts and water pump pulley.
  7. Remove the alternator and power steering pump.
  8. Remove the intake manifold supports, oil filter bracket and power steering bracket.
  9. Loosen the intake manifold retaining bolts in the proper sequence and separate the manifold from the cylinder head.
  10. If necessary, remove the fuel rail and separate the intake collector assembly from the intake manifold.
  11. Remove the intake manifold gasket and clean all the gasket contact surfaces thoroughly with a gasket scraper and suitable solvent. All traces of old gasket material must be removed to ensure proper sealing. Inspect the intake manifold for cracks. Using a metal straightedge, check the surface of the intake manifold for warpage.

To install:
  12. Assemble the collector assembly to the manifold. Torque nuts and bolts in sequence to 13–15 ft. lbs. (18–21 Nm).
  13. Lay the new intake manifold gasket onto the cylinder head and position the intake manifold over the mounting studs and onto the gasket. Install the mounting nuts and torque them to 13–15 ft. lbs. (18–21 Nm), in the proper sequence.
  14. Install all remaining components in the reverse order of removal.

Exhaust Manifold

REMOVAL & INSTALLATION

▸ See Figures 33 thru 42

1982–90 Engines

EXCEPT E15ET ENGINE

➡**If any fuel system components must be removed, make to relieve the fuel system pressure first.**

  1. Disconnect the negative (−) battery cable. Raise and support the vehicle safely.
  2. Remove the under cover and dust covers, if equipped.
  3. Remove the air cleaner or collector assembly, if necessary for access.
  4. Remove the heat shield(s), if equipped.
  5. Disconnect the exhaust pipe from the exhaust manifold.
  6. Remove or disconnect the temperature sensors, oxygen sensors, air induction pipes, brackets and other attachments from the manifold.
  7. Disconnect the EAI and EGR tubes from their fittings if so equipped.
  8. Loosen and remove the exhaust manifold attaching nuts and remove the manifold(s) from the block. Discard the exhaust manifold gaskets and replace with new.
  9. Clean the gasket surfaces and check the manifold for cracks and warpage.

To install:
  10. Install the exhaust manifold with a new gasket. Torque the manifold fasteners from the center outward in several stages to 13–16 ft. lbs. (18–22 Nm), all engines except CA16DE, CA18DE and SR20DE. Torque those engines to 27–35 ft. lbs. (37–48 Nm).
  11. Installation of remaining components is the reverse of removal.

Fig. 33 Removing the exhaust manifold heat shield

Fig. 34 Disconnect the oxygen sensor before lifting heat shield away

Fig. 35 Spraying penetrating oil on the EGR tube. Use penetrating oil on all the nuts and bolts

Fig. 36 If removing the manifold completely you must disconnect the exhaust pipe from the manifold

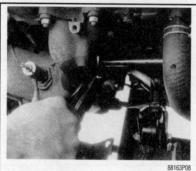

Fig. 37 Loosen the EGR tube while the manifold is still attached to the cylinder head

Fig. 38 Loosening the exhaust manifold nuts

Fig. 39 Slide the exhaust manifold off of the studs carefully to avoid damaging the threads

Fig. 40 Slide the exhaust manifold gaskets off of the studs

Fig. 41 All of the old exhaust manifold gasket must be scraped off before installing new gaskets

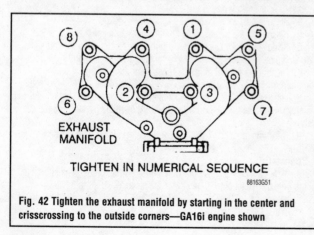

Fig. 42 Tighten the exhaust manifold by starting in the center and crisscrossing to the outside corners—GA16i engine shown

E15ET TURBOCHARGED ENGINE

1. Refer to the Turbocharger Removal and Installation procedure in this section, and remove the turbocharger.

2. Remove the exhaust manifold's heat shields, the exhaust manifold from the cylinder head.

3. Using a putty knife, clean the gasket mounting surfaces.

To install:

4. Use new gaskets and install the manifold. Torque the exhaust manifold-to-cylinder head bolts to 12–15 ft. lbs. (16–20 Nm), the turbocharger-to-exhaust manifold nuts to 22–25 ft. lbs. (30–34 Nm), the exhaust outlet-to-turbocharger nuts to 22–25 ft. lbs. (30–34 Nm), the converter's 10mm mounting bracket bolt to 14–18 ft. lbs. (19–25 Nm) or 8mm mounting bracket bolt to 78–120 inch lbs. (10–14 Nm), the oil pressure tube fitting-to-turbocharger to 14–22 ft. lbs. (19–30 Nm).

5. Install the remaining components.

1991–96 GA16DE and SR20DE Engine

➡If any fuel system components must be removed, be sure to relieve the fuel system pressure first, as described in Section 5.

1. Disconnect the negative (-) battery cable. Raise and support the vehicle safely.
2. Remove the under cover and dust covers, if equipped.
3. Remove the air cleaner or collector assembly, if necessary for access.
4. Remove the heat shield(s), if equipped.
5. Disconnect the exhaust pipe from the exhaust manifold.
6. Remove or disconnect the temperature sensors, oxygen sensors, air induction pipes.
7. Remove manifold support brackets.
8. Disconnect the EAI and EGR tubes from their fittings if so equipped.
9. Loosen and remove the exhaust manifold attaching nuts and remove the manifold(s) from the block. Discard the exhaust manifold gaskets and replace with new.
10. Clean the gasket surfaces and check the manifold for cracks and warpage.

To install:
11. Install the exhaust manifold with a new gasket. Torque the manifold fasteners from the center outward in several stages.

  a. GA16DE engines—Tighten mounting nuts with washers to 12–15 ft. lbs. (16–21 Nm).

  b. SR20DE engines—Tighten mounting nuts with washers to 27–35 ft. lbs. (37–48 Nm).
12. Install or connect the temperature sensors, oxygen sensors and air induction pipes.
13. Connect the EAI and EGR tubes to the connections on the manifold as necessary.
14. Install the manifold support brackets.
15. Connect the exhaust pipe to the manifold using a new gasket. Tighten the manifold nuts to 21–25 ft. lbs. (28–33 Nm) for GA16DE engine models or 32–37 ft. lbs. (43–50 Nm) for SR20DE engine models.
16. Install the remaining components.

Turbocharger

REMOVAL & INSTALLATION

E15ET Engine

1. Disconnect the negative (-) battery cable. Disconnect the air inlet and the outlet pipes from the turbocharger.
2. Disconnect the oil pressure tube and the oil return hose from the turbocharger. Disconnect and mark the high tension wires from the spark plugs.
3. Remove the catalytic converter heat shield, then the converter's mounting bracket.

➡Soak the exhaust pipe outlet bolts with penetrating oil if necessary to loosen them.

4. Remove the exhaust outlet-to-turbocharger mounting nuts and separate the outlet from the turbocharger.
5. Remove the turbocharger-to-exhaust manifold mounting nuts and lift the turbocharger from the exhaust manifold.
6. Using a putty knife, clean the gasket mounting surfaces.

To install:
7. Use new gaskets, install the turbocharger to the exhaust manifold. Observe the following torques:

- Exhaust manifold-to-cylinder head bolts—12–15 ft. lbs. (15–18 Nm)
- Turbocharger-to-exhaust manifold nuts—22–25 ft. lbs. (28–34 Nm)
- Exhaust outlet-to-turbo nuts—22–25 ft. lbs. (28–34 Nm)
- Converter mounting bracket 10mm bolt—14–18 ft. lbs. (16–20 Nm); 8mm bolt—78–120 inch lbs. (10–14 Nm)
- Oil pressure tube fitting-to-turbo—14–22 ft. lbs. (17–30 Nm).

8. Install the remaining components. Connect the negative (-) battery cable and check operation.

Radiator and Cooling Fan

REMOVAL & INSTALLATION

1982–90 Vehicles

◗ See Figure 43

➡Because the cooling fan can run at any time, you should disconnect the negative battery cable for safety.

1. Disconnect the negative (-) battery cable.
2. Drain the cooling system.

✳✳ CAUTION

When draining engine coolant, keep in mind that cats and dogs are attracted to ethylene glycol antifreeze and could drink any that is left in an uncovered container or in puddles on the ground. This will prove fatal in sufficient quantity. Always drain coolant into a sealable container. Coolant should be reused unless it is contaminated or is several years old.

3. Unbolt and set aside the power steering pump if necessary to gain access. DO NOT disconnect the power steering pressure hoses or drain the system.
4. Disconnect the upper and lower radiator hoses, reservoir hose.
5. If equipped with an automatic transaxle, disconnect and cap the cooling lines at the radiator. Disconnect the water temperature switch.
6. Disconnect the fan motor wires and remove the fan assembly. Remove the radiator and cooling fan assembly.

➡Later model vehicles also have a condenser cooling fan, which is the smaller of the two.

7. Remove the fan motor from the shroud if the motor is defective.

To install:
8. Installation is the reverse of removal.
9. Refill the radiator and the automatic transaxle (if equipped). Operate the engine until warm and then check the water level, leaks and fan operation.

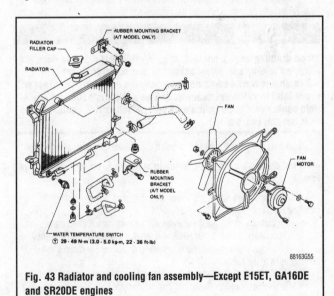

RADIATOR FILLER CAP

RADIATOR

RUBBER MOUNTING BRACKET (A/T MODEL ONLY)

FAN

FAN MOTOR

RUBBER MOUNTING BRACKET (A/T MODEL ONLY)

WATER TEMPERATURE SWITCH
⊕ 29 - 49 N·m (3.0 - 5.0 kg-m, 22 - 36 ft-lb)

88163G55

Fig. 43 Radiator and cooling fan assembly—Except E15ET, GA16DE and SR20DE engines

1991–96 Vehicles

◗ See Figures 44, 45, 46, 47 and 48

➡Because the cooling fan can run at any time, you should disconnect the negative battery cable for safety.

Fig. 44 Make sure the radiator and engine are cool before removing the radiator cap

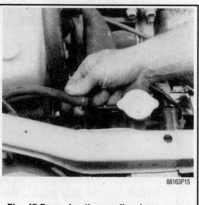

Fig. 45 Removing the overflow hose

Fig. 46 Removing the upper radiator hose

Fig. 47 Removing the lower radiator hose

Fig. 48 After removing all of the retaining bolts, carefully lift radiator from the brackets

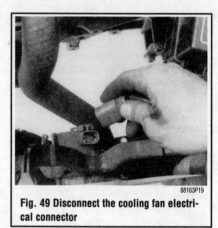

Fig. 49 Disconnect the cooling fan electrical connector

1. Disconnect the negative (-) battery cable.
2. Remove the cap and drain the radiator via the drain plug in the bottom tank. Be sure to only do this when the engine is cold.

✳✳ CAUTION

When draining engine coolant, keep in mind that cats and dogs are attracted to ethylene glycol antifreeze and could drink any that is left in an uncovered container or in puddles on the ground. This will prove fatal in sufficient quantity. Always drain coolant into a sealable container. Coolant should be reused unless it is contaminated or is several years old.

3. If necessary to gain access, unbolt and set aside the power steering pump.

➡Do not disconnect the power steering pressure hoses or drain the system.

4. Disconnect the upper and lower radiator hoses, along with the coolant overflow reservoir hose.
5. If necessary, disconnect the water temperature switch electrical wiring.
6. Disconnect the fan motor wires and remove the fan/shroud assembly.
7. If equipped with an automatic transaxle, disconnect and cap the A/T oil cooling lines at the radiator.
8. Unbolt the radiator support brackets and remove the brackets.
9. Remove the radiator assembly from the vehicle.
To install:

➡Be sure the rubber mounting bushings are in position before the radiator is installed.

10. Install the radiator to the vehicle.
11. Install radiator support brackets and tighten mounting nuts evenly.
12. Install the fan motor and blade to the shroud assembly. Tighten the fan shroud mounting bolts to 29–44 inch lbs. (3–5 Nm).
13. Installation of the remaining components is the reverse of removal.

14. Refill the radiator with the proper coolant/water mixture and bleed the system.
15. Operate the engine until warm and then check for leaks. Check the coolant level and the fan operation.
16. If the A/T oil cooling lines were disconnected, check transaxle fluid level and add fluid as necessary.

Electric Cooling Fan

REMOVAL & INSTALLATION

▶ **See Figures 49, 50 and 51**

➡Because the cooling fan can run at any time, you should disconnect the negative battery cable for safety.

1. Disconnect the negative (-) battery cable.
2. Remove the radiator dynamic damper.
3. On some models it may be necessary to drain some engine coolant and remove the upper radiator hose.

✳✳ CAUTION

When draining engine coolant, keep in mind that cats and dogs are attracted to ethylene glycol antifreeze and could drink any that is left in an uncovered container or in puddles on the ground. This will prove fatal in sufficient quantity. Always drain coolant into a sealable container. Coolant should be reused unless it is contaminated or is several years old.

4. Disconnect the fan electrical connector.
5. Remove the fan guide, fan and motor assembly.
To install:
6. Installation is the reverse of removal.

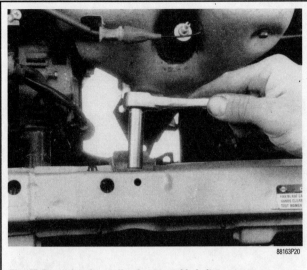

Fig. 50 Removing the cooling fan assembly bolts

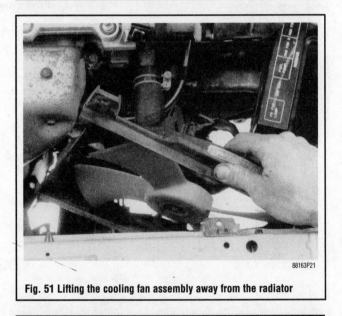

Fig. 51 Lifting the cooling fan assembly away from the radiator

Water Pump

REMOVAL & INSTALLATION

❋❋ CAUTION

When draining engine coolant, keep in mind that cats and dogs are attracted to ethylene glycol antifreeze and could drink any that is left in an uncovered container or in puddles on the ground. This will prove fatal in sufficient quantity. Always drain coolant into a sealable container. Coolant should be reused unless it is contaminated or is several years old.

E-Series Engines

▸ See Figure 52

1. Drain the cooling system.
2. Remove the power steering drive belt and the power steering pump.

➡When removing the power steering pump, do not disconnect the pressure hoses or drain the system.

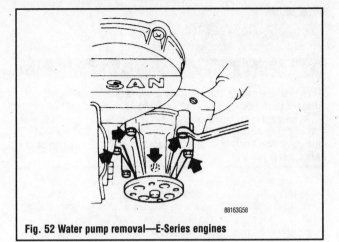

Fig. 52 Water pump removal—E-Series engines

3. Remove the water pump/alternator drive belt.
4. Remove the alternator mounting bolts and move it aside.
5. Remove the water pump pulley, then the water pump and the gasket.

To install:
6. Using a putty knife, clean the gasket mounting surfaces.
7. Install the water pump on the engine, with a new gasket. Torque the water pump bolts evenly to 78–120 inch lbs. (9–13 Nm).
8. Install the water pump pulley, alternator and the power steering pump.
9. Adjust the drive belts and refill the cooling system. Start the engine and check for leaks.

CA16DE and CA18DE Engines

▸ See Figure 53

1. Disconnect the negative (-) battery cable.
2. Drain the engine coolant.
3. Loosen the bolts retaining the fan shroud to the radiator and remove the shroud.
4. Loosen the belt, then remove the fan and pulley from the water pump hub.
5. Remove the bolts retaining the pump and remove the pump together with the gasket from the front cover.

To install:
6. Remove all traces of gasket material and install the pump in the reverse order. Use a new gasket and sealer. Tighten the bolts uniformly and torque to 12–14 ft. lbs. (16–18 Nm).
7. Install the pulley and fan onto the water pump hub.
8. Install and adjust the drive belt and radiator shroud.
9. Connect the negative (-) battery cable.
10. Refill the cooling system and start the engine and check for leaks.

➡The water pump cannot be disassembled and must be replaced as a unit. Be careful not to get coolant on the timing belt

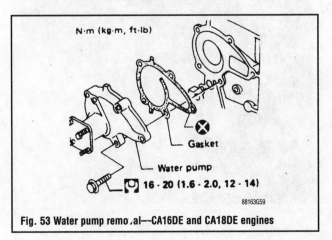

Fig. 53 Water pump removal—CA16DE and CA18DE engines

GA16i Engine

1. Disconnect the negative (-) battery cable.
2. Drain the coolant from the radiator and cylinder block.

✳✳ CAUTION

When draining engine coolant, keep in mind that cats and dogs are attracted to ethylene glycol antifreeze and could drink any that is left in an uncovered container or in puddles on the ground. This will prove fatal in sufficient quantity. Always drain coolant into a sealable container. Coolant should be reused unless it is contaminated or is several years old.

3. Remove all the drive belts.
4. Unbolt the water pump pulley and the water pump attaching bolts.
5. Separate the water pump with the gasket, if installed, from the cylinder block.
6. Remove all gasket material or sealant from the water pump mating surfaces. All sealant must be removed from the groove in the water pump surface also.

To install:

7. Apply a continuous bead of high temperature liquid gasket to the water pump housing mating surface. The housing must be attached to the cylinder block within 5 minutes after the sealant is applied. After the pump housing is bolted to the block, wait at least 30 minutes for the sealant to cure before starting the engine.
8. Position the water pump (and gasket) onto the block and install the attaching bolts. Torque the small retaining bolts to about 60 inch lbs. (10 Nm) and large retaining bolts 12–14 ft. lbs. (16–20 Nm).
9. Install the water pump pulley.
10. Install the drive belts and adjust the tension.
11. Fill the cooling system to the proper level.
12. Connect the negative (-) battery cable.

GA16DE Engine

▶ **See Figures 54, 55, 56 and 57**

1. Disconnect the negative battery cable.
2. Drain the cooling system.

✳✳ CAUTION

When draining engine coolant, keep in mind that cats and dogs are attracted to ethylene glycol antifreeze and could drink any that is left in an uncovered container or in puddles on the ground. This will prove fatal in sufficient quantity. Always drain coolant into a sealable container. Coolant should be reused unless it is contaminated or is several years old.

3. Remove the cylinder head front mounting bracket.
4. Loosen the water pump pulley bolts.
5. Remove the engine drive belts from the A/C compressor, power steering pump and alternator.
6. Remove the belt pulley from the water pump.

Fig. 55 Removing the water pump

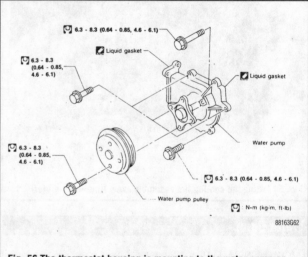

Fig. 56 The thermostat housing is mounting to the water pump on the GA16DE engine

Fig. 54 Removing the water pump retaining bolts

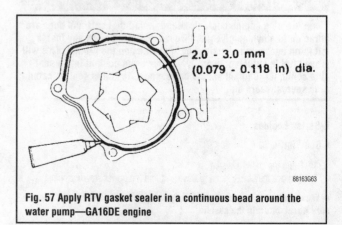

Fig. 57 Apply RTV gasket sealer in a continuous bead around the water pump—GA16DE engine

7. Disconnect electrical connectors and coolant hoses from the thermostat housing.

8. Unbolt and remove the water pump and thermostat housing from the engine.

➡**Remove the thermostat housing with water pump assembly.**

9. Remove the bolts that secure the thermostat housing to the water pump.

10. Remove all traces of gasket material from sealing surfaces.

To install:

11. Apply a continuous bead of liquid sealer to the sealing surface of the thermostat housing. The sealant should be 0.079–0.118 in. (2–3mm) diameter.

12. Install the thermostat housing on the water pump and tighten mounting bolts to 56–73 inch lbs. (7–8 Nm).

13. Apply a continuous bead of liquid sealer to the sealing surface of the water pump. The sealant should be 0.079–0.118 in. (2–3mm) diameter.

14. Install the water pump on the engine and tighten mounting bolts to 56–73 inch lbs. (7–8 Nm).

15. Install the pulley on the water pump and tighten the mounting bolts to 56–73 inch lbs. (7–8 Nm).

16. Connect electrical connectors and coolant hoses to the thermostat housing.

17. Install and adjust the alternator, power steering and A/C compressor drive belts.

18. Refill the cooling system and connect the negative battery cable.

19. Start the engine, bleed the cooling system, warm the engine to full operating temperature, and check for leaks.

20. If necessary, refill the cooling system when the engine has cooled.

SR20DE Engine

▶ **See Figures 58 and 59**

1. Disconnect the negative battery cable.
2. Drain the radiator coolant.

✳✳ CAUTION

When draining engine coolant, keep in mind that cats and dogs are attracted to ethylene glycol antifreeze and could drink any that is left in an uncovered container or in puddles on the ground. This will prove fatal in sufficient quantity. Always drain coolant into a sealable container. Coolant should be reused unless it is contaminated or is several years old.

3. Remove the cylinder block drain plug located at the left front of the engine and drain coolant.
4. Loosen the water pump pulley bolts.
5. Remove the power steering pump, alternator and A/C compressor drive belts (if equipped).
6. Remove the water pump pulley.
7. Note positioning of power steering pump adjusting bracket and remove the power steering pump adjusting bracket from the water pump. If necessary, remove the power steering pump for access to bracket.

➡**When removing the power steering pump, it is not necessary to disconnect the pressure hoses or drain the system. Position or tie the pump aside.**

8. Support the engine and remove the front engine mount.
9. Remove the mounting bolts from the water pump and remove the water pump.
10. Remove all traces of liquid gasket material from sealing surfaces.

To install:

11. Apply a continuous bead of liquid sealer to the mating surface of the water pump. Sealer should be 0.079–0.118 in. (2–3mm) wide.

12. Install the water pump assembly and tighten mounting bolts to 12–15 ft. lbs. (16–21 Nm).

➡**Be sure to properly position the adjusting bracket that was noted during removal.**

13. Install the front engine mount.
14. Install the power steering pump adjusting bracket and install the power steering pump if removed.
15. Install the water pump pulley and tighten mounting bolts to 55–73 inch lbs. (6–8 Nm).
16. Install and adjust the power steering pump, alternator and A/C compressor drive belts (if equipped).
17. Install the cylinder block drain plug located at the left front of the engine and tighten drain plug to 70–104 inch lbs. (8–12 Nm).
18. Refill the cooling system and connect the negative battery cable.
19. Start the engine, bleed the cooling system, and check for leaks.

Cylinder Head

REMOVAL & INSTALLATION

➡**To prevent distortion or warping of the cylinder head, allow the engine to cool completely before removing the head bolts.**

E-Series Engines Except E16i

▶ **See Figures 60, 61, 62 and 63**

➡**If the engine mounting bracket must be removed. Support the engine by placing a jack or equivalent, with a wooden block on top, under the oil pan away from the oil drain plug.**

1. Crank the engine until the No. 1 piston is at Top Dead Center on its compression stroke and disconnect the negative (-) battery cable.
2. Drain the cooling system.

✳✳ CAUTION

When draining engine coolant, keep in mind that cats and dogs are attracted to ethylene glycol antifreeze and could drink any that is left in an uncovered container or in puddles on the ground. This will prove fatal in sufficient quantity. Always drain coolant into a sealable container. Coolant should be reused unless it is contaminated or is several years old.

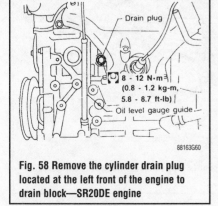

Fig. 58 Remove the cylinder drain plug located at the left front of the engine to drain block—SR20DE engine

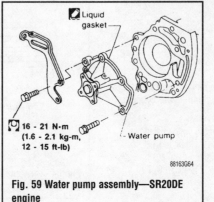

Fig. 59 Water pump assembly—SR20DE engine

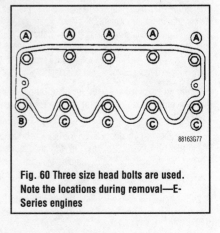

Fig. 60 Three size head bolts are used. Note the locations during removal—E-Series engines

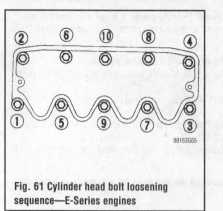

Fig. 61 Cylinder head bolt loosening sequence—E-Series engines

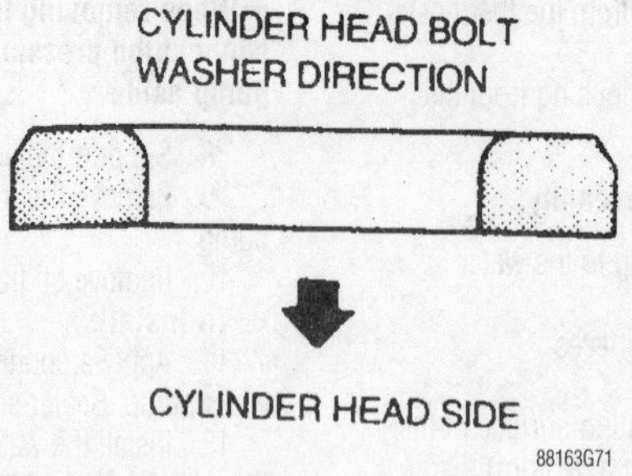

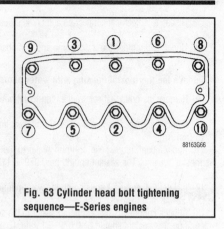

Fig. 62 If cupped washers are used, make certain they are installed in the correct direction

Fig. 63 Cylinder head bolt tightening sequence—E-Series engines

3. Remove the air cleaner assembly.

4. Remove the alternator and all drive belts.

5. Number all spark plug wires as to their respective cylinders, mark and remove the distributor, with all wires attached.

6. Remove the EAI pipes bracket and EGR tube at the right (EGR valve) side. Disconnect the same pipes on the front (exhaust manifold) side from the manifold.

7. Remove the exhaust manifold cover and the exhaust manifold, taking note that the center manifold nut has a different diameter than the other nuts.

8. Remove the air conditioning compressor bracket and the power steering pump bracket (if equipped).

9. Label and disconnect the carburetor throttle linkage, fuel line, and all vacuum and electrical connections.

10. Remove the intake manifold with carburetor or throttle body.

11. Remove the water pump pulley and crankshaft pulley.

12. Remove the rocker (valve) cover.

13. Remove upper and lower dust cover on the camshaft timing belt shroud.

14. With the shroud removed, the cam sprocket, crankshaft sprocket, jack-shaft sprocket, tensioner pulley, and toothed rubber timing belt are exposed.

15. Mark the relationship of the camshaft sprocket to the timing belt and the crankshaft sprocket to the timing belt with paint or a grease pencil. This will make setting everything up during reassembly much easier if the engine is disturbed during disassembly.

16. Remove the belt tensioner pulley.

17. Mark an arrow on the timing belt showing direction of engine rotation, because the belt wears a certain way and should be installed the way it was removed. Slide the belt off the sprockets.

18. Carefully remove the cylinder head from the block, pulling the head up evenly from both ends. If the head seems stuck, DO NOT pry it off. Tap lightly around the lower perimeter of the head with a rubber mallet to help break the seal. Label all head bolts with tape, as they must go back in their original positions. On some engines bolts are different size.

To install:

19. Thoroughly clean both the cylinder block and head mating surfaces. Avoid scratching either. Refer to the engine reconditioning procedures in this section for cleaning and inspection of the cylinder heads.

20. Turn the crankshaft and set the No. 1 cylinder at TDC on its compression stroke. This causes the crankshaft timing sprocket mark to be aligned with the cylinder block cover mark.

21. Align the camshaft sprocket mark with the cylinder head cover mark. This causes the valves for No. 1 cylinder to position at TDC on the compression stroke.

22. Place a new gasket on the cylinder block.

➡**If cupped washers are used for installation, always make sure that the flat side of the washer is facing downward before tightening the cylinder head bolts.**

23. Install the cylinder head on the block and tighten the bolts in stages: first tighten all bolts to 22 ft. lbs. (30 Nm), then retighten them all to 51 ft. lbs. (69 Nm). Next, loosen all bolts completely, and then retighten them again to 22 ft. lbs. (30 Nm). Tighten all bolts to a final torque of 51–54 ft. lbs. (69–74 Nm).

24. Install all remaining components in the reverse order of their removal.

CA16DE and CA18DE Engines

▶ **See Figures 62, 64, 65 and 66**

1. Crank the engine until the No. 1 piston is at Top Dead Center on its compression stroke.

2. Disconnect the negative (-) battery cable.

3. Drain the cooling system and remove the air cleaner assembly and upper radiator hose.

❋❋ CAUTION

When draining engine coolant, keep in mind that cats and dogs are attracted to ethylene glycol antifreeze and could drink any that is left in an uncovered container or in puddles on the ground. This will prove fatal in sufficient quantity. Always drain coolant into a sealable container. Coolant should be reused unless it is contaminated or is several years old.

4. Loosen the alternator and remove all drive belts. Remove the alternator. If necessary remove the right side under cover.

5. Disconnect the air duct at the throttle chamber.

6. Tag and disconnect all lines, hoses and wires which may interfere with cylinder head removal.

7. Remove the 8 screws and lift off the ornament cover.

8. Disconnect the O_2 sensor.

9. Remove the 2 exhaust heat shield covers.

10. Unbolt the exhaust manifold and wire the entire assembly out of the way.

11. Disconnect the EGR tube at the passage cover and then remove the passage cover and its gasket.

12. Disconnect and remove the crank angle sensor from the upper front cover.

➡**Put aligning mark on crank angle sensor and timing belt cover.**

13. Remove the support stay from under the intake manifold assembly.

14. Unbolt the intake manifold and remove it along with the collector and throttle chamber.

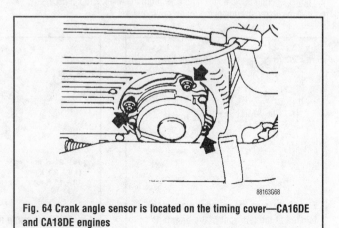

Fig. 64 Crank angle sensor is located on the timing cover—CA16DE and CA18DE engines

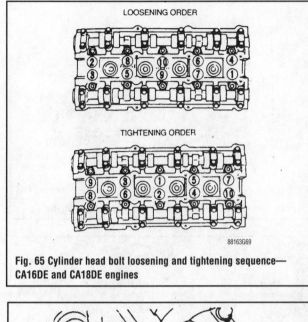

Fig. 65 Cylinder head bolt loosening and tightening sequence—CA16DE and CA18DE engines

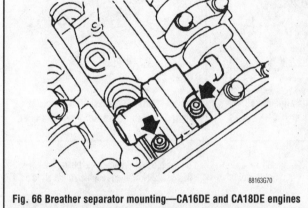

Fig. 66 Breather separator mounting—CA16DE and CA18DE engines

15. Disconnect and remove the fuel injectors as an assembly.
16. Remove the upper and lower front covers.

➡Remove engine mount bracket but support engine under oil pan with wooden blocks or equivalent. Do not position the support near the drain plug.

17. Remove the timing belt and camshaft sprockets.

➡When the timing belt has been removed, NEVER rotate the crankshaft and camshaft separately because the valves will hit the pistons!

18. Remove the camshaft cover.
19. Remove the breather separator.
20. Gradually loosen the cylinder head bolts in several stages, in the sequence illustrated.

21. Carefully remove the cylinder head from the block, pulling the head up evenly from both ends. If the head seems stuck, DO NOT pry it off. Tap lightly around the lower perimeter of the head with a rubber mallet to help break the seal. Label all head bolts with tape or magic marker, as they must go back in their original positions.

To install:

22. Thoroughly clean both the cylinder block and head mating surfaces. Avoid scratching either. Refer to the engine reconditioning procedures in this section for cleaning and inspection of the cylinder heads.

23. Install the cylinder head with bolts on the block. When installing the bolts tighten the two center bolts temporarily to 15 ft. lbs. (20 Nm) and install the head bolts loosely. After the timing belt and front cover have been installed, torque all the head bolts in the torque sequence. Tighten all bolts to 22 ft. lbs. (30 Nm). Re-tighten all bolts to 76 ft. lbs. (103 Nm). Loosen all bolts completely and then re-tighten them once again to 22 ft. lbs. (30 Nm). Tighten all bolts to a final torque of 76 ft. lbs. ((103 Nm).

➡If cupped washers are used for installation, always make sure that the flat side of the washer is facing downward before tightening the cylinder head bolts.

24. Install the camshaft sprocket, timing belt and front covers.
25. The remaining steps of installation are the reverse of removal. Make sure when installing the crank angle sensor to align the sensor with mark that was made before removal.

1987–88 E16i Engine

▶ See Figures 67, 68, 69 and 70

➡Be sure to use new washers when installing the cylinder hea1d bolts.

1. Crank the engine until the No. 1 piston is at TDC on its compression stroke.
2. Relieve the fuel system pressure, as described in Section 5.
3. Disconnect the negative (-) battery cable.
4. Drain the cooling system and remove the air cleaner assembly.

✻✻ CAUTION

When draining engine coolant, keep in mind that cats and dogs are attracted to ethylene glycol antifreeze and could drink any that is left in an uncovered container or in puddles on the ground. This will prove fatal in sufficient quantity. Always drain coolant into a sealable container. Coolant should be reused unless it is contaminated or is several years old.

5. Remove the alternator.
6. Remove the distributor, with all wires attached.
7. Remove the EAI pipe bracket and EGR tube at the right (EGR valve) side. Disconnect the same pipes on the front side of the manifold.
8. Remove the exhaust manifold cover and the exhaust manifold, taking note that the center manifold nut has a different diameter than the other nuts. Label this nut to ensure proper installation.
9. Remove the air conditioning compressor bracket and power steering pump bracket, if equipped.
10. Disconnect the carburetor throttle linkage, fuel line, and all vacuum and electrical connections.

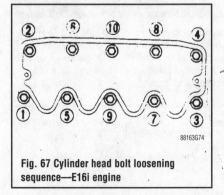

Fig. 67 Cylinder head bolt loosening sequence—E16i engine

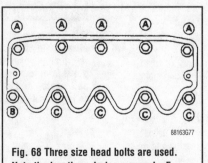

Fig. 68 Three size head bolts are used. Note the locations during removal—E-Series engines

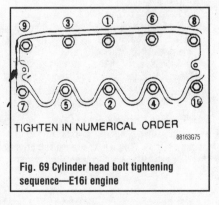

TIGHTEN IN NUMERICAL ORDER

Fig. 69 Cylinder head bolt tightening sequence—E16i engine

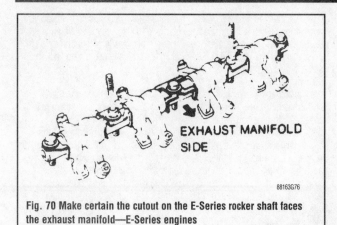

Fig. 70 Make certain the cutout on the E-Series rocker shaft faces the exhaust manifold—E-Series engines

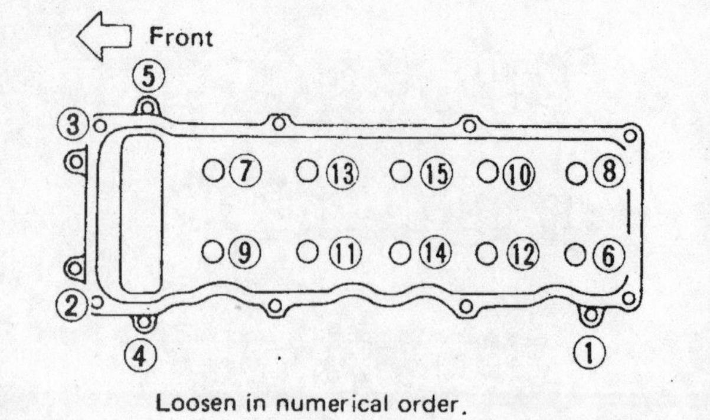

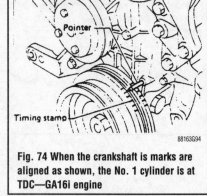

Fig. 71 Cylinder head bolt loosening sequence—GA16i engine

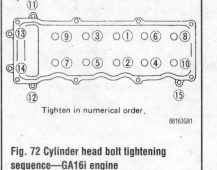

Fig. 72 Cylinder head bolt tightening sequence—GA16i engine

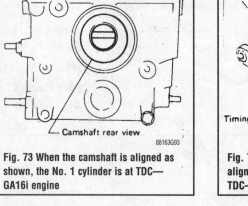

Fig. 73 When the camshaft is aligned as shown, the No. 1 cylinder is at TDC—GA16i engine

Fig. 74 When the crankshaft is marks are aligned as shown, the No. 1 cylinder is at TDC—GA16i engine

11. Remove the intake manifold.
12. Remove water pump drive belt and pulley.
13. Remove crankshaft pulley.
14. Remove the rocker (valve) cover.
15. Remove upper and lower dust cover on the camshaft timing belt shroud.
16. Mark the relationship of the camshaft sprocket to the timing belt and the crankshaft sprocket to the timing belt with paint or a grease pencil. This will make setting everything up during reassembly much easier if the engine is disturbed during disassembly.
17. Remove the belt tensioner pulley.
18. Mark an arrow on the timing belt showing direction of engine rotation and slide the belt off the sprockets.
19. Loosen the head bolts in reverse of the tightening sequence and carefully remove the cylinder head from the block, pulling the head up evenly from both ends. If the head seems stuck, do not pry it off. Tap lightly around the lower perimeter of the head with a rubber mallet to help break the seal. Label all head bolts with tape, as they must go back in their original positions.

To install:
20. Thoroughly clean both the cylinder block and head mating surfaces. Avoid scratching either. Refer to the engine reconditioning procedures in this section for cleaning and inspection of the cylinder heads.
21. Turn the crankshaft and set the No. 1 cylinder at TDC on its compression stroke. This causes the crankshaft timing sprocket mark to be aligned with the cylinder block cover mark.
22. Align the camshaft sprocket mark with the cylinder head cover mark. This causes the valves for No. 1 cylinder to position at TDC on the compression stroke.
23. Place a new gasket on the cylinder block.

➡There are 3 different size head bolts used on the E16i engine. Bolt (A) is 3.74 in. (95mm), bolt (B) is 4.33 in. (110mm) and bolt (C) is 3.15 in. (80mm). Measure the length of each bolt prior to installation and make sure they are installed in their proper locations on the head.

24. Install the cylinder head on the block and tighten the bolts as follows:
   a. Tighten all bolts to 22 ft. lbs. (29 Nm), then retighten them all to 51 ft. lbs. (69 Nm).
   b. Loosen all bolts completely, and then retighten them again to 22 ft. lbs. (29 Nm).
   c. Tighten all bolts to a final torque of 51–54 ft. lbs. (69–74 Nm); if an angle wrench is used, turn each bolt until they have achieved the specified number of degrees—bolts 1, 3, 6, 8 and 9: 45–50°; bolt 7: 55–60°; bolts 2, 4, 5 and 10: 40–45°.
25. The remaining steps of installation are the reverse of removal. When installing the exhaust manifold and exhaust manifold cover. Make sure the center manifold nut, which has a different diameter, is installed in the proper location.

GA16i Engine

▸ **See Figures 71, 72, 73 and 74**

1. Relieve the fuel system pressure, as described in Section 5.
2. Disconnect the negative (-) battery.
3. Drain the cooling.

✳✳ CAUTION

When draining engine coolant, keep in mind that cats and dogs are attracted to ethylene glycol antifreeze and could drink any that is left in an uncovered container or in puddles on the ground. This will prove fatal in sufficient quantity. Always drain coolant into a sealable container. Coolant should be reused unless it is contaminated or is several years old.

4. Disconnect the exhaust tube from the exhaust manifold.
5. Remove the intake manifold support bracket.
6. Remove the air cleaner assembly.
7. Disconnect the center wire from the distributor cap.

8. Remove the rocker arm cover.

9. Remove the distributor.

10. Remove the spark plugs.

11. Set the No. 1 cylinder at TDC of the compression stroke by rotating the engine until the cut out machined in the rear of the camshaft is horizontally aligned with the cylinder head.

12. Hold the camshaft sprocket stationary with the proper tool and loosen the sprocket bolt. Place highly visible and accurate paint or chalk alignment marks on the camshaft sprocket and the timing chain, then slide the sprocket from the camshaft and lift the timing chain from the sprocket. Remove the sprocket. The timing chain will not fall off the crankshaft sprocket unless the front cover is removed. This is due to the cast portion of the front cover located on the lower side of the crankshaft sprocket which acts a stopper mechanism. For this reason a chain stopper (wedge) is not required to remove the cylinder head.

13. Loosen the cylinder bolts in 2–3 stages to prevent warpage and cracking of the head. One of the cylinder head bolts is longer than the rest. Mark this bolt and make a note of its location.

14. Carefully remove the cylinder head from the block, pulling the head up evenly from both ends. If the head seems stuck, do not pry it off. Tap lightly around the lower perimeter of the head with a rubber mallet to help break the seal. The cylinder head and the intake and exhaust manifolds are removed together. Remove the cylinder head gasket.

To install:

15. Thoroughly clean both the cylinder block and head mating surfaces. Avoid scratching either. Refer to the engine reconditioning procedures in this section for cleaning and inspection of the cylinder heads.

16. Turn the crankshaft and set the No. 1 cylinder at TDC on its compression stroke. This is done by aligning the timing pointer with the appropriate timing mark on the pulley. To ensure that the No. 1 piston is at TDC, verify that the knock pin in the front of the camshaft is set at the top.

17. Place a new gasket on the block and lower the head onto the gasket.

➥These engines use different length cylinder head bolts. Bolt (1) is longer than the rest. Bolt (1) is 5.24 in. (133mm) while bolts (2) through (10) are 4.33 in. (110mm). Do not confuse the location of these bolts.

18. Coat the threads and the seating surface of the head bolts with clean engine oil and use a new set of washers. Install the cylinder head bolts in their proper locations and tighten as follows:

   a. Tighten all the bolts in sequence to 22 ft. lbs. (30 Nm).

   b. Tighten all bolts in sequence to 47 ft. lbs. (64 Nm).

   c. Loosen all bolts in reverse of the tightening sequence.

   d. Tighten all bolts again to 22 ft. lbs. (30 Nm).

   e. If an angle torque wrench is not available, torque the bolts in sequence to 43–51 ft. lbs. (58–69 Nm). If using an angle torque wrench for this step, tighten bolt (1) 80–85 degrees clockwise and bolts (6) through (10) 60–65 degrees clockwise.

   f. Finally, tighten bolts (11) through (15) to 55–73 inch lbs. (6.3–8.3 Nm).

19. Place the timing chain on the camshaft sprocket using the alignment marks. Slide the sprocket and timing chain onto the camshaft and install the center bolt.

20. At this point, check the hydraulic valve lifters for proper operation pushing hard on each lifter hard with fingertip pressure. Make sure the rocker arm is not on the cam lobe when making this check. If the valve lifter moves more than 0.04 in. (1mm), air may be inside it.

21. Install the spark plugs.

22. Install the distributor.

23. Install the rocker arm cover.

24. Connect the center wire to the distributor cap.

25. Install the air cleaner assembly.

26. Install the intake manifold support bracket.

27. Fill the cooling system to the proper level and connect the negative (-) battery cable.

28. Make all the necessary engine adjustments. If there was air in the lifters, bleed the air by running the engine at 1000 rpm for 10 minutes. Road test the vehicle for proper operation.

GA16DE Engine

▶ See Figures 75 thru 84

This is a very complex procedure. Before attempting cylinder head service thoroughly review these procedures, as well as the steps required for timing chain and camshaft service. To avoid head gasket leaks later you, should use new cylinder head bolts.

1. Relieve the fuel system pressure as described in Section 5.

2. Disconnect the negative (-) battery cable.

3. Drain the cooling system.

✳✳ CAUTION

When draining engine coolant, keep in mind that cats and dogs are attracted to ethylene glycol antifreeze and could drink any that is left in an uncovered container or in puddles on the ground. This will prove fatal in sufficient quantity. Always drain coolant into a sealable container. Coolant should be reused unless it is contaminated or is several years old.

4. Remove all drive belts. Disconnect the exhaust tube from the exhaust manifold.

5. Remove the power steering bracket.

6. Remove the air duct to intake manifold collector.

7. Remove the front right side wheel, splash cover and front under covers.

8. Remove the front exhaust pipe and engine front mounting bracket.

9. Remove the rocker arm cover.

10. Remove the distributor cap. Remove the spark plugs.

11. Set the No. 1 cylinder at TDC of the compression stroke.

12. Mark and remove the distributor assembly.

13. Remove the cam sprocket cover and gusset. Remove the water pump pulley. Remove the thermostat housing.

14. Remove the chain tensioner, chain guide. Loosen idler sprocket bolt.

15. Remove the camshaft sprocket bolts, camshaft sprocket, camshaft brackets and camshafts. Remove the idler sprocket bolt. These parts should be reassembled in their original position. Bolts should be loosen in 2 or 3 steps.

16. Loosen the cylinder bolts in 2–3 stages to prevent warpage and cracking of the head and note location of all head bolts.

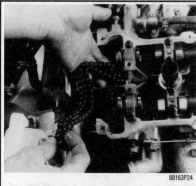

Fig. 75 The timing chain must be removed before performing cylinder head service

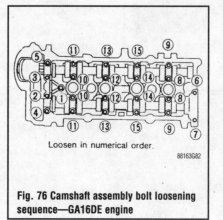

Loosen in numerical order.

Fig. 76 Camshaft assembly bolt loosening sequence—GA16DE engine

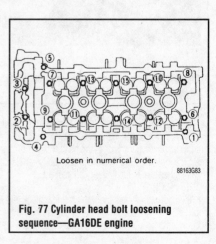

Loosen in numerical order.

Fig. 77 Cylinder head bolt loosening sequence—GA16DE engine

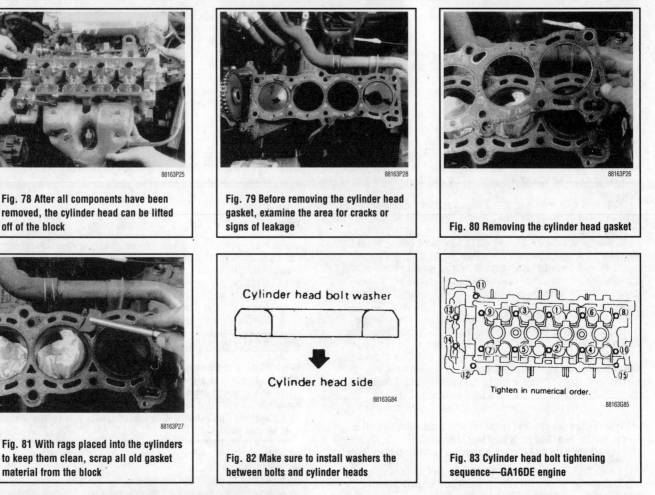

Fig. 78 After all components have been removed, the cylinder head can be lifted off of the block

Fig. 79 Before removing the cylinder head gasket, examine the area for cracks or signs of leakage

Fig. 80 Removing the cylinder head gasket

Fig. 81 With rags placed into the cylinders to keep them clean, scrap all old gasket material from the block

Fig. 82 Make sure to install washers the between bolts and cylinder heads

Fig. 83 Cylinder head bolt tightening sequence—GA16DE engine

Fig. 84 The cylinder head bolts must be tightened with a torque wrench in the proper order

17. Carefully remove the cylinder head from the block, pulling the head up evenly from both ends. If the head seems stuck, do not pry it off. Tap lightly around the lower perimeter of the head with a rubber mallet to help break the seal. The cylinder head and the intake and exhaust manifolds are removed together. Remove the cylinder head gasket.

To install:

18. Thoroughly clean both the cylinder block and head mating surfaces. Avoid scratching either. Refer to the engine reconditioning procedures in this section for cleaning and inspection of the cylinder heads.

19. Coat the threads and the seating surface of the head bolts with clean engine oil, and use a new set of washers as necessary. Install the cylinder head assembly (always replace the head gasket). Install head bolts (with washers) in their proper locations and tighten as follows:

    a. Tighten all the bolts in sequence to 22 ft. lbs. (29 Nm).

    b. Tighten all bolts in sequence to 43 ft. lbs. (59 Nm).

    c. Loosen all bolts in reverse of the tightening sequence.

    d. Tighten all bolts again in sequence to 22 ft. lbs. (29 Nm).

    e. Tighten bolts to 50–55 degrees clockwise in sequence or if angle wrench is not available, tighten bolts to 40–46 ft. lbs. (54–62 Nm) in sequence.

    f. Finally, tighten bolts (11) through (15) to 55–73 inch lbs. (6.3–8.3 Nm).

20. Install the camshaft assembly as outlined in this section, if necessary.

21. Install the upper timing chain assembly.

22. Install all other components in the reverse order of the removal procedure. Refill and check all fluid levels. Road test the vehicle for proper operation.

SR20DE Engine

▶ See Figures 85 thru 90

This is a very complex procedure. Before attempting cylinder head service thoroughly review these procedures, as well as the steps required for timing chain and camshaft service. These are torque-to-yield-design head bolts. To avoid head gasket leaks later, you should use new cylinder head bolts.

1. Release the fuel pressure, as outlined in Section 5.

2. Disconnect the negative (-) battery cable.

3. Raise and safely support the vehicle. Remove the engine under covers.

4. Remove the front right wheel and engine side cover.

5. Drain the cooling system.

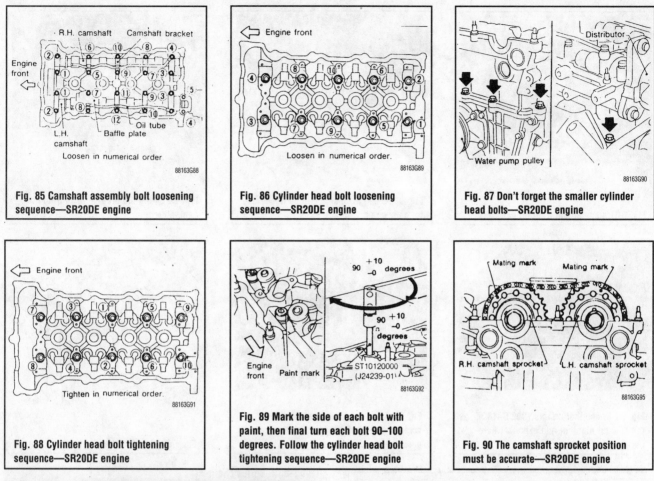

Fig. 85 Camshaft assembly bolt loosening sequence—SR20DE engine

Fig. 86 Cylinder head bolt loosening sequence—SR20DE engine

Fig. 87 Don't forget the smaller cylinder head bolts—SR20DE engine

Fig. 88 Cylinder head bolt tightening sequence—SR20DE engine

Fig. 89 Mark the side of each bolt with paint, then final turn each bolt 90–100 degrees. Follow the cylinder head bolt tightening sequence—SR20DE engine

Fig. 90 The camshaft sprocket position must be accurate—SR20DE engine

✻ CAUTION

When draining engine coolant, keep in mind that cats and dogs are attracted to ethylene glycol antifreeze and could drink any that is left in an uncovered container or in puddles on the ground. This will prove fatal in sufficient quantity. Always drain coolant into a sealable container. Coolant should be reused unless it is contaminated or is several years old.

6. Remove the radiator assembly.
7. Remove the air duct to intake manifold.
8. Remove the drive belts and water pump pulley.
9. Remove the alternator and power steering pump.
10. Remove all vacuum hoses, fuel hoses, wires, electrical connections.
11. Remove all spark plugs.
12. Remove the A.I.V. valve and resonator.
13. Remove the rocker cover and oil separator.
14. Remove the intake manifold supports, oil filter bracket and power steering bracket.
15. Set No. 1 at TDC on the compression stroke. Rotate crankshaft until mating marks on camshaft sprockets are in the correct position.
16. Remove the timing chain tensioner.
17. Mark and remove the distributor assembly. Remove the timing chain guide and camshaft sprockets.
18. Remove the camshafts, camshaft brackets, oil tubes and baffle plate. Keep all parts in order for correct installation.
19. Remove the water hose from the cylinder block and water hose from the heater.
20. Remove the starter motor. Remove the water pipe bolt.
21. Remove the cylinder outside bolts. Remove the cylinder head bolts in 2 or 3 steps. Remove the cylinder head completely with manifolds attached.

To install:
22. Check all components for wear. Replace as necessary. Clean all mating surfaces and replace the cylinder head gasket. Refer to the engine reconditioning procedures in this section for cleaning and inspection of the cylinder heads.

➡You SHOULD use new cylinder head bolts. If the length of any cylinder head bolt exceeds 6.228 in. (158.2mm) you MUST replace the bolts.

23. Install cylinder head. Tighten cylinder head in the following sequence:
   a. Tighten all bolts in sequence to 29 ft. lbs. (39 Nm).
   b. Tighten all bolts in sequence to 58 ft. lbs. (79 Nm).
   c. Loosen all bolts in sequence completely.
   d. Tighten all bolts in sequence to 25–33 ft. lbs. (34–45 Nm).
   e. Tighten all bolts to 90 to 100 degrees clockwise in sequence
   f. Tighten all bolts additional 90 to 100 degrees clockwise in sequence.
   Do not turn any bolt 180 to 200 degrees clockwise all at once.
24. Install all other components in the reverse order of the removal procedure. Refill and check all fluid levels. Road test the vehicle for proper operation.

Oil Pan

REMOVAL & INSTALLATION

◆ **See Figures 91 thru 98**

✻ CAUTION

The EPA warns that prolonged contact with used engine oil may cause a number of skin disorders, including cancer! You should make every effort to minimize your exposure to used engine oil. Protective gloves should be worn when changing the oil. Wash your hands and any other exposed skin areas as soon as possible after exposure to used engine oil. Soap and water, or waterless hand cleaner should be used.

Fig. 91 Removing the front oil pan bolts

Fig. 92 A long extension will be necessary to remove some oil pan bolts

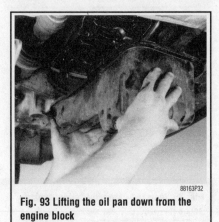

Fig. 93 Lifting the oil pan down from the engine block

Fig. 94 Notice that on this 1992 GA16DE the support member and exhaust where removed for easier access

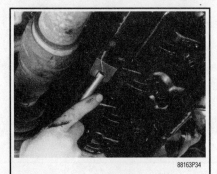

Fig. 95 All of the old gasket must be scraped away before installing the new gasket

Fig. 96 Using a seal cutter on the oil pan

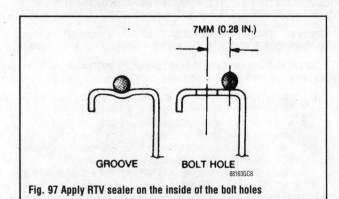

Fig. 97 Apply RTV sealer on the inside of the bolt holes

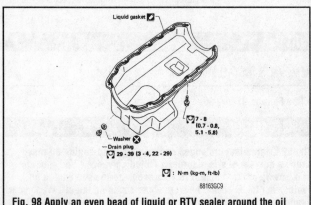

Fig. 98 Apply an even bead of liquid or RTV sealer around the oil pan. Let the RTV set until a thin skin appears, then install—E16i engine shown

1982–88 E-Series Engines

1. If the engine is in the vehicle, attach a lift, support the engine, and remove the engine mounting bolts.
2. Raise the engine slightly, watching to make sure that no hoses or wires are damaged.
3. Drain the engine oil.
4. Remove the oil pan bolts and slide the pan out to the rear.
5. Remove any old gasket material which remains on the pan and/or block.

To install:

6. Use a new gasket, coated on both sides with sealer.
7. Apply a thin bead of silicone seal to the engine block at the junction of the block and front cover, and the junction of the block and rear main bearing cap. Then apply a thin coat of silicone seal to the new oil pan gasket, install the gasket to the block and install the pan.
8. Tighten the pan bolts in a circular pattern from the center to the ends, to 48–84 inch lbs. (6–10 Nm). Overtightening will distort the pan lip, causing leakage.
9. Reinstall the engine mounting bolts.
10. Refill the oil pan to the specified level.

1987–90 CA16DE, CA18DE and GA16i Engines

1. Drain the engine oil.
2. Raise the vehicle and support it with safety stands.
3. Remove the right side splash cover. Remove the right side under cover.
4. Remove the center member.
5. Remove the forward section of the exhaust pipe.
6. Remove the front buffer rod and its bracket.
7. Remove the engine gussets.
8. Insert a seal cutter (SST KV10111100) between the oil pan and the cylinder block.

➡ **DO NOT use a screwdriver!**

9. Tapping the cutter with a hammer, slide it around the oil pan.
10. Remove the oil pan.

To install:

11.   Remove all gasket material from the pan and block mating surfaces.

12.   Apply a continuous bead (3.5–4.5mm) of RTV gasket material around the oil pan. Apply the sealer to the inner surface around the bolt holes where there is no groove.

13.   Install the pan within 5 minutes. Do not allow the sealer to dry. Tighten the pan bolts in a circular pattern from the center to the ends, to 48–84 inch lbs. (6–10 Nm). Overtightening will distort the pan lip, causing leakage.

14.   Install the engine gussets, buffer rod, exhaust pipe and center member.

15.   Install the right side splash cover and the right side under cover.

16.   Refill the oil pan to the specified level. Start engine and check for oil leaks.

1991–96 GA16DE Engine

1.   Disconnect the negative battery cable.
2.   Raise and safely support the vehicle.
3.   Remove the under covers.
4.   Remove the oil pan plug and drain the oil into a container.
5.   Remove the front exhaust tube.
6.   Remove center crossmember assembly.
7.   Remove the support brackets from the sides of the oil pan.
8.   Remove the oil pan mounting bolts. Using the oil pan seal cutter tool KV10111100 or equivalent, separate the oil pan from the engine.

❊❊ WARNING

Do not drive the seal cutter into the oil pump or rear oil seal retainer portion, for the aluminum mating surfaces will be damaged. Do not use a prybar to remove the oil pan; the flange will be deformed.

9.   Clean all the sealing surfaces.

To install:

10.   Apply sealant to the rear oil seal retainer.

11.   Apply a 0.128–0.177 in. (3.5–4.5 mm) continuous bead of liquid gasket to the oil pan mating surface.

12.   Install the oil pan and torque the oil pan mounting bolts/nuts in sequence to 56–73 inch lbs. (6.3–8.3 Nm).

13.   Install the oil pan support brackets.

14.   Install the center crossmember.

15.   Install the front exhaust tube.

16.   Install the under covers.

17.   Using a new gasket, install the oil pan plug and tighten the plug to 21–28 ft. lbs. (28–38 Nm).

18.   Connect the negative battery cable.

19.   After 30 minutes of gasket curing time, refill the oil pan with the specified quantity of clean oil. Operate the engine and check for leaks.

1991–93 SR20DE Engine

▶ **See Figures 99, 100 and 101**

1.   Drain the engine oil.
2.   Raise the vehicle and support it with safety stands.
3.   Remove the right side splash cover. Remove the right side under cover.
4.   Remove the lower oil pan bolts and separate the pan using tool KV10111100.
5.   Remove the baffle plate and front tube.
6.   Place a transmission jack under the transaxle and raise.
7.   Remove the center member and automatic transaxle shift control cable.
8.   Remove the compressor gussets.
9.   Remove the rear cover plate and aluminum oil pan bolts.

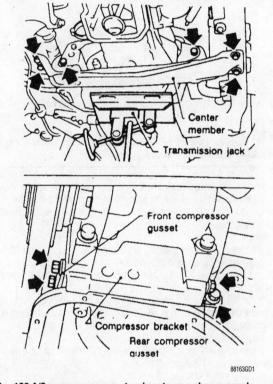

Fig. 100 A/C compressor gusset and center member removal—SR20DE engine shown

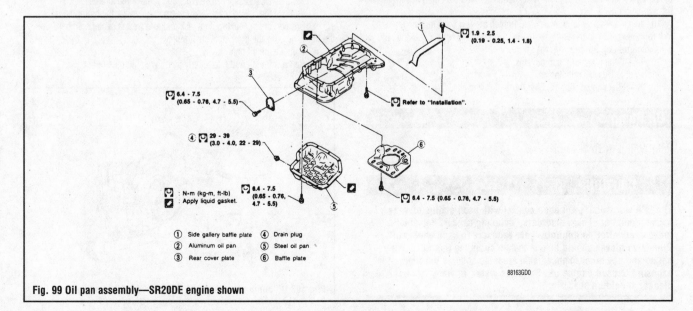

Fig. 99 Oil pan assembly—SR20DE engine shown

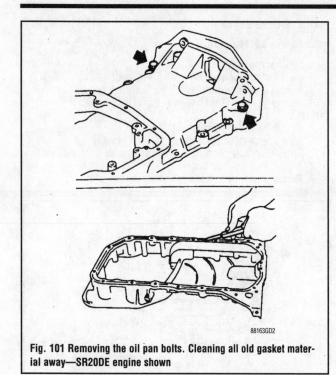

Fig. 101 Removing the oil pan bolts. Cleaning all old gasket material away—SR20DE engine shown

10. Remove the 2 engine-to-transaxle bolts and install them into the vacant holes. Tighten the bolts to release the oil pan from the cylinder block. The oil pan removing tool KV10111100 or equivalent, may have to be used to release the pan from the block.

To install:

11. Remove all old gasket material from the pan and block mating surfaces.

12. Apply a continuous bead (3.5–4.5mm) of RTV gasket material around the oil pan. Apply the sealer to the inner surface around the bolt holes where there is no groove.

13. Install the pan within 5 minutes. Tighten the pan bolts in a circular pattern from the center to the ends, to 48–84 inch lbs. (6–8 Nm). Overtightening will distort the pan lip, causing leakage.

14. Install the 2 transaxle bolts.

15. Install the rear cover, compressor gussets, automatic shift cable, center member and lower the transaxle jack.

16. Install the front tube and baffle plate.

17. Remove all old liquid gasket from the lower pan and upper pan surfaces.

18. Apply a continuous bead (3.5–4.5mm) of RTV gasket material around the oil pan. Apply the sealer to the inner surface around the bolt holes where there is no groove.

19. Install the pan within 5 minutes. Tighten the pan bolts in a circular pattern from the center to the ends, to 48–84 inch lbs. (6–8 Nm). Overtightening will distort the pan lip, causing leakage.

20. Install the remaining components.

21. Wait at least 30 minutes before refilling with oil.

22. Refill the engine with oil. Start the engine and check for leaks.

Oil Pump

REMOVAL & INSTALLATION

✷✷ CAUTION

The EPA warns that prolonged contact with used engine oil may cause a number of skin disorders, including cancer! You should make every effort to minimize your exposure to used engine oil. Protective gloves should be worn when changing the oil. Wash your hands and any other exposed skin areas as soon as possible after exposure to used engine oil. Soap and water, or waterless hand cleaner should be used.

E-Series Engine

▶ **See Figure 102**

1. Disconnect the negative (-) battery cable. Drain the engine oil.
2. Loosen the alternator lower bolts.
3. Remove the alternator belt and adjusting bar bolt.
4. Move the alternator out of the way and support it safely.
5. Disconnect the oil pressure gauge harness.
6. Remove the oil filter.
7. Remove the pump assembly.

To install:

8. Fill the pump with clean engine oil and rotate it several times or pack the pump housing with petroleum jelly.

9. Install the pump on the engine using a new gasket. Torque the pump mounting bolts to 84–108 inch lbs. (10–14 Nm).

10. Install the oil filter and the oil pressure gauge harness connections.

11. Install the alternator, belt and bracket.

12. Start the engine and check for leaks.

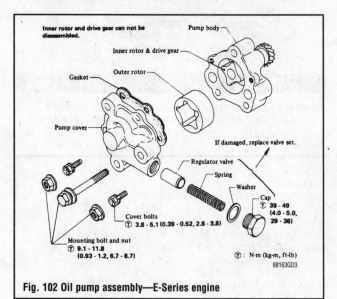

Fig. 102 Oil pump assembly—E-Series engine

CA16DE and CA18DE Engine

▶ **See Figure 103**

1. Disconnect the negative (-) battery cable.
2. Remove all accessory drive belts and remove the alternator.
3. Remove the timing (cam) belt covers and remove the timing belt.
4. Support the transaxle with a jack and remove the center member from the body. Remove the front crankshaft pulley.
5. Remove the oil pan.
6. Remove the oil pump assembly along with the oil strainer.

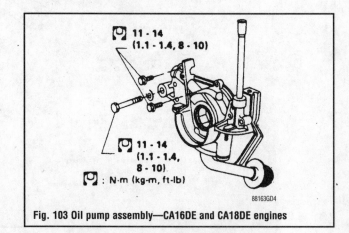

Fig. 103 Oil pump assembly—CA16DE and CA18DE engines

To install:

7. If installing a new or rebuilt oil pump, first pack the pump cavity full of petroleum jelly to prevent the pump from cavitating when the engine is started. Apply RTV sealer to the front oil seal end of the pan prior to installation. Install the pump and the strainer as an assembly, torque the mounting bolts to 9–12 ft. lbs. (12–16 Nm).

➡**Always use a new O-ring when installing the strainer to the pump body.**

8. Install the oil pan and bolt the engine in place.
9. Install the center member if it was removed.
10. Install the timing belt and covers. Install the crankshaft pulley.
11. Install the alternator and all drive belts. Reconnect the negative (-) battery cable.
12. Start engine and check for leaks.

GA16i, GA16DE and SR20DE Engines

◆ **See Figures 104 and 105**

This is a very complex procedure. Before attempting oil pump service thoroughly review these procedures, as well as the steps required for cylinder head, timing chain and camshaft service.

The oil pump is located in the front timing cover.
1. Disconnect the negative (-) battery cable.
2. Drain the engine oil.
3. Remove the drive belts.
4. Remove the cylinder head and oil pan, as outlined in this section.
5. Remove the oil strainer and baffle plate, if so equipped.
6. Remove the front cover assembly.
7. Remove the oil pump retaining bolts and remove the pump gears.
To install:
8. Install the pump gears and torque the cover bolts to 60–84 inch lbs. (7–9 Nm).
9. Remove all traces of gasket material from all gasket mating surfaces.
10. Apply a continuous bead of RVT sealer to the front cover.

➡**When using RTV sealant instead of gaskets, make sure the surface you are working on is very clean and dry before applying the sealant, then apply an even bead. Allow the RTV to dry slightly to form a thin skin. The component MUST be tightened before the RTV dries completely. The bolt torque should be checked again after RTV has completely dried.**

11. Within 5 minutes, install the front cover and torque the front cover bolts to 72 inch lbs. (8 Nm).
12. Install the oil baffle and strainer.

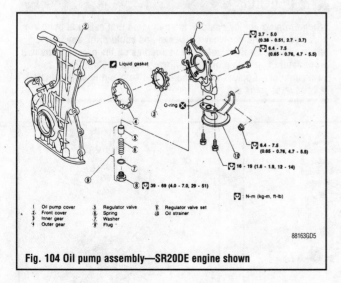

Fig. 104 Oil pump assembly—SR20DE engine shown

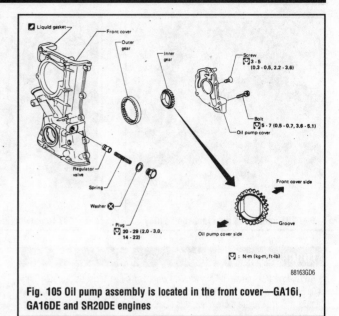

Fig. 105 Oil pump assembly is located in the front cover—GA16i, GA16DE and SR20DE engines

13. Install the oil pans and cylinder head as outlined in this section.
14. Install the drive belts.
15. Connect the negative (-) battery cable.
16. Wait 30 minutes before adding engine oil.
17. Refill with engine oil, start the engine and check for leaks.

Crankshaft Damper

REMOVAL & INSTALLATION

◆ **See Figures 106, 107, 108 and 109**

To remove the crankshaft damper or pulley usually requires a puller. Before proceeding you should check if there is enough clearance in front of the pulley to install the puller. If there is not enough clearance for the puller, you need to remove the engine. Review engine removal steps before proceeding as necessary. The following procedures are for the models that have sufficient clearance for the puller to be used.
1. Disconnect the negative (-) battery cable.
2. Loosen and remove the accessory drive belts.
3. Remove the belt pulleys from the damper, if so equipped.
4. Remove the large center bolt.
5. Using a crankshaft damper puller or equivalent, remove the damper from the crankshaft. Do not use a jaw puller on the damper. The outer ring will be pulled from the inner portion. Replace the damper if this the case.
6. Remove the key way if loose. Be careful not to damage the oil seal.
7. Inspect the oil sealing surface. If a deep grove is present, replace or recondition the damper. Check with the local machine shop to see if a repair sleeve is available.
To install:
8. Install the key way and make sure it is seated properly.
9. Install the damper and bolt. Torque the bolt to the following specifications:
   - 1982 E15— 108–145 ft. lbs. (147–197 Nm)
   - 1983–88 E15 and E16— 83–108 ft. lbs. (133–147 Nm)
   - CA16DE and CA18DE— 105–112 ft. lbs. (143–152 Nm)
   - GA16i— 132–152 ft. lbs. (180–207 Nm)
   - GA16DE— 98–112 ft. lbs. (133–152 Nm)
   - SR20DE—105–122 ft. lbs. (143–166 Nm)
10. Install the belt pulleys, drive belts and connect the battery cable.
11. Start the engine and check for leaks.

Fig. 106 Loosening the crankshaft pulley

Fig. 107 Removing the crankshaft pulley

Fig. 108 Align the keyway when installing the crankshaft pulley

Timing Cover and Seal

To remove front cover the crankshaft damper or pulley must be removed, this usually requires a puller. Before proceeding review the procedures for crankshaft damper and make sure there is enough clearance to install the puller. If there is not enough clearance for the puller, you need to remove the engine. Review engine removal steps before proceeding as necessary.

REMOVAL & INSTALLATION

E-Series Engines

▶ See Figure 110

➡ **The front crankshaft oil seal can only be replaced when the crankshaft sprocket is removed.**

1. Disconnect the battery.
2. Drain the cooling.

❋❋ CAUTION

When draining engine coolant, keep in mind that cats and dogs are attracted to ethylene glycol antifreeze and could drink any that is left in an uncovered container or in puddles on the ground. This will prove fatal in sufficient quantity. Always drain coolant into a sealable container. Coolant should be reused unless it is contaminated or is several years old.

3. Remove the radiator together with the upper and lower radiator hoses.
4. Loosen the air conditioning belt and remove.
5. Loosen the alternator adjusting bolt, and remove the alternator belt. Unbolt the alternator mounting bracket and remove the alternator.
6. Remove the power steering belt (if equipped) by loosening the steering pump adjusting bolt.
7. Remove the water pump pulley.

8. Remove crankshaft pulley. Support the engine and remove the right side engine mount bracket.
9. Loosen and remove the 8 Torx® head bolts securing the timing covers and remove the upper and lower covers.
To install:
10. Install the timing belt covers and torque the belt cover bolts to 36–48 inch lbs. (4–5.5 Nm) and reconnect the engine mounting bracket.
11. Install the crankshaft pulley in place and tighten the crankshaft pulley bolt to the specified torque:
   - 1982 E15—108–145 ft. lbs. (147–197 Nm)
   - 1983–88 E15 and E16—83–108 ft. lbs. (113–147 Nm)
12. Install the water pump pulley.
13. Install the alternator and all the drive belts.
14. Install the radiator and all cooling hoses. Refill the cooling system.
15. Connect the battery cable and start engine.

CA16DE and CA18DE Engines

For removal and installation of the timing belt upper and lower covers, refer to the timing belt procedures later in this section.

GA16i Engine

▶ See Figure 111

1. Disconnect the negative (-) battery cable.
2. Drain the engine coolant.

❋❋ CAUTION

When draining engine coolant, keep in mind that cats and dogs are attracted to ethylene glycol antifreeze and could drink any that is left in an uncovered container or in puddles on the ground. This will prove fatal in sufficient quantity. Always drain coolant into a sealable container. Coolant should be reused unless it is contaminated or is several years old.

Fig. 109 Using a puller to remove the front damper or crankshaft pulley

Fig. 110 Bolt location on the timing belt cover—E-Series engine

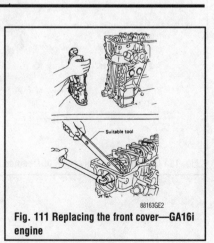

Fig. 111 Replacing the front cover—GA16i engine

3. Remove the oil pan as outlined in this section.

4. Remove all drive belts and power steering pump bracket, if so equipped.

5. Remove the air cleaner.

6. Install an engine lifting device to the front side of the engine. Remove the engine mounting bracket.

7. Remove the water pump as outlined in this section.

8. Remove the timing chain tensioner from the front cover.

9. Remove the rocker arm cover and all spark plugs.

10. Set the No. 1 cylinder to TDC of the compression stroke and remove the crankshaft pulley.

11. Remove the front cover.

To install:

12. Apply RTV sealer to the front cover and install within 5 minutes. Torque the bolts to 60–84 inch lbs. (7–10 Nm).

➡When using RTV sealant instead of gaskets, make sure the surface you are working on is very clean before applying the sealant, then apply an even bead. Allow the RTV to dry slightly to form a thin skin. The component MUST be tightened before the RTV dries completely. The bolt torque should be checked again after RTV has completely dried.

13. Install the crankshaft pulley and torque the bolt to 69–76 ft. lbs. (94–103 Nm).

14. Install the rocker arm cover and all spark plugs.

15. Install the timing chain tensioner to the front cover.

16. Install the water pump as outlined in this section.

17. Install the engine mounting bracket.

18. Install the air cleaner.

19. Install all drive belts and power steering pump bracket, if so equipped.

20. Install the oil pan as outlined in this section.

21. Connect the negative (-) battery cable and refill the engine coolant.

GA16DE Engine

◆ See Figures 112 thru 119

The front oil seal can be replaced by removing the crankshaft damper. Review Crankshaft Damper procedures earlier in this section. Some engines may prove to be difficult to remove the damper or oil seal with front cover and engine installed. It may be helpful to raise and support the car and remove the front wheels. In some cases, it may be necessary to remove the engine or front cover.

1. Relieve the fuel system pressure.

2. Disconnect the negative (-) battery cable.

3. Drain the engine coolant.

❋❋ CAUTION

When draining engine coolant, keep in mind that cats and dogs are attracted to ethylene glycol antifreeze and could drink any that is left in an uncovered container or in puddles on the ground. This will prove fatal in sufficient quantity. Always drain coolant into a sealable container. Coolant should be reused unless it is contaminated or is several years old.

4. Remove the upper radiator hoses and coolant fan connectors.

5. Remove the engine drive belts.

6. Remove the power steering pulley and remove the pump with bracket.

7. Remove the air duct from the intake manifold collector.

8. Disconnect the vacuum hoses, wiring, and harness connectors.

9. Remove the right front wheel and remove the inner wheel covers.

10. Remove the engine under covers.

11. Remove the cylinder head front mounting bracket.

12. Remove the valve cover from the engine. Be sure to loosen in reverse order of installation.

13. Remove the distributor cap and remove the spark plugs, if necessary.

Fig. 112 Removing the crankshaft pulley to gain access to the front cover oil seal—GA16DE shown

Fig. 113 Removing the front oil seal with the cover on the engine—GA16DE shown

Fig. 114 Installing the front cover oil seal with the cover installed—GA16DE shown

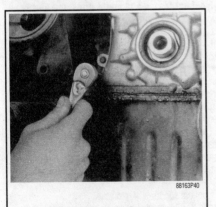

Fig. 115 Removing the front cover bolts

Fig. 116 The front oil pan bolts attach to the front cover

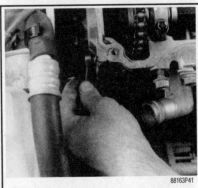

Fig. 117 Removing the upper front cover bolts

Fig. 118 Make sure all bolts are removed and gently pry back the upper front cover

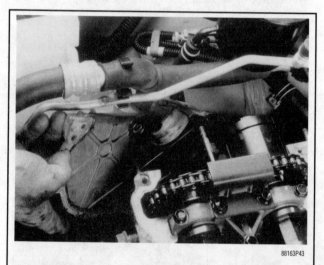

Fig. 119 Removing the front cover and exposing the timing chain

14. Remove the intake manifold supports.
15. Position the No. 1 cylinder to TDC of compression stroke.
16. Matchmark the distributor rotor and the distributor housing. Remove the distributor from the vehicle, if necessary.
17. Remove the water pump pulley from water pump.
18. Remove the complete thermostat housing assembly from the engine.
19. Remove the lower timing chain tensioner.
20. Remove the upper timing chain tensioner and slack side timing chain guide.

To install:
21. Confirm that No. 1 piston is set at TDC on compression stroke.
22. Install the crankshaft sprocket with the marks of the sprocket facing the front of the engine.
23. Install the oil pump drive spacer and install the chain guide.
24. Install the lower timing chain. Set the chain by aligning its mating mark with the one on the crankshaft sprocket. Make sure the sprocket's mating mark faces the front of the engine.

➡The number of links between the alignment marks are the same for the left and the right side.

25. Install the crankshaft sprocket and the lower timing chain. Set the timing chain by aligning its mating mark with the one on the crankshaft sprocket. Make sure sprocket's mating mark faces engine front. The number of links between the alignment marks are the same for the left and right side.

26. Using liquid gasket, install the front cover assembly.
27. Install engine front mounting bracket and install the engine mount.
28. Install the oil strainer, oil pan assembly, and the crankshaft pulley.
29. Install the center crossmember.
30. Set the idler sprocket by aligning the mating mark on the larger sprocket with the silver mating mark on the lower timing chain.
31. If necessary, install the upper timing chain and set it by aligning the mating mark on the smaller sprocket with the silver mating marks on the upper timing chain. Make sure sprocket marks face engine front.
32. Install the upper timing chain tensioner. Before installation of the tensioner, install a suitable pin to hold the tensioner in the relaxed position. After installing the chain tensioner, remove the pin.
33. Install the lower timing chain tensioner. Be sure the notch of the gasket is positioned down.
34. Apply liquid gasket to the thermostat housing and install the housing. Tighten the mounting bolts to 55–73 inch lbs. (7–8 Nm).
35. Install the remaining components. Tighten the water pump mounting bolts to 55–73 inch lbs. (7–8 Nm).
36. Using liquid gasket, install the cylinder head front cover. Tighten the mounting nuts or bolts to 33–44 inch lbs. (4–5 Nm).

➡If any part of the valve assembly or camshafts have been replace, the valve lash clearance will have to be checked.

37. Tighten the valve cover bolts in sequence to 18–35 inch lbs. (2–4 Nm). Be sure to install new gaskets for the spark plug tubes.
38. Tighten the spark plugs to 14–22 ft. lbs. (20–29 Nm). Connect the vacuum hoses, wiring and harness connectors.
39. Install the upper radiator hose and refill the system with coolant.
40. Connect the negative battery cable. Refill all fluid levels. Road test the vehicle for proper operation.

SR20DE Engine

The front oil seal can be replaced by removing the crankshaft damper. Review Crankshaft Damper procedures earlier in this section. Some engines may prove to be difficult to remove damper or oil with front cover and engine installed. It may be helpful to raise and support the car and remove the front wheels. In some cases it may be necessary to remove the engine or front cover.

✱✱ CAUTION

Fuel injection systems remain under pressure after the engine has been turned OFF. Properly relieve the fuel pressure, as outlined in Section 5 before disconnecting any fuel lines. Failure to do so may result in fire or personal injury.

1. Relieve the fuel system pressure.
2. Disconnect the negative (-) battery cable.
3. Drain the engine coolant.

✱✱ CAUTION

When draining engine coolant, keep in mind that cats and dogs are attracted to ethylene glycol antifreeze and could drink any that is left in an uncovered container or in puddles on the ground. This will prove fatal in sufficient quantity. Always drain coolant into a sealable container. Coolant should be reused unless it is contaminated or is several years old.

4. Remove the radiator.
5. Remove the right front wheel and engine side cover.
6. Remove the spark plugs.
7. Rotate the engine and position the No. 1 cylinder to TDC.
8. Remove the air duct to the intake manifold.
9. Remove the drive belts and the water pump pulley.
10. Remove the alternator and the power steering pump from the engine.
11. Label and remove the vacuum hoses, fuel hoses, and the wire harness connectors.
12. Remove the intake manifold supports, if necessary.
13. Unbolt and remove the oil filter bracket and the power steering pump bracket.
14. Remove the timing chain tensioner, as needed.

15. Remove the timing chain guide.

To install:

16. Clean all gasket mating surfaces.

17. If removed, install the crankshaft sprocket. Position the crankshaft so that No. 1 piston is set at TDC (keyway at 12 o'clock, mating mark at 4 o'clock) fit timing chain to crankshaft sprocket so the mating mark is in line with mating mark on crankshaft sprocket. The mating marks on timing chain for the camshaft sprockets should be silver. The mating mark on the timing chain for the crankshaft sprocket should be gold.

18. Install the timing chain to the crankshaft sprocket and install the timing chain guides. Tighten the timing chain guides to 9–14 ft. lbs. (13–19 Nm). Drape the timing chain over the left chain guide.

19. Install the oil pump drive spacer to the crankshaft.

20. Apply a continuous bead of liquid sealant to the front timing cover and install the cover. Torque the front cover mounting bolts to 57–66 inch lbs. (6.4–7.5 Nm).

21. Install right front engine mount.

22. Install the crankshaft pulley and tighten the mounting bolt to 105–112 ft. lbs. (142–152 Nm). Be sure the No. 1 piston is at TDC.

23. Install the oil strainer, baffle plate, and the oil pan assembly.

24. Be sure to apply a bead of sealant to the joint of the block and front timing cover.

25. Using new hose clamps, install the coolant hoses to the engine block.

26. Install the timing chain guide, if removed.

27. Install the chain tensioner. Press the cam stopper down and the press-in sleeve until the hook can be engaged on the pin. When tensioner is bolted in position the hook will release automatically.

➡**Ensure the arrow on the outside of the tensioner faces the front of the engine.**

28. Install the oil filter bracket and the power steering pump bracket.

29. Install the intake manifold supports.

30. Install a continuous bead of sealant to the rocker cover and install the cover. Torque the mounting bolts in sequence as follows:

a. Tighten nuts No. 1, 10, 11, 13 and 8 (in that order) to 35 inch lbs. (4 Nm).

b. Tighten nuts No. 1 through 13 in numerical order to 70–86 inch lbs. (8–10 Nm).

31. Install the remaining components. Install the vacuum hoses, fuel hoses, and the wire harness connectors. Lower the vehicle, connect the negative battery cable, Refill fluid levels, start the engine, and bleed the cooling system. Check for leaks and road test the vehicle for proper operation.

Timing Belt

REMOVAL & INSTALLATION

Refer to section 1 for the manufacturer's recommendations on timing belt replacement schedules. Broken timing belts may cause severe engine damage. It is more cost effective to replace the belt based on maintenance schedule or inspection, rather than wait until it fails. If the belt breaks while the engine is running it may cause additional piston or valve damage.

E-Series Overhead Camshaft Engines

▶ **See Figure 120**

1. Refer to the Timing Belt Cover removal and installation procedures in this section, and remove the timing cover.

2. If necessary, remove the spark plug, then turn the crankshaft to position the No. 1 piston at TDC of the compression stroke.

➡**Note the position of the timing marks on the camshaft sprocket, the timing belt and the crankshaft sprocket (see illustrations).**

3. Loosen and/or remove the timing belt tensioner. Mark the rotation direction of the timing belt, then remove it from the sprockets.

4. To remove the front oil seal, pull off the crankshaft sprocket, then pry out the oil seal with a small prybar (be careful not to scratch the crankshaft).

To install:

5. Clean the oil seal mounting surface.

6. Install a new oil seal, the timing belt and tensioner. Torque the tensioner pulley bolts to 13–16 ft. lbs. (17–22 Nm), the timing cover bolts to 30–48 inch lbs. (3.4–5.4 Nm), the crankshaft pulley bolt to 83–108 ft. lbs. (113–147 Nm).

7. Install the timing belt covers.

8. Start engine and check timing.

CA16DE and CA18DE Engines

▶ **See Figures 121, 122, 123, 124 and 125**

1. Disconnect the negative (-) battery cable.

2. Drain the cooling system.

❊❊❊ CAUTION

When draining engine coolant, keep in mind that cats and dogs are attracted to ethylene glycol antifreeze and could drink any that is left in an uncovered container or in puddles on the ground. This will prove fatal in sufficient quantity. Always drain coolant into a sealable container. Coolant should be reused unless it is contaminated or is several years old.

3. Disconnect the upper radiator hose at the elbow and then position it out of the way.

4. Remove the right side engine under cover.

5. Loosen the power steering pump and the air conditioning compressor and then remove the drive belts.

6. Remove the water pump pulley.

7. Matchmark the crank angle sensor to the upper front cover and the remove it. Carefully position it out of the way.

8. Position a floor jack under the engine and raise it just enough to support the engine.

9. Remove the upper engine mount bracket at the right side of the upper front cover.

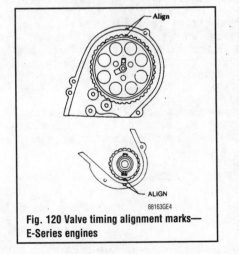

Fig. 120 Valve timing alignment marks—E-Series engines

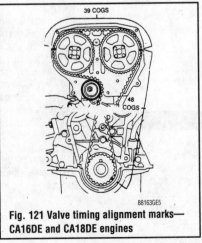

Fig. 121 Valve timing alignment marks—CA16DE and CA18DE engines

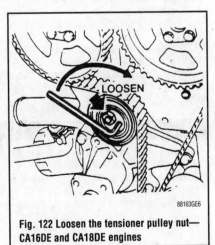

Fig. 122 Loosen the tensioner pulley nut—CA16DE and CA18DE engines

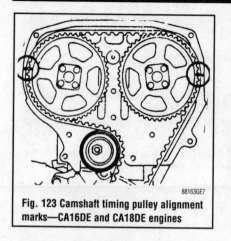

Fig. 123 Camshaft timing pulley alignment marks—CA16DE and CA18DE engines

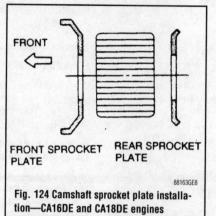

Fig. 124 Camshaft sprocket plate installation—CA16DE and CA18DE engines

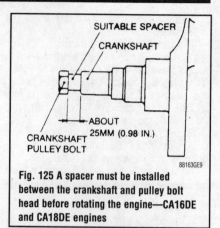

Fig. 125 A spacer must be installed between the crankshaft and pulley bolt head before rotating the engine—CA16DE and CA18DE engines

10. Remove the upper front cover.
11. Align the timing marks on the camshaft pulley sprockets and then remove the crankshaft pulley.

➡ **The crankshaft pulley may be reached by removing the side cover from inside the right-hand wheel opening.**

12. Remove the lower front cover.
13. Loosen the tensioner pulley nut to slacken the timing belt and then slide off the belt.

To install:

➡ **Do not bend or twist the timing belt. NEVER rotate the crankshaft and camshaft separately with the timing belt removed. Be sure the timing belt is free of any oil, water or debris.**

14. Install the crankshaft sprocket with the sprocket plates.
15. Before installing the timing belt, ensure that the No. 1 piston is at TDC of the compression stroke (all sprocket timing marks will be in alignment with the marks on the case).

When the timing belt is on and in position, there should be 39 cogs between the timing mark on each of the camshaft sprocket and 48 cogs between the mark on the right camshaft sprocket and the mark on the crankshaft sprocket.

16. Loosen the timing belt tensioner pulley nut.
17. Temporarily install the crankshaft pulley bolt and then rotate the engine two complete revolutions.

➡ **Fabricate and install a suitable 25mm thick spacer between the end of the crankshaft and the head of the crankshaft pulley bolt to prevent bolt damage.**

18. Tighten the tensioner pulley bolt to 16–22 ft. lbs. (21–30 Nm).
19. Install the upper and lower front covers.
20. Install the crankshaft pulley with its washer and tighten it to 105–112 ft. lbs. (143–152 Nm).
21. Install the engine mount bracket.
22. Install the water pump pulley. Install the crank angle sensor so that the matchmarks made previously line up and tighten the bolts to 61–70 inch lbs. (7–9 Nm).
23. Install all drive belts and adjust.
24. Install the right side engine under cover.
25. Reconnect the radiator hose and refill the radiator.
26. Connect the battery cable and start the engine. Check engine timing and for any leaks. Road test.

Timing Chain

To remove front cover the crankshaft damper or pulley must be removed, this usually requires a puller. Before proceeding review the procedures for Crankshaft Damper and Front Timing Cover. Make sure there is enough clearance to install the puller. If there is not enough clearance for the puller, you will need to remove the engine. Review engine removal steps before proceeding as necessary.

⁕⁕ CAUTION

When draining engine coolant, keep in mind that cats and dogs are attracted to ethylene glycol antifreeze and could drink any that is left in an uncovered container or in puddles on the ground. This will prove fatal in sufficient quantity. Always drain coolant into a sealable container. Coolant should be reused unless it is contaminated or is several years old.

REMOVAL & INSTALLATION

GA16i Engine

▶ **See Figures 126, 127, 128, 129 and 130**

1. Set the No. 1 piston at TDC of the compression stroke.
2. Disconnect the negative (-) battery cable.
3. Remove the front cover.
4. If necessary, define the timing marks with chalk or paint to ensure proper alignment.
5. Hold the camshaft sprocket stationary with a spanner wrench or similar tool and remove the camshaft sprocket bolt.
6. Remove the chain guides.
7. Remove the camshaft sprocket.
8. Remove the oil pump spacer.
9. Remove the crankshaft sprocket and timing chain.

To install:

10. Verify that the No. 1 piston is at TDC of the compression stroke. The crankshaft keyways should be at the 12 o'clock position.
11. Install the camshaft sprocket, bolt and washer. The alignment mark must face towards the front. When installing the washer, place the non-chamfered side of the washer towards the face of camshaft sprocket. Tighten the bolt just enough to hold the sprocket in place.
12. Install the crankshaft sprocket making sure the alignment mark is facing the front.
13. Install the timing chain by aligning the silver links at the 12 o'clock and 6 o'clock positions on the chain with the timing marks on the crankshaft and camshaft sprockets. The number of links between the 2 silver links are the same for the left and the right sides of the chain, so either side of the chain may be used to align the sprocket timing marks.
14. Torque the camshaft sprocket bolt to 72–94 ft. lbs. (98–128 Nm) once the chain is in place and aligned.
15. Install the chain guides and tensioner. Use a new tensioner gasket and torque the tensioner and chain guide bolts to 9–14 ft. lbs. (13–19 Nm). When installing the chain guide, move the guide in the direction that applies tension to the chain.
16. Install the front cover.
17. Connect the negative (-) battery cable. Road test the vehicle for proper operation.

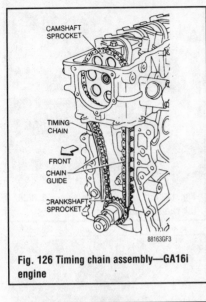

Fig. 126 Timing chain assembly—GA16i engine

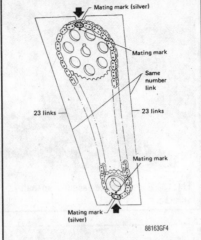

Fig. 127 Timing chain and sprocket alignment marks—GA16i engine

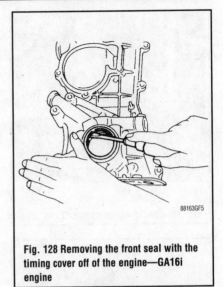

Fig. 128 Removing the front seal with the timing cover off of the engine—GA16i engine

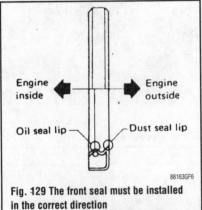

Fig. 129 The front seal must be installed in the correct direction

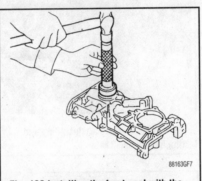

Fig. 130 Installing the front seal with the timing cover off of the engine—GA16i engine

Fig. 131 Removing the chain tensioner

Fig. 132 Removing the top chain guide

Fig. 133 Removing the chain guide

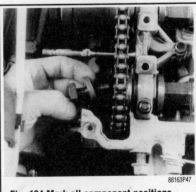

Fig. 134 Mark all component positions before removing the sprockets or chains

GA16DE Engine

♦ See Figures 131 thru 144

1. Relieve the fuel pressure, as outlined in Section 5.
2. Disconnect the negative (–) battery cable.
3. Drain the cooling system.

※※ CAUTION

When draining engine coolant, keep in mind that cats and dogs are attracted to ethylene glycol antifreeze and could drink any that is left in an uncovered container or in puddles on the ground. This will prove fatal in sufficient quantity. Always drain coolant into a sealable container. Coolant should be reused unless it is contaminated or is several years old.

4. Remove the cylinder head assembly.
5. Remove the idle sprocket shaft from the rear side.
6. Remove the upper timing chain assembly.
7. Remove the center member.
8. Remove the oil pan assembly, oil strainer and crankshaft pulley.
9. Support engine and remove the engine front mounting bracket.
10. Remove the front cover. One retaining bolt for the front cover assembly is located on the water pump.

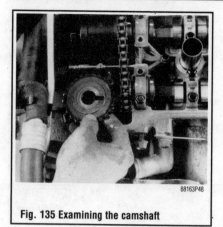

Fig. 135 Examining the camshaft

Fig. 136 Removing the second camshaft sprocket

Fig. 137 Lift the timing chain up and slide the camshaft sprocket out

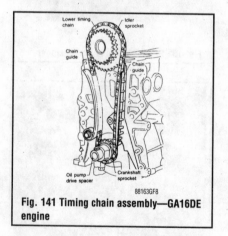

Fig. 138 Examine the tensioners and guides for any damage or wear

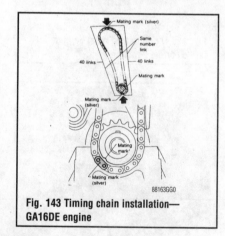

Fig. 139 Take great care installing and aligning the new chain

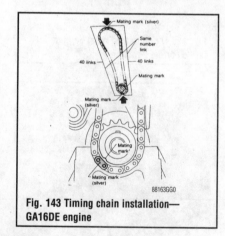

Fig. 140 Inspect the timing chain tensioner for any damage or wear

Fig. 141 Timing chain assembly—GA16DE engine

Fig. 142 Timing chain assembly—GA16DE engine

Fig. 143 Timing chain installation—GA16DE engine

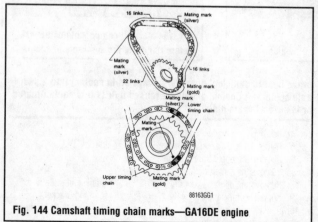

Fig. 144 Camshaft timing chain marks—GA16DE engine

11. Remove the idler sprocket.

12. Remove the lower timing chain assembly, oil pump drive spacer, chain guide, crankshaft sprocket.

To install:

13. Confirm that No. 1 piston is set at TDC on compression stroke. Install the chain guide.

14. Install crankshaft sprocket and lower timing chain. Set timing chain by aligning its mating mark with the one on the crankshaft sprocket. Make sure sprocket's mating mark faces engine front. The number of links between the alignment marks are the same for the left and right side.

15. Install the front cover assembly.

16. Install engine front mounting.

17. Install oil strainer, oil pan assembly and crankshaft pulley.

18. Install center member.

19. Set idler sprocket by aligning the mating mark on the larger sprocket with the silver mating mark on the lower timing chain.

20. Install upper timing chain and set it by aligning the mating mark on the

smaller sprocket with the silver mating marks on the upper timing chain. Make sure sprocket marks face engine front.

21. Install idler sprocket shaft.
22. Install the cylinder head assembly.
23. Install all remaining components in reverse order of removal.
24. Connect the negative (-) battery cable. Refill all fluid levels. Road test the vehicle for proper operation.

SR20DE Engine

▶ See Figures 145, 146 and 147

This is a very complex procedure. Before attempting timing chain service, thoroughly review these procedures, as well as the steps required for front timing cover and camshaft service.

1. Relieve the fuel system pressure, as outlined in Section 5.
2. Disconnect the negative (-) battery cable.
3. Drain the cooling system.

✳✳ CAUTION

When draining engine coolant, keep in mind that cats and dogs are attracted to ethylene glycol antifreeze and could drink any that is left in an uncovered container or in puddles on the ground. This will prove fatal in sufficient quantity. Always drain coolant into a sealable container. Coolant should be reused unless it is contaminated or is several years old.

4. Remove the radiator.
5. Remove the right front wheel and engine side cover.
6. Remove the spark plugs.
7. Rotate the engine and position the No. 1 cylinder to TDC.
8. Remove the air duct to the intake manifold.
9. Remove the drive belts and the water pump pulley.
10. Remove the alternator and the power steering pump from the engine.
11. Label and remove the vacuum hoses, fuel hoses, and the wire harness connectors.
12. Remove the rocker arm cover mounting bolts in the reverse order of installation.
13. Remove the intake manifold supports.
14. Unbolt and remove the oil filter bracket and the power steering pump bracket.
15. Remove the timing chain tensioner.
16. Matchmark the distributor rotor and the distributor housing to the engine block and remove the distributor.
17. Remove the timing chain guide.
18. Holding the flats of the camshaft sprockets, remove the bolts that secure the sprockets.
19. Remove the timing chain sprockets from the camshafts.
20. Remove the oil tubes, baffle plate, camshaft brackets and remove the camshafts from the cylinder head.
21. Remove the starter motor.
22. Remove the coolant hoses from the engine block.
23. Remove the knock sensor harness connector.

24. Remove the EGR tube.
25. Remove the cylinder head assembly.
26. Raise and support the vehicle safely.
27. Remove the oil pan, oil strainer, and the baffle plate.
28. Remove the crankshaft pulley using a suitable puller.
29. Remove the engine front mount.
30. Remove the front cover and oil pump drive spacer.
31. Remove the timing chain guides and timing chain. Check the timing chain for excessive wear at the roller links. Replace the chain if necessary.

To install:
32. Clean all gasket mating surfaces.
33. Install the crankshaft sprocket. Position the crankshaft so that No. 1 piston is set at TDC (keyway at 12 o'clock, mating mark at 4 o'clock) fit timing chain to crankshaft sprocket so the mating mark is in line with mating mark on crankshaft sprocket. The mating marks on timing chain for the camshaft sprockets should be silver. The mating mark on the timing chain for the crankshaft sprocket should be gold.
34. Install the timing chain to the crankshaft sprocket and install the timing chain guides. Tighten the timing chain guides to 9–14 ft. lbs. (13–19 Nm). Drape the timing chain over the left chain guide.
35. Install the oil pump drive spacer to the crankshaft.
36. Apply a continuous bead of liquid sealant to the front timing cover and install the cover. Torque the front cover mounting bolts to 57–66 inch lbs. (6.4–7.5 Nm).
37. Install right front engine mount.

➡**When using RTV sealant instead of gaskets, make sure the surface you are working on is very clean before applying the sealant, then apply an even bead. Allow the RTV to dry slightly to form a thin skin. The component MUST be tightened before the RTV dries completely. The bolt torque should be checked again after RTV has completely dried.**

38. Install the crankshaft pulley and tighten the mounting bolt to 105–112 ft. lbs. (142–152 Nm). Be sure the No. 1 piston is at TDC.
39. Install the oil strainer, baffle plate, and the oil pan assembly.
40. Install the cylinder head assembly. Be sure to apply a bead of sealant to the joint of the block and front timing cover.
41. Install the EGR tube.
42. Install the knock sensor harness connector.
43. Using new hose clamps, install the coolant hoses to the engine block.
44. Install the starter motor.
45. Install the camshafts, camshaft bearing caps, oil tubes, and the baffle plate.

➡**When installing the camshafts, be sure to position the LH and RH camshaft keys at 12 o'clock. Also make sure the camshaft brackets are facing in the correct direction.**

46. Install the camshaft sprockets by lining up the mating marks on the timing chain with the mating marks on the camshaft sprockets. Tighten the camshaft sprocket bolts to 101–116 ft. lbs. (137–157 Nm).
47. Install the timing chain guide and distributor.
48. Install the chain tensioner. Press the cam stopper down and the press-in sleeve until the hook can be engaged on the pin. When tensioner is bolted in position the hook will release automatically.

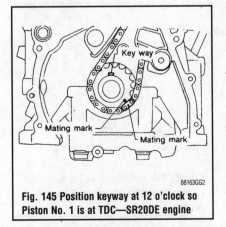

Fig. 145 Position keyway at 12 o'clock so Piston No. 1 is at TDC—SR20DE engine

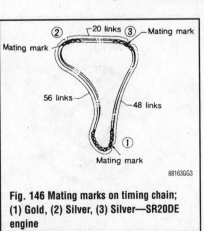

Fig. 146 Mating marks on timing chain; (1) Gold, (2) Silver, (3) Silver—SR20DE engine

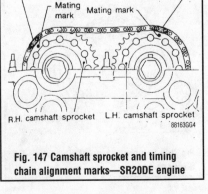

Fig. 147 Camshaft sprocket and timing chain alignment marks—SR20DE engine

➡**Ensure the arrow on the outside of the tensioner faces the front of the engine.**

49. Install the oil filter bracket and the power steering pump bracket.

50. Install the intake manifold supports.

51. Install a continuous bead of sealant to the rocker cover and install the cover. Torque the mounting bolts in sequence as follows:

   a. Tighten nuts No. 1, 10, 11, 13 and 8 (in that order) to 35 inch lbs. (4 Nm).

   b. Tighten nuts No. 1 through 13 in numerical order to 70–86 inch lbs. (8–10 Nm).

52. Install the remaining components. Install the vacuum hoses, fuel hoses, and the wire harness connectors. Lower the vehicle, connect the negative battery cable, Refill fluid levels, start the engine, and bleed the cooling system. Check for leaks and road test the vehicle for proper operation.

Camshaft Sprocket

▶ **See Figure 148**

Before attempting camshaft sprocket service, review the procedures for front timing cover, crankshaft damper and camshaft for your specific engine. The sprocket replacement on many engines is a very complex procedure.

REMOVAL & INSTALLATION

1. Refer to the Timing Belt/Chain Removal and Installation procedures in this section, and remove the timing belt or chain.

2. Remove the sprocket retaining bolt and remove the sprocket from the

88163P50

Fig. 148 Gaining access to most camshaft sprockets involves disassembly of the front of the engine

---

camshaft. On engines with a timing chain the chain and sprocket are removed at the same time.

3. To install, use new gaskets and reverse the removal procedures.

Camshaft and Bearings

REMOVAL & INSTALLATION

1982–88 E-Series Engines

▶ **See Figures 149, 150 and 151**

This is a very complex procedure. Before attempting camshaft service, thoroughly review these procedures, as well as the steps required for front timing cover and cylinder head service.

1. Disconnect the negative (-) battery cable.

2. Drain the engine coolant.

✳ CAUTION

When draining engine coolant, keep in mind that cats and dogs are attracted to ethylene glycol antifreeze and could drink any that is left in an uncovered container or in puddles on the ground. This will prove fatal in sufficient quantity. Always drain coolant into a sealable container. Coolant should be reused unless it is contaminated or is several years old.

3. Remove the cylinder head, as outlined earlier in this section.

4. Remove the rocker shaft along with the rocker arms. Loosen the bolts gradually, in two or three stages.

5. Carefully slide the camshaft out the front of the cylinder head.

6. Check the camshaft run-out, end-play, wear and journal clearance. Refer to the camshaft specifications chart.

To install:

7. Slide the camshaft into the cylinder head carefully and then install a NEW oil seal.

8. Install the cylinder head and rear timing belt cover.

9. Set the camshaft so that the knockpin faces upward and then install the camshaft sprocket so its timing mark aligns with the one on the rear timing cover.

10. Install the timing belt.

11. Coat the rocker shaft and the interior of the rocker arm with engine oil. Install them so the punchmark on the shaft faces forward and the oil holes in the shaft face down. The cut-out in the center retainer on the shaft should face the exhaust manifold side of the engine.

12. Make sure the valve adjusting screws are loosened and then tighten the shaft bolts to 13–15 ft. lbs. (18–20 Nm) in several stages, from the center out. The first and last mounting bolts should have a new bolt stopper installed.

13. Adjust the valves and refill all fluid levels.

14. Start engine, check timing and road test.

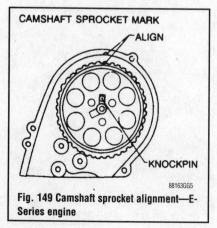

88163GG5

Fig. 149 Camshaft sprocket alignment—E-Series engine

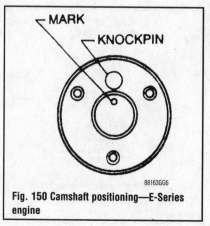

88163GG6

Fig. 150 Camshaft positioning—E-Series engine

88163GG7

Fig. 151 The punch mark on the end of the camshaft must face forward—E-Series engine

1984–89 CA16DE and CA18DE Engines

▶ See Figures 152 thru 158

➥ Since these engines DO NOT use replaceable camshaft bearings, overhaul is performed by replacement of the camshaft or the cylinder head. Check the camshaft bearing surfaces (in the cylinder head) with an internal micrometer and the bearing surfaces (of the camshaft) with a micrometer.

1. Remove the timing belt, as outlined earlier in this section.
2. Disconnect the negative (-) battery cable.
3. Remove the camshaft cover.

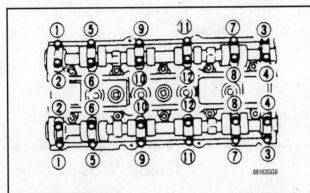

Fig. 152 Camshaft bearing cap loosening sequence—CA16DE and CA18DE engines

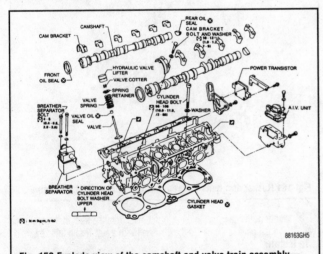

Fig. 153 Explode view of the camshaft and valve train assembly—CA16DE and CA18DE engines

4. Remove the breather separator.
5. Drain the engine coolant.

❋❋ CAUTION

When draining engine coolant, keep in mind that cats and dogs are attracted to ethylene glycol antifreeze and could drink any that is left in an uncovered container or in puddles on the ground. This will prove fatal in sufficient quantity. Always drain coolant into a sealable container. Coolant should be reused unless it is contaminated or is several years old.

6. Remove the cylinder head.
7. While holding the camshaft sprockets, remove the 4 mounting bolts and then remove the sprockets themselves.
8. Remove the timing belt tensioner pulley. Remove the rear timing belt cover.
9. Loosen the camshaft bearing caps in several stages, in the order shown. Remove the bearing caps, but be sure to keep them in order.

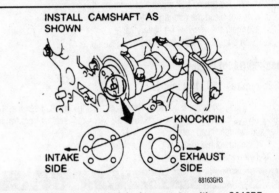

Fig. 157 Installing the camshaft in the correct position—CA16DE and CA18DE engines

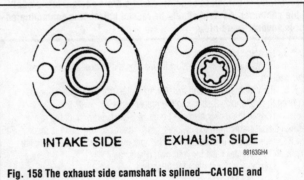

Fig. 158 The exhaust side camshaft is splined—CA16DE and CA18DE engines

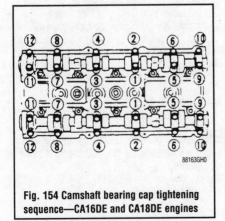

Fig. 154 Camshaft bearing cap tightening sequence—CA16DE and CA18DE engines

Fig. 155 Timing belt tensioner installation—CA16DE and CA18DE engines

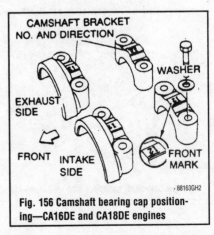

Fig. 156 Camshaft bearing cap positioning—CA16DE and CA18DE engines

10. Remove the front oil seals and then lift out the camshafts.

11. Check the camshaft run-out, end-play, wear and journal clearance. Refer to the camshaft specification chart.

To install:

12. Position the camshafts in the cylinder head so the knockpin on each is on the outboard side.

➡ **The exhaust side camshaft has splines to accept the crank angle sensor.**

13. Position the camshaft bearing caps and finger tighten them. Each cap has an ID mark and a directional arrow stamped into its top surface.

14. Coat a NEW oil seal with engine oil (on the lip) and install it on each camshaft end.

15. Tighten the camshaft bearing cap bolts to 84–108 inch lbs. (10–14 Nm) in the sequence shown.

16. Install the rear timing cover.

17. Install the timing belt tensioner and tighten it to 16–22 ft. lbs. (21–30 Nm).

18. Install the camshaft sprockets and tighten the bolts to 10–14 ft. lbs. (14–20 Nm) while holding the camshaft in place.

19. Install the timing belt and the cylinder head.

20. Fill and bleed the cooling system.

21. Connect the negative (-) battery cable.

22. Start engine, check timing and road test.

1989–90 GA16i Engine

♦ **See Figures 159, 160 and 161**

This is a very complex procedure. Before attempting camshaft service, thoroughly review these procedures, as well as the steps required for front timing cover and cylinder head service.

1. Disconnect the negative (-) battery cable.

2. Drain the engine coolant.

✳ CAUTION

When draining engine coolant, keep in mind that cats and dogs are attracted to ethylene glycol antifreeze and could drink any that is left in an uncovered container or in puddles on the ground. This will prove fatal in sufficient quantity. Always drain coolant into a sealable container. Coolant should be reused unless it is contaminated or is several years old.

3. Remove the timing chain.

4. Remove the cylinder head with manifolds attached, as outline earlier in this section.

5. Remove the intake and exhaust manifolds from the cylinder head. Loosen the bolts in 2–3 stages in the proper sequence.

6. Loosen the rocker arm shaft bolts in 2–3 stages and lift the rocker arm/shaft assembly from the cylinder head. The rocker arm shaft is marked with an **F** to indicate that it faces towards the front of the engine. Place a similar mark on the cylinder head for your own reference.

7. Loosen the thrust plate retaining bolt.

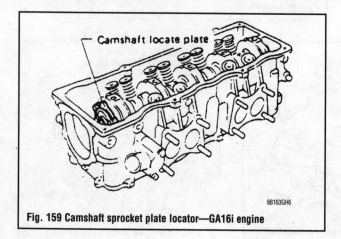

Fig. 159 Camshaft sprocket plate locator—GA16i engine

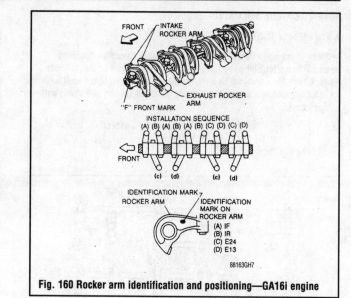

Fig. 160 Rocker arm identification and positioning—GA16i engine

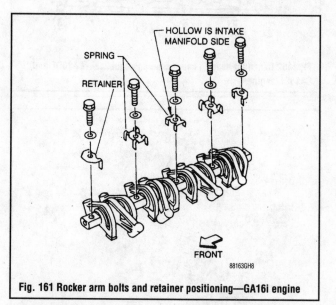

Fig. 161 Rocker arm bolts and retainer positioning—GA16i engine

8. Withdraw the camshaft and the thrust plate from the front of the cylinder head. The thrust plate is located to the camshaft with a key. Retain this key.

To install:

9. Clean all cylinder head, intake and exhaust manifold gasket surfaces. Lubricate the camshaft and rocker arm/shaft assemblies with a liberal coating of clean engine oil. Then, slide the camshaft and thrust plate into the front of the cylinder head. Don't forget to install the thrust plate key.

10. Install the rocker shafts and rocker arms making sure the **F** on the rocker shaft points toward the front of the engine. Install the rocker shaft retaining bolts, spring clips and washers. The center spring clip has a recess cut into one side. When installing the center clip point this recess toward the intake manifold side of the head. Snug the bolts gradually in 2–3 stages starting from the center and working out. Attach the intake and exhaust manifold to the head with new gaskets.

11. Install the cylinder head and timing chain.

12. After the timing chain is in place, set the No. 1 cylinder to TDC of the compression stroke.

13. Torque the No. 1 and No. 2 rocker shaft bolts to 27–30 ft. lbs. (37–41 Nm). Then, set the No. 4 cylinder to TDC and torque the No. 3 and No. 4 rocker shaft bolts to 27–30 ft. lbs. (37–41 Nm).

14. Fill and bleed the cooling system.

15. Connect the negative (-) battery cable.

1991–93 SR20DE Engine

▶ **See Figures 162, 163, 164, 165 and 166**

1. Disconnect the negative (-) battery cable.
2. Remove the rocker cover and oil separator.
3. Rotate the crankshaft until the No. 1 piston is at TDC on the compression stroke. Then rotate the crankshaft until the mating marks on the camshaft sprockets line up with the mating marks on the timing chain.
4. Remove the timing chain tensioner.
5. Remove the distributor.
6. Remove the timing chain guide.
7. Remove the camshaft sprockets. Use a wrench to hold the camshaft while loosening the sprocket bolt.
8. Loosen the camshaft bracket bolts in the opposite order of the torquing sequence.
9. Remove the camshaft.

To install:

10. Clean the left hand camshaft end bracket and coat the mating surface with liquid gasket. Install the camshafts, camshaft brackets, oil tubes and baffle plate. Ensure the left camshaft key is at 12 o'clock and the right camshaft key is at 10 o'clock.
11. The procedure for tightening camshaft bolts must be followed exactly to prevent camshaft damage. Tighten bolts as follows:
   a. Tighten right camshaft bolts 9 and 10 (in that order) to 18 inch lbs. (2 Nm), then tighten bolts 1–8 (in that order) to the same specification.
   b. Tighten left camshaft bolts 11 and 12 (in that order) to 18 inch lbs. (2 Nm), then tighten bolts 1–10 (in that order) to the same specification.
   c. Tighten all bolts in sequence to 54 inch lbs. (6 Nm).
   d. Tighten all bolts in sequence to 78–102 inch lbs. (9–12 Nm) for type A, B and C bolts, and 13–19 ft. lbs. (18–25 Nm) for type D bolts.
12. Line up the mating marks on the timing chain and camshaft sprockets and install the sprockets. Tighten sprocket bolts to 101–116 ft. lbs. (137–157 Nm).
13. Install the timing chain guide, distributor (ensure that rotor head is at 5 o'clock position) and chain tensioner.

14. Clean the rocker cover and mating surfaces and apply a continuous bead of liquid gasket to the mating surface.
15. Install the rocker cover and oil separator. Tighten the rocker cover bolts as follows:
   a. Tighten nuts 1, 10, 11, and 8 in that order to 36 inch lbs. (4 Nm).
   b. Tighten nuts 1–13 as indicated in the figure to 72–84 inch lbs. (8–10 Nm).
16. Connect the negative (-) battery cable. Refill all fluid levels. Road test the vehicle for proper operation.

1990–96 GA16DE Engine

▶ **See Figures 167 thru 179**

This is a very complex procedure. Before attempting camshaft service, thoroughly review these procedures, as well as the steps required for front timing cover and timing chain service.

➡**Modify the service steps as necessary. This is a complete disassembly repair procedure. Review the complete procedure before starting this repair.**

1. Relieve the fuel system pressure, as outlined in Section 5.
2. Disconnect the negative (-) battery.
3. Drain the cooling system.

✶✶ CAUTION

When draining engine coolant, keep in mind that cats and dogs are attracted to ethylene glycol antifreeze and could drink any that is left in an uncovered container or in puddles on the ground. This will prove fatal in sufficient quantity. Always drain coolant into a sealable container. Coolant should be reused unless it is contaminated or is several years old.

4. Remove all drive belts. Disconnect the exhaust tube from the exhaust manifold.

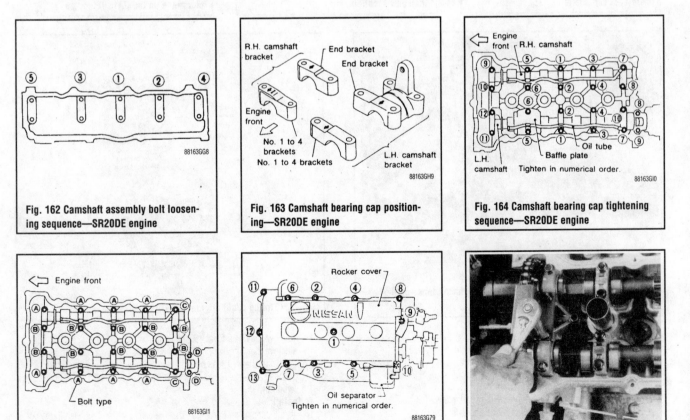

Fig. 162 Camshaft assembly bolt loosening sequence—SR20DE engine

Fig. 163 Camshaft bearing cap positioning—SR20DE engine

Fig. 164 Camshaft bearing cap tightening sequence—SR20DE engine

Fig. 165 Camshaft bolt identification—SR20DE engine

Fig. 166 Rocker cover tightening sequence—SR20DE engine

Fig. 167 Removing the timing chain guide

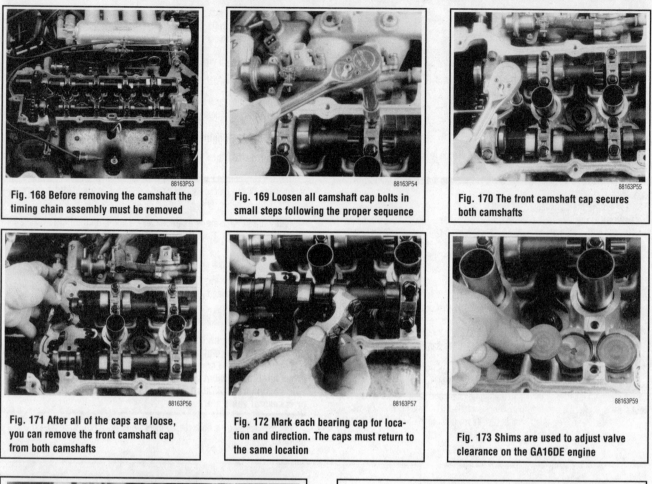

Fig. 168 Before removing the camshaft the timing chain assembly must be removed

Fig. 169 Loosen all camshaft cap bolts in small steps following the proper sequence

Fig. 170 The front camshaft cap secures both camshafts

Fig. 171 After all of the caps are loose, you can remove the front camshaft cap from both camshafts

Fig. 172 Mark each bearing cap for location and direction. The caps must return to the same location

Fig. 173 Shims are used to adjust valve clearance on the GA16DE engine

Fig. 174 The lifters are directly below the camshaft lobes on the GA16DE engine

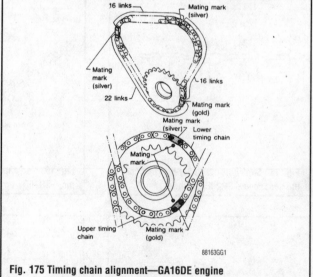

Fig. 175 Timing chain alignment—GA16DE engine

5. Remove the power steering bracket.

6. Remove the air duct to intake manifold collector.

7. Remove the front right side wheel, splash cover and front under covers.

8. Remove the front exhaust pipe and engine front mounting bracket.

9. Remove the rocker arm cover.

10. Remove the distributor cap. Remove the spark plugs.

11. Set the No. 1 cylinder at TDC of the compression stroke.

12. Mark and remove the distributor assembly.

13. Remove the cam sprocket cover and gusset. Remove the water pump pulley. Remove the thermostat housing.

14. Remove the chain tensioner, chain guide. Loosen idler sprocket bolt.

15. Remove the camshaft sprocket bolts, camshaft sprockets, camshaft brackets and camshafts. These parts should be reassembled in their original position. Bolts should be loosen in 2 or 3 steps (loosen bolts in the reverse of the tightening order).

To install:

16. Install camshafts. Make sure that the camshafts are installed in the correct position. Note the identification marks present on the camshafts: **I** for intake camshaft and **E** for exhaust camshaft.

17. Install camshafts brackets. Tighten camshafts brackets bolts in two or

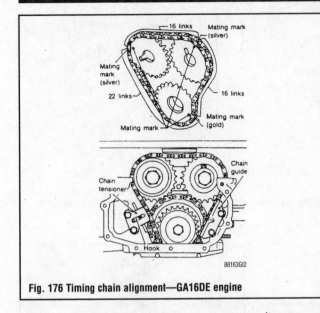

Fig. 176 Timing chain alignment—GA16DE engine

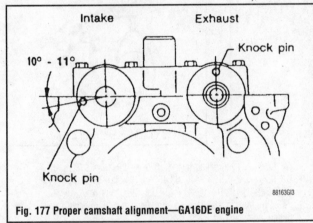

Fig. 177 Proper camshaft alignment—GA16DE engine

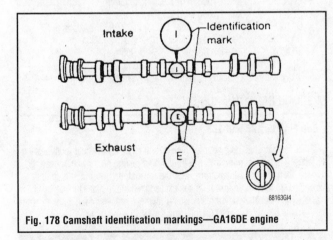

Fig. 178 Camshaft identification markings—GA16DE engine

three steps to 84–108 inch lbs. (9–12 Nm) in the correct sequence. After completing assembly check valve clearance.

18. Assemble camshaft sprocket with chain. Set timing chain by aligning mating marks with those of camshaft sprockets. Make sure sprockets mating marks face engine front.

19. Install camshaft sprocket bolts. Install upper chain tensioner and chain guide.

20. Install lower chain tensioner (make sure that the gasket is installed properly). Check that no problems occur when engine is rotated. Make sure that No. 1 piston is set to TDC on compression stroke.

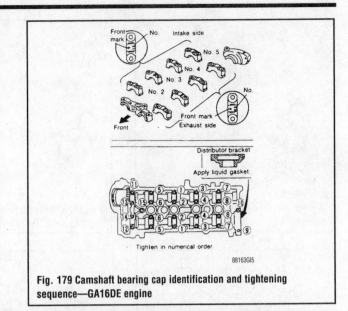

Fig. 179 Camshaft bearing cap identification and tightening sequence—GA16DE engine

21. Install thermostat housing, water pump pulley. Install the distributor assembly.

22. Install cam sprocket cover and rocker cover.

23. Install all remaining components in reverse order of removal.

24. Connect the negative (−) battery cable. Refill all fluid levels. Road test the vehicle for proper operation.

INSPECTION

➡Since these engines DO NOT use replaceable camshaft bearings, overhaul is performed by replacement of the camshaft or the cylinder head. Check the camshaft bearing surfaces (in the cylinder head) with an internal micrometer and the bearing surfaces (of the camshaft) with a micrometer.

E-series Engine

♦ **See Figures 180, 181 and 182**

1. Remove the cylinder head from the vehicle as outlined this section.

2. Remove the camshaft sprocket and front cover assembly.

3. Remove the rocker arm assembly as outlined in this section.

4. Remove the camshaft, being careful not to damage the bearing journals.

5. Using an inside telescope gauge, measure the inside diameter of the

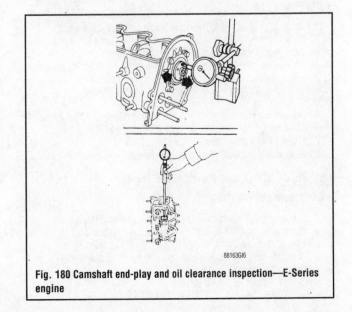

Fig. 180 Camshaft end-play and oil clearance inspection—E-Series engine

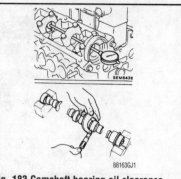

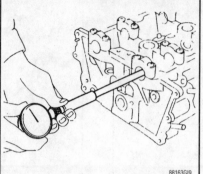

Fig. 181 Front camshaft retaining screws—E-Series engine

Fig. 182 Checking camshaft bearing journal clearance

Fig. 183 Camshaft bearing oil clearance inspection—CA16DE, CA18DE and GA16i engines

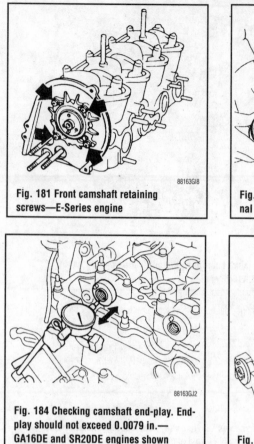

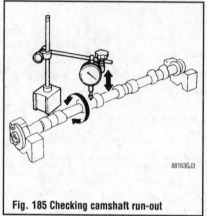

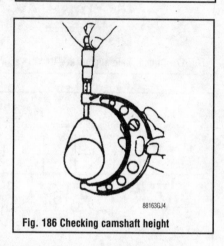

Fig. 184 Checking camshaft end-play. End-play should not exceed 0.0079 in.— GA16DE and SR20DE engines shown

Fig. 185 Checking camshaft run-out

Fig. 186 Checking camshaft height

camshaft bearing. The measurement should be 1.6535–1.6545 in. (42.000–42.025mm).

6. Measure the camshaft bearing journals with a micrometer. The measurement should be 1.6515–1.6522 in. (41.949–41.965mm) for journals 1, 3 and 5. The measurement should be 1.6498–1.6505 in. (41.906–41.922mm) for journals 2 and 4.

7. The maximum oil clearance for 1, 3 and 5 should be 0.0059 (0.15mm) and 0.0079 in. (0.20mm) for 2 and 4.

8. If not within specifications, replace the camshaft and/or cylinder head.

GA16i Engine

♦ See Figure 183

1. Remove the cylinder head from the vehicle as outlined this section.
2. Remove the camshaft sprocket and front cover assembly.
3. Remove the rocker arm assembly as outlined in this section.
4. Remove the camshaft, being careful not to damage the bearing journals.
5. Using an inside telescope gauge, measure the inside diameter of the camshaft bearing. The measurement should be 1.6535–1.6545 in. (42.000–42.025mm).
6. Measure the camshaft bearing journals with a micrometer. The measurement should be 1.6510–1.6518 in. (41.935–41.955mm).
7. The maximum oil clearance is 0.0059 (0.15mm).
8. If not within specifications, replace the camshaft and/or cylinder head.

CA16DE, CA18DE, GA16DE and SR20DE Engines

♦ See Figures 183 and 184

1. Remove the cylinder head from the vehicle as outlined this section.
2. Remove the camshaft, being careful not to damage the bearing journals. Install the camshaft bearing caps and torque to 7–9 ft. lbs. (10–12 Nm).
3. Using an inside telescope gauge, measure the inside diameter of the camshaft bearing. The measurement should be as follows:
- CA18DE— 1.1024–1.1033 in. (28.000–28.025mm)
- CA16DE— 1.1024–1.1033 in. (28.000–28.025mm)

- GA16DE No. 1 journal 1.1024–1.1032 in. (28.000–28.021mm)
- GA16DE No. 2–5— 0.9449–09.457 in. (24.000–24.021mm)
- SR20DE— 1.1024–1.1033 in. (28.000–28.025mm)

4. Measure the camshaft bearing journals with a micrometer. The measurement should be as follows:
- CA18DE— 1.0998–1.1006 in. (27.935–27.955mm)
- CA16DE— 1.0998–1.1006 in. (27.935–27.955mm)
- GA16DE No. 1 journal— 1.0998–1.1006 in. (27.935–27.955mm)
- GA16DE No. 2–5— 0.9423–0.9431 in. (23.935–23.955mm)
- SR20DE— 1.0998–1.1006 in. (27.935–27.955mm)

5. The maximum oil clearance is 0.0059 (0.15mm).
6. If not within specifications, replace the camshaft and/or cylinder head.

CHECKING CAMSHAFT RUN-OUT

♦ See Figures 185 and 186

Place the camshaft on a set of V-blocks, supported by the outermost bearing surfaces. Place a dial micrometer, with its finger resting on the center bearing surface, then turn the camshaft to check the run-out; the run-out should not exceed 0.004 in. (0.010mm), if it does exceed the limit, replace the camshaft.

Check the camshaft bearing surfaces (in the engine) with an internal micrometer and the bearing surfaces (of the camshaft) with a micrometer.

Hydraulic Valve Lifters

REMOVAL & INSTALLATION

GA16i Engine

♦ See Figures 187 and 188

The hydraulic valve lifter is an integral part of the rocker arm assembly. The lifter is not serviced separately.

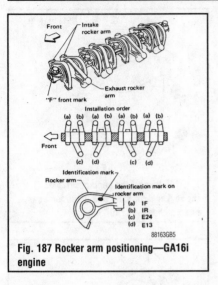

Fig. 187 Rocker arm positioning—GA16i engine

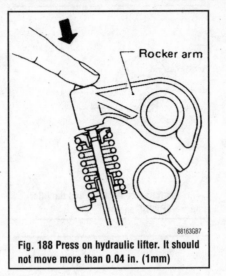

Fig. 188 Press on hydraulic lifter. It should not move more than 0.04 in. (1mm)

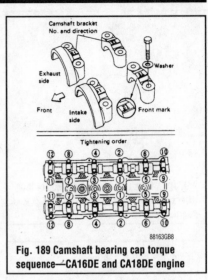

Fig. 189 Camshaft bearing cap torque sequence—CA16DE and CA18DE engine

1. Remove the rocker arm cover and timing chain gear as outlined in this section.
2. Slowly loosen the rocker arm shaft in 3 steps. Be careful not to bend the shaft.
3. Label all components before disassembling the rocker shaft.
4. Remove the retaining bolts and spacers.
5. Remove the rocker arm/lifter assembly from the shaft.
6. If reusing the rocker arm, soak the rocker arm in a pan of oil.

To install:

7. Install the rocker arm/lifters onto the shaft and install the entire assembly.
8. Torque the rocker shaft bolts to 27 ft. lbs. (37 Nm) in 3 steps.
9. Install the timing chain gear and rocker arm cover.
10. Install the remaining components.
11. Start the engine and allow to run with no load at 1000 rpm for 10 minutes to bleed the air out of the lifters.
12. Stop engine, make sure the rocker is in its free position (not on lobe) and press down hard. It should not move more than 0.04 in. (1mm). If it moves to much repeat bleeding procedure above.
13. If after running engine again with no load for 10 minutes to bleed the air out of the lifters, it still moves to much the lifter or other valve components are too worn and must be replaced.

CA16DE and CA18DE Engines

▶ **See Figures 189, 190, 191 and 192**

The hydraulic valve lifter is located under the camshaft lobe. Label all valve components for proper reinstallation. Mark the timing chain and sprocket locations to ensure correct valve timing.
1. Remove the camshaft cover as outlined in this section.
2. Remove the timing chain sprockets and retain valve timing by hanging

the sprocket with a piece of wire and wedge the chain with wood. These procedures are covered earlier in this section.
3. Remove the camshaft bearing cap bolts in the opposite sequence of torquing. This is very important. Remove the camshaft.
4. Remove the valve lifter from the bore by turning and pulling upward.
5. Soak the removed lifters in a pan of clean engine oil before reassembly.

To install:

6. Install the valve lifter into the bore.
7. Install the camshaft and bearing caps.
8. Torque the bolts in sequence to 84–108 inch lbs. (10–12 Nm).
9. Install the timing chain gear and chain in the exact position as removed.
10. Turn the engine to make sure the camshaft is not binding.
11. Install the remaining components.
12. Start the engine and allow to run with no load for 10 minutes to bleed any air in the lifters.

SR20DE Engine

▶ **See Figures 193, 194, 195 and 196**

This is a very complex procedure. Before attempting valve train service thoroughly review these procedures, as well as the steps required for timing chain and camshaft service.

The hydraulic valve lifter is located under the rocker arm in the lifter bore. Label all valve components for exact reassembly. Mark the timing chain the gears for exact valve timing during reinstallation.
1. Remove the camshaft cover as outlined in this section.
2. Remove the timing chain tensioner. Remove the timing chain sprockets and retain valve timing by hanging the sprocket with a piece of wire and wedge the chain with wood. These procedures are covered earlier in this section.

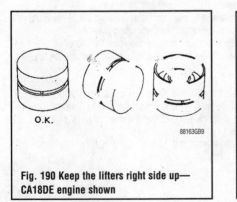

Fig. 190 Keep the lifters right side up— CA18DE engine shown

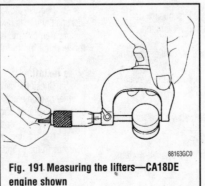

Fig. 191 Measuring the lifters—CA18DE engine shown

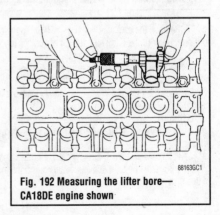

Fig. 192 Measuring the lifter bore— CA18DE engine shown

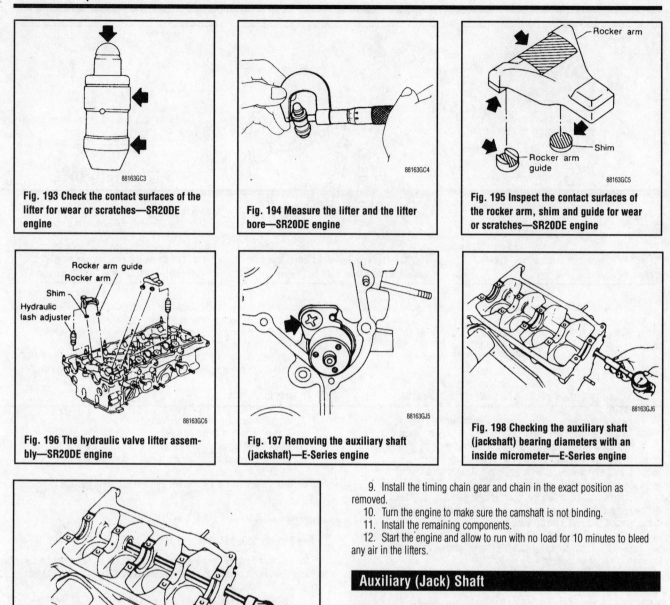

Fig. 193 Check the contact surfaces of the lifter for wear or scratches—SR20DE engine

Fig. 194 Measure the lifter and the lifter bore—SR20DE engine

Fig. 195 Inspect the contact surfaces of the rocker arm, shim and guide for wear or scratches—SR20DE engine

Fig. 196 The hydraulic valve lifter assembly—SR20DE engine

Fig. 197 Removing the auxiliary shaft (jackshaft)—E-Series engine

Fig. 198 Checking the auxiliary shaft (jackshaft) bearing diameters with an inside micrometer—E-Series engine

Fig. 199 Installing the Welsh plug into the block—E-Series engine

9. Install the timing chain gear and chain in the exact position as removed.

10. Turn the engine to make sure the camshaft is not binding.

11. Install the remaining components.

12. Start the engine and allow to run with no load for 10 minutes to bleed any air in the lifters.

Auxiliary (Jack) Shaft

REMOVAL & INSTALLATION

◆ See Figures 197, 198 and 199

1. Refer to the Timing Belt and/or Chain Removal and Installation procedures in this section, and remove the timing belt.

2. Pull the crankshaft sprocket from the crankshaft. Remove the jackshaft sprocket bolts, then separate the sprocket from the jackshaft.

3. Remove the lower locating plate from the cylinder block. Remove the jackshaft and the crankshaft oil seals from the locating plate.

4. Remove the jackshaft retaining plate, then pull the shaft out through the front of the cylinder block. Be careful not to damage the bearings.

To install:

5. Check the jackshaft bearing diameters (in the cylinder block) with an internal micrometer and the bearing diameters (of the jackshaft) with a micrometer; the clearance should not exceed 0.15mm, if it does exceed the limit, replace the jackshaft bearings.

6. Use a hammer and a brass drift, to remove and install the jackshaft bearings in the cylinder block.

3. Remove the camshaft bearing cap bolts in the opposite sequence of torquing. Refer to the Camshaft section of this section. This is very important. Remove the camshaft, oil tubes and baffles.

4. Remove the valve rocker arm, shims, guides and hydraulic lifter from the bore. Document each part for reinstallation.

5. Soak the removed lifters in a pan of clean engine oil during the service procedure.

To install:

6. Install the valve lifter into the bore. Install the guides, shims and rocker arms.

7. Install the camshaft, bearing caps, oil tubes and baffles.

8. Torque the bolts in sequence to the specification in the Camshaft portion of this section.

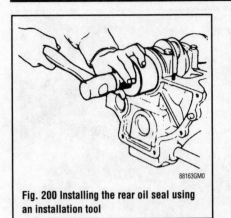

Fig. 200 Installing the rear oil seal using an installation tool

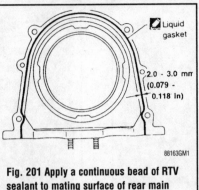

Fig. 201 Apply a continuous bead of RTV sealant to mating surface of rear main seal retainer—SR20DE engine shown

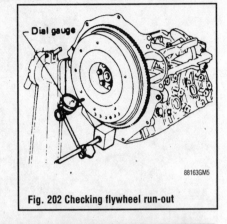

Fig. 202 Checking flywheel run-out

➡Be sure to align the oil hole in the bearing with the hole in the cylinder block. After installation, check the bearing clearances. Using sealant, install a new Welsh plug into the cylinder block.

7. Install the jackshaft in the cylinder block with the retaining plate. Torque the jackshaft sprocket bolts to 6.5–9.0 ft. lbs. (8.8–12.2 Nm), the oil pump bolts to 5.8–7.2 ft. lbs. (8.0–9.8 Nm), the tensioner pulley bolts to 12–15 ft. lbs. (15–20 Nm), the timing cover bolts to 2.5–4.0 ft. lbs. (3.4–6.0 Nm), the crankshaft pulley bolt to 83–108 ft. lbs. (113–147 Nm).

8. Install the lower locating plate on cylinder block with oil new seals.

9. Install both sprockets and the timing belt.

10. Start engine, check timing and road test.

Rear Main Oil Seal

REMOVAL & INSTALLATION

♦ **See Figures 200 and 201**

1. Remove the engine and transaxle assembly from the vehicle.

2. Remove the transaxle from the engine.

3. Remove the clutch/flywheel assembly (manual transaxle) or the drive-plate (automatic transaxle) from the crankshaft.

4. Remove the oil seal retainer, if equipped with a removable retainer.

5. Using a small prybar, pry the rear main oil seal from around the crankshaft.

To install:

6. Apply lithium grease around the sealing lip of the oil seal and install the seal by driving it into the cylinder block using an oil seal installation tool.

7. If applicable, install the oil seal retainer.

8. Install the flywheel or driveplate.

9. Install the transaxle to engine.

10. Install engine and transaxle assembly in the vehicle.

EXHAUST SYSTEM

Inspection

♦ **See Figures 203 thru 209**

➡Safety glasses should be worn at all times when working on or near the exhaust system. Older exhaust systems will almost always be covered with loose rust particles which are more than a nuisance and could injure your eye.

✳ CAUTION

DO NOT perform exhaust repairs or inspection with the engine or exhaust hot. Allow the system to cool completely. Exhaust systems are noted for sharp edges, flaking metal and rusted bolts. Gloves

Flywheel and Ring Gear

REMOVAL & INSTALLATION

♦ **See Figure 202**

1. If equipped with a manual transaxle, refer to the Clutch Removal and Installation procedures in Section 7, then remove the transaxle and the clutch assembly. If equipped with an automatic transaxle, refer to the Automatic Transaxle Removal and Installation procedures in Section 7, then remove the transaxle and the torque converter.

2. For manual transaxles, remove the flywheel-to-crankshaft bolts and the flywheel. For automatic transaxles, remove the drive plate-to-crankshaft bolts and the drive plate.

3. To install, reverse the removal procedures. Torque the flywheel-to-crankshaft bolts to specifications.

RING GEAR REPLACEMENT

Manual Transaxle Only

➡Ring gear replacement should be referred to a qualified engine machine shop.

1. Using a die grinder, cut the ring gear from the flywheel.

✳✳ WARNING

Be careful not to overheat the ring gear, or it will be destroyed.

2. Heat the entire ring gear to cherry red with a torch.

3. Place the ring gear onto the flywheel and allow to cool. Do not cool with water. This will harden the gear. The gear will break when the starter drive makes contact.

4. Install the flywheel to the engine and torque the bolts to specifications in a star pattern.

and eye protection are required. A healthy supply of penetrating oil and rags is highly recommended.

Your vehicle must be raised and supported safely at four points to inspect the exhaust system properly. Start the inspection at the exhaust manifold where the header pipe is attached and work your way to the back of the vehicle. On dual exhaust systems, remember to inspect both sides of the vehicle. Check the complete exhaust system for open seams, holes, loose connections, or other deterioration which could permit exhaust fumes to seep into the passenger compartment. Inspect all mounting brackets and hangers for deterioration, some may have rubber O-rings that can become overstretched and non-supportive (and should be replaced if worn). Many technicians use a pointed tool to poke up into the exhaust system at rust spots to see whether or not they crumble. Most models have heat shield(s) covering certain parts of the exhaust sys-

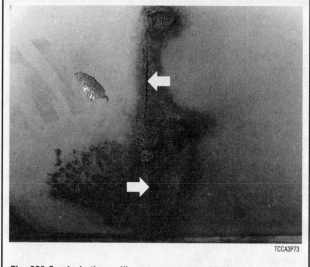

Fig. 203 Cracks in the muffler are a guaranteed leak

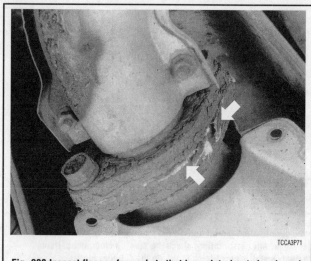

Fig. 208 Inspect flanges for gaskets that have deteriorated and need replacement

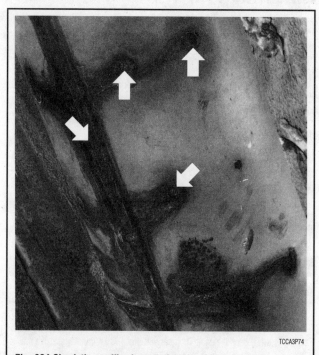

Fig. 204 Check the muffler for rotted spot welds and seams

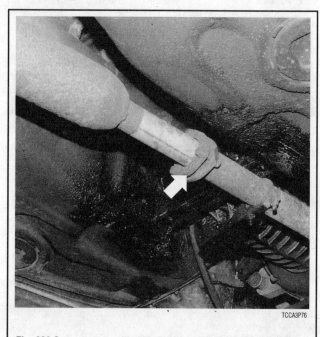

Fig. 209 Some systems, like this one, use large O-rings (donuts) in between the flanges

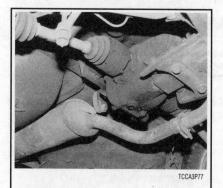

Fig. 205 Make sure the exhaust does contact the body or suspension

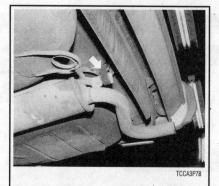

Fig. 206 Check for overstretched or torn exhaust hangers

Fig. 207 Example of a badly deteriorated exhaust pipe

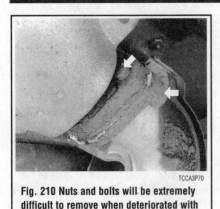

Fig. 210 Nuts and bolts will be extremely difficult to remove when deteriorated with rust

Fig. 211 Example of a flange type exhaust system joint

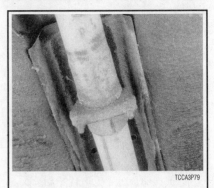

Fig. 212 Example of a common slip joint type system

tem, it is often necessary to remove these shields to visually inspect those components.

REPLACEMENT

♦ See Figures 210, 211 and 212

There are basically two types of exhaust systems. One is the flange type where the component ends are attached with bolts and a gasket in-between. The other exhaust system is the slip joint type. These components slip into one another using clamps to retain them together.

❊ CAUTION

Allow the exhaust system to cool sufficiently before spraying a solvent exhaust fasteners. Some solvents are highly flammable and could ignite when sprayed on hot exhaust components.

Before removing any component of the exhaust system, ALWAYS squirt a liquid rust dissolving agent onto the fasteners for ease of removal. A lot of knuckle skin will be saved by following this rule. It may even be wise to spray the fasteners and allow them to sit overnight.

❊ CAUTION

Do NOT perform exhaust repairs or inspection with the engine or exhaust hot. Allow the system to cool. Exhaust systems are noted for sharp edges, flaking metal and rusted bolts. Gloves and eye protection are required.

1. Raise and support the vehicle safely, as necessary for access. Remember that some longer exhaust pipes may be difficult to wrestle out from under the vehicle if it is not supported high enough.

2. If you haven't already, apply a generous amount of penetrating oil or solvent to any rusted fasteners.

3. On flange joints, carefully loosen and remove the retainers at the flange. If bolts or nuts are difficult to break loose, apply more penetrating liquid and give it some additional time to set. If the fasteners still will not come loose an impact driver may be necessary to jar it loose (and keep the fastener from breaking).

➡ When unbolting the headpipe from the manifold, make sure that the bolts are free before trying to remove them. If you snap a stud in the exhaust manifold, the stud will have to be removed with a bolt extractor, which often means removal of the manifold itself.

4. On slip joint components, remove the mounting U-bolts from around the exhaust pipe you are extracting from the vehicle. Don't be surprised if the U-bolts break while removing the nuts.

5. Loosen the exhaust pipe from any mounting brackets retaining it to the floor pan and separate the components. Slight twisting and turning may be required to remove the component completely from the vehicle. You may need to tap on the component with a rubber mallet to loosen it. If all else fails, use a hacksaw to separate the parts. An oxy-acetylene cutting torch may be faster but the sparks are DANGEROUS near the fuel tank, and at the very least, accidents could happen, resulting in damage to the under-vehicle parts, not to mention yourself.

6. When installing exhaust components, you should loosely position all components before tightening any of the joints. Once you are certain that the system is run correctly, begin tightening the fasteners at the front of the vehicle and work your way back.

ENGINE RECONDITIONING

Determining Engine Condition

Anything that generates heat and/or friction will eventually burn or wear out (for example, a light bulb generates heat, therefore its life span is limited). With this in mind, a running engine generates tremendous amounts of both; friction is encountered by the moving and rotating parts inside the engine and heat is created by friction and combustion of the fuel. However, the engine has systems designed to help reduce the effects of heat and friction and provide added longevity. The oiling system reduces the amount of friction encountered by the moving parts inside the engine, while the cooling system reduces heat created by friction and combustion. If either system is not maintained, a break-down will be inevitable. Therefore, you can see how regular maintenance can affect the service life of your vehicle. If you do not drain, flush and refill your cooling system at the proper intervals, deposits will begin to accumulate in the radiator, thereby reducing the amount of heat it can extract from the coolant. The same applies to your oil and filter; if it is not changed often enough it becomes laden with contaminates and is unable to properly lubricate the engine. This increases friction and wear.

There are a number of methods for evaluating the condition of your engine. A compression test can reveal the condition of your pistons, piston rings, cylinder bores, head gasket(s), valves and valve seats. An oil pressure test can warn you of possible engine bearing, or oil pump failures. Excessive oil consumption, evidence of oil in the engine air intake area and/or bluish smoke from the tailpipe may indicate worn piston rings, worn valve guides and/or valve seals. As a general rule, an engine that uses no more than one quart of oil every 1000 miles is in good condition. Engines that use one quart of oil or more in less than 1000 miles should first be checked for oil leaks. If any oil leaks are present, have them fixed before determining how much oil is consumed by the engine, especially if blue smoke is not visible at the tailpipe.

COMPRESSION TEST

A noticeable lack of engine power, excessive oil consumption and/or poor fuel mileage measured over an extended period are all indicators of internal engine wear. Worn piston rings, scored or worn cylinder bores, blown head gaskets, sticking or burnt valves, and worn valve seats are all possible culprits. A check of each cylinder's compression will help locate the problem.

Gasoline Engines

▶ **See Figure 213**

➡ **A screw-in type compression gauge is more accurate than the type you simply hold against the spark plug hole.**

Although it takes slightly longer to use, it's worth the effort to obtain a more accurate reading.

1. Make sure that the proper amount and viscosity of engine oil is in the crankcase, then ensure the battery is fully charged.
2. Warm-up the engine to normal operating temperature, then shut the engine **OFF**.
3. Disable the ignition system.
4. Label and disconnect all of the spark plug wires from the plugs.
5. Thoroughly clean the cylinder head area around the spark plug ports, then remove the spark plugs.
6. Set the throttle plate to the fully open (wide-open throttle) position. You can block the accelerator linkage open for this, or you can have an assistant fully depress the accelerator pedal.
7. Install a screw-in type compression gauge into the No. 1 spark plug hole until the fitting is snug.

✳✳ WARNING

Be careful not to crossthread the spark plug hole.

8. According to the tool manufacturer's instructions, connect a remote starting switch to the starting circuit.
9. With the ignition switch in the **OFF** position, use the remote starting switch to crank the engine through at least five compression strokes (approximately 5 seconds of cranking) and record the highest reading on the gauge.
10. Repeat the test on each cylinder, cranking the engine approximately the same number of compression strokes and/or time as the first.
11. Compare the highest readings from each cylinder to that of the others. The indicated compression pressures are considered within specifications if the lowest reading cylinder is within 75 percent of the pressure recorded for the highest reading cylinder. For example, if your highest reading cylinder pressure was 150 psi (1034 kPa), then 75 percent of that would be 113 psi (779 kPa). So the lowest reading cylinder should be no less than 113 psi (779 kPa).
12. If a cylinder exhibits an unusually low compression reading, pour a tablespoon of clean engine oil into the cylinder through the spark plug hole and repeat the compression test. If the compression rises after adding oil, it means that the cylinder's piston rings and/or cylinder bore are damaged or worn. If the pressure remains low, the valves may not be seating properly (a valve job is needed), or the head gasket may be blown near that cylinder. If compression in any two adjacent cylinders is low, and if the addition of oil doesn't help raise compression, there is leakage past the head gasket. Oil and coolant in the combustion chamber, combined with blue or constant white smoke from the tailpipe,

are symptoms of this problem. However, don't be alarmed by the normal white smoke emitted from the tailpipe during engine warm-up or from cold weather driving. There may be evidence of water droplets on the engine dipstick and/or oil droplets in the cooling system if a head gasket is blown.

OIL PRESSURE TEST

Check for proper oil pressure at the sending unit passage with an externally mounted mechanical oil pressure gauge (as opposed to relying on a factory installed dash-mounted gauge). A tachometer may also be needed, as some specifications may require running the engine at a specific rpm.

1. With the engine cold, locate and remove the oil pressure sending unit.
2. Following the manufacturer's instructions, connect a mechanical oil pressure gauge and, if necessary, a tachometer to the engine.
3. Start the engine and allow it to idle.
4. Check the oil pressure reading when cold and record the number. You may need to run the engine at a specified rpm, so check the specifications.
5. Run the engine until normal operating temperature is reached (upper radiator hose will feel warm).
6. Check the oil pressure reading again with the engine hot and record the number. Turn the engine **OFF**.
7. Compare your hot oil pressure reading to specification. If the reading is low, check the cold pressure reading against the chart. If the cold pressure is well above the specification, and the hot reading was lower than the specification, you may have the wrong viscosity oil in the engine. Change the oil, making sure to use the proper grade and quantity, then repeat the test.

Low oil pressure readings could be attributed to internal component wear, pump related problems, a low oil level, or oil viscosity that is too low. High oil pressure readings could be caused by an overfilled crankcase, too high of an oil viscosity or a faulty pressure relief valve.

Buy or Rebuild?

Now if you have determined that your engine is worn out, you must make some decisions. The question of whether or not an engine is worth rebuilding is largely a subjective matter and one of personal worth. Is the engine a popular one, or is it an obsolete model? Are parts available? Will it get acceptable gas mileage once it is rebuilt? Is the car it's being put into worth keeping? Would it be less expensive to buy a new engine, have your engine rebuilt by a pro, rebuild it yourself or buy a used engine from a salvage yard? Or would it be simpler and less expensive to buy another car? If you have considered all these matters, and have still decided to rebuild the engine, then it is time to decide how you will rebuild it.

➡ **The editors at Chilton feel that most engine machining should be performed by a professional machine shop. Think of it as an assurance that the job has been done right the first time. There are many expensive and specialized tools required to perform such tasks as boring and honing an engine block or having a valve job done on a cylinder head. Even inspecting the parts requires expensive micrometers and gauges to properly measure wear and clearances. A machine shop can deliver to you clean, and ready to assemble parts, saving you time and aggravation. Your maximum savings will come from performing the removal, disassembly, assembly and installation of the engine and purchasing or renting only the tools required to perform these tasks.**

A complete rebuild or overhaul of an engine involves replacing all of the moving parts (pistons, rods, crankshaft, camshaft, etc.) with new ones and machining the non-moving wearing surfaces of the block and heads. Unfortunately, this may not be cost effective. For instance, your crankshaft may have been damaged or worn, but it can be machined undersize for a minimal fee.

So although you can replace everything inside the engine, it is usually wiser to replace only those parts which are really needed, and, if possible, repair the more expensive ones. Later in this section, we will break the engine down into its two main components: the cylinder head and the engine block. We will discuss each component, and the recommended parts to replace during a rebuild on each.

Engine Overhaul Tips

Most engine overhaul procedures are fairly standard. In addition to specific parts replacement procedures and specifications for your individual engine, this

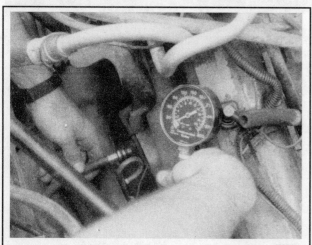

Fig. 213 A screw-in type compression gauge is more accurate and easier to use without an assistant

TCCS3801

section is also a guide to acceptable rebuilding procedures. Examples of standard rebuilding practice are given and should be used along with specific details concerning your particular engine.

Competent and accurate machine shop services will ensure maximum performance, reliability and engine life. In most instances it is more profitable for the do-it-yourself mechanic to remove, clean and inspect the component, buy the necessary parts and deliver these to a shop for actual machine work.

Much of the assembly work (crankshaft, bearings, piston rods, and other components) is well within the scope of the do-it-yourself mechanic's tools and abilities. You will have to decide for yourself the depth of involvement you desire in an engine repair or rebuild.

TOOLS

The tools required for an engine overhaul or parts replacement will depend on the depth of your involvement. With a few exceptions, they will be the tools found in a mechanic's tool kit (see Section 1 of this manual). More in-depth work will require some or all of the following:

- A dial indicator (reading in thousandths) mounted on a universal base
- Micrometers and telescope gauges
- Jaw and screw-type pullers
- Scraper
- Valve spring compressor
- Ring groove cleaner
- Piston ring expander and compressor
- Ridge reamer
- Cylinder hone or glaze breaker
- Plastigage®
- Engine stand

The use of most of these tools is illustrated in this section. Many can be rented for a one-time use from a local parts jobber or tool supply house specializing in automotive work.

Occasionally, the use of special tools is called for. See the information on Special Tools and the Safety Notice in the front of this book before substituting another tool.

OVERHAUL TIPS

Aluminum has become extremely popular for use in engines, due to its low weight. Observe the following precautions when handling aluminum parts:

- Never hot tank aluminum parts (the caustic hot tank solution will eat the aluminum.)
- Remove all aluminum parts (identification tag, etc.) from engine parts prior to the tanking.
- Always coat threads lightly with engine oil or anti-seize compounds before installation, to prevent seizure.
- Never overtighten bolts or spark plugs especially in aluminum threads.

When assembling the engine, any parts that will be exposed to frictional contact must be prelubed to provide lubrication at initial start-up. Any product specifically formulated for this purpose can be used, but engine oil is not recommended as a prelube in most cases.

When semi-permanent (locked, but removable) installation of bolts or nuts is desired, threads should be cleaned and coated with Loctite® or another similar, commercial non-hardening sealant.

CLEANING

▶ **See Figures 214, 215, 216 and 217**

Before the engine and its components are inspected, they must be thoroughly cleaned. You will need to remove any engine varnish, oil sludge and/or carbon deposits from all of the components to insure an accurate inspection. A crack in the engine block or cylinder head can easily become overlooked if hidden by a layer of sludge or carbon.

Most of the cleaning process can be carried out with common hand tools and readily available solvents or solutions. Carbon deposits can be chipped away using a hammer and a hard wooden chisel. Old gasket material and varnish or sludge can usually be removed using a scraper and/or cleaning solvent. Extremely stubborn deposits may require the use of a power drill with a wire brush. If using a wire brush, use extreme care around any critical machined surfaces (such as the gasket surfaces, bearing saddles, cylinder bores, etc.). USE OF A WIRE BRUSH IS NOT RECOMMENDED ON ANY ALUMINUM COMPONENTS. Always follow any safety recommendations given by the manufacturer of the tool and/or solvent.

✳✳ CAUTION

Always wear eye protection during any cleaning process involving scraping, chipping or spraying of solvents.

An alternative to the mess and hassle of cleaning the parts yourself is to drop them off at a local garage or machine shop. They should have the necessary equipment to properly clean all of the parts for a nominal fee.

Remove any oil galley plugs, freeze plugs and/or pressed-in bearings and carefully wash and degrease all of the engine components including the fasteners and bolts. Small parts such as the valves, springs, etc., should be placed in a metal basket and allowed to soak. Use pipe cleaner type brushes, and clean all passageways in the components.

Use a ring expander and remove the rings from the pistons. Clean the piston ring grooves with a special tool or a piece of broken ring. Scrape the carbon off of the top of the piston. You should never use a wire brush on the pistons. After preparing all of the piston assemblies in this manner, wash and degrease them again.

✳✳ WARNING

Use extreme care when cleaning around the cylinder head valve seats. A mistake or slip may cost you a new seat.

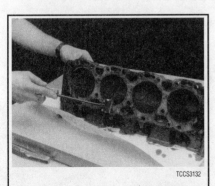

TCCS3132

Fig. 214 Use a gasket scraper to remove the old gasket material from the mating surfaces

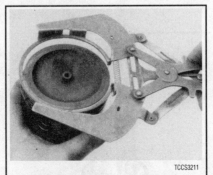

TCCS3211

Fig. 215 Before cleaning and inspection, use a ring expander tool to remove the piston rings

TCCS3208

Fig. 216 Clean the piston ring grooves using a ring groove cleaner tool, or . . .

Fig. 217 . . . use a piece of an old ring to clean the grooves. Be careful, the ring can be quite sharp

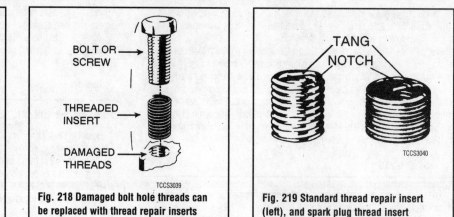

Fig. 218 Damaged bolt hole threads can be replaced with thread repair inserts

Fig. 219 Standard thread repair insert (left), and spark plug thread insert

When cleaning the cylinder head, remove carbon from the combustion chamber with the valves installed. This will avoid damaging the valve seats.

REPAIRING DAMAGED THREADS

▶ See Figures 218, 219, 220, 221 and 222

Several methods of repairing damaged threads are available. Heli-Coil (shown here), Keenserts, and Microdot are among the most widely used. All involve basically the same principle—drilling out stripped threads, tapping the hole and installing a prewound insert—making welding, plugging and oversize fasteners unnecessary.

Two types of thread repair inserts are usually supplied: a standard type for most inch coarse, inch fine, metric course and metric fine thread sizes and a spark lug type to fit most spark plug port sizes. Consult the individual tool manufacturer's catalog to determine exact applications. Typical thread repair kits will contain a selection of prewound threaded inserts, a tap (corresponding to the outside diameter threads of the insert) and an installation tool. Spark plug inserts usually differ because they require a tap equipped with pilot threads and a combined reamer/tap section. Most manufacturers also supply blister-packed thread repair inserts separately in addition to a master kit containing a variety of taps and inserts plus installation tools.

Before attempting to repair a threaded hole, remove any snapped, broken or damaged bolts or studs. Penetrating oil can be used to free frozen threads. The offending item can usually be removed with locking pliers or using a screw/stud extractor. After the hole is clear, the thread can be repaired as shown in the kit manufacturer's instructions.

Engine Preparation

To properly rebuild an engine, you must first remove it from the vehicle, then disassemble and diagnose it. Ideally you should place your engine on an engine stand. This affords you the best access to the engine components. Remove the flywheel or flexplate before installing the engine to the stand.

Now that you have the engine on a stand, and assuming that you have drained the oil and coolant from the engine, it's time to strip it of all but the necessary components. Before you start disassembling the engine, you may want to take a moment to draw some pictures, or fabricate some labels or containers to mark the locations of various components and the bolts and/or studs which fasten them. Modern day engines use a lot of little brackets and clips which hold wiring harnesses and such, and these holders are often mounted on studs and/or bolts that can be easily mixed up. The manufacturer spent a lot of time and money designing your vehicle, and they wouldn't have wasted any of it by haphazardly placing brackets, clips or fasteners on the vehicle. If it's present when you disassemble it, put it back when you assemble, you will regret not remembering that little bracket which holds a wire harness out of the path of a rotating part.

You should begin by unbolting any accessories still attached to the engine, such as the water pump, power steering pump, alternator, etc. Then, unfasten any manifolds (intake or exhaust) which were not removed during the engine removal procedure. Finally, remove any covers remaining on the engine such as the rocker arm, front or timing cover and oil pan. Some front covers may require the vibration damper and/or crank pulley to be removed beforehand. The idea is to reduce the engine to the bare necessities of cylinder head(s), valve train, engine block, crankshaft, pistons and connecting rods, plus any other `in block' components such as oil pumps, balance shafts and auxiliary shafts.

Finally, remove the cylinder head(s) from the engine block and carefully place on a bench. Disassembly instructions for each component follow later in this section.

Cylinder Head

There are two basic types of cylinder heads used on today's automobiles: the Overhead Valve (OHV) and the Overhead Camshaft (OHC). The latter can also be broken down into two subgroups: the Single Overhead Camshaft (SOHC) and the Dual Overhead Camshaft (DOHC). Generally, if there is only a single camshaft on a head, it is just referred to as an OHC head. Also, an engine with an OHV cylinder head is also known as a pushrod engine.

Fig. 220 Drill out the damaged threads with the specified size bit. Be sure to drill completely through the hole or to the bottom of a blind hole

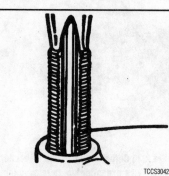

Fig. 221 Using the kit, tap the hole in order to receive the thread insert. Keep the tap well oiled and back it out frequently to avoid clogging the threads

Fig. 222 Screw the insert onto the installer tool until the tang engages the slot. Thread the insert into the hole until it is ¼–½ turn below the top surface, then remove the tool and break off the tang using a punch

Most cylinder heads these days are made of an aluminum alloy due to its light weight, durability and heat transfer qualities. However, cast iron was the material of choice in the past, and is still used on many vehicles. Whether made from aluminum or iron, all cylinder heads have valves and seats. Some use two valves per cylinder, while the more hi-tech engines will utilize a multi-valve configuration using 3, 4 and even 5 valves per cylinder. When the valve contacts the seat, it does so on precision machined surfaces, which seals the combustion chamber. All cylinder heads have a valve guide for each valve. The guide centers the valve to the seat and allows it to move up and down within it. The clearance between the valve and guide can be critical. Too much clearance and the engine may consume oil, lose vacuum and/or damage the seat. Too little, and the valve can stick in the guide causing the engine to run poorly if at all, and possibly causing severe damage. The last component all automotive cylinder heads have are valve springs. The spring holds the valve against its seat. It also returns the valve to this position when the valve has been opened by the valve train or camshaft. The spring is fastened to the valve by a retainer and valve locks (sometimes called keepers). Aluminum heads will also have a valve spring shim to keep the spring from wearing away the aluminum.

An ideal method of rebuilding the cylinder head would involve replacing all of the valves, guides, seats, springs, etc. with new ones. However, depending on how the engine was maintained, often this is not necessary. A major cause of valve, guide and seat wear is an improperly tuned engine. An engine that is running too rich, will often wash the lubricating oil out of the guide with gasoline, causing it to wear rapidly. Conversely, an engine which is running too lean will place higher combustion temperatures on the valves and seats allowing them to wear or even burn. Springs fall victim to the driving habits of the individual. A driver who often runs the engine rpm to the redline will wear out or break the springs faster then one that stays well below it. Unfortunately, mileage takes it toll on all of the parts. Generally, the valves, guides, springs and seats in a cylinder head can be machined and re-used, saving you money. However, if a valve is burnt, it may be wise to replace all of the valves, since they were all operating in the same environment. The same goes for any other component on the cylinder head. Think of it as an insurance policy against future problems related to that component.

Unfortunately, the only way to find out which components need replacing, is to disassemble and carefully check each piece. After the cylinder head(s) are disassembled, thoroughly clean all of the components.

DISASSEMBLY

OHC Heads

▶ See Figures 223 and 224

Whether it is a single or dual overhead camshaft cylinder head, the disassembly procedure is relatively unchanged. One aspect to pay attention to is careful labeling of the parts on the dual camshaft cylinder head. There will be an intake camshaft and followers as well as an exhaust camshaft and followers and they must be labeled as such. In some cases, the components are identical and could easily be installed incorrectly. DO NOT MIX THEM UP! Determining which is which is very simple; the intake camshaft and components are on the same side of the head as was the intake manifold. Conversely, the exhaust camshaft and components are on the same side of the head as was the exhaust manifold.

CUP TYPE CAMSHAFT FOLLOWERS

▶ See Figures 225, 226 and 227

Most cylinder heads with cup type camshaft followers will have the valve spring, retainer and locks recessed within the follower's bore. You will need a C-clamp style valve spring compressor tool, an OHC spring removal tool (or equivalent) and a small magnet to disassemble the head.

1. If not already removed, remove the camshaft(s) and/or followers. Mark their positions for assembly.
2. Position the cylinder head to allow use of a C-clamp style valve spring compressor tool.

➡It is preferred to position the cylinder head gasket surface facing you with the valve springs facing the opposite direction and the head laying horizontal.

3. With the OHC spring removal adapter tool positioned inside of the follower bore, compress the valve spring using the C-clamp style valve spring compressor.

TCCA3P54

Fig. 223 Exploded view of a valve, seal, spring, retainer and locks from an OHC cylinder head

TCCA3P62

Fig. 224 Example of a multi-valve cylinder head. Note how it has 2 intake and 2 exhaust valve ports

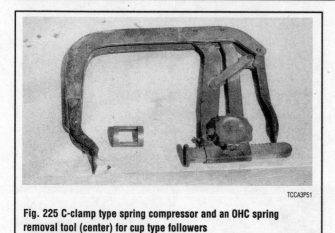

Fig. 225 C-clamp type spring compressor and an OHC spring removal tool (center) for cup type followers

Fig. 226 Most cup type follower cylinder heads retain the camshaft using bolt-on bearing caps

Fig. 227 Position the OHC spring tool in the follower bore, then compress the spring with a C-clamp type tool

Fig. 228 Example of the shaft mounted rocker arms on some OHC heads

4. Remove the valve locks. A small magnetic tool or screwdriver will aid in removal.
5. Release the compressor tool and remove the spring assembly.
6. Withdraw the valve from the cylinder head.
7. If equipped, remove the valve seal.

➡Special valve seal removal tools are available. Regular or needlenose type pliers, if used with care, will work just as well. If using ordinary pliers, be sure not to damage the follower bore. The follower and its bore are machined to close tolerances and any damage to the bore will effect this relationship.

8. If equipped, remove the valve spring shim. A small magnetic tool or screwdriver will aid in removal.
9. Repeat Steps 3 through 8 until all of the valves have been removed.

ROCKER ARM TYPE CAMSHAFT FOLLOWERS

♦ See Figures 228 thru 236

Most cylinder heads with rocker arm-type camshaft followers are easily disassembled using a standard valve spring compressor. However, certain models may not have enough open space around the spring for the standard tool and may require you to use a C-clamp style compressor tool instead.

1. If not already removed, remove the rocker arms and/or shafts and the camshaft. If applicable, also remove the hydraulic lash adjusters. Mark their positions for assembly.
2. Position the cylinder head to allow access to the valve spring.
3. Use a valve spring compressor tool to relieve the spring tension from the retainer.

➡Due to engine varnish, the retainer may stick to the valve locks. A gentle tap with a hammer may help to break it loose.

4. Remove the valve locks from the valve tip and/or retainer. A small magnet may help in removing the small locks.
5. Lift the valve spring, tool and all, off of the valve stem.

Fig. 229 Another example of the rocker arm type OHC head. This model uses a follower under the camshaft

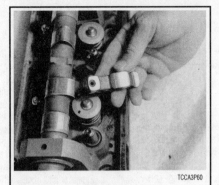

Fig. 230 Before the camshaft can be removed, all of the followers must first be removed . . .

Fig. 231 . . . then the camshaft can be removed by sliding it out (shown), or unbolting a bearing cap (not shown)

Fig. 232 Compress the valve spring . . .

Fig. 233 . . . then remove the valve locks from the valve stem and spring retainer

Fig. 234 Remove the valve spring and retainer from the cylinder head

Fig. 235 Remove the valve seal from the guide. Some gentle prying or pliers may help to remove stubborn ones

Fig. 236 All aluminum and some cast iron heads will have these valve spring shims. Remove all of them as well

6. If equipped, remove the valve seal. If the seal is difficult to remove with the valve in place, try removing the valve first, then the seal. Follow the steps below for valve removal.

7. Position the head to allow access for withdrawing the valve.

➡ Cylinder heads that have seen a lot of miles and/or abuse may have mushroomed the valve lock grove and/or tip, causing difficulty in removal of the valve. If this has happened, use a metal file to carefully remove the high spots around the lock grooves and/or tip. Only file it enough to allow removal.

8. Remove the valve from the cylinder head.

9. If equipped, remove the valve spring shim. A small magnetic tool or screwdriver will aid in removal.

10. Repeat Steps 3 though 9 until all of the valves have been removed.

INSPECTION

Now that all of the cylinder head components are clean, it's time to inspect them for wear and/or damage. To accurately inspect them, you will need some specialized tools:

- A 0–1 in. micrometer for the valves
- A dial indicator or inside diameter gauge for the valve guides
- A spring pressure test gauge

If you do not have access to the proper tools, you may want to bring the components to a shop that does.

Valves

◆ **See Figures 237 and 238**

The first thing to inspect are the valve heads. Look closely at the head, margin and face for any cracks, excessive wear or burning. The margin is the best place to look for burning. It should have a squared edge with an even width all around the diameter. When a valve burns, the margin will look melted and the edges rounded. Also inspect the valve head for any signs of tulipping. This will show as a lifting of the edges or dishing in the center of the head and will usually not occur to all of the valves. All of the heads should look the same, any that seem dished more than others are probably bad. Next, inspect the valve lock grooves and valve tips. Check for any burrs around the lock grooves, especially if you had to file them to remove the valve. Valve tips should appear flat, although slight rounding with high mileage engines is normal. Slightly worn valve tips will need to be machined flat. Last, measure the valve stem diameter with the micrometer. Measure the area that rides within the guide, especially towards the tip where most of the wear occurs. Take several measurements along its length and compare them to each other. Wear should be even along the length with little to no taper. If no minimum diameter is given in the specifications, then the stem should not read more than 0.001 in. (0.025mm) below the unworn portion of the stem. Any valves that fail these inspections should be replaced.

Springs, Retainers and Valve Locks

◆ **See Figures 239 and 240**

The first thing to check is the most obvious, broken springs. Next check the free length and squareness of each spring. If applicable, insure to distinguish between intake and exhaust springs. Use a ruler and/or carpenter's square to measure the length. A carpenter's square should be used to check the springs for squareness. If a spring pressure test gauge is available, check each springs rating and compare to the specifications chart. Check the readings against the specifications given. Any springs that fail these inspections should be replaced.

The spring retainers rarely need replacing, however they should still be checked as a precaution. Inspect the spring mating surface and the valve lock retention area for any signs of excessive wear. Also check for any signs of cracking. Replace any retainers that are questionable.

Valve locks should be inspected for excessive wear on the outside contact area as well as on the inner notched surface. Any locks which appear worn or broken and its respective valve should be replaced.

Cylinder Head

There are several things to check on the cylinder head: valve guides, seats, cylinder head surface flatness, cracks and physical damage.

VALVE GUIDES

◆ **See Figure 241**

Now that you know the valves are good, you can use them to check the guides, although a new valve, if available, is preferred. Before you measure anything, look at the guides carefully and inspect them for any cracks, chips or breakage. Also if the guide is a removable style (as in most aluminum heads), check them for any looseness or evidence of movement. All of the guides should appear to be at the same height from the spring seat. If any seem lower (or higher) from another, the guide has moved. Mount a dial indicator onto the spring side of the cylinder head. Lightly oil the valve stem and insert it into the cylinder head. Position the dial indicator against the valve stem near the tip and zero the gauge. Grasp the valve stem and wiggle towards and away from the dial indicator and observe the readings. Mount the dial indicator 90 degrees from the initial point and zero the gauge and again take a reading. Compare the two readings for an out of round condition. Check the readings against the specifications given. An Inside Diameter (I.D.) gauge designed for valve guides will give you an accurate valve guide bore measurement. If the I.D. gauge is used, compare the readings with the specifications given. Any guides that fail these inspections should be replaced or machined.

VALVE SEATS

A visual inspection of the valve seats should show a slightly worn and pitted surface where the valve face contacts the seat. Inspect the seat carefully for severe pitting or cracks. Also, a seat that is badly worn will be recessed into the cylinder head. A severely worn or recessed seat may need to be replaced. All cracked seats must be replaced. A seat concentricity gauge, if available, should be used to check the seat run-out. If run-out exceeds specifications the seat must be machined (if no specification is available given use 0.002 in. or 0.051mm).

CYLINDER HEAD SURFACE FLATNESS

◆ **See Figures 242 and 243**

After you have cleaned the gasket surface of the cylinder head of any old gasket material, check the head for flatness.

Place a straightedge across the gasket surface. Using feeler gauges, determine the clearance at the center of the straightedge and across the cylinder head at several points. Check along the centerline and diagonally on the head surface. If the warpage exceeds 0.003 in. (0.076mm) within a 6.0 in. (15.2cm) span, or 0.006 in. (0.152mm) over the total length of the head, the cylinder head must be resurfaced. After resurfacing the heads of a V-type engine, the intake manifold flange surface should be checked, and if necessary, milled proportionally to allow for the change in its mounting position.

CRACKS AND PHYSICAL DAMAGE

Generally, cracks are limited to the combustion chamber, however, it is not uncommon for the head to crack in a spark plug hole, port, outside of the head or in the valve spring/rocker arm area. The first area to inspect is always the hottest: the exhaust seat/port area.

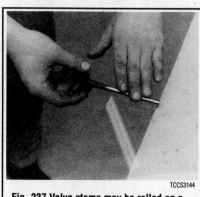

Fig. 237 Valve stems may be rolled on a flat surface to check for bends

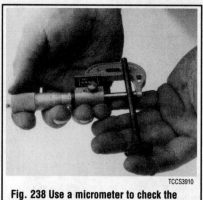

Fig. 238 Use a micrometer to check the valve stem diameter

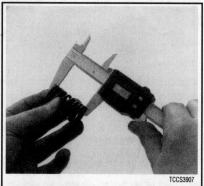

Fig. 239 Use a caliper to check the valve spring free-length

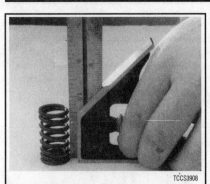

Fig. 240 Check the valve spring for squareness on a flat surface; a carpenter's square can be used

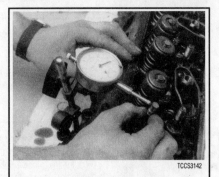

Fig. 241 A dial gauge may be used to check valve stem-to-guide clearance; read the gauge while moving the valve stem

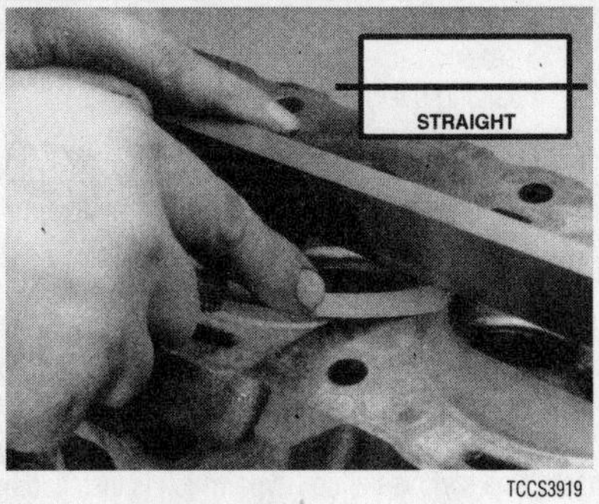

Fig. 242 Check the head for flatness across the center of the head surface using a straightedge and feeler gauge

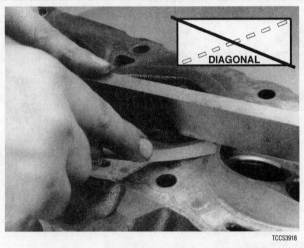

Fig. 243 Checks should also be made along both diagonals of the head surface

A visual inspection should be performed, but just because you don't see a crack does not mean it is not there. Some more reliable methods for inspecting for cracks include Magnaflux®, a magnetic process or Zyglo®, a dye penetrant. Magnaflux® is used only on ferrous metal (cast iron) heads. Zyglo® uses a spray on fluorescent mixture along with a black light to reveal the cracks. It is strongly recommended to have your cylinder head checked professionally for cracks, especially if the engine was known to have overheated and/or leaked or consumed coolant. Contact a local shop for availability and pricing of these services.

Physical damage is usually very evident. For example, a broken mounting ear from dropping the head or a bent or broken stud and/or bolt. All of these defects should be fixed or, if unrepairable, the head should be replaced.

Camshaft and Followers

Inspect the camshaft(s) and followers as described earlier in this section.

REFINISHING & REPAIRING

Many of the procedures given for refinishing and repairing the cylinder head components must be performed by a machine shop. Certain steps, if the inspected part is not worn, can be performed yourself inexpensively. However, you spent a lot of time and effort so far, why risk trying to save a couple bucks if you might have to do it all over again?

Valves

Any valves that were not replaced should be refaced and the tips ground flat. Unless you have access to a valve grinding machine, this should be done by a

machine shop. If the valves are in extremely good condition, as well as the valve seats and guides, they may be lapped in without performing machine work.

It is a recommended practice to lap the valves even after machine work has been performed and/or new valves have been purchased. This insures a positive seal between the valve and seat.

LAPPING THE VALVES

➡**Before lapping the valves to the seats, read the rest of the cylinder head section to insure that any related parts are in acceptable enough condition to continue. Also, remember that before any valve seat machining and/or lapping can be performed, the guides must be within factory recommended specifications.**

1. Invert the cylinder head.
2. Lightly lubricate the valve stems and insert them into the cylinder head in their numbered order.
3. Raise the valve from the seat and apply a small amount of fine lapping compound to the seat.
4. Moisten the suction head of a hand-lapping tool and attach it to the head of the valve.
5. Rotate the tool between the palms of both hands, changing the position of the valve on the valve seat and lifting the tool often to prevent grooving.
6. Lap the valve until a smooth, polished circle is evident on the valve and seat.
7. Remove the tool and the valve. Wipe away all traces of the grinding compound and store the valve to maintain its lapped location.

✳✳ WARNING

Do not get the valves out of order after they have been lapped. They must be put back with the same valve seat with which they were lapped.

Springs, Retainers and Valve Locks

There is no repair or refinishing possible with the springs, retainers and valve locks. If they are found to be worn or defective, they must be replaced with new (or known good) parts.

Cylinder Head

Most refinishing procedures dealing with the cylinder head must be performed by a machine shop. Read the sections below and review your inspection data to determine whether or not machining is necessary.

VALVE GUIDE

➡**If any machining or replacements are made to the valve guides, the seats must be machined.**

Unless the valve guides need machining or replacing, the only service to perform is to thoroughly clean them of any dirt or oil residue.

There are only two types of valve guides used on automobile engines: the replaceable-type (all aluminum heads) and the cast-in integral-type (most cast iron heads). There are four recommended methods for repairing worn guides.

- Knurling
- Inserts
- Reaming oversize
- Replacing

Knurling is a process in which metal is displaced and raised, thereby reducing clearance, giving a true center, and providing oil control. It is the least expensive way of repairing the valve guides. However, it is not necessarily the best, and in some cases, a knurled valve guide will not stand up for more than a short time. It requires a special knurlizer and precision reaming tools to obtain proper clearances. It would not be cost effective to purchase these tools, unless you plan on rebuilding several of the same cylinder head.

Installing a guide insert involves machining the guide to accept a bronze insert. One style is the coil-type which is installed into a threaded guide. Another is the thin-walled insert where the guide is reamed oversize to accept a split-sleeve insert. After the insert is installed, a special tool is then run through the guide to expand the insert, locking it to the guide. The insert is then reamed to the standard size for proper valve clearance.

Reaming for oversize valves restores normal clearances and provides a true valve seat. Most cast-in type guides can be reamed to accept an valve with an oversize stem. The cost factor for this can become quite high as you will need to purchase the reamer and new, oversize stem valves for all guides which were reamed. Oversizes are generally 0.003–0.030 in. (0.076–0.762mm), with 0.015 in. (0.381mm) being the most common.

To replace cast-in type valve guides, they must be drilled out, then reamed to accept replacement guides. This must be done on a fixture which will allow centering and leveling off of the original valve seat or guide, otherwise a serious guide-to-seat misalignment may occur making it impossible to properly machine the seat.

Replaceable-type guides are pressed into the cylinder head. A hammer and a stepped drift or punch may be used to install and remove the guides. Before removing the guides, measure the protrusion on the spring side of the head and record it for installation. Use the stepped drift to hammer out the old guide from the combustion chamber side of the head. When installing, determine whether or not the guide also seals a water jacket in the head, and if it does, use the recommended sealing agent. If there is no water jacket, grease the valve guide and its bore. Use the stepped drift, and hammer the new guide into the cylinder head from the spring side of the cylinder head. A stack of washers the same thickness as the measured protrusion may help the installation process.

VALVE SEATS

➡ **Before any valve seat machining can be performed, the guides must be within factory recommended specifications. If any machining occurred or if replacements were made to the valve guides, the seats must be machined.**

If the seats are in good condition, the valves can be lapped to the seats, and the cylinder head assembled. See the valves section for instructions on lapping.

If the valve seats are worn, cracked or damaged, they must be serviced by a machine shop. The valve seat must be perfectly centered to the valve guide, which requires very accurate machining.

CYLINDER HEAD SURFACE

If the cylinder head is warped, it must be machined flat. If the warpage is extremely severe, the head may need to be replaced. In some instances, it may be possible to straighten a warped head enough to allow machining. In either case, contact a professional machine shop for service.

➡ **Any OHC cylinder head that shows excessive warpage should have the camshaft bearing journals align bored after the cylinder head has been resurfaced.**

✳ WARNING

Failure to align bore the camshaft bearing journals could result in severe engine damage including but not limited to: valve and piston damage, connecting rod damage, camshaft and/or crankshaft breakage.

CRACKS AND PHYSICAL DAMAGE

Certain cracks can be repaired in both cast iron and aluminum heads. For cast iron, a tapered threaded insert is installed along the length of the crack. Aluminum can also use the tapered inserts, however welding is the preferred method. Some physical damage can be repaired through brazing or welding. Contact a machine shop to get expert advice for your particular dilemma.

ASSEMBLY

The first step for any assembly job is to have a clean area in which to work. Next, thoroughly clean all of the parts and components that are to be assembled. Finally, place all of the components onto a suitable work space and, if necessary, arrange the parts to their respective positions.

OHC Engines

▶ **See Figure 244**

CUP TYPE CAMSHAFT FOLLOWERS

To install the springs, retainers and valve locks on heads which have these components recessed into the camshaft follower's bore, you will need a small screwdriver-type tool, some clean white grease and a lot of patience. You will also need the C-clamp style spring compressor and the OHC tool used to disassemble the head.

1. Lightly lubricate the valve stems and insert all of the valves into the cylinder head. If possible, maintain their original locations.
2. If equipped, install any valve spring shims which were removed.
3. If equipped, install the new valve seals, keeping the following in mind:
- If the valve seal presses over the guide, lightly lubricate the outer guide surfaces.
- If the seal is an O-ring type, it is installed just after compressing the spring but before the valve locks.
4. Place the valve spring and retainer over the stem.
5. Position the spring compressor and the OHC tool, then compress the spring.
6. Using a small screwdriver as a spatula, fill the valve stem side of the lock with white grease. Use the excess grease on the screwdriver to fasten the lock to the driver.
7. Carefully install the valve lock, which is stuck to the end of the screwdriver, to the valve stem then press on it with the screwdriver until the grease squeezes out. The valve lock should now be stuck to the stem.
8. Repeat Steps 6 and 7 for the remaining valve lock.

TCCA3P64

Fig. 244 Once assembled, check the valve clearance and correct as needed

9. Relieve the spring pressure slowly and insure that neither valve lock becomes dislodged by the retainer.

10. Remove the spring compressor tool.

11. Repeat Steps 2 through 10 until all of the springs have been installed.

12. Install the followers, camshaft(s) and any other components that were removed for disassembly.

ROCKER ARM TYPE CAMSHAFT FOLLOWERS

1. Lightly lubricate the valve stems and insert all of the valves into the cylinder head. If possible, maintain their original locations.

2. If equipped, install any valve spring shims which were removed.

3. If equipped, install the new valve seals, keeping the following in mind:

• If the valve seal presses over the guide, lightly lubricate the outer guide surfaces.

• If the seal is an O-ring type, it is installed just after compressing the spring but before the valve locks.

4. Place the valve spring and retainer over the stem.

5. Position the spring compressor tool and compress the spring.

6. Assemble the valve locks to the stem.

7. Relieve the spring pressure slowly and insure that neither valve lock becomes dislodged by the retainer.

8. Remove the spring compressor tool.

9. Repeat Steps 2 through 8 until all of the springs have been installed.

10. Install the camshaft(s), rockers, shafts and any other components that were removed for disassembly.

Engine Block

GENERAL INFORMATION

A thorough overhaul or rebuild of an engine block would include replacing the pistons, rings, bearings, timing belt/chain assembly and oil pump. For OHV engines also include a new camshaft and lifters. The block would then have the cylinders bored and honed oversize (or if using removable cylinder sleeves, new sleeves installed) and the crankshaft would be cut undersize to provide new wearing surfaces and perfect clearances. However, your particular engine may not have everything worn out. What if only the piston rings have worn out and the clearances on everything else are still within factory specifications? Well, you could just replace the rings and put it back together, but this would be a very rare example. Chances are, if one component in your engine is worn, other components are sure to follow, and soon. At the very least, you should always replace the rings, bearings and oil pump. This is what is commonly called a "freshen up".

Cylinder Ridge Removal

Because the top piston ring does not travel to the very top of the cylinder, a ridge is built up between the end of the travel and the top of the cylinder bore.

Pushing the piston and connecting rod assembly past the ridge can be difficult, and damage to the piston ring lands could occur. If the ridge is not removed before installing a new piston or not removed at all, piston ring breakage and piston damage may occur.

➡️ It is always recommended that you remove any cylinder ridges before removing the piston and connecting rod assemblies. If you know that new pistons are going to be installed and the engine block will be bored oversize, you may be able to forego this step. However, some ridges may actually prevent the assemblies from being removed, necessitating its removal.

There are several different types of ridge reamers on the market, none of which are inexpensive. Unless a great deal of engine rebuilding is anticipated, borrow or rent a reamer.

1. Turn the crankshaft until the piston is at the bottom of its travel.

2. Cover the head of the piston with a rag.

3. Follow the tool manufacturers instructions and cut away the ridge, exercising extreme care to avoid cutting too deeply.

4. Remove the ridge reamer, the rag and as many of the cuttings as possible. Continue until all of the cylinder ridges have been removed.

DISASSEMBLY

▶ See Figures 245 and 246

The engine disassembly instructions following assume that you have the engine mounted on an engine stand. If not, it is easiest to disassemble the engine on a bench or the floor with it resting on the bell housing or transmission mounting surface. You must be able to access the connecting rod fasteners and turn the crankshaft during disassembly. Also, all engine covers (timing, front, side, oil pan, whatever) should have already been removed. Engines which are seized or locked up may not be able to be completely disassembled, and a core (salvage yard) engine should be purchased.

OHC Engines

If not done during the cylinder head removal, remove the timing chain/belt and/or gear/sprocket assembly. Remove the oil pick-up and pump assembly and, if necessary, the pump drive. If equipped, remove any balance or auxiliary shafts. If necessary, remove the cylinder ridge from the top of the bore. See the cylinder ridge removal procedure earlier in this section.

All Engines

Rotate the engine over so that the crankshaft is exposed. Use a number punch or scribe and mark each connecting rod with its respective cylinder number. The cylinder closest to the front of the engine is always number 1. However, depending on the engine placement, the front of the engine could either be the flywheel or damper/pulley end. Generally the front of the engine faces the front of the vehicle. Use a number punch or scribe and also mark the main bearing caps from front to rear with the front most cap being number 1 (if there are five caps, mark them 1 through 5, front to rear).

✳️✳️ WARNING

Take special care when pushing the connecting rod up from the crankshaft because the sharp threads of the rod bolts/studs will score the crankshaft journal. Insure that special plastic caps are installed over them, or cut two pieces of rubber hose to do the same.

Again, rotate the engine, this time to position the number one cylinder bore (head surface) up. Turn the crankshaft until the number one piston is at the bottom of its travel, this should allow the maximum access to its connecting rod. Remove the number one connecting rods fasteners and cap and place two lengths of rubber hose over the rod bolts/studs to protect the crankshaft from damage. Using a sturdy wooden dowel and a hammer, push the connecting rod

TCCS3803

Fig. 245 Place rubber hose over the connecting rod studs to protect the crankshaft and cylinder bores from damage

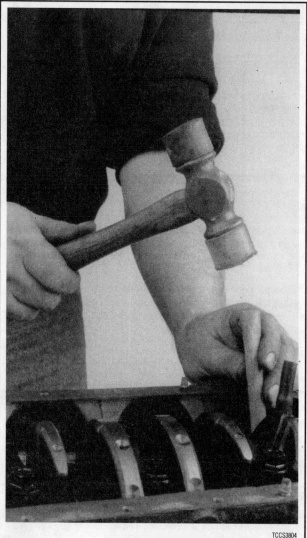

TCCS3804

Fig. 246 Carefully tap the piston out of the bore using a wooden dowel

up about 1 in. (25mm) from the crankshaft and remove the upper bearing insert. Continue pushing or tapping the connecting rod up until the piston rings are out of the cylinder bore. Remove the piston and rod by hand, put the upper half of the bearing insert back into the rod, install the cap with its bearing insert installed, and hand-tighten the cap fasteners. If the parts are kept in order in this manner, they will not get lost and you will be able to tell which bearings came form what cylinder if any problems are discovered and diagnosis is necessary. Remove all the other piston assemblies in the same manner. On V-style engines, remove all of the pistons from one bank, then reposition the engine with the other cylinder bank head surface up, and remove that banks piston assemblies.

The only remaining component in the engine block should now be the crankshaft. Loosen the main bearing caps evenly until the fasteners can be turned by hand, then remove them and the caps. Remove the crankshaft from the engine block. Thoroughly clean all of the components.

INSPECTION

Now that the engine block and all of its components are clean, it's time to inspect them for wear and/or damage. To accurately inspect them, you will need some specialized tools:

- Two or three separate micrometers to measure the pistons and crankshaft journals
- A dial indicator
- Telescoping gauges for the cylinder bores
- A rod alignment fixture to check for bent connecting rods

If you do not have access to the proper tools, you may want to bring the components to a shop that does.

Generally, you shouldn't expect cracks in the engine block or its components unless it was known to leak, consume or mix engine fluids, it was severely overheated, or there was evidence of bad bearings and/or crankshaft damage. A visual inspection should be performed on all of the components, but just because you don't see a crack does not mean it is not there. Some more reliable methods for inspecting for cracks include Magnaflux®, a magnetic process or Zyglo®, a dye penetrant. Magnaflux® is used only on ferrous metal (cast iron). Zyglo® uses a spray on fluorescent mixture along with a black light to reveal the cracks. It is strongly recommended to have your engine block checked professionally for cracks, especially if the engine was known to have overheated and/or leaked or consumed coolant. Contact a local shop for availability and pricing of these services.

Engine Block

ENGINE BLOCK BEARING ALIGNMENT

Remove the main bearing caps and, if still installed, the main bearing inserts. Inspect all of the main bearing saddles and caps for damage, burrs or high spots. If damage is found, and it is caused from a spun main bearing, the block will need to be align-bored or, if severe enough, replacement. Any burrs or high spots should be carefully removed with a metal file.

Place a straightedge on the bearing saddles, in the engine block, along the centerline of the crankshaft. If any clearance exists between the straightedge and the saddles, the block must be align-bored.

Align-boring consists of machining the main bearing saddles and caps by means of a flycutter that runs through the bearing saddles.

DECK FLATNESS

The top of the engine block where the cylinder head mounts is called the deck. Insure that the deck surface is clean of dirt, carbon deposits and old gasket material. Place a straightedge across the surface of the deck along its centerline and, using feeler gauges, check the clearance along several points. Repeat the checking procedure with the straightedge placed along both diagonals of the deck surface. If the reading exceeds 0.003 in. (0.076mm) within a 6.0 in. (15.2cm) span, or 0.006 in. (0.152mm) over the total length of the deck, it must be machined.

CYLINDER BORES

◆ See Figure 247

The cylinder bores house the pistons and are slightly larger than the pistons themselves. A common piston-to-bore clearance is 0.0015–0.0025 in. (0.0381mm–0.0635mm). Inspect and measure the cylinder bores. The bore should be checked for out-of-roundness, taper and size. The results of this inspection will determine whether the cylinder can be used in its existing size and condition, or a rebore to the next oversize is required (or in the case of removable sleeves, have replacements installed).

The amount of cylinder wall wear is always greater at the top of the cylinder than at the bottom. This wear is known as taper. Any cylinder that has a taper of 0.0012 in. (0.305mm) or more, must be rebored. Measurements are taken at a number of positions in each cylinder: at the top, middle and bottom and at two points at each position; that is, at a point 90 degrees from the crankshaft centerline, as well as a point parallel to the crankshaft centerline. The measurements are made with either a special dial indicator or a telescopic gauge and micrometer. If the necessary precision tools to check the bore are not available, take the block to a machine shop and have them mike it. Also if you don't have the tools to check the cylinder bores, chances are you will not have the necessary devices to check the pistons, connecting rods and crankshaft. Take these components with you and save yourself an extra trip.

For our procedures, we will use a telescopic gauge and a micrometer. You will need one of each, with a measuring range which covers your cylinder bore size.

1. Position the telescopic gauge in the cylinder bore, loosen the gauges lock and allow it to expand.

➡**Your first two readings will be at the top of the cylinder bore, then proceed to the middle and finally the bottom, making a total of six measurements.**

Fig. 247 Use a telescoping gauge to measure the cylinder bore diameter—take several readings within the same bore

Fig. 248 Measure the piston's outer diameter, perpendicular to the wrist pin, with a micrometer

2. Hold the gauge square in the bore, 90 degrees from the crankshaft centerline, and gently tighten the lock. Tilt the gauge back to remove it from the bore.

3. Measure the gauge with the micrometer and record the reading.

4. Again, hold the gauge square in the bore, this time parallel to the crankshaft centerline, and gently tighten the lock. Again, you will tilt the gauge back to remove it from the bore.

5. Measure the gauge with the micrometer and record this reading. The difference between these two readings is the out-of-round measurement of the cylinder.

6. Repeat steps 1 through 5, each time going to the next lower position, until you reach the bottom of the cylinder. Then go to the next cylinder, and continue until all of the cylinders have been measured.

The difference between these measurements will tell you all about the wear in your cylinders. The measurements which were taken 90 degrees from the crankshaft centerline will always reflect the most wear. That is because at this position is where the engine power presses the piston against the cylinder bore the hardest. This is known as thrust wear. Take your top, 90 degree measurement and compare it to your bottom, 90 degree measurement. The difference between them is the taper. When you measure your pistons, you will compare these readings to your piston sizes and determine piston-to-wall clearance.

Crankshaft

Inspect the crankshaft for visible signs of wear or damage. All of the journals should be perfectly round and smooth. Slight scores are normal for a used crankshaft, but you should hardly feel them with your fingernail. When measuring the crankshaft with a micrometer, you will take readings at the front and rear of each journal, then turn the micrometer 90 degrees and take two more readings, front and rear. The difference between the front-to-rear readings is the journal taper and the first-to-90 degree reading is the out-of-round measurement. Generally, there should be no taper or out-of-roundness found, however, up to 0.0005 in. (0.0127mm) for either can be overlooked. Also, the readings should fall within the factory specifications for journal diameters.

If the crankshaft journals fall within specifications, it is recommended that it be polished before being returned to service. Polishing the crankshaft insures that any minor burrs or high spots are smoothed, thereby reducing the chance of scoring the new bearings.

Pistons and Connecting Rods

PISTONS

♦ See Figure 248

The piston should be visually inspected for any signs of cracking or burning (caused by hot spots or detonation), and scuffing or excessive wear on the skirts. The wrist pin attaches the piston to the connecting rod. The piston should move freely on the wrist pin, both sliding and pivoting. Grasp the connecting rod securely, or mount it in a vise, and try to rock the piston back and forth along the centerline of the wrist pin. There should not be any excessive play evident between the piston and the pin. If there are C-clips retaining the pin in the piston then you have wrist pin bushings in the rods. There should not be any excessive play between the wrist pin and the rod bushing. Normal clearance for the wrist pin is approx. 0.001–0.002 in. (0.025mm–0.051mm).

Use a micrometer and measure the diameter of the piston, perpendicular to the wrist pin, on the skirt. Compare the reading to its original cylinder measurement obtained earlier. The difference between the two readings is the piston-to-wall clearance. If the clearance is within specifications, the piston may be used as is. If the piston is out of specification, but the bore is not, you will need a new piston. If both are out of specification, you will need the cylinder rebored and oversize pistons installed. Generally if two or more pistons/bores are out of specification, it is best to rebore the entire block and purchase a complete set of oversize pistons.

CONNECTING ROD

You should have the connecting rod checked for straightness at a machine shop. If the connecting rod is bent, it will unevenly wear the bearing and piston, as well as place greater stress on these components. Any bent or twisted connecting rods must be replaced. If the rods are straight and the wrist pin clearance is within specifications, then only the bearing end of the rod need be checked. Place the connecting rod into a vice, with the bearing inserts in place, install the cap to the rod and torque the fasteners to specifications. Use a telescoping gauge and carefully measure the inside diameter of the bearings. Compare this reading to the rods original crankshaft journal diameter measurement. The difference is the oil clearance. If the oil clearance is not within specifications, install new bearings in the rod and take another measurement. If the clearance is still out of specifications, and the crankshaft is not, the rod will need to be reconditioned by a machine shop.

➡**You can also use Plastigage® to check the bearing clearances. The assembling section has complete instructions on its use.**

Camshaft

Inspect the camshaft and lifters/followers as described earlier in this section.

Bearings

All of the engine bearings should be visually inspected for wear and/or damage. The bearing should look evenly worn all around with no deep scores or pits. If the bearing is severely worn, scored, pitted or heat blued, then the bearing, and the components that use it, should be brought to a machine shop for inspection. Full-circle bearings (used on most camshafts, auxiliary shafts, balance shafts, etc.) require specialized tools for removal and installation, and should be brought to a machine shop for service.

Oil Pump

➡The oil pump is responsible for providing constant lubrication to the whole engine and so it is recommended that a new oil pump be installed when rebuilding the engine.

Completely disassemble the oil pump and thoroughly clean all of the components. Inspect the oil pump gears and housing for wear and/or damage. Insure that the pressure relief valve operates properly and there is no binding or sticking due to varnish or debris. If all of the parts are in proper working condition, lubricate the gears and relief valve, and assemble the pump.

REFINISHING

▶ See Figure 249

Almost all engine block refinishing must be performed by a machine shop. If the cylinders are not to be rebored, then the cylinder glaze can be removed with a ball hone. When removing cylinder glaze with a ball hone, use a light or penetrating type oil to lubricate the hone. Do not allow the hone to run dry as this may cause excessive scoring of the cylinder bores and wear on the hone. If new pistons are required, they will need to be installed to the connecting rods. This should be performed by a machine shop as the pistons must be installed in the correct relationship to the rod or engine damage can occur.

Pistons and Connecting Rods

▶ See Figures 250, 251, 252 and 253

Only pistons with the wrist pin retained by C-clips are serviceable by the home-mechanic. Press fit pistons require special presses and/or heaters to remove/install the connecting rod and should only be performed by a machine shop.

All pistons will have a mark indicating the direction to the front of the engine and the must be installed into the engine in that manner. Usually it is a notch or arrow on the top of the piston, or it may be the letter F cast or stamped into the piston.

ASSEMBLY

Before you begin assembling the engine, first give yourself a clean, dirt free work area. Next, clean every engine component again. The key to a good assembly is cleanliness.

Mount the engine block into the engine stand and wash it one last time using water and detergent (dishwashing detergent works well). While washing it, scrub the cylinder bores with a soft bristle brush and thoroughly clean all of the oil passages. Completely dry the engine and spray the entire assembly down with an anti-rust solution such as WD-40® or similar product. Take a clean lint-free rag and wipe up any excess anti-rust solution from the bores, bearing saddles, etc. Repeat the final cleaning process on the crankshaft. Replace any freeze or oil galley plugs which were removed during disassembly.

Crankshaft

▶ See Figures 254, 255, 256 and 257

1. Remove the main bearing inserts from the block and bearing caps.
2. If the crankshaft main bearing journals have been refinished to a definite undersize, install the correct undersize bearing. Be sure that the bearing inserts and bearing bores are clean. Foreign material under inserts will distort bearing and cause failure.

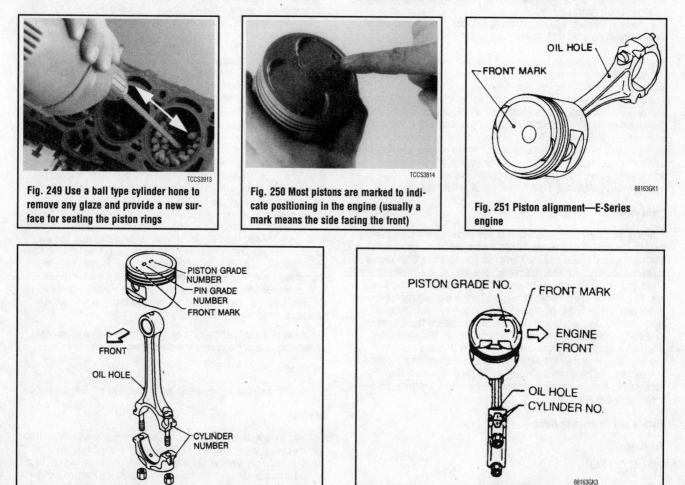

Fig. 249 Use a ball type cylinder hone to remove any glaze and provide a new surface for seating the piston rings

Fig. 250 Most pistons are marked to indicate positioning in the engine (usually a mark means the side facing the front)

Fig. 251 Piston alignment—E-Series engine

Fig. 252 Piston and connecting rod positioning—GA16i, CA16DE, CA18DE, GA16DE and SR20DE engines

Fig. 253 Piston and rod alignment—CA16DE and CA18DE engines

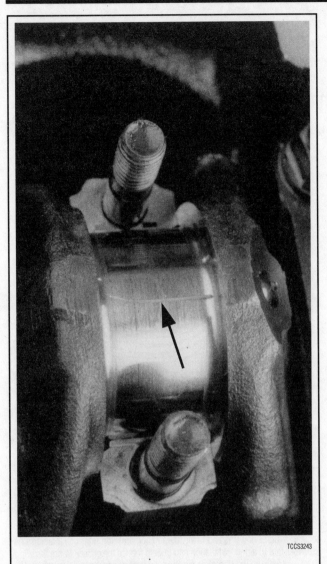

Fig. 254 Apply a strip of gauging material to the bearing journal, then install and torque the cap

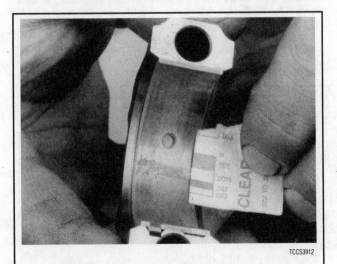

Fig. 255 After the cap is removed again, use the scale supplied with the gauging material to check the clearance

Fig. 256 A dial gauge may be used to check crankshaft end-play

Fig. 257 Carefully pry the crankshaft back and forth while reading the dial gauge for end-play

3. Place the upper main bearing inserts in bores with tang in slot.

➡The oil holes in the bearing inserts must be aligned with the oil holes in the cylinder block.

4. Install the lower main bearing inserts in bearing caps.
5. Clean the mating surfaces of block and rear main bearing cap.
6. Carefully lower the crankshaft into place. Be careful not to damage bearing surfaces.
7. Check the clearance of each main bearing by using the following procedure:

a. Place a piece of Plastigage® or its equivalent, on bearing surface across full width of bearing cap and about ¼ in. off center.

b. Install cap and tighten bolts to specifications. Do not turn crankshaft while Plastigage® is in place.

c. Remove the cap. Using the supplied Plastigage® scale, check width of Plastigage® at widest point to get maximum clearance. Difference between readings is taper of journal.

d. If clearance exceeds specified limits, try a 0.001 in. or 0.002 in. undersize bearing in combination with the standard bearing. Bearing clearance must be within specified limits. If standard and 0.002 in. undersize bearing does not bring clearance within desired limits, refinish crankshaft journal, then install undersize bearings.

8. Install the rear main seal.

9. After the bearings have been fitted, apply a light coat of engine oil to the journals and bearings. Install the rear main bearing cap. Install all bearing caps except the thrust bearing cap. Be sure that main bearing caps are installed in original locations. Tighten the bearing cap bolts to specifications.

10. Install the thrust bearing cap with bolts finger-tight.

11. Pry the crankshaft forward against the thrust surface of upper half of bearing.

12. Hold the crankshaft forward and pry the thrust bearing cap to the rear. This aligns the thrust surfaces of both halves of the bearing.

13. Retain the forward pressure on the crankshaft. Tighten the cap bolts to specifications.

14. Measure the crankshaft end-play as follows:

a. Mount a dial gauge to the engine block and position the tip of the gauge to read from the crankshaft end.

b. Carefully pry the crankshaft toward the rear of the engine and hold it there while you zero the gauge.

c. Carefully pry the crankshaft toward the front of the engine and read the gauge.

d. Confirm that the reading is within specifications. If not, install a new thrust bearing and repeat the procedure. If the reading is still out of specifications with a new bearing, have a machine shop inspect the thrust surfaces of the crankshaft, and if possible, repair it.

15. Rotate the crankshaft so as to position the first rod journal to the bottom of its stroke.

Pistons and Connecting Rods

♦ **See Figures 258 thru 267**

1. Before installing the piston/connecting rod assembly, oil the pistons, piston rings and the cylinder walls with light engine oil. Install connecting rod bolt protectors or rubber hose onto the connecting rod bolts/studs. Also perform the following:

a. Select the proper ring set for the size cylinder bore.

b. Position the ring in the bore in which it is going to be used.

c. Push the ring down into the bore area where normal ring wear is not encountered.

d. Use the head of the piston to position the ring in the bore so that the ring is square with the cylinder wall. Use caution to avoid damage to the ring or cylinder bore.

e. Measure the gap between the ends of the ring with a feeler gauge. Ring gap in a worn cylinder is normally greater than specification. If the ring gap is greater than the specified limits, try an oversize ring set.

f. Check the ring side clearance of the compression rings with a feeler gauge inserted between the ring and its lower land according to specification. The gauge should slide freely around the entire ring circumference without binding. Any wear that occurs will form a step at the inner portion of the lower land. If the lower lands have high steps, the piston should be replaced.

2. Unless new pistons are installed, be sure to install the pistons in the cylinders from which they were removed. The numbers on the connecting rod and bearing cap must be on the same side when installed in the cylinder bore. If a connecting rod is ever transposed from one engine or cylinder to another, new bearings should be fitted and the connecting rod should be numbered to corre-

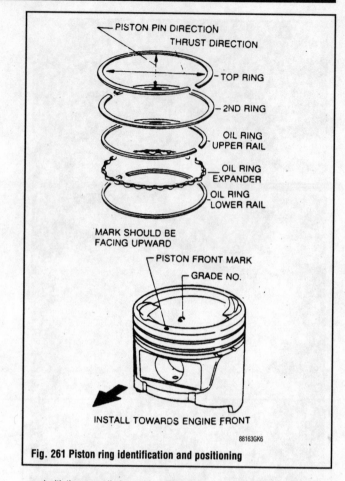

Fig. 261 Piston ring identification and positioning

spond with the new cylinder number. The notch on the piston head goes toward the front of the engine.

3. Install all of the rod bearing inserts into the rods and caps.

4. Install the rings to the pistons. Install the oil control ring first, then the second compression ring and finally the top compression ring. Use a piston ring expander tool to aid in installation and to help reduce the chance of breakage.

5. Make sure the ring gaps are properly spaced around the circumference of the piston. Fit a piston ring compressor around the piston and slide the piston and connecting rod assembly down into the cylinder bore, pushing it in with the wooden hammer handle. Push the piston down until it is only slightly below the top of the cylinder bore. Guide the connecting rod onto the crankshaft bearing journal carefully, to avoid damaging the crankshaft.

6. Check the bearing clearance of all the rod bearings, fitting them to the crankshaft bearing journals. Follow the procedure in the crankshaft installation above.

Fig. 258 Checking the piston ring-to-ring groove side clearance using the ring and a feeler gauge

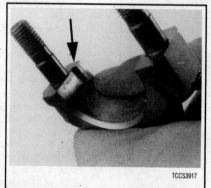

Fig. 259 The notch on the side of the bearing cap matches the tang on the bearing insert

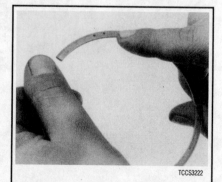

Fig. 260 Most rings are marked to show which side of the ring should face up when installed to the piston

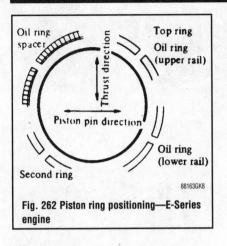

Fig. 262 Piston ring positioning—E-Series engine

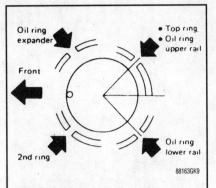

Fig. 263 Piston ring positioning—Gasoline engines except E-Series

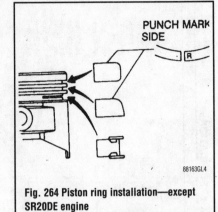

Fig. 264 Piston ring installation—except SR20DE engine

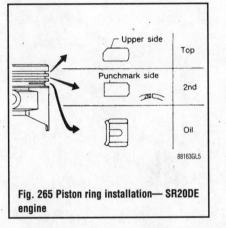

Fig. 265 Piston ring installation— SR20DE engine

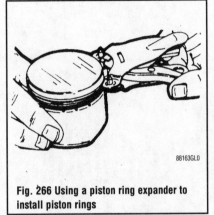

Fig. 266 Using a piston ring expander to install piston rings

Fig. 267 Install the piston and rod assembly into the block using a ring compressor and the handle of a hammer

7. After the bearings have been fitted, apply a light coating of assembly oil to the journals and bearings.

8. Turn the crankshaft until the appropriate bearing journal is at the bottom of its stroke, then push the piston assembly all the way down until the connecting rod bearing seats on the crankshaft journal. Be careful not to allow the bearing cap screws to strike the crankshaft bearing journals and damage them.

9. After the piston and connecting rod assemblies have been installed, check the connecting rod side clearance on each crankshaft journal.

10. Prime and install the oil pump and the oil pump intake tube.

11. Install the auxiliary/balance shaft(s)/assembly(ies).

OHC Engines

CYLINDER HEAD(S)

1. Install the cylinder head(s) using new gaskets.
2. Install the timing sprockets/gears and the belt/chain assemblies.

Engine Covers and Components

Install the timing cover(s) and oil pan. Refer to your notes and drawings made prior to disassembly and install all of the components that were removed. Install the engine into the vehicle.

Engine Start-up and Break-in

STARTING THE ENGINE

Now that the engine is installed and every wire and hose is properly connected, go back and double check that all coolant and vacuum hoses are connected. Check that your oil drain plug is installed and properly tightened. If not already done, install a new oil filter onto the engine. Fill the crankcase with the proper amount and grade of engine oil. Fill the cooling system with a 50/50 mixture of coolant/water.

1. Connect the vehicle battery.
2. Start the engine. Keep your eye on your oil pressure indicator; if it does not indicate oil pressure within 10 seconds of starting, turn the vehicle **OFF**.

❋❋ WARNING

Damage to the engine can result if it is allowed to run with no oil pressure. Check the engine oil level to make sure that it is full. Check for any leaks and if found, repair the leaks before continuing. If there is still no indication of oil pressure, you may need to prime the system.

3. Confirm that there are no fluid leaks (oil or other).
4. Allow the engine to reach normal operating temperature (the upper radiator hose will be hot to the touch).
5. At this point any necessary checks or adjustments can be performed, such as ignition timing.
6. Install any remaining components or body panels which were removed.

BREAKING IT IN

Make the first miles on the new engine, easy ones. Vary the speed but do not accelerate hard. Most importantly, do not lug the engine, and avoid sustained high speeds until at least 100 miles. Check the engine oil and coolant levels frequently. Expect the engine to use a little oil until the rings seat. Change the oil and filter at 500 miles, 1500 miles, then every 3000 miles past that.

KEEP IT MAINTAINED

Now that you have just gone through all of that hard work, keep yourself from doing it all over again by thoroughly maintaining it. Not that you may not have maintained it before, heck you could have had one to two hundred thousand miles on it before doing this. However, you may have bought the vehicle used, and the previous owner did not keep up on maintenance. Which is why you just went through all of that hard work. See?

ENGINE MECHANICAL SPECIFICATIONS

Component	U.S.	Metric
CYLINDER HEAD		
Surface Warpage		
All engines	0.0-0.004 in.	0.0-0.10 mm
Valve		
Stem diameter		
E15 and E16		
intake:	0.2744-0.2750 in.	6.970-6.985 mm
exhaust:	0.2734-0.2740 in.	6.945-6.960 mm
CD17		
intake:	0.2742-0.2748 in.	6.965-6.980 mm
exhaust:	0.2734-0.2740 in.	6.945-6.950 mm
CA16DE and CA18DE		
GA16i and SR20DE		
intake:	0.2348-0.2354 in.	5.965-5.980 mm
exhaust:	0.2341-0.2346 in.	5.945-5.960 mm
GA16DE		
intake:	0.2152-0.2157 in.	5.465-5.480 mm
exhaust:	0.2144-0.2150 in.	5.445-5.460 mm
Face angle		
E15 and E16	45 degrees 30min.	
CD17	45 degrees 30 min.	
CA16DE and CA18DE	45 degrees 30 min.	
GA16i	45 degrees 30 min.	
GA16DE and SR20DE	45 degrees 30 min.	45 degrees 30 min.
Valve margin		
E15, E16, GA16i		
CD17 and SR20DE	0.020 in.	0.50 mm
CA16DE and CA18DE	0.020 in.	0.50 mm
intake:	0.051 in.	1.30 mm
exhaust:	0.059 in.	1.50 mm
GA16DE	0.035-0.043 in.	0.90-1.10 mm

88163GN5

ENGINE MECHANICAL SPECIFICATIONS

Component	U.S.	Metric
Valve		
Valve tip removal limit		
E15 and E16	0.008 in.	0.20 mm
CD17	0.020 in.	0.50 mm
CA16DE and CA18DE	0.020 in.	0.50 mm
GA16i	0.020 in.	0.50 mm
GA16DE and SR20DE	0.008 in.	0.20 mm
Valve Spring		
Free height		
E15 and E16	1.8386 in.	46.70 mm
CD17	1.8268 in.	46.40 mm
outer;		
inner;		
CA16DE and CA18DE	1.7009 in.	43.20 mm
GA16i and GA16DE	1.6970 in.	43.10 mm
intake:	2.0709 in.	52.60 mm
exhaust:	2.1543 in.	54.72 mm
SR20DE	1.9433 in.	49.36 mm
Assembled height		
E15 and E16	1.543 in.@51.66 lb.	39.2mm@229.78N
CD17		
outer;	1.555 in.@33.70 lb.	39.5mm@150.00N
inner;	1.417 in.@19.20 lb.	36.0mm@85.00N
CA16DE and CA18DE	162.00 in.	28.4 mm
GA16i	1.634 in.@49.70 lb.	41.7mm@221.05N
intake:	1.705 in.@54.00 lb.	43.4mm@240.17N
exhaust:	1.331 in.@110.00 lb.	33.8mm@489.40N
intake:	1.346 in.@122.60 lb.	34.2mm@545.30N
exhaust:	1.181 in.@135.25 lb.	30.0mm@625.00N
SR20DE		
Out of square		
E15 and E16	0.079 in.	2.00 mm
CD17	0.083 in.	2.10 mm
CA16DE and CA18DE	0.071 in.	1.80 mm
GA16i and GA16DE	0.091 in.	2.30 mm
intake:	0.094 in.	2.40 mm
exhaust:	0.087 in.	2.20 mm
SR20DE		
Valve Guide		
Outer diameter		
E15 and E16	0.4825-0.4832 in.	12.256-12.274 mm
CD17	0.4418-0.4423 in.	11.223-11.234 mm
CA16DE, CA18DE and SR20DE	0.3946-0.3950 in.	10.023-10.034 mm
GA16i	0.3946-0.3950 in.	10.023-10.034 mm
intake:	0.4182-0.4187 in.	10.623-10.634 mm
exhaust:	0.3749-0.3754 in.	9.523-9.534 mm
GA16DE		
Inner diameter		
E15 and E16	0.2758-0.2764 in.	7.005-7.020 mm
CD17	0.2756-0.2762 in.	7.000-7.015 mm
CA16DE, CA18DE and SR20DE	0.2362-0.2369 in.	6.000-6.018 mm
GA16i	0.2362-0.2368 in.	6.000-6.015 mm
intake:	0.2598-0.2604 in.	6.600-6.615 mm
exhaust:	0.2165-0.2175 in.	5.500-5.515 mm
GA16DE		

88163GN6

ENGINE MECHANICAL SPECIFICATIONS

Component	U.S.	Metric
Valve Guide		
Stem-to-guide clearance		
E15 and E16		
intake:	0.0008-0.0040 in.	0.020-0.100 mm
exhaust:	0.0018-0.0040 in.	0.045-0.100 mm
CD17		
intake:	0.0008-0.0040 in.	0.020-0.100 mm
exhaust:	0.0016-0.0040 in.	0.040-0.100 mm
CA16DE and CA18DE		
intake:	0.0008-0.0021 in.	0.020-0.053 mm
exhaust:	0.0016-0.0029 in.	0.040-0.074 mm
GA16i		
intake:	0.0008-0.0020 in.	0.020-0.050 mm
exhaust:	0.0012-0.0022 in.	0.030-0.057 mm
GA16DE and SR20DE		
intake:	0.0008-0.0020 in.	0.020-0.050 mm
exhaust:	0.0016-0.0028 in.	0.040-0.070 mm
Deflection limit		
E15 and E16	0.008 in.	0.20 mm
CD17	0.004 in.	0.10 mm
GA16i, GA16DE and SR20DE	0.008 in.	0.20 mm
Valve seat		
Angle		
E15 and E16		
intake:	30, 45, 50 degrees	
exhaust:	45, 50 degrees	
CD17 45 degrees		
CA16DE and CA18DE		
intake:	30, 45, 60 degrees	
exhaust:	15, 45, 60 degrees	
GA16i		
intake:	30, 45, 60 degrees	
exhaust:	10, 45 degrees	
GA16DE		
intake:	30, 45, 60 degrees	
exhaust:	10, 45, 60 degrees	
SR20DE	44 deg. 53 min. -45 deg. 07 min.	
Camshaft and Bearings		
Bearing clearance		
E15 and E16		
No. 1,3,5	0.0014-0.0059 in.	0.035-0.150 mm
No. 2,4	0.0031-0.0079 in.	0.078-0.200 mm
CD17	0.0018-0.0059 in.	0.020-0.150 mm
CA16DE, CA18DE, GA16i, GA16DE and SR20DE	0.0018-0.0047 in.	0.045-0.120 mm
Journal diameter		
E15 and E16		
No. 1,3,5	1.6515-1.6522 in.	41.949-41.965 mm
No. 2,4	1.6498-1.6505 in.	41.906-41.922 mm
CD17	1.1795-1.1803 in.	29.960-29.980 mm
CA16DE and CA18DE	1.0998-1.1006 in.	27.935-27.955 mm
GA16i	1.6510-1.6518 in.	41.935-41.955 mm
GA16DE		
No. 1:	1.0998-1.1006 in.	27.935-27.955 mm
No. 2-5:	0.9423-0.9431 in.	23.935-23.955 mm
SR20DE	1.0998-1.1006 in.	27.935-27.955 mm
Camshaft out of round		
E15 and E16	0.0040 in. max.	0.10 mm
CD17	0.0020 in. max.	0.05 mm
CA16DE and CA18DE	0.0020 in. max.	0.05 mm
GA16i, GA16DE and SR20DE	0.0040 in. max.	0.10 mm

88163GN7

ENGINE MECHANICAL SPECIFICATIONS

Component	U.S.	Metric
Camshaft and Bearings		
Endplay		
E15 and E16	0.0160 max. in.	0.40 mm
CD17	0.0024-0.0067 in.	0.06-0.17 mm
CA16DE and CA18DE	0.0028-0.0059 in.	0.07-0.15 mm
GA16i	0.0012-0.0079 in.	0.03-0.20 mm
GA16DE	0.0045-0.0079 in.	0.115-0.200 mm
SR20DE	0.0022-0.0079 in.	0.055-0.200 mm
Lobe height		
E15 and E16		
intake:	1.4128-1.4226 in.	35.884-36.134 mm
exhaust:	1.4031-1.4130 in.	35.640-35.890 mm
CD17		
intake:	1.7500-1.7520 in.	44.450-44.500 mm
exhaust:	1.7894-1.7913 in.	45.450-45.500 mm
CA16DE and CA18DE	1.5931-1.5951 in.	40.485-40.515 mm
GA16i		
intake:	1.4147-1.4222 in.	35.933-36.123 mm
exhaust:	1.4073-1.4148 in.	35.746-35.936 mm
GA16DE		
intake:	1.5984-1.6059 in.	40.600-40.790 mm
exhaust:	1.5701-1.5776 in.	39.880-40.070 mm
SR20DE		
intake:	1.5121-1.5196 in.	38.408-38.598 mm
exhaust:	1.4921-1.5004 in.	37.920-38.110 mm
Lobe wear limit		
E15 and E16	0.0079 max. in.	0.20 mm
CD17		
intake:	1.7441 max. in.	44.300 mm
exhaust:	1.7835 max. in.	45.300 mm
CA16DE, CA18DE and SR20DE	0.0080 max. in.	0.20 mm
GA16i and GA16DE	0.0079 max. in.	0.20 mm
JACK SHAFT AND BEARING		
Journal clearance		
E15 and E16	0.0008-0.0059 in.	0.020-0.150 mm
End play		
E15 and E16	0.0018-0.0041 in.	0.045-0.105 mm
Fuel pump lobe height		
E15 and E16	1.094-1.098 in.	27.80-27.90 mm
ENGINE BLOCK		
Deck Warpage		
All engines	0.0059 max. in.	0.150 mm
Cylinder out of round		
E15 and E16	0.0006 max. in.	0.015 mm
CD17	0.0080 max. in.	0.200 mm
CA16DE, CA18DE, GA16i, GA16DE and SR20DE	0.0006 max. in.	0.015 mm
Cylinder taper		
E15 and E16	0.0008 max. in.	0.020 mm
CD17	0.0080 max. in.	0.200 mm
CA16DE, CA18DE, GA16i, GA16DE and SR20DE	0.0004 max. in.	0.010 mm
Piston to cylinder clearance		
E15 and E16	0.0009-0.0017 in.	0.023-0.043 mm
CD17	0.0020-0.0028 in.	0.050-0.070 mm
CA16DE, CA18DE, GA16i and GA16DE	0.0006-0.0014 in.	0.015-0.035 mm
SR20DE	0.0004-0.0012 in.	0.010-0.030 mm

88163GN8

ENGINE MECHANICAL SPECIFICATIONS

Component	U.S.	Metric
PISTON AND RINGS		
Piston pin hole diameter		
E15 and E16	0.7481-0.7485 in.	19.003-19.012 mm
CD17	0.9445-0.9448 in.	23.991-23.999 mm
CA16DE and CA18DE	0.7869-0.7874 in.	19.987-19.999 mm
GA16i and GA16DE	0.7475-0.7480 in.	18.987-18.999 mm
SR20DE	0.8656-0.8661 in.	21.987-21.999 mm
Ring side clearance		
E15 and E16		
top	0.0016-0.0080 in.	0.040-0.200 mm
2nd	0.0012-0.0080 in.	0.030-0.200 mm
oil	0.0020-0.0057 in.	0.050-0.145 mm
CD17		
top	0.0008-0.0080 in.	0.020-0.200 mm
2nd	0.0016-0.0059 in.	0.040-0.150 mm
oil	0.0012-0.0040 in.	0.030-0.100 mm
CA16DE and CA18DE		
top	0.0016-0.0400 in.	0.040-0.100 mm
2nd	0.0012-0.0400 in.	0.030-0.100 mm
oil	0.0010-0.0400 in.	0.025-0.100 mm
GA16i and GA16DE		
top	0.0016-0.0080 in.	0.040-0.200 mm
2nd	0.0012-0.0080 in.	0.030-0.200 mm
oil	snug	snug
SR20DE		
top	0.0018-0.0080 in.	0.045-0.200 mm
2nd	0.0012-0.0080 in.	0.030-0.200 mm
oil	snug	snug
Ring gap		
E15 and E16		
top	0.0079-0.0138 in.	0.200-0.350 mm
2nd	0.0059-0.0118 in.	0.150-0.300 mm
oil	0.0118-0.0354 in.	0.300-0.900 mm
CD17		
top	0.0079-0.0390 in.	0.200-1.000 mm
2nd	0.0079-0.0280 in.	0.200-0.700 mm
oil	0.0118-0.0240 in.	0.300-0.600 mm
CA16DE and CA18DE		
top	0.0087-0.0390 in.	0.220-1.000 mm
2nd	0.0075-0.0390 in.	0.190-1.000 mm
oil	0.0079-0.0390 in.	0.200-1.000 mm
GA16i and GA16DE		
top	0.0079-0.0390 in.	0.200-1.000 mm
2nd	0.0146-0.0390 in.	0.370-1.000 mm
oil	0.0079-0.0390 in.	0.200-1.000 mm
SR20DE		
top	0.0079-0.0390 in.	0.200-1.000 mm
2nd	0.0138-0.0390 in.	0.350-1.000 mm
oil	0.0079-0.0390 in.	0.200-1.000 mm
Piston pin diameter		
E15 and E16	0.7478-0.7480 in.	18.995-19.000 mm
CD17	0.9446-0.9449 in.	23.994-24.000 mm
CA16DE and CA18DE	0.7870-0.7874 in.	19.989-20.001 mm
GA16i and GA16DE	0.7476-0.7481 in.	18.989-19.001 mm
SR20DE	0.8656-0.8661 in.	21.987-21.999 mm
Piston pin clearance		
E15 and E16	0.0003-0.0005 in.	0.008-0.012 mm
CD17 and GA16DE	0.0000-0.0002 in.	0.000-0.004 mm
CA16DE, CA18DE and GA16i	0.0002-0.0007 in.	0.005-0.017 mm
SR20DE	0.0002-0.0009 in.	0.005-0.023 mm

88163GN9

ENGINE MECHANICAL SPECIFICATIONS

Component	U.S.	Metric
CONNECTING ROD		
Rod bend		
E15 and E16	0.0020 max. in.	0.050 mm
CD17, GA16i and GA16DE	0.0059 max. in.	0.150 mm
CA16DE and CA18DE	0.0040 max. in.	0.100 mm
SR20DE	0.0059 max. in.	0.150 mm
Big end play		
E15 and E16	0.020 max. in.	0.50 mm
CD17	0.012 max. in.	0.30 mm
CA16DE and CA18DE	0.016 max. in.	0.40 mm
CRANKSHAFT		
Main journal diameter		
E15 and E16	1.9663-1.9671 in.	49.943-49.964 mm
CD17	2.0847-2.0852 in.	52.951-52.964 mm
CA16DE and CA18DE	2.0847-2.0856 in.	52.951-52.975 mm
GA16i and GA16DE		
grade 0:	1.9668-1.9671 in.	49.956-49.964 mm
grade 1:	1.9665-1.9668 in.	49.948-49.956 mm
grade 2:	1.9661-1.9665 in.	49.940-49.948 mm
SR20DE		
grade 0:	2.1643-2.1646 in.	54.974-54.980 mm
grade 1:	2.1641-2.1643 in.	54.968-54.974 mm
grade 2:	2.1639-2.1641 in.	54.962-54.968 mm
grade 3:	2.1636-2.1639 in.	54.956-54.962 mm
Rod journal diameter		
E15 and E16	1.5730-1.5738 in.	39.954-39.974 mm
CD17	1.7701-1.7706 in.	44.961-44.974 mm
CA16DE and CA18DE	1.7698-1.7706 in.	44.954-44.974 mm
GA16i	1.5731-1.5738 in.	39.956-39.974 mm
GA16DE		
grade 0:	1.5735-1.5738 in.	39.968-39.974 mm
grade 1:	1.5733-1.5735 in.	39.962-39.968 mm
grade 2:	1.5731-1.5733 in.	39.956-39.962 mm
SR20DE		
grade 0:	1.8885-1.8887 in.	47.968-47.974 mm
grade 1:	1.8883-1.8885 in.	47.962-47.968 mm
grade 2:	1.8880-1.8883 in.	47.956-47.962 mm
Journal out of round		
E15, E16, CD17	0.0012 max. in.	0.030 mm
CA16DE, CA18DE, GA16i, GA16DE and SR20DE	0.0002 max. in.	0.005 mm
Crankshaft end play		
E15, E16, CD17 and SR20DE	0.0118 max. in.	0.300 mm
CA16DE, CA18DE, GA16i and GA16DE	0.0120 max. in.	0.300 mm
Main bearing clearance		
E15 and E16		
No. 1,5	0.0012-0.0039 in.	0.031-0.100 mm
No. 2,3,4	0.0012-0.0039 in.	0.031-0.100 mm
CD17	0.0015-0.0047 in.	0.039-0.120 mm
CA16DE, CA18DE and GA16i	0.0008-0.0040 in.	0.021-0.100 mm
GA16DE	0.0007-0.0040 in.	0.018-0.100 mm
SR20DE	0.0002-0.0020 in.	0.004-0.050 mm
Rod bearing clearance		
E15 and E16	0.0012-0.0039 in.	0.031-0.100 mm
CD17	0.0009-0.0047 in.	0.024-0.120 mm
CA16DE and CA18DE	0.0007-0.0040 in.	0.018-0.100 mm
GA16i and GA16DE	0.0004-0.0040 in.	0.010-0.100 mm
SR20DE	0.0008-0.0035 in.	0.020-0.090 mm

88163GP0

TORQUE SPECIFICATIONS

Component	U.S.	Metric
Belt/Chain Tensioner		
E15 and E16	12-15 ft. lbs.	14-20 Nm
CA16DE and CA18DE	23-31 ft. lbs.	31-42 Nm
GA16i	9-14 ft. lbs.	13-19 Nm
GA16DE	4-9 ft. lbs.	6-12 Nm
SR20DE	5-6 ft. lbs.	6-8 Nm
CD17	27-34 ft. lbs.	36-44 Nm
Camshaft Bearing Cap		
CA16DE and CA18DE	7-9 ft. lbs.	10-12 Nm
GA16DE	7-9 ft. lbs.	10-12 Nm
SR20DE		
1st step:	1.4 ft. lbs.	2 Nm
2nd step:	4.3 ft. lbs.	6 Nm
3rd step:		
bolts A,B,C:	7-9 ft. lbs.	9-12 Nm
bolt D:	13-19 ft. lbs.	18-25 Nm
CD17	13-16 ft. lbs.	18-22 Nm
Camshaft Pulley		
E15 and E16	4-6 ft. lbs.	5-8 Nm
CA16DE and CA18DE	4-6 ft. lbs.	5-8 Nm
GA16i	72-94 ft. lbs.	98-127 Nm
GA16DE	72-94 ft. lbs.	98-127 Nm
SR20DE upper:	32-43 ft. lbs.	43-58 Nm
SR20DE lower:	101-116 ft. lbs.	137-157 Nm
CD17	68-75 ft. lbs.	92-102 Nm
Cylinder Head		
1982-83 E15 and E16		
1st step:	33 ft. lbs.	44 Nm
2nd step:	51-54 ft. lbs.	69-74 Nm
1984-86 E15ET and E16		
1st step:	10 ft. lbs.	14 Nm
2nd step:	20 ft. lbs.	28 Nm
3rd step:	30 ft. lbs.	41 Nm
4th step:	40 ft. lbs.	52 Nm
5th step:	51-54 ft. lbs.	69-74 Nm
1987-88 E16i		
1st step:	22 ft. lbs.	30 Nm
2nd step:	51 ft. lbs.	69 Nm
3rd step:	loosen all bolts completely	
4th step:	22 ft. lbs.	30 Nm
5th step:	51-54 ft. lbs.	69-74 Nm
CA16DE and CA18DE		
1st step:	22 ft. lbs.	30 Nm
2nd step:	76 ft. lbs.	103 Nm
3rd step:	loosen all bolts completely	
4th step:	22 ft. lbs.	30 Nm
5th step:	76 ft. lbs.	103 Nm
6th step:	turn bolts (1) 80-85 degrees and (2-10) 60-65 degrees	
GA16i		
1st step:	22 ft. lbs.	30 Nm
2nd step:	47 ft. lbs.	64 Nm
3rd step:	loosen all bolts completely	
4th step:	22 ft. lbs.	30 Nm
5th step:	turn bolts (11-15) to 4.6-6.1 ft. lbs.	
6th step:	plus or not plus an additional 85-90 degrees	
GA16DE		
1st step:	22 ft. lbs.	30 Nm
2nd step:	43 ft. lbs.	60 Nm
3rd step:	loosen all bolts completely	
4th step:	22 ft. lbs.	30 Nm
5th step:	plus an additional 50-55 degrees	

88163GP1

TORQUE SPECIFICATIONS

Component	U.S.	Metric
Cylinder Head		
SR20DE		
1st step:	29 ft. lbs.	39 Nm
2nd step:	58 ft. lbs.	79 Nm
3rd step:	loosen all bolts completely	
4th step:	25-33 ft. lbs.	35-45 Nm
5th step:	turn bolts 90-100 degrees	
6th step:	turn bolts 90-100 degrees	
CD17		
1st step:	29 ft. lbs.	39 Nm
2nd step:	58 ft. lbs.	79 Nm
3rd step:	72-80 ft. lbs.	98-108 Nm
Connecting Rod		
E15, E16, CD17	23-27 ft. lbs.	31-37 Nm
CA16DE, CA18DE, GA16i	30-33 ft. lbs.	41-48 Nm
GA16DE, SR20DE		
1st step:	10-12 ft. lbs.	14-16 Nm
2nd step: GA16DE	turn bolts an additional 40 degrees	38-45 Nm
SR20DE	turn bolts, 60 degrees	
Crankshaft Bearing Cap		
E15 and E16	36-43 ft. lbs.	49-59 Nm
CA16DE, CA18DE, CD17	33-40 ft. lbs.	44-54 Nm
GA16i and GA16DE	34-38 ft. lbs.	46-53 Nm
SR20DE	51-61 ft. lbs.	69-83 Nm
Crankshaft Damper		
E15		
1983-87 E15ET and E16	108-145 ft. lbs.	147-197 Nm
1988-89 E16	83-108 ft. lbs.	113-147 Nm
CA16DE and CA18DE	80-94 ft. lbs.	109-128 Nm
GA16i	105-112 ft. lbs.	145-152 Nm
GA16DE	132-152 ft. lbs.	179-207 Nm
SR20DE	98-112 ft. lbs.	133-152 Nm
CD17	90-98 ft. lbs.	122-133 Nm
Flywheel		
1982-87 E15 and E16	58-65 ft. lbs.	78-88 Nm
1988-89 E16		
M/T:	58-65 ft. lbs.	78-88 Nm
A/T:	69-76 ft. lbs.	94-103 Nm
CA16DE, CA18DE and SR20DE	61-69 ft. lbs.	83-94 Nm
GA16i	69-76 ft. lbs.	94-103 Nm
GA16DE		
M/T:	61-69 ft. lbs.	83-94 Nm
A/T:	69-76 ft. lbs.	94-103 Nm
CD17	72-80 ft. lbs.	98-108 Nm
Intake Manifold		
1982-83 E15 and E16	11-14 ft. lbs.	14-20 Nm
1984-91 E16, GA16i and GA16DE	12-15 ft. lbs.	16-22 Nm
CA16DE and CA18DE	14-19 ft. lbs.	19-26 Nm
SR20DE	13-15 ft. lbs.	18-22 Nm
CD17	13-16 ft. lbs.	18-24 Nm
Intake Plenum		
All EFI engines	13-15 ft. lbs.	18-22 Nm
Exhaust Manifold		
All engines, except	12-15 ft. lbs.	16-22 Nm
CA16DE, CA18DE and SR20DE	27-35 ft. lbs.	34-48 Nm
GA16DE	16-21 ft. lbs.	22-25 Nm
Exhaust Manifold-to-Pipe		
All engines	14-31 ft. lbs.	20-43 Nm

88163GP2

TORQUE SPECIFICATIONS

Component	U.S.	Metric
Oil Pump Bolts		
E15 and E16	7-9 ft. lbs.	10-12 Nm
CA16DE and CA18DE	5-6 ft. lbs.	7-8 Nm
GA16i	5-6 ft. lbs.	7-8 Nm
GA16DE	5-6 ft. lbs.	7-8 Nm
SR20DE	5-6 ft. lbs.	7-8 Nm
CD17	4-5 ft. lbs.	5-7 Nm
Spark Plug		
All engines	11-14 ft. lbs.	15-20 Nm
Water Pump		
E15 and E16	7-10 ft. lbs.	10-14 Nm
CA16DE and CA18DE	8-12 ft. lbs.	11-15 Nm
GA16i	5-6 ft. lbs.	6-8 Nm
GA16DE	6-8 ft. lbs.	8-10 Nm
SR20DE	5-6 ft. lbs.	6-8 Nm
CD17	12-14 ft. lbs.	16-20 Nm
Water Pump Pulley		
E15, E16, CA16DE and CA18DE	3-4 ft. lbs.	4-5 Nm
GA16i	6-8 ft. lbs.	8-10 Nm
GA16DE	6-8 ft. lbs.	8-10 Nm
SR20DE	5-6 ft. lbs.	6-8 Nm
CD17	6-8 ft. lbs.	8-10 Nm
Thermostat Housing		
E15 and E16	3-4 ft. lbs.	4-5 Nm
CA16DE and CA18DE	5-6 ft. lbs.	7-8 Nm
GA16i	6-8 ft. lbs.	8-10 Nm
GA16DE	6-8 ft. lbs.	8-10 Nm
SR20DE	6-8 ft. lbs.	8-10 Nm
CD17	6-8 ft. lbs.	8-10 Nm
Front Cover		
E15 and E16	3-4 ft. lbs.	4-5 Nm
CA16DE and CA18DE	4-5 ft. lbs.	6-7 Nm
GA16i	5-6 ft. lbs.	6-8 Nm
GA16DE	5-6 ft. lbs.	6-8 Nm
SR20DE	5-6 ft. lbs.	6-8 Nm
CD17	5-6 ft. lbs.	6-8 Nm
Jack Shaft Pulley		
E15 and E16	4-6 ft. lbs.	5-8 Nm
Oil Pan		
E15 and E16	3-4 ft. lbs.	4-5 Nm
CA16DE and CA18DE	5-6 ft. lbs.	6-8 Nm
GA16i	5-6 ft. lbs.	6-8 Nm
GA16DE	5-6 ft. lbs.	6-8 Nm
SR20DE	5-6 ft. lbs.	6-8 Nm
CD17	5-6 ft. lbs.	6-8 Nm
Rocker Arm Shaft		
E15 and E16	12-15 ft. lbs.	14-20 Nm
GA16i	27-30 ft. lbs.	37-41 Nm

88163GP3

USING A VACUUM GAUGE

White needle = steady needle   *Dark needle = drifting needle*

The vacuum gauge is one of the most useful and easy-to-use diagnostic tools. It is inexpensive, easy to hook up, and provides valuable information about the condition of your engine.

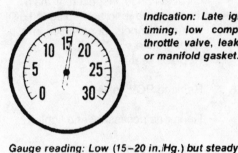

Indication: *Normal engine in good condition*

Gauge reading: Steady, from 17–22 in./Hg.

Indication: *Sticking valve or ignition miss*

Gauge reading: Needle fluctuates from 15–20 in./Hg. at idle

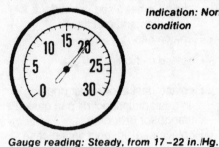

Indication: *Late ignition or valve timing, low compression, stuck throttle valve, leaking carburetor or manifold gasket.*

Gauge reading: Low (15–20 in./Hg.) but steady

Indication: *Improper carburetor adjustment, or minor intake leak at carburetor or manifold*

NOTE: *Bad fuel injector O-rings may also cause this reading.*

Gauge reading: Drifting needle

Indication: *Weak valve springs, worn valve stem guides, or leaky cylinder head gasket (vibrating excessively at all speeds).*

NOTE: *A plugged catalytic converter may also cause this reading.*

Gauge reading: Needle fluctuates as engine speed increases

Indication: *Burnt valve or improper valve clearance. The needle will drop when the defective valve operates.*

Gauge reading: Steady needle, but drops regularly

Indication: *Choked muffler or obstruction in system. Speed up the engine. Choked muffler will exhibit a slow drop of vacuum to zero.*

Gauge reading: Gradual drop in reading at idle

Indication: *Worn valve guides*

Gauge reading: Needle vibrates excessively at idle, but steadies as engine speed increases

TCCS3C01

Troubleshooting Engine Mechanical Problems

Problem	Cause	Solution
External oil leaks	• Cylinder head cover RTV sealant broken or improperly seated	• Replace sealant; inspect cylinder head cover sealant flange and cylinder head sealant surface for distortion and cracks
	• Oil filler cap leaking or missing	• Replace cap
	• Oil filter gasket broken or improperly seated	• Replace oil filter
	• Oil pan side gasket broken, improperly seated or opening in RTV sealant	• Replace gasket or repair opening in sealant; inspect oil pan gasket flange for distortion
	• Oil pan front oil seal broken or improperly seated	• Replace seal; inspect timing case cover and oil pan seal flange for distortion
	• Oil pan rear oil seal broken or improperly seated	• Replace seal; inspect oil pan rear oil seal flange; inspect rear main bearing cap for cracks, plugged oil return channels, or distortion in seal groove
	• Timing case cover oil seal broken or improperly seated	• Replace seal
	• Excess oil pressure because of restricted PCV valve	• Replace PCV valve
	• Oil pan drain plug loose or has stripped threads	• Repair as necessary and tighten
	• Rear oil gallery plug loose	• Use appropriate sealant on gallery plug and tighten
	• Rear camshaft plug loose or improperly seated	• Seat camshaft plug or replace and seal, as necessary
Excessive oil consumption	• Oil level too high	• Drain oil to specified level
	• Oil with wrong viscosity being used	• Replace with specified oil
	• PCV valve stuck closed	• Replace PCV valve
	• Valve stem oil deflectors (or seals) are damaged, missing, or incorrect type	• Replace valve stem oil deflectors
	• Valve stems or valve guides worn	• Measure stem-to-guide clearance and repair as necessary
	• Poorly fitted or missing valve cover baffles	• Replace valve cover
	• Piston rings broken or missing	• Replace broken or missing rings
	• Scuffed piston	• Replace piston
	• Incorrect piston ring gap	• Measure ring gap, repair as necessary
	• Piston rings sticking or excessively loose in grooves	• Measure ring side clearance, repair as necessary
	• Compression rings installed upside down	• Repair as necessary
	• Cylinder walls worn, scored, or glazed	• Repair as necessary

TCCS3C01

Troubleshooting Engine Mechanical Problems

Problem	Cause	Solution
Excessive oil consumption (cont.)	· Piston ring gaps not properly staggered · Excessive main or connecting rod bearing clearance	· Repair as necessary · Measure bearing clearance, repair as necessary
No oil pressure	· Low oil level · Oil pressure gauge, warning lamp or sending unit inaccurate · Oil pump malfunction · Oil pressure relief valve sticking · Oil passages on pressure side of pump obstructed · Oil pickup screen or tube obstructed · Loose oil inlet tube	· Add oil to correct level · Replace oil pressure gauge or warning lamp · Replace oil pump · Remove and inspect oil pressure relief valve assembly · Inspect oil passages for obstruction · Inspect oil pickup for obstruction · Tighten or seal inlet tube
Low oil pressure	· Low oil level · Inaccurate gauge, warning lamp or sending unit · Oil excessively thin because of dilution, poor quality, or improper grade · Excessive oil temperature · Oil pressure relief spring weak or sticking · Oil inlet tube and screen assembly has restriction or air leak · Excessive oil pump clearance · Excessive main, rod, or camshaft bearing clearance	· Add oil to correct level · Replace oil pressure gauge or warning lamp · Drain and refill crankcase with recommended oil · Correct cause of overheating engine · Remove and inspect oil pressure relief valve assembly · Remove and inspect oil inlet tube and screen assembly. (Fill inlet tube with lacquer thinner to locate leaks.) · Measure clearances · Measure bearing clearances, repair as necessary
High oil pressure	· Improper oil viscosity · Oil pressure gauge or sending unit inaccurate · Oil pressure relief valve sticking closed	· Drain and refill crankcase with correct viscosity oil · Replace oil pressure gauge · Remove and inspect oil pressure relief valve assembly
Main bearing noise	· Insufficient oil supply · Main bearing clearance excessive · Bearing insert missing · Crankshaft end-play excessive · Improperly tightened main bearing cap bolts · Loose flywheel or drive plate · Loose or damaged vibration damper	· Inspect for low oil level and low oil pressure · Measure main bearing clearance, repair as necessary · Replace missing insert · Measure end-play, repair as necessary · Tighten bolts with specified torque · Tighten flywheel or drive plate attaching bolts · Repair as necessary

TCCS3C01

Troubleshooting Engine Mechanical Problems

Problem	Cause	Solution
Connecting rod bearing noise	• Insufficient oil supply	• Inspect for low oil level and low oil pressure
	• Carbon build-up on piston	• Remove carbon from piston crown
	• Bearing clearance excessive or bearing missing	• Measure clearance, repair as necessary
	• Crankshaft connecting rod journal out-of-round	• Measure journal dimensions, repair or replace as necessary
	• Misaligned connecting rod or cap	• Repair as necessary
	• Connecting rod bolts tightened improperly	• Tighten bolts with specified torque
Piston noise	• Piston-to-cylinder wall clearance excessive (scuffed piston)	• Measure clearance and examine piston
	• Cylinder walls excessively tapered or out-of-round	• Measure cylinder wall dimensions, rebore cylinder
	• Piston ring broken	• Replace all rings on piston
	• Loose or seized piston pin	• Measure piston-to-pin clearance, repair as necessary
	• Connecting rods misaligned	• Measure rod alignment, straighten or replace
	• Piston ring side clearance excessively loose or tight	• Measure ring side clearance, repair as necessary
	• Carbon build-up on piston is excessive	• Remove carbon from piston
Valve actuating component noise	• Insufficient oil supply	• Check for: (a) Low oil level (b) Low oil pressure (c) Wrong hydraulic tappets (d) Restricted oil gallery (e) Excessive tappet to bore clearance
	• Rocker arms or pivots worn	• Replace worn rocker arms or pivots
	• Foreign objects or chips in hydraulic tappets	• Clean tappets
	• Excessive tappet leak-down	• Replace valve tappet
	• Tappet face worn	• Replace tappet; inspect corresponding cam lobe for wear
	• Broken or cocked valve springs	• Properly seat cocked springs; replace broken springs
	• Stem-to-guide clearance excessive	• Measure stem-to-guide clearance, repair as required
	• Valve bent	• Replace valve
	• Loose rocker arms	• Check and repair as necessary
	• Valve seat runout excessive	• Regrind valve seat/valves
	• Missing valve lock	• Install valve lock
	• Excessive engine oil	• Correct oil level

TCCS3C01

4

DRIVEABILITY AND EMISSION CONTROLS

EMISSION CONTROLS

♦ See Figure 1

There·are three types of automotive pollutants: crankcase fumes, exhaust gases and gasoline evaporation. The components used to control these pollutants, make up the emission control system. Emission system components vary greatly according to engine type, application and model year, refer to the vehicle emissions label for specific application information.

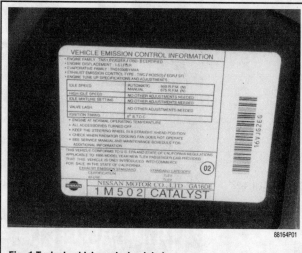

Fig. 1 Typical vehicle emission label

Automatic Temperature Controlled (ATC) Air Cleaner

OPERATION

♦ See Figures 2 and 3

Carbureted and Throttle Body Injected Engines

The rate of fuel atomization varies with the temperature of the air that the fuel is being mixed with, Cold air being drawn into the engine causes a denser and richer air/fuel mixture, inefficient fuel atomization, thus, more hydrocarbons in the exhaust gas. Hot air being drawn into the engine causes a leaner air/fuel mixture and more efficient atomization and combustion for less hydrocarbons in the exhaust gases.

The automatic temperature controlled air cleaner is designed so that the temperature of the ambient air being drawn into the engine is automatically controlled, to hold temperature, consequently, the fuel/air ratio at a constant rate for efficient fuel combustion.

A temperature sensing vacuum switch controls the vacuum applied to a vacuum motor, operating a valve in the intake snorkel of the air cleaner. When the engine is cold or the air being drawn into the engine is cold, the vacuum motor opens the valve, allowing air heated by the exhaust manifold to be drawn into the engine. As the engine warms up, the temperature sensing unit shuts off the vacuum applied to the vacuum motor which allows the valve to close, shutting off the heated air and allowing cooler, outside (under hood) air to be drawn into the engine.

INSPECTION & TESTING

System Inspection

When the air around the temperature sensor of the unit mounted inside the air cleaner housing reaches 100°F (38°C), the sensor should block the flow of vacuum to the air control valve vacuum motor. When the temperature around the temperature sensor is below 100°F (38°C), the sensor should allow vacuum to pass onto the air valve vacuum motor thus blocking off the air cleaner snorkel to under hood (unheated) air.

When the temperature around the sensor is above 118°F (48°C), the air control valve should be completely open to under hood air.

If the air cleaner fails to operate correctly, check for loose or broken vacuum hoses. If the hoses are not the cause, proceed to temperature and/or vacuum motor testing.

Temperature Sensor Testing

♦ See Figures 4 and 5

➡This procedure must be started when the engine is completely cold; if not use dry ice to cool the temperature sensor.

1. Disconnect·the vacuum hose from the vacuum motor.
2. Using a vacuum T-type connector, connect a vacuum gauge in series with the vacuum motor. Reconnect the hose to the vacuum motor.
3. Place a thermometer on the air cleaner housing, as close as possible to temperature sensor.
4. Start the engine and observe the vacuum gauge and air door position, at the following temperatures:
   • Temperature below 118°F (48°C) the vacuum gauge should read at least 4 inches of vacuum—Door fully open (fully raised)
   • Temperature between 100–118°F (38–48°C) the vacuum gauge should read approximately 4 inches of vacuum—Door ½ open (partially raised)
   • Temperature above 100°F (38°C) the vacuum gauge should read approximately 2 inches of vacuum—Door fully closed (completely down)
5. If the door does not perform as specified, remove the vacuum supply hose from the temperature sensor. Verify that at least 4 inches of vacuum is available to the sensor.
   • If there an adequate vacuum supply to the temperature sensor, replace the ATC temperature sensor
   • If there is not an adequate vacuum supply to the temperature sensor, check and repair vacuum source problem

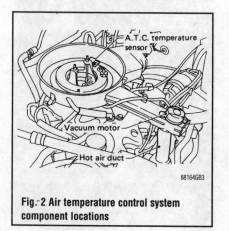

Fig.·2 Air temperature control system component locations

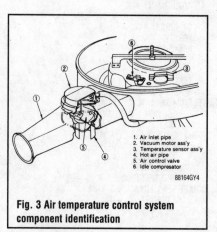

1. Air inlet pipe
2. Vacuum motor ass'y
3. Temperature sensor ass'y
4. Hot air pipe
5. Air control valve
6. Idle compressor

Fig. 3 Air temperature control system component identification

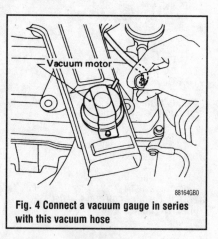

Fig. 4 Connect a vacuum gauge in series with this vacuum hose

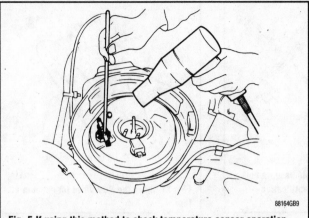

Fig. 5 If using this method to check temperature sensor operation, use extreme care when heating the sensor. Damage to the sensor can occur if it is exposed to extreme heat

Vacuum Motor Testing

1. Disconnect the rubber hose from the vacuum motor.
2. Connect a vacuum pump to the motor and apply vacuum.
3. The motor should hold vacuum indefinitely.
  - If the motor moves the air door and holds vacuum, the vacuum motor is operating properly.
  - If the motor holds vacuum, but does not move, proceed to the next step.
  - If the motor does not hold vacuum, replace the vacuum motor.
4. Inspect the ATC system air door for sticking or binding.
  - If a problem is found with the door, repair as required.
  - If no problems are found with the door, replace the vacuum motor.

Air Induction (Injection) System

OPERATION

The air induction system is used to send fresh secondary air to the exhaust manifold. During normal engine operation, the exhaust pressure usually pulsates in response to the opening and closing of the exhaust valves. By utilizing the vacuum created by the exhaust pulsation, secondary air can be drawn into the exhaust manifold, in proportion with the vacuum supply. The additional air helps complete the combustion of unburned emissions in the exhaust manifold, thereby reducing CO and HC emissions. The secondary air also increases the efficiency of the TWC converter, further reducing emissions.

The system consists of an air induction valve assembly, a filter, hoses and the connecting tubes. The induction valves contain either one or two reed valve assemblies. The reed valves prevent exhaust from flowing back through the system, into the air cleaner. Some early systems use a thermal vacuum valve to prevent system operation during extreme cold conditions and after the engine has reached operating temperature. Later model engines, use a solenoid, which is controlled by the ECM, to perform this function. ECM controlled systems operate only when the engine is cold or when hot and idling.

Some engines may use an addition valve assembly to prevent backfire, during the initial period of deceleration. This valve is known as the Anti-backfire (AB) valve.

TESTING

Anti-Backfire (AB) Valve

◆ See Figure 6

1. Warm the engine to normal operating temperature.
2. Disconnect the hose from the air cleaner and place a finger near the outlet.
3. Run the engine at about 3000 rpm under no load, then return to idle. A suction should be felt. If no vacuum is felt, replace the AB valve.

Air Induction Valve (AIV)

MODELS WITHOUT AIV CONTROL SOLENOID

Disconnect the air induction tube from the tube leading to the exhaust manifold. Place the tube to your mouth, then suck on the tube (air should move freely through the valve); try to blow through the tube (air should not flow through it). If the valve does not respond correctly, replace it.

MODELS WITH AIV CONTROL SOLENOID

◆ See Figures 7 and 8

1. Check the air valve and control valve for binding or damage. Repair or replace the valve, if required.
2. Disconnect the injection hose. At the exhaust tube side, suck and blow into the hose and make sure that air flow does not exist.
3. Connect a vacuum pump to the air injection control valve located at the bottom of the valve case.
4. With vacuum applied to the valve, repeat Step 1. Air should flow freely to the exhaust pipe, and should not flow in the opposite direction.
5. If the valve fails to perform as specified replace the AIV valve assembly.

AIV Control Solenoid

◆ See Figures 9 and 10

1. Mark and tag all vacuum lines attached to the control valve. Once marked, remove the hoses from the control assembly.
2. Apply 12V to terminal **2**, and ground to terminal **1**.
3. With the solenoid energized, check for air passage between vacuum fittings as follows:
  - Ports A and B—Passage open—air should pass freely
  - Ports B and C—Passage blocked—no air should not pass
4. Disconnect the 12V power supply. With the solenoid de-energized check for air passages between the vacuum fittings as follows:
  - Ports A and B —Passage blocked—no air should not pass
  - Ports B and C —Passage open—air should pass freely

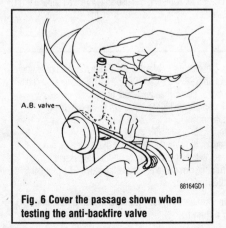

Fig. 6 Cover the passage shown when testing the anti-backfire valve

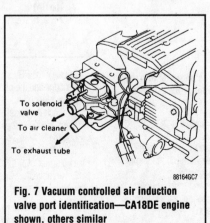

Fig. 7 Vacuum controlled air induction valve port identification—CA18DE engine shown, others similar

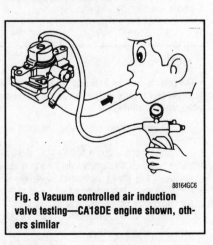

Fig. 8 Vacuum controlled air induction valve testing—CA18DE engine shown, others similar

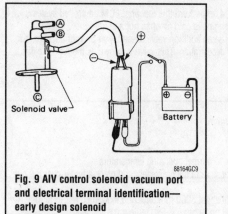

Fig. 9 AIV control solenoid vacuum port and electrical terminal identification—early design solenoid

88164GC9

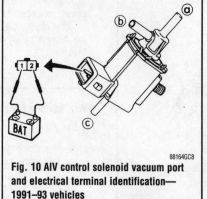

Fig. 10 AIV control solenoid vacuum port and electrical terminal identification—1991–93 vehicles

88164GC8

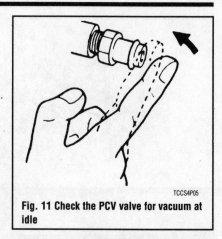

Fig. 11 Check the PCV valve for vacuum at idle

TCCS4P05

5. If the solenoid did not perform as specified, replace the EGR/EVAP solenoid/valve assembly.

AIV Thermal Vacuum Valve

1. Remove the thermal vacuum valve from the engine.
2. Plug one of the vacuum ports.
3. Apply vacuum to the air cleaner port; it should allow vacuum to pass. Repeat the test for other port. If either port was closed, replace the vacuum valve.

✴✴ WARNING

Do not allow water to enter the vacuum passages when testing, or the valve may be damaged.

4. Place the valve in a container of water with a thermometer. Heat the water and Repeat Steps 2 and 3. Observe the valve operation at the following temperature.

- Below 59°F (15°C)—valve should be closed (vacuum should not pass)
- Between 59–140°F (15–60°C)—valve should be open (vacuum should pass)
- Above 140°F (60°C)—valve should be closed (vacuum should not pass)

5. If the thermal vacuum valve did not perform as specified, replace the valve.

Catalyst Warm-up System

OPERATION

This system was used on 1982–85 vehicles with carburetors. The MPG models are controlled by the ECU.

The catalyst warm-up system increases engine speed during warm-up periods to raise the temperature of the catalyst, thereby decreasing exhaust emissions.

The system consists of a vacuum switching valve, temperature sensor, neutral switch and vacuum delay valve. This system uses the throttle opener servo diaphragm as described earlier in this section.

TESTING & INSPECTION

1. Start the engine.

➡**The engine must be between 59–104°F (15–40°C) to begin testing. Accurate test results will not be obtained if engine temperatures are not within specifications.**

2. Shift gears to make sure that engine speed increases when gear is in neutral.

3. Warm the engine above 104°F (40°C) and make sure the engine rpm decreases and does not change when the gear is shifted to neutral. If the engine speed does not vary at all, disconnect the vacuum switching valve.

4. With the engine running, apply 12 volts to the valve and make sure the engine speed increases and ignition timing retards. If no change occurs, test the vacuum switch, opener servo, distributor and vacuum hoses.

Crankcase Ventilation System

OPERATION

▶ **See Figures 11, 12 and 13**

When the engine is running, a small portion of the gases which are formed in the combustion chamber during combustion, leak by the piston rings and enter the crankcase. Since these gases are under pressure they tend to escape from the crankcase and enter into the atmosphere. If these gases were allowed to remain in the crankcase for any length of time, they would contaminate the engine oil and cause sludge to build up. If the gases are allowed to escape into the atmosphere, they would pollute the air, for they contain unburned hydrocarbons. The crankcase emission control equipment recycles these gases back into the engine combustion chamber where they are burned.

Crankcase gases are recycled in the following manner: when the engine is running, clean filtered air (from the carburetor air filter) is drawn into the crankcase or the rocker cover, through a hose. As the air passes through the crankcase it mixes with combustion gases, then carries them (out of the crankcase) through the PCV valve and into the intake manifold. After they enter the intake manifold they are drawn into the combustion chamber and burned.

The most critical component in the system is the PCV valve. This vacuum controlled valve regulates the amount of gases which are recycled into the combustion chamber. At low engine speeds, the valve is partially closed, limiting the flow of gases into the intake manifold. At increased engine speeds, the valve opens to admit greater quantities of the gases into the intake manifold. If the valve should become blocked or plugged, the gases will be prevented from escaping from the crankcase by the normal route. Since these gases are under pressure, they will find their own way out of the crankcase. This alternate route is usually a weak oil seal or gasket in the engine. As the gas escapes by the gasket, it also creates an oil leak. Besides causing oil leaks, a clogged PCV valve also allows these gases to remain in the crankcase for an extended period of time, promoting the formation of sludge in the engine.

The crankcase emission control equipment consists of a positive crankcase ventilation valve (PCV), an oil filler cap (sealed) and hoses (connected to the equipment). The CA16DE, CA18DE and SR20DE engines use an external oil separator (in the PCV line) to keep excess oil in the crankcase, away from the PCV valve.

TESTING

To check the PCV system, inspect the PCV valve, the air filter(s), the hoses, the connections and the oil separator (SR20DE, CA16DE and CA18DE engines); check for leaks, plugged valve(s) and/or filters, then replace or tighten, as necessary.

To check the hoses, use compressed air to free them or replace them. If the air filters are dirty, replace them.

Test the PCV valve as follows:

1. Pull the PCV valve out of the cylinder head with the engine running. Place a finger over the valve inlet. A strong vacuum should be present.

2. Remove the valve from the hose. Lightly shake the valve. The plunger should be audible as it rattles inside.

➡**If the valve fails to function as outlined, replace it with a new one; DO NOT attempt to clean or adjust it.**

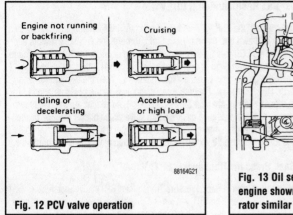

Fig. 12 PCV valve operation

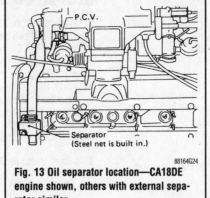

Fig. 13 Oil separator location—CA18DE engine shown, others with external separator similar

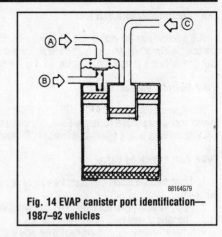

Fig. 14 EVAP canister port identification—1987–92 vehicles

REMOVAL & INSTALLATION

PCV Valve

1. Disconnect the valve from the PCV hose.
2. Unscrew the PCV valve out of the rocker cover.
3. Screw the valve into the rocker cover and carefully tighten the valve.

✳✳ WARNING

Do not overtighten the valve. The valve will seal with a light amount of torque.

4. Connect the vacuum hose to the valve and secure with the retaining clamp.

PCV Filter

Replace the PCV filter inside the air cleaner, at the recommended maintenance intervals, or more frequently if operating in dusty or smoggy conditions.

To replace the PCV filter, remove the air cleaner cover and remove the filter cartridge.

Evaporative Emission Controls

OPERATION

During system operation, fuel vapors and/or liquid are routed to the liquid/vapor separator or check valve, where liquid fuel is directed back into the fuel tank as fuel vapors flow into the charcoal filled canister. The charcoal absorbs and stores the fuel vapors when the engine is not running or at idle. When the throttle plates are opened, vacuum from above the throttle plate (ported vacuum) is routed through a vacuum signal line, to the purge control valve on the canister. The control valve opens, the fuel vapors move from the canister through a purge line, into the intake manifold and the combustion chambers.

All models use a sealed fuel tank, carbon canister/vapor vent line, fuel check valve, vacuum signal line, a canister purge line and a fuel tank vacuum relief valve. Carbureted engines have an additional vent line and switching valve, which are connected to the carburetor float bowl vent. Depending on the specific application, the system will use either thermal control valve or a purge control valve/solenoid, to prevent system operation during engine warm-up. Early systems use a thermal control valve to close off the vacuum signal to the purge control valve until engine temperature is above 122°F (50°C). On later systems, this function is controlled by the ECM, through the EGR/Canister Control Solenoid. The ECM also prevents operation during idle and when high engine speeds.

TESTING

Check the hoses for proper connections and damage. Replace as necessary. Check the vapor separator tank for fuel leaks, distortion and dents, then replace as necessary.

EVAP Carbon Canister/Purge Control Valve

1982–86 VEHICLES

The carbon canister has an air filter in the bottom of the canister. The filter element should be checked once a year or every 12,000 miles (19,000 km); more frequently if the car is operated in dusty areas. Replace the filter by pulling it out of the bottom of the canister and installing a new one.

1. Disconnect the rubber hose between the canister control valve and the T-fitting, at the T-fitting.
2. Apply vacuum to the hose leading to the control valve (upper vacuum port).
3. The valve should hold vacuum indefinitely. If the control valve leaks, remove the top cover of the valve and check for a dislocated or cracked diaphragm. If the diaphragm is damaged, a repair kit containing a new diaphragm, retainer and spring is available, replace it.

1987–92 VEHICLES

▶ See Figure 14

1. Disconnect the canister and remove if necessary.
2. Blow air into port **A** and ensure that there is no leakage.
3. Blow air into ports **B** and ensure that there is leakage.

1993–96 VEHICLES

▶ See Figure 15

1. Disconnect the canister and remove if necessary.
2. Blow air into port **A** and ensure that there is no leakage. If leakage occurs, replace the canister assembly.
3. Apply 4–6 in. Hg (13.5–20 kPa) of vacuum to port **A**.
4. Cover port **D** with your hand while blowing air into port **C**. Air should flow freely from port **C** to port **B**.
5. If the canister/purge valve assembly does not perform as specified, replace the assembly.

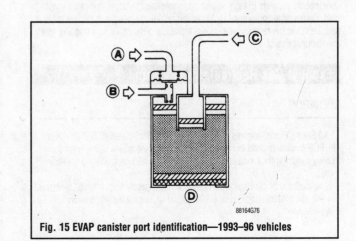

Fig. 15 EVAP canister port identification—1993–96 vehicles

EVAP Control Solenoid Valve

This solenoid cuts the vacuum to the EGR valve and EVAP purge valve on the charcoal canister off at both low and high RPM. For testing information refer to EGR Control Solenoid testing information found in this Section.

EVAP Thermal Vacuum Valve

This valve cuts the vacuum to the EGR valve, EVAP purge valve and the distributor during cold engine operation. For testing information refer to EGR Thermal Vacuum Valve testing information found in this section.

EVAP Vent Switching Valve

1. Disconnect the rubber hose from the vent valve control port (upper vacuum port).
2. Apply vacuum to the hose leading to the control valve.
3. The valve should hold vacuum indefinitely.
• If the valve holds vacuum, proceed to the next step.
• If the control valve leaks, remove the top cover of the valve and check for a dislocated or cracked diaphragm. Repair or replace as necessary.
4. Disconnect the vent line from the carburetor float bowl.
5. Connect a vacuum pump to the switching valve vent line port.
6. With the engine **OFF**, apply vacuum to vent line hose. The valve should NOT hold vacuum.
7. Start the engine and apply vacuum to the to the vent line, vacuum should hold.
8. Replace the Vent switching valve if it does not perform as specified.

Fuel Tank Vacuum Relief Valve

Wipe the valve housing clean. Suck air through the cap. A slight resistance indicates that the valve is in good condition. Resistance should disappear when the valve clicks. If the valve is clogged or if no resistance is felt, replace the fuel cap.

Fuel Check Valve

1. Blow air through the connector on the tank side. A considerable resistance should be felt and a portion of air flow should be directed toward the canister.
2. Blow air through the connector on the canister side. Air flow should be smoothly directed toward the fuel tank.
3. If the valve does not perform as specified replace the fuel check valve.
4. If the valve is equipped with an internal rollover valve, test the rollover function as follows:
   a. Tilt the valve to 90° and repeat Steps 1 and 2.
   b. Tilt the valve to 180°and repeat Steps 1 and 2.
   c. Air should not be allowed to pass in either test. If air does pass when the valve is rotated, replace the fuel check valve assembly.

REMOVAL & INSTALLATION

Removal and installation of the various evaporative emission control system components consists of tagging and disconnecting the hoses from the component. Remove the component by loosening retaining screws and removing the part. Install in the reverse order. When replacing hose, make sure that it is fuel and vapor resistant.

Exhaust Gas Recirculation System

OPERATION

All Sentra/Pulsar engines use an Exhaust Gas Recirculation (EGR) system. The EGR system is used to reduce combustion temperatures in the engine, thereby reducing the oxides of nitrogen emissions and controlling detonation (ping).
The methods of controlling this function, vary greatly from engine-to-engine. For specific system usage, refer to the engine vacuum schematics provide in this section.

Exhaust Gas Recirculation (EGR) Valve

On all engines, the EGR valve is mounted on the intake manifold. The recycled exhaust gas is drawn into the intake manifold, through the exhaust manifold and controlled by the EGR valve. As the throttle valve is opened, vacuum is applied to the EGR valve vacuum diaphragm. The diaphragm moves a tapered valve, that allows exhaust gas to pass into the intake manifold. When the vacuum reaches about 2 in. Hg (7 kPa), the diaphragm moves against spring pressure and is in a fully up (open) position at about 8 in. Hg (27 kPa) of vacuum. As the diaphragm moves up, it opens the exhaust gas metering valve which allows exhaust gas to be pulled into the engine intake manifold. The system does not operate when the engine is idling because the exhaust gas recirculation would cause a rough idle.

EGR Back Pressure Transducer (BPT) Valve

Some engines have a Back Pressure Transducer (BPT) valve installed between the EGR valve. The BPT valve has a diaphragm which is raised or lowered by exhaust back pressure. The diaphragm opens or closes an air bleed, which is connected into the EGR vacuum line. High exhaust pressure raises the diaphragm, closing off the air bleed. When the air bleed is closed, more vacuum reaches the EGR valve, thus opening the valve further.

Exhaust Gas Recirculation (EGR) Control Solenoid

On most later carbureted engines and all fuel injected engines, the EGR control solenoid replaces the thermal vacuum switch. The control solenoid operation is controlled by the ECM, which uses inputs received from the CPS, MAF, ECT and ignition switch to determine if the EGR system should be enabled. When the ECM energizes the solenoid, the plunger in the solenoid cuts the vacuum supply to the EGR valve and EVAP purge valve off. When EGR function is desired, the ECM de-energizes the solenoid.

Exhaust Gas Recirculation (EGR) Temperature Sensor

The sensor sends a voltage signal to the ECM proportional to the EGR passage temperature. As the exhaust flow increases, the EGR passage temperature increases, causing the EGR temperature sensor resistance to decreases. The decrease in resistance causes the sensor reference line voltage to drop. The ECM can calculate the EGR system efficiency, by monitoring voltage changes in the temperature sensor circuit.

Exhaust Gas Recirculation (EGR) Thermal Vacuum Valve

Many early systems use a thermal vacuum valve inserted in the engine thermostat housing which prevents EGR operation when the engine is cold. The valve controls the application of the vacuum to the EGR valve, according to engine temperature. When the engine coolant reaches a predetermined temperature, the thermal vacuum valve opens and allows vacuum to be routed to the EGR valve. Below the predetermined temperature, the thermal vacuum valve closes and blocks vacuum to the EGR valve.

Exhaust Gas Recirculation (EGR) Venturi Vacuum Transducer (VVT)

1982 1.5L engines use a Venturi Vacuum Transducer (VVT) valve. The VVT valve monitors exhaust pressure and carburetor vacuum in order to activate the diaphragm which controls the throttle vacuum applied to the EGR control valve. This system expands the operating range of the EGR unit, as well as increasing the EGR flow rate.

TESTING

Exhaust Gas Recirculation (EGR) Valve

▶ See Figure 16

1. Remove the EGR valve and apply enough vacuum to the diaphragm to open the valve.
2. The valve should remain open for over 30 seconds after the vacuum is removed.
• If the valve holds vacuum, proceed to the next step.
• If the valve does not hold vacuum, replace the valve assembly.
3. Check the valve for damage, such as warpage, cracks and excessive wear around the valve and seat. If necessary, clean the seat with a brush and compressed air, then remove any deposits from around the valve and port (seat).

Exhaust Gas Recirculation (EGR) Back Pressure Transducer Valve

▶ See Figure 17

1. Disconnect the two vacuum hoses from the valve. Plug one of the ports.
2. While applying pressure to the bottom of the valve, apply vacuum to the unplugged port and check for leakage. If any leakage exists, replace the valve.

Exhaust Gas Recirculation (EGR) Control Solenoid

▶ See Figures 18, 19 and 20

1. Mark and tag all vacuum lines attached to the control valve. Once marked, remove the hoses from the control assembly.

2. Apply 12V to terminal **2**, and ground to terminal **1**.
3. With the solenoid energized, check for air passage between vacuum fittings as follows:
   - Ports A and B 1987–96 engines—Passage open—air should pass freely
   - Ports B and C 1987–94 engines—Passage blocked—no air should not pass
   - Ports A and C 1995–96 engines—Passage blocked—no air should not pass
4. Disconnect the 12V power supply. With the solenoid de-energized check for air passages between the vacuum fittings as follows:
   - Ports A and B 1987–96 engines—Passage blocked—no air should not pass
   - Ports B and C 1987–94 engines—Passage open—air should pass freely
   - Ports A and C 1995–96 engines—Passage open—air should pass freely
5. If the solenoid did not perform as specified, replace the EGR/EVAP solenoid/valve assembly.

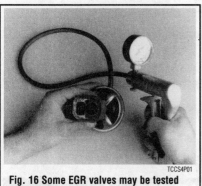

Fig. 16 Some EGR valves may be tested using a vacuum pump by watching for diaphragm movement

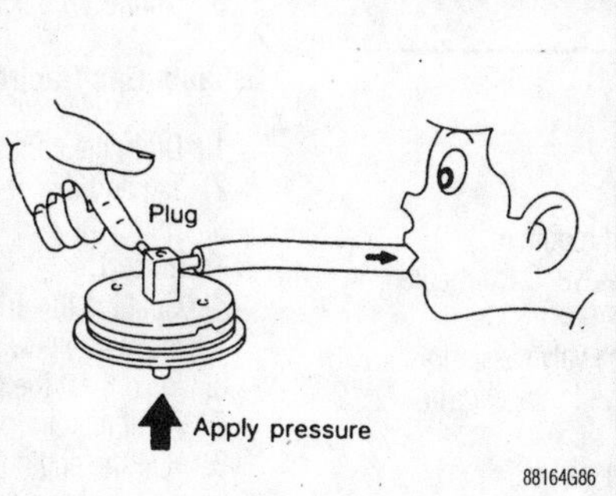

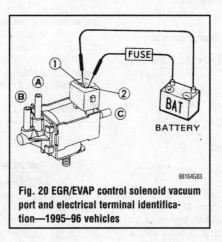

Fig. 17 EGR-BPT valve testing

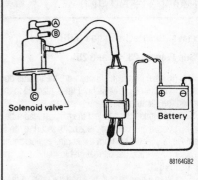

Fig. 18 EGR/EVAP control solenoid vacuum port identification—1987–90 vehicles

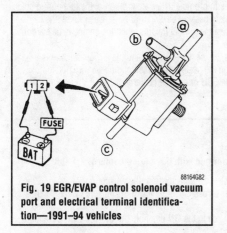

Fig. 19 EGR/EVAP control solenoid vacuum port and electrical terminal identification—1991–94 vehicles

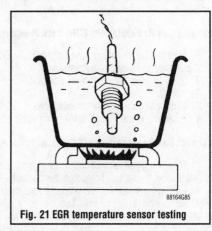

Fig. 20 EGR/EVAP control solenoid vacuum port and electrical terminal identification—1995–96 vehicles

Fig. 21 EGR temperature sensor testing

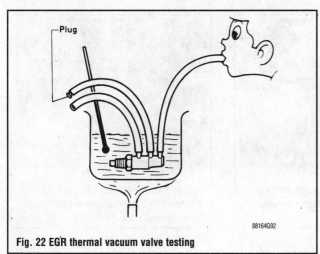

Fig. 22 EGR thermal vacuum valve testing

Exhaust Gas Recirculation (EGR) Temperature Sensor

▶ See Figure 21

1. Disconnect the EGR temperature sensor harness connector
2. Remove the EGR temperature sensor from the engine.
3. Place the sensor in water.
4. Heat the water to boiling and measure the resistance across the EGR temperature sensor connector terminals
5. Resistance should be 76–94 kilo-ohms with the EGR temperature sensor at 212°F (100°C).

Exhaust Gas Recirculation (EGR) Thermal Vacuum Valve

▶ See Figure 22

1. Remove the EGR thermal vacuum valve from the engine.
2. Connect a vacuum pump to the air cleaner port (upper port).
3. Plug either of the remaining ports.
4. Apply vacuum to the air cleaner port; it should allow vacuum to pass. Repeat the test for other port. If either port was closed, replace the vacuum valve.

Do not allow water to enter the vacuum passages when testing, or the valve may be damaged.

5. Place the valve in a container of water with a thermometer and heat the water. When the temperature of the water reaches approximately 122°F (50°C). Repeat the above test procedure. Vacuum should not pass through either passage, if it does replace the valve.

Exhaust Gas Recirculation (EGR) Venturi Vacuum Transducer (VVT)

To check the VVT valve, disconnect the top and bottom center hoses and apply a vacuum to the top hose. Check for leaks. If a leak is present, replace the valve.

REMOVAL & INSTALLATION

Exhaust Gas Recirculation (EGR) Valve

♦ **See Figures 23, 24 and 25**

1. Remove the air inlet hose from the throttle housing, if required.
2. Mark and tag any vacuum lines attached to the EGR valve. Once marked, unplug the vacuum hoses.
3. If equipped, disconnect the exhaust feed tube from the valve assembly.
4. Loosen and remove the 2 bolts securing the EGR valve to the engine. Remove the EGR valve from the engine compartment.
5. Remove any gasket material from the mating surfaces.
To install:
6. Using a new gasket, position the valve to the intake and secure with the retaining bolts. Tighten the bolts completely with a suitable wrench.
7. Connect the exhaust feed tube to the valve, if removed.
8. Attach the vacuum hoses to the EGR valve, in their correct order.
9. Connect the air inlet hose, if removed.

Exhaust Gas Recirculation (EGR) Back Pressure Transducer Valve

1. Mark and tag all vacuum hose attached to the BPT valve. Once tagged, remove the vacuum hoses from the assembly.
2. Slide the valve from its mounting bracket.
To install:
3. Slide valve back into the mounting bracket.
4. Reconnect vacuum hoses to the appropriated port.

Exhaust Gas Recirculation (EGR) Control Solenoid

1. Mark and tag all vacuum hose attached to the control solenoid. Once tagged, remove the vacuum hoses from the assembly.
2. Unplug the sensor harness connector from the control solenoid.
3. Remove the control solenoid from the engine compartment by either unfastening the retaining bolts which secure the control solenoid and bracket, or remove the solenoid from the bracket by loosening the tabs at the rear of the unit.

To install:
4. Depending on how the control solenoid was removed, install the valve by either inserting the bracket into the tabs at the rear of the unit, or secure the control solenoid and bracket using the retaining bolts.
5. Plug the sensor harness connector into the control solenoid.
6. Connect the vacuum hoses to their original locations.

Exhaust Gas Recirculation (EGR) Temperature Sensor

1. Disconnect the negative battery cable.
2. Disconnect the wiring harness.
3. Unscrew the EGR sensor.
To install:
4. Install the EGR sensor and torque to 11 ft. lbs. (15 Nm).
5. Connect the wire harness.
6. Connect the negative battery cable.

Exhaust Gas Recirculation (EGR) Thermal Vacuum Valve

1. Drain the engine coolant.
2. Tag and disconnect the vacuum hoses from the valve.
3. Using the correct size wrench, remove the sensor.
To install:
4. Coat the threads of the new valve with an approved anti-seize compound.
5. Install the new sensor using the correct size wrench.
6. Reconnect the vacuum hoses to the appropriate fitting.
7. Refill the engine coolant.
8. Run the engine until the cooling fans operate and check for leaks.

Fuel Mixture Heating System

♦ **See Figure 26**

The system's purpose is to promote better atomization of the fuel during cold engine operation. The system uses an electric grid style heater under the carburetor or throttle body, to heat the air/fuel mixture when the engine is below normal operating temperature.

When the engine starts, the heater energizes and the air/fuel mixture is heated as it passes through the heater grid. When engine warm-up is complete, the current is cut off by the ECU or mixture heater relay.

TESTING & INSPECTION

System Inspection

➡ **This test must be performed with the engine below 122°F (50°C).**

1. Disconnect the electrical connector from the mixture heater.
2. Connect a voltmeter across the terminals of the mixture heater electrical connector.
3. Turn the ignition switch to the **ON** position, but do NOT start the engine. Observe the reading on the voltmeter.

Fig. 23 With the air cleaner inlet hose removed, disconnect the vacuum supply hose from the EGR valve

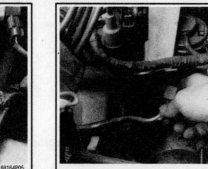

Fig. 24 Disconnect the exhaust inlet pipe from the manifold, then detach the pipe from the EGR valve

Fig. 25 Remove the two nuts from the mounting studs and remove the EGR valve from the intake manifold

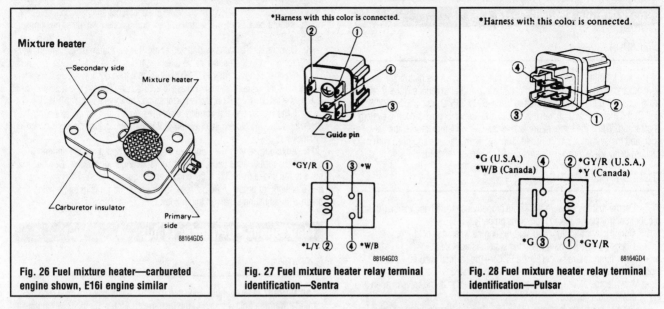

Fig. 26 Fuel mixture heater—carbureted engine shown, E16i engine similar

Fig. 27 Fuel mixture heater relay terminal identification—Sentra

Fig. 28 Fuel mixture heater relay terminal identification—Pulsar

• If the reading is approximately battery voltage, proceed to the next step.

• If the reading is not approximately battery voltage, inspect the mixture heater relay, choke relay, water temperature switch and power supply circuitry for a fault.

4. Connect an ohmmeter across the mixture heater terminals. Check the continuity between the heater terminals. If continuity does not exist (open), replace the carburetor insulator assembly.

Mixture Relay Testing

▶ **See Figures 27 and 28**

1. Remove the relay from the vehicle.
2. Connect an ohmmeter across terminals **3** and **4**. Continuity should not exist.
3. Connect a 12 volt battery source across terminals **1** and **2**. Continuity should now exist across the terminals.
4. If the relay did not perform as specified, replace the relay and recheck system operation.

Fuel Shut-Off System

OPERATION

The 1982 and later carbureted engines, use the fuel shut-off system to reduce exhaust emissions during deceleration. The system is operated by an anti-dieseling solenoid valve in the carburetor which is controlled by a vacuum switch or ECU on later ECCS vehicles. When the intake manifold vacuum increases to an extremely high level (which it does during deceleration), the fuel flow of the slow system is shut off by the anti-dieseling solenoid valve. When the intake manifold vacuum drops to a low level, the fuel flow of the slow system is resupplied. The solenoid is energized when the clutch pedal is depressed or the vehicle is placed in neutral.

The fuel shut-off system is further controlled by the clutch switch and gear position switches such as the neutral switch (manual transaxle) and the inhibitor switch (automatic transaxle) to ensure that fuel cannot be shut off even it the manifold vacuum is high enough to trigger the normal fuel shut-off operation.

TESTING & INSPECTION

1. ECU controlled systems. Check the clutch and neutral switches for continuity.

2. Turn the ignition switch **OFF** and disconnect the ECU connector, if so equipped. Turn the ignition **ON** and check for continuity at terminals 4 and 5 to ground. There should be continuity. If not, check the harness.

3. Non ECU controlled systems. Disconnect the fuel shut-off relay at the relay center and turn the ignition **ON**. Check for voltage at the green/red and black terminals. Should be 12 volts with the clutch disengaged and 0 volts with the clutch engaged (tree).

4. Disconnect the vacuum hose from the vacuum switch. Apply vacuum with a vacuum pump and check continuity through the vacuum switch.

5. All systems: Disconnect the solenoid electrical connector and vacuum connector. The engine should stall. If not, replace the solenoid.

Mixture Ratio Rich/Lean and EGR Large/Small Exchange System

This system is used only on 1982 California engines. The system controls the air/fuel mixture ratio and the amount of recirculated exhaust gas (manual transaxle models only) in accordance with the engine coolant temperature and car speed. The system consists of a vacuum switching valve, a power valve, a speed detecting switch located in the speedometer, a speed detecting switch amplifier and a water temperature switch.

When road speed is above 40 mph (64 km/h) and the engine coolant temperature is above 122°F (50°C), the vacuum switching valve is ON. When the coolant temperature is above 122°F (50°C) but the vehicle is traveling less than 40 mph (65 km/h), the vacuum switching valve is OFF, thus enriching the fuel mixture. When coolant temperature is below 122°F (50°C), the vacuum switching valve is always ON, thereby causing the fuel mixture to lean down.

TESTING

Warm up the engine and raise the drive wheels off the ground; support the raised end of the vehicle with jack stands and block the wheels still on the ground. Start the engine, shift the transaxle into TOP speed and maintain a speedometer speed higher than 50 mph (80 km/h). Pinch off the vacuum switching valve-to-air cleaner hose, then see if the engine speed decreases and operates erratically. Shift the transaxle into 3rd speed and run the vehicle at a speed lower than 30 mph (48 km/h). Disconnect the vacuum switching valve-to-power valve hose, at the power valve and plug the open end with your finger. The engine should operate erratically. If the expected engine reaction in both of these tests does not happen, check all of the wiring connections and hoses for breaks and/or blockage.

Spark Timing Control System

OPERATION

The spark timing control system is designed to control the distributor vacuum advance under various driving conditions in order to reduce HC and NOx emissions. With the water temperature below 59° F (15°C) and above 122°F (50°C) the thermal vacuum valve is closed and the spark timing control system is activated. When the temperature is between the two temperatures, the valve is open and the system is not activated. Some early models are equipped with a vacuum delay valve, but all systems operate basically the same.

TESTING & INSPECTION

1. Ensure that the vacuum hoses are properly connected and the distributor vacuum controller and linkage functions properly.
2. Connect a timing light and start the engine when it is cold.
3. Check the spark timing when the system is activated.
• Water temperature below 59°F (15°C)—the thermal vacuum valve is closed and the spark timing control system is activated
• Water temperature is between 59–122°F (15–50°C), the valve is open and the system is not activated.
• Water temperature is above 122°F (50°C)—the thermal vacuum valve is closed and the spark timing control system is activated
4. If the timing does not change as specified, check the thermal vacuum valve.

Throttle Opener Control System

The Throttle Opener Control System (TOCS) is used on E-series engines. The purpose of the system is to reduce hydrocarbon emissions during coasting conditions.

OPERATION

High manifold vacuum during coasting prevents the complete combustion of the air/fuel mixture because of the reduced amount of air. This condition will result in a large amount of HC emission. Leaning the air/fuel mixture for a short time (during the high vacuum condition) will reduce the emission of the HC. However, changing the air/fuel mixture with the mixture adjusting screw will cause poor engine idle and increase emissions during normal idle conditions.

The TOC system consists of a servo diaphragm, vacuum control valve, throttle opener solenoid valve, speed detecting switch and amplifier on manual transaxle models. Automatic transaxle models use an inhibitor and inhibitor relay in place of the speed detecting switch and amplifier. At the moment when the manifold vacuum increases, as during deceleration, the vacuum control valve opens to transfer the manifold vacuum to the servo diaphragm chamber and the carburetor throttle valve opens slightly. Under this condition, the proper amount of fresh air is sucked into the combustion chamber. As a result, a more complete ignition takes place, burning much of the HC in the exhaust gases.

TESTING & INSPECTION

When the engine is idling too high and does not drop to idling speed, the TOC system should be checked.
1. Check for continuity between the green/red and black terminals of the function check connector with the ignition **OFF**. If no continuity exists, the solenoid may be at fault. Replace the valve assembly.
2. Manual transaxle vehicles: remove the speedometer cable and spin the speedometer in the combination meter to confirm that the pointer indicates more than 10 mph (16 km/h). The voltage at the function check connector green/red and black terminals should read 0 volts above 10 mph (16 km/h) and 12 volts below 10 mph (16 km/h). If not the amplifier or speed detecting switch may be at fault.

3. Automatic transaxle vehicles: voltage at the function check connector terminals should be 12 volts in Neutral or Park and 0 volts in all other positions. See Step 2.
4. Disconnect the harness at the solenoid. Tee a vacuum gauge into the vacuum hose going to the opener servo diaphragm.
5. Warm the engine and run to 3000–3500 rpm then quickly close the throttle. At this time, the vacuum should increase to 23.6 in. Hg or above and then decrease to the level set at idling. If not the temperature control valve may be at fault.
6. If the pressure is not correct, lower the level by turning the adjusting screw or not in the clockwise direction. If it is the higher, turn the screw counterclockwise.
7. Adjusting servo stroke: connect a tachometer and warm the engine. Disconnect the rubber hose between the diaphragm and control valve. Connect the hose to the intake manifold. If the engine speed goes to 1650–1850 rpm, the servo is working properly. Adjust the engine speed until it is in range using the diaphragm adjusting screw on the link lever.

Maintenance Reminder Lights

OPERATION

All 1982–87 models equipped with a oxygen sensor have maintenance reminder warning light, located in the instrument cluster. The light will illuminate at approximately 30,000 miles (48,000 km). At this time, the oxygen sensor should be inspected and/or replaced and the entire emission system should be inspected. After the oxygen sensor and emission system have been serviced and repaired as necessary, the maintenance warning light must be reset. There two methods of resetting the lamp. The method will depend upon the vehicle model, year, engine and engine calibration.

Beginning in 1988, maintenance resets where no longer used. The CHECK ENGINE light will come on indicating a malfunction and a trouble code will be stored in the ECU memory. The light will extinguish when the problem is corrected.

RESETTING

Without Relay

On most early systems, the oxygen sensor lamp is reset, by disconnecting a wiring harness connector, located behind the instrument panel. The reminder light will no longer function.

WARNING LIGHT CONNECTOR LOCATIONS

▶ **See Figure 29**

• 1983–86 Pulsar—light green and black with a light green tracer or black and white wires, located near the fuse box
• 1987 Pulsar—red and black, red and blue wires, located above the fuse box.
• 1982–83 Sentra—green and yellow or green and black wires, located above the fuse box.
• 1984 Sentra—light green and black with a light green tracer wires, located near the hood release handle.
• 1985–86 Sentra—light green and black wires, located above the fuse box.
• 1987 Sentra—red and black, red and blue wires, located above the fuse box.

With Relay

Some later production models may be equipped with a sensor relay. The relay is reset by either depressing a button on the relay or by inserting a small screwdriver into the reset hole. Reset relay at 30,000 miles (48,000 km) and 60,000 miles (96,000 km). At 90,000 miles (145,000 km), locate and disconnect warning light wire connector.

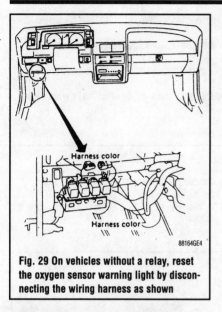

Fig. 29 On vehicles without a relay, reset the oxygen sensor warning light by disconnecting the wiring harness as shown

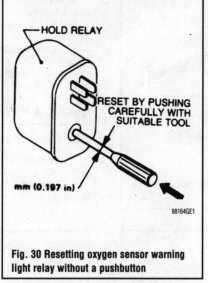

Fig. 30 Resetting oxygen sensor warning light relay without a pushbutton

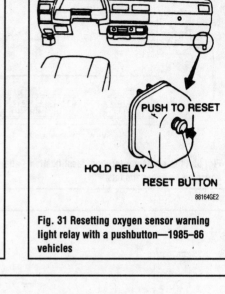

Fig. 31 Resetting oxygen sensor warning light relay with a pushbutton—1985–86 vehicles

WARNING LIGHT RELAY LOCATIONS

▶ See Figures 30, 31 and 32

• 1986 Pulsar—the reset relay is located behind the right kick panel. At 90,000 miles (145,000 km), disconnect the connector with the red/black wire and red/blue wire located above the fuse box.

• 1987 Pulsar—the reset relay is located behind the left kick panel. At 90,000 miles (145,000 km), disconnect the connector with the red/black wire and red/blue wire located above the fuse box.

• 1985–86 Sentra—the reset relay is located behind the right kick panel. At 90,000 miles (145,000 km), disconnect the connector with the light green and black wire located near the hood release handle.

• 1987 Sentra—the reset relay is located behind the right kick panel. At 90,000 miles (145,000 km), disconnect the connector with the red/black wire and red/blue wire located above the fuse box.

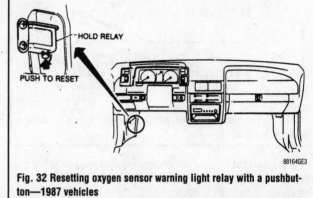

Fig. 32 Resetting oxygen sensor warning light relay with a pushbutton—1987 vehicles

ELECTRONIC ENGINE CONTROLS—CARBURETED ENGINES

Mixture Ratio Feedback System

GENERAL OPERATION

The need for better fuel economy, combined with increasingly strict emission control regulations, required a more exact control of the engine air/fuel mixture. The manufacturer has developed this system which is installed on most 1984 and later models. The system consists of the following sensors.

• Air Temperature Sensor
• Air/Fuel Mixture Solenoid
• Crank Angle Sensor
• Inhibitor Switch
• Neutral/Clutch Switch
• Oxygen Sensor
• Throttle Valve Switch
• Vacuum Sensor
• Vehicle Speed Sensor
• Water Temperature Sensor

The principle of the system is to control the air/fuel mixture exactly, so that a more complete combustion can occur in the engine and more thorough oxidation and reduction of the exhaust gases can occur in the catalytic converter. The object is to maintain a stoichiometric air/fuel mixture, which is chemically correct for theoretically complete combustion.

It should be noted that proper operation of the system is entirely dependent on the oxygen sensor. Thus, if the sensor is not replaced at the correct interval or if the sensor fails during normal operation, the engine fuel mixture will be incorrect, resulting in poor fuel economy, starting problems or stumbling and stalling of the engine when warm.

PRELIMINARY TESTING

▶ See Figures 33 and 34

✳ WARNING

Make sure the ignition switch is OFF before disconnecting any harness connectors. Disconnect the negative battery cable before disconnecting the ECU harness connector. Voltage spikes can damage the electronic components. Make sure the ECU (Electronic Control Unit) connector is fully seated during inspection.

➡Do not condemn the electronic engine controls before fully checking the basics. Many electronic parts are replaced only to find out it is something simple. Electronic parts are usually not returnable. Make sure the component is defective before purchasing.

1. Check the engine for air and vacuum leaks. Most engines should draw about 15–20 inch Hg. at idle. The needle should be steady.

2. Check the air filter for clogging.

3. Inspect the dipstick, AB valve hose, air induction hose, intake manifold gasket, valve cover gasket, EGR gasket and oil filler cap for leaks.

4. Check the EGR valve seat and operation. A malfunction EGR can cause no or abnormal idle.

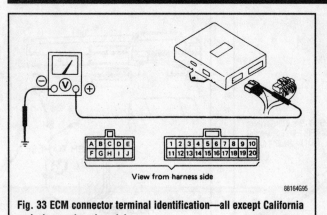

Fig. 33 ECM connector terminal identification—all except California emission equipped models

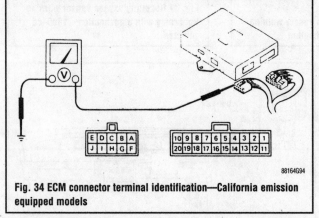

Fig. 34 ECM connector terminal identification—California emission equipped models

5. Check the fuel supply to the carburetor and make sure the fuel is at the proper octane. Old fuel can cause driveability problems that are difficult to diagnose.

6. Check the fuel filter for clogging.

7. With the engine idling, check the fuel level through the glass window on the carburetor bowl. The level should be at the middle dot. If not correct, remove the top of the carburetor and adjust the float level as outlined in Section 5.

8. Perform ignition tests with an oscilloscope. All firing voltages should be in the same range. Check the secondary ignition system with a spark tester.

9. Check and adjust the ignition to the proper specification in Section 2.

10. Check all engine related electrical harness connectors, including the ECU. Loose or corroded terminals can cause many driveability problems.

Air/Fuel Mixture Solenoid

OPERATION

The air/fuel mixture solenoid provides a method of controlling the amount of fuel supplied to the engine, throughout all engine operating conditions. By monitoring the inputs from various sensors, the ECM can vary the **ON** or **OFF** time of the solenoid; this in known as the duty cycle. By continually adjusting the duty cycle every 65 milli-seconds, the optimum air/fuel mixture, for all engine conditions, can be provided.

TESTING

1. Turn off ignition and disconnect air/fuel ratio solenoid harness connector.

2. Measure the resistance of the solenoid. The resistance should be 30–50 ohms. If air/fuel solenoid resistance is out of specification, replace solenoid assembly.

3. If solenoids are within specifications, reconnect solenoid harness connectors.

4. Disconnect ECM 10 pin connector from control unit and disconnect alternator **L** terminal.

5. Turn ignition switch ON and measure voltage between terminal **F** and ground.

- If battery voltage is not present, check and (if necessary) repair/replace harness.
- If voltage is within specification, check and (if necessary) replace control unit.

REMOVAL & INSTALLATION

♦ **See Figures 35 and 36**

1. Drain approximately one quart of engine coolant.
2. Remove carburetor from engine.
3. Disconnect harness from harness connector and cut the harness cover at the connector.

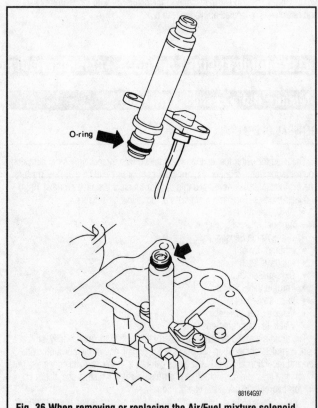

Fig. 35 Remove the two mounting screws and pull the solenoid from the carburetor housing

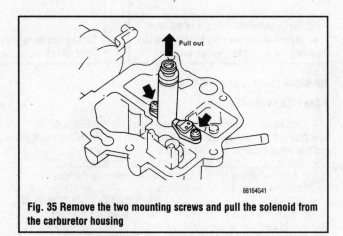

Fig. 36 When removing or replacing the Air/Fuel mixture solenoid, always install new O-rings

4. Remove choke chamber assembly from carburetor.

5. Remove air/fuel ratio solenoid from choke chamber.

To install:

6. Use new O-rings on solenoid and apply a light coating of oil to O-rings.

7. Install solenoid and torque mounting bolts to 12–36 inch lbs. (1.5–4 Nm).

8. Install choke chamber assembly.

9. Install new boots and terminal ends to harness with terminal pliers, and then place terminals in connector.

Anti-Dieseling Solenoid

OPERATION

▶ **See Figures 37 and 38**

The anti-diesel solenoid is used to prevent engine run-on after the ignition switch is turned **OFF**. The system uses a valve to shut off the supply of fuel to the primary low speed circuit, when the engine is turned off. The solenoid is normally closed and when energized, the needle assembly retracts, allowing fuel to flow through the primary low speed circuit.

TESTING

1. Turn off ignition and disconnect air/fuel ratio solenoid harness connector.

2. Measure the resistance of the solenoid. The resistance should be 25–45 ohms.

- If the solenoid resistance is within specification, proceed to the next step.
- If the solenoid resistance is out of specification, replace solenoid assembly.

3. Reconnect solenoid harness connectors.

4. Disconnect ECM 10 pin connector from control unit and disconnect alternator **L** terminal.

5. Turn ignition switch ON and measure voltage between terminal **G** and ground.

- If battery voltage is not present, check and (if necessary) repair/replace harness.
- If voltage is within specification, check and (if necessary) replace control unit.

REMOVAL & INSTALLATION

✳ CAUTION

Observe all fuel system safety precautions when performing this procedure.

1. Allow engine to complete cool.

2. Remove the air cleaner assembly.

3. Disconnect harness from harness connector and remove the solenoid wires from the connector.

4. Place a rag below the solenoid and unscrew the solenoid from the carburetor housing.

To install:

5. Install a new gasket to the solenoid.

6. Carefully screw the solenoid into the carburetor housing. Tighten the solenoid to 13 ft. lbs. (18 Nm)

7. Properly route the wires away from moving components and install the wiring into the connector.

8. Start the engine and verify no fuel leakage.

9. Install the air cleaner assembly.

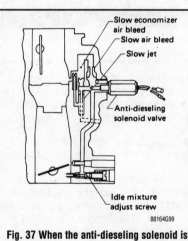

Fig. 37 When the anti-dieseling solenoid is de-energized, the solenoid plunger blocks off the primary slow (low speed) system

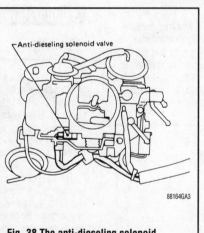

Fig. 38 The anti-dieseling solenoid threads into the side of the carburetor at the mounting location shown

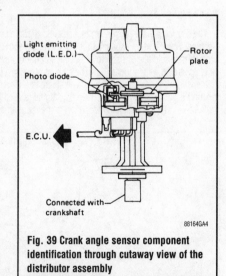

Fig. 39 Crank angle sensor component identification through cutaway view of the distributor assembly

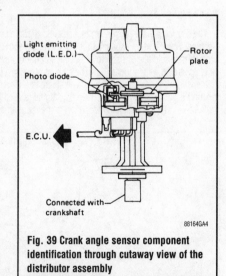

Fig. 40 Crank angle sensor plate and related components

Crank Angle Sensor

OPERATION

▶ **See Figures 39 and 40**

The crank angle sensor detects engine rpm and the crank angle (piston position). It also sends a signal to the control unit to control various operations. This sensor is built into the distributor.

The signal rotor plate has 360 slits at 1° intervals on its outer periphery. It also has four slits at 90° intervals. These four slits are used to detect the crank angle, that is, the position of each piston. The teeth are used to provide the 1° signal that is necessary to control engine rpm and ignition timing.

The crank angle sensor has two diodes and a wave forming circuit. When a signal rotor plate passes the space between the light emitting diode (LED) and photo diode, the slit of the signal rotor plate alternately cuts the light which is sent to the photo diode from the LED. This causes an alternative voltage and it is then converted into an on-off pulse by the wave forming circuit, which is sent to the control unit.

TESTING

Crank angle sensor testing, requires complete testing of the ignition system. For information, refer to ignition system testing in Section 2.

REMOVAL & INSTALLATION

The crank angle sensor is an integral part of the distributor and must be replaced as an assembly. Refer to Section 2 for distributor removal and installation procedures.

Inhibitor Switch

The Inhibitor Switch is used in vehicles equipped with automatic transaxle. For testing and other service information, refer to Section 7.

Neutral/Clutch Switch

The Neutral/Clutch Switch is used in vehicles equipped with automatic transaxle. For testing and other service information, refer to Section 7.

Oxygen Sensor

OPERATION

▶ **See Figure 41**

The oxygen sensor (O_2sensor) is a ceramic zirconia bulb which produces an electrical voltage when exposed to the oxygen. The sensor is mounted in the exhaust manifold and is used to detect the amount of oxygen present in the exhaust stream. When there is a large amount of oxygen present (lean mixture), the sensor produces a low voltage. When there is a lesser amount present (rich mixture) it produces a higher voltage. The signal is used by the ECU to pulse the Air/Fuel mixture solenoid, according to the requirements of the engine.

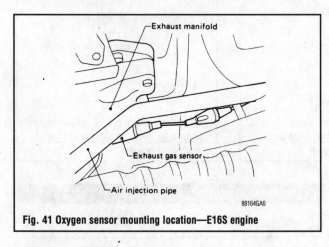

Fig. 41 Oxygen sensor mounting location—E16S engine

TESTING

1. Start the engine and allow it to reach operating temperature. Turn the engine **OFF**.
2. Connect the positive lead of a multimeter to the O_2 sensor signal wire and the negative lead to the engine ground.
3. Start the engine and run at 2000 rpm for two minutes.
4. Return the engine to idle and the voltage reading should be fluctuating between 100 and 900 millivolts, as the O_2 sensor detects varying levels of oxygen in the exhaust stream.

➡**Under normal conditions the O_2 sensor should fluctuate high and low. If the O_2 sensor voltage does not fluctuate, the sensor may be defective or mixture could be extremely out of range.**

5. Prior to condemning the O_2 sensor, check the sensor response to changes in the fuel mixture as follows:
   a. Force the system rich by closing the choke plate. If the O_2 sensor reads now reads above 550 millivolts, the sensor is operating properly and the problems is elsewhere in the system. If the sensor fails to respond, replace the sensor and retest.
   b. Force the system lean by removing a vacuum line. If this causes the oxygen sensor voltage to read below 350 millivolts the sensor is operating properly and the problems is elsewhere in the system. If the sensor fails to respond, replace the sensor and retest.

➡**Before installing a new oxygen sensor, perform a visual inspection. Black sooty deposits on the O_2 sensor tip may indicate a rich air/fuel mixture. White gritty deposits could be an internal antifreeze leak. Brown deposits indicate oil consumption. All of these contaminants can damage a new sensor.**

REMOVAL & INSTALLATION

The oxygen sensor is installed in the exhaust manifold and is removed in the same manner as a spark plug. Always remove electrical connection before trying to remove the sensor. Exercise care when handling the sensor do not drop or handle the sensor roughly; the electrical connector and louvered end must be kept free of grease and dirt. Use an anti-seize compound when installing. Make sure to coat just the threads of the sensor and care should be used not to get compound on the sensor itself. Torque the sensor to 13–17 ft. lbs. (18–27 Nm).

Temperature Sensors

OPERATION

All models use a water temperature sensor input, to provide an accurate temperature signal to the ECM. The sensor screws into a coolant passage in the engine and detect changes in engine temperature. The coolant temperature sensor is a primary input in determining the duty cycle, as well as engaging closed loop operation.

Some systems also use an air temperature sensor, located in the air cleaner housing. Both sensors are used to control various emission control devices.

The coolant and air temperature sensing units, use a thermistor which is sensitive to the changes in temperature. Electrical resistance of the thermistor decreases in response to the temperature rise. This change will cause a change in voltage on the sensor reference line. The ECM will use the reference line voltage to determine engine temperature.

TESTING

▶ **See Figures 42 and 43**

1. Disconnect ECM 20 pin connector from control unit.
2. Measure the sensor resistance as follows:
• Coolant temperature sensor—between terminal **8** and **19** of ECM 20 pin connector.
• Air temperature sensor—between terminal **1** and **19** of ECM 20 pin connector.
3. Compare the readings to the resistance chart and proceed as follows:
• If both resistance's are within specification, check/replace ECM control unit.
• If resistance is not within specification, proceed to the next step.
4. Remove and check the appropriate temperature sensor and measure the resistance across the terminals.
• If temperature sensor is not within specification, replace sensor.
• If sensor is within specifications, check and (if necessary) repair/replace harness.

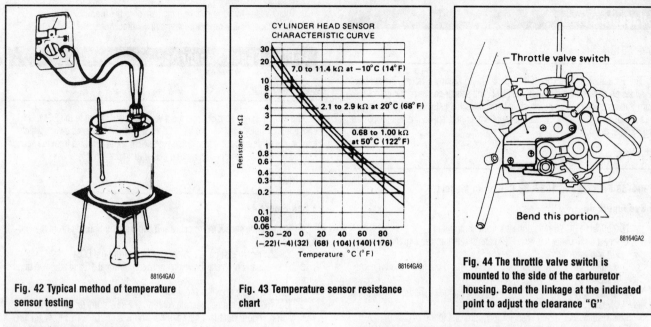

Fig. 42 Typical method of temperature sensor testing

Fig. 43 Temperature sensor resistance chart

Fig. 44 The throttle valve switch is mounted to the side of the carburetor housing. Bend the linkage at the indicated point to adjust the clearance "G"

REMOVAL & INSTALLATION

Water Temperature Sensor

1. Drain the engine coolant.
2. Disconnect the harness connector.
3. Using the correct size wrench, remove the sensor.

To install:

4. Coat the threads of the new sensor with an approved anti-seize compound.
5. Install the new sensor using the correct size wrench.
6. Reconnect ECT harness connector.
7. Refill the engine coolant.
8. Run the engine until the cooling fans operate and check for leaks.

Throttle Valve Switch

OPERATION

♦ **See Figure 44**

The throttle valve switch is attached to the carburetor throttle plate and operates in response to accelerator pedal movement. The switch is used to control the operation of the anti-dieseling solenoid.

TESTING

1. Turn the ignition switch to the **OFF** position.
2. Disconnect the carburetor electrical connector.
3. Connect jumper wires between the anti-dieseling solenoid terminals as follows:
    a. Connect the carburetor harness RED wire to the vehicle harness GRAY wire.
    b. Connect the carburetor harness BLACK wire to the vehicle harness BLUE wire.
4. Connect an ohmmeter across the throttle switch wires, on the carburetor wiring harness. Continuity should not exist.
   • If continuity does not exist, proceed to the next step.
   • If continuity is present, attempt to adjust the switch. If unable to adjust, replace the switch.
5. Start the engine and run at 2000 rpm. Observe the ohmmeter reading.
   • If continuity is present, proceed to the next step.
   • If continuity does not exist, first attempt to adjust the switch. If unable to adjust, replace the switch

6. Gradually decrease the engine speed to 1000–1700 rpms on manual transaxles, and 900–1600 rpms on automatic transaxles. Observe the ohmmeter reading.
   • If continuity does not exist, the switch is functioning properly.
   • If continuity is present, attempt to adjust the switch. If unable to adjust, replace the switch.
7. Remove the jumper wires and reconnect the carburetor wiring harness.

ADJUSTMENT

♦ **See Figures 44 and 45**

1. Drain approximately one quart of engine coolant.
2. Remove carburetor from engine.
3. Open throttle manually.
4. Then, close throttle opening manually until ohmmeter indicates an open circuit.
5. At this point, check clearance **G**; the clearance gap between throttle valve and inner carburetor wall. The throttle gap should be as follows:
   • 1986 Federal—0.0118 ± 0.0028 (0.30 ± 0.07mm)
   • 1986 California—0.0146 ± 0.0028 in. (0.37 ± 0.07mm)
   • 1987–88 All—0.0146 ± 0.0028 in. (0.37 ± 0.07mm)
6. Adjustment is made by bending plate until ohmmeter indicates an open circuit.

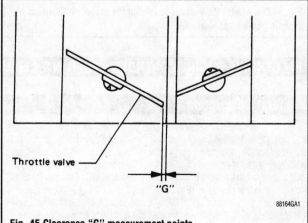

Fig. 45 Clearance "G" measurement points

Vacuum Sensor

OPERATION

The vacuum sensor is part of the Spark Timing Control System. The sensor provides an engine load signal to the ECM. The sensor converts manifold vacuum into an electrical signal, which is transmitted to the ECM. The ECM uses this signal, along with coolant temperature and engine speed inputs, to optimize the ignition timing.

TESTING

1984–88 Federal and 1987–88 California Models

▶ See Figure 46

1. Disconnect ECC 20 pin connector from control unit.
2. Connect a voltmeter between ECC control unit harness terminal **9** and a known good engine ground.
3. Disconnect vacuum hose for vacuum sensor and connect vacuum pump to vacuum sensor.
4. With no vacuum applied to the sensor, the voltmeter should read approximately 4.0 volts.
   • If the reading was within specifications, proceed to the next step.
   • If the reading was not within specifications, check power supply and wiring to sensor. If okay, replace the sensor and retest.
5. Using the vacuum pump, apply 25.0 in. Hg to the sensor. The voltage measurement should be approximately 0.5 volts.
   • If the reading was within specifications, the sensor is okay.
   • If the reading was not within specifications, replace the sensor and retest.

REMOVAL & INSTALLATION

1. Disconnect the vacuum hose from the sensor.
2. Disconnect the electrical connector from the sensor.

3. Remove the two bolt securing the sensor to the firewall.
4. Installation is the reverse of the removal procedure.

Vehicle Speed Sensor

OPERATION

The vehicle speed sensor provides a vehicle speed signal to the ECM. On conventional speedometers, the speed sensor consists of a reed switch which transforms vehicle speed into a pulse signal. The input received from the sensor is used to regulate ignition timing and decell fuel shut off.

TESTING

▶ See Figure 47

1. Remove the speedometer cable and cable pinion housing, from the transaxle.
2. Disconnect the 20 pin electrical connector from the ECM.
3. Connect an ohmmeter between connector terminal 10 and a known good ground.
4. Turn the ignition switch to the **ON** position.
5. Observe the ohmmeter while rotating the speedometer drive gear. The reading should fluctuate between continuity and open, twice per revolution.
6. If the sensor did not perform as specified, inspect the wiring between the instrument cluster and the ECM. If the wiring is okay, replace the VSS.

REMOVAL & INSTALLATION

The instrument panel mounted VSS is integral part of the vehicle speed sensor. Refer to Section 6 for speedometer head Removal and Installation information.

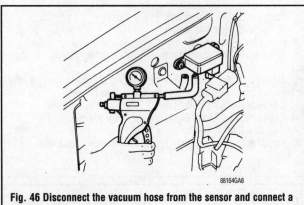

Fig. 46 Disconnect the vacuum hose from the sensor and connect a vacuum pump as shown

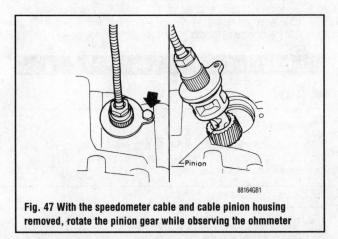

Fig. 47 With the speedometer cable and cable pinion housing removed, rotate the pinion gear while observing the ohmmeter

ELECTRONIC ENGINE CONTROLS—FUEL INJECTED ENGINES

General Description

As automotive emissions standards tightened, and fuel economy became more important, the widespread use of Electronic Fuel Injection increased dramatically. As a result engine performance also improved. The Sentra and Pulsar models use two different types of electronic fuel injection. The first type uses a single fuel injector mounted in the throttle body housing. This system is known as Throttle Body Fuel Injection (TBI). The TBI system is used on E16i and GA16i engines.

The E15ET, CA16DE, CA18DE, GA16DE and SR20DE engines use Multi-port Fuel Injection (MFI). The MFI system uses one fuel injector for each cylinder.

The injectors are mounted in the intake manifold and are controlled by the engine control module. The injectors are pulsed together or in pairs depending on the specific application.

On all fuel injected engines a mixture ratio feedback system is used for optimum three-way catalyst action. The engine control module (ECM) consists of a microcomputer, inspection lamps, a diagnostic mode selector and connectors for signal input, output, and power supply. The ECM controls the amount of fuel injected, ignition timing, mixture ratio feedback, idle speed, fuel pump operation, air injection valve (AIV) operation, exhaust gas recirculation (EGR) and evaporative emission canister (EVAP canister) purge operation.

The air/fuel ratio is fine tuned using a heated oxygen sensor (HO$_2$S) or oxygen sensor (O$_2$S) and the ECM varies the injection pulse width to maintain the mixture inside the stoichiometric window. When the ECM uses the HO$_2$S or O$_2$S as the primary source of feedback information, this is called "closed loop" control. Under certain conditions the ECM may ignore the HO$_2$S or O$_2$S. Some of these conditions are:

- Deceleration
- High speed or high-load conditions such as towing
- Engine idling
- HO$_2$S or O$_2$S or circuit malfunction
- Engine starting
- HO$_2$S or O$_2$S temperature is too cold for accurate measurement

Without constant adjustment, the ideal mixture (called the stoichiometric window) is rarely obtained from any car, because certain factors such as: manufacturing variations, worn parts and the operating environment may cause the mixture ratio to change. For this reason, the actual fuel setting and theoretical fuel setting is measured by the ECM and recorded. The ECM uses this data to return the fuel mixture to the "learned" setting rather than the factory setting. This ability to "learn" the ideal setting is called "fuel trim." The data for fuel trim is stored in the volatile memory of the ECM. The contents of the fuel trim data may change under certain conditions: if ECM power is lost for approximately 24 hours, the operating adjustments change for an extended period of time, or there is a component malfunction.

Electronic Service Precautions

- Do not disconnect the engine control module (ECM) harness connectors before the battery ground cable has been disconnected.
- Make sure all ECM connectors are fastened securely. A poor connection can cause a high voltage surge from the coil and condenser, which will damage integrated circuits.
- Keep the ECM harness at least 4 inches away from adjacent harnesses to prevent an ECM system malfunction due to external electronic interference.
- Keep all parts and harnesses dry during service.
- Before attempting to remove any parts, turn the ignition switch to the **OFF** position and disconnect the battery ground cable.
- Always use a 12V battery as a power source.
- Do not disconnect the battery cables with the engine running.
- Do not press the gas pedal when starting the engine.
- Do not race up the engine immediately after starting and just before shutdown.
- Do not disassemble the ECM for any reason.
- If the battery is disconnected, the memory will return to default Read Only Memory values.
- Engine operation may vary slightly, but this is not an indication of a defective component.
- If a 2-way radio is installed, keep the antenna as far as possible away from the ECM. Keep the antenna cable at least 8 inches away from the ECM harness, and do not let them run parallel for a long distance. Make sure the radio chassis is grounded to the vehicle body.
- Make sure the ignition switch is **OFF** and the negative (-) battery connection is disconnected before connecting or disconnecting ECM connectors.
- When performing ECM input/output signal diagnosis, remove the pin terminal retainer from the 20 and 16 pin connectors to make it easier to insert tester probes into the connector.
- When connecting or disconnecting any terminals from the ECM, take care not to bend or break any pin terminals. Check that there are no bends or breaks on ECM pin terminals before attempting any connections.
- Before replacing any ECM, perform the ECM input/output signal diagnosis to make sure the ECM is functioning properly or not.
- After performing the electronic control system inspection, perform the ECM self-diagnosis and driving test.
- When measuring the supply voltage of ECM-controlled components with a circuit tester, separate 1 tester probe from another. If the 2 tester probes accidentally make contact with each other during measurement, a short circuit will result, causing damage to the power transistor in the ECM.
- All connector symbols in wiring diagrams are shown from the terminal side. The connector guides for male terminals are shown in black, and female terminals are shown in white in wiring diagrams.

Air Flow Meter

OPERATION

Only the 1984 E15ET engine uses an air flow meter sensor. All other fuel injected engines use a mass air flow type sensor. The air flow meter measures the amount of air entering the intake manifold and sends a voltage signal to the control unit. As air enters the intake, the incoming air moves the sensor flap. A potentiometer is connected to the sensor flap. allowing sensor flap movement to be converted into a voltage signal. Since air flow is directly proportional to engine load, this signal is the principal input for determining fuel injection duration.

TESTING

1. Disconnect the air flow sensor electrical connector.
2. Connect an ohmmeter between terminals **33** and **26**. Then between terminals **33** and **26**. The measurement obtained in both tests should be 280–400 ohms.
   - If the both measurements were within specifications, proceed to the next step.
   - If either measurement was not within specifications, replace the VAF sensor and retest.
3. Connect the ohmmeter between terminal **33** and **31** of the air flow sensor. Operate the flap manually. The door should move smoothly, without binding or sticking. The resistance must increase and decrease smoothly and without any wide fluctuations. Open and close the vane slowly several times while observing the ohmmeter closely.
   - If there are any major fluctuations in the readings or the readings indicates an open or a short, replace the air flow meter and retest.
   - If the air flow meter operates correctly, examine the connector and wiring harness for corrosion or damage.

Camshaft Position (CMP)/Crank Angle Sensor

OPERATION

In order to properly function Nissan engines equipped with electronic fuel injection require an engine speed input, as well as a piston position or TDC input. Early systems call this sensor a Crank Angle sensor, however the more commonly accepted term is Camshaft Position (CMP) Sensor. The CMP or Crank Angle sensor are essentially the same sensor, therefore the sensor will be referred to as the more commonly recognized CMP sensor. All engines except the CA16DE and CA18DE engines, receive this input from the distributor. The CA16DE and CA18DE engines do not have a distributor, but instead these engines use a distributor like component which is driven by the exhaust camshaft. Both types of CMP sensors function essentially the same.

The CMP sensor sends a signal to the ECM as both a position (the timing) reference and RPM reference. This signal is used by the ECM to calculate ignition timing and other functions. The CMP sensor has a rotor plate and a wave forming circuit. The signal rotor plate has 360 slits for 1 degree signal (angle signal) and 4 slits for 180 degree signal (the engine speed signal). Light emitting diodes (LEDs) and photo diodes are built in the wave forming circuit. When the rotor plate passes the space between the LED and the photo diode, the slits of the rotor plate continually cut the light, which is sent to the photo diode from the LED, causing rough shaped pulses. These pulses are converted into on/off signals by the wave forming circuit and sent to the control unit as input signals.

TESTING

E16i, CA16DE and CA18DE Engines

▶ **See Figures 48, 49 and 50**

1. Disconnect the CMP electrical connector.
2. Turn the ignition switch to the **ON** position.

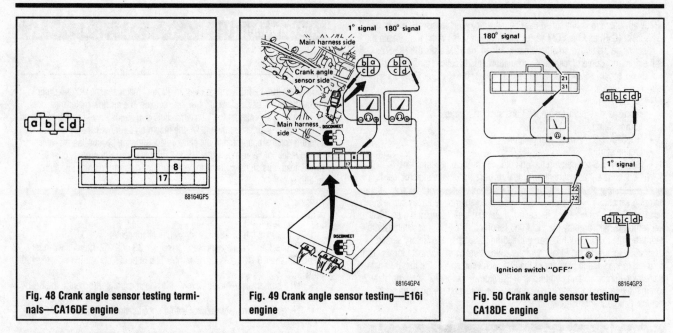

Fig. 48 Crank angle sensor testing terminals—CA16DE engine

Fig. 49 Crank angle sensor testing—E16i engine

Fig. 50 Crank angle sensor testing—CA18DE engine

3. Using a voltmeter and check the CMP power source between terminal **B** and a known good engine ground. The voltmeter should read approximately battery voltage.
   - If reading is as specified, proceed to the next step.
   - If reading is not as specified, check power supply circuitry.
4. Turn the ignition switch to the **OFF** position.
5. Using an ohmmeter, check the CMP sensor ground circuit, by connecting the meter between a known good engine ground and terminal:
   - E16i engine— terminal **D**.
   - CA16DE and CA18DE engines— terminal **A**.
6. Continuity should exist.
   - If continuity does not exist, repair open in ground circuit.
   - If continuity does exist, proceed to the next step.
7. Start the engine.
8. To test the sensor 180° signal, connect a logic probe between the following terminals:
   - E16i and CA18DE engines—ECU terminal **17** and a known good engine ground.
   - CA18DE engine—ECU terminals **21, 31** and a known good engine ground.
9. To test the sensor 1° signal, connect a logic probe between the following terminals:
   - E16i and CA18DE engines—ECU terminal **8** and a known good engine ground.
   - CA18DE engine—ECU terminals **22, 32** and a known good engine ground.
10. The logic probe should indicate that a pulse signal exists in both tests. If a pulse signal was not present, inspect wiring. If wiring is okay, replace the crank angle sensor.

GA16i, 1991–94 GA16DE and SR20DE Engines

♦ **See Figures 51, 52, 53 and 54**

➡ **Testing the CMP will require loosening and removing the distributor, which will disturb the ignition timing. Refer to Sections 2 for more information.**

1. Remove the distributor from the engine.

➡ **Do not disconnect the wiring harness.**

2. Disconnect the ignition wires, from the distributor cap and connect the coil wire to a known good engine ground.
3. Visually inspect the signal plate in the distributor for damage or dust. Clean or replace if necessary.
4. Turn the ignition switch **ON**.
5. To test the sensor 180° signal, rotate the distributor shaft with a voltmeter connected between the following terminals:
   - GA16DE engine—between distributor connector terminal **1** and a known good ground.
   - GA16i and SR20DE engines—between distributor connector terminal **A** and a known good ground.
6. To test the No. 1 cylinder signal, place the ignition switch in the **ON** position. Rotate the distributor and with a voltmeter connected between the following terminals:
   - GA16i engine—between distributor connector terminal **B** and a known good ground.
   - GA16DE engine—between distributor connector terminal **2** and a known good ground.
   - SR20DE engine—between distributor connector terminal **D** and a known good ground.

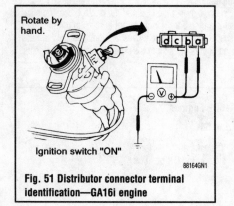

Fig. 51 Distributor connector terminal identification—GA16i engine

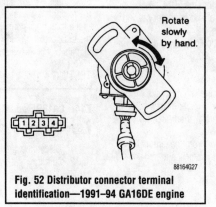

Fig. 52 Distributor connector terminal identification—1991–94 GA16DE engine

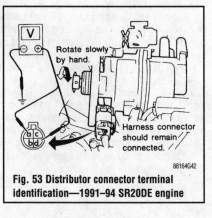

Fig. 53 Distributor connector terminal identification—1991–94 SR20DE engine

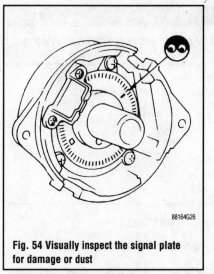

Fig. 54 Visually inspect the signal plate for damage or dust

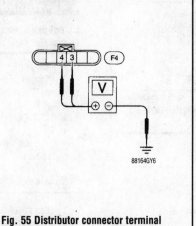

Fig. 55 Distributor connector terminal identification—1995–96 GA16DE and SR20DE engines

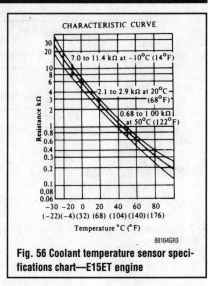

Fig. 56 Coolant temperature sensor specifications chart—E15ET engine

7. The reading in both tests should fluctuate between 0 and 5 volts. If the voltage reading does not register within this range, replace the distributor assembly.

1995–96 GA16DE and SR20DE Engines

◗ See Figure 55

1. Remove the distributor cap and visually inspect the signal plate in the distributor for damage or dust. Clean or replace if necessary. If okay, proceed to the next step.
2. Connect a voltmeter between terminal **3** and a known good engine ground. Set the meter to the AC range.

➡**Do not disconnect the wiring harness.**

3. Start the engine and checking the voltage reading.
4. With the engine still running, connect a voltmeter between terminal **4** and a known good engine ground.
5. The reading in both tests should be approximately 2.7 volts (AC). If the voltage reading in not within specifications, replace the distributor assembly.

REMOVAL & INSTALLATION

The CMP sensor is an integral part of the distributor assembly; if it is found to be defective, replace the distributor assembly.

Coolant Temperature (ECT) Sensor

OPERATION

The ECT sensor is a temperature-sensitive resistor that monitors the coolant temperature. The sensor is threaded into a coolant passage. As the coolant heats from the engine use, the resistance of thermistor inside the ECT sensor decreases. The resistance change, causes the sensor reference line voltage to drop in proportion with the resistance change. The ECM detects the temperature change and adjusts the air/fuel mixture to compensate for the change.

TESTING

◗ See Figures 56 thru 61

1. Disconnect the ECT sensor connector.
2. Place a known, accurate thermometer in water to verify temperature.
3. Place the ECT sensor in water and heat the water while measuring resistance.
4. Compare resistance with the appropriate specifications chart.
5. Replace the ECT sensor if the resistance readings are not within specifications.

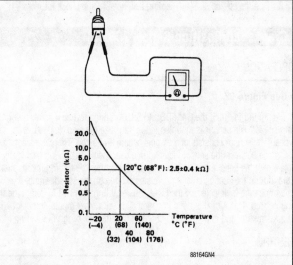

Fig. 57 Coolant temperature sensor specifications—all 1987–90 engines

Temperature °C (°F)	Resistance kΩ
20 (68)	2.3 - 2.7
90 (194)	0.24 - 0.26
110 (230)	0.14 - 0.15

Fig. 58 Coolant temperature sensor specifications chart—1991–94 GA16DE engine

Temperature °C (°F)	Resistance kΩ
20 (68)	2.1 - 2.9
50 (122)	0.68 - 1.0
80 (176)	0.30 - 0.33

Fig. 59 Coolant temperature sensor specifications chart—1991–94 SR20DE engine

Engine coolant temperature °C (°F)	Voltage (V)	Resistance (kΩ)
−10 (14)	4.4	7.0 – 11.4
20 (68)	3.5	2.1 – 2.9
50 (122)	2.2	0.68 – 1.00
90 (194)	1.0	0.236 – 0.260

88164G55

Fig. 60 Coolant temperature sensor specifications chart—1995–96 GA16DE and SR20DE engines

REMOVAL & INSTALLATION

1. Drain the engine coolant.
2. Remove harness connector.
3. Using the correct size wrench, remove the ECT sensor.

To install:

4. Coat the threads of the new ECT sensor with an approved sealing compound.
5. Install the new ECT sensor using the correct size wrench.
6. Reconnect ECT harness connector to the new ECT sensor.
7. Refill the engine coolant.
8. Run the engine until the cooling fans operate and check for leaks.

Crankshaft Position Sensor (CKPS)

OPERATION

▶ See Figure 62

Beginning in 1995, the GA16DE and SR20DE engines use a crankshaft position sensor. The sensor is mounted to the transaxle housing, just above the flywheel. The sensor consists of a magnet, a core and a coil. There is preset clearance between the sensor face and ring gear teeth. As the ring gear teeth rotate past the sensor, the air gap (clearance) changes, disrupting the magnetic field around the sensor, creating a voltage change on the sensor signal line. The rate of change is detected by the ECM, thus enabling the ECM to determine the engine rpm. This signal is used in conjunction with other inputs, to detect an engine misfire, and is not used to control either the fuel or ignition timing.

TESTING

▶ See Figures 63 and 64

1. Remove the crankshaft position sensor from the transaxle housing.
2. Visually inspect the sensor tip for dirt build-up or damage.

➡**On vehicles equipped with a manual transaxle, dirt build-up from clutch material is a common cause of failure.**

- If the sensor is okay, proceed to the next step.
- If the sensor has excessive dirt build-up, carefully clean the sensor.

※ **WARNING**

Do not use a wire brush or any other abrasive material to clean the sensor tip.

- If the sensor is damaged, replace the sensor and retest.
3. Connect an ohmmeter across the sensor terminals and measure the resistance. The resistance reading at 77°F (25°C) should be as follows:
- GA16DE engine with M/T—432–528 ohms
- GA16DE engine with A/T—166–204 ohms
- SR20DE engine—166–204 ohms
4. If the measured value is not within specifications, replace the crankshaft position sensor.

REMOVAL & INSTALLATION

1. Disconnect the electrical connector from the sensor.
2. Remove the mounting bolt and lift the sensor its bore.
3. Installation is the reverse of the removal procedure.

Engine Control Module (ECM)

OPERATION

The ECM consists of a microcomputer, inspection lamps, a diagnostic mode selector and connectors for signal input and output, and for power supply. The unit has control of the injected fuel amount, ignition timing, mixture ratio feedback, idle speed, fuel pump operation, mixture heating, AIV operation, and EGR and canister purge operation.

TESTING

There are no methods currently available to test the ECM in the field. Most testing of the ECM, usually involves testing the components associated with the ECM and if all components are okay, substituting a know good unit is the common practice.

REMOVAL & INSTALLATION

1984–90 Vehicles

1. Disconnect the negative battery cable.
2. Locate the ECM under either front seat.
3. Slide the seat assembly fully in either direction in order to gain access.
4. Disconnect the ECM harness connectors.
5. Remove the bolts securing the ECM to the vehicle floor.

To install:

6. Position the ECM on the vehicle floor. Install and tighten the retaining bolts.
7. Connect the electrical connectors to the ECM.
8. Connect the negative battery cable.

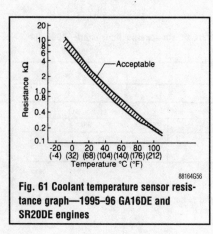

Fig. 61 Coolant temperature sensor resistance graph—1995–96 GA16DE and SR20DE engines

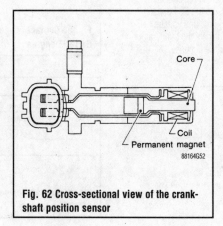

Fig. 62 Cross-sectional view of the crankshaft position sensor

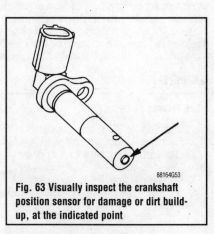

Fig. 63 Visually inspect the crankshaft position sensor for damage or dirt build-up, at the indicated point

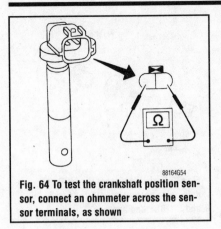

Fig. 64 To test the crankshaft position sensor, connect an ohmmeter across the sensor terminals, as shown

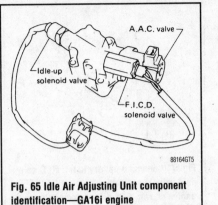

Fig. 65 Idle Air Adjusting Unit component identification—GA16i engine

Fig. 66 Idle Air Adjusting Unit component identification—1991–94 GA16DE and all SR20DE engines

1991–96 Vehicles

1. Disconnect the negative battery cable.
2. Remove the center shift console side undercover panels as outlined in Section 10.
3. Disconnect the ECM harness connectors.
4. Remove the bolts securing the ECM to the vehicle floor.

To install:

5. Position the ECM on the vehicle floor. Install and tighten the retaining bolts.
6. Connect the ECM harness connector to the ECM monitor.
7. Position and secure the center shift console side undercover panels.
8. Connect the negative battery cable.

Idle Air Adjusting (IAA) Unit

OPERATION

▶ **See Figures 65, 66 and 67**

GA16i, CA16DE, CA18DE, GA16DE and SR20DE engines all use the Idle Air Adjusting (IAA) Unit to maintain the idle speed at a predetermined range. The IAA unit is made up of Fast Idle Control Device (FICD) solenoid valve and the Auxiliary Air Control (AAC) valve. Only the GA16i engine uses an Idle-up solenoid.

The Auxiliary Air Control valves are used to control the engine idle speed, by regulating the amount of air flow allowed to bypass the throttle plates. The valve assembly is controlled by on/off pulses received from the ECM. By energizing the valve longer, more air will bypass the throttle plates, thus the engine speed will increase.

The FIC system is used to bypass additional air, when the AAC valve may not be able to compensate. The FICD solenoid is energized, when an additional load is placed on the engine, such as; high power steering effort or when the A/C compressor clutch is engaged. The GA16i engine uses both a FICD and an Idle-up solenoid to perform this function.

TESTING

Auxiliary Air Valve (AAV)

EXCEPT 1995–96 1.6L (GA16DE) ENGINE

▶ **See Figures 68 and 69**

1. Disconnect the IAC auxiliary air control harness connector.
2. Measure resistance between the IAC auxiliary air control terminals. The resistance should be approximately 10 ohms.

➡ **If resistance is not within specifications, replace the IAC control valve**

3. Visually inspect the valve plunger for sticking or binding. Check the valve spring for damage and replace if necessary.

1995–96 1.6L (GA16DE) ENGINE

▶ **See Figure 70**

1. Disconnect the electrical connector from the IACV-AAC valve.
2. Connect an ohmmeter across AAC valve terminals **2** and **3**. Measure the resistance across the terminals.
3. Connect an ohmmeter across AAC valve terminals **3** and **4**. Measure the resistance across the terminals.
4. The resistance measurement in both tests should be 50–100 ohms at 77°F (25°C). If the resistance is not within specifications, replace the IACV-AAC valve assembly.

Fast Idle Control Device (FICD) and Idle-up Valve

EXCEPT 1995–96 1.6L (GA16DE) ENGINE

▶ **See Figures 71, 72 and 73**

1. Unplug the harness connector.

➡ **On the GA16i engine, make certain to properly identify the connector terminals before applying voltage to the valve. All other engines will use a two terminal connector.**

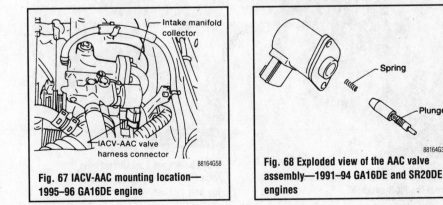

Fig. 67 IACV-AAC mounting location—1995–96 GA16DE engine

Fig. 68 Exploded view of the AAC valve assembly—1991–94 GA16DE and SR20DE engines

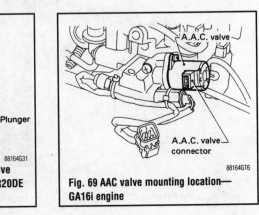

Fig. 69 AAC valve mounting location—GA16i engine

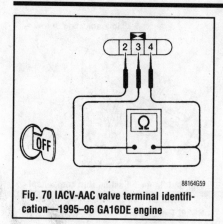

Fig. 70 IACV-AAC valve terminal identification—1995–96 GA16DE engine

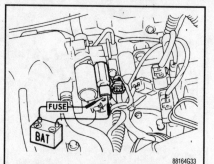

Fig. 71 Connect a battery to the FICD solenoid valve, as shown—1991–94 GA16DE engine shown, SR20DE engine similar

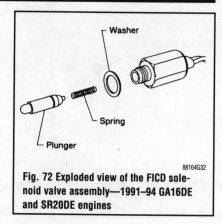

Fig. 72 Exploded view of the FICD solenoid valve assembly—1991–94 GA16DE and SR20DE engines

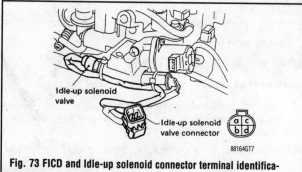

Fig. 73 FICD and Idle-up solenoid connector terminal identification—GA16i engine

2. Apply 12V to the harness connector terminals (IAA unit side). On GA16i engines, use terminals A and B for FICD testing and terminals C and D for Idle-up solenoid testing.

3. Listen for a clicking sound when 12V is applied.

4. If no sound is present, check the plunger for sticking or a broken spring.

1995–96 1.6L (GA16DE) ENGINE

▶ See Figure 74

1. Disconnect the electrical connector from the IACV-FICD solenoid.
2. Connect an ohmmeter across FICD solenoid terminals **1** and **5**.
3. Measure the resistance across the terminals. Resistance should be 75–125 ohms. If the resistance is not within specifications, replace the IACV-FICD solenoid assembly.

REMOVAL & INSTALLATION

▶ See Figures 75 and 76

1. Disconnect the harness connector from the idle air adjusting unit.

2. Unfasten the retaining bolts securing the IAA unit to the intake manifold, and remove the unit.

3. Remove any gasket material from the mating surface.

To install:

4. Position the IAA unit to the intake. Using a new gasket on the engine and secure with the retaining bolts.

5. Connect the wiring harness to the IAA unit.

ADJUSTMENT

The IAC auxiliary air control and the IAC valve fast idle control device are mounted on a common component called the idle air adjusting unit (IAA). The fast idle speed is adjusted by turning the idle adjusting screw which is located on the idle air adjusting unit. See Section 1 for more specific information.

Idle Air Control Valve (IACV) Air Regulator

OPERATION

▶ See Figures 77 and 78

The IACV-air regulator is used on CA16DE, CA18DE, GA16DE and SR20DE engines to provide increased idle speed during cold engine operation. The valve contains bimetal spring, that is connected to a rotary shutter. The shutter opens, when the engine is cold, allowing additional air to bypass the throttle plates, thus increasing the engine speed. During warm-up, an electrical current supplied to the valve, heats the bimetal spring, closing off the port.

TESTING

▶ See Figures 79 and 80

1. Turn the ignition switch to the **OFF** position.
2. Disconnect the IACV-air regulator electrical connector.

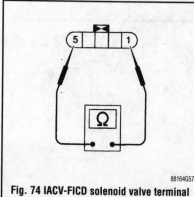

Fig. 74 IACV-FICD solenoid valve terminal identification—1995–96 GA16DE engine

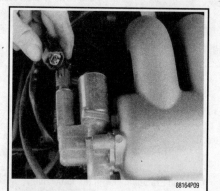

Fig. 75 Detach the electrical connector from the FICD solenoid

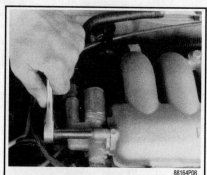

Fig. 76 Remove the IAA unit from the intake manifold by unfastening the mounting bolt and nut

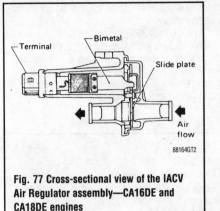

Fig. 77 Cross-sectional view of the IACV
Air Regulator assembly—CA16DE and
CA18DE engines

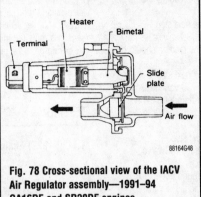

Fig. 78 Cross-sectional view of the IACV
Air Regulator assembly—1991–94
GA16DE and SR20DE engines

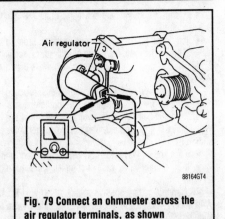

Fig. 79 Connect an ohmmeter across the
air regulator terminals, as shown

3. Connect a voltmeter between terminal **A** and a known good engine ground.

4. Turn the ignition switch **ON**. Battery voltage should be present.
- If battery voltage is present, proceed to the next step.
- If battery voltage is not present, check power supply circuitry.

5. Turn the ignition switch **OFF**.

6. Connect an ohmmeter from terminal **B** to a known good engine ground. Continuity should exist.
- If continuity is present, proceed to the next step.
- If continuity is not present, check ground circuit for opens.

7. Connect an ohmmeter across the IACV-air regulator terminals.

8. Measure the resistance between the terminals. The resistance should be approximately 70–80 ohms. If resistance is not within specifications, replace the IAC control valve

9. Visually inspect the rotary shutter for clogging, sticking or binding. Clean shutter or replace the valve assembly if necessary.

Idle Speed Control (ISC) Valve

OPERATION

The ISC valve is used on E16i engine to maintain idle speed during all phases of engine operation. The valve contains rotary solenoid valve which is controlled by the ECM. The ECM uses on/off pulses to control the position of the shutter on the valve. By energizing the valve longer, more air will bypass the throttle plates, thus the engine speed will increase.

TESTING

▶ See Figures 81, 82, 83, 84 and 85

1. Turn the ignition switch to the **OFF** position.
2. Disconnect the ISC valve electrical connector.

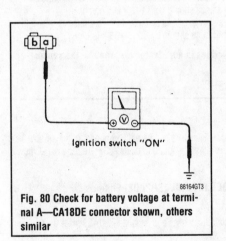

Fig. 80 Check for battery voltage at terminal A—CA18DE connector shown, others similar

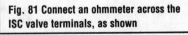
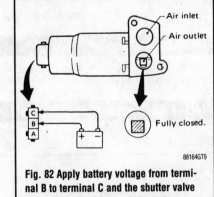

Fig. 81 Connect an ohmmeter across the ISC valve terminals, as shown

Fig. 82 Apply battery voltage from terminal B to terminal C and the shutter valve should be fully closed—E16i engine

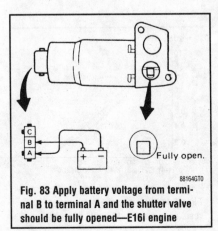

Fig. 83 Apply battery voltage from terminal B to terminal A and the shutter valve should be fully opened—E16i engine

Fig. 84 With no voltage applied, inspect the shutter valve clearance—E16i engine

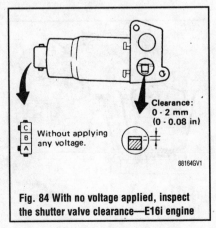

Fig. 85 ISC valve mounting bolt identification

3. Connect an ohmmeter between terminals **B** and **C**. The reading should be 8.5–9.5 ohms.
   • If the reading was within specifications, proceed to the next step.
   • If the reading was not within specifications, replace the ISC valve assembly.
4. Connect an ohmmeter between terminals **B** and **A**. The reading should be 9.5–10.5 ohms.
   • If the reading was within specifications, proceed to the next step.
   • If the reading was not within specifications, replace the ISC valve assembly.
5. Connect battery positive voltage to terminal **B** and ground terminal **A**. With battery voltage applied, observe the shutter valve position. The valve should be fully closed.
   • If the shutter valve was fully closed, proceed to the next step.
   • If the shutter valve was not completely closed, replace the ISC valve assembly.
6. Connect battery positive voltage to terminal **B** and ground terminal **C**. With battery voltage applied, observe the shutter valve position. The valve should be fully open.
   • If the shutter valve was fully opened, proceed to the next step.
   • If the shutter valve was not completely open, replace the ISC valve assembly.
7. Disconnect the battery from the ISC valve. With no voltage applied to the ISC valve, there should be a 0–0.08 in. (0–2mm) opening clearance between the shutter valve and the housing.
   • If the measurement was within specifications, proceed to the next step.
   • If the measurement was not within specifications, replace the ISC valve assembly.
8. Visually inspect the rotary shutter for clogging, sticking or binding. Clean shutter or replace if necessary.

REMOVAL & INSTALLATION

1. Disconnect the electrical connector from the ISC valve assembly.
2. Remove the mounting bolts in the reverse order of the tightening sequence.
3. Remove the valve assembly from the side of the throttle body housing.
To install:
4. Position the ISC valve to the side of the throttle body housing.
5. Tighten the mounting bolts in the following sequence: A—B—C to 36 inch lbs. (4.5 Nm).
6. Connect the electrical connector to the ISC valve.

Inhibitor Switch

The inhibitor switch is used in vehicles equipped with automatic transaxle. For testing and other service information Refer to Section 7.

Intake Air Temperature (IAT) Sensor

OPERATION

♦ See Figure 86

There are two different types of intake air temperature sensors. The 1984 E15ET uses an air temperature sensor located, in the air flow meter assembly. The sensor measures the temperature of the incoming air and transmits a volt-

age signal to the ECM. The ECM will use this input to optimize the fuel mixture, according to the specific air temperature.

Beginning in 1995, the GA16DE and SR20DE engines use an IAT sensor. The sensor is mounted in air cleaner housing and detects changes in the intake air temperature. As the temperature of the incoming air increases the resistance of the sensor decreases proportionally. Changes in temperature are transmitted to the ECM and are used to detect problems with the On Board Diagnostic system. The sensor has no direct affect on the engine control system.

TESTING

1.5L (E15ET) Engine

1. Disconnect the air flow meter electrical connector.
2. Connect an ohmmeter between **30** and a known good engine ground.
3. The resistance measurement should be as follows:
   • Below 68°F (20°C)—Above 2.1 k-ohms
   • Above 68°F (20°C)—Below 2.9 k-ohms
4. If the value obtained is not within specifications, replace the air flow meter assembly.

1.6L (GA16DE) and 2.0L (SR20DE) Engines

♦ See Figures 87 and 88

1. Disconnect IAT sensor electrical connector.
2. Remove the IAT sensor from the air cleaner housing.
3. Place the sensor bulb in a pot of water.

❈❈ WARNING

Place only the temperature sensing portion of the sensor in the water. Do NOT submerge the entire sensor in the water.

4. Connect an ohmmeter across the IAT sensor terminals.
5. Heat the water and measure the resistance at different temperatures.
   • At 68°F (20°C) resistance should be 2.1–2.9 kilo ohms.
   • At 122°F (50°C) resistance should be 0.68–1.0 kilo ohms.
   • At 176°F (80°C) resistance should be 0.27–0.38 kilo ohms.

➡If sensor resistance values is not parameters, replace the sensor.

REMOVAL & INSTALLATION

1.5L (E15ET) Engine

The intake air temperature sensor is an integral component of the air flow meter. If the air temperature sensor is found to be defective, replace the air flow meter assembly.

1995–96 1.6L (GA16DE) and 2.0L (SR20DE) Engines

1. Disconnect the IAT sensor electrical connector.
2. Remove the two retaining screws and separate the IAT sensor from the air cleaner housing.

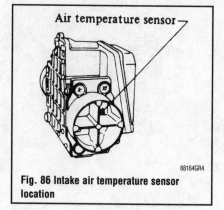

Fig. 86 Intake air temperature sensor location

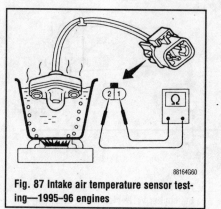

Fig. 87 Intake air temperature sensor testing—1995–96 engines

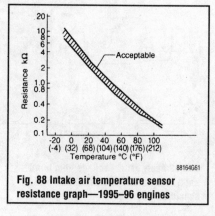

Fig. 88 Intake air temperature sensor resistance graph—1995–96 engines

To install:

3. Position the sensor to the air cleaner housing and secure in place using the two retaining screws.

4. Reconnect the wiring harness.

Knock Sensor (KS)

OPERATION

▶ See Figure 89

Some engines use a knock sensor mounted in the engine block to prevent internal engine damage caused by engine detonation. The sensor contains a piezoelectric crystal which emits a voltage signal when it is subjected to shock or vibration caused by detonation. The ECM receives this signal and retards the ignition timing.

TESTING

1991–94 2.0L (SR20DE) Engine

▶ See Figure 90

1. Disconnect the KS connector.
2. Using a high-impedance ohmmeter (at least 10 meg-ohm), check the resistance between KS terminal **A** and a known good engine ground
3. Replace the KS if continuity is not present.

✳✳ WARNING

Replace the KS if it falls or is struck.

1995–96 1.6L (GA16DE) and 2.0L (SR20DE) Engines

▶ See Figure 91

1. Disconnect the KS connector.
2. Using a high-impedance ohmmeter (at least 10 meg-ohm), check the resistance between KS terminal **2** and a known good engine ground

3. Resistance should be 500–620 ohms at 77°F (25°C). If resistance is not within specifications, replace the knock sensor.

✳✳ WARNING

Replace the KS if it falls or is struck.

REMOVAL & INSTALLATION

1. Disconnect the electrical connector from the sensor.
2. Remove the KS from the engine block.
To install:
3. Position and secure the KS to the engine block using the retaining bolt.
4. Connect the electrical connector to the KS.

Mass Air Flow (MAF) Sensor

OPERATION

▶ See Figures 92, 93 and 94

All Sentra/Pulsar fuel injected engines, except the E15ET engine use a MAF sensor input to calculate engine load. The sensor is mounted either in the air cleaner housing on MFI engines or in the throttle body housing on TBI engines.

The MAF uses a heated wire or film which is stretched across the incoming air flow. The element requires more electrical current to maintain its temperature, as the amount of intake air flow increases. By measuring the amount of current necessary to maintain the temperature of the wire or film, the control unit can calculate the volume of air entering the engine. Since the volume of air entering the engine is directly proportional to the amount of engine load, the ECM can determine the operating load of the engine, by monitoring the MAF signal wire.

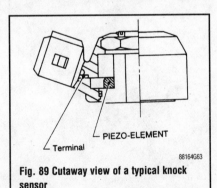

Fig. 89 Cutaway view of a typical knock sensor

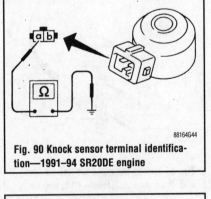

Fig. 90 Knock sensor terminal identification—1991–94 SR20DE engine

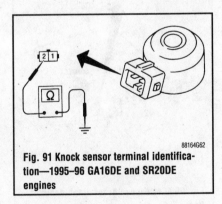

Fig. 91 Knock sensor terminal identification—1995–96 GA16DE and SR20DE engines

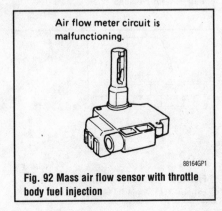

Fig. 92 Mass air flow sensor with throttle body fuel injection

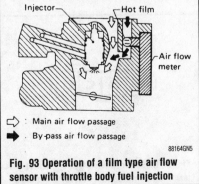

Fig. 93 Operation of a film type air flow sensor with throttle body fuel injection

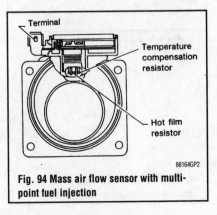

Fig. 94 Mass air flow sensor with multi-point fuel injection

TESTING

E16i Engine

METHOD A

▶ See Figure 95

1. Pull back the mass air flow sensor harness protective cover, exposing the wire terminal ends.
2. Turn the ignition **ON**.
3. Connect a voltmeter between MAF sensor connector **E** and a known good engine. Battery voltage should exist.
   - If battery voltage does not exist, check the MAF sensor power-supply circuitry.
   - If battery voltage does exist, proceed to the next step.
4. Connect a voltmeter between ECM connector **31** and a known good engine ground.
5. Start the engine and allow it to fully warm up before continuing.
6. The voltage reading should change by racing the engine with the accelerator pedal, from 0 to approximately 5.0 volts. If the voltage is not as specified, check the wiring between the MAF sensor and the ECM. If the wiring is okay, replace the MAF sensor.

METHOD B

▶ See Figure 96

1. Remove the MAF sensor from the vehicle.
2. Connect positive (+) battery voltage to sensor terminal **E**. Connect terminal **C** to battery ground (−).
3. Connect a voltmeter between sensor terminals **A** and **D**. The meter should read 1.5–2.0 volts.

- If battery voltage was within specifications, proceed to the next step.
- If battery voltage was not within specifications, replace the MAF sensor.
4. With the meter and battery connected as in the previous step, blow across the sensor film. The meter should read between 2.5–4.0 volts. If the reading is not within specifications, replace the MAF sensor.

CA16DE Engine

▶ See Figure 97

1. Visually inspect the MAF sensor hot wire for dirt, dust, or damage. Clean or replace if necessary.
2. Pull back the mass air flow sensor harness protective cover, exposing the wire terminal ends.
3. Turn the ignition **ON**.
4. Connect a voltmeter between MAF sensor connector **B** and a known good engine. Battery voltage should exist.
   - If battery voltage does not exist, check MAF sensor power supply circuitry.
   - If battery voltage does exist, proceed to the next step.
5. Connect a voltmeter between ECM connector **31** and a known good engine ground.
6. Start the engine and allow it to fully warm up before continuing.
7. The voltage reading should be approximately 1.5 volts at idle. If the voltage is not as specified, check the wiring between the MAF sensor and the ECM. If the wiring is okay, replace the MAF sensor.

GA16i and CA18DE Engines

▶ See Figures 98, 99 and 100

1. Visually inspect the MAF sensor hot wire for dirt, dust, or damage. Clean or replace if necessary.

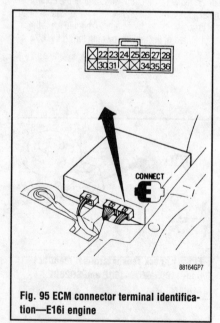

Fig. 95 ECM connector terminal identification—E16i engine

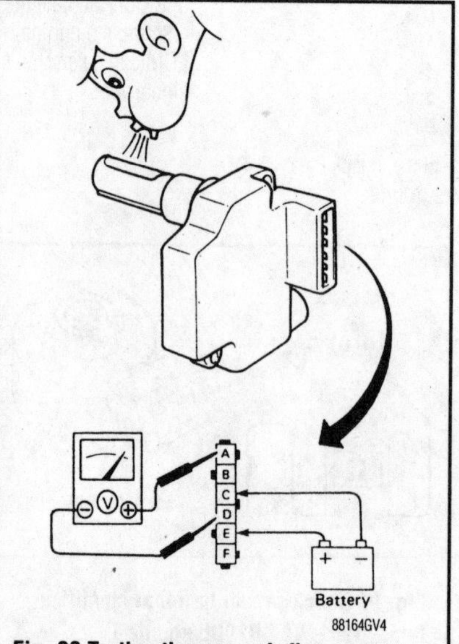

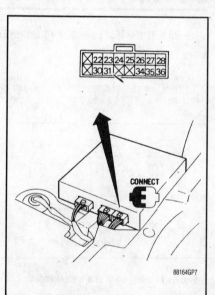

Fig. 96 Testing the mass air flow sensor, with the sensor removed—E16i engine

Fig. 97 ECM connector terminal identification—CA16DE engine

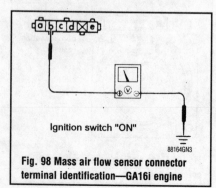

Fig. 98 Mass air flow sensor connector terminal identification—GA16i engine

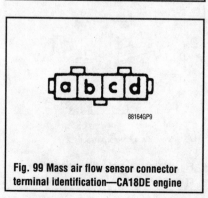

Fig. 99 Mass air flow sensor connector terminal identification—CA18DE engine

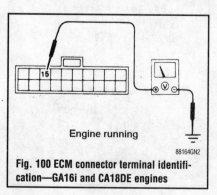

Fig. 100 ECM connector terminal identification—GA16i and CA18DE engines

2. Pull back the mass air flow sensor harness protective cover, exposing the wire terminal ends.

3. Turn the ignition **ON**.

4. Connect a voltmeter between the MAF sensor connector **B** and a known good engine. Battery voltage should exist.

- If battery voltage does not exist, check MAF sensor power supply circuitry.

- If battery voltage does exist, proceed to the next step.

5. Connect a voltmeter between ECM connector **15** and a known good engine ground.

6. Start the engine. Allow the engine to fully warm up before continuing.

7. The voltage reading at idle should be approximately 1.0 volt for the GA16i engine, or 1.5 volts for the GA18DE engine. If the voltage is out of range, before replacing the sensor, check the wiring between the MAF sensor and the ECM.

1.6L (GA16DE) and 2.0L (SR20DE) Engines

♦ See Figures 101 thru 108

1. Pull back the mass air flow sensor harness protective cover, exposing the wire terminal ends.

2. Turn the ignition **ON** and start the engine. Allow the engine to fully warm up before continuing.

3. Turn the ignition **OFF**.

4. Connect a voltmeter between MAF sensor connector **A** and a known good

engine ground on 1991–94 vehicles. For testing of 1995–95 vehicles, make connection between MAF terminal **1** and a known good engine ground.

5. Turn the ignition **ON**, but do not start the engine. The voltage reading should be less than 1.0 volt.

6. Start the engine and observe the voltmeter. Compare the readings to the specifications give on the MAF sensor parameter chart.

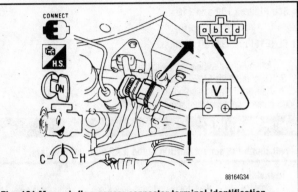

Fig. 101 Mass air flow sensor connector terminal identification—1991–94 GA16DE engine

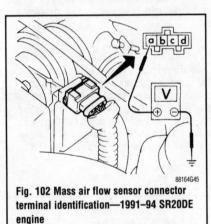

Fig. 102 Mass air flow sensor connector terminal identification—1991–94 SR20DE engine

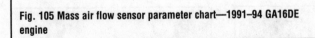

Fig. 103 Inspect the heated wire for damage, dust or dirt build-up—1991–94 GA16DE engine

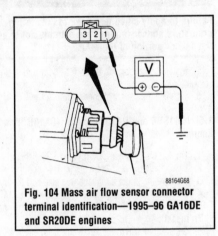

Fig. 104 Mass air flow sensor connector terminal identification—1995–96 GA16DE and SR20DE engines

Conditions	Voltage V
Ignition switch "ON" (Engine stopped.)	Less than 1.0
Idle (Engine is warm-up sufficiently.)	0.7 - 1.1

Fig. 105 Mass air flow sensor parameter chart—1991–94 GA16DE engine

Conditions	Voltage V
Ignition switch "ON" (Engine stopped.)	Less than 1.0
Idle (Engine is warm-up sufficiently.)	1.3 - 1.7V

Fig. 106 Mass air flow sensor parameter chart—1991–94 SR20DE engine

Conditions	Voltage V
Ignition switch "ON" (Engine stopped.)	Less than 1.0
Idle (Engine is warmed-up sufficiently.)	1.0 - 1.7
Idle to about 4,000 rpm*	1.0 - 1.7 to Approx. 4.0

*: Check for linear voltage rise in response to increases to about 4,000 rpm in engine speed.

Fig. 107 Mass air flow sensor parameter chart—1995–96 GA16DE engine

Conditions	Voltage V
Ignition switch "ON" (Engine stopped.)	Less than 1.0
Idle (Engine is warmed-up sufficiently.)	1.3 - 1.7
Idle to about 4,000 rpm*	1.3 - 1.7 to Approx. 4.0

*: Check for linear voltage rise in response to increases to about 4,000 rpm in engine speed.

Fig. 108 Mass air flow sensor parameter chart—1995–96 SR20DE engine

➡If the voltages are out of range, perform the following checks before replacing the MAF sensor:

7. Visually inspect the MAF sensor hot wire for dirt, dust, or damage. Clean if necessary. If okay, check wiring and power supply circuitry.

REMOVAL & INSTALLATION

♦ **See Figures 109 and 110**

1.6L (E16i and GA16i) Engines

1. Remove the throttle valve switch for access.
2. Disconnect the MAF sensor electrical connector.
3. Remove the two retaining screws and slide the sensor from the throttle body, pulling it outward vertically.

❊❊ WARNING

Never touch the sensor portion of the MAF with your fingers.

To install:
4. Coat the sensor-to-throttle body mating surface with silicone grease. This will provide proper heat dissipation.

❊❊ WARNING

Failure to apply silicone grease to the mating surface will cause premature sensor failure. Use extreme not to get the grease onto the sensor portion of the MAF.

5. Install the sensor into the throttle body and secure with the retaining screws.
6. Connect the electrical connector.

1.6L (CA16DE and GA16DE), 1.8L (CA18DE) and 2.0L (SR20DE) Engines

1. Unplug the wire harness from the MAF sensor.
2. Disconnect the duct between the MAF and the intake manifold.
3. Remove the upper air cleaner housing and the MAF as an assembly.
4. Remove the retaining bolts which secure the MAF to the air cleaner.
5. Remove any gasket material from the mating surfaces.
To install:
6. Secure the MAF to the air cleaner, with a new gasket, using the retaining bolts.
7. Install the upper air cleaner housing.
8. Connect the duct to the intake valve from the MAF.
9. Plug the wire harness into the MAF.

Neutral Position Switch

The neutral position switch is used in vehicles equipped with manual transaxle. Refer to Section 7 for service information.

Oxygen Sensor (O2S)

OPERATION

♦ **See Figures 111 and 112**

The oxygen sensor (O2sensor) is a ceramic zirconia bulb which produces an electrical voltage when exposed to the oxygen. The sensor is mounted in the exhaust manifold and is used to detect the amount of oxygen present in the exhaust stream. When there is a large amount of oxygen present (lean mixture), the sensor produces a low voltage. When there is a lesser amount present (rich mixture) it produces a higher voltage.

The O2S must reach an operating temperature of approximately 600°F (315°C), in order to function properly. Some sensors contain an electrical heating element to speed up the warm-up time during cold engine operation, and to ensure the sensor remains functional during all phases of engine operation. Sensors using an internal heater are commonly referred to as Heated Oxygen Sensors or HO2S.

Front Mounted Sensors

The ECM uses the signal received from the front mounted oxygen sensor, to maintain an ideal fuel mixture of 14.7:1. Since the oxygen sensor is able to rapidly detect oxygen changes in the exhaust and convert it to electrical voltage, the sensor acts as a rich-lean switch. The ECM continually monitors the oxygen sensor's signal and corrects the air/fuel mixture accordingly, thus maintaining the optimum air/fuel mixture.

Rear Mounted Sensors

Beginning in 1995, the GA16DE and SR20DE engines use a second oxygen sensor, mounted after the TWC converter assembly. This sensor, known as a Rear HO2S, uses the same operating principles as front mounted sensors mounted. The major difference between the sensors is the purpose they serve. Unlike front mounted sensors, rear mounted sensors have no effect on the fuel management system. The On Board Diagnostic (OBD) system uses the signal received from the rear mounted sensor is to detect the efficiency of the TWC converter.

TESTING

Performance Test

FRONT MOUNTED SENSOR

1. Set the ECM to **Mode II**.
2. Start the engine and warm it up until the engine coolant indicator points in the middle of the gauge.
3. Run the engine at about 2000 rpm for 2 minutes under a no-load condition.
4. Observe the Green LED on 1987–90 vehicles, the Red LED on 1991–94 vehicles, or the instrument panel Malfunction Indicator Lamp (MIL) on 1995–96 vehicles. Make sure the lamp, cycles between **ON** (Lean) and **OFF** (Rich) more

Fig. 109 With the upper air cleaner housing cover off, unfasten the MAF sensor outer mounting bolts

Fig. 110 Some sensors may also be fastened from inside the air cleaner housing

Fig. 111 Non-heated type oxygen sensor connector

than 5 times every 10 seconds, measured at 2000 rpm under no-load conditions.

- If the lamp operation was as specified, the sensor is operating properly.
- If the sensor did not perform as specified proceed to the next step.

5. Recheck the harness connections and the ECM pin terminals for damage. Reconnect the ECM harness and repeat the test. If the test results did not change proceed to the next step.

➡**Before condemning the sensor, it is important to determine whether the sensor is defective or a fault somewhere else, is causing an improper air/fuel mixture.**

6. If the light is fixed **ON**, the fuel mixture could be too lean, causing the sensor to continuously produce a lean signal. Before replacing the sensor, verify no other fault codes exist and check the following items:
- Vacuum leaks
- Exhaust leaks, before the sensor
- Engine Misfire

7. If the light is fixed **OFF**, the fuel mixture could be too rich, causing the sensor to continuously produce a rich signal. Before replacing the sensor, verify no other fault codes exist and check the following items:
- Leaking injectors
- Fuel return system restriction
- EVAP System fault

REAR MOUNTED SENSOR

▸ **See Figure 113**

1. Connect a voltmeter between ECM terminals **52** (sensor signal) and **43** (engine ground).

➡**Do NOT disconnect the connector from the ECM.**

2. Start the engine and allow it to reach normal operating temperature.
3. While observing the voltmeter, rev-up the engine, under no load, between idle speed and 4000 rpm, at least 10 times.

➡**To achieve best results, depress and release the accelerator as quickly as possible.**

- If the sensor remained below 0.55 volts and went above 0.6 volts at least once during the test, the sensor is functioning properly.
- If the sensor voltage remained above 0.6 volts and did not go below 0.55 volts, proceed to the next step.

4. While observing the voltmeter, perform one or more of the following tests to attempt to determine the sensors low range operation.
   a. Allow the engine to idle for 10 minutes.
   b. Roadtest the vehicle. When vehicle is coasting, in 3rd gear, at 50 mph (80 km/h).
   c. Rev-up the engine, under no load, between idle speed and 6000 rpms.
   d. The voltmeter should have dropped below 0.55 volts at least once during testing.
- If the sensor performed as specified, the Rear HO2S is functioning properly.

- If the sensor did not perform as specified, replace the Rear HO2S and retest.

Heater Test

1991–94 VEHICLES

▸ **See Figure 114**

➡**1991–93 GA16DE engines do not use a heated oxygen sensor.**

1. Disconnect the HO2S connector.
2. Measure the resistance across the heater terminals **A** and **C**.

※※ **WARNING**

Make certain to properly identify the oxygen sensor terminals, before attempting to test the sensor. Testing across the wrong terminals can damage the sensor.

3. Resistance should be 3–1000 ohms.
4. If resistance is not as specified, replace the HO2S.

1995–96 VEHICLES

▸ **See Figure 115**

1. Disconnect the HO2S connector.
2. Measure the resistance across the heater terminals **1** and **3**.

※※ **WARNING**

Make certain to properly identify the oxygen sensor terminals, before attempting to test the sensor. Testing across the wrong terminals can damage the sensor.

3. Resistance should be as follows:
- Front sensor—3.3–6.3 ohms at 77°F (25°C)
- Rear sensor—5.2–8.2 ohms at 77°F (25°C)
4. If resistance is not as specified, replace the HO2S.

REMOVAL & INSTALLATION

▸ **See Figure 116**

1. Disconnect the electrical connector and remove the O2sensor from the exhaust manifold using the proper socket.

➡**The oxygen sensor will be easier to remove when the exhaust manifold is warm.**

To install:
2. Install the O2sensor in the exhaust manifold. Torque the sensor to 30–37 ft. lbs. (40–50 Nm).
3. Connect the electrical connector and make sure the wire does not touch any part of the exhaust system.

Fig. 112 A three-wire connector indicates that the oxygen sensor is a heated type

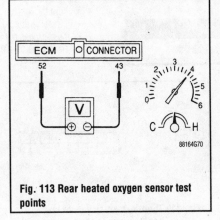

Fig. 113 Rear heated oxygen sensor test points

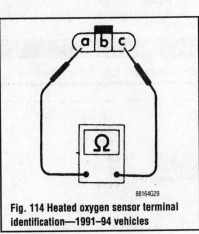

Fig. 114 Heated oxygen sensor terminal identification—1991–94 vehicles

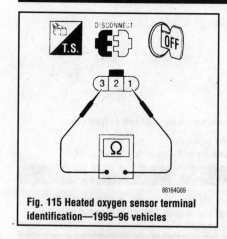

Fig. 115 Heated oxygen sensor terminal identification—1995–96 vehicles

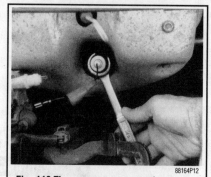

Fig. 116 The oxygen sensor can be removed using a wrench or a special socket

Fig. 117 Power steering switch mounting location—1991–94 SR20DE engine shown, others similar

Power Steering Pressure (PSP) Switch

OPERATION

In order to prevent stalling when power steering load becomes excessive, some engines use an oil pressure switch, attached to the power steering high pressure line, to detect the power steering load. When power steering load reaches a predetermined level, the switch closes, sending a signal to the control unit. The control unit will then send a command to the idle controlling device to increase idle speed. When steering loads return to normal level, the switch will open and the idle up command will cease.

TESTING

▶ **See Figure 117**

1. Disconnect the PSP switch connector.
2. Start the engine and allow to idle.
3. Check for continuity between across the terminals.
4. With the steering wheel straight, there should be no continuity. With the steering wheel being turned, there should be continuity between the terminals. If the switch does not perform as specified replace the switch and retest.

REMOVAL & INSTALLATION

1. Partially drain the power steering fluid.
2. Disconnect the wiring connector from the Power Steering Pressure switch (PSP).
3. Remove the power steering pressure switch using 2 suitable wrenches to prevent twisting the pressure line.
4. Plug the line opening with a clean rag to prevent entry of dirt or contamination.

To install:

5. Install the power steering pressure switch with a new seal and tighten securely.

✳✳ WARNING

Be careful not to damage the pressure line.

6. Connect the wiring connector.
7. Fill the power steering fluid to the proper level.
8. Start the engine and turn the wheel right to left and check for leaks.
9. Following proper procedures, bleed air from the power steering system.

Throttle Position Sensor (TPS) and Throttle Position (TP) Switch Assembly

OPERATION

▶ **See Figure 118**

All engines use a throttle position sensor to detect changes in the throttle plate angle. An additional switch assembly, to detect idle and full throttle conditions, may also be used. The TPS identifies the position of the throttle plate by transforming the throttle valve position into output voltage and feeding the voltage signal to the control unit. In addition, the TPS detects the opening or closing speed of the throttle valve and feeds the rate of voltage change to the ECM.

Some engines incorporate a throttle switch or switches into the TPS. The TP closed throttle switch closes when the throttle valve is positioned at idle and opens when it is in any other position. The TP wide-open throttle switch closes when the throttle pedal is fully depressed and opens when it is in any other position.

TESTING

Throttle Position Sensor

ALL 1987–90 ENGINES

▶ **See Figures 119 and 120**

1. Disconnect the TP sensor wire harness connector.
2. Connect a voltmeter between the TP sensor terminal **F** and a known good engine ground.
3. Turn the ignition switch to the **ON** position.
   • If meter reads 5.0 volts, proceed to the next step.
   • If meter does not read 5.0 volts, check TP sensor power supply circuitry.
4. Reconnect the TP sensor electrical connector.

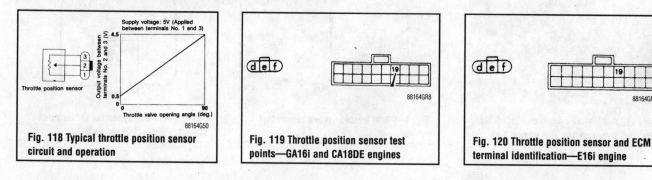

Fig. 118 Typical throttle position sensor circuit and operation

Fig. 119 Throttle position sensor test points—GA16i and CA18DE engines

Fig. 120 Throttle position sensor and ECM terminal identification—E16i engine

5. Connect voltmeter between ECM terminal **19** and a known good engine ground.

6. Measure the voltage while opening and closing the throttle. The readings should be approximately 0.4 volts with the throttle at rest and 4.0 volts with the throttle plates fully opened. The sensor voltage should be rise and fall smoothly (linear), with no sharp changes in voltage.

7. If the sensor does not perform as specified, first attempt to adjust the sensor. If unable to adjust, replace the sensor and retest.

GA16DE ENGINE

▶ See Figures 121 and 122

1. Disconnect the TP sensor wire harness connector.
2. Connect an ohmmeter between the following TP sensor terminals:
- 1991–94 engines—terminals **A** and **B**.
- 1995–96 engines—terminals **2** and **3**.
3. Measure the resistance between the TP sensor terminals while opening and closing the throttle plates. The readings should be as follows:
- With the throttle at rest, (idle position), the resistance should be approximately 0.5 kilo-ohms.
- With the throttle at wide-open position, (pedal depressed fully), the resistance should be approximately 4.0 kilo-ohms.
- With the throttle between idle and full throttle, the resistance should be between 0.5–4.0 kilo-ohms.
4. If the sensor does not perform as specified, attempt to adjust the sensor. If unable to adjust, replace the sensor and retest.

SR20DE ENGINE

▶ See Figures 123 and 124

1. Disconnect the TP sensor wire harness connector.
2. Connect an ohmmeter between TP sensor terminals **A** and **B** on 1991–94 vehicles, or terminals **2** and **3** for 1995–96 vehicles.
3. Measure the resistance between the TP sensor terminals while opening and closing the throttle plates. The readings should be as follows:
- With the throttle at rest, (idle position), the resistance should be approximately 1 kilo-ohm.
- With the throttle at wide-open position, (pedal depressed fully), the resistance should be approximately 10 kilo-ohms.

- With the throttle between idle and full throttle, the resistance should be between 1–10 kilo-ohms.
4. If the sensor does not perform as specified, attempt to adjust the sensor. If unable to adjust, replace the sensor and retest.

Closed Throttle (Idle) Switch

E15ET ENGINE

▶ See Figure 125

1. Disconnect the idle switch harness connector.
2. Check for continuity between switch terminals **18** and **25**.
3. Continuity should be present with the throttle plate fully closed. When the gas pedal is depressed, continuity should disappear. If switch fails to perform as specified, replace the idle switch.

ALL 1987–90 ENGINES

▶ See Figure 126

➡ All GA16i engines use an idle switch, but these engines do not use a wide-open throttle switch.

1. Disconnect the idle switch harness connector.
2. Check for continuity between switch terminals **A** and **B**.
3. Continuity should be present with the throttle plate fully closed. When the gas pedal is depressed, continuity should disappear. If switch fails to perform as specified, replace the idle switch.

SR20DE ENGINE WITH AUTOMATIC TRANSAXLE

▶ See Figures 127 and 128

1. Disconnect the closed TP switch harness connector.
2. Check for continuity between the switch terminals:
- 1991–94 vehicles—1 and 2
- 1995–96 vehicles—2 and 3
3. Continuity should be present with the throttle plate fully closed. When the gas pedal is depressed, continuity should disappear. If switch fails to perform as specified, replace the switch.

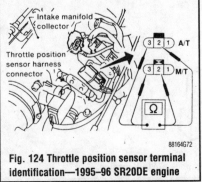

Fig. 121 Throttle position sensor terminal identification—1991–94 GA16DE engine

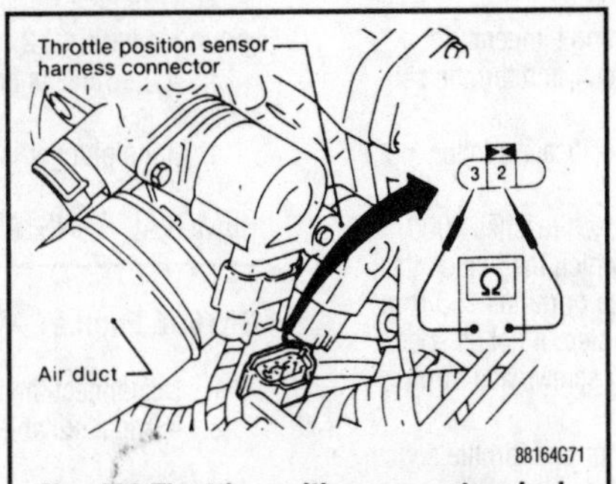

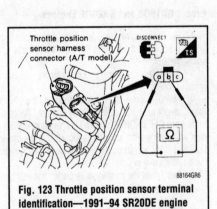

Fig. 122 Throttle position sensor terminal identification—1995–96 GA16DE engine

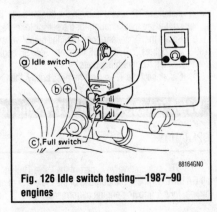

Fig. 123 Throttle position sensor terminal identification—1991–94 SR20DE engine

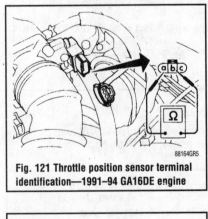

Fig. 124 Throttle position sensor terminal identification—1995–96 SR20DE engine

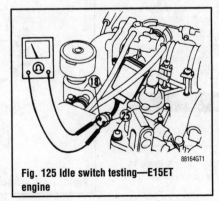

Fig. 125 Idle switch testing—E15ET engine

Fig. 126 Idle switch testing—1987–90 engines

Wide-Open Throttle Switch

SR20DE ENGINE WITH AUTOMATIC TRANSAXLE

♦ See Figures 129 and 130

1. Disconnect the closed TP switch harness connector.
2. Check for continuity between the switch terminals:
- 1991–94 vehicles—2 and 3
- 1995–96 vehicles—1 and 2
3. No continuity should be present with the throttle plate closed. When the gas pedal is fully depressed, continuity should exist. If switch fails to perform as specified, replace the switch.

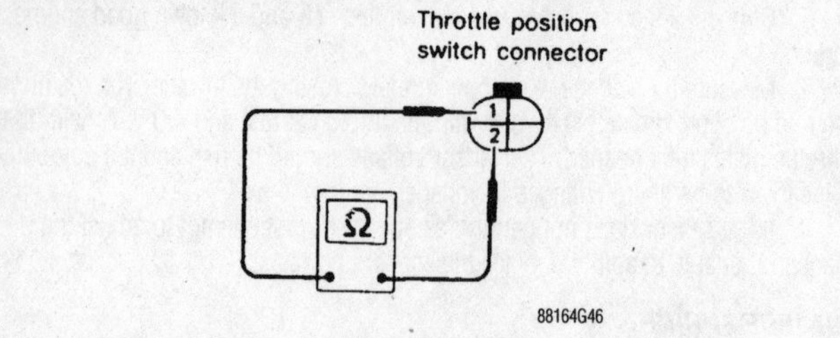

Fig. 127 Closed throttle switch testing—1991–94 SR20DE engine

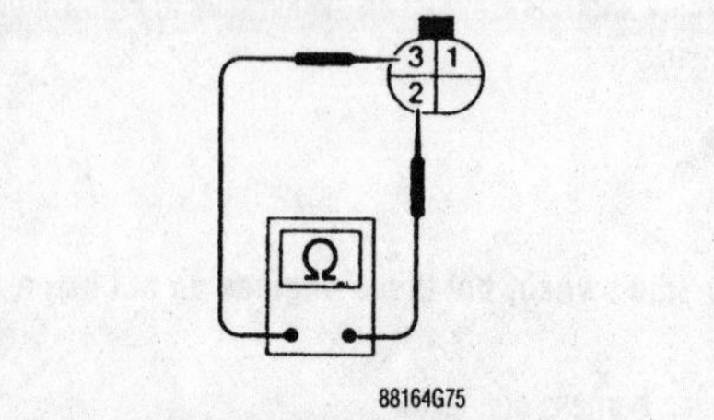

Fig. 128 Closed throttle switch testing—1995–96 SR20DE engine

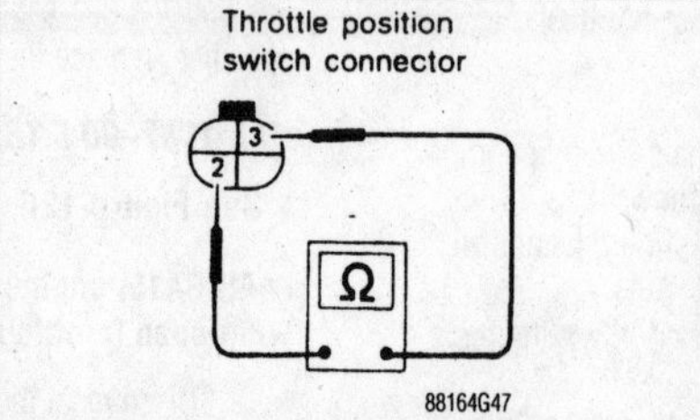

Fig. 129 Wide-open switch testing—1991–94 SR20DE engine

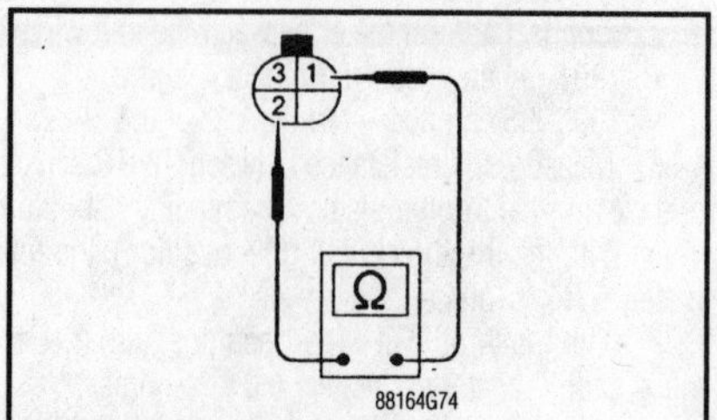

Fig. 130 Wide-open switch testing—1995–96 SR20DE engine

REMOVAL & INSTALLATION

1. Disconnect the wiring connector at the Throttle Position Sensor (TP).
2. Remove the two mounting screws and the sensor.
To install:
3. Install the sensor on the throttle body but leave the mounting screws loose enough to rotate the sensor.
4. Connect the wiring connector.
5. Adjust the sensor and tighten the screws.

ADJUSTMENT

Except GA16DE and SR20DE Engines

1. Start the engine and allow it to reach normal operating temperature.
2. Disconnect the throttle valve switch harness connector and throttle sensor harness connector.
3. Check the idle speed and if necessary, adjust to specification following proper procedures.
4. Manually open the throttle valve until the engine speed reaches 2000 rpm. Lower the engine speed slowly and note the rpm at which the idle contact turns from OFF to ON. It should be approximately 300 plus or minus 150 rpm over whatever engine speed was recorded in the previous step. If not as specified, adjust by loosening the throttle valve switch securing screws and turning the throttle valve switch.
5. Reconnect the throttle valve switch harness connector and throttle sensor harness connector.

GA16DE and SR20DE Engines

1. Install the TP sensor body in the throttle body. If the retaining bolts are tightened, loosen them enough for the sensor to move.
2. Rotate the TP sensor body until the output voltage is 0.45–0.55 volts on 1991–94 engines or 0.35–0.65 volts on 1995–96 engines.
3. Tighten the mounting bolts.
4. Disconnect the TP sensor harness briefly, then reconnect the harness.

Valve Timing Control (VTC) Solenoid Valve

OPERATION

The VTC solenoid valve is part of the Valve Timing Control System, found on all GA16DE engines. The purpose of the system is to achieve optimum valve timing, thus improving engine performance.

The system will vary the intake valve timing according to engine speed, and other inputs received from the coolant temperature and throttle position sensors. The ECM controls the position of the intake camshaft, by controlling the oil pressure to the intake camshaft pulley hub. When the ECM energizes the solenoid, oil pressure is supplied to the pulley hub, changing the position of the hub, thereby advancing the intake valve timing.

TESTING

GA16DE Engine

♦ See Figure 131

1. Remove the VTC valve from the vehicle.
2. Using a fused jumper wire, apply battery voltage to terminal **1**, and ground to terminal **2**.
3. If the valve is functioning correctly, the plunger shaft in the valve should be extended.
4. If the plunger is not extended, replace the VTC solenoid.

REMOVAL & INSTALLATION

GA16DE Engine

1. Disconnect the wiring harness connector from the VTC valve.
2. Using a suitable wrench, remove the VTC from the cylinder head.

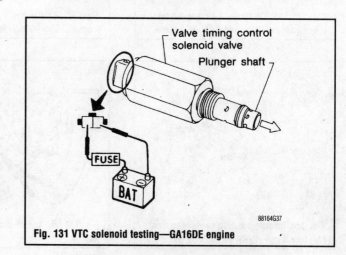

Fig. 131 VTC solenoid testing—GA16DE engine

To install:
3. Install the VTC in to the cylinder head, by first hand tightening, then using a wrench.
4. Plug the wire harness connector into the VTC valve.

Vehicle Speed Sensor (VSS)

OPERATION

The vehicle speed signal is generated from the vehicle speed sensor. Sentra/Pulsar models use two different type sensors.

Reed Switch Type

♦ **See Figure 132**

Reed switch type sensors are used on early systems, through 1990. Beginning in 1991, the reed switch type sensors are only used with analogue (needle) type instrument clusters.

The reed switch type VSS is part of the speedometer assembly, mounted to the rear of the instrument cluster. The shaft of the reed switch is turned by the speedometer cable connected to the rear of the instrument cluster. The reed switch has a small magnet attached to it which causes the reed switch to close every time the magnet sweeps past the reed switch. The typical reed switch VSS is connected to a regulated 5V direct current supply, resulting in a switching direct current (DC) square-wave output signal. The VSS output signal frequency will be directly proportional to vehicle speed and is carried to the ECM through the wiring harness.

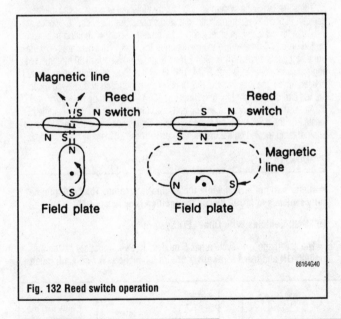

Fig. 132 Reed switch operation

Magnetic Impulse Type

♦ **See Figure 133**

Magnetic impulse type VSS sensors are used on digital type instrument clusters, beginning in 1991, and all vehicles beginning in 1993.

These sensors use a two wire sensor, located at the transaxle. The shaft of the VSS is turned by the transaxle output shaft. The shaft is attached to a ferromagnetic toothed wheel, which spins in close proximity to a permanent magnet wrapped with many turns of fine wire. As the magnetic field is distorted by the passing teeth of the ferromagnetic wheel, the movement induces a voltage into the coil around the magnet. The voltage produced by the coil will be alternating (AC), and the frequency will be proportional to the RPM of the shaft.

TESTING

Reed Switch Type

♦ **See Figures 134, 135 and 136**

1. Check the speedometer operation.
•   If the speedometer is not functioning, check speedometer cable and begin with speedometer assembly testing. Repair or replace necessary components.
•   If the speedometer is functioning properly, proceed to the next step.
2. Remove the instrument cluster from the vehicle.
3. Connect a continuity tester across the VSS connector terminals.
4. Turn the VSS pinion gear by hand.
5. As the VSS shaft is turned, the continuity tester should alternate between open and shorted.
6. If the VSS does not switch back and forth between open and shorted as the VSS shaft is turned, replace the VSS.

Magnetic Impulse Type

♦ **See Figure 133**

1. Remove the Vehicle Speed Sensor (VSS).
2. Connect a voltmeter across the VSS terminals.
3. Set the voltmeter to read low range alternating current.
4. Spin the VSS pinion gear fast and measure the voltage.
5. Voltage should be about 0.5V AC with the VSS spinning.
•   If there is no output from the VSS when spun, replace the VSS.
•   If the VSS tests okay, check wiring to the instrument cluster and from cluster to the ECM.

REMOVAL & INSTALLATION

Reed Switch Type

The instrument panel mounted VSS is integral part of the vehicle speed sensor. Refer to Section 6 for Speedometer Head removal and installation information.

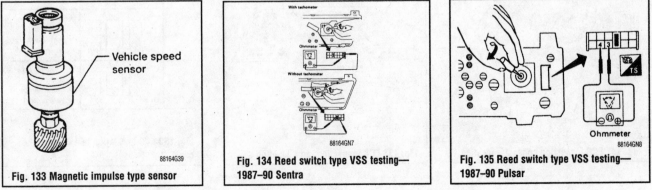

Fig. 133 Magnetic impulse type sensor

Fig. 134 Reed switch type VSS testing—1987–90 Sentra

Fig. 135 Reed switch type VSS testing—1987–90 Pulsar

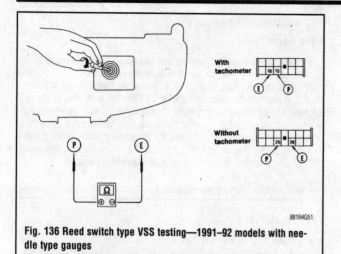

Fig. 136 Reed switch type VSS testing—1991–92 models with needle type gauges

Magnetic Impulse Type

1. Locate the VSS at the transaxle housing.
2. If equipped with speedometer cable, disconnect the cable from the sensor.
3. Disconnect the wire harness connector at the VSS.
4. Remove the hardware which secures the VSS to the transaxle. Once the hardware is removed, lift the VSS out of transaxle hole.

To install:

5. Carefully lower the VSS into its mounting hole in the transaxle. Do not force the piece. Allow it the mesh with the transaxle gears.
6. Secure the VSS with the attaching hardware.
7. If removed, connect the speedometer cable.
8. Connect the wiring harness connector to the VSS.

SELF-DIAGNOSTIC SYSTEMS

Electronic Controlled Carburetor (ECC) Engines

▶ See Figures 137, 138 and 139

Engines equipped with an electronically controlled carburetor use an ECM that does not store trouble codes. However, the system does provide some self-diagnostic capabilities. By observing the ECC system inspection lamp, located on the instrument panel, some basic system operating information can be obtained. Use the following procedure to evaluate system operation.

1. Check the ECU and oxygen sensor harness connector for damage or corrosion.
2. Verify the ECC the inspection harness connector is disconnected.
3. Turn the ignition switch **ON** and check the ECC inspection light on the instrument panel. If the bulb does not light, replace the bulb or repair wiring.
4. If the light stays **ON**, start the engine and warm.
5. Run the engine to 2000 rpm, for about 5 minutes. If the light goes **OFF**, there is no trouble.
6. If the light stays **ON**, turn the engine **OFF** and connect the Electronic Controlled Carburetor (ECC) test connector near the wiper motor.
7. Run the engine at idle to receive lighting intervals. If no light exists, check for an opening in the oxygen sensor circuit.
8. If the light comes **ON**, check the lighting intervals and compare the reading to the ECC inspection lamp diagnostic chart.
9. Proceed with testing of the appropriate components, according to the results received in Step 7.

Fuel Injected Engines

SYSTEM OPERATION

The self-diagnostic system used on all fuel injected engines is capable of detecting specific system malfunctions and storing trouble codes. All codes are available for examination unless codes have been erased, or ignition has been cycled on/off 50 times since the malfunction last occurred. There are two variations of the this system. The 1984 E15ET engine and all 1987–90 fuel injected engines, use a dual LED type ECM. This ECM has 5 diagnostic modes. The LED is used for diagnostics and troubleshooting. A malfunction is displayed by both the red and green Light Emitting Diodes (LED's), if so equipped.

All 1991–96 vehicles use an Engine Control Module (ECM) with a single LED located on the side. The ECM lamp will blink simultaneously with the "Check Engine" lamp located on the instrument panel. These ECMs only have 2 modes.

READING CODES

➥Modes will not switch while the engine is running. The ECM automatically switches to MODE I when the ignition is switched OFF.

1984–90 Vehicles With Dual LED System

The self-diagnostic system has 5 modes. To switch modes, switch the ignition **ON** and use a screwdriver to turn the mode select switch through

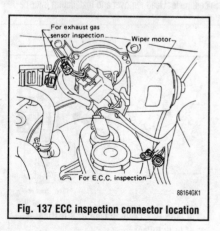

Fig. 137 ECC inspection connector location

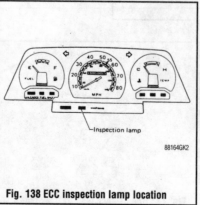

Fig. 138 ECC inspection lamp location

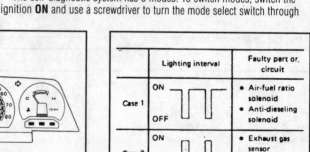

	Lighting interval	Faulty part or circuit
Case 1	ON ⎍⎍⎍ OFF	• Air-fuel ratio solenoid • Anti-dieseling solenoid
Case 2	ON ⎍⎍ OFF	• Exhaust gas sensor • Water temperature sensor

Fig. 139 ECC inspection lamp diagnostic chart

the access port on the ECM. The inspection lights will begin to flash. When the desired mode has been entered, turn the screwdriver fully counterclockwise. The red LED and green LED perform different functions in different modes.

Mode I—This is the normal vehicle operating mode. The green LED will indicate loop status. If the green LED is not blinking when the engine is running, the vehicle is in open loop, or the HO2S, O2S, or sensor circuit has a malfunction. If the green LED is blinking, the vehicle is in closed loop. If a malfunction takes place, the red LED and the MIL will glow, indicating a malfunction has occurred.

Mode II—Both the red LED and green LED are used to monitor mixture ratio feedback control. The green LED will function as described in MODE I. If vehicle is in open loop, the red LED and green LED will remain on or off. In order for results to be valid, vehicle must be in closed loop. In closed loop, the red LED remains off if the system is running rich, comes on if the system is running lean, and blinks at the same time with the green LED if system is within 5% of the exact air/fuel ratio.

Mode III—When this mode is accessed, the codes stored in the ECM's memory will be flashed by the green LED and red LED on the side of the ECM. The red LED will light first. This is the first digit of the trouble code; the green LED will flash next, showing the second digit of the code. For example: 2 flashes of the red LED followed by 1 flash of the green LED corresponds to Code 21.

Mode IV—This mode is used for checking the throttle plate (TP) switch, starter, and vehicle speed switch status. When the TP switch or starter switch is activated, the red LED will briefly flash as the status changes. For VSS status, the green LED will remain off when vehicle speed is less than 12 mph (19 km/h) and come on when vehicle speed is greater than 12 mph (19 km/h).

Mode V—This mode represents a real-time diagnostic test of the crank angle sensor, ignition signal and the mass airflow signal. The malfunction code will be displayed only when the malfunction occurs and will not be stored in memory. The output code will appear as a single or short string of pulses. Count the number of pulses for the malfunction code.

- 1 pulse—CMP sensor signal lost or noise in signal
- 2 pulses—MAF Sensor signal abnormal
- 3 pulses—Fuel pump circuit shorted or open
- 4 pulses—Ignition signal lost

1991–96 Engines With Single LED System

▶ See Figures 140, 141, 142, 143 and 144

➡**Modes will not switch while the engine is running. The ECM automatically switches to MODE I when the ignition is switched OFF.**

To switch modes, turn the ignition on and use a screwdriver to turn the mode select switch through the access port on the ECM. Turn the mode select switch clockwise and hold for 2 seconds before turning the screwdriver counterclockwise.

Mode I (Normal/Malfunction Warning)—On California models, if a malfunction occurs with the engine running, the red LED and the MIL will glow. This indicates an ECM malfunction has occurred, and a code has been stored. On Federal models, codes are stored, and the red LED will glow only when the CPU in the ECM malfunctions.

Mode II (Self-Diagnostics)—When mode is accessed (the engine OFF), ECM memory codes will be flashed by the MIL and the red LED on the side of the ECM. Long flashes (0.6 second) represent the first digit of the code. Short flashes (0.3 second) represent the second digit of the code. For example: 4 long flashes followed by 3 short flashes of the MIL (or the red LED) would indicate a Code 43.

Mode II (HO2S or O2S monitor)—When this mode is used (while the engine is running), both the red LED and the MIL are used to monitor air/fuel mixture feedback control. For accurate results, the vehicle must be in closed loop. In closed loop, the red LED will indicate if system is running rich (light off), lean (light on) or at ideal air/fuel ratio (blinking at 5 times in 10 seconds).

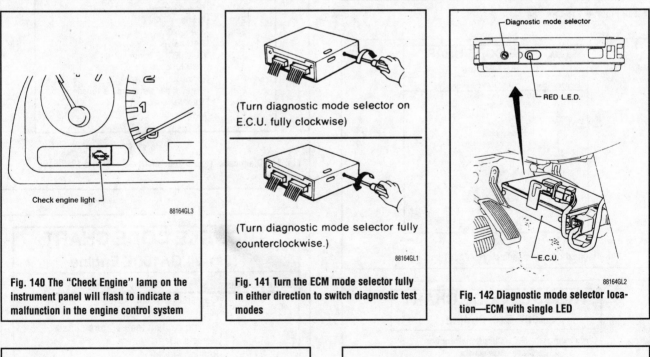

Fig. 140 The "Check Engine" lamp on the instrument panel will flash to indicate a malfunction in the engine control system

Fig. 141 Turn the ECM mode selector fully in either direction to switch diagnostic test modes

Fig. 142 Diagnostic mode selector location—ECM with single LED

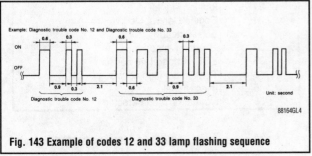

Fig. 143 Example of codes 12 and 33 lamp flashing sequence

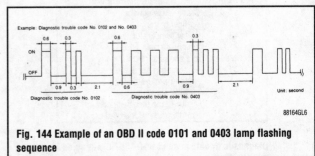

Fig. 144 Example of an OBD II code 0101 and 0403 lamp flashing sequence

CLEARING CODES

Dual LED System

▶ See Figure 145

Switch from diagnostic Mode III to Mode IV with the engine off by turning the diagnostic mode selector clockwise. Turning the test selector fully clockwise will cause the diagnostic modes to cycle until a mode is selected. Also, disconnecting the battery for no less than 24 hours will clear codes.

Single LED System

Switch from diagnostic Mode II to Mode I with the engine off by turning the diagnostic mode selector fully clockwise. The diagnostic mode selector is located on the side of the engine control module (ECM). Wait for 2 seconds before turning the mode selector counterclockwise. Also, disconnecting the battery for at least 24 hours will clear codes.

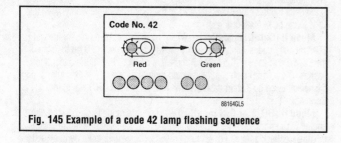

Fig. 145 Example of a code 42 lamp flashing sequence

DIAGNOSTIC TROUBLE CODES

▶ See Figurse 146 thru 154

TROUBLE CODE CHART
E15ET Engine

Code Number	Circuit malfunction
11	Crank angle sensor
12	Air flow meter
13	Water temperature sensor
14	Speed sensor
21	Ignition signal
23	Throttle valve switch
31	Fast Idle Control Device (with A/C)
31	ECU (ECCS control unit with A/C)
32	Starter signal
33	Exhaust gas sensor
34	Detonation sensor
41	Air temperature sensor
42	Barometric pressure sensor
43	Battery voltage too low or high
44	ECCS working properly

88164GM1

Fig. 146 Diagnostic trouble code chart—E15ET engine

TROUBLE CODE CHART
1987 E16i Engine

Code Number	Circuit malfunction
11	Crank angle sensor
12	Air flow meter
13	Water temperature sensor
21	Ignition signal
22	Idle speed control
33	Exhaust gas sensor
41	Air temperature sensor
42	Throttle sensor circuit
43	Mixture ratio feedback control
44	No malfunction detected

88164GM2

Fig. 147 Diagnostic trouble code chart—1987 E16i engine

TROUBLE CODE CHART
CA16DE & CA18DE Engines

Code Number	Circuit malfunction
11	Crank angle sensor
12	Air flow meter
13	Water temperature sensor
14	Speed sensor
21	Ignition signal
23	Idle switch
31	ECU (ECCS control unit)
32	EGR function
33	Exhaust gas sensor
34	Detonation sensor
35	Exhaust gas temperature sensor
42	Throttle sensor
44	Throttle valve switch (CA16DE)
45	Injector leak
55	No malfunction detected

88164GM3

Fig. 148 Diagnostic trouble code chart—CA16DE and CA18DE engines

TROUBLE CODE CHART
GA16i & 1988 E16i Engines

Code Number	Circuit malfunction
11	Crank angle sensor
12	Air flow meter
13	Water temperature sensor
14	Speed sensor
21	Ignition signal
23	Idle switch
25	AAC valve
31	ECU (ECCS control unit)
32	EGR function
33	Exhaust gas sensor
35	Exhaust gas temperature sensor
42	Throttle sensor
45	Injector leak
55	No malfunction detected

88164GM4

Fig. 149 Diagnostic trouble code chart—GA16i and 1988 E16i engines

TROUBLE CODE CHART
1991-94 GA16DE Engine

Code Number	Circuit malfunction
11	Camshaft position sensor
12	Mass air flow sensor
13	Engine coolant temperature sensor
14	Vehicle speed sensor
21	Ignition signal
31	Engine Control Module
32	EGR function
33	Oxygen sensor
35	EGR temperature sensor
43	Throttle position sensor
45	Injector leak
55	No malfunction detected

88164GM5

Fig. 150 Diagnostic trouble code chart—1991–94 GA16DE engine

TROUBLE CODE CHART
1991-94 SR20DE Engine

Code Number	Circuit malfunction
11	Camshaft position sensor
12	Mass air flow sensor
13	Engine coolant temperature sensor
14	Vehicle speed sensor
21	Ignition signal
25	IACV-AAC valve
28	Overheat
31	Engine Control Module
32	EGR function
33	Heated oxygen sensor
34	Knock sensor
35	EGR temperature sensor
43	Throttle position sensor
45	Injector leak
55	No malfunction detected

Fig. 151 Diagnostic trouble code chart—1991-94 SR20DE engine

TROUBLE CODE CHART
1995 GA16DE Engine

Code Number	Circuit malfunction
11	Camshaft position sensor
12	Mass air flow sensor
13	Engine coolant temperature sensor
14	Vehicle speed sensor
21	Ignition signal - primary
25	IACV-AAC valve
28	Overheat
31	Engine Control Module
32	EGR system
33	Front oxygen sensor
34	Knock sensor
35	EGR temperature sensor
36	EGRC-BPT valve
37	Closed loop
41	Intake air temperature sensor
43	Throttle position sensor
55	No self-diagnostic failure indicated
65	Cylinder #4 misfire
66	Cylinder #3 misfire
67	Cylinder #2 misfire
68	Cylinder #1 misfire
71	Random misfire
72	TWC system
76	Fuel injection system
77	Rear oxygen sensor
82	Crankshaft position sensor
85	VTC solenoid valve
91	Front oxygen sensor heater
94	Torque converter clutch solenoid
95	Crank P/S (OBD) cog
98	Coolant temperature sensor
103	Park/Neutral switch
105	EGRC solenoid

Fig. 152 Diagnostic trouble code chart—1995 GA16DE engine

TROUBLE CODE CHART
1995 SR20DE Engine

Code Number	Circuit malfunction	Code Number	Circuit malfunction
11	Camshaft position sensor	76	Fuel injection system
12	Mass air flow sensor	77	Rear oxygen sensor
13	Engine coolant temperature sensor	82	Crankshaft position sensor
14	Vehicle speed sensor	84	A/T diagnostic comm line
21	Ignition signal - primary	91	Front oxygen sensor heater
25	IACV-AAC valve	95	Crank P/S (OBD) cog
28	Overheat	98	Coolant temperature sensor
31	Engine Control Module	103	Park/Neutral switch
32	EGR system	105	EGRC solenoid
33	Front oxygen sensor	111	Inhibitor switch
34	Knock sensor	112	Vehicle speed sensor - A/T
35	EGR temperature sensor	113	A/T 1st signal
36	EGRC-BPT valve	114	A/T 2st signal
37	Closed loop	115	A/T 3st signal
41	Intake air temperature sensor	116	A/T 4st signal
43	Throttle position sensor	118	Shift solenoid A
55	No self-diagnostic failure indicated	121	Shift solenoid B
65	Cylinder #4 misfire	123	Overrun clutch switch
66	Cylinder #3 misfire	124	Torque converter clutch switch
67	Cylinder #2 misfire	125	Line pressure S/V
68	Cylinder #1 misfire	126	Throttle position sensor A/T
71	Random misfire	127	Engine speed signal
72	TWC system	128	Fluid temperature sensor

Fig. 153 Diagnostic trouble code chart—1995 SR20DE engine

TROUBLE CODE CHART
1996 GA16DE & SR20DE Engines

Code Number	Circuit malfunction	Code Number	Circuit malfunction
0101	Camshaft position sensor	0605	Cylinder #4 misfire
0102	Mass air flow sensor	0606	Cylinder #3 misfire
0103	Engine coolant temperature sensor	0607	Cylinder #2 misfire
0104	Vehicle speed sensor	0608	Cylinder #1 misfire
0201	Ignition signal - primary	0701	Multiple cylinder misfire
0205	IACV-AAC valve	0702	TWC system
0208	Cooling fan circuit (overheat)	0706	Fuel injection system
0301	Engine Control Module	0707	Rear oxygen sensor
0302	EGR system function	0802	Crankshaft position sensor (OBD)
0303	Front oxygen sensor	0804	A/T diagnostic communication signal
0304	Knock sensor	0805	VTC solenoid valve
0305	EGR temperature sensor	0901	Front oxygen sensor heater
0306	EGRC-BPT valve	0904	Torque converter clutch solenoid
0307	Closed loop	0905	Crankshaft position sensor
0401	Intake air temperature sensor	0908	Coolant temperature sensor
0403	Throttle position sensor	1003	Park/Neutral switch
0505	No self-diagnostic failure indicated	1005	EGR/EVAP canister purge solenoid

Fig. 154 Diagnostic trouble code chart—1996 GA16DE and SR20DE engines

COMPONENT LOCATIONS

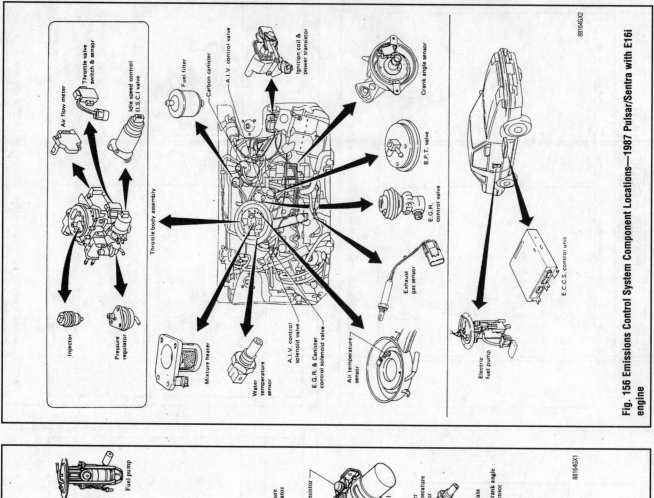

Fig. 156 Emissions Control System Component Locations—1987 Pulsar/Sentra with E16i engine

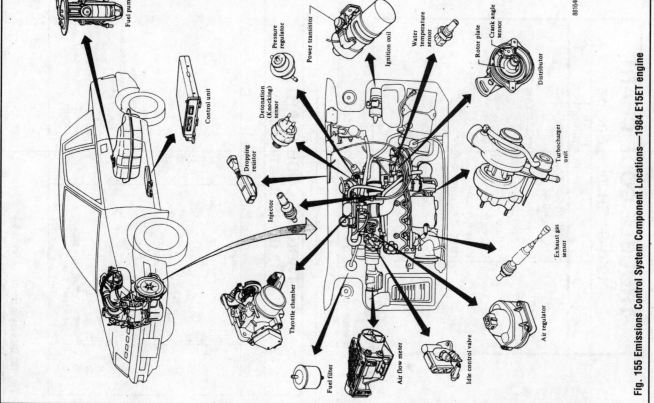

Fig. 155 Emissions Control System Component Locations—1984 E15ET engine

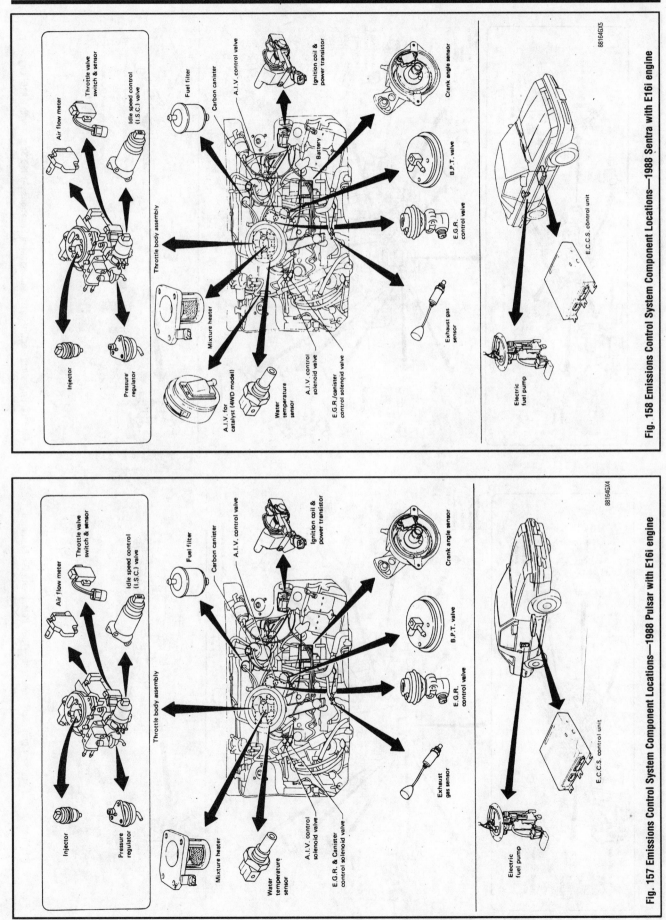

Fig. 158 Emissions Control System Component Locations—1988 Sentra with E16i engine

Fig. 157 Emissions Control System Component Locations—1988 Pulsar with E16i engine

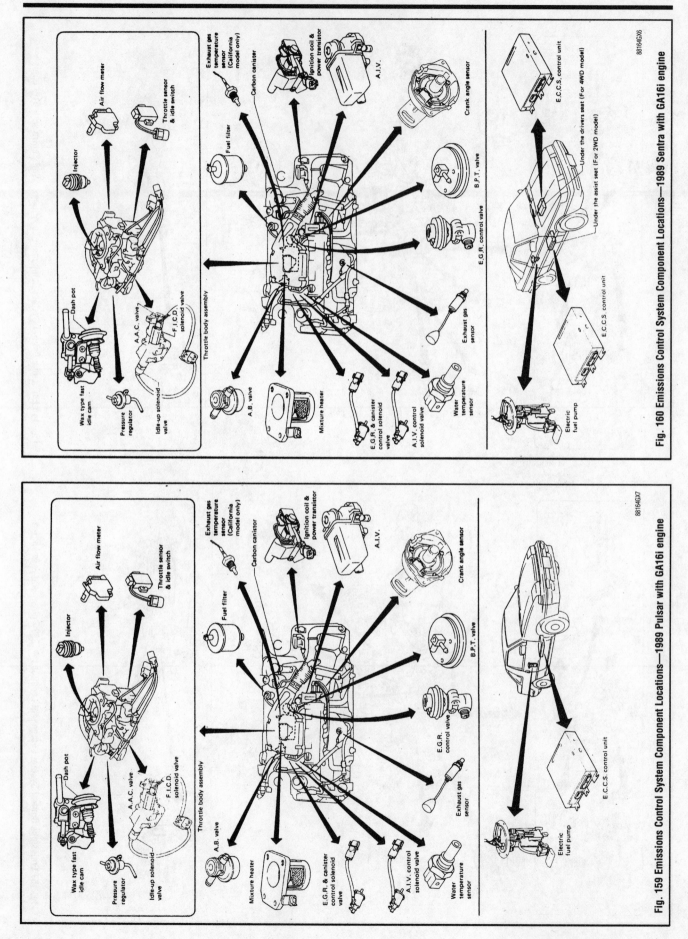

Fig. 160 Emissions Control System Component Locations—1989 Sentra with GA16i engine

Fig. 159 Emissions Control System Component Locations—1989 Pulsar with GA16i engine

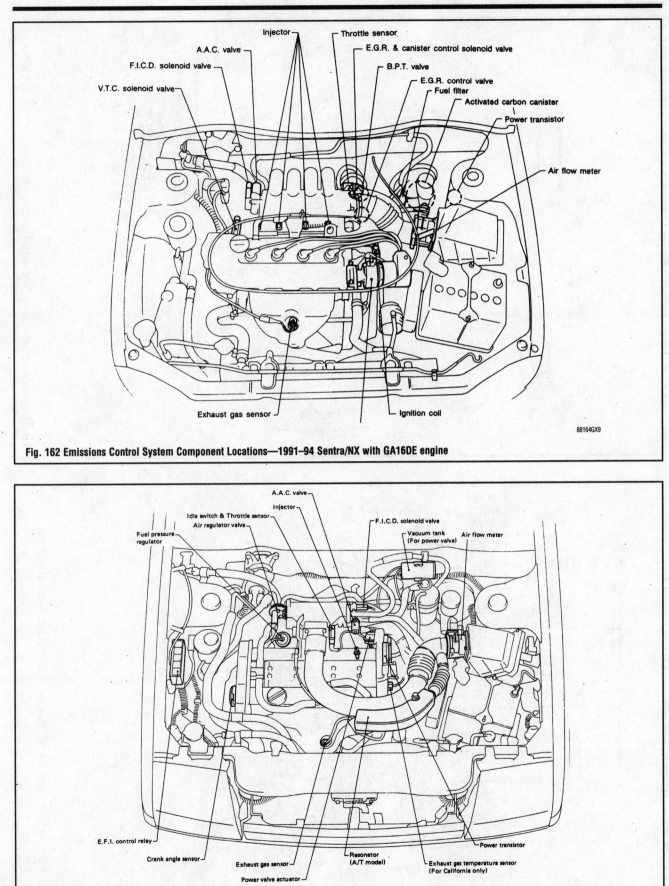

Fig. 162 Emissions Control System Component Locations—1991–94 Sentra/NX with GA16DE engine

Fig. 161 Emissions Control System Component Locations—1989 Pulsar with CA18DE engine, CA16DE engine similar

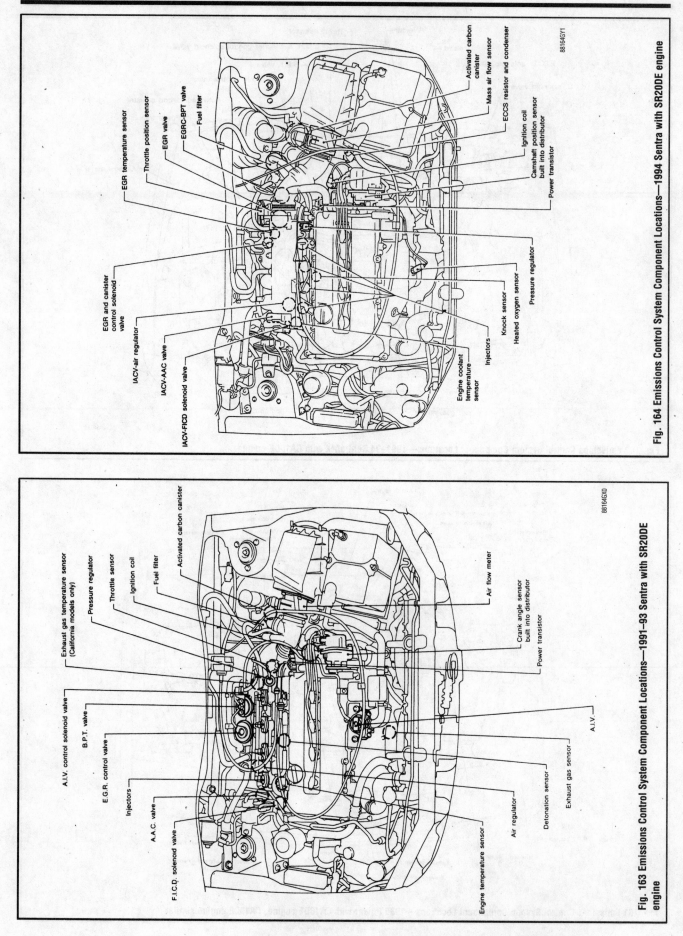

Fig. 164 Emissions Control System Component Locations—1994 Sentra with SR20DE engine

Fig. 163 Emissions Control System Component Locations—1991–93 Sentra with SR20DE engine

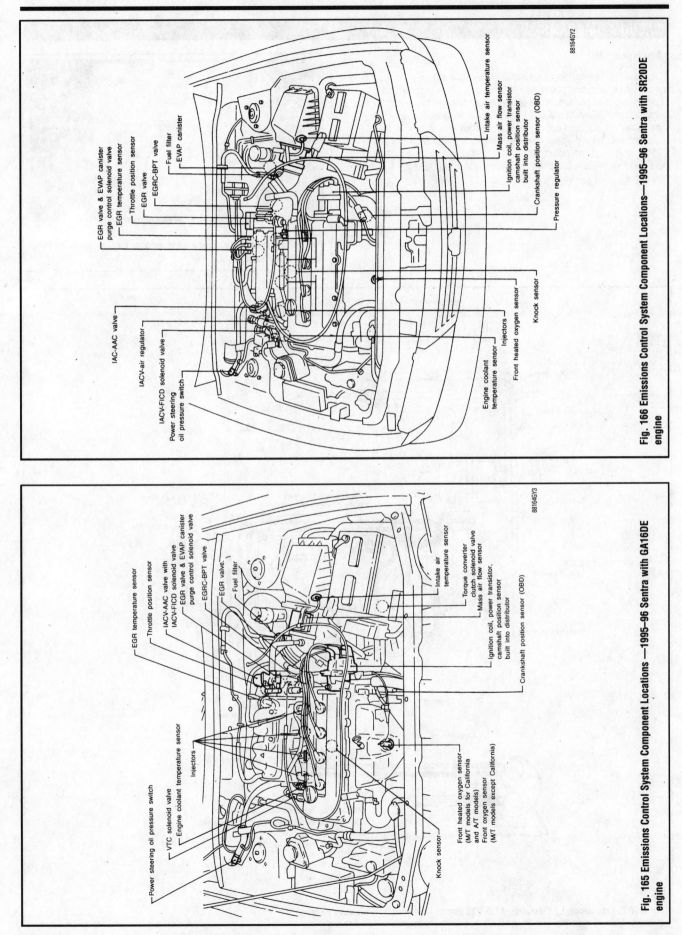

88164GY2

Fig. 166 Emissions Control System Component Locations—1995–96 Sentra with SR20DE engine

EGR valve & EVAP canister purge control solenoid valve
EGR temperature sensor
Throttle position sensor
EGR valve
EGRC-BPT valve
Fuel filter
EVAP canister
Intake air temperature sensor
Mass air flow sensor
Ignition coil, power transistor camshaft position sensor built into distributor
Crankshaft position sensor (OBD)
Pressure regulator

IAC-AAC valve
IACV-air regulator
IACV-FICD solenoid valve
Power steering oil pressure switch
Engine coolant temperature sensor
Front heated oxygen sensor
Injectors
Knock sensor

88164GY3

Fig. 165 Emissions Control System Component Locations —1995–96 Sentra with GA16DE engine

EGR temperature sensor
Throttle position sensor
IACV-AAC valve with IACV-FICD solenoid valve
EGR valve & EVAP canister purge control solenoid valve
EGRC-BPT valve
EGR valve
Fuel filter
Intake air temperature sensor
Torque converter clutch solenoid valve
Mass air flow sensor
Ignition coil, power transistor, camshaft position sensor built into distributor
Crankshaft position sensor (OBD)

Power steering oil pressure switch
VTC solenoid valve
Engine coolant temperature sensor
Injectors
Knock sensor
Front heated oxygen sensor (M/T models for California and A/T models)
Front oxygen sensor (M/T models except California)

VACUUM DIAGRAMS

♦ **See Figure 146**

Following are vacuum diagrams for most of the engine and emissions package combinations covered by this manual. Because vacuum circuits will vary based on various engine and vehicle options, always refer first to the vehicle emission control information label, if present. Should the label be missing, or should vehicle be equipped with a different engine from the vehicle's original equipment, refer to the diagrams below for the same or similar configuration.

If you wish to obtain a replacement emissions label, most manufacturers make the labels available for purchase. The labels can usually be ordered from a local dealer.

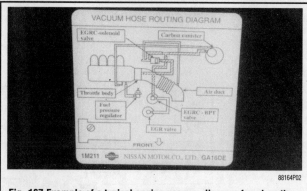

Fig. 167 Example of a typical engine vacuum diagram found on the inner engine hood panel

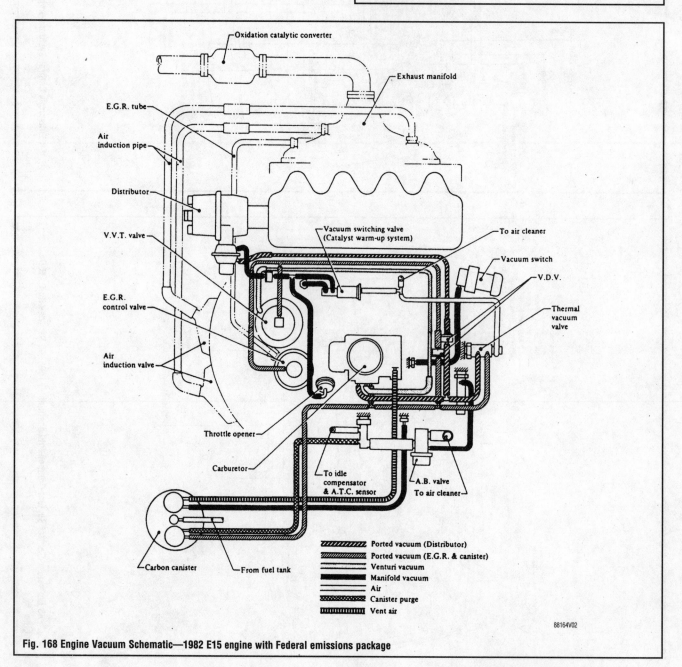

Fig. 168 Engine Vacuum Schematic—1982 E15 engine with Federal emissions package

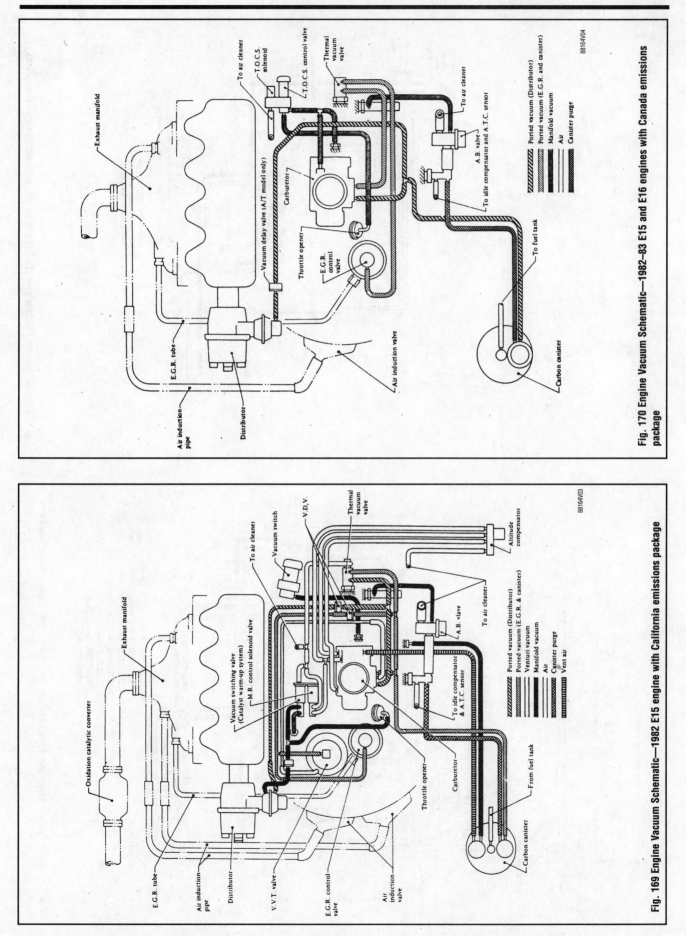

Fig. 170 Engine Vacuum Schematic—1982-83 E15 and E16 engines with Canada emissions package

Fig. 169 Engine Vacuum Schematic—1982 E15 engine with California emissions package

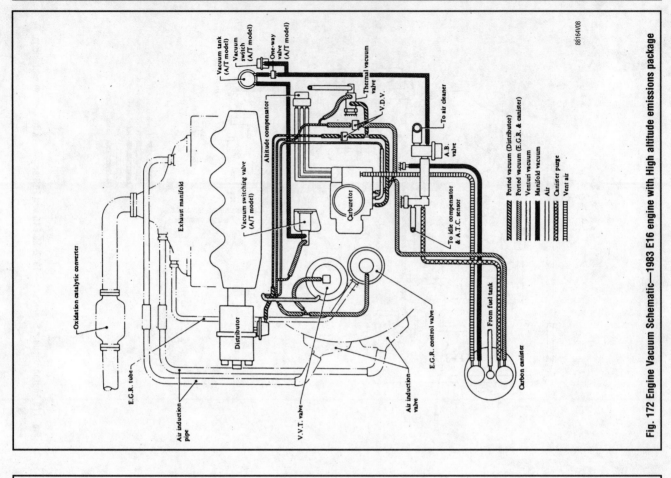

Fig. 172 Engine Vacuum Schematic—1983 E16 engine with High altitude emissions package

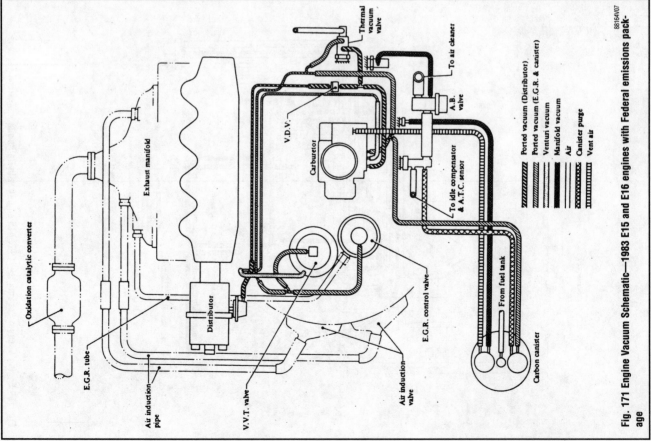

Fig. 171 Engine Vacuum Schematic—1983 E15 and E16 engines with Federal emissions package

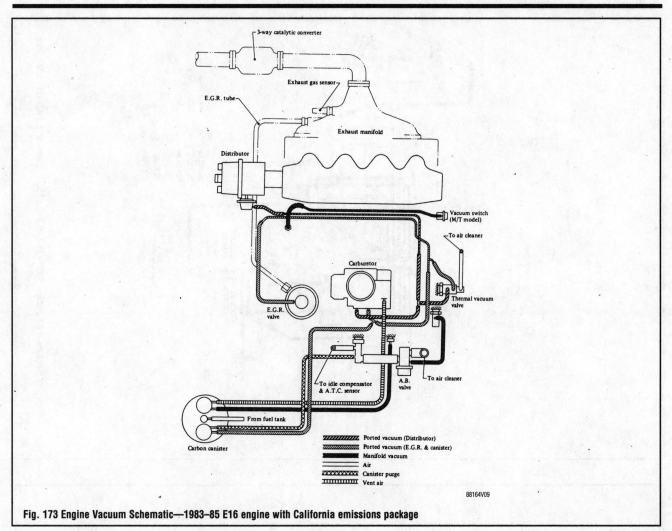

Fig. 173 Engine Vacuum Schematic—1983–85 E16 engine with California emissions package

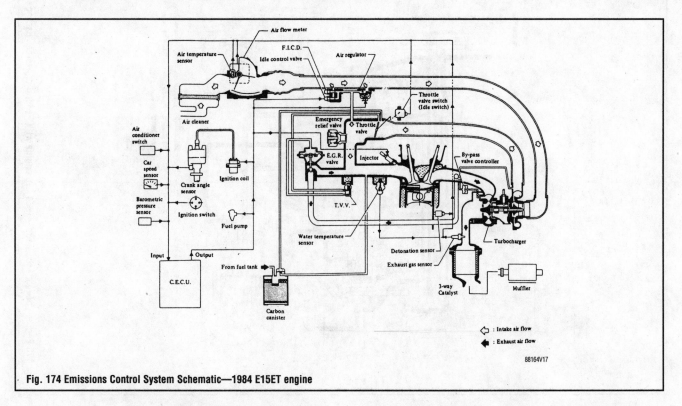

Fig. 174 Emissions Control System Schematic—1984 E15ET engine

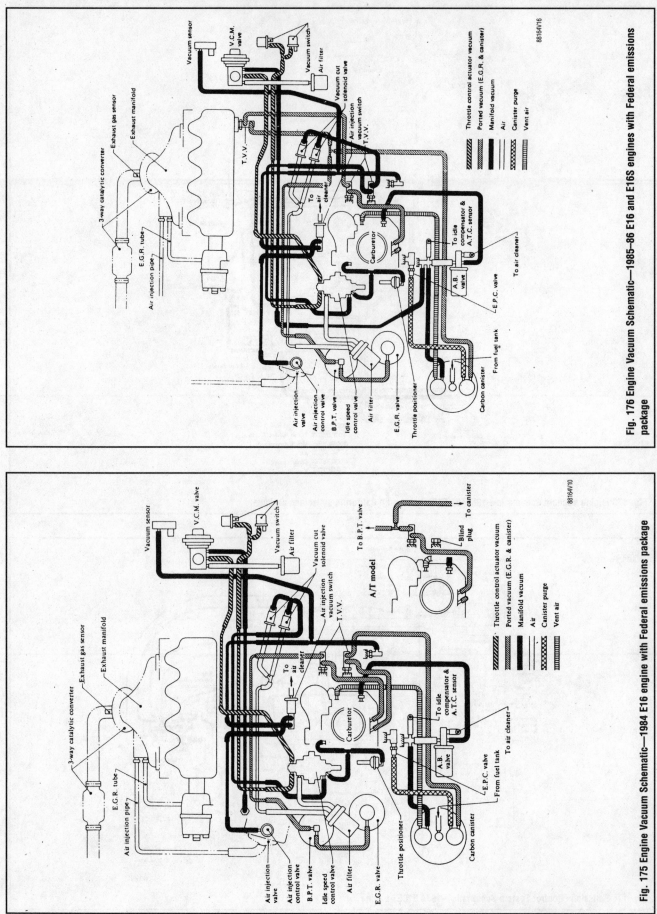

Fig. 176 Engine Vacuum Schematic—1985-86 E16 and E16S engines with Federal emissions package

Fig. 175 Engine Vacuum Schematic—1984 E16 engine with Federal emissions package

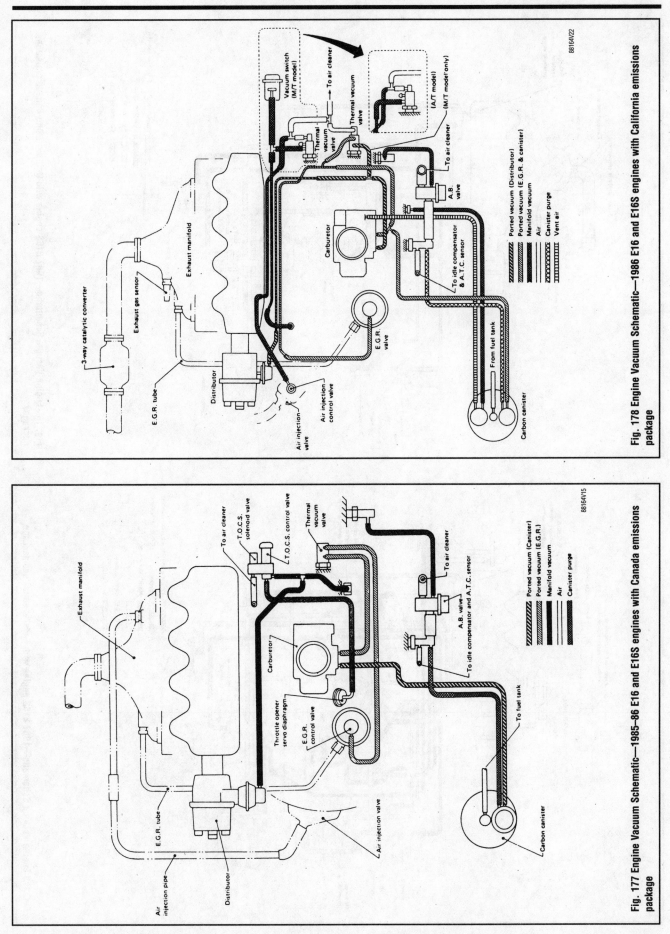

8816A/V22

Fig. 178 Engine Vacuum Schematic—1986 E16 and E16S engines with California emissions package

8816A/V15

Fig. 177 Engine Vacuum Schematic—1985–86 E16 and E16S engines with Canada emissions package

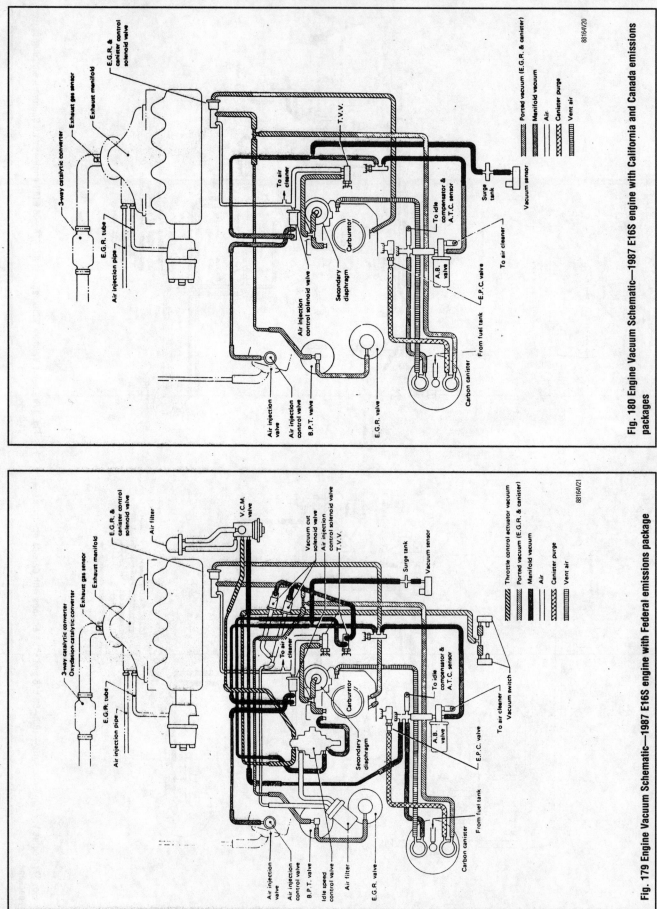

Fig. 180 Engine Vacuum Schematic—1987 E16S engine with California and Canada emissions packages

Fig. 179 Engine Vacuum Schematic—1987 E16S engine with Federal emissions package

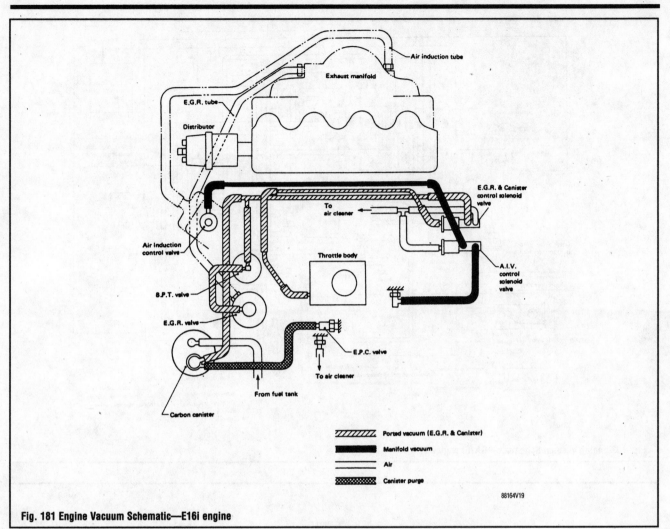

Fig. 181 Engine Vacuum Schematic—E16i engine

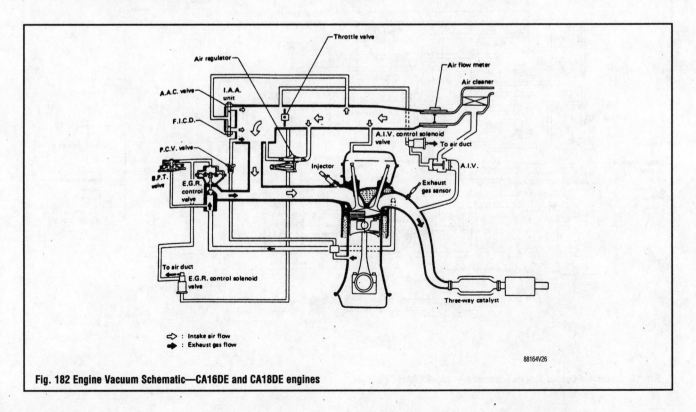

Fig. 182 Engine Vacuum Schematic—CA16DE and CA18DE engines

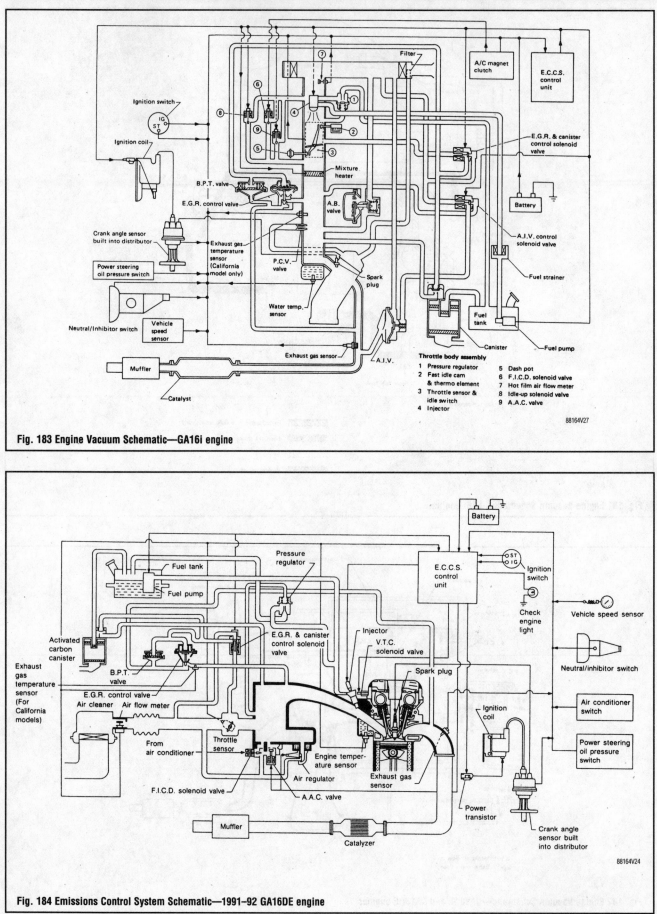

Throttle body assembly

1 Pressure regulator
2 Fast idle cam & thermo element
3 Throttle sensor & idle switch
4 Injector
5 Dash pot
6 F.I.C.D. solenoid valve
7 Hot film air flow meter
8 Idle-up solenoid valve
9 A.A.C. valve

88164V27

Fig. 183 Engine Vacuum Schematic—GA16i engine

88164V24

Fig. 184 Emissions Control System Schematic—1991–92 GA16DE engine

System Diagram

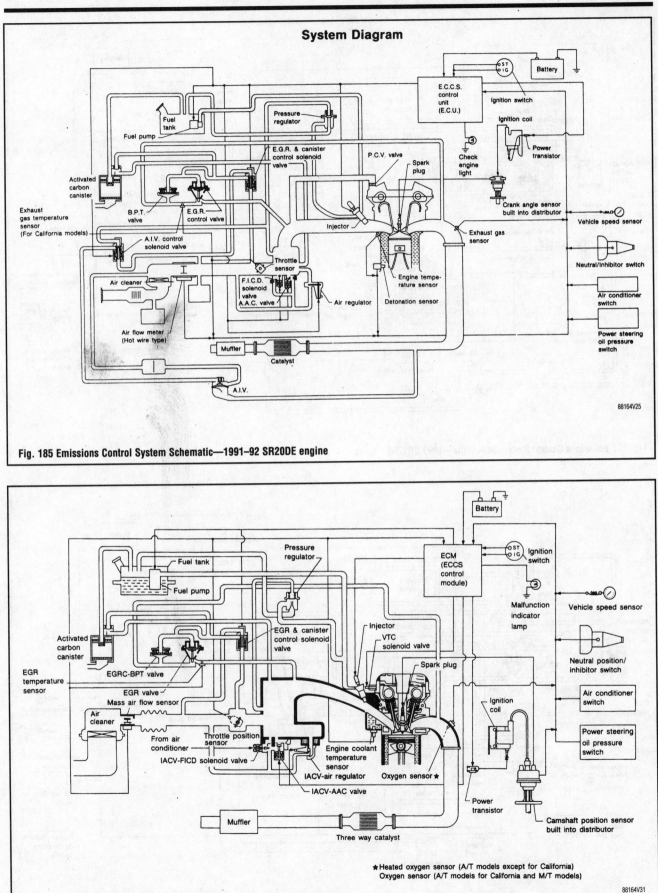

Fig. 185 Emissions Control System Schematic—1991–92 SR20DE engine

★ Heated oxygen sensor (A/T models except for California)
Oxygen sensor (A/T models for California and M/T models)

Fig. 186 Emissions Control System Schematic—1993–94 GA16DE engine

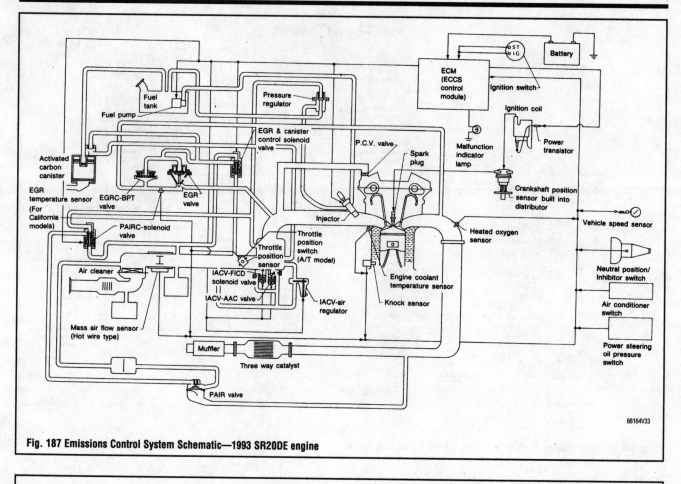

Fig. 187 Emissions Control System Schematic—1993 SR20DE engine

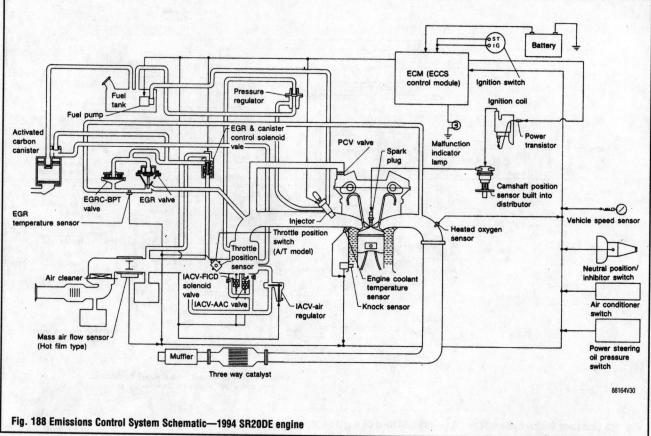

Fig. 188 Emissions Control System Schematic—1994 SR20DE engine

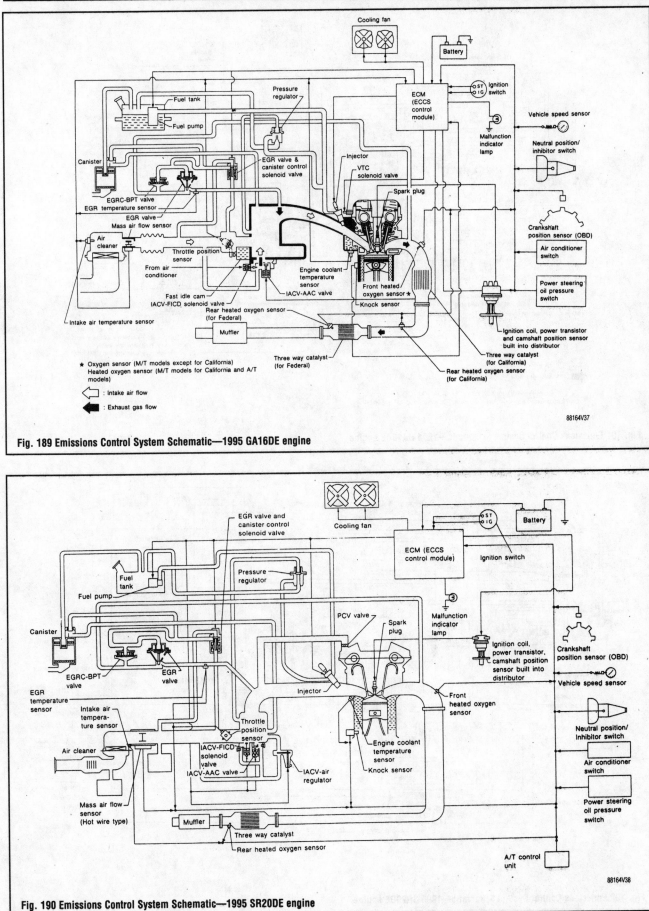

Fig. 189 Emissions Control System Schematic—1995 GA16DE engine

Fig. 190 Emissions Control System Schematic—1995 SR20DE engine

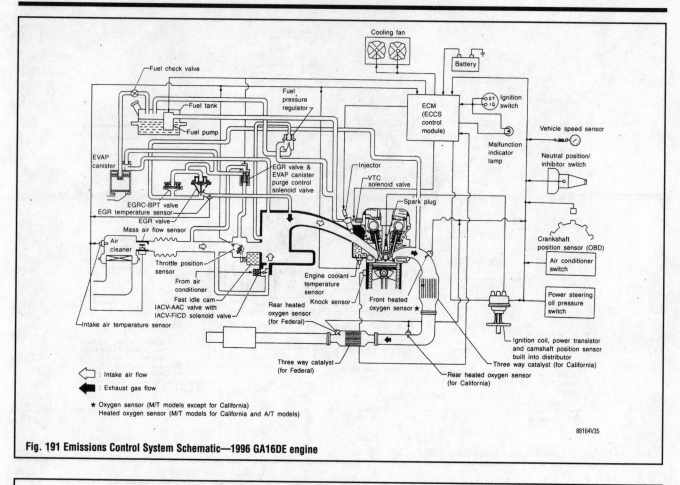

Fig. 191 Emissions Control System Schematic—1996 GA16DE engine

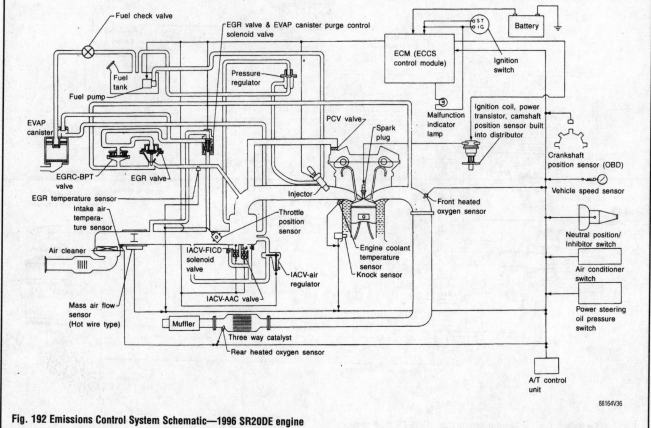

Fig. 192 Emissions Control System Schematic—1996 SR20DE engine

5

FUEL SYSTEM

BASIC FUEL SYSTEM DIAGNOSIS

Gasoline Engines

When there is a problem starting or driving a vehicle, two of the most important checks involve the ignition and the fuel systems. The questions most mechanics attempt to answer first, "is there spark?" and ``is there fuel?" will often lead to solving most basic problems. For ignition system diagnosis and testing, please refer to the information on engine electrical components and ignition systems found earlier in this manual. If the ignition system checks out (there is spark), then you must determine if the fuel system is operating properly (is there fuel?).

NO-START TESTING

Preliminary Inspection

†. Connect a voltmeter across the battery terminals. If battery voltage is not at least 12 volts, charge and test the battery before proceeding.

2. Turn the key to the **START** position, and observe the voltmeter. If the engine turned over and battery voltage remained above 9.6 volts, go to the next step. If the engine failed to crank and/or voltage was below 9.6 volts, proceed as follows:
  • If the instrument panel lights dim, load test the battery, check the battery terminals and cables, test the starter motor, and verify that the engine turns.
  • If the instrument panel lights do not dim, check the battery terminal connections, the ignition switch/wiring, and the starter.

3. Using a spark tester as described in Section 2, check for spark at two or more spark plugs.
  • If a normal spark is observed, continue testing following the appropriate fuel system diagnostic procedures.
  • If the spark test result is not okay, isolate and relate the faulty ignition system component, as described in Section 2.

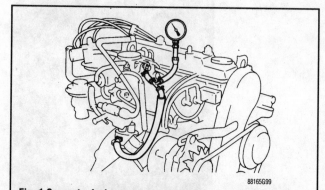

Fig. 1 Connect a fuel pressure gauge as shown, to check fuel pressure on carbureted vehicles

Fuel System Diagnosis

CARBURETED ENGINES

▶ See Figure 1

1. Remove the air cleaner assembly.
2. Operate the accelerator pump, while watching for fuel discharge from the port in the throttle barrel. If fuel is not discharged from the pump, proceed to next step. If accelerator pump operates, refer to the appropriate section and check the following items:
  • Remove spark plugs and verify the engine is not flooded.
  • Check for proper fuel type and quality (no water etc.).
  • Check for large vacuum leaks mechanical
  • Check for a mechanical engine defect such as a broken timing belt, leaking cylinder head gasket, etc.
  • Recheck the ignition system operation for correct ignition timing and spark quality.
3. Verify adequate fuel in the tank. If okay inspect visually inspect the fuel supply system components. Check for damaged lines, clogged fuel filter, etc.; if okay proceed to the next step.

➡Most fuel pressure specifications are given at idle speed. It may be necessary to compensate the reading obtained; verify that adequate pressure exists to unseat the float and fill the carburetor.

4. Connect a fuel pressure gauge and check fuel pressure and volume. If fuel pressure and/or volume is not within specifications, replace the fuel pump and retest.

✳✳ WARNING

Do NOT use a glass or Styrofoam container when checking fuel pump volume.

FUEL INJECTED ENGINES

▶ See Figures 2, 3, 4 and 5

1. Cycle the ignition switch **ON** and **OFF**, several times, while listening for fuel pump operation.
  • If fuel pump operates, proceed to next step.
  • If fuel pump does not operate begin testing of the fuel pump circuit.
2. Verify adequate fuel in the tank, then connect a fuel pressure gauge and check fuel pressure.
  • If fuel pressure is within specifications, proceed to next step.
  • If the pressure is not within specifications, continue checking the fuel pump and supply system.
3. Disconnect the fuel injector connector and connect a noid light to the wiring harness. Crank the engine, while watching the light. Perform this test on at least two injectors before proceeding.
  • If the light does not flash, go to the next step.

Fig. 2 Fuel pressure can be checked using an inexpensive pressure/vacuum gauge

Fig. 3 A noid light can be attached to the fuel injector harness in order to test for injector pulse

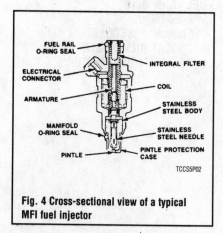

Fig. 4 Cross-sectional view of a typical MFI fuel injector

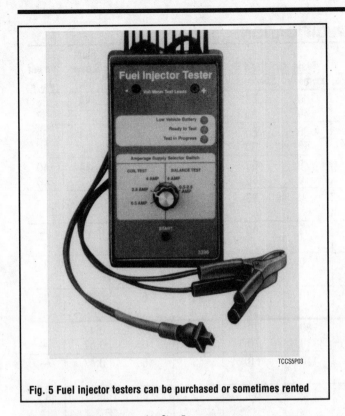

Fig. 5 Fuel injector testers can be purchased or sometimes rented

- If the light flashes, proceed to Step 5.
4. Check and verify the MIL lamp is operating properly.
- If the light does not operate, check the ECM and related wiring.
- If the MIL lamp is operational, check the injector wiring and circuitry.

5. Check the engine valve timing and overall mechanical condition of the engine. If okay, items such as; poor fuel quality, faulty injectors and computer controlled devices should be checked. Although these items are less likely, a shorted TPS or faulty coolant temperature sensor, are also possible causes of a no-start condition.

Fuel System Service Precautions

Safety is the most important factor when performing fuel system maintenance, as well as any type of maintenance involving fuel system components. Failure to conduct maintenance and repairs in a safe manner may result in serious personal injury or death. Maintenance and testing of the vehicle's fuel system components can be accomplished safely and effectively by adhering to the following rules and guidelines.

- To avoid the possibility of fire and personal injury, always disconnect the negative battery cable unless the repair or test procedure requires that battery voltage be applied.
- Always relieve the fuel system pressure prior to disconnecting any fuel system component (injector, fuel rail, pressure regulator, etc.), fitting or fuel line connection. Exercise extreme caution whenever relieving fuel system pressure to avoid exposing skin, face and eyes to fuel spray. Please be advised that fuel under pressure may penetrate the skin or any part of the body that it contacts.
- Always place a shop towel or cloth around the fitting or connection prior to loosening to absorb any excess fuel due to spillage. Ensure that all fuel spillage (should it occur) is quickly removed from engine surfaces. Ensure that all fuel soaked cloths or towels are deposited into a suitable waste container.
- Always keep a dry chemical (Class B) fire extinguisher near the work area.
- Do not allow fuel spray or fuel vapors to come into contact with a spark or open flame.
- Always use a backup wrench when loosening and tightening fuel line connection fittings. This will prevent unnecessary stress and torsion to fuel line piping. Always follow the proper torque specifications.
- Always replace worn fuel fitting O-rings with new. Do not substitute fuel hose or equivalent, where fuel pipe is installed.

CARBURETED FUEL SYSTEMS

➡**This section pertains to the removal, installation and adjustment of fuel system related components. For comprehensive diagnostic and testing of the emission and fuel systems, refer to Section 4.**

Mechanical Fuel Pump

▶ **See Figure 6**

OPERATION

The fuel pump is a mechanically operated, diaphragm type driven by the fuel pump eccentric on the camshaft. The pump is located on the lower right side of the engine.

The pump cannot be disassembled. If it fails either the pressure or the volume test, replace the unit.

REMOVAL & INSTALLATION

❋ CAUTION

Never smoke when working around gasoline! Avoid all sources of sparks or ignition. Gasoline vapors are EXTREMELY volatile!

1. Disconnect the fuel lines from the fuel pump.

➡**Be sure to plug the line leading from the fuel tank to prevent the excess loss of fuel.**

2. Remove the two fuel pump mounting nuts and the fuel pump assembly from the right side of the engine.
   To install:

3. Clean gasket mating surfaces.
4. Use a new gasket and/or sealant and mount the pump to the engine block. Torque the fuel pump bolts to 84–108 inch lbs. (10–13 Nm).
5. Connect the fuel lines to the fuel pump.
6. Start the engine and check for fuel leaks.

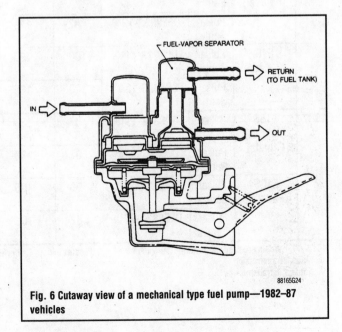

Fig. 6 Cutaway view of a mechanical type fuel pump—1982–87 vehicles

CARBURETOR SPECIFICATIONS

Year	Model	Vehicle Model	Carb Model	Main Jet #		Main Air Bleed #		Slow Jet #		Float Level (in.)	Power Jet #
				Primary	Secondary	Primary	Secondary	Primary	Secondary		
1982	E15 (Federal)	Sentra	DCR 306-132①	117	125	60	80	45	50	NA	38
			DCR 306-133②	115	125	60	80	45	50		38
	E15 (California)	Sentra	DCR 306-142①	115	125	80	80	45	50	NA	38
			DCR 306-143②	114	125	80	80	45	50		35
	E15 (Canada)	Sentra	DCR 306-152①	100	130	70	60	43	80	NA	40
			DCR 306-153②	100	130	70	60	43	80		40
	E15 (MPG)	Sentra	DFP 306-2	98	135	60	80	43	55	NA	—
1983	E16 (Calif.)	Pulsar Sentra	DFC328-1① DFC328-2②	91	130	105	60	43	70	0.47	—
	E16 (Federal)	Pulsar Sentra	DCZ328-1① DCZ328-2②	106	133	100	60	43	55	0.47	35
	E16 (Canada)	Pulsar Sentra	DCZ328-11① DCZ328-12②	100	135	110	60	43	65	0.47	35
1984	E16 (Federal)	Pulsar Sentra	DFE2832-1①	90	105	80	70	43	65	0.47	—
			DFE2832-2②	82	105	110	70	45	65	0.47	—
	E16 (Calif.)	Pulsar Sentra	DFC328-1F② DFC328-2F②	91	130	110	60	43	65	0.47	—
	E16 (Canada)	Pulsar Sentra	DCZ328-11F① DCZ328-12F②	100	135	110	60	43	65	0.47	35
1985	E16 (Federal)	Pulsar Sentra	DFE2832-5①	90	105	80	70	43	65	0.47	—
			DFE2832-2②	82	105	110	70	45	65	0.47	—
	E16 (Calif.)	Pulsar Sentra	DFC328-1F② DFC328-2F②	91	130	110	60	43	65	0.47	—
	E16 (Canada)	Pulsar Sentra	DCZ328-11F① DCZ328-12G②	100	135	110	60	43	65	0.47	35
1986	E16 (Calif.)	Pulsar Sentra	DFC328-3①	91	130	110	60	43	80	0.650–0.689	—
		Pulsar Sentra	DFC328-4②	91	130	110	60	43	80	0.650–0.689	—
	E16 (Federal)	Pulsar Sentra	DFE2832-11①	90	115	80	70	43	65	0.650–0.689	—
		Pulsar Sentra	DFE2832-12②	82	115	110	70	45	65	0.650–0.689	—
	E16 (Canada)	Pulsar Sentra	DCZ328-11①	100	135	110	60	43	80	0.650–0.689	—
		Pulsar Sentra	DCZ328-12②	100	135	110	60	43	80	0.650–0.689	—
1987	E16S (Calif. &) Canada	Pulsar Sentra	DRC328-11①	87	130	110	60	43	80	0.650–0.689	—
		Pulsar Sentra	DFC328-12②	87	130	100	60	43	80	0.650–0.689	—
	E16S (Federal)	Pulsar Sentra	DFE2832-21①	90	105	80	70	43	65	0.650–0.689	—
		Pulsar Sentra	DFE2832-22②	82	105	110	70	45	65	0.650–0.689	—

NOTE: FU models are 5-speed Hatchbacks sold in the United States except California.
① Manual transmission
② Automatic transmission

88165C01

TESTING

Static Pressure

> **❊❊ CAUTION**
>
> **Never smoke when working around gasoline! Avoid all sources of sparks or ignition. Gasoline vapors are EXTREMELY volatile!**

1. Disconnect the fuel line at the carburetor. Using a T-connector, attach two rubber hoses to the connector, then install it between the fuel line and the carburetor fitting.

➡ **When disconnecting the fuel line, be sure to place a container under the line to catch the excess fuel in the line.**

2. Connect a fuel pump pressure gauge to the T-connector and secure it with a clamp.
3. Start the engine and check the pressure at various speeds. The pressure should be 3.0–3.8 psi (20.7–26.2 kPa) for 1982–83 or 2.8–3.8 psi (19.3–26.2 kPa) for 1984 and later. There is usually enough gasoline in the float bowl to perform this test.
4. If the pressure is okay, perform a capacity test. Remove the gauge and the T-connector assembly, then reinstall the fuel line to the carburetor.

Capacity

1. Disconnect the fuel line from the carburetor and place the line in a graduated container.

> **❊❊ WARNING**
>
> **Do NOT use a glass or styrofoam container when checking fuel pump volume.**

2. Fill the carburetor float bowl with gas.
3. Start the engine and run it for one minute at about 600 rpm. The pump should deliver 44.0 oz. (1300 ml) per minute.

Carburetor

The carburetor used is a 2-barrel down-draft type with a low speed (primary) side and a high speed (secondary) side.

An electrically operated anti-dieseling solenoid is used on all engines. When the ignition switch is turned OFF, the valve is de-energized, shutting off the supply of fuel to the idle circuit.

All 1984 and later USA carbureted models are equipped with the ECC. System (Electronic Controlled Carburetor). The ECC control unit consists of a microcomputer, connectors for signal input and output and power supply, and an exhaust gas sensor monitor lamp. The control unit senses and controls various carburetor operations.

On all non-California models, the conventional choke valve and fast idle cam has been replaced with a duty-controlled solenoid valve for fuel enrichment and an idle speed control actuator (ISCA). These devices are controlled according to the engine speed, amount of intake air, and objective engine speed. Also, the air-fuel ratio and ignition timing are controlled according to the engine water temperature, atmospheric pressure, vehicle speed and transaxle gear position. In addition, this system controls the ignition timing and the idle speed according to applied electric loads such as a cooler, thereby achieving better emission control, fuel economy etc.

On California models the carburetor is equipped with an air-fuel ratio control on-off valve instead of a power valve. This on-off valve opens or closes the compensating air bleed and main jet to compensate for rich/lean air-fuel ratio, depending on varying conditions, such as acceleration, deceleration, low coolant temperature, low voltage, etc. These varying conditions are detected by various sensors which transmit corresponding signals to provide air-fuel ratio compensation.

ADJUSTMENTS

Throttle Linkage

1. Disconnect the negative battery cable.
2. Remove the air cleaner.
3. Open the automatic choke valve by hand, while turning the throttle valve by pulling the throttle lever, then set the choke valve in the open position.

➡ **If equipped with a vacuum controlled throttle positioner, use a vacuum hand pump to retract the throttle positioner rod.**

4. Adjust the throttle cable at the carburetor bracket, so that 1.0–2.0mm of pedal free-play exists.

Dashpot

▸ **See Figures 7 and 8**

A dashpot is used on carburetors of automatic transaxle equipped vehicles, as well as some manual transaxle models. The dashpot slowly closes the throttle on automatic transaxle equipped vehicles to prevent stalling, and serves as an emission control device on all late model vehicles.

The dashpot should be adjusted to contact the throttle lever on deceleration at approximately 2,300–2,500 rpm (E15) engines, 1,900–2,100 rpm (E16, automatic transaxle) or 2,250–2,450 (E16, manual transaxle).

➡ **Before attempting to adjust the dashpot, make sure the idle speed, timing and mixture adjustments are correct.**

1. Loosen the locknut (turn the dashpot, if necessary) and make sure the engine speed drops smoothly from 2,000 rpm to 1,000 rpm in 3 seconds.
2. If the dashpot has been removed from the carburetor, it must be adjusted when installed. Adjust the gap between the primary throttle valve and the inner carburetor wall, when the dashpot stem comes in contact with the throttle arm. The dashpot gap is 0.66–0.86mm (manual transaxle) or 0.49–0.69mm (automatic transaxle).

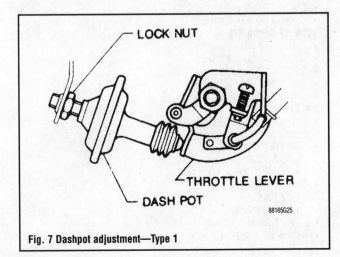

Fig. 7 Dashpot adjustment—Type 1

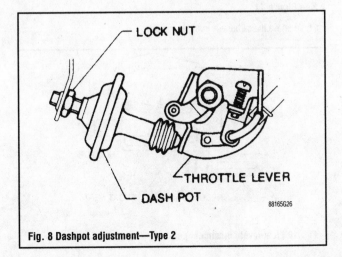

Fig. 8 Dashpot adjustment—Type 2

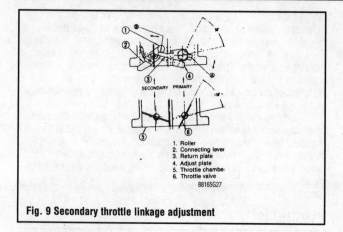

Fig. 9 Secondary throttle linkage adjustment

1. Roller
2. Connecting lever
3. Return plate
4. Adjust plate
5. Throttle chamber
6. Throttle valve

88165G27

Secondary Throttle Linkage

♦ See Figure 9

All carburetors discussed in this book are two stage type carburetors. On this type of carburetor, the engine runs on the primary barrel most of the time, with the secondary barrel being used for acceleration purposes. When the throttle valve on the primary side opens to an angle of approximately 50° (from its fully closed position), the secondary throttle valve is pulled open by the connecting linkage. The 50° angle of throttle valve opening works out to a clearance measurement of 5.7–6.9mm between the throttle valve and the carburetor body. The easiest way to measure this is to use a drill bit. Drill bits from sizes H to P (standard letter size drill bits) should fit. Check the appendix in the back of the book for the exact size of the various drill bits. If an adjustment is necessary, bend the connecting link between the two linkage assemblies.

➡The carburetor is equipped with a tang on the adjusting link, bend the tang to adjust the clearance.

Float Level

♦ See Figure 10

The fuel level is normal if it is within the lines or dot on the window glass of the float chamber (or the sight glass) when the vehicle is resting on level ground and the engine is off.

If the fuel level is outside the lines, remove the float housing cover. Have an absorbent cloth under the cover to catch the fuel from the fuel bowl. Adjust the float level by bending the needle seat on the float.

The needle valve should have an effective stroke of about 1.5mm. When necessary, the needle valve stroke can be adjusted by bending the float stopper.

➡Be careful not to bend the needle valve rod when installing the float and baffle plate, if removed.

Fast Idle

♦ See Figure 11

1. Remove the carburetor from the vehicle.

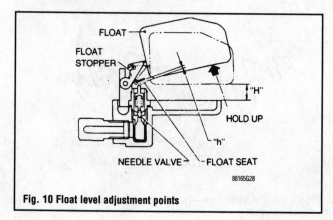

Fig. 10 Float level adjustment points

88165G28

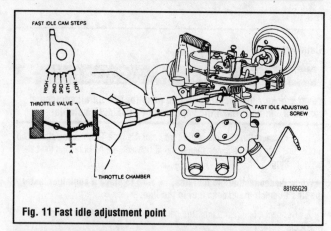

Fig. 11 Fast idle adjustment point

88165G29

➡On some California engines, disconnect the harness cover from the automatic choke heater cover, the vacuum hose from the vacuum break diaphragm (install a plug after pushing the vacuum break stem toward the diaphragm), then move the throttle lever counterclockwise (fully). Go to Step 4.

2. Remove the choke cover, then place the fast idle arm on the 2nd step of the fast idle cam. Using the correct wire gauge, measure the clearance **A** between the throttle valve and the wall of the throttle valve chamber (at the center of the throttle valve). Check it against the following specifications:
- 1982–88 Sentra with manual transaxle—0.80–0.87mm
1982–88 Sentra with automatic transaxle—1.07–1.14mm
- 1983 Pulsar (USA) with manual transaxle—0.79–0.93mm
- 1983 Pulsar (USA) with automatic transaxle—1.08–1.22mm
- 1983 Pulsar (Canada) with manual transaxle—0.65–0.79mm
- 1983 Pulsar (Canada) with automatic transaxle—0.93–1.07mm
- 1984–87 Pulsar (USA) with manual transaxle—0.76–0.96mm
- 1984–87 Pulsar (USA) with automatic transaxle—1.05–1.25mm
- 1984–87 Pulsar (Canada) with manual transaxle—0.54–0.82mm
- 1984–87 Pulsar (Canada) with automatic transaxle—0.90–1.10mm

➡The first step of the fast idle adjustment procedure is not absolutely necessary.

3. Install the carburetor on the engine.
4. Start the engine, warm it to operating temperatures and check the fast idle rpm. The cam should be at the 2nd step.

1982–83 Sentra E15—
- Federal: 2,400–3,200 rpm
- Calif.: 2,300–3,100 rpm
- Canada MT: 1,900–2,700 rpm
- Canada AT: 2,400–3,200 rpm

1984–87 Sentra E16—
- Federal: Not adjustable
- Calif. MT: 2,600–3,400 rpm
- Calif. AT: 2,900–3,700 rpm
- Canada MT: 1,900–2,700 rpm
- Canada AT: 2,400–3,200 rpm

1983 Pulsar—
- Federal MT: 2,400–3,200 rpm
- Federal AT: 2,700–3,500 rpm
- Calif. MT: 2,600–3,400 rpm
- Calif. AT: 2,900–3,700 rpm
- Canada MT: 1,900–2,700 rpm
- Canada AT: 2,400–3,200 rpm

1984–87 Pulsar—
- Calif. MT: 2,600–3,400 rpm
- Calif. AT: 2,900–3,700 rpm
- Canada MT: 1,900–2,700 rpm

- Canada AT: 2,400–3,200 rpm

5. To adjust the fast idle speed, turn the fast idle adjusting screw counterclockwise to increase the fast idle speed and clockwise to decrease the fast idle speed.

Primary and Secondary Throttle Valve Interlock Opening

♦ See Figure 12

With the carburetor removed from the engine, turn the throttle arm until the adjusting plate comes in contact with the lock lever at point **A** and check clearance **G**. The clearance should be 0.25 in. (6.3mm).

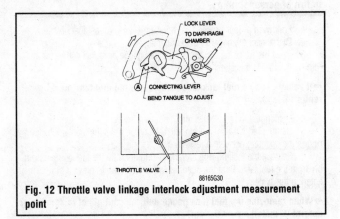

Fig. 12 Throttle valve linkage interlock adjustment measurement point

Choke Unloader

➡ **The choke must be cold for this adjustment. This adjustment does not apply to 1984 and later non-California USA models, nor to 1987 California/Canada models.**

1. Close the choke valve completely.
2. Hold the choke valve closed by stretching a rubber band between the choke piston lever and a stationary part of the carburetor.
3. Open the throttle lever fully.

➡ **The unloader cam is located next to the choke plate adjusting lever.**

4. Adjustment is made by bending the unloader tongue. Gauge the gap between the choke plate and the carburetor body to:
   - Pulsar—2.96mm
   - 1982–83 Sentra—2.36mm
   - 1984–87 Sentra—3.00mm

Vacuum Break (Choke Pull-Off)

♦ See Figure 13

1. With the engine cold, close the choke completely.
2. Pull the vacuum break stem straight up as far as it will go.
3. Check the clearance between the choke plate and the carburetor wall. Clearance should be:

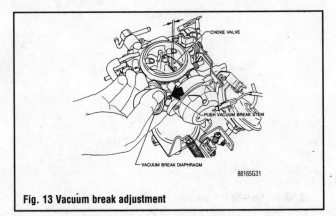

Fig. 13 Vacuum break adjustment

- 1.33–1.73mm (below 63°F)
- 2.40–2.80mm (above 75°F)

4. Adjustment is made by bending the tang at the choke plate lever assembly.

➡ **Remove the choke cover, then connect a rubber band to the choke lever to hold it shut.**

Accelerator Pump

♦ See Figure 14

If a smooth, constant stream of fuel is not injected into the carburetor bore when the throttle is opened, the accelerator pump needs adjusting.
1. Remove the carburetor from the engine.
2. Check the gap between the primary throttle valve and the inner wall of the carburetor when the pump lever comes in contact with the piston pin. This is the stroke limiter gap. It should be 1.3mm. If not, bend the stroke limiter.
3. Fill the carburetor bowl with fuel.
4. Fully open the choke.
5. Place a calibrated container under the throttle bore. Slowly open and close the throttle (full open to full closed) ten times keeping the throttle open 3 seconds each time. Measure the amount of fuel in the container. The amount should be 0.3–0.5 ml. If not, and the stroke limiter gap is correct, replace the accelerator pump unit.

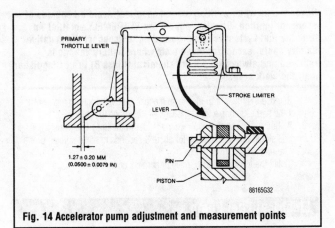

Fig. 14 Accelerator pump adjustment and measurement points

Anti-Dieseling Solenoid

Check this valve if the engine continues to run after the key has been turned off.
1. Run the engine at idle speed and disconnect the lead wire at the anti-dieseling solenoid. The engine should stop.
2. If the engine does not stop, check the harness for current at the solenoid. If current is present, replace the solenoid. Installation torque for the solenoid is 13–16 ft. lbs. (18–22 Nm).

REMOVAL & INSTALLATION

1. Remove the air cleaner.
2. Disconnect the electrical connector(s), the fuel and the vacuum hoses from the carburetor.
3. Remove the throttle lever.
4. Remove the four nuts and washers retaining the carburetor to the manifold.
5. Lift the carburetor from the manifold.
6. Remove and discard the gasket used between the carburetor and the manifold.
   To install:
7. Install carburetor on the manifold, use a new base gasket and torque the carburetor mounting nuts to 9–13 ft. lbs. (11–18 Nm).
8. Install the throttle lever.
9. Connect the electrical connector(s), the fuel and the vacuum hoses to the carburetor.
10. Install the air cleaner.
11. Start engine, warm engine and adjust as necessary.

THROTTLE BODY FUEL INJECTION SYSTEMS

General Description

The Throttle Body Fuel Injection (TBI) system consists of a single fuel injector mounted inside the throttle body. The fuel delivery system provides a constant supply of pressurized fuel to the fuel injector. The amount of injected fuel is controlled by the Engine Control Module (ECM).

During system operation, the ECM uses various sensors to convert the engine's operating conditions into electronic signals. Sensor inputs are used by the ECM to determine the specific fuel requirements of the engine and to calculate the optimum air/fuel mixture.

The ECM controls the amount of fuel supplied to the engine using the fuel injector. By varying the electric pulse to the injector, the duration of time the fuel injector remains open can be controlled. This allows the ECM to precisely meter the fuel supplied to the engine, providing the optimum air/fuel mixture to the engine, under various operating conditions.

Relieving Fuel System Pressure

➧ See Figure 15

⁂ CAUTION

Never smoke when working around gasoline! Avoid all sources of sparks or ignition. Gasoline vapors are EXTREMELY volatile! Any time the fuel system is being worked on, disconnect the negative battery cable, except for those tests where battery voltage is required and always keep a dry chemical (Class B) fire extinguisher near the work area.

1. Remove the fuel pump fuse from the fuse block, fuel pump relay or disconnect the harness connector at the tank while engine is running.
2. It should run and then stall when the fuel in the lines is exhausted. When the engine stops, crank the starter for about 3 seconds to make sure all pressure in the fuel lines is released.
3. Install the fuel pump fuse, relay or harness connector after repair is made.

Electrical Fuel Pump

All fuel injected models use an in-tank type pump. The fuel pumps are of a wet type, where the vane rollers are directly coupled to the motor, which is filled with fuel. A relief valve in the pump is designed to open, should a malfunction arise in the system.

➡Before disconnecting the fuel lines or any of the fuel system components, refer to Fuel Pressure Release procedures, in this section and release the fuel pressure.

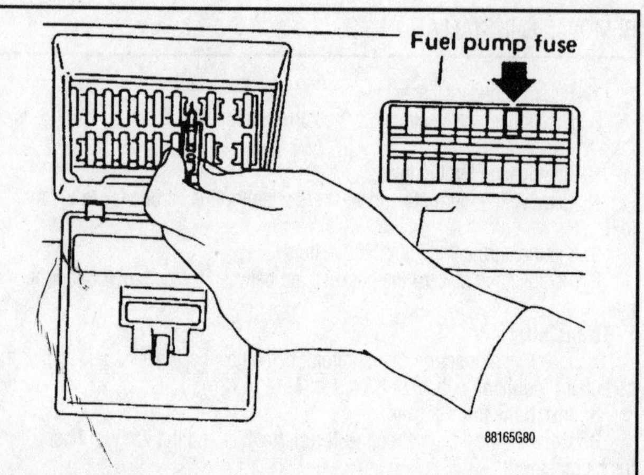

Fig. 15 Fuel pump fuse location—1987–90 vehicles

REMOVAL & INSTALLATION

⁂ CAUTION

Fuel injection systems remain under pressure after the engine has been turned OFF. Properly relieve fuel pressure before disconnecting any fuel lines. Also observe all safety practices outlined earlier in the Fuel System Safety Precautions. Failure to do so may result in fire or personal injury.

1. Following proper procedures, relieve fuel system residual pressure.
2. Disconnect the negative battery cable.
3. Open the trunk lid, disconnect the fuel gauge electrical connector and remove the fuel tank inspection cover.

➡If vehicle has no fuel tank inspection cover the fuel tank must be removed.

4. Disconnect the fuel outlet and the return hoses.
5. Using a large brass drift pin and a hammer, drive the fuel tank locking ring in the counterclockwise direction.
6. Remove the locking ring and the O-ring, then lift the fuel pump assembly from the fuel tank. Plug the opening with a clean rag to prevent dirt from entering the system.

➡When removing the fuel tank gauge unit, be careful not to damage or deform it. Install a new O-ring.

To install:

7. Install fuel pump assembly in tank. With a new O-ring install the fuel tank locking ring in place.
8. Reconnect the fuel lines and the electrical connection.
9. Install the fuel tank inspection cover.
10. Connect battery cable, start engine and check for leaks.

TESTING

➧ See Figure 16

1. Disconnect the fuel hose at the throttle body inlet hose; this is the hose leading from the fuel filter. Install Pressure Gauge tool J–25400–34 or equivalent, in series with the hose running between the fuel filter and the throttle body. Place the gauge, so it can be read from the driver's seat.
2. Start the engine and read the fuel pressure, it should be as follows:
   - E16i—14 psi (96.5 kPa) for 2WD and 36.6 psi (252.3 kPa) for 4WD at idle
   - GA16i—34.0 psi (234.4 kPa) with regulator vacuum hose connected
   - GA16i—43.4 psi (299.2 kPa) with regulator vacuum hose disconnected

➡If the reading is not correct, replace the pressure regulator and repeat the checking procedure. If the pressure is below specifications, check for clogged or deformed fuel lines; if necessary, replace the fuel pump or check valve.

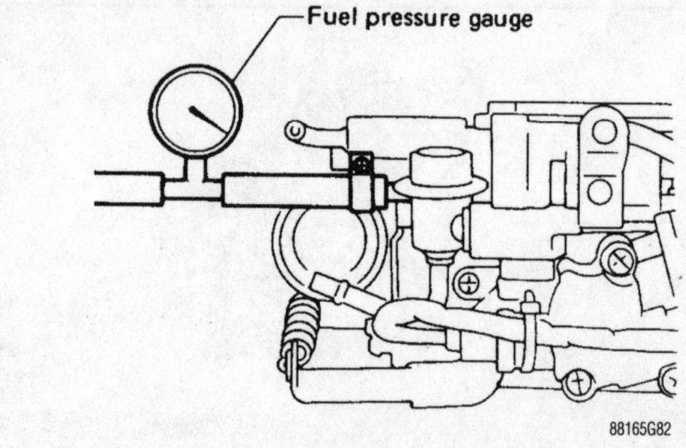

Fig. 16 Connect the fuel pressure gauge as shown

Throttle Body

REMOVAL & INSTALLATION

E16i and GA16i Engines

❊❊ CAUTION

Fuel injection systems remain under pressure after the engine has been turned OFF. Properly relieve fuel pressure before disconnecting any fuel lines. Also, observe all safety practices outlined above in the Fuel System Safety Precautions. Failure to do so may result in fire or personal injury.

1. Following proper procedures, relieve fuel system residual pressure.
2. Release the fuel pump pressure and disconnect the negative battery cable.
3. Disconnect the vacuum hoses, fuel line and the electrical connections from the throttle body. Disconnect the accelerator cable from the throttle body.
4. Remove the mounting bolts and the throttle body from the intake manifold.
5. To install, use a new gasket and reverse the removal procedures. Torque the throttle chamber bolts to 15–20 ft. lbs. (20–27 Nm). Adjust the throttle cable if necessary.

ADJUSTMENTS

Throttle Switch

E16I & GA16I ENGINES

▶ **See Figure 17**

1. Connect an approved tachometer and warm up the engine.
2. Disconnect the throttle switch connector. Check the idle speed and adjust as necessary, according to the Tune-Up specifications chart in Section 1.
3. Manually open the throttle to about 2000 rpm, lower the engine speed slowly and read the engine speed at which the idle contact turns ON and OFF. The ON/OFF rpm should be 900–1200 rpm.
4. If not within specifications, turn the throttle switch until the correct ON/OFF rpm is reached.
5. Tighten the switch screws and install the air cleaner.

Fuel Injector

REMOVAL & INSTALLATION

E16i and GA16i Engines

▶ **See Figures 18, 19 and 20**

❊❊ CAUTION

Fuel injection systems remain under pressure after the engine has been turned OFF. Properly relieve fuel pressure before disconnecting any fuel lines. Also observe all safety practices outlined earlier in the Fuel System Safety Precautions. Failure to do so may result in fire or personal injury.

1. Following proper procedures, relieve fuel system residual pressure.
2. Remove injector cover and pull out injector straight upward. Take care not to break or bend injector terminal.
3. Install a new lower injector O-ring in the throttle body.
4. Install the fuel injector and push it down using a suitable tool. Align the direction of the injector terminals. Take care not to break or bend injector terminal.
5. Install a new upper injector O-ring in the throttle body.

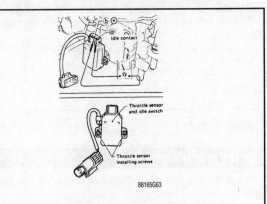

Fig. 17 Throttle switch adjustment—E16i and GA16i engines

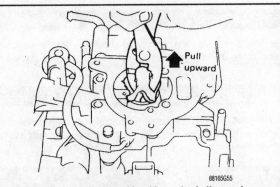

Fig. 18 Grasp the injector assembly with a pair of pliers and remove the injector from the throttle body housing

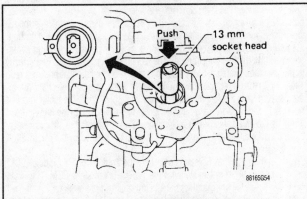

Fig. 19 Use a 13mm socket to press the injector into position

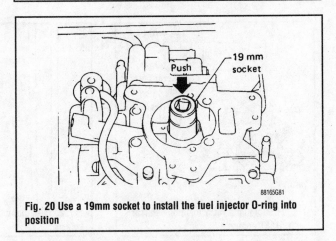

Fig. 20 Use a 19mm socket to install the fuel injector O-ring into position

6. Install upper plate and injector cover with rubber plug removed.

7. Make sure that two O-rings (small one and big one) are installed in the injector cover.

8. Check for proper connection between injector terminal and injector cover terminal, then install rubber plug.

9. Start engine and check for fuel leaks.

TESTING

Refer to Section 4 for all electronic fuel injection testing and diagnostics.

Fuel Pressure Regulator

The pressure regulator is located under the throttle body assembly on Throttle Body Injected (TBI models).

REMOVAL & INSTALLATION

✳✳ CAUTION

Fuel injection systems remain under pressure after the engine has been turned OFF. Properly relieve fuel pressure before disconnecting any fuel lines. Also, observe all safety practices outlined previously in the Fuel System Safety Precautions. Failure to do so may result in fire or personal injury.

1. Following proper procedures, relieve fuel system residual pressure.
2. Remove the air inlet tube assembly.
3. Disconnect the vacuum hose and return line from the fuel pressure regulator.
4. Loosen the retaining screw(s).
5. Carefully remove the regulator from the throttle body assembly.

To install:

6. Install new O-rings on the regulator assembly. Lightly lubricate the O-rings with gasoline.
7. Install the regulator to the throttle body housing and secure with retaining screw(s).
8. Connect the vacuum hose and return line to the fuel pressure regulator.
9. Pressurize the fuel system and check for leaks.
10. Install the air inlet tube assembly.

MULTI-POINT FUEL INJECTION SYSTEMS

➡**This section covers the removal, installation and adjustment of fuel injection system components. For comprehensive diagnostic and testing of the emission and fuel systems, refer to Section 4.**

General Information

The electronic fuel injection system consists of 2 subsystems, the fuel delivery system supplies fuel to the fuel injectors at a specified pressure. The electronic control system regulates the flow of fuel from the injectors into the engine.

The fuel delivery system consists of an electric fuel pump, fuel filters, fuel pressure regulator an fuel injectors. The electric fuel pump, mounted in the fuel tank, draws fuel through a filter screen attached to the fuel pump/sending unit assembly. The fuel is then pumped to the engine compartment, through another filter and into the fuel injection rail. The fuel injection rail supplies fuel directly to the injectors. Constant fuel pressure is maintained by the fuel pressure regulator. The pressure regulator is mounted at the end of the fuel injection rail, downstream from the fuel injectors. Excess fuel supplied by the fuel pump is relieved by the regulator and returned to the fuel tank through the fuel return line. The fuel injectors spray a metered quantity of fuel into the intake air stream when they are energized. The quantity of fuel is determined by the electronic control system.

The electronic control system consists of the Engine Control Module (ECM) and the engine sensors and switches that provide input to the ECM. The Mass Air Flow (MAF) sensor monitors the amount of air flow into the engine, measures air temperature, controls the electric fuel pump and supplies this information to the ECM. Information is also supplied to the ECM regarding engine coolant temperature, engine speed and exhaust gas oxygen content. Based on the input information, the ECM computes the required fuel flow rate and determines the needed injector pulse width, then outputs an command to the fuel injector to meter the exact quantity of fuel.

Relieving Fuel System Pressure

◆ **See Figures 21, 22 and 23**

✳✳ CAUTION

Never smoke when working around gasoline! Avoid all sources of sparks or ignition. Gasoline vapors are EXTREMELY volatile! Any time the fuel system is being worked on, disconnect the negative battery cable, except for those tests where battery voltage is required and always keep a dry chemical (Class B) fire extinguisher near the work area.

1. Remove the fuel pump fuse from the fuse block or disconnect the fuel pump relay, while engine is running.
2. Crank the engine. It should run and then stall when the fuel in the lines is exhausted. When the engine stops, crank the starter for about 3 seconds to make sure all pressure in the fuel lines is released.
3. Turn the ignition switch to the **OFF** position.
4. Install the fuel pump fuse, relay or harness connector after repair is made.

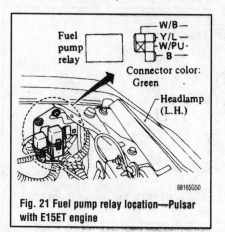

Fig. 21 Fuel pump relay location—Pulsar with E15ET engine

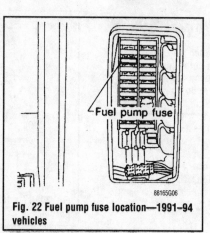

Fig. 22 Fuel pump fuse location—1991–94 vehicles

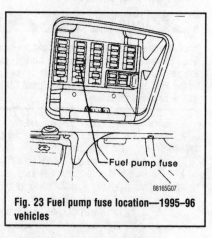

Fig. 23 Fuel pump fuse location—1995–96 vehicles

➥On all fuel injected Pulsar and Sentra models, if the fuse box is equipped with a fuse for fuel pump, this fuse can be removed instead of detaching the electrical connector from the fuel pump or relay.

Electric Fuel Pump

All fuel injected models use an in-tank type pump. The fuel pumps are of a wet type, where the vane rollers are directly coupled to the motor, which is filled with fuel. A relief valve in the pump is designed to open, should a malfunction arise in the system.

➥Before disconnecting the fuel lines or any of the fuel system components, refer to Fuel Pressure Release procedures in this section, and release the fuel pressure.

REMOVAL & INSTALLATION

✳✳ CAUTION

Fuel injection systems remain under pressure after the engine has been turned OFF. Properly relieve fuel pressure before disconnecting any fuel lines. Also observe all safety practices outlined earlier in the Fuel System Safety Precautions. Failure to do so may result in fire or personal injury.

E15ET Engine

The 1984 Pulsar uses an in-tank fuel pump assembly which is similar to the one used on the Throttle Body Fuel Injected vehicles. Refer to the procedure outlined for those vehicles, in the Throttle Body Fuel injection portion of this section.

GA16DE and SR20DE Engines

▸ See Figures 24 thru 29

➥This procedure should be done with a half tank or less. Fuel may spill out of the fuel pump/sender opening when removed.

1. Following proper procedures, relieve fuel system residual pressure.
2. Disconnect the negative battery cable and relieve the fuel pressure.
3. Remove the rear seat and inspection hole cover located beneath the rear seat.
4. Disconnect the fuel supply hose, fuel return hose and wiring harness connections.
5. Remove the 6 retaining screws and lift the fuel module assembly from the tank.
6. On 1991–94 vehicles, remove the fuel pump from the chamber assembly as follows:
    a. Pull up on the top (connection end) of the pump.
    b. Slide the pump out of the chamber assembly.
7. On 1995–96 vehicles, remove the fuel pump from the chamber assembly as follows:
    a. Pull up the front of the fuel pump chamber and slide the chamber cover toward the top (connection end) of the pump.
    b. Remove the fuel pump from the chamber.

To install:
8. Install the fuel pump into the chamber assembly.
9. Install the 6 retaining screws and torque as follows:
- 1991–94 vehicles—26–35 inch lbs. (3.2–4.2 Nm).
- 1995–96 vehicles—17–22 inch lbs. (2.0–2.5 Nm).
10. Connect the fuel lines and the wiring harness.
11. Install the inspection hole cover located beneath the rear seat and seat.
12. Connect the negative battery cable, turn the ignition **ON** and check for leaks.

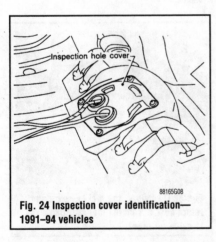

88165G08

Fig. 24 Inspection cover identification— 1991–94 vehicles

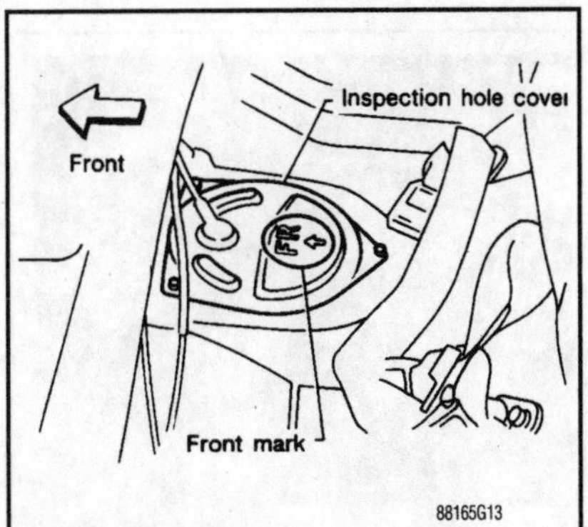

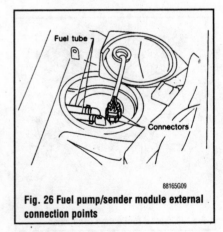

88165G13

Fig. 25 Inspection cover identification— 1995–96 vehicles

88165G09

Fig. 26 Fuel pump/sender module external connection points

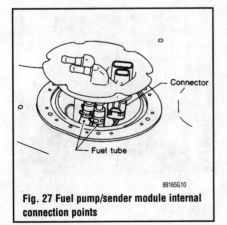

88165G10

Fig. 27 Fuel pump/sender module internal connection points

88165G11

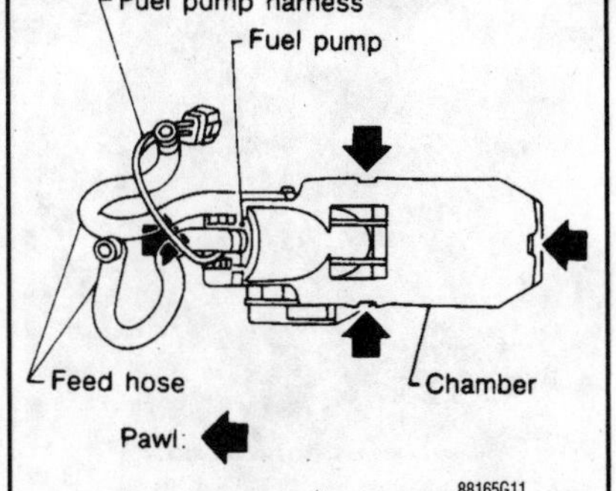

Fig. 28 Removing the fuel pump from the chamber assembly—1995–96 vehicles

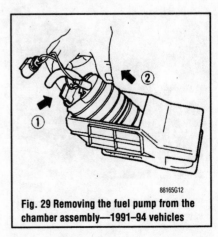

88165G12

Fig. 29 Removing the fuel pump from the chamber assembly—1991–94 vehicles

TESTING

▶ **See Figures 30 and 31**

1. Properly release the fuel system residual pressure.
2. Disconnect the fuel hose from between the fuel filter and the fuel rail.

➡ **Make the connection in series with the fuel filter line leading to the engine.**

3. Install fuel pressure Gauge J–25400–34 or equivalent, between the metal pipe and the fuel filter hose. Place the gauge, so it can be read from the driver's seat.
4. Start the engine and read the fuel pressure, it should be as follows:
   • E15ET Turbo—30 psi (206.85 kPa) at idle
   • E15ET Turbo—37 psi (255 kPa) engine accelerated
   • GA16DE and SR20DE—36.0 psi (248.2 kPa) with the regulator vacuum hose connected
   • GA16DE and SR20DE—43.0 psi (296.5 kPa) with the regulator vacuum hose disconnected

➡ **If the reading is not correct, check the pressure regulator, fuel pump, fuel filter. Also check for clogged or damaged fuel pressure and return lines; if necessary, replace the faulty component(s) and retest.**

Throttle Body

ADJUSTMENTS

Throttle Switch

E15ET TURBO ENGINE

1. Connect an approved tachometer and warm up the engine.
2. Disconnect the throttle switch connector. Check the idle speed and adjust as necessary, according to the Tune-Up specifications chart in Section 1.

3. Connect an ohmmeter between terminals **18 and 25** and make sure continuity exists.
4. Manually open the throttle to about 2000 rpm, lower the engine speed slowly and read the engine speed at which the idle contact turns the switch ON and OFF. The ON/OFF rpm should be about 1100 rpm.
5. If not within specifications, turn the throttle switch until the continuity changes from ON to OFF at 1100 rpm with no load.
6. Tighten the switch screws and install the air cleaner tube.

Fuel Injectors

REMOVAL & INSTALLATION

▶ **See Figures 32 thru 42**

✳✳ CAUTION

Fuel injection systems remain under pressure after the engine has been turned OFF. Properly relieve fuel pressure before disconnecting any fuel lines. Also observe all safety practices outlined previously in the Fuel System Safety Precautions. Failure to do so may result in fire or personal injury.

E15ET Turbo Engine

▶ **See Figures 43 and 44**

1. Following proper procedures, relieve fuel system residual pressure.
2. Remove the air inlet pipe and the hose.
3. Disconnect the accelerator wire and (if equipped with an automatic transaxle) the throttle wire.
4. Disconnect the throttle valve switch electrical harness connector, the mounting bolts and the throttle chamber.
5. Remove the PCV valve and the hose.

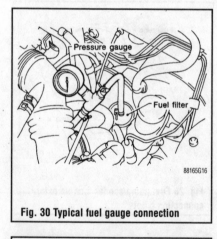

Fig. 30 Typical fuel gauge connection

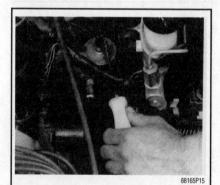

Fig. 31 The fuel gauge should be connected in series with this hose

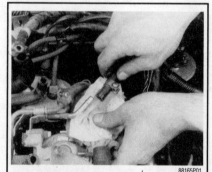

Fig. 32 Disconnect the fuel pressure and return hoses, from the fuel rail. Use a rag to catch spillage

Fig. 33 Detach the fuel injector electrical connectors

Fig. 34 Remove the fuel rail retaining bolts

Fig. 35 Remove the fuel rail and fuel injectors as an assembly

Fig. 36 Be careful, so not to lose the two fuel rail spacers during removal and installation

Fig. 37 Replace the insulators whenever the fuel rail has been removed

Fig. 38 Once the fuel rail has been removed, the fuel injector cover screws can be removed

Fig. 39 Although it is not recommended, individual injectors can be removed with the rail assembly intact

Fig. 40 Before installing the injector cover, make certain that the injector is properly aligned

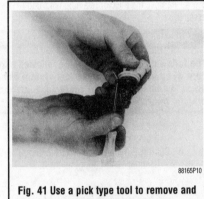

Fig. 41 Use a pick type tool to remove and install the fuel injector upper O-ring

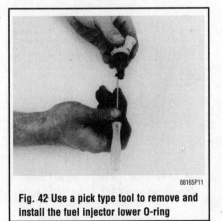

Fig. 42 Use a pick type tool to remove and install the fuel injector lower O-ring

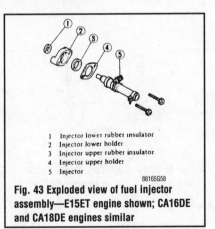

1 Injector lower rubber insulator
2 Injector lower holder
3 Injector upper rubber insulator
4 Injector upper holder
5 Injector

Fig. 43 Exploded view of fuel injector assembly—E15ET engine shown; CA16DE and CA18DE engines similar

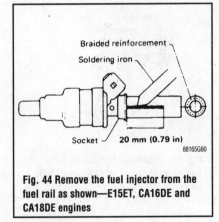

Fig. 44 Remove the fuel injector from the fuel rail as shown—E15ET, CA16DE and CA18DE engines

6. Loosen the clamps at both ends of the air pipe.
7. Disconnect the IVC and the air regulator harness connectors.
8. Remove the air pipe.
9. Disconnect the harness connectors from the injectors. Remove the fuel hoses. Remove the fuel rail mounting bolts and the fuel injector mounting screws.
10. Remove the fuel rail assembly by pulling out the fuel rail and the injectors.
11. Unfasten the fuel injector-to-fuel rail hose clamp and pull the injector from the fuel rail.

✳✳ WARNING

The following procedure must be followed carefully. Use extreme care when using heat around fuel system components. DO NOT allow the soldering iron to cut through the hose; cut only the braided reinforcement, from the hose.

12. Remove the injectors from the rail as follows:
   a. Heat a 150 watt soldering iron.
   b. Cut (melt) a line in the braided reinforcement, starting at the injector socket, extending 19mm (long) up the hose.

➡**Be careful not to damage the socket plastic connector with the soldering iron.**

   c. Pull the rubber hose off by hand.
To install:
13. To install a new fuel hose, clean the injector tail section, wet the inside of the new hose with fuel, push the hose into the fuel injector hose socket (as far as it will go). Assemble the injector(s) onto the fuel rail.

14. Install injectors on fuel rail.
15. Install fuel rail to engine. Always use new O-rings on injectors.
16. Install fuel lines to fuel rail and electrical connections to injectors.
17. Install the air pipe.
18. Reconnect the IVC and the air regulator harness connectors.
19. Install PCV valve and hose.
20. Install the throttle chamber and attaching parts.
21. Install the air inlet pipe and hose.
22. Start engine and check for fuel leaks.

CA16DE and CA18DE Engines

♦ **See Figures 45 and 46**

1. Release the fuel system pressure and disconnect the negative battery cable.
2. Remove the throttle chamber, intake manifold stay, IAA unit and intake side rocker cover.
3. Disconnect all fuel and vacuum hoses and electrical harnesses from the pressure regulator and fuel rail (charging assembly).
4. Remove the injector retaining bolts and remove the injector/fuel rail assembly.

✳✳ WARNING

The following procedure must be followed carefully. Use extreme care when using heat around fuel system components. DO NOT allow the soldering iron to cut through the hose; cut only the braided reinforcement, from the hose.

5. Remove the injectors from the rail as follows:
   a. Heat a 150 watt soldering iron.
   b. Cut (melt) a line in the braided reinforcement, starting at the injector socket, extending 19mm (long) up the hose.

➡**Be careful not to damage the socket plastic connector with the soldering iron.**

   c. Pull the rubber hose off by hand.
   To install:
6. Wet the new injector hose with clean fuel and push the rubber hose onto the injector tail piece by hand as far as it will go.
7. Install the injector/fuel rail assembly and torque the injector retaining bolts to 35 inch lbs. (4.0 Nm).
8. Reconnect all fuel and vacuum hoses and electrical harnesses.
9. Install the remaining components.
10. Connect the battery cable, start the engine and check for leaks before road testing.

GA16DE Engine

♦ **See Figures 47, 48, 49 and 50**

1. Relieve the fuel system pressure and disconnect the negative battery cable.
2. Disconnect the fuel injector wiring harness connectors and the vacuum line from the fuel pressure regulator.
3. Disconnect the electrical connectors from each injector.
4. Disconnect the vacuum hose from the fuel pressure regulator.
5. Disconnect the fuel pressure and return lines from the fuel rail.
6. Remove the bolts that secure the fuel rail to the intake, in proper sequence.
7. Remove the injectors with the fuel rail assembly.
8. Remove the individual injector by removing the two bolts that secure the cap to the injector.
9. Remove the injector from the fuel rail by pushing the injector from the bottom and discard the O-rings.

✳✳ WARNING

DO NOT remove the injector by pulling on the electrical connector housing.

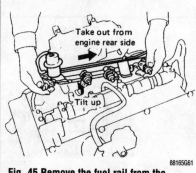

Fig. 45 Remove the fuel rail from the engine as shown—CA16DE and CA18DE engines

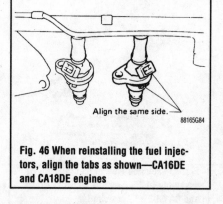

Fig. 46 When reinstalling the fuel injectors, align the tabs as shown—CA16DE and CA18DE engines

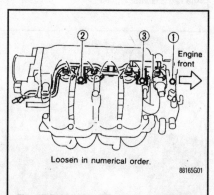

Fig. 47 Fuel rail bolt loosening and tightening sequence—1991–94 GA16DE engine

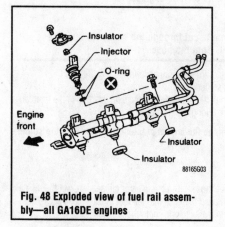

Fig. 48 Exploded view of fuel rail assembly—all GA16DE engines

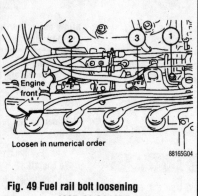

Fig. 49 Fuel rail bolt loosening sequence—1995–96 GA16DE engine

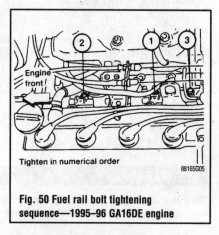

Fig. 50 Fuel rail bolt tightening sequence—1995–96 GA16DE engine

To install:

10. Install new O-rings onto the injectors and coat the O-rings with a light coating non-silicone based oil.

11. Install the injector into the fuel rail assembly and install the cap that secures the injector. Tighten the cap bolts to 26–33 inch lbs. (2.9–3.8 Nm).

12. Install the insulators, injectors, and the fuel rail assembly to the intake manifold. Torque the retaining bolts in sequence and in two (2) steps. Torque the bolts to 12–15 ft. lbs. (16–21 Nm).

13. Connect the fuel lines to the fuel rail, using new clamps.

14. Connect the fuel injector wiring harness connectors and the vacuum line to the fuel pressure regulator.

15. Connect the negative battery cable.

16. Start the engine and check for fuel leaks after the installation is complete.

SR20DE Engine

▶ **See Figures 51, 52 and 53**

1. Release the fuel system residual pressure.

2. Disconnect the negative battery cable.

3. Remove the intake manifold plenum (collector) assembly, follow the procedures outlined in Section 3.

4. Disconnect the vacuum hose from the pressure regulator.

5. Disconnect the fuel pressure and return lines from the fuel rail.

6. Disconnect the electrical connectors from each injector.

7. Remove the three bolts that secure the fuel rail to the intake, in proper sequence.

8. Remove the injector/fuel rail assembly.

9. Remove the individual injector by removing the two bolts that secure the cap to the injector.

10. Push out the injector from the bottom of the fuel rail assembly.

✳✳ WARNING

DO NOT remove the injector by pulling on the electrical connector housing.

To install:

11. Install new O-rings onto the injectors and coat the O-rings with a light coating non-silicone based oil.

12. Install the injectors to the fuel rail and tighten the cap that secures the injector to 26–33 inch lbs. (2.9–3.8 Nm). Install the rail onto intake manifold.

13. Torque the fuel rail bolts as follows:
   a. Tighten all bolts in sequence to 96 inch lbs. (11 Nm).
   b. Tighten all bolts in sequence to 15–20 ft. lbs. (21–26 Nm).

14. Connect the fuel hoses to the fuel rail, using new clamps.

15. Connect the vacuum line to the fuel pressure regulator.

16. Connect the injector wiring harness.

17. Connect the battery cable, start the engine, and check for leaks before road testing.

TESTING

Refer to Section 4 for all electronic fuel injection testing and diagnostics.

Fuel Pressure Regulator

The pressure regulator is located on the fuel return side of the fuel injection rail.

REMOVAL & INSTALLATION

▶ **See Figures 54, 55, 56 and 57**

✳✳ CAUTION

Fuel injection systems remain under pressure after the engine has been turned OFF. Properly relieve fuel pressure before disconnecting any fuel lines. Also observe all safety practices outlined previously in the Fuel System Safety Precautions. Failure to do so may result in fire or personal injury.

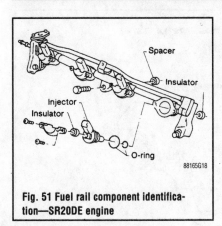

Fig. 51 Fuel rail component identification—SR20DE engine

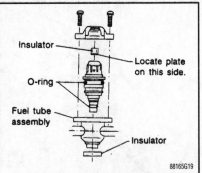

Fig. 52 Exploded view of the fuel injector assembly—SR20DE engine

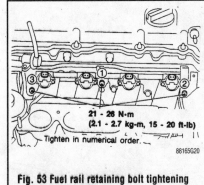

Fig. 53 Fuel rail retaining bolt tightening sequence—SR20DE engine

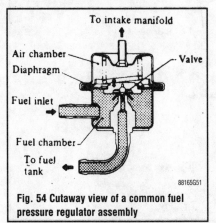

Fig. 54 Cutaway view of a common fuel pressure regulator assembly

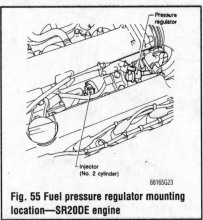

Fig. 55 Fuel pressure regulator mounting location—SR20DE engine

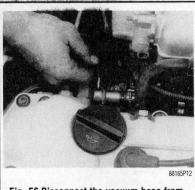

Fig. 56 Disconnect the vacuum hose from the pressure regulator nipple

Fig. 57 Remove the two screws securing the pressure regulator to the fuel rail

1. Following proper procedures, relieve fuel system residual pressure.
2. Disconnect the vacuum hose from the fuel pressure regulator.
3. Disconnect the fuel return line from the pressure regulator.
4. Loosen the retaining screw(s).
5. Carefully remove the regulator from the fuel rail assembly.

To install:

6. Install new O-rings on the regulator assembly. Lightly lubricate the O-rings with gasoline.
7. Install the regulator to the fuel rail and secure with retaining screw(s).
8. Connect the vacuum hose to the fuel pressure regulator.
9. Pressurize the fuel system and check for leaks.

FUEL TANK

Tank Assembly

REMOVAL & INSTALLATION

1983–90 Pulsar

▶ See Figures 58 and 59

1. Following proper procedures, relieve fuel system residual pressure.
2. Drain the fuel tank.

3. Remove the rear seat cushion.
4. Remove the inspection cover.
5. Disconnect the fuel gauge electrical harness connector.
6. Disconnect the fuel filler and the ventilation hoses. Disconnect the fuel outlet, return and evaporation hoses, at the front of the tank. Plug open fuel lines.

➡ Remove the tank protector, if so equipped.

7. Remove the fuel tank mounting bolts and the tank from the vehicle.

To install:

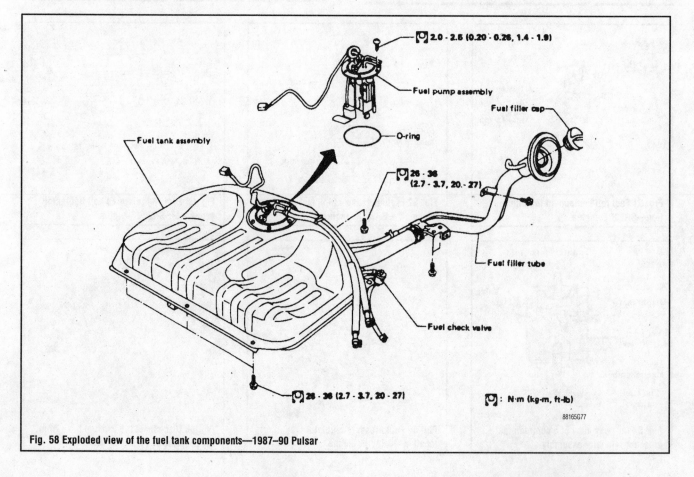

Fig. 58 Exploded view of the fuel tank components—1987–90 Pulsar

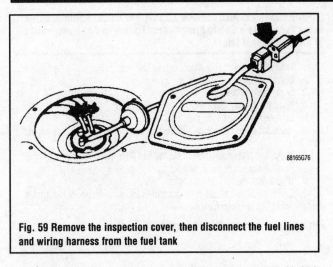

Fig. 59 Remove the inspection cover, then disconnect the fuel lines and wiring harness from the fuel tank

8. Install the fuel tank to vehicle and torque the mounting bolts to 20–27 ft. lbs. (27–37 Nm).
9. Reconnect all fuel lines, ventilation hoses and the electrical connection.
10. Install the inspection cover and rear seat cushion.
11. Start engine and check for fuel leaks.

1982–90 Sentra

2WD MODELS

▶ See Figure 60

❈❈ CAUTION

Fuel injection systems remain under pressure after the engine has been turned OFF. Properly relieve fuel pressure before disconnect-

ing any fuel lines. Also observe all safety practices outlined earlier in the Fuel System Safety Precautions. Failure to do so may result in fire or personal injury.

1. Following proper procedures, relieve fuel system residual pressure.
2. Disconnect the negative battery cable. Drain fuel into a safe, enclosed, metal container.
3. Remove inspection cover and disconnect fuel tank gauge unit harness connector.
4. Disconnect fuel filler and ventilation tubes.

➡Plug hose and pipe openings to prevent entry of dust and dirt.

5. Disconnect fuel outlet, return and evaporation hoses.
6. Place a suitable jack under the tank to support. Remove 6 bolts attaching fuel tank flange to the body and then lower the fuel tank.
   To install:
7. Raise the tank and install the 6 bolts attaching fuel tank flange to the body. Torque the bolts to 20–27 ft. lbs. (27–34 Nm).
8. Connect fuel outlet, return and evaporation hoses.
9. Connect fuel filler and ventilation tubes.
10. Connect the fuel gauge and pump harness connectors. Install inspection cover.
11. Refill the fuel tank and check for leaks. Connect the negative battery cable, start the engine and check for leaks.

4WD MODELS

❈❈ CAUTION

Fuel injection systems remain under pressure after the engine has been turned OFF. Properly relieve fuel pressure before disconnecting any fuel lines. Also observe all safety practices outlined earlier in the Fuel System Safety Precautions. Failure to do so may result in fire or personal injury.

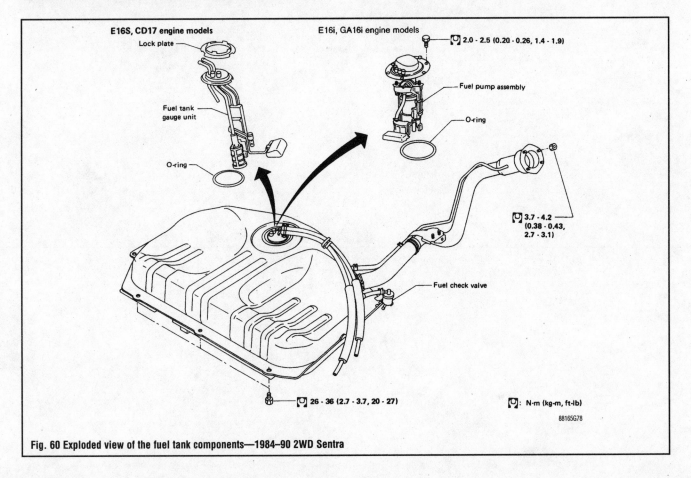

Fig. 60 Exploded view of the fuel tank components—1984–90 2WD Sentra

1. Following proper procedures, relieve fuel system residual pressure.
2. Disconnect the negative battery cable. Drain fuel into a safe, enclosed, metal container.
3. Remove inspection cover and disconnect fuel tank gauge unit harness connector.
4. Disconnect fuel filler and ventilation tubes.

➡**Plug hose and pipe openings to prevent entry of dust and dirt.**

5. Disconnect the fuel outlet, return and evaporation hoses.
6. Raise the car and support it securely. Support the tank securely from underneath. Remove the bolt from the rear end of the support strap on either side (the bolts screw in upward). You may twist the strap 90° an pull it out of the fitting in the body where it connects, if necessary for clearance or to replace it if damaged.
7. Lower the tank and remove it.

To install:

8. If the tank is being replaced, remove the fuel pump mounting bolts and remove the pump. Install it with a new O-ring, torquing the bolts to 17–23 inch lbs. (1.9–2.6 Nm).
9. Inspect the straps and, if they are bent or show cracks anywhere along their length, replace them. They can be installed by inserting the inner end into the body fitting with the outer end turned outboard and then turning them 90° so they run from front to rear.
10. Raise the tank into position. Then, raise the rear ends of the straps into position so the bolt holes in the straps line up with those in the body. Install the attaching bolts and torque them to 20–27 ft. lbs. (27–34 Nm).
11. Reconnect the fuel lines, evaporative emissions system, tank filler and electrical connectors in reverse of the removal procedure.

1991–96 Sentra

�֍֍ **CAUTION**

Fuel injection systems remain under pressure after the engine has been turned OFF. Properly relieve fuel pressure before disconnecting any fuel lines. Also observe all safety practices outlined earlier in the Fuel System Safety Precautions. Failure to do so may result in fire or personal injury.

1. Following proper procedures, relieve fuel system residual pressure.
2. Disconnect the negative battery cable.
3. Drain the fuel tank.
4. Remove the rear seat cushion.
5. Remove the inspection cover.
6. Disconnect the fuel gauge and the fuel pump electrical harness connector.
7. At the fuel filler door, disconnect the fuel filler tube from the body.
8. Raise and support the vehicle safely.
9. Disconnect the ventilation hoses.
10. Disconnect the fuel outlet, return and evaporation hoses, at the front of the tank and plug the open fuel lines.

➡**If equipped, remove the tank protector.**

11. Support the tank, remove the fuel tank mounting bolts, and lower the tank from the vehicle.

To install:

➡**If the sending unit or the fuel pump are removed, a new O-ring must be installed.**

12. Install the fuel tank to vehicle and torque the mounting bolts to 20–26 ft. lbs. (27–37 Nm). If removed, install the fuel tank protector.
13. Connect all the fuel lines and ventilation hoses.
14. Lower the vehicle and connect the filler tube to the vehicle body.
15. Connect the fuel gauge and fuel pump electrical connections.
16. Install the inspection cover and rear seat cushion.
17. Pour fuel back into fuel tank.
18. Connect the negative battery cable.
19. Start engine and check for fuel leaks.

6

CHASSIS ELECTRICAL

UNDERSTANDING AND TROUBLESHOOTING ELECTRICAL SYSTEMS

Basic Electrical Theory

♦ See Figure 1

For any 12 volt, negative ground, electrical system to operate, the electricity must travel in a complete circuit. This simply means that current (power) from the positive (+) terminal of the battery must eventually return to the negative (-) terminal of the battery. Along the way, this current will travel through wires, fuses, switches and components. If, for any reason, the flow of current through the circuit is interrupted, the component fed by that circuit will cease to function properly.

Perhaps the easiest way to visualize a circuit is to think of connecting a light bulb (with two wires attached to it) to the battery—one wire attached to the negative (-) terminal of the battery and the other wire to the positive (+) terminal. With the two wires touching the battery terminals, the circuit would be complete and the light bulb would illuminate. Electricity would follow a path from the battery to the bulb and back to the battery. It's easy to see that with longer wires on our light bulb, it could be mounted anywhere. Further, one wire could be fitted with a switch so that the light could be turned on and off.

The normal automotive circuit differs from this simple example in two ways. First, instead of having a return wire from the bulb to the battery, the current travels through the frame of the vehicle. Since the negative (-) battery cable is attached to the frame (made of electrically conductive metal), the frame of the vehicle can serve as a ground wire to complete the circuit. Secondly, most automotive circuits contain multiple components which receive power from a single circuit. This lessens the amount of wire needed to power components on the vehicle.

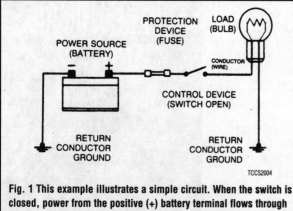

Fig. 1 This example illustrates a simple circuit. When the switch is closed, power from the positive (+) battery terminal flows through the fuse and the switch, and then to the light bulb. The light illuminates and the circuit is completed through the ground wire back to the negative (-) battery terminal. In reality, the two ground points shown in the illustration are attached to the metal frame of the vehicle, which completes the circuit back to the battery

HOW DOES ELECTRICITY WORK: THE WATER ANALOGY

Electricity is the flow of electrons—the subatomic particles that constitute the outer shell of an atom. Electrons spin in an orbit around the center core of an atom. The center core is comprised of protons (positive charge) and neutrons (neutral charge). Electrons have a negative charge and balance out the positive charge of the protons. When an outside force causes the number of electrons to unbalance the charge of the protons, the electrons will split off the atom and look for another atom to balance out. If this imbalance is kept up, electrons will continue to move and an electrical flow will exist.

Many people have been taught electrical theory using an analogy with water. In a comparison with water flowing through a pipe, the electrons would be the water and the wire is the pipe.

The flow of electricity can be measured much like the flow of water through a pipe. The unit of measurement used is amperes, frequently abbreviated as amps (a). You can compare amperage to the volume of water flowing through a pipe.

When connected to a circuit, an ammeter will measure the actual amount of current flowing through the circuit. When relatively few electrons flow through a circuit, the amperage is low. When many electrons flow, the amperage is high.

Water pressure is measured in units such as pounds per square inch (psi); The electrical pressure is measured in units called volts (v). When a voltmeter is connected to a circuit, it is measuring the electrical pressure.

The actual flow of electricity depends not only on voltage and amperage, but also on the resistance of the circuit. The higher the resistance, the higher the force necessary to push the current through the circuit. The standard unit for measuring resistance is an ohm. Resistance in a circuit varies depending on the amount and type of components used in the circuit. The main factors which determine resistance are:

• Material—some materials have more resistance than others. Those with high resistance are said to be insulators. Rubber materials (or rubber-like plastics) are some of the most common insulators used in vehicles as they have a very high resistance to electricity. Very low resistance materials are said to be conductors. Copper wire is among the best conductors. Silver is actually a superior conductor to copper and is used in some relay contacts, but its high cost prohibits its use as common wiring. Most automotive wiring is made of copper.

• Size—the larger the wire size being used, the less resistance the wire will have. This is why components which use large amounts of electricity usually have large wires supplying current to them.

• Length—for a given thickness of wire, the longer the wire, the greater the resistance. The shorter the wire, the less the resistance. When determining the proper wire for a circuit, both size and length must be considered to design a circuit that can handle the current needs of the component.

• Temperature—with many materials, the higher the temperature, the greater the resistance (positive temperature coefficient). Some materials exhibit the opposite trait of lower resistance with higher temperatures (negative temperature coefficient). These principles are used in many of the sensors on the engine.

OHM'S LAW

There is a direct relationship between current, voltage and resistance. The relationship between current, voltage and resistance can be summed up by a statement known as Ohm's law.

Voltage (E) is equal to amperage (I) times resistance (R): $E = I \times R$
Other forms of the formula are $R = E/I$ and $I = E/R$

In each of these formulas, E is the voltage in volts, I is the current in amps and R is the resistance in ohms. The basic point to remember is that as the resistance of a circuit goes up, the amount of current that flows in the circuit will go down, if voltage remains the same.

The amount of work that the electricity can perform is expressed as power. The unit of power is the watt (w). The relationship between power, voltage and current is expressed as:

Power (w) is equal to amperage (I) times voltage (E): $W = I \times E$

This is only true for direct current (DC) circuits; The alternating current formula is a tad different, but since the electrical circuits in most vehicles are DC type, we need not get into AC circuit theory.

Electrical Components

POWER SOURCE

Power is supplied to the vehicle by two devices: The battery and the alternator. The battery supplies electrical power during starting or during periods when the current demand of the vehicle's electrical system exceeds the output capacity of the alternator. The alternator supplies electrical current when the engine is running. Just not does the alternator supply the current needs of the vehicle, but it recharges the battery.

The Battery

In most modern vehicles, the battery is a lead/acid electrochemical device consisting of six 2 volt subsections (cells) connected in series, so that the unit is capable of producing approximately 12 volts of electrical pressure. Each sub-section consists of a series of positive and negative plates held a short distance apart in a solution of sulfuric acid and water.

The two types of plates are of dissimilar metals. This sets up a chemical reaction, and it is this reaction which produces current flow from the battery when its positive and negative terminals are connected to an electrical load . The power removed from the battery is replaced by the alternator, restoring the battery to its original chemical state.

The Alternator

On some vehicles there isn't an alternator, but a generator. The difference is that an alternator supplies alternating current which is then changed to direct current for use on the vehicle, while a generator produces direct current. Alternators tend to be more efficient and that is why they are used.

Alternators and generators are devices that consist of coils of wires wound together making big electromagnets. One group of coils spins within another set and the interaction of the magnetic fields causes a current to flow. This current is then drawn off the coils and fed into the vehicles electrical system.

GROUND

Two types of grounds are used in automotive electric circuits. Direct ground components are grounded to the frame through their mounting points. All other components use some sort of ground wire which is attached to the frame or chassis of the vehicle. The electrical current runs through the chassis of the vehicle and returns to the battery through the ground (-) cable; if you look, you'll see that the battery ground cable connects between the battery and the frame or chassis of the vehicle.

➡It should be noted that a good percentage of electrical problems can be traced to bad grounds.

PROTECTIVE DEVICES

▶ **See Figure 2**

It is possible for large surges of current to pass through the electrical system of your vehicle. If this surge of current were to reach the load in the circuit, the surge could burn it out or severely damage it. It can also overload the wiring,

causing the harness to get hot and melt the insulation. To prevent this, fuses, circuit breakers and/or fusible links are connected into the supply wires of the electrical system. These items are nothing more than a built-in weak spot in the system. When an abnormal amount of current flows through the system, these protective devices work as follows to protect the circuit:

• Fuse—when an excessive electrical current passes through a fuse, the fuse "blows" (the conductor melts) and opens the circuit, preventing the passage of current.

• Circuit Breaker—a circuit breaker is basically a self-repairing fuse. It will open the circuit in the same fashion as a fuse, but when the surge subsides, the circuit breaker can be reset and does not need replacement.

• Fusible Link—a fusible link (fuse link or main link) is a short length of special, high temperature insulated wire that acts as a fuse. When an excessive electrical current passes through a fusible link, the thin gauge wire inside the link melts, creating an intentional open to protect the circuit. To repair the circuit, the link must be replaced. Some newer type fusible links are housed in plug-in modules, which are simply replaced like a fuse, while older type fusible links must be cut and spliced if they melt. Since this link is very early in the electrical path, it's the first place to look if nothing on the vehicle works, yet the battery seems to be charged and is properly connected.

✳✳ CAUTION

Always replace fuses, circuit breakers and fusible links with identically rated components. Under no circumstances should a component of higher or lower amperage rating be substituted.

SWITCHES & RELAYS

▶ **See Figures 3 and 4**

Switches are used in electrical circuits to control the passage of current. The most common use is to open and close circuits between the battery and the various electric devices in the system. Switches are rated according to the amount of amperage they can handle. If a sufficient amperage rated switch is not used in a circuit, the switch could overload and cause damage.

Some electrical components which require a large amount of current to operate use a special switch called a relay. Since these circuits carry a large amount of current, the thickness of the wire in the circuit is also greater. If this large wire were connected from the load to the control switch, the switch would have to carry the high amperage load and the fairing or dash would be twice as large to accommodate the increased size of the wiring harness. To prevent these problems, a relay is used.

Relays are composed of a coil and a set of contacts. When the coil has a current passed though it, a magnetic field is formed and this field causes the contacts to move together, completing the circuit. Most relays are normally open, preventing current from passing through the circuit, but they can take any elec-

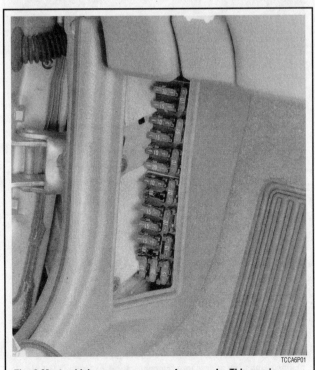

Fig. 2 Most vehicles use one or more fuse panels. This one is located on the driver's side kick panel

TCCA6P01

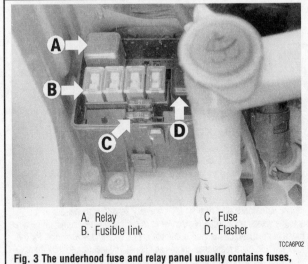

| A. Relay | C. Fuse |
| B. Fusible link | D. Flasher |

TCCA6P02

Fig. 3 The underhood fuse and relay panel usually contains fuses, relays, flashers and fusible links

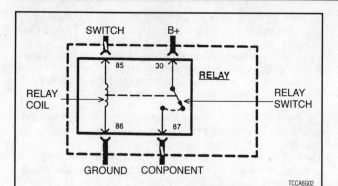

Fig. 4 Relays are composed of a coil and a switch. These two components are linked together so that when one operates, the other operates at the same time. The large wires in the circuit are connected from the battery to one side of the relay switch (B+) and from the opposite side of the relay switch to the load (component). Smaller wires are connected from the relay coil to the control switch for the circuit and from the opposite side of the relay coil to ground

trical form depending on the job they are intended to do. Relays can be considered "remote control switches." They allow a smaller current to operate devices that require higher amperages. When a small current operates the coil, a larger current is allowed to pass by the contacts. Some common circuits which may use relays are the horn, headlights, starter, electric fuel pump and other high draw circuits.

LOAD

Every electrical circuit must include a "load" (something to use the electricity coming from the source). Without this load, the battery would attempt to deliver its entire power supply from one pole to another. This is called a "short circuit." All this electricity would take a short cut to ground and cause a great amount of damage to other components in the circuit by developing a tremendous amount of heat. This condition could develop sufficient heat to melt the insulation on all the surrounding wires and reduce a multiple wire cable to a lump of plastic and copper.

WIRING & HARNESSES

The average vehicle contains meters and meters of wiring, with hundreds of individual connections. To protect the many wires from damage and to keep them from becoming a confusing tangle, they are organized into bundles, enclosed in plastic or taped together and called wiring harnesses. Different harnesses serve different parts of the vehicle. Individual wires are color coded to help trace them through a harness where sections are hidden from view.

Automotive wiring or circuit conductors can be either single strand wire, multi-strand wire or printed circuitry. Single strand wire has a solid metal core and is usually used inside such components as alternators, motors, relays and other devices. Multi-strand wire has a core made of many small strands of wire twisted together into a single conductor. Most of the wiring in an automotive electrical system is made up of multi-strand wire, either as a single conductor or grouped together in a harness. All wiring is color coded on the insulator, either as a solid color or as a colored wire with an identification stripe. A printed circuit is a thin film of copper or other conductor that is printed on an insulator backing. Occasionally, a printed circuit is sandwiched between two sheets of plastic for more protection and flexibility. A complete printed circuit, consisting of conductors, insulating material and connectors for lamps or other components is called a printed circuit board. Printed circuitry is used in place of individual wires or harnesses in places where space is limited, such as behind instrument panels.

Since automotive electrical systems are very sensitive to changes in resistance, the selection of properly sized wires is critical when systems are repaired. A loose or corroded connection or a replacement wire that is too small for the circuit will add extra resistance and an additional voltage drop to the circuit.

The wire gauge number is an expression of the cross-section area of the conductor. Vehicles from countries that use the metric system will typically describe the wire size as its cross-sectional area in square millimeters. In this method, the larger the wire, the greater the number. Another common system for expressing wire size is the American Wire Gauge (AWG) system. As gauge number increases, area decreases and the wire becomes smaller. An 18 gauge wire is smaller than a 4 gauge wire. A wire with a higher gauge number will carry less current than a wire with a lower gauge number. Gauge wire size refers to the size of the strands of the conductor, not the size of the complete wire with insulator. It is possible, therefore, to have two wires of the same gauge with different diameters because one may have thicker insulation than the other.

It is essential to understand how a circuit works before trying to figure out why it doesn't. An electrical schematic shows the electrical current paths when a circuit is operating properly. Schematics break the entire electrical system down into individual circuits. In a schematic, usually no attempt is made to represent wiring and components as they physically appear on the vehicle; switches and other components are shown as simply as possible. Face views of harness connectors show the cavity or terminal locations in all multi-pin connectors to help locate test points.

CONNECTORS

◆ See Figures 5 and 6

Three types of connectors are commonly used in automotive applications—weatherproof, molded and hard shell.

• Weatherproof—these connectors are most commonly used where the connector is exposed to the elements. Terminals are protected against moisture and dirt by sealing rings which provide a weathertight seal. All repairs require the use of a special terminal and the tool required to service it. Unlike standard blade type terminals, these weatherproof terminals cannot be straightened once they are bent. Make certain that the connectors are properly seated and all of the sealing rings are in place when connecting leads.

• Molded—these connectors require complete replacement of the connector if found to be defective. This means splicing a new connector assembly into the harness. All splices should be soldered to insure proper contact. Use care

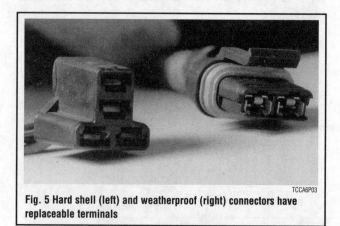

Fig. 5 Hard shell (left) and weatherproof (right) connectors have replaceable terminals

Fig. 6 Weatherproof connectors are most commonly used in the engine compartment or where the connector is exposed to the elements

when probing the connections or replacing terminals in them, as it is possible to create a short circuit between opposite terminals. If this happens to the wrong terminal pair, it is possible to damage certain components. Always use jumper wires between connectors for circuit checking and NEVER probe through weatherproof seals.

• Hard Shell—unlike molded connectors, the terminal contacts in hard-shell connectors can be replaced. Replacement usually involves the use of a special terminal removal tool that depresses the locking tangs (barbs) on the connector terminal and allows the connector to be removed from the rear of the shell. The connector shell should be replaced if it shows any evidence of burning, melting, cracks, or breaks. Replace individual terminals that are burnt, corroded, distorted or loose.

Test Equipment

Pinpointing the exact cause of trouble in an electrical circuit is most times accomplished by the use of special test equipment. The following describes different types of commonly used test equipment and briefly explains how to use them in diagnosis. In addition to the information covered below, the tool manufacturer's instructions booklet (provided with the tester) should be read and clearly understood before attempting any test procedures.

JUMPER WIRES

> ### ※ CAUTION
>
> **Never use jumper wires made from a thinner gauge wire than the circuit being tested. If the jumper wire is of too small a gauge, it may overheat and possibly melt. Never use jumpers to bypass high resistance loads in a circuit. Bypassing resistance's, in effect, creates a short circuit. This may, in turn, cause damage and fire. Jumper wires should only be used to bypass lengths of wire or to simulate switches.**

Jumper wires are simple, yet extremely valuable, pieces of test equipment. They are basically test wires which are used to bypass sections of a circuit. Although jumper wires can be purchased, they are usually fabricated from lengths of standard automotive wire and whatever type of connector (alligator clip, spade connector or pin connector) that is required for the particular application being tested. In cramped, hard-to-reach areas, it is advisable to have insulated boots over the jumper wire terminals in order to prevent accidental grounding. It is also advisable to include a standard automotive fuse in any jumper wire. This is commonly referred to as a "fused jumper". By inserting an in-line fuse holder between a set of test leads, a fused jumper wire can be used for bypassing open circuits. Use a 5 amp fuse to provide protection against voltage spikes.

Jumper wires are used primarily to locate open electrical circuits, on either the ground (-) side of the circuit or on the power (+) side. If an electrical component fails to operate, connect the jumper wire between the component and a good ground. If the component operates only with the jumper installed, the ground circuit is open. If the ground circuit is good, but the component does not operate, the circuit between the power feed and component may be open. By moving the jumper wire successively back from the component toward the power source, you can isolate the area of the circuit where the open is located. When the component stops functioning, or the power is cut off, the open is in the segment of wire between the jumper and the point previously tested.

You can sometimes connect the jumper wire directly from the battery to the "hot" terminal of the component, but first make sure the component uses 12 volts in operation. Some electrical components, such as fuel injectors or sensors, are designed to operate on about 4 to 5 volts, and running 12 volts directly to these components will cause damage.

TEST LIGHTS

▶ **See Figure 7**

The test light is used to check circuits and components while electrical current is flowing through them. It is used for voltage and ground tests. To use a 12 volt test light, connect the ground clip to a good ground and probe wherever necessary with the pick. The test light will illuminate when voltage is detected. This does not necessarily mean that 12 volts (or any particular amount of volt-

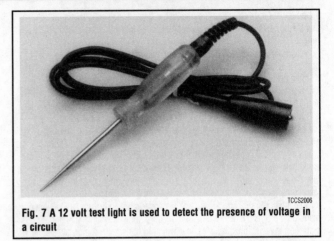

Fig. 7 A 12 volt test light is used to detect the presence of voltage in a circuit

TCCS2006

age) is present; it only means that some voltage is present. It is advisable before using the test light to touch its ground clip and probe across the battery posts or terminals to make sure the light is operating properly.

> ### ※ WARNING
>
> **Do not use a test light to probe electronic ignition, spark plug or coil wires. Never use a pick-type test light to probe wiring on computer controlled systems unless specifically instructed to do so. Any wire insulation that is pierced by the test light probe should be taped and sealed with silicone after testing.**

Like the jumper wire, the 12 volt test light is used to isolate opens in circuits. But, whereas the jumper wire is used to bypass the open to operate the load, the 12 volt test light is used to locate the presence of voltage in a circuit. If the test light illuminates, there is power up to that point in the circuit; if the test light does not illuminate, there is an open circuit (no power). Move the test light in successive steps back toward the power source until the light in the handle illuminates. The open is between the probe and a point which was previously probed.

The self-powered test light is similar in design to the 12 volt test light, but contains a 1.5 volt penlight battery in the handle. It is most often used in place of a multimeter to check for open or short circuits when power is isolated from the circuit (continuity test).

The battery in a self-powered test light does not provide much current. A weak battery may not provide enough power to illuminate the test light even when a complete circuit is made (especially if there is high resistance in the circuit). Always make sure that the test battery is strong. To check the battery, briefly touch the ground clip to the probe; if the light glows brightly, the battery is strong enough for testing.

➡**A self-powered test light should not be used on any computer controlled system or component. The small amount of electricity transmitted by the test light is enough to damage many electronic automotive components.**

MULTIMETERS

Multimeters are an extremely useful tool for troubleshooting electrical problems. They can be purchased in either analog or digital form and have a price range to suit any budget. A multimeter is a voltmeter, ammeter and ohmmeter (along with other features) combined into one instrument. It is often used when testing solid state circuits because of its high input impedance (usually 10 megaohms or more). A brief description of the multimeter main test functions follows:

• Voltmeter—the voltmeter is used to measure voltage at any point in a circuit, or to measure the voltage drop across any part of a circuit. Voltmeters usually have various scales and a selector switch to allow the reading of different voltage ranges. The voltmeter has a positive and a negative lead. To avoid damage to the meter, always connect the negative lead to the negative (-) side of the circuit (to ground or nearest the ground side of the circuit) and connect the positive lead to the positive (+) side of the circuit (to the power source or the nearest power source). Note that the negative voltmeter lead will always be black and that the positive voltmeter will always be some color other than black (usually red).

• Ohmmeter—the ohmmeter is designed to read resistance (measured in ohms) in a circuit or component. Most ohmmeters will have a selector switch which permits the measurement of different ranges of resistance (usually the selector switch allows the multiplication of the meter reading by 10, 100, 1,000 and 10,000). Some ohmmeters are "auto-ranging" which means the meter itself will determine which scale to use. Since the meters are powered by an internal battery, the ohmmeter can be used like a self-powered test light. When the ohmmeter is connected, current from the ohmmeter flows through the circuit or component being tested. Since the ohmmeter's internal resistance and voltage are known values, the amount of current flow through the meter depends on the resistance of the circuit or component being tested. The ohmmeter can also be used to perform a continuity test for suspected open circuits. In using the meter for making continuity checks, do not be concerned with the actual resistance readings. Zero resistance, or any ohm reading, indicates continuity in the circuit. Infinite resistance indicates an opening in the circuit. A high resistance reading where there should be none indicates a problem in the circuit. Checks for short circuits are made in the same manner as checks for open circuits, except that the circuit must be isolated from both power and normal ground. Infinite resistance indicates no continuity, while zero resistance indicates a dead short.

❋❋ WARNING

Never use an ohmmeter to check the resistance of a component or wire while there is voltage applied to the circuit.

• Ammeter—an ammeter measures the amount of current flowing through a circuit in units called amperes or amps. At normal operating voltage, most circuits have a characteristic amount of amperes, called "current draw" which can be measured using an ammeter. By referring to a specified current draw rating, then measuring the amperes and comparing the two values, one can determine what is happening within the circuit to aid in diagnosis. An open circuit, for example, will not allow any current to flow, so the ammeter reading will be zero. A damaged component or circuit will have an increased current draw, so the reading will be high. The ammeter is always connected in series with the circuit being tested. All of the current that normally flows through the circuit must also flow through the ammeter; if there is any other path for the current to follow, the ammeter reading will not be accurate. The ammeter itself has very little resistance to current flow and, therefore, will not affect the circuit, but it will measure current draw only when the circuit is closed and electricity is flowing. Excessive current draw can blow fuses and drain the battery, while a reduced current draw can cause motors to run slowly, lights to dim and other components to not operate properly.

Troubleshooting Electrical Systems

When diagnosing a specific problem, organized troubleshooting is a must. The complexity of a modern automotive vehicle demands that you approach any problem in a logical, organized manner. There are certain troubleshooting techniques, however, which are standard:

• Establish when the problem occurs. Does the problem appear only under certain conditions? Were there any noises, odors or other unusual symptoms? Isolate the problem area. To do this, make some simple tests and observations, then eliminate the systems that are working properly. Check for obvious problems, such as broken wires and loose or dirty connections. Always check the obvious before assuming something complicated is the cause.

• Test for problems systematically to determine the cause once the problem area is isolated. Are all the components functioning properly? Is there power going to electrical switches and motors. Performing careful, systematic checks will often turn up most causes on the first inspection, without wasting time checking components that have little or no relationship to the problem.

• Test all repairs after the work is done to make sure that the problem is fixed. Some causes can be traced to more than one component, so a careful verification of repair work is important in order to pick up additional malfunctions that may cause a problem to reappear or a different problem to arise. A blown fuse, for example, is a simple problem that may require more than another fuse to repair. If you don't look for a problem that caused a fuse to blow, a shorted wire (for example) may go undetected.

Experience has shown that most problems tend to be the result of a fairly simple and obvious cause, such as loose or corroded connectors, bad grounds or damaged wire insulation which causes a short. This makes careful visual inspection of components during testing essential to quick and accurate troubleshooting.

Testing

OPEN CIRCUITS

▶ **See Figure 8**

This test already assumes the existence of an open in the circuit and it is used to help locate the open portion.
1. Isolate the circuit from power and ground.
2. Connect the self-powered test light or ohmmeter ground clip to the ground side of the circuit and probe sections of the circuit sequentially.
3. If the light is out or there is infinite resistance, the open is between the probe and the circuit ground.
4. If the light is on or the meter shows continuity, the open is between the probe and the end of the circuit toward the power source.

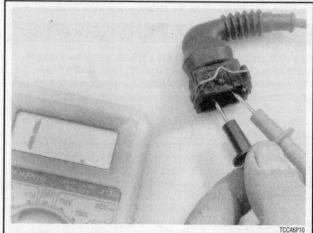

TCCA6P10

Fig. 8 The infinite reading on this multimeter indicates that the circuit is open

SHORT CIRCUITS

➡ **Never use a self-powered test light to perform checks for opens or shorts when power is applied to the circuit under test. The test light can be damaged by outside power.**

1. Isolate the circuit from power and ground.
2. Connect the self-powered test light or ohmmeter ground clip to a good ground and probe any easy-to-reach point in the circuit.
3. If the light comes on or there is continuity, there is a short somewhere in the circuit.
4. To isolate the short, probe a test point at either end of the isolated circuit (the light should be on or the meter should indicate continuity).
5. Leave the test light probe engaged and sequentially open connectors or switches, remove parts, etc. until the light goes out or continuity is broken.
6. When the light goes out, the short is between the last two circuit components which were opened.

VOLTAGE

This test determines voltage available from the battery and should be the first step in any electrical troubleshooting procedure after visual inspection. Many electrical problems, especially on computer controlled systems, can be caused by a low state of charge in the battery. Excessive corrosion at the battery cable terminals can cause poor contact that will prevent proper charging and full battery current flow.

1. Set the voltmeter selector switch to the 20V position.
2. Connect the multimeter negative lead to the battery's negative (-) post or terminal and the positive lead to the battery's positive (+) post or terminal.
3. Turn the ignition switch **ON** to provide a load.
4. A well charged battery should register over 12 volts. If the meter reads below 11.5 volts, the battery power may be insufficient to operate the electrical system properly.

VOLTAGE DROP

▶ **See Figure 9**

When current flows through a load, the voltage beyond the load drops. This voltage drop is due to the resistance created by the load and also by small resistance's created by corrosion at the connectors and damaged insulation on the wires. The maximum allowable voltage drop under load is critical, especially if there is more than one load in the circuit, since all voltage drops are cumulative.

1. Set the voltmeter selector switch to the 20 volt position.
2. Connect the multimeter negative lead to a good ground.
3. Operate the circuit and check the voltage prior to the first component (load).
4. There should be little or no voltage drop in the circuit prior to the first component. If a voltage drop exists, the wire or connectors in the circuit are suspect.
5. While operating the first component in the circuit, probe the ground side of the component with the positive meter lead and observe the voltage readings. A small voltage drop should be noticed. This voltage drop is caused by the resistance of the component.
6. Repeat the test for each component (load) down the circuit.
7. If a large voltage drop is noticed, the preceding component, wire or connector is suspect.

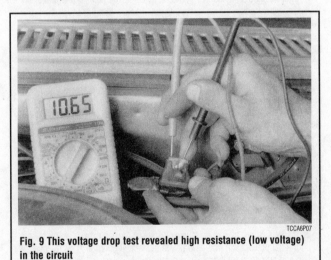

Fig. 9 This voltage drop test revealed high resistance (low voltage) in the circuit

RESISTANCE

▶ **See Figures 10 and 11**

❋❋❋ WARNING

Never use an ohmmeter with power applied to the circuit. The ohmmeter is designed to operate on its own power supply. The normal 12 volt electrical system voltage could damage the meter!

1. Isolate the circuit from the vehicle's power source.
2. Ensure that the ignition key is **OFF** when disconnecting any components or the battery.
3. Where necessary, also isolate at least one side of the circuit to be checked, in order to avoid reading parallel resistance's. Parallel circuit resistance's will always give a lower reading than the actual resistance of either of the branches.

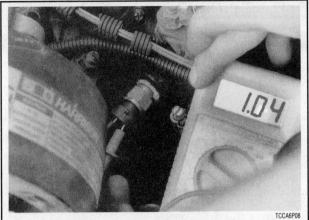

Fig. 10 Checking the resistance of a coolant temperature sensor with an ohmmeter. Reading is 1.04 kilohms

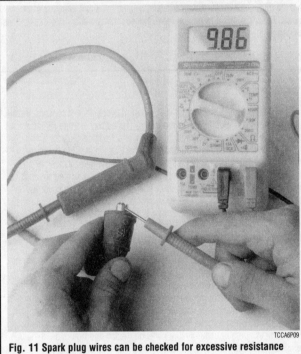

Fig. 11 Spark plug wires can be checked for excessive resistance using an ohmmeter

4. Connect the meter leads to both sides of the circuit (wire or component) and read the actual measured ohms on the meter scale. Make sure the selector switch is set to the proper ohm scale for the circuit being tested, to avoid misreading the ohmmeter test value.

Wire and Connector Repair

Almost anyone can replace damaged wires, as long as the proper tools and parts are available. Wire and terminals are available to fit almost any need. Even the specialized weatherproof, molded and hard shell connectors are now available from aftermarket suppliers.

Be sure the ends of all the wires are fitted with the proper terminal hardware and connectors. Wrapping a wire around a stud is never a permanent solution and will only cause trouble later. Replace wires one at a time to avoid confusion. Always route wires exactly the same as the factory.

➡**If connector repair is necessary, only attempt it if you have the proper tools. Weatherproof and hard shell connectors require special tools to release the pins inside the connector. Attempting to repair these connectors with conventional hand tools will damage them.**

SUPPLEMENTAL RESTRAINT SYSTEM

General Information

SYSTEM OPERATION

The Supplemental Restraint System (SRS) is used on 1990 and later Pulsar and Sentra models. In the event of a substantial front end collision, the SRS is designed to provide additional protection for the driver, and on 1995 and later models the front seat passenger. The SRS assists the normal seat belt restraining system by deploying an air bag assembly, via the steering wheel or passenger side dash pad.

The SRS utilizes an air bag module, front impact sensors, a spiral cable, a warning lamp, and a control module. All SRS wiring and connectors are yellow coated to identify them; never probe or disconnect any SRS electrical circuit without first disabling the SRS system.

With the battery cables connected, the SRS system is energized and monitoring the front impact sensors and the safing sensor for collision confirmation messages. When the vehicle strikes, or is struck by, another object (such as a tree, wall, another vehicle, etc.), the front impact sensors and safing sensor signals the diagnostic module, which determines the force and direction of the impact. Based on this information the diagnostic module either deploys or does not deploy the air bag(s).

SYSTEM COMPONENTS

Air Bag Module

The air bag module is the most visible part of the system. It contains the air bag cushion and its supporting components. The air bag module contains a housing to which the cushion and inflator are attached and sealed.

The inflator assembly is mounted to the back of the module housing. When supplied with the proper electrical signal, the inflator assembly produces a gas which discharges directly into the cushion. A protective cover is fitted to the front of the air bag module and forms a decorative cover in the center of the steering wheel. The air bag module is mounted directly to the steering wheel.

Front Impact Sensors

The driver-side air bag system is a safety device designed to reduce the risk of fatality or serious injury, caused by a frontal impact of the vehicle.

The impact sensors provide verification of the direction and severity of the impact. Three impact sensors are used. One is called a safing sensor. It is located inside the diagnostic module which is mounted on the floor pan, just forward of the center console. The other two sensors are mounted on the upper crossmember of the radiator closure panel on the left and right side of the vehicle under the hood.

The impact sensors are threshold sensitive switches that complete an electrical circuit when an impact provides a sufficient G force to close the switch. The sensors are calibrated for the specific vehicle and react to the severity and direction of the impact.

Spiral Cable

The spiral cable is mounted on the steering column behind the steering wheel and is used to maintain a continuous electrical circuit between the wiring harness and the driver's air bag module. This assembly consists of a flat ribbon-like electrically conductive tape which winds and unwinds with the steering wheel rotation.

Diagnostic Module

The Air Bag System Diagnostic Module (ASDM) contains the safing sensor, G-sensor, CPU and energy reserve capacitor. The ASDM monitors the system to determine the system readiness. The ASDM will store sufficient energy to deploy the air bag for only two minutes after the battery is disconnected. The ASDM contains on-board diagnostics and will illuminate the AIR BAG warning lamp in the cluster when a fault occurs.

SERVICE PRECAUTIONS

➡**All SRS electrical wiring harnesses and connectors are covered with YELLOW outer insulation. Do not use electrical test equipment on any circuit related to the SRS (air bag) sensors. When installing SRS components, always install with the arrow marks facing the front of the vehicle.**

Several precautions must be observed when handling the inflator module to avoid accidental deployment and possible personal injury.
- Before attempting to diagnose, remove or install the air bag system components, you must first disconnect and isolate the negative (-) battery cable. Failure to do so could result in accidental deployment and possible personal injury.
- Never carry the inflator module by the wires or connector on the underside of the module.
- When carrying a live inflator module, hold securely with both hands, and ensure that the bag and trim cover are pointed away.
- Place the inflator module on a bench or other surface with the bag and trim cover facing up.
- With the inflator module on the bench, never place anything on or close to the module which may be thrown in the event of an accidental deployment.
- The fasteners, screws, and bolts originally used for the SRS have special coatings and are specifically designed for the SRS. They must never be replaced with any substitutes. Anytime a new fastener is needed, replace with the correct fasteners provided in the service package or fasteners listed in the parts books.

Handling A Live Air Bag Module

At no time should any source of electricity be permitted near the inflator on the back of the module. When carrying a live module, the trim cover should be pointed away from the body to minimize injury in the event of accidental deployment. In addition, if the module is placed on a bench or other surface, the plastic trim cover should be face up to minimize movement in case of accidental deployment.

When handling a steering column with an air bag module attached, never place the column on the floor or other surface with the steering wheel or module face down.

Handling A Deployed Air Bag Module

The vehicle interior may contain a very small amount of sodium hydroxide powder, a by-product of air bag deployment. Since this powder can irritate the skin, eyes, nose or throat, be sure to wear safety glasses, rubber gloves and long sleeves during cleanup.

If you find that the cleanup is irritating your skin, run cool water over the affected area. Also, if you experience nasal or throat irritation, exit the vehicle for fresh air until the irritation ceases. If irritation continues, see a physician.

Begin the cleanup by putting tape over the two air bag exhaust vents so that no additional powder will find its way into the vehicle interior. Then remove the air bag and air bag module from the vehicle.

Use a vacuum cleaner to remove any residual powder from the vehicle interior. Work from the outside in so that you avoid kneeling or sitting in an uncleaned area.

Be sure to vacuum the heater and A/C outlets as well. In fact it's a good idea to run the blower on low and to vacuum up any powder expelled from the plenum. You may need to vacuum the interior of the car a second time to recover all of the powder.

Check with the local authorities before disposing of the deployed bag and module in your trash.

After an air bag has been deployed, the air bag module and spiral cable must be replaced because they cannot be reused. Other air bag system components should be replaced with new ones if damaged.

DISARMING THE SYSTEM

To disarm the SRS system turn the ignition switch to **OFF** position. Then disconnect the both battery cables starting with the negative cable first and wait at least 10 minutes after the cables are disconnected. Be sure to insulate the battery terminal ends.

ARMING THE SYSTEM

To arm the SRS system turn the ignition switch to **OFF** position. Connect the both battery cables starting with the positive cable first.

HEATER

Heater Blower Motor

REMOVAL & INSTALLATION

1982–87 Vehicles

♦ See Figure 12

➡The blower motor is located behind the glove box, facing the floor.

1. Disconnect the electrical harness from the blower motor.
2. Remove the retaining bolts from the bottom of the blower unit and lower the blower motor from the case.
3. To install, reverse the removal procedures.

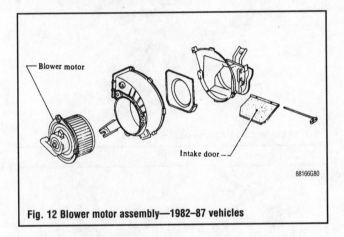

Fig. 12 Blower motor assembly—1982–87 vehicles

1988–96 Vehicles

➡The blower motor is located behind the glove box.

1. Disconnect the negative battery cable.
2. Remove the glove box assembly.
3. Disconnect the electrical harness from the blower motor.
4. Remove the retaining bolts from the bottom of the blower unit and lower the blower motor from the case.

To install:

5. Install the blower motor assembly and secure with retaining bolts.
6. Connect the electrical harness to the blower motor.
7. Install the glove box assembly.
8. Connect the negative battery cable.

Heater Assembly

REMOVAL & INSTALLATION

✳✳ CAUTION

When draining the coolant, keep in mind that cats and dogs are attracted by the ethylene glycol antifreeze, and are quite likely to drink any that is left in an uncovered container or in puddles on the

➡The SRS or air bag system is equipped with a self-diagnostic operation. After turning the ignition key to the ON or START position, the AIR BAG warning lamp will illuminate for 7 seconds. After 7 seconds, the AIR BAG lamp will extinguish if no malfunction is detected. If the AIR BAG lamp does not extinguish after 7 seconds, check the SRS self diagnostic system for a malfunction.

ground. This will prove fatal in sufficient quantity. Always drain the coolant into a sealable container. Coolant should be reused unless it is contaminated or several years old.

1983–90 Pulsar

Since the air conditioning evaporator is located between the blower motor and the heater core, the heater core can be removed without disturbing the air conditioning evaporator.

1. Set the TEMP lever to the maximum **HOT** position and drain the engine coolant.
2. Disconnect the heater assembly hoses in the engine compartment.
3. Remove the instrument panel assembly as outlined in Section 10.
4. Remove the heater control assembly.
5. Remove the heater unit assembly.

To install:

6. Install the heater unit in the vehicle.
7. Install the control assembly and instrument panel as outlined in Section 10.
8. Reconnect the heater hoses and refill the cooling system.
9. Start engine and check system for proper operation.

1982–86 Sentra

1. Disconnect the negative battery cable. Set TEMP lever to maximum **HOT** position and drain engine coolant.
2. Disconnect the heater hoses at the engine compartment.
3. Remove the instrument panel assembly as outlined in Section 10.
4. Support the unit and remove the bolt from the mounting bracket located on the top right. Then, loosen the two bolts that support the unit via slotted brackets at the bottom. Lift the unit so the slots clear these bolts and remove it.

To install:

5. Install the heater unit onto the firewall by positioning it on the 2 lower bolts and then installing and tightening the upper bolt. Tighten the lower bolt.
6. Reconnect the heater hoses and clamp them securely.
7. With a helper, put the instrument panel into position and hold it there. Then, install the 4 bolts that fasten the unit at the top.
8. Install the 4 bolts that fasten the unit at the bottom. Install the bolt covers on the top of the panel.
9. Install the glove box and adjacent instrument panel section by reversing the removal procedure.
10. Install the heater control, connect the cables, and adjust them. Connect the electrical connector.
11. Install the radio by reversing the removal procedure.
12. Install the ash tray slider and the ashtray.
13. Install the instrument cluster in reverse of the removal procedure. Install the instrument hood.
14. Connect the choke control cable, harness connectors, hood latch control cable, speedometer cable, and radio aerial cable.
15. Refill the engine with coolant. Reconnect the battery. Start the engine and check for leaks. Refill the cooling system after the engine has reached operating temperature and has then been allowed to cool.

1987–92 Sentra

1. Disconnect the negative battery cable. Remove the upper defroster grilles by gently pulling them upward to free the 8 clips fastening each of them in place.
2. Slide a thin, flat instrument in to release the clips by depressing the

tangs on top and on the bottom of the center and right side air discharge grilles. Then, slide them out of the instrument panel.

3. Remove the instrument panel assembly as outlined in Section 10.

4. Drain the cooling system into a clean container. Disconnect the heater hoses in the engine compartment.

5. Loosen the two bolts, located in slots, that support the unit on either side. Then, holding the unit against the firewall, remove the bolt from the hanger at the top. Raise the unit slightly so it will clear the lower mounting bolts and remove it from the firewall.

To install:

6. First raise the unit into position and locate it so the grooves in the lower mounts fit over the 2 lower supporting bolts. Then install and tighten the upper mounting bolts. Tighten the lower mounting bolts.

7. Install and connect the heater hoses and clamps.

8. Install the instrument panel assembly as outlined in Section 10.

9. Install the hood release and fuse block. Connect the Super Multiple Junction connector and install its mounting bolt.

10. Install the radio and the heater control.

11. Install the ashtray slider and ashtray.

12. Install the front console and then the rear console. Install the gearshift knob.

13. Put the instrument cluster into position, connect all the electrical connectors and install it.

14. Install the instrument cluster bezel.

15. Install the instrument panel cover.

16. Install the center and right air discharge grilles.

17. Install the upper defroster grilles. Reconnect the battery and refill the cooling system.

1993–94 Sentra

1. Be sure that the ignition switch is in the **OFF** position. Disconnect the negative battery cable. Wait 10 minutes before continuing with this procedure so that the SRS (air bag system) will have a sufficient amount of time to discharge.

2. Remove the steering wheel.

3. Remove the steering column cover.

4. Remove the instrument panel assembly as outlined in Section 10.

5. Remove the lower knee protector.

6. Drain the cooling system into a clean container. Disconnect the heater hoses in the engine compartment.

7. Loosen the 2 mounting bolts, located in slots, that support the heater unit on either side. Then, holding the unit against the firewall, remove the mounting bolt from the hanger at the top. Raise the unit slightly so it will clear the lower mounting bolts and remove it from the firewall.

To install:

8. First raise the heater unit into position and locate it so the grooves in the lower mounts fit over the 2 lower supporting bolts. Then install and tighten the upper mounting bolts. Tighten the lower mounting bolts.

9. Install and connect the heater hoses and clamps.

10. Install the instrument panel assembly as outlined in Section 10.

11. Install the steering column cover.

12. Install the steering wheel.

13. Reconnect the negative battery cable. Refill the cooling system.

1995–96 Sentra

1. Be sure that the ignition switch is in the **OFF** position. Disconnect the negative battery cable, then disconnect the positive battery cable. Wait 10 minutes before continuing with this procedure so that the SRS (air bag system) will have a sufficient amount of time to discharge.

2. Drain the cooling system.

3. Discharge the air conditioning system.

4. Remove the steering wheel.

5. Remove the instrument panel assembly as outlined in Section 10.

6. Remove the instrument panel reinforcement.

7. Remove the mounting fasteners that mount the heating and cooling assembly to the interior side of the firewall.

8. Remove the cooling unit and heater unit from the vehicle.

To install:

9. Place the heater unit and cooling unit into proper position in the vehicle against the interior side of the firewall. Install and tighten the heater and cooling unit mounting fasteners.

10. Install the instrument panel reinforcement.

11. Install the instrument panel assembly as outlined in Section 10.

12. Install the steering wheel.

13. Reconnect the positive battery cable, then reconnect the negative battery cable.

14. Refill the cooling system.

15. Recharge the air conditioning system.

Heater Core

REMOVAL & INSTALLATION

▶ **See Figures 13 and 14**

1. Refer to the Heater Assembly removal and installation procedures in this section, and remove the heater assembly from the vehicle.

2. Remove the heater assembly case bolts and separate the cases, then pull the heater core from the case.

3. To install, reverse the removal procedures. Refill the cooling system.

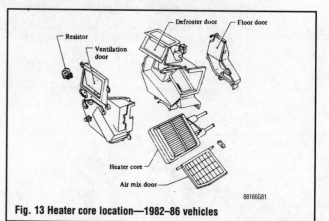

Fig. 13 Heater core location—1982–86 vehicles

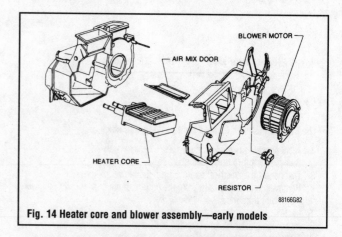

Fig. 14 Heater core and blower assembly—early models

Heater Control Head

REMOVAL & INSTALLATION

Except 1991–96 Sentra

▶ **See Figures 15 and 16**

1. Disconnect the negative battery cable.

2. Remove the control cables by unfastening clamps at door levers.

3. Remove the center finish panel screws and pull the bezel out. Later models also have metal retaining clips. Refer to the Instrument Panel in Section 10.

4. Disconnect the electrical connector and remove the heater control head

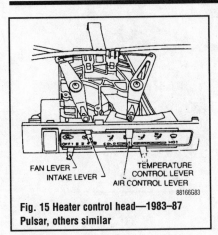

Fig. 15 Heater control head—1983–87 Pulsar, others similar

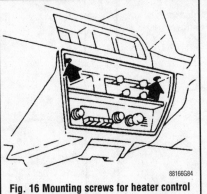

Fig. 16 Mounting screws for heater control head—1983–86 Pulsar

Fig. 17 Removal of center trim panel mounting screws—1992 Sentra shown

assembly mounting bolts. Remove the ground wire from intake box, if so equipped.

5. Remove the heater control head assembly.

To install:

6. Install the heater control and reconnect the control cables and electrical connectors.

7. Install the center finish panel and check operation.

1991–94 Sentra

▶ See Figures 17 and 18

1. Disconnect the negative battery cable.
2. Remove the center trim panel and shift cover.
3. Disconnect the temperature control cable at the heater unit side.
4. Disconnect the fresh vent control cable at the heater unit side.
5. Remove the 6 bracket screws.
6. Pull the control assembly out and disconnect the control harness and remove.

To install:

7. Install the control assembly and reconnect the harnesses.
8. Connect all cables and harnesses.
9. Adjust the temperature control cable by moving the control lever to **max. hot** and set the air door in the **full hot** mode. Pull the outer cable until all slack is taken out. Test the operation before going further.
10. Install the trim panel and shift cover.
11. Connect the battery cable and check operation.

1995–96 Sentra

▶ See Figure 19

1. Disconnect the negative battery cable.
2. Using a small, flat-bladed screwdriver, gently pry out the upper mask of the center instrument cluster bezel.
3. Remove the center instrument cluster bezel upper mounting screw and remove the center instrument cluster bezel by prying out with a small, flat-bladed screwdriver.
4. Remove the heater-A/C control unit mounting screws.
5. Disconnect the temperature and mode control cables from the heater-A/C control unit side.
6. Disconnect the wiring connectors from behind the heater-A/C control unit.

To install:

7. Place the control assembly into the instrument panel and reconnect the temperature and mode control cables to the back of the control unit. Reconnect the wiring connectors to the back of the control unit.
8. Install and tighten the heater-A/C control unit mounting screws.
9. Install the center instrument cluster bezel onto the instrument panel and install the center bezel upper mounting screw. Install the center bezel upper mask onto the cluster bezel making certain all 4 retaining pawls are engaged.
10. Turn the mode control knob to the **DEFROST** position. Set the side link in the **DEFROST** position by hand.
11. Pull on the cable cover in the direction of the arrow, then clamp the cable cover.

Fig. 18 Removal of center trim panel—1992 Sentra shown

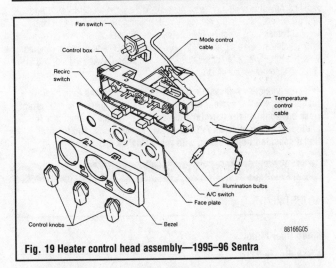

Fig. 19 Heater control head assembly—1995–96 Sentra

12. Reconnect the negative battery cable and check the heater-A/C system for proper operation.

Blower Motor Switch

REMOVAL & INSTALLATION

Control Knob Type Only

▶ See Figure 20

1. Disconnect the negative battery cable.
2. Remove the heater-A/C control assembly from the instrument panel.
3. Pull the fan control dial off of the front of the control assembly.

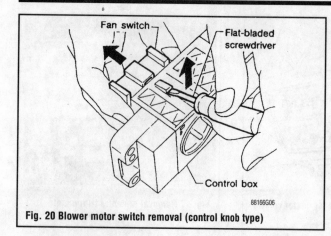

Fig. 20 Blower motor switch removal (control knob type)

4. Using a small, flat-bladed screwdriver, remove the blower motor switch out from behind the control unit.

To install:

5. Install the blower motor switch into the heater-A/C control unit. Be sure to engage the switch retaining clips.

6. Install the fan control dial onto the front of the control assembly.

7. Install the heater-A/C control assembly into the instrument panel.

8. Reconnect the negative battery cable. Check the blower motor switch for proper operation.

Air Conditioning Components

REMOVAL & INSTALLATION

Repair or service of air conditioning components is not covered by this manual, because of the risk of personal injury or death, and because of the legal ramifications of servicing these components without the proper EPA certification and experience. Cost, personal injury or death, environmental damage, and legal considerations (such as the fact that it is a federal crime to vent refrigerant into the atmosphere), dictate that the A/C components on your vehicle should be serviced only by a Motor Vehicle Air Conditioning (MVAC) trained, and EPA certified automotive technician.

➡ **If your vehicle's A/C system uses R-12 refrigerant and is in need of recharging, the A/C system can be converted over to R-134a refrigerant (less environmentally harmful and expensive). Refer to Section 1 for additional information on R-12 to R-134a conversions, and for additional considerations dealing with your vehicle's A/C system.**

Push Button Control Cables and Actuators

ADJUSTMENTS

Mode Door Motor

▶ See Figure 21

The mode door determines the air flow through the air distribution system depending on the mode selected (vent, defrost, etc.). The door linkage is located on the left side of the housing and is controlled by a motor. The motor has a built-in position sensor and will stop at the position called for by the controls. The adjustment procedure starts with the motor removed from the housing.

1. With the motor removed from the housing, connect the motor wiring and set the controls to the **VENT** mode.

2. Turn the ignition switch **ON**, let the motor go to its vent position, then turn the ignition **OFF**.

3. Manually move the linkage on the housing to the vent position, install the motor and attach the linkage.

4. With the ignition switch **ON**, cycle the system through all the modes and check the operation of the linkage.

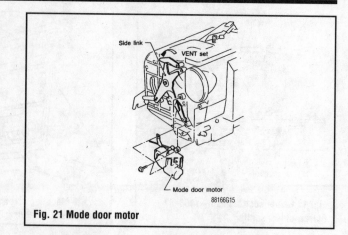

Fig. 21 Mode door motor

Mode Control Cable—1995–96 Sentra

▶ See Figure 22

1. Turn the mode control knob to the **DEFROST** position.

2. Place the side link in the **DEFROST** position by hand.

3. Pull the cable cover down away from the side link and then clamp the cable cover.

4. After adjusting the control cable, check the system for proper operation.

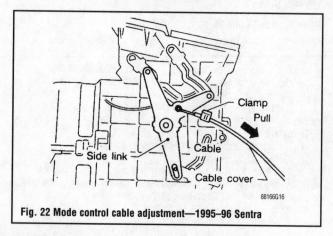

Fig. 22 Mode control cable adjustment—1995–96 Sentra

Air Intake Door Motor—Except 1995–96 Sentra

▶ See Figure 23

1. With the door motor removed but wiring connected, turn the ignition switch **ON** and set the controls to recirculate by pushing the **REC** button.

2. Install the motor onto the blower housing.

3. Hold the door in the recirculate position and attach the linkage. Turn the **REC** button **ON** and **OFF** to check operation of the door.

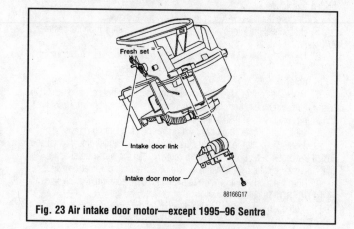

Fig. 23 Air intake door motor—except 1995–96 Sentra

Air Intake Door Motor—1995–96 Sentra

♦ **See Figure 24**

1. Install the air intake door motor onto the intake unit. Be sure that the intake door motor lever is installed into the slit portion of the intake door link.
2. Connect the air intake door motor electrical connector.
3. Turn the ignition switch to the **ON** position.
4. Check that the air intake door motor operates correctly when the **REC** switch is turned **ON** and **OFF**.

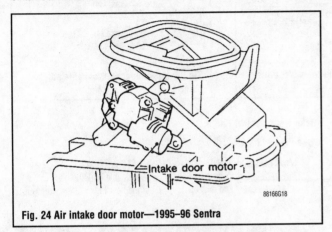

Fig. 24 Air intake door motor—1995–96 Sentra

Water Cock Control Rod—1995–96 Sentra

♦ **See Figure 25**

When adjusting the control rod, first disconnect the temperature control cable from the air mix door lever. Reconnect and adjust the temperature control cable.

1. Move the air mix door lever to the left.
2. Pull the control rod toward the air mix door lever to a clearance of about 0.080 in. (2.0mm) between the ends of control rod and link lever.
3. Reconnect the control rod to the door lever.
4. After the control rod is connected, check the control for proper operation.

Temperature Control Cable—Except 1995–96 Sentra

This cable operates the air mix door inside the air distribution system. A control rod connects the air mix door lever and the water valve link lever on the heater core. The control rod should be adjusted first.

1. To adjust the control rod, disconnect the temperature control cable from the door lever.
2. The valve end of the rod is attached to the valve with a wire loop. With the rod loose at the air mix door end, move the air mix door lever and the valve lever all the way in the direction that would pull the rod away from the valve lever.
3. Gently pull the rod so there is about 0.80 in. (2mm) gap between the rod and valve lever and secure the rod at the door lever.

4. When attaching the temperature control lever, adjust the cable housing so the full **COLD** lever position will completely shut off the heat.

Temperature Control Cable—1995–96 Sentra

♦ **See Figure 26**

1. Move the temperature control knob to the full **HOT** position.
2. Disconnect the temperature control cable.
3. Place the air mix door lever in the full **HOT** position.
4. Pull on the cable cover in direction away from the air mix door lever. Clamp the cable cover.
5. After adjustment, check system for proper operation.

Slide Lever Control Cables and Actuators

ADJUSTMENT

If the linkage has been disassembled, it should be adjusted as an assembly rather than trying to adjust only one part. First, adjust the rods and levers, then connect and adjust the cables to the linkage.

Ventilator Door Control Rod

1. Viewed from the driver's side, rotate the side link fully clockwise.
2. With the upper and lower door levers pushed down, connect the lower rod first, then the upper rod.

Defroster Door Control Rod

1. Rotate the side link fully counterclockwise.
2. Push the defroster door lever towards the firewall and connect the rod.

Air Control Cable

♦ **See Figure 27**

1. Rotate the side link fully clockwise.
2. With the control lever in the **DEFROST** position, hook the cable to the side link.
3. Take up the slack in the cable housing by pushing it gently away from the firewall and secure the housing.

Water Valve Control Rod

♦ **See Figure 28**

1. To adjust the control rod, disconnect the temperature control cable from the door lever.
2. The valve end of the rod is attached to the valve with a wire loop. With the rod loose at the air mix door end, move the air mix door lever and the valve link lever all the way in the direction that would pull the rod away from the valve lever.
3. Gently pull the rod so there is about 0.080 in. (2mm) gap between the rod and valve lever and secure the rod at the door lever.

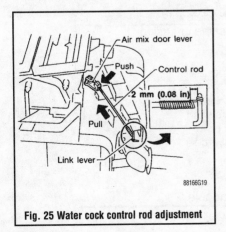

Fig. 25 Water cock control rod adjustment

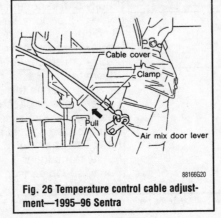

Fig. 26 Temperature control cable adjustment—1995–96 Sentra

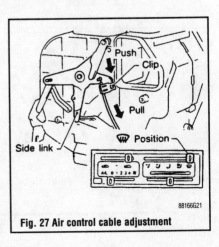

Fig. 27 Air control cable adjustment

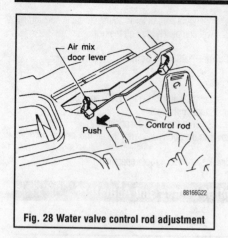

Fig. 28 Water valve control rod adjustment

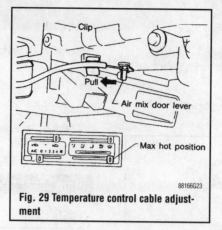

Fig. 29 Temperature control cable adjustment

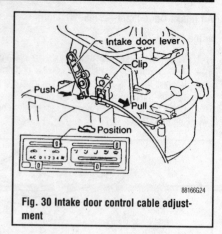

Fig. 30 Intake door control cable adjustment

Temperature Control Cable

♦ See Figure 29

1. Move the control levers to the full **HOT** position.
2. Rotate the air mix door linkage towards the full **HOT** position.
3. Attach the cable and take up the slack in the cable housing before securing it with the clip.

Intake Door Control Cable

♦ See Figure 30

1. Move the control lever to the **RECIRCULATE** position.
2. Move the intake door lever fully towards the cable housing clip.
3. Attach the cable and take up the slack in the housing before securing it with the clip.

CRUISE CONTROL

General Description

Nissan refers to their cruise control as the Automatic Speed Control Device (ASCD) system. The ASCD system maintains a desired speed of the vehicle under normal driving conditions. The cruise control system's main parts are the control switches, control unit, actuator, speed sensor, vacuum pump, vacuum pump relay, vacuum switch, vacuum tank, electrical release switches and electrical harness.

➡The use of the speed control is not recommended when driving conditions do not permit maintaining a constant speed, such as in heavy traffic or on roads that are winding, icy, snow covered or slippery.

CRUISE CONTROL TROUBLESHOOTING

Problem	Possible Cause
Will not hold proper speed	Incorrect cable adjustment
	Binding throttle linkage
	Leaking vacuum servo diaphragm
	Leaking vacuum tank
	Faulty vacuum or vent valve
	Faulty stepper motor
	Faulty transducer
	Faulty speed sensor
	Faulty cruise control module
Cruise intermittently cuts out	Clutch or brake switch adjustment too tight
	Short or open in the cruise control circuit
	Faulty transducer
	Faulty cruise control module
Vehicle surges	Kinked speedometer cable or casing
	Binding throttle linkage
	Faulty speed sensor
	Faulty cruise control module
Cruise control inoperative	Blown fuse
	Short or open in the cruise control circuit
	Faulty brake or clutch switch
	Leaking vacuum circuit
	Faulty cruise control switch
	Faulty stepper motor
	Faulty transducer
	Faulty speed sensor
	Faulty cruise control module

Note: Use this chart as a guide. Not all systems will use the components listed.

TCCA6C01

ENTERTAINMENT SYSTEMS

RADIO

REMOVAL & INSTALLATION

1982–86 Vehicles

▶ See Figures 31 and 32

1. Remove the ash tray and the ash tray bracket.
2. Remove the radio mounting bolts.
3. Remove the instrument panel cover surrounding the radio.
4. Disconnect the electrical harness connector and the antenna plug from the radio.
5. To install, reverse the removal procedures.

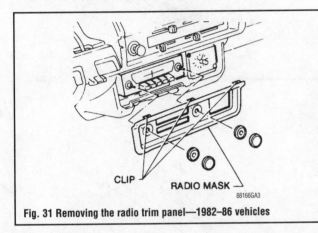

Fig. 31 Removing the radio trim panel—1982–86 vehicles

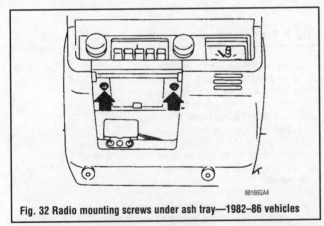

Fig. 32 Radio mounting screws under ash tray—1982–86 vehicles

1987–94 Vehicles

▶ See Figures 33, 34 and 35

➡Some late model radio assemblies have an auxiliary fuse located in the rear of the radio. If all other power sources check OK, remove the radio and check the fuse.

1. Disconnect the negative battery cable.
2. Remove the cluster center trim panel screws. Pull the trim panel straight out to disengage the clips.
3. Remove the radio retaining bolts and pull the radio out far enough to disconnect the antenna and electrical wiring.

To install:

4. Position the radio and connect the electrical connectors.
5. Install the retaining bolts and torque to 24 inch lbs. (1.36 Nm).
6. Install the center cluster trim panel.
7. Connect the negative battery cable and check operation.

1995–96 Sentra

1. Disconnect the negative battery cable.
2. Using a small, flat-bladed screwdriver, gently pry out the upper mask of the center instrument cluster bezel.
3. Remove the center instrument cluster bezel upper mounting screw and remove the center instrument cluster bezel by prying out with a small, flat-bladed screwdriver.
4. Remove the radio unit mounting screws and pull the radio unit from the center of the instrument panel.
5. Disconnect the antenna and electrical wiring connectors from behind the radio unit and remove the radio from the vehicle.

To install:

6. Install the radio unit into the center of the instrument panel and reconnect the wiring connectors to the radio unit.
7. Install and tighten the radio unit mounting screws.
8. Install the center instrument cluster bezel into the instrument panel and install the center bezel upper mounting screw.
9. Install the center bezel upper mask onto the center instrument cluster bezel making certain that all 4 retaining pawls are engaged.
10. Reconnect the negative battery cable. Turn on the radio and check for proper operation.

Speakers

REMOVAL & INSTALLATION

Instrument Panel Mount

Remove the speaker grille by removing the retaining screw or release the retaining clips with a plastic pry tool. Remove the speaker retaining screws and disconnect the wiring. Be careful not to damage the instrument panel.

Fig. 33 Removal of radio unit mounting screws—1992 Sentra pictured, others similar

Fig. 34 Pulling radio unit out from instrument panel center console

Fig. 35 Disconnecting antenna lead from back of radio unit

Door Mount

▶ **See Figures 36 and 37**

Remove the door panel as outlined in Section 10. Remove the speaker from the door. If no sound is coming from the speaker, check the door wiring for continuity before condemning the speaker. The speaker wire may break after years of opening and closing the door.

Fig. 36 Removal of door speaker mounting screws

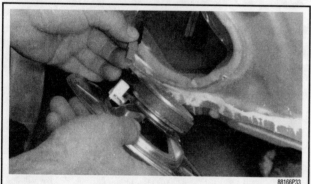

Fig. 37 Detaching the electrical connector from the back of the speaker

Rear Deck Mount

Open the hatch or trunk and remove the speaker retaining screws from underneath the deck panel.

Antenna

REMOVAL & INSTALLATION

1982–86 Vehicles

▶ **See Figure 38**

1. Disconnect the negative battery cable.
2. Remove the radio and disconnect the antenna lead as outlined in this section.

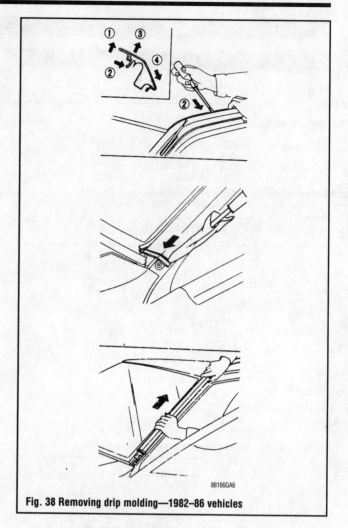

Fig. 38 Removing drip molding—1982–86 vehicles

3. Remove the drip molding as follows:
   a. Depress the clip pawl.
   b. Remove the molding end cap and seal.
   c. Slide the molding off by pulling upward
4. Disconnect the antenna rod from the base.
5. Remove the antenna rod from the clip.
6. Remove the body seal grommet from the door post and pull the antenna wire through the mounting hole. Be careful not to pull too hard. The antenna jack may become caught under the instrument panel.
   To install:
7. Fish the antenna wire through the mounting hole to the radio.
8. Mount the antenna with the retaining screws.
9. Install the drip molding. Put the molding in place and tap it lightly by hand. Be sure to align the cowl panel with the end of the molding end cap and seal.
10. Install the radio as outlined in this section.

1987–94 Vehicles

The radio antenna is part of the rear window defogger.

WINDSHIELD WIPER AND WASHERS

Blade and Arm

REMOVAL & INSTALLATION

♦ **See Figures 39, 40, 41 and 42**

1. Some models have covers that are hinged to the arm. Pull these upward at the end of the arm opposite the blade. Other models have covers that fit over the end of the linkage shaft and the arm; simply pull these off. If necessary, turn the ignition switch **ON** and turn the wipers **ON** and then **OFF** again to bring them to the full park position.

2. Hold the wiper arm against the torque and loosen the nut which attaches the arm to the linkage shaft with a socket wrench. Remove the nut.

3. Note or measure the distance between the blade and the lower edge of

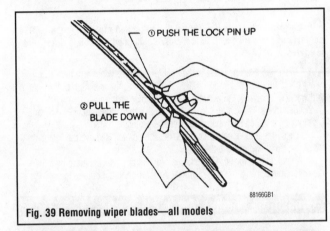

Fig. 39 Removing wiper blades—all models

① PUSH THE LOCK PIN UP

② PULL THE BLADE DOWN

Fig. 40 Windshield wiper linkage shaft-to-arm retaining nut cover removal

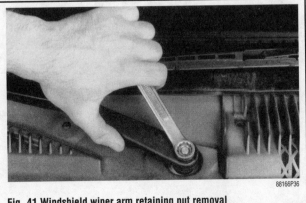

Fig. 41 Windshield wiper arm retaining nut removal

Fig. 42 Windshield wiper arm removal

the windshield, which is usually about 1 in. (25mm). The blade is usually parallel with the bottom of the windshield. Then, turn the arm outward on its hinges so its spring pressure is removed from the lower end. Pull the lower end of the arm straight off the splines on the shaft.

To install:

4. First line up the wiper blade with the bottom of the windshield at the proper clearance. Then, install the end of the arm over the end of the shaft, turning it slightly, if necessary, in either direction so the splines will engage.

5. Install the attaching nut. Hold the arm to minimize torque on the driveshaft and torque the nut to 12–17 ft. lbs. (17–23 Nm). Install decorative caps or covers in reverse of removal.

Wiper Motor and Linkage

REMOVAL & INSTALLATION

1983–90 Pulsar

♦ **See Figure 43**

The wiper motor is on the firewall under the hood. The operating linkage is on the firewall inside the car.

1. Disconnect the negative battery terminal and remove the motor wiring connection.

2. Unbolt the motor from the body.

3. Disconnect the wiper linkage from the motor and remove the motor.

4. Disconnect linkage from the pivot.

5. To install, reverse the removal procedures.

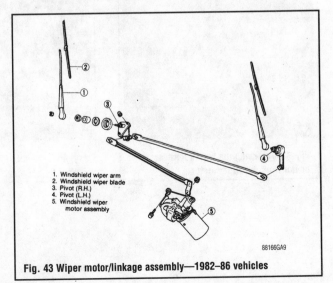

1. Windshield wiper arm
2. Windshield wiper blade
3. Pivot (R.H.)
4. Pivot (L.H.)
5. Windshield wiper motor assembly

Fig. 43 Wiper motor/linkage assembly—1982–86 vehicles

1982–90 Sentra

The wiper motor is on the firewall under the hood. The operating linkage is on the firewall inside the car.

1. Disconnect the negative battery cable. Detach the motor wiring plug.
2. Inside the car, remove the nut connecting the linkage to the wiper shaft. Slide the linkage off the shaft. If there is a lot of resistance, use a small puller or force the linkage lever off the shaft with a pair of pliers.

➡**Don't tap on the motor shaft with a hammer!**

3. Unbolt and remove the wiper motor from the firewall.
4. Remove the nut that attaches each wiper arm driveshaft unit to the cowl. Then, work the shaft downward and into the cowl interior.
5. Work the linkage out of the access holes and remove it from the vehicle.

To install:
6. Work the linkage into the access holes.
7. Install the nut that attaches each wiper arm driveshaft unit to the cowl. Torque the nuts to 10 ft. lbs. (13 Nm).
8. Install the wiper motor on the firewall.
9. Inside the car, install the nut connecting the linkage to the wiper shaft. Torque the nut to 60 inch lbs. (7 Nm).
10. Connect the negative battery cable. Attach the motor wiring plug.

1991–96 Sentra

▶ **See Figures 44, 45, 46 and 47**

The wiper motor is on the firewall under the hood. The operating linkage is on the firewall inside the vehicle.

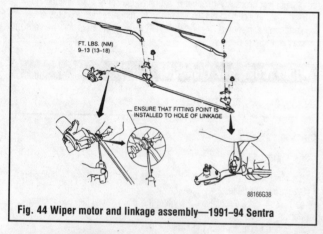

Fig. 44 Wiper motor and linkage assembly—1991–94 Sentra

1. Disconnect negative battery cable. Detach the motor wiring plug.
2. Remove the cowl panel assembly at the base of the windshield.
3. Working from inside the vehicle, remove the nut connecting the linkage to the wiper shaft.
4. Unbolt and remove the wiper motor from the firewall.

➡**Don't tap on the motor shaft with a hammer!**

To install:
5. Install the wiper motor and linkage assembly in the same order of removal.
6. To reduce wiper arm looseness, prior to connecting the wiper arm, make sure the motor spline shaft and pivot area is completely free of debris and corrosion. Wire brush as necessary.

Rear Wiper Motor

REMOVAL & INSTALLATION

➡**To perform this procedure, you will need a soft material (such as RTV sealer) used to seal the plastic watershields used in vehicle doors and tailgates.**

1. Disconnect the negative battery cable. Bend the wiper arm to raise the wiper blade off the rear window glass. Then, remove the attaching bolt or nut and washers and work the wiper arm off the motor shaft.
2. Remove the attaching screws and remove the tailgate inner finish panel. Carefully peel the plastic water shield off the sealer.
3. Disconnect the electrical connector at the motor. Remove the motor mounting bolts and remove the motor.
4. Install the motor in reverse of the removal procedure. Before installing the water shield, run a fresh ring of RTV sealer around the outer edge.

Windshield Washer Motor

REMOVAL & INSTALLATION

Front and Rear

Remove the washer reservoir/motor assembly from the vehicle and drain it into a suitable container. Pull the motor from the rubber grommet. If you're having difficulty, lubricate the grommet with penetrating oil and try again. Apply petroleum jelly to the grommets to install the motor.

Fig. 45 Detaching the wiring harness connector from the wiper motor

Fig. 46 Removal of wiper motor mounting bolts

Fig. 47 Removal of wiper motor from the firewall

INSTRUMENTS AND SWITCHES

❊❊ CAUTION

To avoid rendering the SRS (Supplemental Restraint System) inoperative, which could lead to personal injury or death in the event of a severe frontal collision, extreme caution must be taken when servicing the electrically related systems. All SRS electrical wiring harnesses and connectors are covered with YELLOW outer insulation. Do not use electrical test equipment on any circuit related to the SRS (air bag).

Air Bag

DISARMING

On vehicles equipped with an air bag, turn the ignition switch to the **OFF** position. The negative battery cable must be disconnected (also disconnect the positive battery cable for 1995–96 Sentra) and wait 10 minutes after the cable is disconnected before working on the system. SRS sensors must always be installed with the arrow marks facing the front of the vehicle.

Instrument Cluster

REMOVAL & INSTALLATION

1983–90 Pulsar

1. Disconnect the negative battery terminal.
2. Loosen the tilt adjusting lever and completely lower the steering column.
3. Remove the steering column cover.
4. Remove the mounting screws and the instrument cluster hood.
5. Remove the instrument cluster screws, pull the cluster forward, then disconnect the speedometer cable and the harness connectors.
6. Remove the instrument cluster from the vehicle.

To install:
7. Install the instrument cluster and attaching screws.
8. Reconnect all electrical connections and speedometer cable.
9. Reconnect steering column and cover.
10. Connect the battery cable.
11. Start engine and check for proper operation of all components.

1982–86 Sentra

1. Disconnect the battery negative cable. Remove the 2 screws from the lower side of the instrument hood and remove it.
2. Remove the 2 screws from the top of the instrument cluster, pull it out to disconnect the electrical connectors, and remove it.
3. Install the cluster in reverse of the removal procedure.

1987–90 Sentra

1. Disconnect the battery negative cable. Remove the 2 screws from underneath the cluster bezel and the 2 from the underside of the cluster hood. Then, use a thin, flat object to depress the locking pawl in the fastener located at the top left of the cluster bezel; then, slide this fastener out of the dash. Now, slide the cluster bezel out of the dash.
2. Remove the mounting screws from the underside and front of the instrument cluster and then pull it out of the dash panel far enough for you to gain access to the electrical connectors. Disconnect these connectors and then remove the cluster by sliding it out of the dash.
3. Install the cluster by reversing the removal procedure.

1991–94 Sentra

1. Disconnect the negative battery cable.

❊❊ CAUTION

To avoid rendering the SRS (Supplemental Restraint System) inoperative, which could lead to personal injury or death in the event of a severe frontal collision, extreme caution must be taken when servicing the electrical related systems. All SRS electrical wiring harnesses and connectors are covered with YELLOW outer insulation. Do not use electrical test equipment on any circuit related to the SRS (air bag).

2. Remove the steering wheel and the steering column covers as outlined in Section 8.
3. Remove the instrument cluster lid by removing its screws.
4. Remove the instrument cluster screws.
5. Gently withdraw the cluster from the instrument pad and disconnect all wiring and speedometer cable. Make sure the wires are marked clearly to avoid confusion during installation. Be careful not to damage the printed circuit.
6. Remove the cluster.

To install:
7. Install the cluster and connect all wiring and the speedometer cable.
8. Install the instrument cluster screws.
9. Install the instrument cluster lid and its screws.
10. Install the steering wheel and the steering column covers.
11. Connect the negative battery cable and check operation.

1995–96 Sentra

1. Disconnect the negative battery cable, then the positive battery cable. Wait 10 minutes before continuing with this procedure so that the SRS (air bag system) will have sufficient time to discharge.
2. Remove the steering wheel.
3. Remove the upper and lower steering column covers.
4. Remove the combination switch mounting screws and disconnect the wiring connectors to the switch. Remove the combination switch from the steering column.
5. Remove the 2 instrument cluster bezel mounting screws. Using a small, flat-bladed screwdriver, disengage the cluster bezel retaining pawls and metal clips. Remove the cluster bezel from the instrument panel.
6. Remove the instrument cluster mounting screws and pull the cluster out of the instrument panel far enough to disconnect the wiring harness connectors from behind the assembly. Remove the cluster assembly from the vehicle.

To install:
7. Place the instrument cluster into the instrument panel and reconnect the wiring harness connectors behind the cluster assembly. Place the cluster into position, install and tighten the mounting screws.
8. Install the cluster bezel into the instrument panel. Be sure to engage the 5 retaining pawls and 2 metal clips. Install and tighten the 2 bezel mounting screws.
9. Install the combination switch onto the steering column and reconnect the wiring connectors to the switch. Install and tighten the 3 mounting screws.
10. Install the upper and lower steering column covers and tighten the mounting screws.
11. Install the steering wheel.
12. Reconnect the positive battery cable, then reconnect the negative battery cable.

Speedometer

➡**If equipped with a digital speedometer, the entire cluster assembly must be replaced if the speedometer is faulty.**

REMOVAL & INSTALLATION

Analog (Needle Type) Speedometers

1. Disconnect the negative battery cable.
2. Remove the instrument cluster assembly from instrument panel far enough to disconnect the gauge connections.

3. Disconnect the speedometer cable (or speed sensor connector) and remove it from the vehicle.

4. Remove the speedometer fasteners and carefully remove the speedometer from the cluster. Be careful not to damage the printed circuit board.

5. Installation is the reverse of the removal procedure.

Tachometer, Fuel Gauge and Temperature Gauge

REMOVAL & INSTALLATION

1. Disconnect the negative battery cable.

2. Remove the instrument cluster assembly from the instrument panel far enough to disconnect the wiring connections from the back of the gauges.

3. Remove the instrument cluster assembly from the vehicle.

4. Remove the mounting fasteners from the gauge requiring removal.

5. Carefully remove the gauge from the cluster assembly. Be careful not to damage the circuit board.

6. Installation is the reverse of removal.

Windshield Wiper Switch

REMOVAL & INSTALLATION

1982–83 Vehicles

1. Remove the steering wheel and the steering column cover as outlined in Section 8.

2. Disconnect all of the combination switch wires.

3. Loosen the retaining screw and remove the combination switch wires.

4. To install, reverse the removal procedures.

1984–96 Vehicles

▶ See Figures 48 and 49

The wiper switch can be removed without removing the combination switch from the steering column.

1. Remove the steering column cover.

2. Disconnect the wiper switch electrical connector.

3. Remove the wiper switch to combination switch retaining screws.

4. To install, reverse the removal procedures.

➡On the 1987–88 Pulsar models, the wiper switch is located in the dash. To remove this switch, detach the electrical connector and remove the retaining screw.

Rear Window Wiper Switch

REMOVAL & INSTALLATION

1. Remove the instrument cluster.

2. Remove the nut that attaches the combination switch to the dash.

3. Disconnect the electrical connectors from the rear of the switch, then remove it.

4. Installation is the reverse of the removal procedure.

Headlight Switch

REMOVAL & INSTALLATION

1982–83 Sentra and 1983 Pulsar

1. Place the ignition switch in the **OFF** position and disconnect the negative battery terminal.

2. Remove the steering wheel and the steering column cover.

3. Disconnect the wiring harness from the combination switch.

4. Loosen the retaining screws and remove the combination switch.

5. To install, reverse the removal procedures.

1984–96 Vehicles

EXCEPT 1987–90 PULSAR

▶ See Figure 50

The headlight switch can be removed without removing the combination switch from the steering column.

1. Remove the steering column cover.

2. Disconnect the headlight switch electrical connector.

3. Remove the headlight switch to combination switch retaining screws.

4. To install, reverse the removal procedures.

1987–90 PULSAR

The headlight switch is located on the dashboard.

1. Disconnect the negative battery cable.

2. Remove the headlight switch retaining screw.

3. Pull the headlight switch out from the dash just far enough to disconnect the electrical connector from behind the switch.

4. Remove the switch from the vehicle.

5. To install, reverse the removal procedure.

Ignition Switch

Ignition switch removal and installation procedures are covered in Section 8.

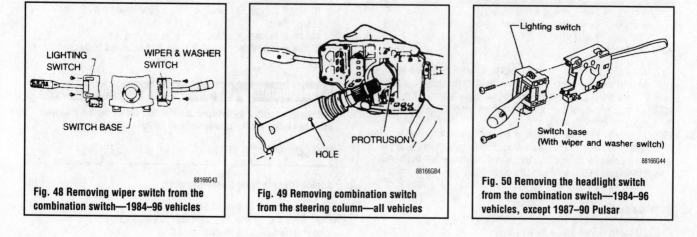

LIGHTING SWITCH WIPER & WASHER SWITCH SWITCH BASE

88166G43

Fig. 48 Removing wiper switch from the combination switch—1984–96 vehicles

HOLE PROTRUSION

88166GB4

Fig. 49 Removing combination switch from the steering column—all vehicles

Lighting switch Switch base (With wiper and washer switch)

88166G44

Fig. 50 Removing the headlight switch from the combination switch—1984–96 vehicles, except 1987–90 Pulsar

LIGHTING

Sealed Beam Type Headlights

REMOVAL & INSTALLATION

Sentra

1. Remove the grille, if necessary.
2. Remove the headlight retaining ring screws. These are the 3 or 4 short screws in the assembly. There are also 2 longer screws at the top and side of the headlight which are used to aim the headlight. Do not tamper with these or the headlight will have to be re-aimed.
3. Remove the ring on the headlights.
4. Pull the headlight bulb from its socket and disconnect the electrical plug.

To install:

5. Connect the plug to the new bulb.
6. Position the headlight in the shell. Make sure that the word **TOP** is, indeed, at the top and that the knobs in the headlight lens engage the slots in the mounting shell.
7. Place the retaining ring over the bulb and install the screws.
8. Install the grille, if removed.

Pulsar

♦ See Figure 51

1. Utilizing the manual headlight door openers, open the headlights.
2. Remove the screws and the clip, then headlight cover.
3. Remove the retaining ring cover.
4. Pull out the headlight, remove the rubber cap and the wiring connector. Remove the headlight.
5. To install, reverse the removal procedures.

Composite Type Headlights

REMOVAL & INSTALLATION

Except 1995–96 Sentra

➥Grasp only the plastic base when handling the bulb. Never touch the glass portion of the bulb. When the bulb is ON, the finger oil can cause the bulb to burst. If the bulb is touched, it MUST be cleaned with alcohol before installation.

1. Open the engine hood.
2. Disconnect the negative battery cable.
3. Turn the bulb retaining ring counterclockwise until it is free from the headlight reflector.
4. Disconnect the wiring harness from the backside of the bulb.
5. Remove the bulb from the retainer carefully.

To install:

6. Install the bulb into the retainer.
7. Apply electrically conductive grease to the harness connector and install the assembly.
8. Install the bulb into the reflector and turn clockwise until it stops.
9. Reconnect the negative battery cable.
10. Close the hood and check operation.

1995–96 Sentra

♦ See Figures 52, 53 and 54

➥Grasp only the plastic base when handling the bulb. Never touch the glass portion of the bulb. When the bulb is ON, the finger oil can cause the bulb to burst.

1. Open the hood.
2. Disconnect the negative battery cable.
3. If the right side (passenger's side) headlight bulb is being replaced, reposition the engine coolant reservoir out of the way for access.
4. Disconnect the headlight bulb electrical connector.

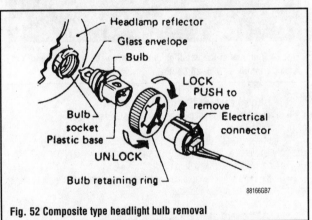

Fig. 52 Composite type headlight bulb removal

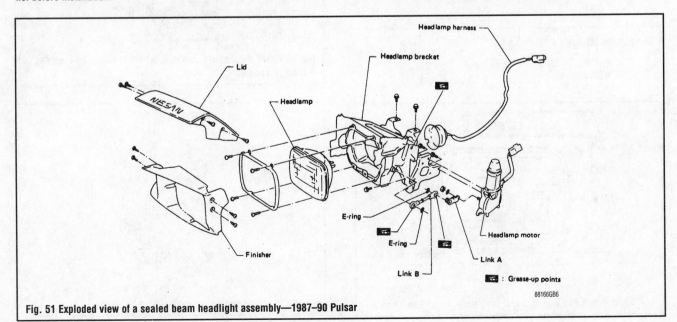

Fig. 51 Exploded view of a sealed beam headlight assembly—1987–90 Pulsar

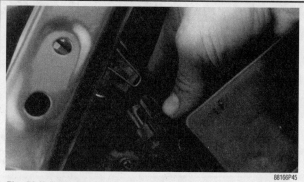

Fig. 53 Unfastening the wiring terminal connector from the headlight bulb—1995–96 Sentra

Fig. 54 Removal of the headlight bulb from the back of the headlight body assembly—1995–96 Sentra

5. Push down the headlight bulb retainer spring.
6. Pull out the headlight bulb and socket as an assembly.

To install:

7. Install the headlight bulb and socket assembly into the headlight body assembly and engage the headlight bulb spring retainer.
8. Connect the headlight bulb electrical connector.
9. If the right side headlight bulb was replaced, install the engine coolant reservoir back to its proper location.
10. Reconnect the negative battery cable.
11. Close the hood and check headlight operation.

HEADLIGHT AIMING

▶ **See Figures 55 thru 60**

1. Raise the headlight doors on 1983–90 Pulsar.
2. Turn the low beam **ON**.

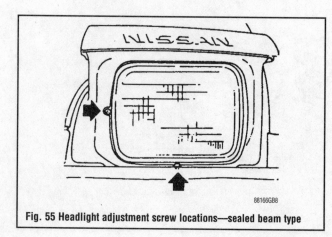

Fig. 55 Headlight adjustment screw locations—sealed beam type

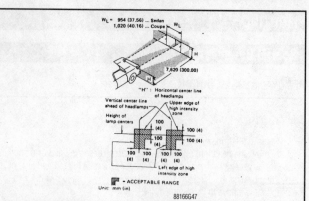

Fig. 56 Headlight aiming, except for 1991–94 Sentra—refer to text for procedures

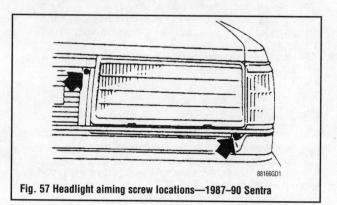

Fig. 57 Headlight aiming screw locations—1987–90 Sentra

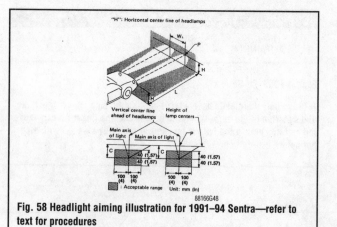

Fig. 58 Headlight aiming illustration for 1991–94 Sentra—refer to text for procedures

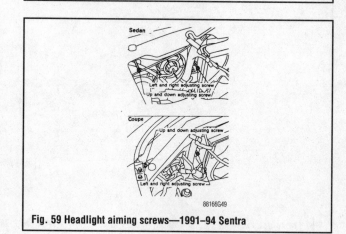

Fig. 59 Headlight aiming screws—1991–94 Sentra

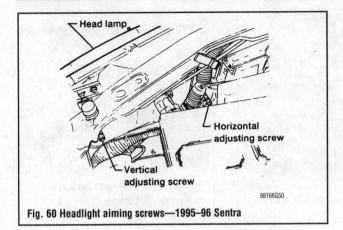

Fig. 60 Headlight aiming screws—1995–96 Sentra

3. Use the adjusting screws to perform aiming adjustment. The screw on the side is for side to side adjustment and the screw on the bottom is for up and down adjustment.

4. Park the vehicle in front of bare wall. Refer to the illustration.

5. Adjust the headlights so that the upper edge and left edge of the high intensity zone are within the acceptable range.

6. The dotted lines in the illustration show the center of the headlights. **H** equals horizontal center line of headlights and **WL** equals the distance between each headlight center.

MANUAL OPERATION OF HEADLIGHTS

Pulsar

♦ See Figure 61

1. Turn **OFF** both headlight switch and retractable headlight switch.
2. Remove the motor shaft cap.
3. Turn the motor shaft counterclockwise by hand until the headlights are opened or closed.
4. Reinstall the motor shaft cap and connect the battery cable.

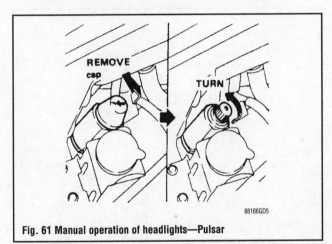

Fig. 61 Manual operation of headlights—Pulsar

Signal and Marker Lights

REMOVAL & INSTALLATION

♦ See Figures 62 thru 68

Front Turn Signal And Parking Lights

1. Remove turn signal/parking light lens with retaining screws.
2. Slightly depress the bulb and turn it counterclockwise to release it.

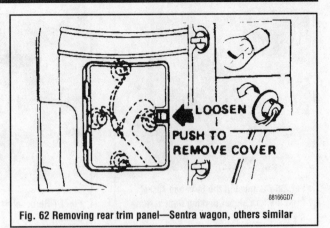

Fig. 62 Removing rear trim panel—Sentra wagon, others similar

Fig. 63 Removal of the turn signal/parking light lens retaining screw—1992 Sentra shown

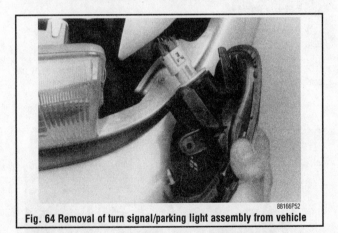

Fig. 64 Removal of turn signal/parking light assembly from vehicle

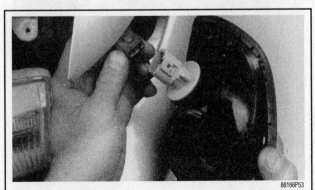

Fig. 65 Detaching the wiring harness connector from the turn signal/parking light bulb socket

Fig. 66 Removal of the bulb and socket from the turn signal/parking light assembly

Fig. 67 Removal of light bulb from the socket

Fig. 68 Unfasten the retaining screws, then remove the marker light housing—1992 Sentra shown

3. To install the bulb carefully push down and turn bulb clockwise at the same time.
4. Install the turn signal/parking light lens with retaining screws.

Side Marker Lights

➡Rear side marker light bulbs on 1995–96 Sentra are located in the same taillight housing as the rear turn signal, brake and parking lights. Refer to that procedure if replacing the rear side marker bulb(s).

1. Remove side marker light lens with retaining screws.
2. Turn the bulb socket counterclockwise to release it from the lens.
3. Pull the bulb straight out.
4. To install the bulb carefully push it straight in.
5. Turn the bulb socket clockwise to install it in lens.
6. Install the side marker light lens with the retaining screws.

Rear Turn Signal, Brake And Parking Lights

▶ **See Figure 69**

1. Remove the rear trim panel in the rear of vehicle to gain access to the bulb socket.
2. Slightly depress the bulb and turn it counterclockwise to release it.
3. To install the bulb carefully push down and turn the bulb clockwise at the same time.
4. Install the trim panel.
5. Check the rear turn signal, brake and parking lights for proper operation.

Fig. 69 Rear light bulb replacement

High-Mount Brake Light

▶ **See Figures 70, 71, 72 and 73**

DECK LID OR SPOILER MOUNTED

1. Disconnect the negative battery cable.
2. Open up the deck lid.
3. Remove the light bulb socket from inside the deck lid at the brake light housing.
4. Remove the light bulb from the socket.
To install:
5. Install the new brake light bulb.
6. Install the light bulb and socket into the brake light housing in the deck-lid or spoiler (if equipped).
7. Reconnect the negative battery cable and check the brake light for proper operation.

INTERIOR/REAR PACKAGE SHELF MOUNTED

1. Disconnect the negative battery cable.
2. Working from inside the vehicle, remove the brake light housing from the

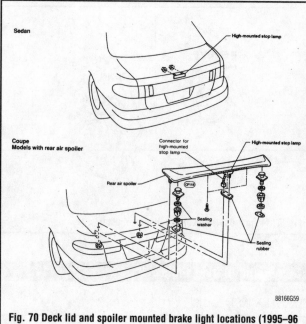

Fig. 70 Deck lid and spoiler mounted brake light locations (1995–96 Sentra pictured)

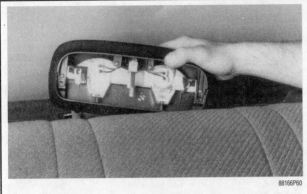

Fig. 71 Removal of brake light housing from the rear package shelf

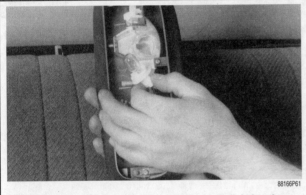

Fig. 72 Removal of light bulb socket from the brake light housing

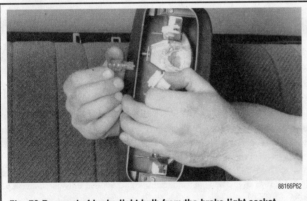

Fig. 73 Removal of brake light bulb from the brake light socket

rear package shelf far enough to remove the light bulb socket requiring bulb replacement.

3. Remove the brake light bulb.

To install:

4. Install the replacement bulb(s).
5. Install the bulb socket(s) into the brake light housing.
6. Install the brake light housing back into correct position on the rear package shelf.
7. Reconnect the negative battery cable and check the brake light for proper operation.

Dome Light

▶ See Figures 74 and 75

1. Remove the dome light lens by disengaging the retaining pawls.
2. Remove the dome light bulb.

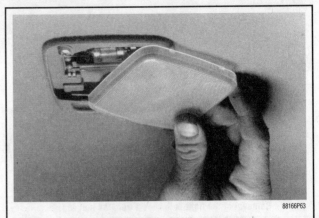

Fig. 74 Removal of the dome light lens

Fig. 75 Dome light bulb removal

3. Installation is the reverse of removal.
4. Check the dome light for proper operation.

License Plate Light

▶ See Figures 76, 77 and 78

1. Remove the license plate light bulb housing retaining screws.
2. Remove the light bulb requiring replacement and socket from the housing.
3. Remove the light bulb from the socket.
4. Installation is the reverse of removal.
5. Check license plate light for proper operation.

Fig. 76 License plate bulb housing mounting screw removal—1992 Sentra shown

Fig. 77 Removal of the light bulb socket from the housing

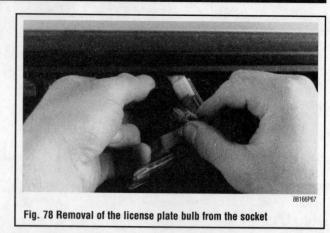

Fig. 78 Removal of the license plate bulb from the socket

TRAILER WIRING

Wiring the car for towing is fairly easy. There are a number of good wiring kits available and these should be used, rather than trying to design your own. All trailers will need brake lights and turn signals as well as tail lights and side marker lights. Most states require extra marker lights for overwide trailers. Also, most states have recently required back-up lights for trailers, and most trailer manufacturers have been building trailers with back-up lights for several years.

Additionally, some Class I, most Class II and just about all Class III trailers will have electric brakes.

Add to this number an accessories wire, to operate trailer internal equipment or to charge the trailer's battery, and you can have as many as seven wires in the harness.

Determine the equipment on your trailer and buy the wiring kit necessary. The kit will contain all the wires needed, plus a plug adapter set which included the female plug, mounted on the bumper or hitch, and the male plug, wired into, or plugged into the trailer harness.

When installing the kit, follow the manufacturer's instructions. The color coding of the wires is standard throughout the industry.

One point to note: most imported vehicles have separate turn signals, in which the brake lights and turn signals do not operate with the same bulb. Some, however, do not. For those vehicles without separate turn signals, you can purchase an isolation unit so that the brake lights won't blink whenever the turn signals are operated, or you can go to your local electronics supply house and buy four diodes to wire in series with the brake and turn signal bulbs. Diodes will isolate the brake and turn signals. The choice is yours. The isolation units are simple and quick to install, but far more expensive than the diodes. The diodes, however, require more work to install properly, since they require the cutting of each bulb's wire and soldering in place of the diode.

One final point, the best kits are those with a spring loaded cover on the vehicle mounted socket. This cover prevents dirt and moisture from corroding the terminals. Never let the vehicle socket hang loosely. Always mount it securely to the bumper or hitch.

CIRCUIT PROTECTION

Fuses

On all vehicles, the fuse block is located under the left side of the instrument panel. Later model vehicles have auxiliary fuse and relay boxes located in the engine compartment.

REMOVAL & INSTALLATION

The fuses can be easily inspected to see if they are blown. Simply pull the fuse from the block, inspect it and replace it with a new one, if necessary.

➡When replacing a blown fuse, be certain to replace it with one of the correct amperage.

Fusible Links

A fusible link(s) is a protective device used in an electrical circuit. When current increases beyond a certain amperage, the fusible metal wire of the link

melts, thus breaking the electrical circuit and preventing further damage to the other components and wiring. Whenever a fusible link is melted because of a short circuit, correct the cause before installing a new link.

All fusible links are the plug in kind. To replace them, simply unplug the bad link and insert the new one.

Circuit Breakers

Circuit breakers are also located in or near the fuse block. A circuit breaker is an electrical switch which breaks the circuit during an electrical overload. The circuit breaker will remain open until the short or overload condition in the circuit is corrected.

Flasher

To replace the flasher, carefully pull it from the electrical connector. If necessary, remove any component that restricts removal.

WIRING DIAGRAMS

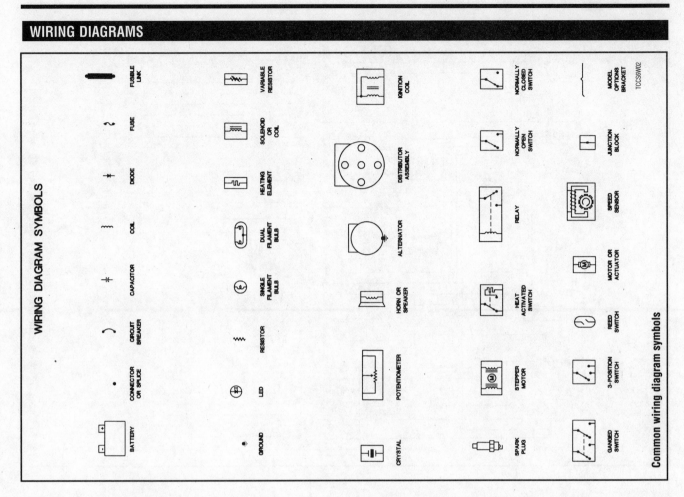

Common wiring diagram symbols

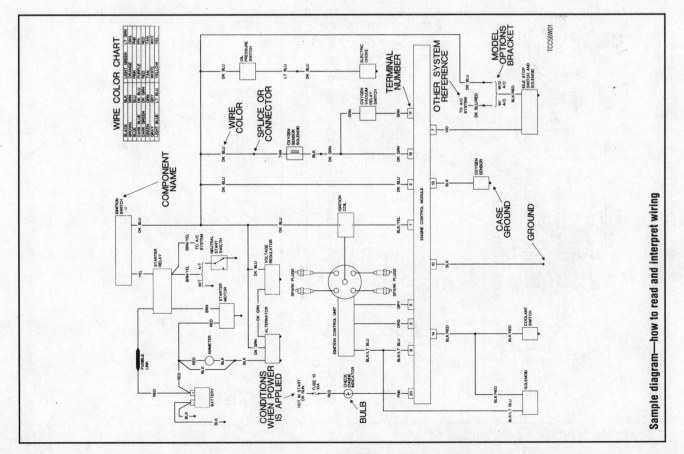

Sample diagram—how to read and interpret wiring

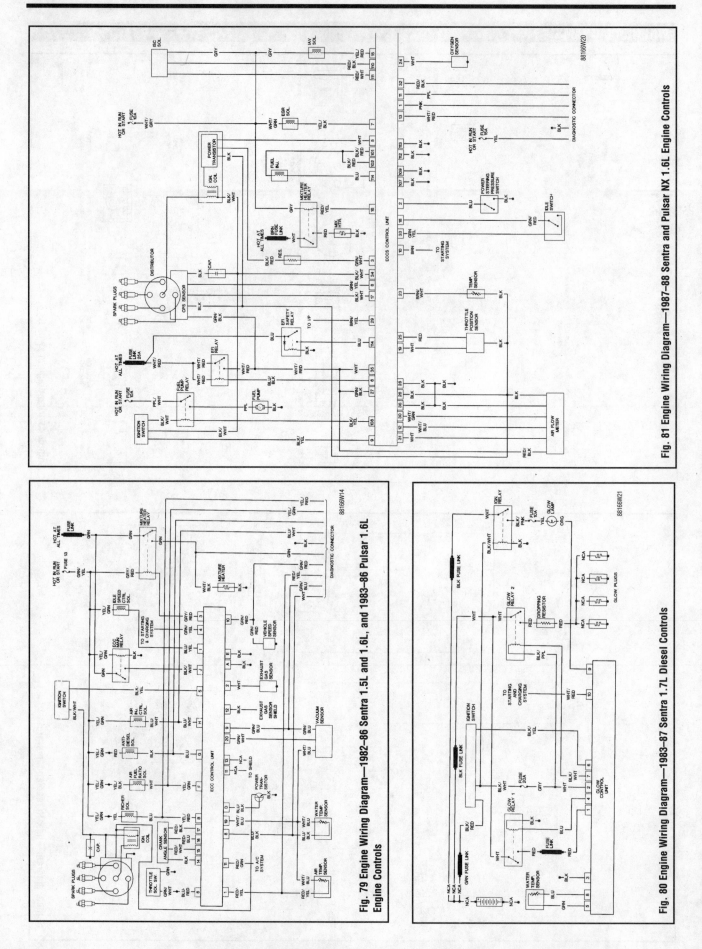

Fig. 81 Engine Wiring Diagram—1987–88 Sentra and Pulsar NX 1.6L Engine Controls

Fig. 79 Engine Wiring Diagram—1982–86 Sentra 1.5L and 1.6L, and 1983–86 Pulsar 1.6L Engine Controls

Fig. 80 Engine Wiring Diagram—1983–87 Sentra 1.7L Diesel Controls

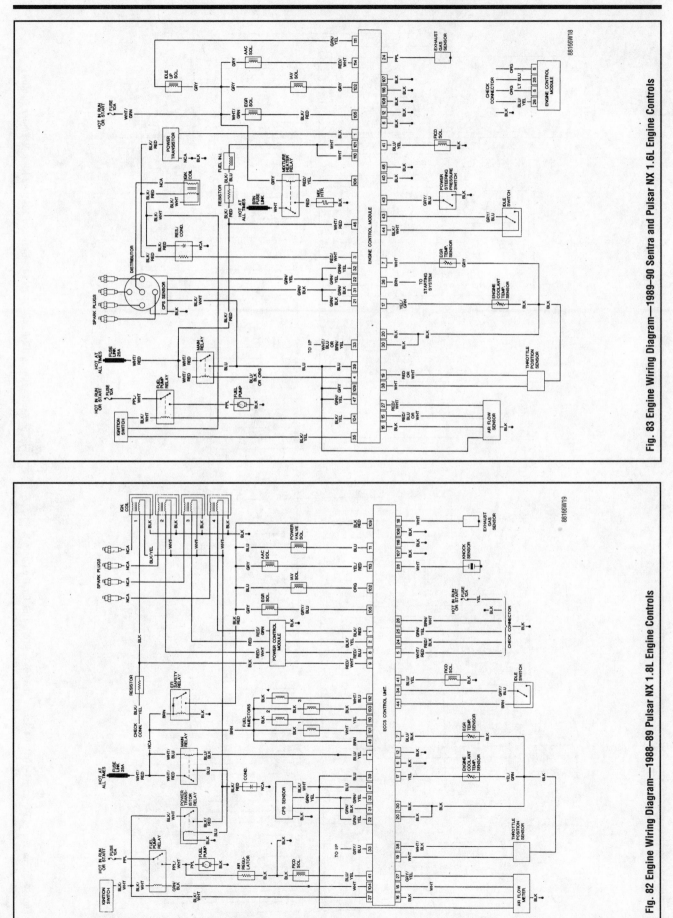

Fig. 83 Engine Wiring Diagram—1989-90 Sentra and Pulsar NX 1.6L Engine Controls

Fig. 82 Engine Wiring Diagram—1988-89 Pulsar NX 1.8L Engine Controls

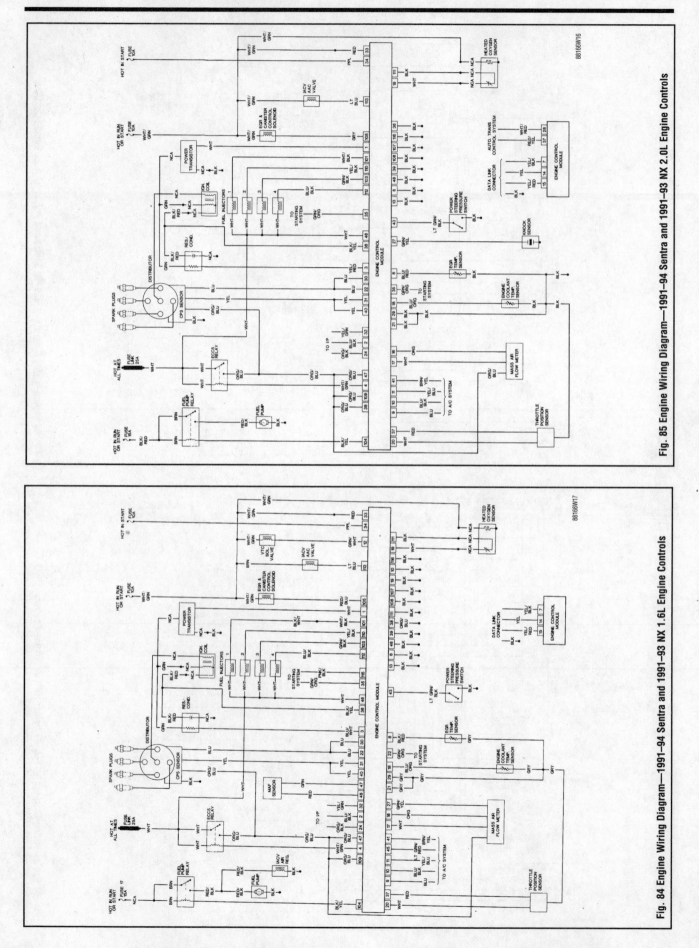

Fig. 85 Engine Wiring Diagram—1991–94 Sentra and 1991–93 NX 2.0L Engine Controls

Fig. 84 Engine Wiring Diagram—1991–94 Sentra and 1991–93 NX 1.6L Engine Controls

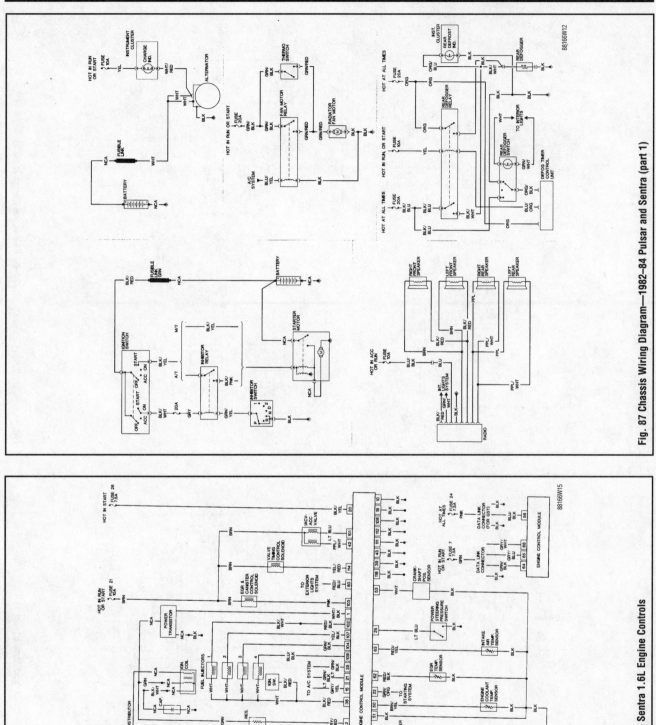

88166W12

Fig. 87 Chassis Wiring Diagram—1982–84 Pulsar and Sentra (part 1)

88166W15

Fig. 86 Engine Wiring Diagram—1995–96 Sentra 1.6L Engine Controls

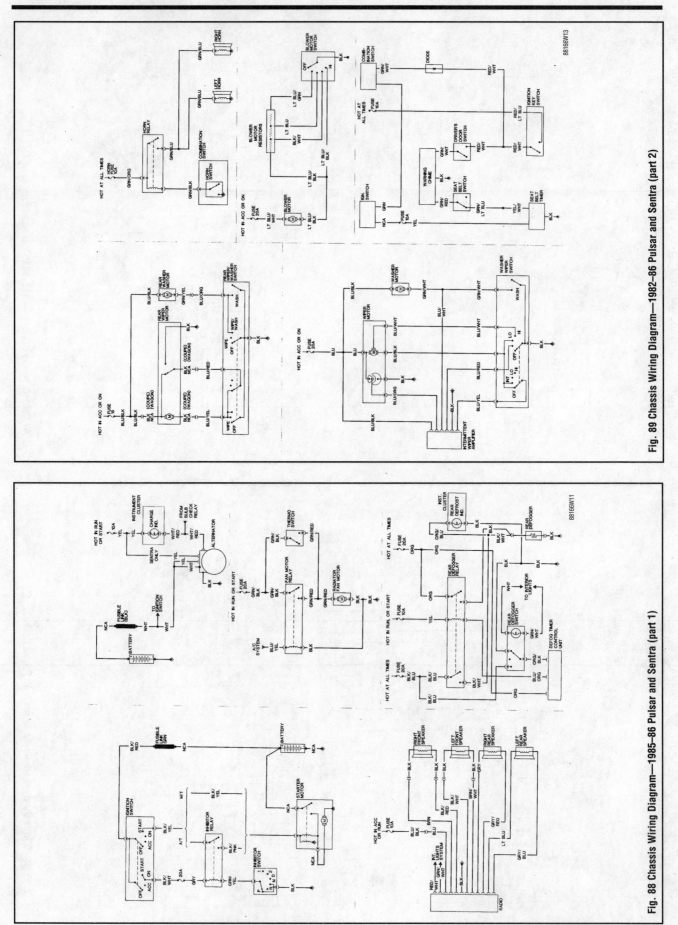

Fig. 89 Chassis Wiring Diagram—1982–86 Pulsar and Sentra (part 2)

Fig. 88 Chassis Wiring Diagram—1985–86 Pulsar and Sentra (part 1)

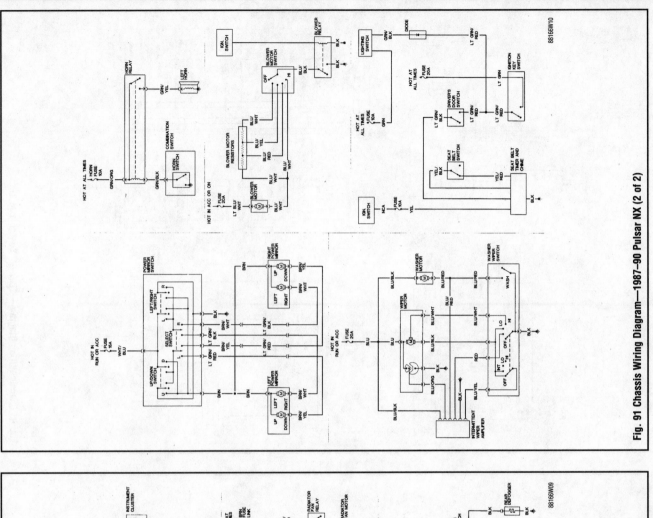

Fig. 91 Chassis Wiring Diagram—1987–90 Pulsar NX (2 of 2)

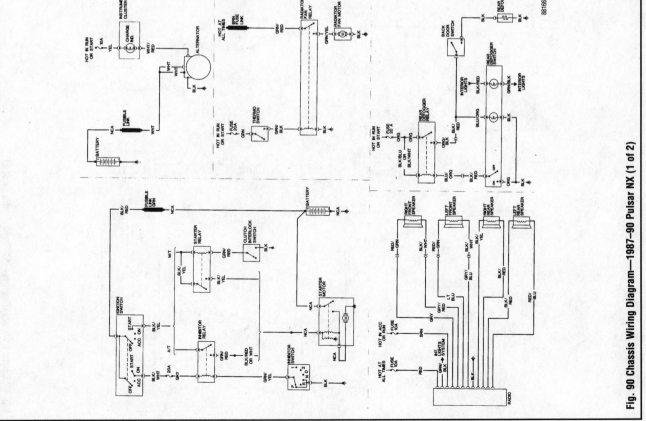

Fig. 90 Chassis Wiring Diagram—1987–90 Pulsar NX (1 of 2)

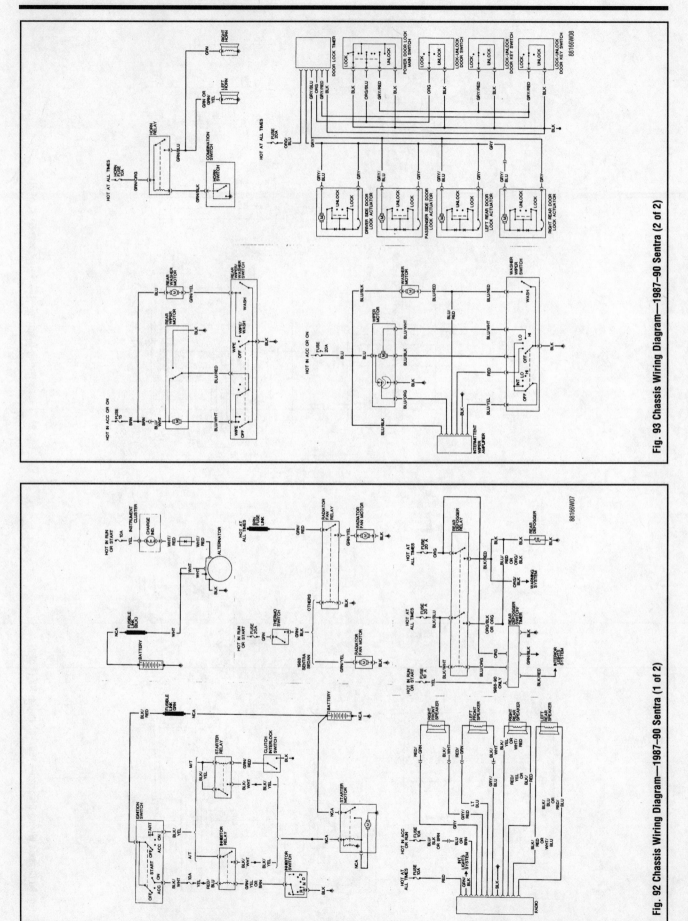

Fig. 93 Chassis Wiring Diagram—1987-90 Sentra (2 of 2)

Fig. 92 Chassis Wiring Diagram—1987-90 Sentra (1 of 2)

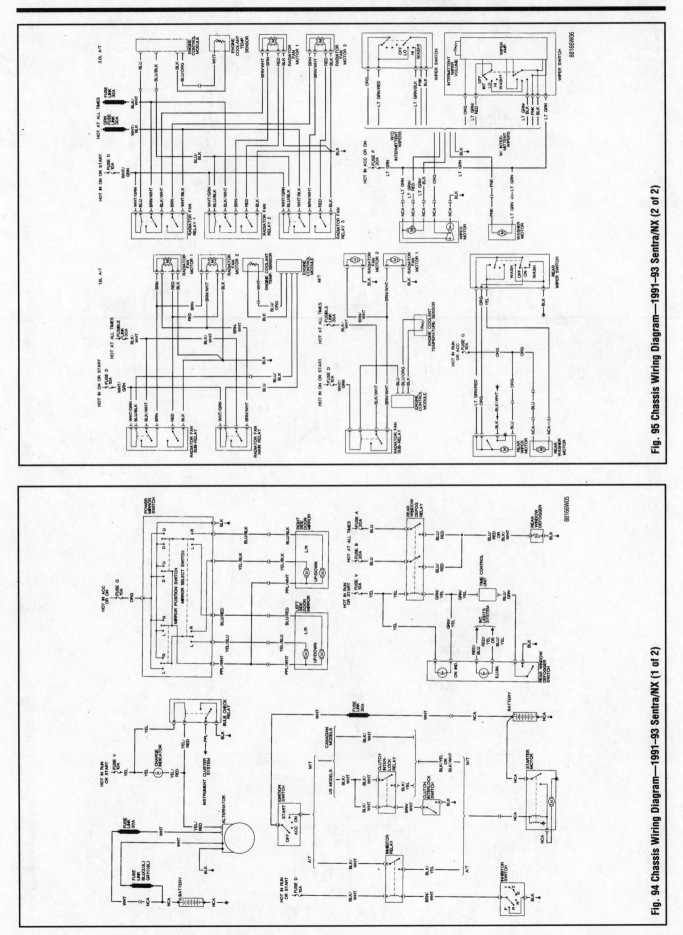

Fig. 95 Chassis Wiring Diagram—1991–93 Sentra/NX (2 of 2)

Fig. 94 Chassis Wiring Diagram—1991–93 Sentra/NX (1 of 2)

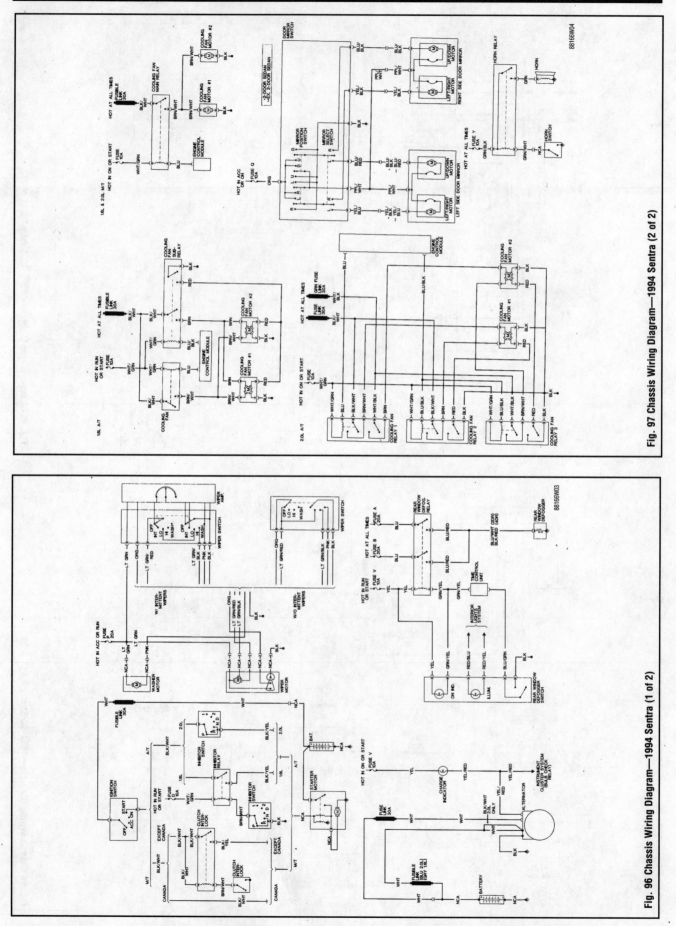

Fig. 97 Chassis Wiring Diagram—1994 Sentra (2 of 2)

Fig. 96 Chassis Wiring Diagram—1994 Sentra (1 of 2)

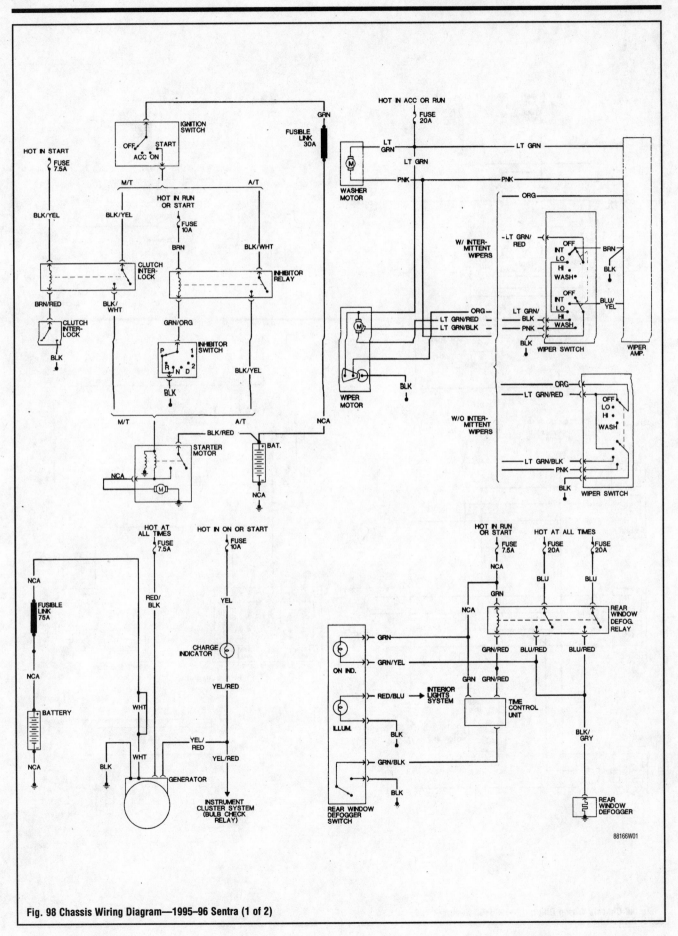

Fig. 98 Chassis Wiring Diagram—1995–96 Sentra (1 of 2)

88166W01

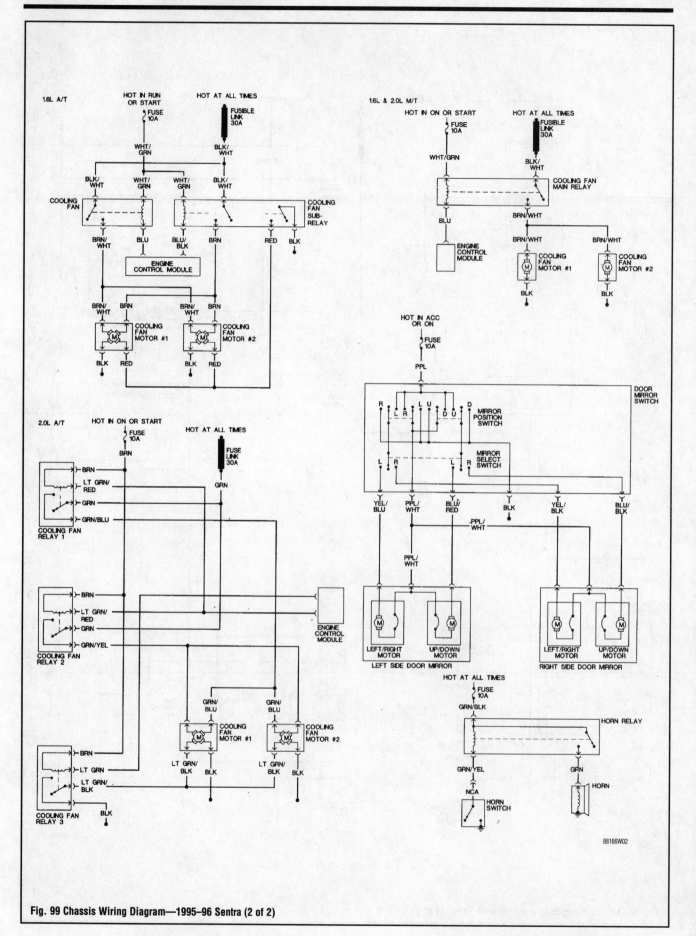

Fig. 99 Chassis Wiring Diagram—1995–96 Sentra (2 of 2)

88166W02

7

DRIVE
TRAIN

MANUAL TRANSAXLE

Understanding the Manual Transaxle

Because of the way an internal combustion engine breathes, it can produce torque, or twisting force, only within a narrow speed range. Most modern, overhead valve pushrod engines must turn at about 2500 rpm to produce their peak torque. By 4500 rpm they are producing so little torque that continued increases in engine speed produce no power increases. The torque peak on overhead camshaft engines is generally much higher, but much narrower.

The manual transaxle and clutch are employed to vary the relationship between engine speed and the speed of the wheels so that adequate engine power can be produced under all circumstances. The clutch allows engine torque to be applied to the transaxle input shaft gradually, due to mechanical slippage. Consequently, the vehicle may be started smoothly from a full stop. The transaxle changes the ratio between the rotating speeds of the engine and the wheels by the use of gears. The gear ratios allow full engine power to be applied to the wheels during acceleration at low speeds and at highway/passing speeds.

In a front wheel drive transaxle, power is usually transmitted from the input shaft to a mainshaft or output shaft located slightly beneath and to the side of the input shaft. The gears of the mainshaft mesh with gears on the input shaft, allowing power to be carried from one to the other. All forward gears are in constant mesh and are free from rotating with the shaft unless the synchronizer and clutch is engaged. Shifting from one gear to the next causes one of the gears to be freed from rotating with the shaft and locks another to it. Gears are locked and unlocked by internal dog clutches which slide between the center of the gear and the shaft. The forward gears employ synchronizers; friction members which smoothly bring gear and shaft to the same speed before the toothed dog clutches are engaged.

Adjustments

‣ **See Figures 1 and 2**

SHIFTER LINKAGE

➡ **On 1982–86 models shifter linkage adjustment is possible. On models from 1987-96 there are no provisions for linkage adjustment.**

1. Raise and support the front of the vehicle on jackstands.
2. Under the vehicle, at the shift control area, loosen the select stopper securing bolts.
3. Shift the gear selector into 1st gear.
4. Adjust the clearance between the control lever and select stopper by sliding the select stopper so that the clearance is 1.00mm.
5. Torque the stopper securing bolts to 28–44 inch lbs. (3–5 Nm). Check that the control lever can be shifted without binding or dragging.

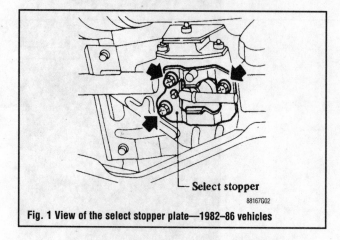

Fig. 1 View of the select stopper plate—1982–86 vehicles

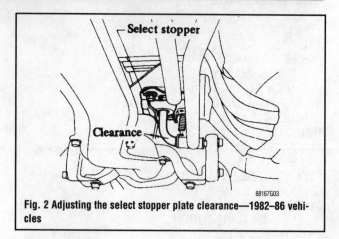

Fig. 2 Adjusting the select stopper plate clearance—1982–86 vehicles

SHIFTER ASSEMBLY

On 1982–86 models all shifter adjustments are performed by adjusting the shift linkage. On 1987 and later models the shifter and shift linkage is not adjustable. If a problem is suspected with the shift mechanism locate and replace the worn or damaged component.

CLUTCH SWITCH

‣ **See Figure 3**

➡**This procedure applies to all models equipped with a clutch interlock switch**

1. Pull the carpet up and back from underneath the clutch pedal assembly.
2. Verify that the clutch pedal height is properly adjusted. The measurement is from the floor pan to the top of the pedal pad.
3. Inspect the clearance between the end of the clutch switch threads and the rubber stopper. This clearance is referred to as clearance **C**. The measured clearance should be 0.012–0.039 in. (0.3–1.0mm).
4. If clearance **C** is not within specifications, the switch can be adjusted by loosening the locknut and screwing the clutch switch in and out.

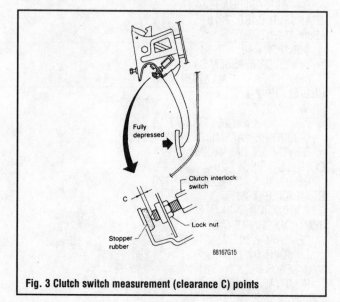

Fig. 3 Clutch switch measurement (clearance C) points

5. Once proper clearance is obtained, tighten the switch locknut to 9 ft. lbs. (13 Nm).

6. Place the carpet down underneath the clutch pedal assembly.

⁂ WARNING

Make sure that carpet is completely pushed down or pedal binding can occur.

7. Replace the floor mats.
8. Check the clutch switch for proper operation.

Back-Up Light Switch

REMOVAL & INSTALLATION

1. Raise vehicle and support safely.
2. Disconnect the electrical connections.
3. Remove switch from transaxle housing, when removing place drain pan under transaxle to catch fluid.

To install:

4. Apply sealer to the switch and torque to 14–22 ft. lbs. (20–29 Nm).
5. Connect the electrical connector.
6. Check and if necessary, refill transaxle with fluid.

Transaxle Assembly

REMOVAL & INSTALLATION

◆ **See Figures 4 thru 17**

1982–86 Vehicles

1. Remove the battery.

➡**On the Pulsar, remove the battery holding plate and the radiator reservoir.**

2. Drain the lubricant from the transaxle.
3. Remove the driveshafts from the transaxle.

➡**Take care not to damage the seal lips. After the driveshafts are removed, Insert a dummy shaft Into each opening so that the side gears don't fall into the case.**

4. Remove the distributor, the air induction tube, the EGR tube and the exhaust manifold cover.
5. Remove the heater hose clamp.
6. Remove the clutch control cable from the lever.
7. Disconnect the speedometer cable at the case.
8. Disconnect all wiring from the case. Remove the wheel well liner.
9. Separate the control and support rods from the case. Disconnect the exhaust pipe at the manifold.
10. Place a jackstand under the engine oil pan to take up the engine weight.
11. Take up the transaxle weight with a floor jack.
12. Remove the engine gusset bolts. On the Pulsar, remove the transaxle protector.
13. On 5-speed models, remove the engine right side and rear mounting brackets and the starter.
14. Attach a shop crane to the transaxle at the clutch control cable bracket.
15. Unbolt the transaxle from the engine. On 5-speed models, pull the engine to the right and slide the transaxle away from the engine.
16. Lower the transaxle from the vehicle.

To Install:

17. Install the transaxle in the vehicle. Note the following points:
   a. Clean all mating surfaces.
   b. Apply EP chassis lube to the splines on the clutch disc and input shaft.
   c. Fill transaxle with 80W-90 gear oil. Apply sealant to the threads of the filler and drain plugs.

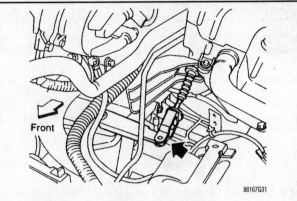

Fig. 4 Disconnect the clutch cable at the point indicated

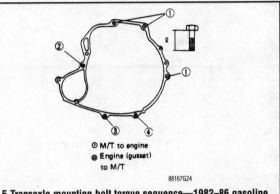

Fig. 5 Transaxle mounting bolt torque sequence—1982–86 gasoline engines

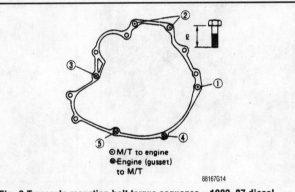

Fig. 6 Transaxle mounting bolt torque sequence—1983–87 diesel engines

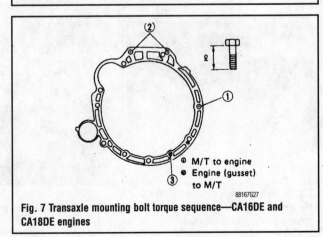

Fig. 7 Transaxle mounting bolt torque sequence—CA16DE and CA18DE engines

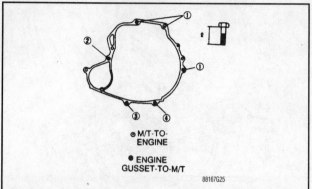

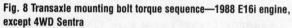

Fig. 8 Transaxle mounting bolt torque sequence—1988 E16i engine, except 4WD Sentra

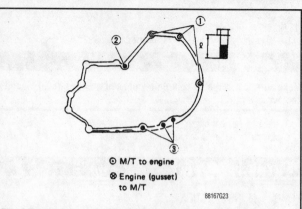

Fig. 9 Transaxle mounting bolt torque sequence—1988 4WD Sentra

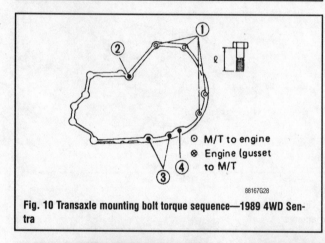

Fig. 10 Transaxle mounting bolt torque sequence—1989 4WD Sentra

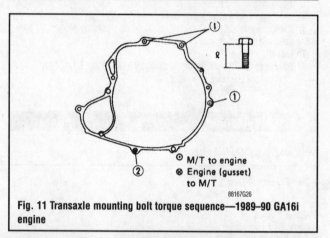

Fig. 11 Transaxle mounting bolt torque sequence—1989–90 GA16i engine

Fig. 12 Drain the transaxle assembly, before removing

Fig. 13 Disconnect the clutch cable from the release lever

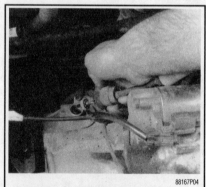

Fig. 14 Remove the speedometer cable from the transaxle housing

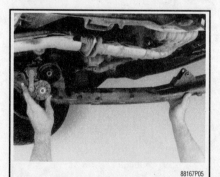

Fig. 15 With the engine/transaxle assembly properly supported from above, remove the front crossmember

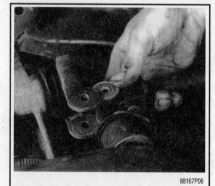

Fig. 16 Disconnect the shifter control rod at the transaxle

Fig. 17 Carefully pry the halfshaft from the transaxle

18. Install the driveshafts for the transaxle.
19. Install all brackets and the protector cover, if equipped.
20. Tighten transaxle to engine bolts as follows:
- With E16 engine—12–15 ft. lbs. (16–21 Nm)
- With CD17 engine and 7T transaxle—22–30 ft. lbs. (30–40 Nm)
- With CD17 engine and 9T transaxle—32–43 ft. lbs. (43–58 Nm)
21. Tighten engine gusset to transaxle bolts to 12–15 ft. lbs. (16–21 Nm)
22. Install the remaining components in the reverse order of removal.

1987–90 Vehicles

1. Disconnect the negative battery cable.
2. Remove the battery and battery bracket.
3. Remove the air duct, air cleaner box and air flow meter.
4. Raise the front of the vehicle and support safely.
5. Drain the transaxle oil.
6. On Sentra (4WD) vehicles, remove the transfer case.
7. Withdraw the halfshafts from the transaxle.

➡When removing halfshafts, use care not to damage the lip of the oil seal. After shafts are removed, Insert a steel bar or wooden dowel of suitable diameter to prevent the side gears from rotating and falling into the differential case.

8. Remove the wheel well protector(s).
9. Separate the control rod and support rod from the transaxle.
10. Remove the engine gusset securing bolt and the engine mounting.
11. Remove the clutch control cable from the operating lever.
12. Disconnect speedometer cable from the transaxle.
13. Disconnect the wires from the reverse (back-up), neutral and overdrive switches. Disconnect the speed and position switch sensors from the transaxle also, if so equipped.
14. Support the engine by placing a jack under the oil pan, with a wooden block placed between the jack and pan for protection.
15. Support the transaxle with a hydraulic floor jack.
16. Remove the engine mounting securing bolts.

➡Most of the transaxle mounting bolts are different lengths. Tagging the bolts upon removal will facilitate proper tightening during installation.

17. Remove the bolts attaching the transaxle to the engine.
18. Using the hydraulic floor jack as a carrier, carefully lower the transaxle down and away from the engine.
To install:
19. Before installing, clean the mating surfaces on the engine rear plate and clutch housing. On Sentra (4WD), apply sealant KP51000150 or equivalent.
20. Apply a light coat of a lithium-based grease to the spline parts of the clutch disc and the transaxle input shaft.
21. Raise the transaxle into place and bolt it to the engine. Install the engine mounts. Torque the transaxle mounting bolts as follows:
- 1987–88 Pulsar/Sentra (E16S and E16i)—tighten bolts (1) and (3) to 12–15 ft. lbs. (16–22 Nm). Tighten bolts (2) and (4) to 14–22 ft. lbs. (20–29 Nm). Bolts (3) and (4) are found all Sentra models.
- 1987–88 Pulsar (CA18DE)—On CA18DE engines, tighten bolts (1) and (2) to 32–43 ft. lbs. (43–58 Nm) and bolts (3) to 22–30 ft. lbs. (30–40 Nm).
- 1989 Pulsar (CA18DE)—tighten bolts (1) and (2) to 32–43 ft. lbs. (43–58 Nm) and bolt (3) to 22–30 ft. lbs. (30–40 Nm).
- Pulsar and 2WD Sentra—tighten all bolts to 12–15 ft. lbs. (16–21 Nm).
- Sentra 4WD—torque all the bolts to 22–30 ft. lbs. (29–41 Nm).
22. Install all the remaining components in the reverse order of removal.

1991–93 Vehicles

1. Disconnect the negative and positive battery cables.
2. Remove the battery and battery bracket.
3. Remove the air duct, air cleaner box and the air flow meter.
4. Raise the front of the vehicle and support it safely.
5. Drain the transaxle oil.
6. Withdraw the halfshafts from the transaxle.

➡When removing the halfshafts, be careful not to damage the lip of the oil seal. After shafts are removed, insert a steel bar or wooden dowel of a suitable diameter to prevent the side gears from rotating and falling into the differential case.

7. Remove the wheel well protector(s).
8. Separate the control rod and support rod from the transaxle.
9. Remove the engine gusset securing bolt and the engine mounting.
10. Remove the clutch control cable from the operating lever.
11. Disconnect the speedometer cable from the transaxle.
12. Disconnect the wires from the reverse (back-up), neutral and overdrive switches. Disconnect the speed and position switch sensors from the transaxle also, if so equipped.
13. Support the engine by placing a jack under the oil pan, with a wooden block placed between the jack and pan for protection.
14. Support the transaxle with a jack.
15. Remove the engine mounting securing bolts.

➡Most of the transaxle mounting bolts are different lengths. Tagging the bolts upon removal will facilitate proper tightening during installation.

16. Remove the bolts attaching the transaxle to the engine.
17. Carefully lower the transaxle down and away from the engine.
To install:
18. Before installing, clean the mating surfaces on the engine rear plate and clutch housing.
19. Apply a light coat of a lithium-based grease to the spline parts of the clutch disc and the transaxle input shaft.
20. Raise the transaxle into place and bolt it to the engine. Install the engine mounts. Torque the transaxle mounting bolts.

➡For bolt identification, tightening specifications and sequence, refer to the appropriate graphic.

21. Install all remaining components in the reverse order of removal.

➡When filling the transaxle make certain that the fluid meets API GL-4 specifications. For specific weight information, refer to your owners manual or Section 1 of this book.

22. Remove the filler plug and fill the transaxle to the proper level. Fill to the level of the plug hole. Apply a thread sealant to the threads of the filler plug and install the plug in the transaxle case.

1994–96 Vehicles

▶ **See Figures 18 and 19**

1. Disconnect the negative and positive battery cables.
2. Remove the battery and battery tray.
3. Remove the air duct, air cleaner box and the air flow meter.
4. Raise the front of the vehicle and support it safely.
5. Remove the clutch control cable from the operating lever.
6. Disconnect the speedometer cable from the transaxle.
7. Disconnect the wires from the reverse (back-up), neutral and ground harness connectors.
8. Disconnect the vehicle speed sensor and the crankshaft position sensor from the transaxle.
9. Remove the starter motor from the transaxle.
10. Remove the through bolts that secure shift control rod and the support rod from the transaxle. Disconnect the rods from the transaxle.

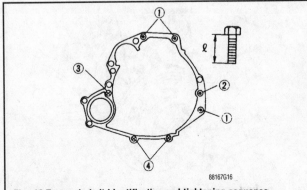

88167G16

Fig. 18 Transaxle bolt identification and tightening sequence— 1991–96 GA16DE engine

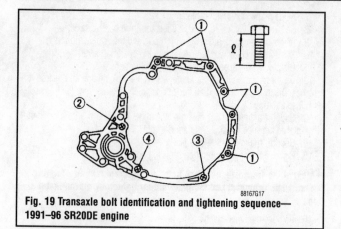

Fig. 19 Transaxle bolt identification and tightening sequence—1991–96 SR20DE engine

11. Drain the transaxle oil.
12. Remove the exhaust front tube.
13. Withdraw the halfshafts from the transaxle.

➡When removing the halfshafts, be careful not to damage the lip of the oil seal. After shafts are removed, insert a steel bar or wooden dowel of a suitable diameter to prevent the side gears from rotating and falling into the differential case.

14. Support the engine by placing a jack under the oil pan; with a wooden block placed between the jack and pan for protection.
15. Support the transaxle with a jack and remove the rear and left side engine mounts.

➡Most of the transaxle mounting bolts are different lengths. Tagging the bolts upon removal will facilitate proper tightening during installation.

16. Remove the bolts attaching the transaxle to the engine.
17. Slide the transaxle away from the engine and carefully lower the transaxle down and away from the engine.

To install:

18. Before installing, clean the mating surfaces on the engine rear plate and clutch housing.
19. Apply a light coat of a lithium-based grease to the spline parts of the clutch disc and the transaxle input shaft.
20. Raise the transaxle into place and bolt it to the engine. Install the engine mounts. Torque the transaxle mounting bolts to specifications.

➡For bolt identification, tightening specifications and sequence, refer to the appropriate graphic.

21. Install the remaining components in the reverse order of removal.
22. Remove the filler plug and fill the transaxle to the proper level. Fill to the level of the plug hole. Apply a thread sealant to the threads of the filler plug and install the plug in the transaxle case.

Halfshafts

REMOVAL & INSTALLATION

1982–90 Vehicles

▶ **See Figures 20, 21, 22 and 23**

➡Installation of the halfshafts may require a special tool for the spline alignment of the halfshaft end and the transaxle case. Do not perform this procedure without access to this tool. The Kent Moore tool Number is J-34296 and J-34297

1. Raise the front of the vehicle and support it on jackstands, then remove the wheel and the tire assembly.
2. Remove the cotter pin from the drive axle.

Fig. 20 Inspect the halfshaft CV-boots for cracks and leakage

Fig. 21 Carefully pry the halfshaft from the transaxle housing

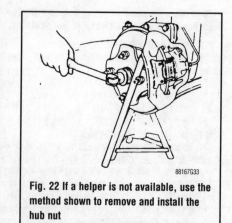

Fig. 22 If a helper is not available, use the method shown to remove and install the hub nut

3. Have a helper firmly apply the brakes, and loosen the hub nut.
4. Remove the caliper assembly.

➡It is not necessary to disconnect the brake hose from the caliper. Position the caliper out of the way and secure with mechanics wire.

5. Using the removal tool HT72520000 or equivalent, remove the tie rod ball joint from the steering knuckle.
6. On 1982–86 vehicles, disconnect the ball joint from the lower control arm, by removing the mounting nuts from the bottom of the control arm.
7. On 1987–90 vehicles, disconnect the ball joint from the steering knuckle, using removal tool HT72520000 or equivalent.
8. Using a block of wood and a mallet, separate the halfshaft from the hub/steering knuckle assembly. If the assembly is difficult to separate it may be necessary to use a press/puller tool.

➡In order to protect the halfshaft from damage, it is a good idea when striking the halfshaft, to temporarily install the hub nut.

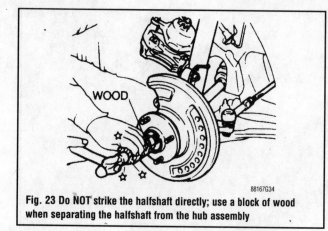

Fig. 23 Do NOT strike the halfshaft directly; use a block of wood when separating the halfshaft from the hub assembly

9. Drain the lubricant from the transaxle.
10. Support the engine properly and remove support bracket if so equipped.
11. Remove the halfshaft from the right side on automatic transaxle equipped vehicles and on all manual transaxles as follows:
    a. Insert a suitable prybar between the inner CV-joint and the transaxle.
    b. Carefully pry the halfshaft from the transaxle.

➥**When removing the driveshaft from the transaxle, do not pull on the driveshaft. The driveshaft will separate at the sliding joint (damaging the boot).**

12. Remove the left side halfshaft on automatic transaxles as follows:
    a. Remove the right side halfshaft as outlined above.
    b. Insert a slotted screwdriver, from the right side of the transaxle. .

➥**Make certain that the screwdriver is properly aligned into the slot in the halfshaft.**

    c. Tap the screwdriver with a mallet to remove the left side halfshaft from the transaxle.
13. Pull the hub/steering knuckle assembly away from the vehicle and remove the halfshaft from the transaxle.

➥**After removing the halfshaft from the transaxle, be sure to install a holding tool to hold the side gear in place while the axle is removed.**

To install:

14. Always use a new circlip on the driveshaft and install a new oil seal to the transaxle.
15. Install the halfshaft into the transaxle.

➥**When installing the driveshaft into the transaxle, use oil seal protector tool KV38105500 or equivalent to protect the oil seal from damage; after installation, remove the tool.**

16. Align the halfshaft with the hub/knuckle assembly and connect the lower control arm-to-ball joint.
17. On 1982–86 vehicles, connect the lower control arm to the ball joint and tighten the control arm-to-ball joint nuts to 40–47 ft. lbs. (54–64 Nm).
18. On 1987–90 vehicles, connect the lower ball joint to the steering knuckle and tighten the stud nut to 43–54 ft. lbs. (59–74 Nm).
19. Connect the tie rod to the steering knuckle and torque the tie rod stud nut to 22–36 ft. lbs. (30–49 Nm).
20. Install then hub nut and tighten to 87–145 ft. lbs. (118–197 Nm).
21. Install new cotter pin in drive axle and mount the caliper assembly.
22. Install the wheel and tire assembly.
23. Road test for proper operation.

1991–96 Vehicles

♦ **See Figures 20, 21, 24 thru 29**

➥**The halfshafts will require a special tool for the spline alignment of the halfshaft end into the transaxle case. Do not perform this procedure without access to this tool. The Kent Moore tool Number is J–34296 and J–34297**

1. Raise the front of the vehicle and support it on jackstands, then remove the wheel and the tire assembly.
2. Remove the cotter pin from the drive axle.
3. Have a helper firmly apply the brakes, and loosen the hub nut.
4. Remove the clip and separate the brake hose from the strut.
5. Remove the caliper assembly and support it with a wire. Do not allow the caliper to hang from the brake hose.

➥**It is not necessary to disconnect the brake hose from the caliper. Position the caliper out of the way and secure with mechanics wire.**

6. Remove the bolts that secure the strut to the steering knuckle.

➥**Cover the halfshaft boots with shop towels to protect them during removal of the shaft.**

7. Separate the halfshaft from the knuckle by lightly tapping it with a hammer. If it is hard to remove, use a puller.
8. Remove the right halfshaft from the transaxle as follows:
    a. Models without support bearing—Pry the halfshaft from the transaxle.
    b. Models with support bearing—Remove the support bearing bolts and pull the halfshaft from transaxle.

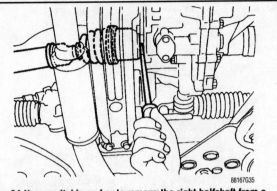
Fig. 24 Use a suitable prybar to remove the right halfshaft from a transaxle without a support bearing—1991–96 vehicles

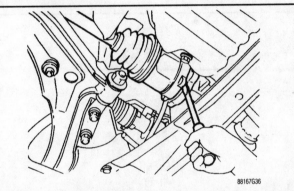
Fig. 25 Removing the right halfshaft from a transaxle with a support bearing—1991–96 vehicles

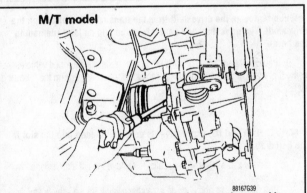
Fig. 26 Removing the right halfshaft from the transaxle assembly—1982–90 vehicles

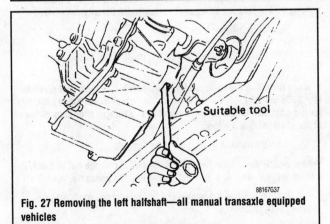
Fig. 27 Removing the left halfshaft—all manual transaxle equipped vehicles

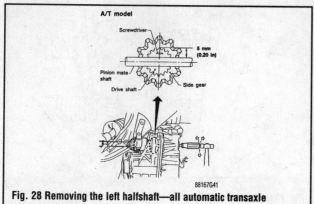

Fig. 28 Removing the left halfshaft—all automatic transaxle equipped vehicles

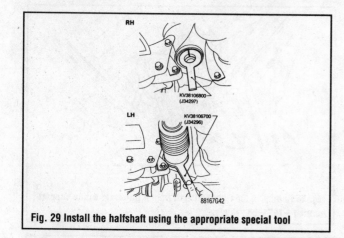

Fig. 29 Install the halfshaft using the appropriate special tool

➡**When removing the driveshaft from the transaxle, do not pull on the driveshaft. The driveshaft will separate at the sliding joint (damaging the boot).**

9. Remove the left side halfshaft on manual transaxle equipped vehicles, using a prybar. On vehicles equipped automatic transaxles perform the following steps:

   a. Remove the right side halfshaft as outlined above.

   b. Insert a slotted screwdriver, from the right side of the transaxle.

➡**Make certain that the screwdriver is properly aligned into the slot in the halfshaft.**

   c. Tap the screwdriver with a mallet to remove the left side halfshaft from the transaxle.

10. Pull the hub/steering knuckle assembly away from the vehicle and remove the halfshaft from the transaxle.

➡**After removing the halfshaft from the transaxle, be sure to install a holding tool to hold the side gear in place while the axle is removed.**

11. Remove the halfshaft from the vehicle.

To install:

12. Use a new circlip on the halfshaft and install a new oil seal to the transaxle.

➡**When installing the halfshaft into the transaxle, use oil seal protector tool KV38106700 (J34296) for the left side or tool KV38106800 (J34297) for the right side to protect the oil seal from damage; after installation of the shaft remove the tool.**

13. Install the halfshaft assembly into the transaxle.

➡**After installation of the halfshaft, try to pull the flange out by hand. If it pulls out, the circular clip is not locked into the transaxle.**

14. If removed, install the support bearing bracket bolts and tighten the mounting bolts to 19–26 ft. lbs. (25–35 Nm).

15. Lubricate the splines of the halfshaft and insert the shaft through the steering knuckle.

16. Align the steering knuckle with the lower strut mount and install the mounting bolts. Tighten the mounting bolts to 68–82 ft. lbs. (92–111 Nm).

17. Install the disc brake caliper and connect the brake hose to the strut with the clip.

18. Install the washer and hub nut to the halfshaft. Tighten the hub nut to 145–202 ft. lbs. (197–274 Nm).

19. Install the adjusting cap and a new cotter pin in drive axle.

20. Install the wheel and tire assembly and lower the vehicle.

21. Road test the vehicle for proper operation.

CV-JOINT OVERHAUL

◆ **See Figures 30, 31 and 32**

The Pulsar/Sentra models use 4 different type CV-joints, which vary according to the engine/transaxle application. Make certain to properly identify which type of joint(s) your vehicle is equipped with, before attempting to service the CV-joint assembly.

➡**When installing the new boots, tape the splines of the axle shaft to protect the boots.**

Transaxle Side

TRIPOD JOINT

◆ **See Figures 33, 34 and 35**

1. Remove the halfshaft from the vehicle.

2. Place the halfshaft securely in a soft-jawed vise.

3. Remove the boot bands.

4. Matchmark the slide joint housing to the halfshaft and remove the slide joint housing.

5. Remove the snapring and matchmark the spider assembly to the halfshaft.

6. Press the spider assembly from the halfshaft.

7. Remove the CV-joint boot.

To install:

8. Install the boot and a new small clamp on the halfshaft.

➡**Cover the halfshaft serration with tape, so as not to damage the new boot during installation.**

9. Place the halfshaft in a soft-jawed vise.

10. Align the matchmarks and using a suitable driver, press the spider assembly onto the halfshaft. Install the spider assembly with the serrated chamfered edge facing the shaft.

11. Install a new snapring. The round surface should face the spider assembly.

12. Pack the slide joint housing with the following specified amounts of Nissan genuine grease or equivalent:

- 1985–86 Sentra and Pulsar NX Left side joint — 6.70 oz. (190g)
- 1985–86 Sentra and 1985 Pulsar NX Right side joint — 7.58 oz. (215g)
- 1987–90 Sentra (Except Coupe) — 6.35–7.05 oz. (180–200g)

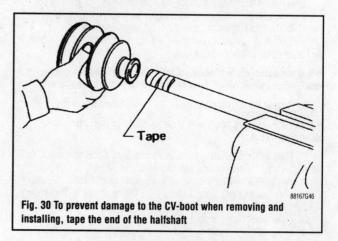

Fig. 30 To prevent damage to the CV-boot when removing and installing, tape the end of the halfshaft

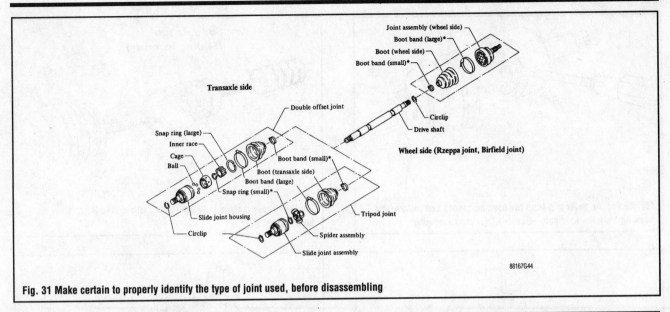

Fig. 31 Make certain to properly identify the type of joint used, before disassembling

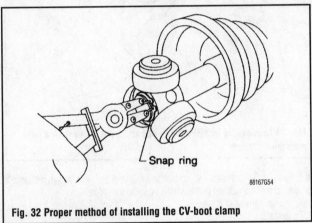

Fig. 32 Proper method of installing the CV-boot clamp

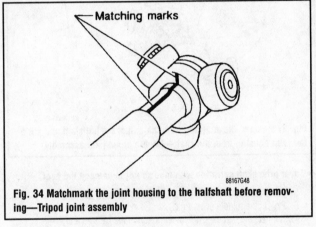

Fig. 34 Matchmark the joint housing to the halfshaft before removing—Tripod joint assembly

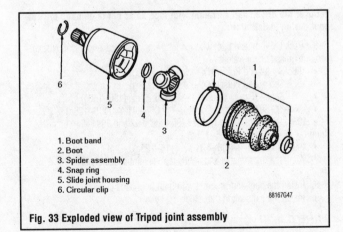

1. Boot band
2. Boot
3. Spider assembly
4. Snap ring
5. Slide joint housing
6. Circular clip

Fig. 33 Exploded view of Tripod joint assembly

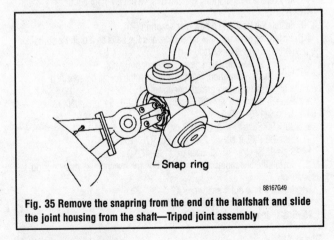

Fig. 35 Remove the snapring from the end of the halfshaft and slide the joint housing from the shaft—Tripod joint assembly

- 1987–90 Sentra (Coupe) and Pulsar NX — 7.76–8.46 oz. (220–240g)
- 1991–94 Sentra/NX Coupe — 7.94–8.29 oz. (225–235g)
- 1995–96 Sentra with GA16DE engine—5.47–5.82 oz. (155–165g)
- 1995–96 Sentra with SR20DE engine—4.59–5.29 oz. (130–150g)

13. Align the matchmarks and install the slide joint housing.

14. Slide the CV-joint boot over the slide joint housing and install the large boot clamp. Secure the boot with both clamps.

15. Install the halfshaft into the vehicle.

DOUBLE OFFSET JOINT

▶ See Figures 36 and 37

1. Remove the halfshaft assembly from the vehicle.
2. Remove the boot bands.
3. Before separating the joint assembly from the halfshaft, matchmark the slide joint housing and inner race.
4. Pry off the outer snapring (**A**) and pull out the slide joint housing.

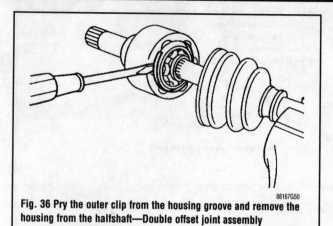

Fig. 36 Pry the outer clip from the housing groove and remove the housing from the halfshaft—Double offset joint assembly

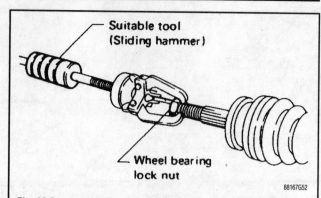

Fig. 38 Proper method of removing the wheel side joints from the halfshaft

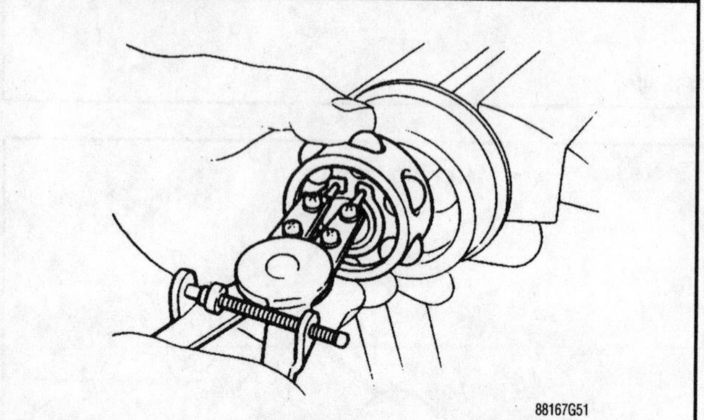

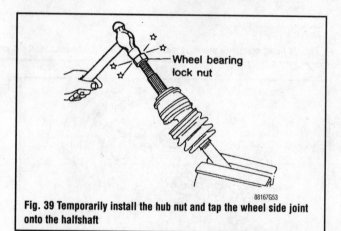

Fig. 37 Remove the snapring from the end of the halfshaft and slide the joint housing from the shaft—Double offset joint assembly

Fig. 39 Temporarily install the hub nut and tap the wheel side joint onto the halfshaft

➥Cover driveshaft serration with tape so not to damage the boot.

5. Place matchmarks on the inner race and the halfshaft.
6. Pry off the middle snapring (C).
7. Remove the ball cage, the inner race, and the balls as a unit.
8. Pry off the rear snapring (B) and remove the CV-joint boot.

To install:

9. Install the boot and a new rear snapring (**B**).
10. Install the ball cage, the inner race, and the balls as a unit. Be sure that the matchmarks on the inner race and
halfshaft are aligned; install a new middle snapring (**C**).
11. Pack the CV-joint housing and boot with the following specified amounts of Nissan genuine grease or equivalent:
   • 1985–87 Sentra, 1987–89 Pulsar NX and 1991–94 Sentra/NX Coupe —
4.94–5.64 oz. (140–160g)
   • 1988–90 Sentra — 3.17–3.88 oz. (90–110g)
   • 1985–86 Pulsar NX — 2.47–3.53 oz. (70–100g)
   • 1995–96 Sentra—4.59–5.29 oz. (130–150g)
12. Install the slide joint housing and align the matchmarks made during disassembly.
13. Install a new outer snapring (**A**).
14. Install the boot and secure with the boot bands.
15. Install the halfshaft in the vehicle.

Wheel Side

♦ **See Figures 38 and 39**

RZEPPA JOINT

➥The joint on the wheel side cannot be disassembled.

1. Remove the halfshaft from the vehicle.
2. Matchmark the halfshaft and the joint assembly.
3. Separate the joint assembly from the halfshaft by placing the halfshaft

securely in a vise and place the locknut on the end of the joint. Attach a slide hammer to the locknut and pull the joint from the halfshaft.
4. Remove the boot bands.

To install:

5. Install the boot with new boot bands.

➥Cover the drive shaft serration with tape so as not to damage the new boot during installation.

6. Pack CV-joint and boot with the following specified amounts of Nissan genuine grease or equivalent:
   • 1985 Sentra and Pulsar NX— 3.88 oz. (110g)
   • 1986 Sentra and Pulsar NX— 4.94 oz. (140g)
   • 1987 Sentra (Except Coupe) — 4.59–5.29 oz. (130–150g)
   • 1988–90 Sentra (Except Coupe) — 4.06–4.41 oz. (115–125g)
   • 1987–90 Sentra (Coupe), 1987–90 Pulsar NX and 1991–94 Sentra/NX Coupe — 5.47–6.17 oz. (155–175g)
   • 1995–96 Sentra—4.06–4.41 oz. (115–125g)
7. Align the matchmarks and lightly tap the joint assembly onto the shaft.
8. Install the boot and secure it with both boot band clamps.
9. Install the halfshaft in the vehicle.

BIRFIELD JOINT

➥The joint on the wheel side cannot be disassembled.

1. Remove the halfshaft from the vehicle.
2. Matchmark the halfshaft and the joint assembly.
3. Separate the joint assembly from the halfshaft by placing the halfshaft securely in a vise and place the locknut on the
end of the joint. Attach a slide hammer to the locknut and pull the joint from the halfshaft.
4. Remove the boot bands.

To install:

5. Install the boot with new boot bands.

6. Pack CV-joint and boot with the following specified amounts of Nissan genuine grease or equivalent:
- 1985–87 Sentra and 1987–89 Pulsar NX — 3.88–4.59 oz. (110–130g)
- 1985–86 Pulsar NX — 2.47–3.53 oz. (70–100g)
- 1988–90 Sentra — 3.00–3.70 oz. (85–105g)
- 1991–96 Sentra/NX Coupe — 3.70–4.41 oz. (105–125g)

CLUTCH

Understanding The Clutch

❋❋ CAUTION

The clutch driven disc may contain asbestos, which has been determined to be a cancer causing agent. Never clean clutch surfaces with compressed air! Avoid inhaling any dust from any clutch surface! When cleaning clutch surfaces, use a commercially available brake cleaning fluid.

The purpose of the clutch is to disconnect and connect engine power at the transaxle. A vehicle at rest requires a lot of engine torque to get all that weight moving. An internal combustion engine does not develop a high starting torque (unlike steam engines) so it must be allowed to operate without any load until it builds up enough torque to move the vehicle. Torque increases with engine rpm. The clutch allows the engine to build up torque by physically disconnecting the engine from the transaxle, relieving the engine of any load or resistance.

The transfer of engine power to the transaxle (the load) must be smooth and gradual; if it weren't, drive line components would wear out or break quickly. This gradual power transfer is made possible by gradually releasing the clutch pedal. The clutch disc and pressure plate are the connecting link between the engine and transaxle. When the clutch pedal is released, the disc and plate contact each other (the clutch is engaged) physically joining the engine and transaxle. When the pedal is pushed inward, the disc and plate separate (the clutch is disengaged) disconnecting the engine from the transaxle.

Most clutches utilize a single plate, dry friction disc with a diaphragm-style spring pressure plate. The clutch disc has a splined hub which attaches the disc to the input shaft. The disc has friction material where it contacts the flywheel and pressure plate. Torsion springs on the disc help absorb engine torque pulses. The pressure plate applies pressure to the clutch disc, holding it tight against the surface of the flywheel. The clutch operating mechanism consists of a release bearing, fork and cylinder assembly.

The release fork and actuating linkage transfer pedal motion to the release bearing. In the engaged position (pedal released) the diaphragm spring holds the pressure plate against the clutch disc, so engine torque is transmitted to the input shaft. When the clutch pedal is depressed, the release bearing pushes the diaphragm spring center toward the flywheel. The diaphragm spring pivots the fulcrum, relieving the load on the pressure plate. Steel spring straps riveted to the clutch cover lift the pressure plate from the clutch disc, disengaging the engine drive from the transaxle and enabling the gears to be changed.

The clutch is operating properly if:
1. It will stall the engine when released with the vehicle held stationary.
2. The shift lever can be moved freely between 1st and reverse gears when the vehicle is stationary and the clutch disengaged.

Adjustments

FREE-PLAY

♦ See Figures 40, 41 and 42

All models use a cable actuated mechanical clutch. The free-play is adjusted at the cable bracket, located near the clutch release lever on the transaxle.

➥When adjusting the free-play after replacing the clutch cable, depress the clutch pedal 50 times as a break in procedure before adjusting the free-play.

1. Loosen the adjusting knob at the transaxle as much that is needed to obtain a proper adjustment.
2. Adjust the pedal free-play by turning the adjusting knob at the transaxle.

7. Align the matchmarks and lightly tap the joint assembly onto the shaft.

➥Be sure to position the axle nut on the end of the CV-joint to protect the threads when tapping the joint on to the axle, to protect the threads.

8. Install the boot and secure it with both boot band clamps.
9. Install the halfshaft in the vehicle.

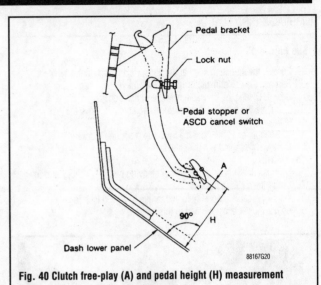

Fig. 40 Clutch free-play (A) and pedal height (H) measurement points

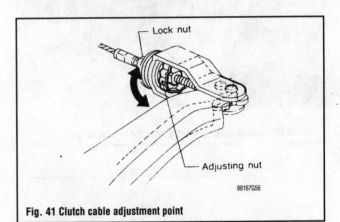

Fig. 41 Clutch cable adjustment point

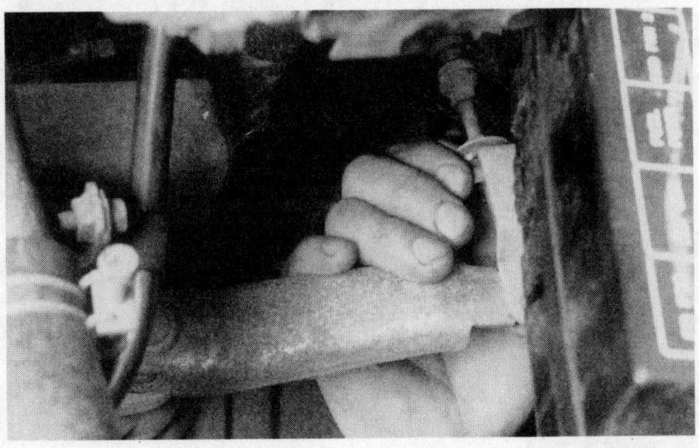

Fig. 42 Adjust the clutch free-play using the adjusting nut, located at the transaxle cable end

3. Measure the distance from the pedal resting position to the end of the free travel. The distance (measurement **A**) should be as follows:
- 1982–84 vehicles—0.43–0.83 in. (11–21mm)
- 1985–90 vehicles—0.49–0.69 in. (12.5–17.5mm)
- 1991–96 vehicles—0.42–0.59 in. (10.5–15mm)

4. Road test vehicle for proper operation.

Clutch Cable

REMOVAL & INSTALLATION

▶ **See Figure 43**

1. Loosen the adjusting knob at the transaxle as much that is needed.
2. Remove the cable insulator nuts at the clutch pedal mount, in engine compartment. Disengage the cable from the clutch pedal.
3. Lubricate the rubber grommet to ease removal. Remove the grommet from the firewall.
4. Disengage the cable from the transaxle mounting bracket.
5. Remove the cable from the vehicle.

To Install:

6. Lubricate the rubber grommets and moving parts with heavy grease.
7. Install the cable to the vehicle.
8. Install the cable bracket nuts and torque to 72–96 inch lbs. (8–11 Nm).
9. Adjust the cable as outlined in this section.

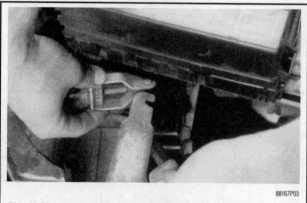

Fig. 43 Disconnect the clutch cable from the release lever

Driven Disc and Pressure Plate

REMOVAL & INSTALLATION

▶ **See Figures 44 thru 49**

1. Following the procedures outlined earlier in this section, remove the manual transaxle assembly.
2. Insert a clutch disc centering tool KV30101000 or equivalent, into the clutch disc hub for support.
3. Loosen the pressure plate bolts evenly in reverse order of the tightening sequence, a little at a time to prevent distortion.
4. Remove the clutch pressure plate and disc together as an assembly.
5. Remove the throwout bearing from the clutch lever, by pulling the bearing retainers outward.

To install:

➡ **The entire clutch assembly (disc, pressure plate and release bearing) should be replaced or reconditioned at this time. The clutch release mechanism, pilot bearing (if applicable) and flywheel should be carefully inspect prior to reassembly.**

6. Before continuing, compare the replacement parts with the old components, verifying that they are exactly the same.
7. Inspect the flywheel for cracks, discoloration and warpage. Minor imperfections can be corrected by lightly sanding with emery paper. Serious defects require resurfacing or replacement of the flywheel.
8. Apply a light coating of a high temperature chassis lubricant to the clutch disc splines, input shaft and pilot bearing. Install the disc and pressure plate. Use a disc centering tool to aid installation. Torque the pressure plate bolts in sequence and in several steps to 16–22 ft. lbs. (20–26 Nm).
9. Install the new throwout bearing in the clutch release lever. Remove the clutch disc centering tool.
10. Install the transaxle into the vehicle. If the mating surfaces will not come together, do not force the units together perform the following steps:
    a. Remove the transaxle and recheck that the disc is centered.
    b. Clean dowel pins and alignment holes.

※ WARNING

NEVER attempt to draw the transaxle to the engine with the bolts. This may damage the clutch and/or transaxle.

11. After the transaxle is installed, connect the clutch cable and check operation before complete reassembly.
12. Adjust the clutch pedal as necessary.

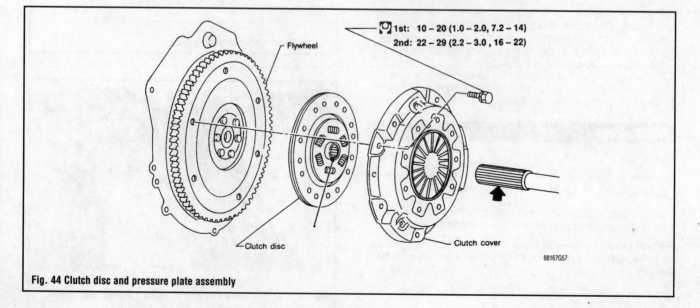

Fig. 44 Clutch disc and pressure plate assembly

Fig. 45 Clutch pressure plate tightening sequence

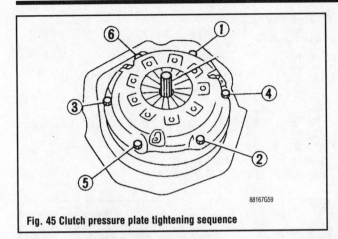

Fig. 46 Remove the clutch disc and pressure plate as an assembly

Fig. 47 Always replace the release bearing when replacing the clutch assembly

Fig. 48 Leave the aligning (arbor) tool inserted while tightening the pressure plate mounting bolts

Fig. 49 Before installing the transaxle, use an arbor tool to verify that the disc is properly aligned

AUTOMATIC TRANSAXLE

Understanding the Automatic Transaxle

The automatic transaxle allows engine torque and power to be transmitted to the front wheels within a narrow range of engine operating speeds. It will allow the engine to turn fast enough to produce plenty of power and torque at very low speeds, while keeping it at a sensible rpm at high vehicle speeds (and it does this job without driver assistance). The transaxle uses a light fluid as the medium for the transmission of power. This fluid also works in the operation of various hydraulic control circuits and as a lubricant. Because the transaxle fluid performs all of these functions, trouble within the unit can easily travel from one part to another.

Adjustments

CONTROL CABLE

1982–90 Vehicles

♦ See Figures 50 and 51

1. Place the control lever In **P**.
2. Connect the control cable end to the lever in the transaxle unit and tighten the cable securing bolt.
3. Move the lever to the **No.1** position. Make sure that the lever works smoothly and quietly.
4. Place the control lever in **P**.

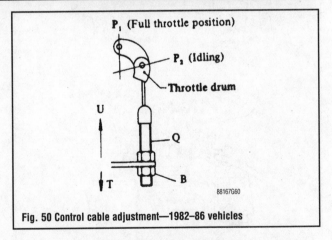

Fig. 50 Control cable adjustment—1982–86 vehicles

5. . Make sure that the lever locks in Park. Remove the cable adjusting outer nut and loosen the inner nut. Connect the control cable to the trunnion and install the outer nut.
6. Pull on the cable a couple of times, then tighten the outer nut until it just contacts the bracket. Tighter the inner nut securely. The length of the cable between the inner end of the rubber boot and the outer end of the rod should be 120.5mm.
7. Check all parts to ensure smooth working order. Check the cable spring cotter pin to make sure that it is assembled as shown.

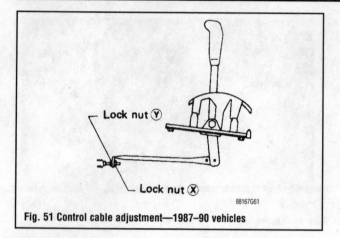

Fig. 51 Control cable adjustment—1987–90 vehicles

1991–92 Vehicles

♦ **See Figure 52**

1. Place the shift selector in **P**.
2. Loosen the control cable locknut and place the manual shaft in the **P** position.
3. Adjust the cable using the long hole in the control cable at the transaxle end.
4. Tighten the locknut.
5. Move the selector from **P** to **1** and make sure that the selector lever can be moved smoothly and without any sliding noise.
6. Apply heavy grease to all moving parts.

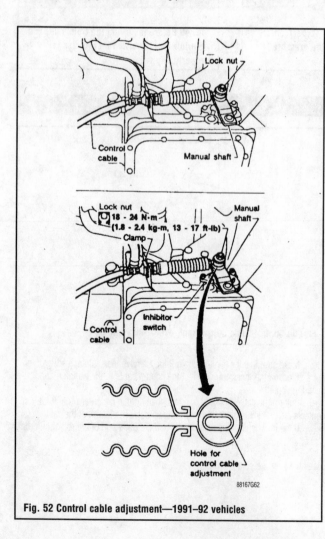

Fig. 52 Control cable adjustment—1991–92 vehicles

1993–96 Vehicles

♦ **See Figure 53**

1. Place the shift selector in **P**.
2. Loosen the control cable locknut and place the manual shaft in the **P** position.
3. Pull the control cable in the direction of extending the cable with 1.5 lbs. (6.9 N) of force.
4. Retract the control cable 0.039 in. (1.0mm) and tighten the control cable locknut.
5. Move the selector from **P** to **1** and make sure that the selector lever can be moved smoothly and without any sliding noise.
6. Apply heavy grease to all moving parts.

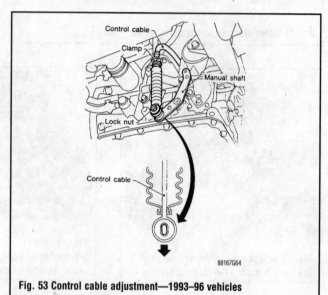

Fig. 53 Control cable adjustment—1993–96 vehicles

THROTTLE CABLE (WIRE)

1982–90 Vehicles

♦ **See Figure 54**

The throttle wire is adjusted by means of double nuts on the carburetor or throttle body side. Refer to the illustration for details. If this adjustment is out of range, the transaxle shift patterns will change. This can affect the durability and driveability of the transaxle.

1. Loosen the throttle wire double nuts **A** and **B** on the carburetor side.
2. With the throttle drum set at **P1** (fully open), move the fitting **Q** fully in the direction **T** and tighten nut **B** in direction **U**.
3. Reverse nut **B** 1 to 1.5 turns in direction **T** and tighten nut a while holding the throttle in the full open position.
4. Make sure the throttle wire stroke **L** is within the range of 1.079–1.236 in. (27.431.4mm).

1991–96 Vehicles

♦ **See Figure 55**

The throttle wire is adjusted by means of double nuts on the throttle body side. Refer to the illustration for details. If this adjustment is out of range, the transaxle shift patterns will change. This can affect the durability and driveability of the transaxle.

➙**This procedure applies only to the RL4F03A transaxle. The RE4FO3V transaxles do NOT use a throttle wire input.**

1. Turn the ignition switch **OFF**. Mark the throttle wire to aid in measurement.
2. While pressing the lock plate, move the adjusting tube in the direction **T**.
3. Return the lock plate. The adjusting tube is locked at this time.

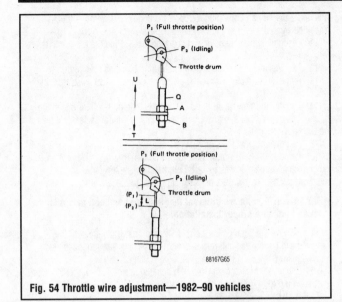

Fig. 54 Throttle wire adjustment—1982–90 vehicles

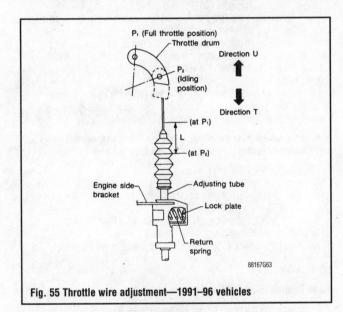

Fig. 55 Throttle wire adjustment—1991–96 vehicles

4. Move the throttle drum from **P2** to **P1** quickly. The adjusting tube moves in direction **U** while depressing the lock plate.

5. Make sure the throttle wire stroke **L** is within the range of 1.079-1.236 in. (27.431.4mm) between full throttle and idle.

Inhibitor Switch (Back-Up/Neutral Safety)

The inhibitor switch, contains both the back-up and neutral safety switches. The switch allows the back-up lights to work when the transaxle is placed in Reverse range. It also act as a Neutral Safety switch, by allowing the current to pass to the starter when the transaxle is placed in Neutral or Park. The switch may be at fault is the starter motor will not crank.

REMOVAL & INSTALLATION

1. Raise and support the vehicle on jackstands.
2. At the transaxle, disconnect the manual control cable from the manual shaft.
3. Remove the three retaining screws and the switch from transaxle.
To install:
4. Install the inhibitor switch to the transaxle. Do not tighten the adjusting screws.
5. Following proper procedures, adjust the inhibitor switch.

6. Connect the manual control cable and adjust as required.
7. Lower the vehicle to the ground.

ADJUSTMENT

♦ **See Figure 56**

1. Raise and support the vehicle on jackstands.
2. At the transaxle, disconnect the manual control cable from the manual shaft.
3. Place the select lever in the **Neutral** position.
4. Loosen the inhibitor switch adjusting screws.
5. Using a 0.098 in. (2.5mm) diameter pin for 1982–92 vehicles and a 0.157 in. (4mm) pin for 1993 and later vehicles, adjust the switch as follows:
a. Place the pin into the manual shaft adjustment hole.
b. Rotate the inhibitor switch until the pin can be inserted through the manual shaft and into the inhibitor switch alignment hole.
c. Tighten the adjusting screws to 17–23 inch lbs. (2.0-2.6 Nm).
d. Check the switch for continuity. Continuity should exist only when the manual shaft is in the **P** and **Neutral** positions.
6. Connect the manual control cable and adjust as required.
7. Lower the vehicle to the ground.

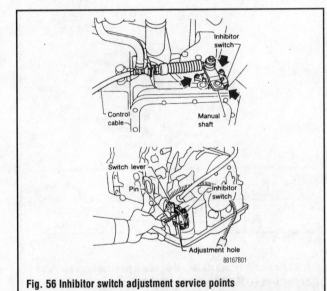

Fig. 56 Inhibitor switch adjustment service points

Transaxle

REMOVAL & INSTALLATION

1982–90 Vehicles

♦ **See Figures 57, 58 and 59**

1. Disconnect the negative battery cable.
2. Raise and support the vehicle safely.
3. Remove the left front tire.
4. Drain the transaxle fluid.
5. Remove the left side fender protector and remove the halfshafts.

➡**Be careful not to damage the oil seals when removing the halfshafts. After removing the halfshafts, install a suitable bar so the side gears will not rotate and fall into the differential case.**

6. On Sentra Wagon, disconnect and remove the forward exhaust pipe.
7. Disconnect the speedometer cable.
8. Disconnect the throttle wire (cable) connection.
9. Remove the control cable rear end from the unit and remove the oil level gauge tube.
10. Place a suitable jack under the transaxle and engine. Do not place the

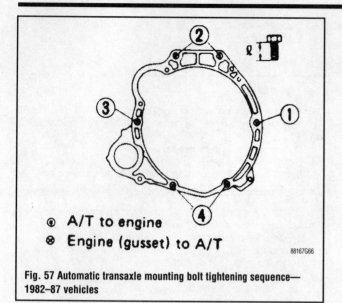

Fig. 57 Automatic transaxle mounting bolt tightening sequence—1982–87 vehicles

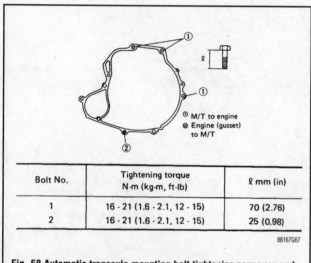

Bolt No.	Tightening torque N·m (kg-m, ft-lb)	ℓ mm (in)
1	16 - 21 (1.6 - 2.1, 12 - 15)	70 (2.76)
2	16 - 21 (1.6 - 2.1, 12 - 15)	25 (0.98)

Fig. 58 Automatic transaxle mounting bolt tightening sequence and specifications—1988–90 vehicles with GA16i engine

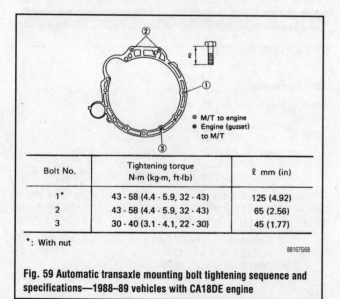

Bolt No.	Tightening torque N·m (kg-m, ft-lb)	ℓ mm (in)
1*	43 - 58 (4.4 - 5.9, 32 - 43)	125 (4.92)
2	43 - 58 (4.4 - 5.9, 32 - 43)	65 (2.56)
3	30 - 40 (3.1 - 4.1, 22 - 30)	45 (1.77)

*: With nut

Fig. 59 Automatic transaxle mounting bolt tightening sequence and specifications—1988–89 vehicles with CA18DE engine

jack under the oil pan drain plug. Support the engine with wooden blocks placed between the engine and the center member.

11. Disconnect the oil cooler and charging tubes. Plug the tube ends to prevent leakage.

12. Remove the engine motor mount securing bolts, as required.

13. Remove the starter motor and disconnect all electrical wires from the transaxle.

14. Loosen and remove all but 3 of the bolts holding the transaxle to the engine. Leave the 3 bolts in to support the weight of the transaxle while removing the converter bolts.

15. Remove the driveplate or dust covers.

16. Remove the bolts holding the torque converter to the driveplate. Rotate the crankshaft to gain access to each bolt. Before separating the torque converter, place chalk marks on 2 parts for alignment purposes during installation.

➡**The transaxle bolts are different lengths. Tag each bolt according to location to ensure proper installation.**

17. Remove the 3 temporary bolts. Move the jack gradually until the transaxle can be lowered and removed from the vehicle through the left side wheel housing.

18. Check the driveplate run-out with a dial indicator. Run-out must be no more than 0.020 in. (0.5mm).

To install:

19. If the torque converter was removed from the engine for any reason, after it is installed, the distance from the face of the converter to the edge of the transaxle housing (distance **A**) must be checked prior to installing the transaxle. This is done to ensure proper installation of the torque converter. Check the distance and make sure it is as follows: RL3F01A transaxles should be 0.831 in. (21mm) or more, RL4F03A and RL4F03V transaxles should be 0.748 in. (19mm) or more.

20. Raise the transaxle onto the engine and install the torque converter-to-driveplate bolts. Torque the bolts to specification. Install 3 bolts to support the transaxle while tighten the converter bolts.

➡**After the converter Is Installed, rotate the crankshaft several times to make sure the transaxle rotates freely and does not bind.**

21. Install the driveplate or dust covers.

22. Install the transaxle mounting bolts and tighten as follows:
• 1982–89 vehicles, tighten bolts (1), (2) and (3) to 29–36 ft. lbs. (39–49 Nm and bolts (4) to 22–30 ft. lbs. (30–40 Nm).
• 1990 vehicles, tighten bolts (1) to 29–36 ft. lbs. (39–49 Nm) and bolts (2) to 22–30 ft. lbs. (30–40 Nm).

23. Install the remaining components in the reverse order of removal.

1991–96 Vehicles

▶ See Figures 60, 61, 62 and 63

1. Disconnect the negative and positive battery cables.
2. Remove the battery and bracket from the vehicle.
3. Remove the air duct between the throttle body and the air cleaner.
4. Disconnect the solenoid harness connector, inhibitor switch harness connector and the revolution speed sensor harness connector.

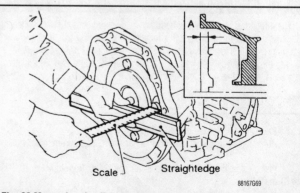

Fig. 60 Measuring the distance from the face of the converter to the edge of the transaxle housing (distance A)

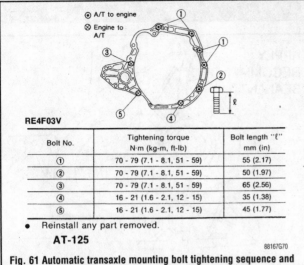

RE4F03V

Bolt No.	Tightening torque N·m (kg-m, ft-lb)	Bolt length "ℓ" mm (in)
①	70 - 79 (7.1 - 8.1, 51 - 59)	55 (2.17)
②	70 - 79 (7.1 - 8.1, 51 - 59)	50 (1.97)
③	70 - 79 (7.1 - 8.1, 51 - 59)	65 (2.56)
④	16 - 21 (1.6 - 2.1, 12 - 15)	35 (1.38)
⑤	16 - 21 (1.6 - 2.1, 12 - 15)	45 (1.77)

● Reinstall any part removed.

AT-125

88167G70

Fig. 61 Automatic transaxle mounting bolt tightening sequence and specifications—1991–96 vehicles with RL4F03A transaxle

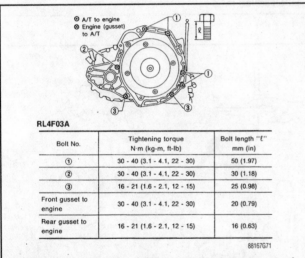

RL4F03A

Bolt No.	Tightening torque N·m (kg-m, ft-lb)	Bolt length "ℓ" mm (in)
①	30 - 40 (3.1 - 4.1, 22 - 30)	50 (1.97)
②	30 - 40 (3.1 - 4.1, 22 - 30)	30 (1.18)
③	16 - 21 (1.6 - 2.1, 12 - 15)	25 (0.98)
Front gusset to engine	30 - 40 (3.1 - 4.1, 22 - 30)	20 (0.79)
Rear gusset to engine	16 - 21 (1.6 - 2.1, 12 - 15)	16 (0.63)

88167G71

Fig. 62 Automatic transaxle mounting bolt tightening sequence and specifications—1994–96 vehicles with RE4F03V transaxle

5. Disconnect the torque converter clutch solenoid harness connector and the vehicle speed sensor harness connector.
6. If equipped, remove the crankshaft position sensor from the transaxle.
7. For RL4F03A transaxles, disconnect the throttle wire at the engine side.
8. Drain the fluid from the transaxle.
9. Disconnect the control cable from the transaxle.
10. Disconnect the oil cooler lines from the transaxle.
11. Remove the halfshafts from the transaxle.
12. Remove the intake manifold support brackets.
13. Remove the starter motor from the transaxle.
14. Remove the upper bolts that secure the transaxle to the engine.
15. Using a block of wood, support the transaxle with a jack.
16. Remove the center crossmember.
17. On vehicles with GA16DE engines, remove the front and rear gussets.
18. Remove the rear plate cover.
19. Remove the torque converter mounting bolts. It will be necessary to rotate the engine by hand to gain access to all bolts.

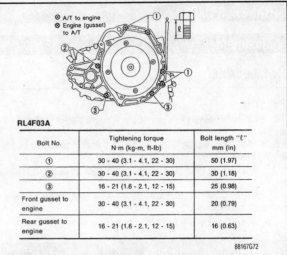

RL4F03A

Bolt No.	Tightening torque N·m (kg-m, ft-lb)	Bolt length "ℓ" mm (in)
①	30 - 40 (3.1 - 4.1, 22 - 30)	50 (1.97)
②	30 - 40 (3.1 - 4.1, 22 - 30)	30 (1.18)
③	16 - 21 (1.6 - 2.1, 12 - 15)	25 (0.98)
Front gusset to engine	30 - 40 (3.1 - 4.1, 22 - 30)	20 (0.79)
Rear gusset to engine	16 - 21 (1.6 - 2.1, 12 - 15)	16 (0.63)

88167G72

Fig. 63 Automatic transaxle mounting bolt tightening sequence and specifications—1991–92 vehicles with RL3F01A transaxle

20. Remove the rear transaxle to engine bracket.
21. Remove the rear transaxle mount.
22. Remove the lower transaxle to engine mounting bolts.
23. Slide the transaxle away from the engine and lower the transaxle assembly.

To install:
When connecting the torque converter to the transaxle, be sure to measure the distance between the mounting lug of the converter and the front edge of the transaxle.
24. The measured distance between the converter and the front of the transaxle (distance **A**) should be:
   a. 0.831 in. (21.1mm) or more for GA16DE engine vehicles
   b. 0.626 in. (15.9mm) or more for SR20DE engine vehicles
25. Raise the transaxle and install to engine driveplate.
26. Install the transaxle mounting bolts in the proper location as noted during removal. Torque the bolts to specifications.

➡**For bolt identification, tightening specifications and sequence, refer to the appropriate graphic.**

27. Install the rear transaxle mount.
28. Install the rear transaxle to engine bracket.
29. Install the torque converter mounting bolts and torque the four bolts to 33–43 ft. lbs. (44–59 Nm).
30. Install the remaining components in the reverse order of removal.

Halfshafts

REMOVAL & INSTALLATION

Refer to the Manual Transaxle procedures with this exception: When removing both halfshafts from 4WD equipped models, insert a dowel or equivalent through the right side halfshaft hole and use a small mallet to tap the left halfshaft out of the transaxle case. Withdraw the shaft from the steering knuckle and remove it. Be careful not to damage the pinion mating shaft and the side gear while tapping the left halfshaft out of the transaxle case.

CV-JOINT OVERHAUL

Refer to the Manual Transaxle section procedures.

TRANSFER CASE

Adjustment

CONTROL CABLE

1. Place the shift selector in **P**.
2. Loosen the control cable locknut and place the manual shaft in the **P** position.
3. Pull the control cable in the direction of extending the cable with 1.5 lbs. (6.9 N) of force.
4. Retract the control cable 0.039 in. (1.0mm) and tighten the control cable locknut.
5. Move the selector from **P** to **1.** and make sure that the selector lever can be moved smoothly and without any sliding noise.
6. Apply heavy grease to all moving parts.

Transfer Case Assembly

REMOVAL & INSTALLATION

◆ **See Figures 64, 65 and 66**

1. Drain the gear oil from the transaxle and the transfer case.
2. Disconnect and remove the forward exhaust pipe.
3. Using chalk or paint, matchmark the flanges on the driveshaft and then unbolt and remove the driveshaft from the transfer case.
4. Unbolt and remove the transfer control actuator from the side of the transfer case.
5. Disconnect and remove the right side halfshaft.
6. Unscrew and withdraw the speedometer pinion gear from the transfer case. Position it out of the way and secure it with wire.
7. Unbolt and remove the front, rear and side transfer case gussets (support members).
8. Use a hydraulic floor jack and a block of wood to support the transfer case, remove the transfer case-to-transaxle mounting bolts and then remove the case itself. Be careful when moving it while supported on the jack.

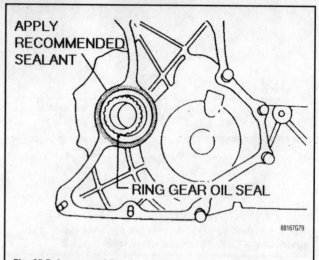

Fig. 65 Before assembling the transfer case to the transaxle, apply proper sealant to the point shown

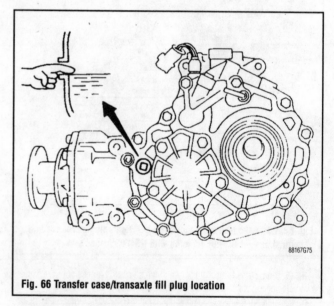

Fig. 66 Transfer case/transaxle fill plug location

To install:

9. Apply Nissan KP510-00150 sealant or equivalent to transaxle case mating surface.
10. Install the transfer case in the vehicle. Tighten the transfer case-to-transaxle mounting bolts and the transfer case gusset mounting bolts to 22–30 ft. lbs. (30–40 Nm).
11. Be sure to use a multi-purpose grease to lubricate all oil seal surfaces prior to reinstallation.
12. Install the remaining components in the reverse order of removal.

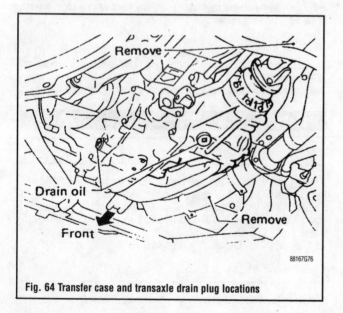

Fig. 64 Transfer case and transaxle drain plug locations

DRIVELINE

Driveshaft

REMOVAL & INSTALLATION

Sentra 4WD

▶ **See Figures 67 and 68**

These models use a driveshaft with 3 U-joints and a center support bearing. The driveshaft is balanced as an assembly. It is not recommended that it be disassembled.

☀ WARNING

It is extremely important to matchmark the driveshaft components to their mating surfaces, prior to disassembly. Failure to due so may result in a severe vibration problem, due to the misalignment of the driveline components.

1. Raise and properly support the vehicle.
2. Mark the relationship of the driveshaft flange to the differential flange.
3. Unbolt the center bearing bracket.
4. Unbolt the driveshaft flange from the differential flange.
5. Pull the driveshaft back under the rear axle.

To install:

6. Align the mating marks made in Step 1 and install the driveshaft. Tighten the flange bolts to 17–24 ft. lbs. (22–30 Nm).
7. Install the center bearing bracket and tighten the fasteners to 26–35 ft. lbs. (35–45 Nm).
8. Lower the vehicle.

U-JOINT REPLACEMENT

▶ **See Figure 69**

The driveshaft universal joints are not serviceable. Inspect the journal axial play and if it exceeds 0.00 inches, replace the driveshaft assembly.

DRIVESHAFT BALANCING

▶ **See Figure 70**

If vibration is present at high speed, inspect the driveshaft run-out first.

1. Raise the vehicle and support safely.
2. Measure the driveshaft run-out at several points by rotating the final drive companion flange by hand.
3. If the run-out exceeds 0.024 in. (0.6mm), disconnect the driveshaft at the final drive and rotate the companion flange 180 degrees and reinstall.
4. If the run-out still exists, run the driveshaft at about 30 miles per hour (48 kp/h) with the rear wheels off the ground and support safely.
5. Use a jackstand to steady a light colored pencil.

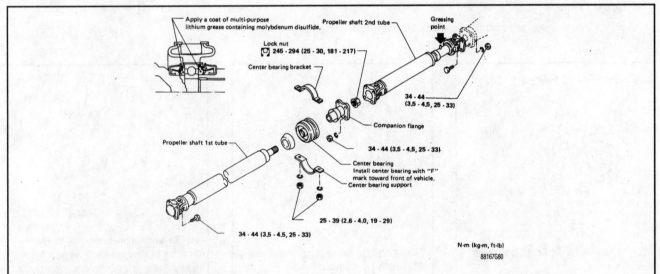

Fig. 67 Exploded view of the driveshaft assembly

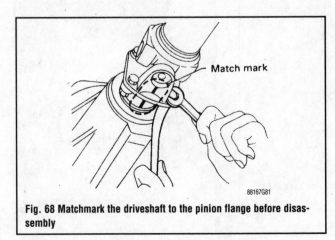

Fig. 68 Matchmark the driveshaft to the pinion flange before disassembly

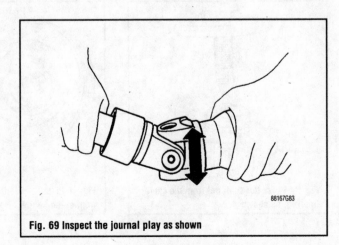

Fig. 69 Inspect the journal play as shown

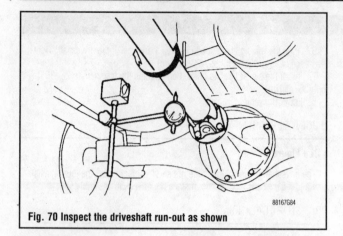

Fig. 70 Inspect the driveshaft run-out as shown

6. As the driveshaft rotates, mark the high spots on the driveshaft.

7. Place 2 hose clamps around the driveshaft opposite the high spot and recheck. Move the clamps around to try to balance the shaft.

8. If 2 clamps does not correct the vibration, replace the driveshaft, center bearing or U-joints.

Center Bearing

REMOVAL & INSTALLATION

▶ **See Figures 71 thru 76**

The center bearing is a sealed unit which must be replaced as an assembly if defective.

It is extremely important to matchmark the driveshaft components to their mating surfaces, prior to disassembly. Failure to due so may result in a severe vibration problem, due to the misalignment of the driveline components.

1. Remove the driveshaft.

2. Paint a matchmark across where the flanges behind the center yoke are joined. This is for assembly purposes. If you don't paint or somehow mark the relationship between the 2 shafts, they may be out of balance when you put them back together.

3. Remove he bolts and separate the shafts. Make a matchmark on the front driveshaft half which lines up with the mark on the flange half.

4. Hold the driveshaft using special tool ST38060002 or equivalent, while unbolting the companion flange from the front driveshaft. Do not place the front driveshaft tube in a vise. The best way is to grip the flange while loosening the nut. It is going to require some strength to remove.

5. Press the companion flange off the front driveshaft and press the center bearing from its mount.

To install:

6. The new bearing is already lubricated. Install it into the mount, making sure that the seals and so on are facing the same way as when removed.

7. Slide the companion flange, onto the front driveshaft, aligning the marks made during removal. Install the washer and locknut. If the washer and locknut are separate pieces, tighten them to 145–175 ft. lbs. (197–238 Nm). If they are a unit, tighten it to 180–217 ft. lbs. (245–295 Nm). Check that the bearing rotates freely around the driveshaft. Stake the nut.

8. Connect the companion flange to the other half of the driveshaft, aligning the marks made during removal. Tighten the bolts securely.

9. Install the driveshaft.

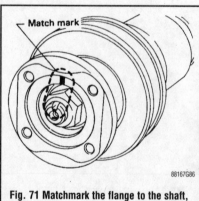

Fig. 71 Matchmark the flange to the shaft, as shown

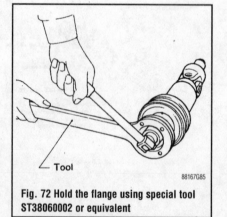

Fig. 72 Hold the flange using special tool ST38060002 or equivalent

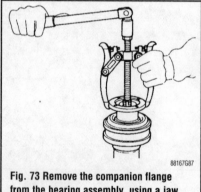

Fig. 73 Remove the companion flange from the bearing assembly, using a jaw type puller

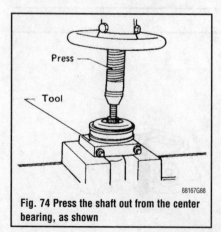

Fig. 74 Press the shaft out from the center bearing, as shown

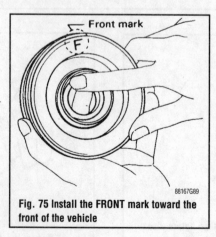

Fig. 75 Install the FRONT mark toward the front of the vehicle

Fig. 76 Stake the flange nut to the shaft

REAR AXLE

Identification

The 1988–89 Sentra 4WD uses a model R160 final drive unit with independent halfshaft assemblies.

Rear Halfshafts

REMOVAL & INSTALLATION

Sentra 4WD

▶ **See Figures 77 and 78**

1. Raise the rear of the vehicle and support it with jackstands.
2. Remove the wheel and tire assembly.
3. Pull out the wheel bearing cotter pin and then remove the adjusting cap and insulator.
4. Set the parking brake and then remove the wheel bearing locknut.
5. Disconnect and plug the hydraulic brake lines. Disconnect the parking brake cable.
6. Using a block of wood and a small mallet, carefully tap the halfshaft out of the knuckle/ backing plate assembly.
7. Unbolt the radius rod and the transverse link at the wheel end.

➡ **Before removing the transverse link mounting bolt, matchmark the toe-in adjusting plate to the link.**

8. Using a suitable prybar, carefully remove the halfshaft from the final drive.
To install:
9. Position the halfshaft into the knuckle and then insert it into the final drive; making sure the serration's are properly aligned.

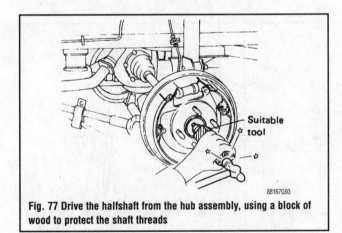

Fig. 77 Drive the halfshaft from the hub assembly, using a block of wood to protect the shaft threads

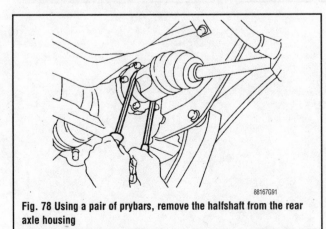

Fig. 78 Using a pair of prybars, remove the halfshaft from the rear axle housing

10. Push the shaft into the final drive and then press-fit the circlip on the halfshaft into the groove on the side gear.
11. After insertion, pull the halfshaft by hand to be certain that it is properly seated in the side gear and will not come out.
12. Install the remaining components in the reverse order of removal.
13. Bleed the brake system.

CV-JOINT OVERHAUL

▶ **See Figure 79**

Wheel Side Joint

➡ **The joint on the wheel side cannot be disassembled.**

1. Remove the halfshaft from the vehicle.
2. Matchmark the halfshaft and the joint assembly.
3. Separate the joint assembly from the halfshaft by placing the halfshaft securely in a vise and place the locknut on the end of the joint. Attach a slide hammer to the locknut and pull the joint from the halfshaft.
4. Remove the boot bands.
To install:
5. Install the boot with new boot bands.

➡ **Cover the halfshaft serration with tape so as not to damage the new boot during installation.**

6. Pack CV-joint and boot with Nissan genuine grease or equivalent:
7. Align the matchmarks and lightly tap the joint assembly onto the shaft.
8. Install the boot and secure it with both boot band clamps.
9. Install the halfshaft in the vehicle.

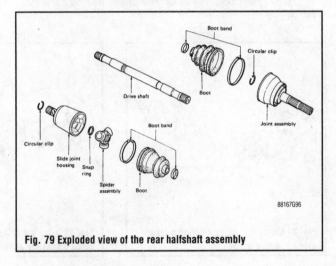

Fig. 79 Exploded view of the rear halfshaft assembly

Axle Housing Side Joint

1. Remove the halfshaft from the vehicle.
2. Place the halfshaft securely in a soft-jawed vise.
3. Remove the boot bands.
4. Matchmark the slide joint housing to the halfshaft and remove the slide joint housing.
5. Remove the snapring and matchmark the spider assembly to the halfshaft.
6. Press the spider assembly from the halfshaft.
7. Remove the CV-joint boot.
To install:
8. Install the boot and a new small clamp on the halfshaft.

➡ **Cover the halfshaft serration with tape so as not to damage the new boot during installation.**

9. Place the halfshaft in a soft-jawed vise.

10. Align the matchmarks and using a suitable driver, press the spider assembly onto the halfshaft. Install the spider assembly with the serrated chamfered edge facing the shaft.

11. Install a new snapring. The round surface should face the spider assembly.

12. Pack the slide joint housing with Nissan genuine grease or equivalent:

13. Align the matchmarks and install the slide joint housing.

14. Slide the CV-joint boot over the slide joint housing and install the large boot clamp. Secure the boot with both clamps.

15. Install the halfshaft into the vehicle.

Axle Seals

REMOVAL & INSTALLATION

▶ **See Figure 80**

1. Following the procedures outlined above, remove the appropriate half-shaft from the vehicle.

2. Remove the seal from the case using a suitable prybar.

To install:

3. Press the seal into the case using a seal installer J25809 or equivalent.

4. Install the halfshaft assembly.

5. Recheck the fluid level in the differential and fill if necessary.

Pinion Seal

REMOVAL & INSTALLATION

▶ **See Figures 81, 82 and 83**

1. Following the procedures outlined in this section, remove the driveshaft assembly.

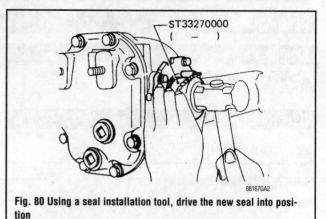

Fig. 80 Using a seal installation tool, drive the new seal into position

2. Remove the pinion nut and pull the pinion flange off using a gear puller.

3. Pry the seal from the case using a suitable prybar.

To install:

4. Install the new pinion seal using a seal installer ST30720000 or equivalent.

5. Install the pinion flange and nut. While holding the pinion flange using special tool J34311 or equivalent, tighten the nut to 123–145 ft. lbs. (167–196 Nm).

6. Using an inch lbs. torque wrench, turn the drive pinion in both directions, several times, and measure bearing preload. The preload should be 6.5–13.5 inch lbs. (0.74–1.52 Nm).

➡**In order to accurately check bearing preload, both rear halfshafts must be disconnected from rear axle housing.**

7. Install the driveshaft assembly.

8. Check the differential fluid level and fill if necessary.

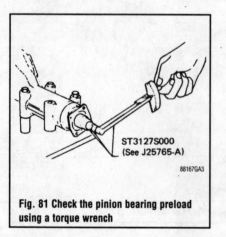

Fig. 81 Check the pinion bearing preload using a torque wrench

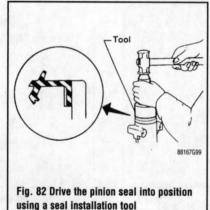

Fig. 82 Drive the pinion seal into position using a seal installation tool

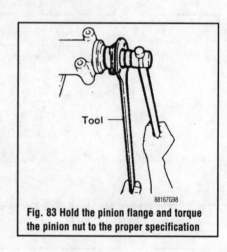

Fig. 83 Hold the pinion flange and torque the pinion nut to the proper specification

8

SUSPENSION AND STEERING

FRONT SUSPENSION

♦ **See Figure 1**

The independent front suspension system on all models covered uses MacPherson struts. Each strut combines the function of coil spring and shock absorber. The spindle is mounted to the lower part of the strut which has a single ball joint. No upper suspension arm is required in this design. The spindle and lower suspension transverse link (control arm) are located fore and aft by the tension rods to the front part of the chassis on most models. A cross-chassis sway bar is used on all models.

MacPherson Strut

REMOVAL & INSTALLATION

♦ **See Figures 2, 3, 4 and 5**

1. Raise and safely support the vehicle on jackstands.
2. Remove the wheel.

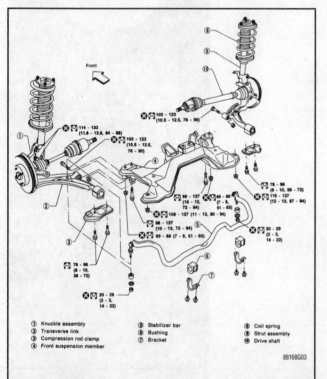

① Knuckle assembly
② Transverse link
③ Compression rod clamp
④ Front suspension member
⑤ Stabilizer bar
⑥ Bushing
⑦ Bracket
⑧ Coil spring
⑨ Strut assembly
⑩ Drive shaft

88168G03

Fig. 1 Front suspension assembly—1991–96 vehicles

3. Detach the brake tube from the strut. Disconnect the ABS wiring from the strut, if so equipped.
4. Support the transverse link with a jackstand.
5. Detach the steering knuckle from the strut.
6. Support the strut and remove the three upper attaching nuts. Remove the strut from the vehicle.

To install:

7. Install the strut assembly on the vehicle and torque the strut-to-body nuts to 23–31 ft. lbs. (32–42 Nm), the piston rod locknut to 43–54 ft. lbs. (58–73 Nm) and the strut-to-knuckle bolts to 72–87 ft. lbs. (98–118 Nm).
8. If brake line was removed, bleed brakes and install the wheel.

OVERHAUL

♦ **See Figures 6 thru 15**

❊❊ CAUTION

The coil springs are under considerable tension and can exert enough force to cause serious injury. Disassemble the struts only if the proper tools are available and use extreme caution.

The coil springs on all models must be removed with the aid of a coil spring compressor. If you don't have one, don't try to improvise by using something else; you could risk serious personal injury. The coil spring compressor is Special Tool ST35652001, or variations of that number. Basically, they are all the same tool. These are the recommended compressors, although they are probably not the only spring compressors which will work. Always follow manufacturer's instructions when operating a spring compressor. You can now buy cartridge type shock absorbers for some models; installation procedures are not the same as those given here. In this case, follow the instructions that come with the shock absorbers.

To remove the coil spring, you must first remove the strut assembly from the vehicle. Refer to the previous procedure.

1. Secure the strut assembly in a vise.
2. Attach the spring compressor to the spring. On springs with more than six coils, leave the top few coils free.
3. Remove the dust cap from the top of the strut to expose the center nut, if a dust cap is provided.
4. Compress the spring just far enough to permit the strut insulator to be turned by hand. Remove the self-locking center nut.
5. Take out the strut mounting insulator and bracket, thrust bearing, upper spring seat and bound bumper rubber from the top of the strut. Note their removal sequence and be sure to assemble them in the reverse order.
6. Remove the spring with the spring compressor still attached.

To install:

The strut assembly may be sealed from the factory with a welded piston retainer/seal. If this is the case, the complete hydraulic unit will have to be replaced. These can be purchased from a local parts retailer.

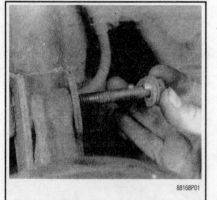

88168P01

Fig. 2 Remove the attaching bolts and . . .

88168P02

Fig. 3 . . . detach the steering knuckle from the strut

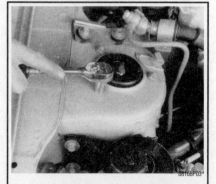

88168P03

Fig. 4 Unfasten the three nuts which secure the top of the strut . . .

Fig. 5 . . . and remove the strut from the vehicle

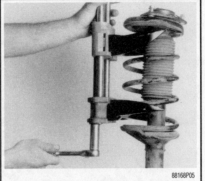

Fig. 6 With the strut secured in a vise, properly position a spring compressor

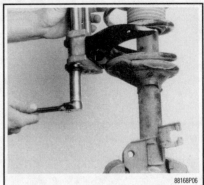

Fig. 7 Use a socket wrench to turn the compressor's adjusting rod

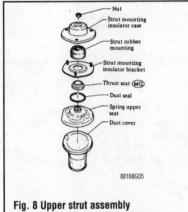

Fig. 8 Upper strut assembly

- Nut
- Strut mounting insulator case
- Strut rubber mounting
- Strut mounting insulator bracket
- Thrust seat (MG)
- Dust seal
- Spring upper seat
- Dust cover

Fig. 9 With the spring sufficiently compressed, remove the center nut at the top

Fig. 10 Remove the strut mounting insulator and bracket from the upper spring seat

Fig. 11 Remove the upper spring seat

Fig. 12 While still compressed, remove the spring . . .

Fig. 13 . . . followed by the bound bumper rubber . . .

Fig. 14 . . . and the rubber seat

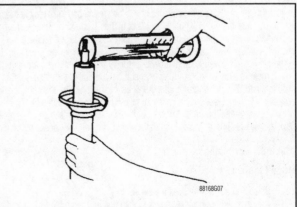

Fig. 15 Filling the strut assembly with hydraulic oil

Reassemble the strut assembly and observe the following. Make sure you assemble the unit with the shock absorber piston rod fully extended. When assembling, take care that the rubber spring seats, both top and bottom, and the spring are positioned in their grooves before releasing the spring.

7. To remove the shock absorber: Remove the dust cap (if equipped) and push the piston rod down until it bottoms. With the piston in this position, loosen and remove the gland packing shock absorber retainer. This calls for the Special Tool ST35500001, but you should be able to loosen it either with a pipe wrench or by tapping it around with a drift.

➡**If the gland tube is dirty, clean it before removing it to prevent dirt from contaminating the fluid inside the strut tube.**

8. Remove the O-ring from the top of the piston guide and lift out the piston rod together with the cylinder. Drain all of the fluid from the strut and shock components into a suitable container. Clean all parts.

➡**The piston rod, piston rod guide and cylinder are a matched set: single parts of this shock assembly should not be exchanged with parts of other assemblies.**

Assemble the shock absorber into the strut assembly with the following notes:

After installing the cylinder and piston rod assembly (the shock absorber kit) in the outer casing, remove the piston rod guide (if equipped) from the cylinder and pour the correct amount of new fluid into the cylinder and strut outer casing. To find this amount, consult the instructions with your shock absorber kit. The amount of oil should be listed. Use only Genuine Strut Oil or its equivalent.

➡**It is important that the correct amount of fluid be poured into the strut to assure correct shock absorber damping force.**

Install the O-ring, fluid and any other cylinder components. Fit the gland packing and tighten it after greasing the gland packing-to-piston rod mating surfaces.

➡**When tightening the gland packing, extend the piston rod about 3–5 in. (7.6–12.7cm) from the end of the outer casing to expel most of the air from the strut.**

After the kit is installed, bleed the air from the system in the following manner: hold the strut with its bottom end facing down. Pull the piston rod out as far as it will go. Turn the strut upside down and push the piston in as far as it will go. Repeat this procedure several times until an equal pressure is felt on both the pullout and the push in strokes of the piston rods. The remaining assembly is the reverse of disassembly.

Lower Ball Joint

INSPECTION

The lower ball joint should be replaced when play becomes excessive. The manufacturer does not publish specifications on just what constitutes excessive play, relying instead on a method of determining the force (in inch lbs.) required to keep the ball joint turning. This method is not very helpful to the backyard mechanic since it involves removing the ball joint, which is what we are trying to avoid in the first place. An effective way to determine ball joint play is to jack up the car until the wheel is just a couple of inches (about 5 centimeters) off the ground and the ball joint is unloaded (meaning you can't jack directly underneath the ball joint). Place a long bar under the tire and move the wheel and tire assembly up and down. Keep one hand on top of the tire while you are doing this. If there is over ¼ in. (6mm) of play at the top of the tire, the ball joint is probably bad. This is assuming that the wheel bearings are in good shape and properly adjusted. As a double check on this, have someone watch the ball joint while you move the tire up and down with the bar. If you can see considerable play, besides feeling play at the top of the wheel, the ball joint needs replacing.

Dial Indicator Method

♦ See Figure 16

1. Raise and safely support the vehicle.
2. Clamp a dial indicator to the transverse link and place the tip of the dial on the lower edge of the brake caliper.

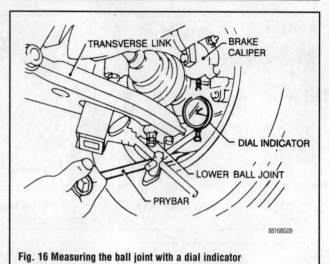

Fig. 16 Measuring the ball joint with a dial indicator

3. Zero the indicator.
4. Make sure the front wheels are facing straight-ahead and the brake pedal is fully depressed.
5. Insert a long prybar between the transverse link and the inner rim of the wheel.
6. Push down and release the prybar and observe the reading (deflection) on the dial indicator. Take several readings and use the maximum dial indicator deflection as the ball joint vertical end-play. Make sure to **0** the indicator after each reading. If the reading is not within specifications, replace the transverse link or the ball joint. Ball joint vertical end-play specifications are as follows:
   • 1983–88 Pulsar: 0.098 in. (2.5mm) or less
   • 1989–90 Pulsar: 0 in. (0mm)
   • 1982–96 Sentra: 0 in. (0mm)

REMOVAL & INSTALLATION

➡**On most late model vehicles, the transverse link (lower control arm) must be removed and then the ball joint pressed out. The ball joint should be greased every 30,000 miles (48,300km). There is a plugged hole in the bottom of the joint for installation of a grease fitting.**

1. Refer to the Drive Axle removal and installation procedures in Section 7, and remove the drive axle.
2. Remove the ball joint-to-control arm nut. Using Ball Joint Remover tool HT72520000 or equivalent, separate the ball joint from the control arm.
3. Remove the other ball joint bolts from the control arm and the ball joint from the vehicle.

To install:
4. Install the ball joint in the control arm and tighten the ball stud attaching nut (from ball joint-to-steering knuckle) to 40–51 ft. lbs. (54–69 Nm), and the ball joint to transverse link bolts to 40–47 ft. lbs. (54–64 Nm).
5. Install the drive axle.

Lower Control Arm (Transverse Link)

REMOVAL & INSTALLATION

1982–86 Vehicles

♦ See Figures 17 and 18

➡**Always use a new nut when installing the ball joint to the control arm.**

1. Raise and safely support the vehicle on jackstands.
2. Remove the wheel.
3. Matchmark the control arm's eccentric washer and the mount.
4. Remove the lower ball joint bolts from the control arm.

➡**If equipped with a stabilizer bar, disconnect it from the control arm.**

5. Remove the control arm-to-body bolts.

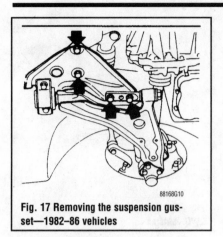

Fig. 17 Removing the suspension gusset—1982–86 vehicles

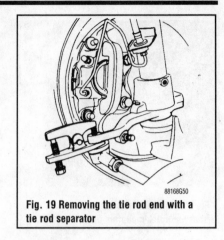

Fig. 18 Removing the transverse link—1982–86 vehicles

Fig. 19 Removing the tie rod end with a tie rod separator

6. Remove the gusset.

7. Remove the control arm from the vehicle.

To install:

➡**Failure to properly position the matchmarked washer will alter the front end alignment setting.**

8. Install the lower control arm with the eccentric washer on the vehicle, being careful to align the matchmarks. Tighten the gusset-to-body bolts to 65–87 ft. lbs. (88–118 Nm); the control arm securing nut to 72–87 ft. lbs. (98–118 Nm); the lower ball joint-to-control arm nuts to 40–47 ft. lbs. (54–64 Nm); and the stabilizer bar-to-control arm to 80–100 inch lbs. (9–11 Nm) for 2WD Sentra and Pulsar or 12–16 ft. lbs. (16–21 Nm) for 4WD Sentra.

9. Reconnect the stabilizer if so equipped to the control arm.

10. Install the wheel.

➡**When installing the link, tighten the nut securing the link spindle to the gusset. Final tightening should be made with the weight of the car on the wheels.**

1987–96 Vehicles

◗ **See Figures 19, 20, 21, 22 and 23**

➡**A ball joint removal tool will be required for this operation.**

1. Raise the vehicle and safely support it with jackstands. Remove the wheel.

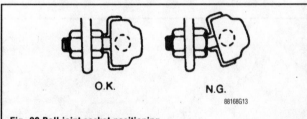

Fig. 20 Ball joint socket positioning

2. Remove the wheel bearing locknut.

3. Remove the tie rod ball joint with a puller.

4. Remove the lower strut-to-knuckle mounting bolts and separate the strut from the knuckle.

5. Separate the outer end of the halfshaft from the steering knuckle by carefully tapping it with a rubber mallet.

➡**Be sure to cover the CV-joints with a shop rag.**

6. Using a ball joint removal tool, separate the lower ball joint stud from the steering knuckle.

7. Matchmark the control arm's eccentric washer and the mount.

8. Unbolt and remove the transverse link and ball joint as an assembly.

To install:

➡**Failure to properly position the matchmarked washer will alter the front end alignment setting.**

9. Install the lower control arm to the vehicle, being careful to align the matchmarks on the eccentric washer and mount.

10. Reconnect the ball joint and halfshaft.

11. Connect the strut to the knuckle.

12. Install the tie rod ball joint.

13. Tighten the wheel bearing locknut.

14. Install the wheel and make sure the tab on the transverse link clamp is pointing in the proper direction. Final tightening of all bolts should take place with the weight of the vehicle on the wheels. Check wheel alignment.

Stabilizer Bar

REMOVAL & INSTALLATION

◗ **See Figures 24, 25, 26 and 27**

1. On the Sentra wagon, disconnect the parking brake cable at the equalizer.

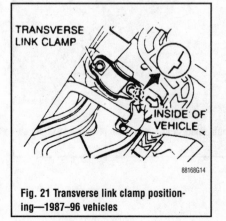

Fig. 21 Transverse link clamp positioning—1987–96 vehicles

Fig. 22 Matchmark the transverse link's eccentric washer and mount

Fig. 23 Use two wrenches to unfasten the mounting bolt

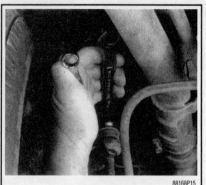

Fig. 24 Unfasten the stabilizer bar-to-transverse link mounting bolts

Fig. 25 Also unfasten the stabilizer bar mounting bracket bolts

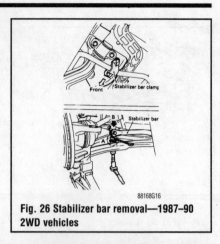

Fig. 26 Stabilizer bar removal—1987–90 2WD vehicles

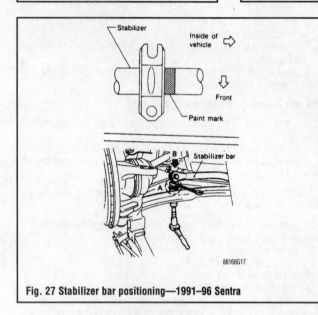

Fig. 27 Stabilizer bar positioning—1991–96 Sentra

2. On the Sentra wagon (4WD), remove the mounting nuts for the transaxle support rod and the transaxle control rod.

3. Disconnect the front exhaust pipe at the manifold and position it out of the way.

4. On the Sentra wagon (4WD), matchmark the flanges and then separate the driveshaft from the transfer case.

5. Remove the stabilizer bar-to-transverse link (lower control arm) mounting bolts.

6. Remove the 4 stabilizer bar mounting bracket bolts and then pull the bar out, around the link and exhaust pipe.

To install:

7. Install the stabilizer bar and mounting brackets. Never fully tighten the mounting bolts unless the car is resting on the ground with normal weight upon the wheels. On the 1987–90 Pulsar, be sure the stabilizer bar ball joint socket is properly positioned.

➡️When installing the stabilizer bar, make sure that the paint mark and clamp face in their correct directions (1987–96 vehicles).

8. Install the driveshaft to the transfer case if it was removed.

9. Reconnect the front exhaust pipe at the manifold.

10. Connect the parking brake cables and install any other bolts that were removed.

11. Final tightening of all bolts should take place with the weight of the vehicle on the wheels.

Front Axle Hub, Knuckle and Bearing

REMOVAL & INSTALLATION

♦ **See Figures 28, 29, 30, 31 and 32**

1982–90 Vehicles

1. Raise and support the front of the vehicle safely, then remove the wheels.
2. Remove wheel bearing locknut.
3. Remove brake clip assembly. Make sure not to twist the brake hose.
4. Remove tie rod ball joint.

➡️Cover axle boots with waste cloth or equivalent so as not to damage them when removing driveshaft. Make a matching mark on strut housing and adjusting pin before removing them.

5. Separate halfshaft from the knuckle by slightly tapping it.
6. Mark and remove the strut mounting bolts.
7. Remove the lower ball joint from the knuckle.
8. Remove the knuckle from the lower control arm.

➡️To replace the wheel bearings and races they must be pressed in and out of the knuckle assembly. To pack the wheel bearings, they will have to be removed from the knuckle assembly.

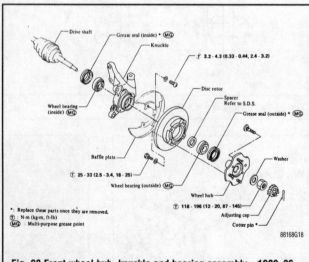

Fig. 28 Front wheel hub, knuckle and bearing assembly—1982–86 vehicles

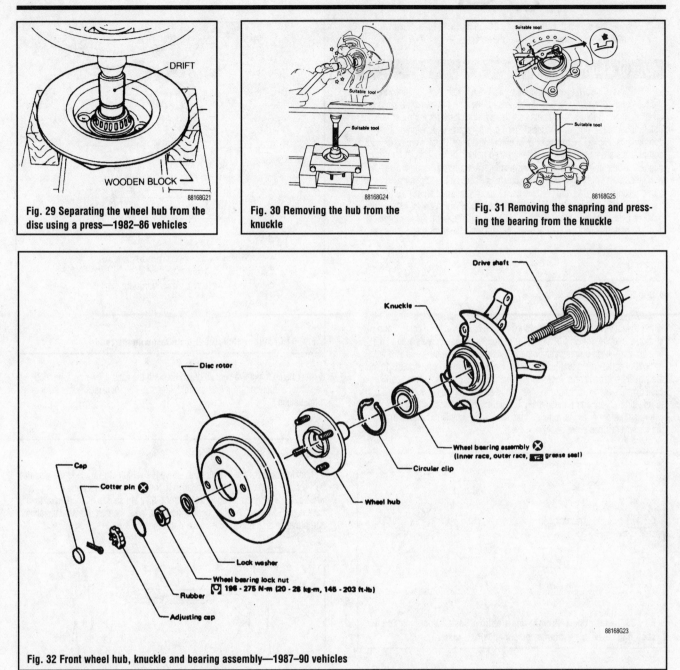

Fig. 29 Separating the wheel hub from the disc using a press—1982–86 vehicles

Fig. 30 Removing the hub from the knuckle

Fig. 31 Removing the snapring and pressing the bearing from the knuckle

Fig. 32 Front wheel hub, knuckle and bearing assembly—1987–90 vehicles

9. Install the knuckle to the lower control arm and connect the ball joint.
10. Connect the knuckle to the strut and to the halfshaft.
11. Install the tie rod ball joint.
12. Install the brake caliper assembly.
13. Install the wheel bearing locknut and torque hub nut to 145–203 ft. lbs. (197–276 Nm).
14. Install the front wheels.

1991–96 Sentra

1. Raise the vehicle and support safely. Remove the front wheel.
2. Remove the wheel bearing locknut while depressing the brake pedal.
3. Remove the brake caliper and hang with a piece of wire instead of the brake hose.
4. Remove the tie rod end using a tie rod removing tool J25730A or equivalent.
5. Separate the halfshaft from the knuckle by slightly tapping with a soft hammer.
6. Remove the strut-to-knuckle retaining bolts and separate.

7. Loosen the lower ball joint nut and separate using a ball joint separator J25730A or equivalent.
8. Place the assembly in a vise. Drive the hub with the inner race from the knuckle with a suitable tool. Remove the inner and outer grease seals.
9. Remove the bearing inner race and outer grease seal.
10. Remove the snapring and press out the bearing outer race.

To install:
11. Press a new wheel bearing into the knuckle assembly not exceeding 3.3 tons (3,000 kg) pressure.
12. Install the snapring and pack the grease seals with chassis grease.
13. Install the inner and outer grease seals.
14. Press the wheel hub into the knuckle not exceeding 3.3 tons (3,000 kg) pressure.
15. Check bearing operation and force the assembly into the knuckle to 3.9–5.5 tons (7,800–5,000 kg) pressure.
16. Make sure the bearings rotate freely.
17. Install the knuckle and wheel hub. Torque the wheel bearing locknut to 145–203 ft. lbs. (196–275 Nm).
18. Install the lower ball joint and torque the nut to 43–54 ft. lbs. (59–74 Nm).

19. Install the strut bolts and torque to 84–98 ft. lbs. (114–133 Nm).
20. Install the front wheels and lower the vehicle.

Wheel Alignment

If the tires are worn unevenly, if the vehicle is not stable on the highway or if the handling seems uneven in spirited driving, the wheel alignment should be checked. If an alignment problem is suspected, first check for improper tire inflation and other possible causes. These can be worn suspension or steering components, accident damage or even unmatched tires. If any worn or damaged components are found, they must be replaced before the wheels can be properly aligned. Wheel alignment requires very expensive equipment and involves minute adjustments which must be accurate; it should only be performed by a trained technician. Take your vehicle to a properly equipped shop.

Following is a description of the alignment angles which are adjustable on most vehicles and how they affect vehicle handling. Although these angles can apply to both the front and rear wheels, usually only the front suspension is adjustable.

CASTER

▶ **See Figure 33**

Looking at a vehicle from the side, caster angle describes the steering axis rather than a wheel angle. The steering knuckle is attached to a control arm or strut at the top and a control arm at the bottom. The wheel pivots around the line between these points to steer the vehicle. When the upper point is tilted back, this is described as positive caster. Having a positive caster tends to make the wheels self-centering, increasing directional stability. Excessive positive caster makes the wheels hard to steer, while an uneven caster will cause a pull to one side. Overloading the vehicle or sagging rear springs will affect caster, as will raising the rear of the vehicle. If the rear of the vehicle is lower than normal, the caster becomes more positive.

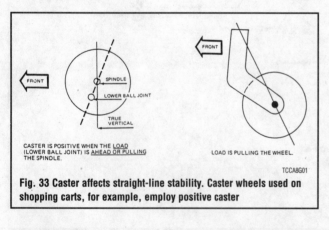

Fig. 33 Caster affects straight-line stability. Caster wheels used on shopping carts, for example, employ positive caster

CAMBER

▶ **See Figure 34**

Looking from the front of the vehicle, camber is the inward or outward tilt of the top of wheels. When the tops of the wheels are tilted in, this is negative camber; if they are tilted out, it is positive. In a turn, a slight amount of negative

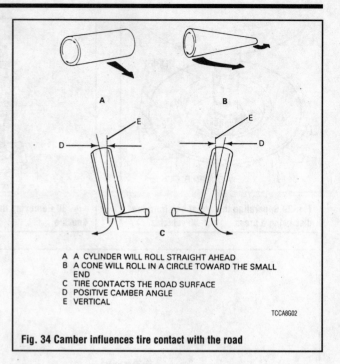

A A CYLINDER WILL ROLL STRAIGHT AHEAD
B A CONE WILL ROLL IN A CIRCLE TOWARD THE SMALL END
C TIRE CONTACTS THE ROAD SURFACE
D POSITIVE CAMBER ANGLE
E VERTICAL

Fig. 34 Camber influences tire contact with the road

camber helps maximize contact of the tire with the road. However, too much negative camber compromises straight-line stability, increases bump steer and torque steer.

TOE

▶ **See Figure 35**

Looking down at the wheels from above the vehicle, toe angle is the distance between the front of the wheels, relative to the distance between the back of the wheels. If the wheels are closer at the front, they are said to be toed-in or to have negative toe. A small amount of negative toe enhances directional stability and provides a smoother ride on the highway.

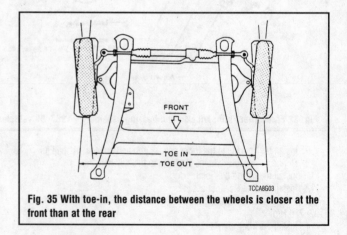

Fig. 35 With toe-in, the distance between the wheels is closer at the front than at the rear

REAR SUSPENSION

▶ **See Figures 36 and 37**

Coil Springs

REMOVAL & INSTALLATION

1982–86 Vehicles

1. Raise and safely support the rear of the vehicle with jackstands, then remove the wheel.

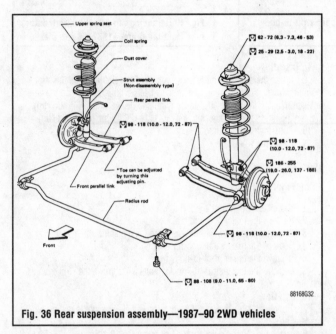

Fig. 36 Rear suspension assembly—1987–90 2WD vehicles

2. Support the lower end of the rear arm with a jackstand.
3. Remove the lower end bolt from the shock absorber.
4. Slowly, lower the jack and remove the coil spring.
5. To install, reverse the removal procedures. Tighten the shock absorber's lower bolt to 51–65 ft. lbs. (69–88 Nm).

Shock Absorber

REMOVAL & INSTALLATION

1982–86 Vehicles

1. Raise and support the rear of the vehicle on jackstands.
2. Remove the upper nut and the lower mounting bolt form the shock absorber.
3. Remove the shock absorber from the vehicle.
4. To install, reverse the removal procedures. Tighten the upper shock absorber nut to 78–104 inch lbs. (9–12 Nm) and the lower shock absorber bolt to 51–65 ft. lbs. (69–88 Nm).

TESTING

▶ **See Figure 38**

The purpose of the shock absorber is simply to limit the motion of the spring during compression and rebound cycles. If the vehicle is not equipped with these motion dampers, the up and down motion would multiply until the vehicle was alternately trying to leap off the ground and to pound itself into the pavement.

Contrary to popular rumor, the shocks do not affect the ride height of the vehicle. This is controlled by other suspension components such as springs and tires. Worn shock absorbers can affect handling; if the front of the vehicle is rising or falling excessively, the "footprint" of the tires changes on the pavement and steering is affected.

The simplest test of the shock absorber is simply push down on one corner of the unladen vehicle and release it. Observe the motion of the body as it is released. In most cases, it will come up beyond it original rest position, dip

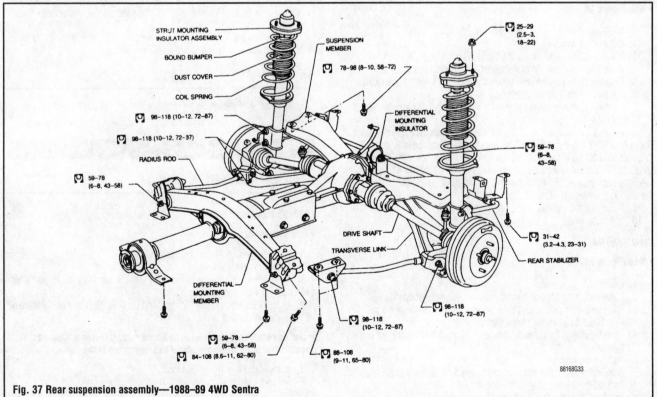

Fig. 37 Rear suspension assembly—1988–89 4WD Sentra

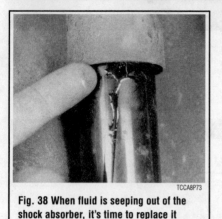

Fig. 38 When fluid is seeping out of the shock absorber, it's time to replace it

TCCA8P73

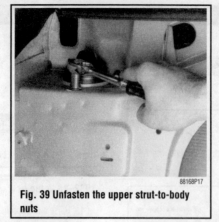

Fig. 39 Unfasten the upper strut-to-body nuts

88168P17

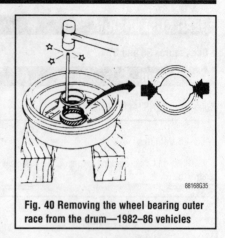

Fig. 40 Removing the wheel bearing outer race from the drum—1982–86 vehicles

88168G35

back below it and settle quickly to rest. This shows that the damper is controlling the spring action. Any tendency to excessive pitch (up-and-down) motion or failure to return to rest within 2-3 cycles is a sign of poor function within the shock absorber. Oil-filled shocks may have a light film of oil around the seal, resulting from normal breathing and air exchange. This should NOT be taken as a sign of failure, but any sign of thick or running oil definitely indicates failure. Gas filled shocks may also show some film at the shaft; if the gas has leaked out, the shock will have almost no resistance to motion.

While each shock absorber can be replaced individually, it is recommended that they be changed as a pair (both front or both rear) to maintain equal response on both sides of the vehicle. Chances are quite good that if one has failed, its mate is weak also.

MacPherson Struts

REMOVAL & INSTALLATION

1987–90 Vehicles

EXCEPT 4WD SENTRA

▶ See Figure 36

1. Raise and safely support the rear of the vehicle on jackstands.
2. Remove the wheel.
3. Disconnect the brake tube and parking brake cable.
4. If necessary, remove the brake assembly and wheel bearing.
5. Disconnect the parallel links and radius rod from the strut or knuckle.
6. Support the strut with a jackstand.
7. Remove the strut upper end nuts and then remove the strut from the vehicle.

To install:

8. Install the strut assembly to the vehicle and tighten the strut-to-parallel link nuts to 65–87 ft. lbs. (88–118 Nm), the strut-to-radius rod nuts to 54–69 ft. lbs. (64–94 Nm) and the strut-to-body nuts to 23–31 ft. lbs. (31–42 Nm). Torque the radius rod-to-knuckle nuts to 43–61 ft. lbs. (58–83 Nm), the strut-to-knuckle and parallel link-to-knuckle bolts to 72–87 ft. lbs. (98–118 Nm) and the strut-to-body nuts to 18–22 ft. lbs. (25–30 Nm).

9. Reconnect the brake tube and parking brake cable.
10. Install the wheel.

4WD SENTRA

▶ See Figure 37

1. Block the front wheels.
2. Raise and safely support the rear of the vehicle with jackstands.
3. Position a floor jack under the transverse link on the side of the strut to be removed. Raise it just enough to support the strut.
4. Open the rear of the car and remove the 3 nuts that attach the top of the strut to the body.
5. Remove the wheel.
6. Remove the brake line from its bracket and position it out of the way.
7. Remove the 2 lower strut-to-knuckle mounting bolts.
8. Carefully lower the floor jack and remove the strut.

To install:

9. Install the strut assembly in the vehicle. Final tightening of the strut mounting bolts should take place with the wheels on the ground and the vehicle unladen. Tighten the upper strut-to-body nuts to 33–40 ft. lbs. (45–60 Nm). Tighten the lower strut-to-knuckle bolts to 111–120 ft. lbs. (151–163 Nm).

10. Connect the brake line.
11. Install the wheel.

1991–96 Sentra

▶ See Figure 39

1. Raise the vehicle and support it safely.
2. Remove the rear wheel and brake caliper.
3. Disconnect the parallel link, radius rod and stabilizer hardware.
4. Remove the rear seat and trim panel.
5. Remove the upper strut-to-body nuts.
6. Remove the lower strut-to-knuckle bolts and remove the strut from the vehicle.

To install:

7. Tighten all suspension bolts when the vehicle's weight is resting on the suspension.

8. Install the strut and tighten the upper nuts to 18–22 ft. lbs. (25–29 Nm), lower strut bolts to 72–98 ft. lbs. (98–133 Nm) and parallel link bolts to 72–98 ft. lbs. (98–133 Nm).

9. Install the rear seat and trim panel.
10. Lower the vehicle and have the rear end aligned.

OVERHAUL

Refer to the MacPherson Strut procedure in the Front Suspension portion of this section.

Rear Wheel Bearings

REMOVAL & INSTALLATION

1982–86 Vehicles

▶ See Figure 40

1. Raise and support the vehicle safely.
2. Remove the rear wheels.
3. Work off center hub cap by using thin tool. If necessary tap around it with a soft hammer while removing.
4. Using needlenose pliers, straighten and pull out the cotter pin, then take off the adjusting cap and wheel bearing locknut.

➥**During removal, be careful to avoid damaging O-ring in dust cap. A circular clip holds the inner wheel bearing in the brake hub.**

5. Remove drum with bearing inside.
6. Remove bearing outer race from drum using long brass drift pin or equivalent.

To install:

7. Install the bearing outer race as follows: Grind about 0.010 in. (2.5mm) from the outside circumference of the old outer bearing race. Use this home-made tool as a race installer tool. Install the inner bearing and grease seal in the brake drum and install the drum on the vehicle.

➡️**The rear wheel bearings must be adjusted after installation.**

8. Install the outer bearing assembly, wheel bearing locknut, adjusting cap and a new cotter pin.

9. Install the center cap and the wheel assembly. To remove the wheel bearing races, knock them out of the brake drum using a suitable brass punch.

1987–96 Vehicles

EXCEPT 4WD SENTRA

♦ **See Figures 41 and 42**

➡️To perform this procedure, a large 3-ton (3,000 kg) press and special tools ST33220000, J25804–01 and J26082, or equivalent, are required. The press must be able to measure pressure. You might be able to engage the services of a machine shop to perform this procedure.

> ※※ **CAUTION**
>
> **Since brake linings may contain asbestos, a known carcinogen, don't use compressed air to remove brake dust from these parts. Use of compressed air can cause you to inhale asbestos fibers.**

1. Raise the car and support it securely via the body. Remove the rear wheels.

2. Remove the brake caliper and hang by a piece of wire (1991–92 Sentra). Remove the wheel bearing locknut. Then, remove the brake drum/hub or disc/hub and bearing assembly from the spindle.

3. Invert the brake drum or disc and carefully pry the circlip out of the inside diameter of the drum. Then, utilize ST33220000 J25804–01 and a press to force the bearing assembly down and out of the brake drum by pressing it toward the inside of the drum or disc with the drum suspended on blocks.

To install:

4. Check the circlip for cracks or any sign that it has been sprung (bent inward). Have the hub inspected for cracks by a machine shop equipped with a magnetic or dye test. Do the same with the spindle.

5. Apply multipurpose grease to the seal lip. Then, press a new bearing assembly into the hub from the inside using the press and ST33220000 J26082. Be sure not to press the inner race of the wheel bearing assembly and to carefully avoid damaging the grease seal. If the bearing cannot be pressed in with a pressure of 3 tons (3,000 kg), replace the hub.

6. Install a new circlip into the groove in the drum/hub or disc.

7. Install the hub onto the spindle. Install the wheel bearing locknut and tighten it to 137–188 ft. lbs. (186–256 Nm).

4WD SENTRA

➡️To perform this procedure, you will need special tools designed to be used with a hammer to drive inner and outer bearing races from the rear knuckles of 4WD Sentras. You will also need a large press, and a tool designed to transfer the power of that press to the bearing to install it. Also needed is a special tool to transfer the power of a 5.5 ton (5,000 kg) press to the bearing and such a press to apply pressure to the bearing to test preload.

> ※※ **CAUTION**
>
> **Since brake linings may contain asbestos, a known carcinogen, don't use compressed air to remove brake dust from these parts. Use of compressed air can cause you to inhale asbestos fibers.**

1. Raise the car and support it by the body. Remove the rear wheels.

2. Disconnect the brake line at the connection and plug the openings.

3. Cover the driveshaft rubber boots with rags. Tap the end of the driveshaft very lightly with a hammer, block of wood, and a suitable broad ended punch to free the driveshaft from the knuckle.

4. Matchmark the rear bolt installation angle to retain alignment. Then, remove the nuts and bolts fastening the control arm to the knuckle. Unbolt the radius rod from the knuckle. Unbolt the knuckle from the strut and remove it.

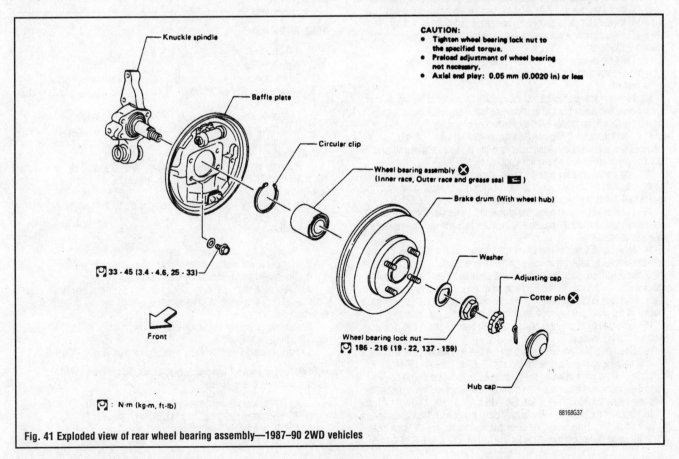

CAUTION:
- Tighten wheel bearing lock nut to the specified torque.
- Preload adjustment of wheel bearing not necessary.
- Axial end play: 0.05 mm (0.0020 in) or less

Knuckle spindle
Baffle plate
Circular clip
Wheel bearing assembly ✕
(Inner race, Outer race and grease seal ▤)
Brake drum (With wheel hub)
Washer
Adjusting cap
Cotter pin ✕
Wheel bearing lock nut
186 - 216 (19 - 22, 137 - 159)
Hub cap
Front
33 - 45 (3.4 - 4.6, 25 - 33)
: N·m (kg-m, ft-lb)

88168G37

Fig. 41 Exploded view of rear wheel bearing assembly—1987–90 2WD vehicles

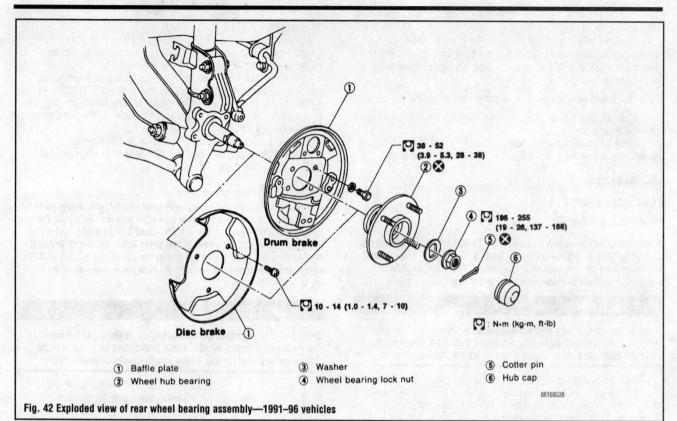

Drum brake

Disc brake

38 - 52
(3.9 - 5.3, 28 - 38)

186 - 255
(19 - 26, 137 - 186)

10 - 14 (1.0 - 1.4, 7 - 10)

N·m (kg-m, ft-lb)

① Baffle plate ③ Washer ⑤ Cotter pin
② Wheel hub bearing ④ Wheel bearing lock nut ⑥ Hub cap

88168G38

Fig. 42 Exploded view of rear wheel bearing assembly—1991–96 vehicles

5. Mount the knuckle in a vise and drive the hub out of the knuckle via the inner race with a tool such as J25804–01 and hammer.

6. Use a press to force the outboard bearing inner race from the hub. You will need blocks, a press, and ST30031000. Remove the other grease seal.

7. With the knuckle in a vise, drive the bearing inner race and grease seal out of the knuckle. Use an appropriate, cone shaped special tool and hammer.

8. Cautiously remove the inner and outer circlips from the knuckle with pointed instruments.

9. Drive the bearing outer race out of the knuckle with a hammer and appropriate, cone shaped special tool.

To install:

10. Have a machine shop inspect the knuckle for cracks with a magnetic or dye process. Replace radius rod or transverse link bushings, if necessary. Inspect the C-clips and replace if they are cracked or sprung.

11. Install the inner C-clip into the knuckle, making sure it seats in its groove. Then, press a new bearing outer race into the knuckle with a suitable tool and press, without using any lubricant.

12. Apply wheel bearing grease to each bearing, working the grease thoroughly into the areas between the rollers. Also apply the grease to the lip of the grease seal. Install the bearings and grease seal into the knuckle.

13. Install the outer C-clip into the groove in the knuckle. Then, use an appropriate tool to apply the pressure to the outer race and tap it to install the race into the hub.

14. Now, install a special tool onto the top of the hub that will drive the hub onto the knuckle by applying pressure on the inner race only. Support the hub at the center only. Then, place the assembly in a press and press the hub into the knuckle with about 3 tons (3,000 kg) force. Now, increase the pressure on the press to 5.5 tons (5,000 kg). Spin the knuckle several turns in each direction to make sure the wheel bearing operates smoothly (preload is not excessive).

15. Coat the lips of the inner grease seal with bearing grease and then install it into the knuckle.

16. Slide the driveshaft splines through the center of the wheel hub. Bolt the knuckle onto the strut and torque the bolts to 72–87 ft. lbs. (98–118 Nm).

17. Install the bolts attaching the transverse link to the steering knuckle. Align the matchmarks made earlier to maintain rear wheel alignment. Install the nuts and torque them to 72–87 ft. lbs. (98–118 Nm).

18. Connect the brake line. Thoroughly bleed the brake system as described in the next section. Then, install the wheel bearing locknut, have a helper hold the brake pedal down, and torque the locknut to 174–231 ft. lbs. (237–314

Nm). Check wheel bearing axial (end) play with a dial indicator. It should be 0.05mm or less. Install the wheels.

ADJUSTMENT

1982–86 Vehicles

1. Raise the rear of the vehicle and support it on jackstands.
2. Remove the wheel.
3. Remove the bearing dust cap with a pair of channel locks pliers.
4. Remove the cotter pin and retaining nut cap (if equipped), dispose of the cotter pin.
5. Tighten the wheel bearing nut to 18–22 ft. lbs. (25–30 Nm).
6. Rotate the drum back and forth a few revolutions to snug down the bearing.
7. After turning the wheel, recheck the torque of the nut, then loosen it 90° from its position.
8. Install the retaining nut cap (if equipped). Align the cotter pin holes in the nut or nut cap with the hole in the spindle by turning the nut no more than 15° to align the holes.
9. Install the cotter pin, bend up its ends and install the dust cap.

4WD Sentra

1. Raise and support the vehicle safely.
2. Remove wheel bearing locknut while depressing brake pedal.
3. Disconnect brake hydraulic line and parking brake cable.
4. Separate driveshaft from knuckle by slightly tapping it with suitable tool. Cover axle boots with waste cloth so as not to damage them when removing driveshaft.
5. Remove all knuckle retaining bolts and nuts. Make a matchmark before removing the adjusting pin.
6. Remove knuckle and inner and outer circular clips. Remove wheel bearings.

➡**To remove the wheel bearing races, knock them out of the knuckle using a suitable brass punch.**

7. Install the knuckle with wheel bearings to the driveshaft.
8. Connect brake hydraulic line and parking brake cable.
9. Install the wheel bearing locknut.
10. Bleed the brakes.

STEERING

Steering Wheel

☀ CAUTION

To avoid rendering the SRS (Supplemental Restraint System) inoperative, which could lead to personal injury or death in the event of a severe frontal collision, extreme caution must be taken when servicing the electrical related systems. All SRS electrical wiring harnesses and connectors are covered with YELLOW outer insulation. Do not use electrical test equipment on any circuit related to the SRS (air bag).

Fig. 43 With the wheels pointing straight ahead, the steering wheel should be centered

REMOVAL & INSTALLATION

Without Air Bag (SRS)

♦ See Figures 43 thru 50

1. Position the wheels in the straight ahead direction. The steering wheel should be right side up and level.
2. Disconnect the battery ground cable.
3. Some models have countersunk screws on the back of the steering wheel; remove these screws and pull off the horn pad.

➡ Some models have a horn wire running from the pad to the steering wheel; disconnect it.

Fig. 44 Unfasten the screws from the back of the steering wheel

Fig. 45 Disconnect the horn wire between the pad and steering wheel

Fig. 46 Use a socket wrench to unfasten . . .

Fig. 47 . . . and remove the steering wheel attaching nut

Fig. 48 Before removal, matchmark the top of the steering column shaft and wheel flange

Fig. 49 Attach a steering wheel puller and tighten the center bolt . . .

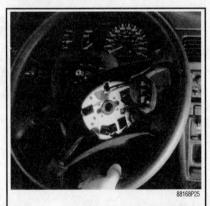

Fig. 50 . . . to remove the steering wheel

4. Remove the rest of the horn switching mechanism, noting the relative location of the parts. Remove the mechanism only if it hinders subsequent wheel removal procedures.

5. Matchmark the top of the steering column shaft and the steering wheel flange.

6. Remove the attaching nut. Using Steering Wheel Remover tool ST27180001 or equivalent, pull the steering wheel from the steering column.

➡ **Do not strike the shaft with a hammer, which may cause the column to collapse.**

7. Install the steering wheel in the reverse order of removal, aligning the punch marks; DO NOT drive or hammer the wheel.

8. Tighten the steering wheel nut to 29–40 ft. lbs. (39–54 Nm).

9. Reinstall the horn button, pad or ring.

With Air Bag (SRS)

◆ **See Figures 51, 52 and 53**

❋❋❋ CAUTION

To avoid rendering the SRS (Supplemental Restraint System) inoperative, which could lead to personal injury or death in the event of a severe frontal collision, extreme caution must be taken when servicing the electrical related systems. All SRS electrical wiring harnesses and connectors are covered with YELLOW outer insulation. Do not use electrical test equipment on any circuit related to the SRS.

1. Position the wheels in the straight ahead direction. The steering wheel should be right side up and level.

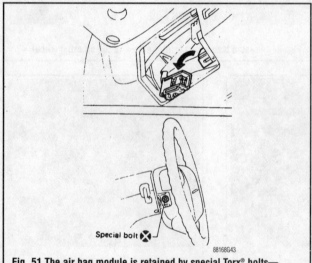

Fig. 51 The air bag module is retained by special Torx® bolts— 1991–96 Sentra

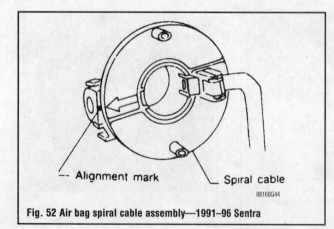

Fig. 52 Air bag spiral cable assembly—1991–96 Sentra

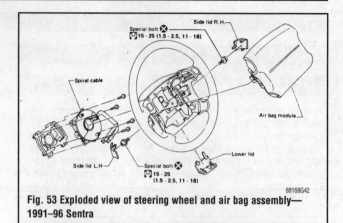

Fig. 53 Exploded view of steering wheel and air bag assembly— 1991–96 Sentra

2. Disconnect the battery ground cable, then wait at least 10 minutes to disarm the SRS, as described in Section 6.

3. Some models have countersunk screws on the back of the steering wheel; if so equipped, remove the screws and pull off the horn pad.

➡ **Some models have a horn wire running from the pad to the steering wheel; if so equipped, disconnect it.**

4. Remove the rest of the horn switching mechanism, noting the relative location of the parts. Remove the mechanism only if it hinders subsequent wheel removal procedures.

5. Matchmark the top of the steering column shaft and the steering wheel flange.

6. Remove the attaching nut. Using Steering Wheel Remover tool ST27180001 or equivalent, pull the steering wheel from the steering column.

➡ **Do not strike the shaft with a hammer; doing so may cause the column to collapse.**

7. Install the steering wheel in the reverse order of removal, aligning the punch marks; DO NOT drive or hammer the wheel.

8. Tighten the steering wheel nut to 29–40 ft. lbs. (39–54 Nm).

9. Reinstall the horn button, pad or ring.

10. Arm the SRS, as described in Section 6.

Turn Signal Switch

REMOVAL & INSTALLATION

On many later models, the turn signal switch is part of a combination switch. The whole unit is removed together.

1982–86 Sentra

1. Refer to the Steering Wheel removal and installation procedures in this section, and remove the steering wheel.

2. Remove the steering column cover(s).

3. Disconnect the electrical connectors from the switch.

4. Remove the retaining screws and the switch from the steering column.

5. To install, reverse the removal procedures.

➡ **Many models have turn signal switches with a tab that must fit into a hole in the steering shaft, in order for the system to return the switch to the neutral position after the turn has been made. Be sure to align the tab and the hole when installing.**

1983–90 Pulsar and 1987–96 Sentra

1. Disconnect the negative battery terminal.

2. Remove the steering column covers.

3. Disconnect the electrical connector from the turn signal side of the combination switch.

4. Remove the retaining screws and separate the turn signal switch from the combination switch.

5. To install, reverse the removal procedures.

Ignition Switch and Lock Cylinder

REMOVAL & INSTALLATION

The steering lock/ignition switch assembly is attached to the steering column by special screws whose heads shear off on installation. The screws must be drilled out to remove the assembly.

1. Refer to the Steering Wheel removal and installation procedures in this section, and remove the steering wheel.
2. Remove the steering column cover(s).
3. Using a drill, drill out the self-shear type screws of the steering lock retainer.

➡ **The 1991–96 Sentra models use only 2 self-shearing screws to hold the steering lock onto the steering column. All other models use 2 self-shearing screws and 2 regular screws.**

4. Remove the screws and the steering lock from the steering column.
To install:
5. Use new self-shearing screws. Tighten the self-shearing type screws until the heads break off.
6. Install the steering column cover and steering wheel as outlined in this section.

Tie Rod Ends (Steering Side Rods)

REMOVAL & INSTALLATION

⬧ **See Figures 54 thru 59**

1. Raise the front of the vehicle and support it on jackstands. Remove the wheel.
2. Locate the faulty tie rod end. It will have a lot of play in it and the dust cover will probably be ripped.

3. Remove the cotter pin and the tie rod ball joint stud nut. Note the position of the steering linkage.
4. Loosen the tie rod end-to-steering gear (tie rod) locknut.
5. Using the Ball Joint Remover tool HT72520000, remove the tie rod ball joint from the strut or steering knuckle.
6. Unscrew the tie rod end from the tie rod, counting the number of turns it takes to completely free it.
To install:
7. Install the new tie rod end, turning it in exactly as far as you screwed out the old one. Make sure it is correctly positioned in relationship to the steering gear.
8. Fit the ball joint and nut, tighten them and install a new cotter pin. Tighten the ball joint stud nut to 22–36 ft. lbs. (30–49 Nm) and the ball joint-to-tie rod end locknut to 27–34 ft. lbs. (37–46 Nm).

➡ **Before finally tightening the tie rod locknut or clamp, adjust the toe-in of the vehicle to a rough setting, as described under Front Suspension. Have a qualified alignment technician align the front end.**

Manual Steering Gear

REMOVAL & INSTALLATION

⬧ **See Figure 60**

1982–86 Vehicles

1. Raise and support the car on jackstands.
2. Using the Ball Joint Remover tool HT72520000, remove the tie rod from the knuckle.
3. Loosen, but do not remove, the steering gear mounting bolts.
4. Remove the steering column lower joint.
5. Unbolt and remove the gear.
To install:
6. Install the steering gear assembly to the vehicle. Torque the tie rod-to-steering knuckle nut to 26–35 ft. lbs. (34–48 Nm), the steering gear-to-frame

Fig. 54 Use a pair of needlenose pliers to straighten and remove the cotter pin

Fig. 55 Use a wrench to remove the tie rod ball joint stud nut

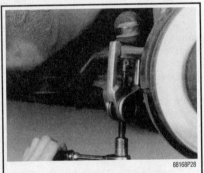

Fig. 56 Use a ball joint removal tool to press the ball joint from the steering knuckle

Fig. 57 Unthread the tie rod end from the tie rod

Fig. 58 To ease installation, matchmark the location of the tie rod end locknut . .

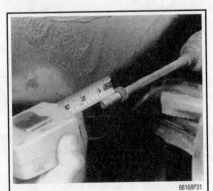

Fig. 59 . . . or note the length of the tie rod's exposed threads

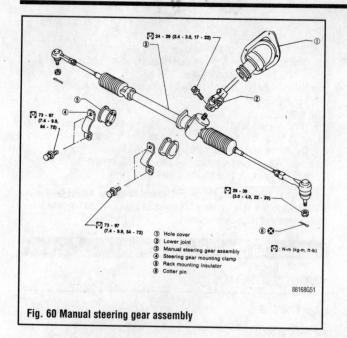

① Hole cover
② Lower joint
③ Manual steering gear assembly
④ Steering gear mounting clamp
⑤ Rack mounting insulator
⑥ Cotter pin

N·m (kg-m, ft-lb)

88168G51

Fig. 60 Manual steering gear assembly

clamp bolts to 43–58 ft. lbs. (58–78 Nm), the lower joint-to-pinion gear bolt to 22–29 ft. lbs. (29–39 Nm) and the lower joint-to-steering column bolt to 22–29 ft. lbs. (29–39 Nm).

➡**When installing the lower steering joint to the steering gear, make sure that the wheels are aligned with the vehicle and that the steering joint slot is aligned with the steering gear cap or spacer mark.**

1987–96 Vehicles

1. Raise and support the vehicle safely and remove the wheels.
2. Disconnect the tie rod from the steering knuckle and loosen the steering gear attaching bolts.
3. Remove the bolt securing the lower joint to the steering gear pinion and remove the lower joint from the pinion
.4. Remove the bolts holding the steering gear housing to the body, and remove the steering gear and linkage assembly from the vehicle.
  To install:
5. Install the assembly into the vehicle. When fitting the lower U-joint, make sure the attaching bolt is aligned perfectly with the cut out in the splined end of the steering column shaft.
6. Tighten the steering gear mounting clamp bolts to 54–72 ft. lbs. (73–97 Nm). Tighten the tie rod end nuts to 22–29 ft. lbs. (29–39 Nm).
7. Have the front end aligned by a qualified alignment technician.

ADJUSTMENTS

1982–86 Vehicles

1. Remove the steering gear from the car as previously outlined. Disconnect the tie rod ends and remove the boots.
2. Turn the pinion shaft to neutral (centered) position. This puts the spacer at –38.3° to –25.3° on 1982–84 models, and –33.52 to –46.5° on 1985 models; it sets the guide chip at 43.5° to 56.5° on 1986 models.
3. On 1982–84 models, measure pinion rotating torque with an inch lb. torque wrench working on the pinion shaft. It must be 13 inch lbs. (1.5 Nm) or less. Measure rack starting force with a spring scale. Rack starting force must be 18–40 lb. (8–18 kg) Loosen the locknut and adjust the retainer adjusting screw as necessary.
4. On 1985 and 1986 models, measure the pinion shaft rotating torque with an inch lb. torque wrench on the pinion shaft. Rotate the shaft slowly from its neutral or centered position 180° in both directions, watching for the spot where torque is at its greatest level. Loose en the adjusting screw with the pinion at this position and then hand-tighten the adjusting screw until its end touches the retainer. Hold the adjustment and tighten the locknut.
5. On 1985 and 1986 models, now rotate the pinion from its centered posi-

tion to the end of the rack and make sure torque is no more than 13 inch lbs. (1.5 Nm) on 1985 models and 16 inch lbs. (1.8 Nm) on 1986 models.
6. Reassemble the steering gear linkage and install the gear in the car.

1987–90 Vehicles

1. Remove the steering gear from the car as previously outlined. Disconnect the tie rod ends and remove the boots.
2. Turn the pinion shaft to neutral (centered) position. This puts the guide chip at neutral position (6° either side of center).
3. Loosen the locknut. Tighten the adjusting screw to 43 inch lbs. (4.9 Nm). Then, loosen it and tighten it to this torque again.
4. Loosen the adjusting screw and torque it to 1.7 inch lbs. (0.19 Nm).
5. Rotate the pinion to move the rack back and forth all the way through two full cycles. Then, return it to neutral position.
6. Slowly rotate the pinion and measure rotating torque through the entire 180° range either side of neutral. Find the point where rotating force is at its maximum. Loosen the adjusting screw at this point. Then, torque it to 26 inch lbs. (3.0 Nm).
7. Now check the pinion rotating torque. Traveling 100° either side of neutral position, it should average 6.1–10.4 inch lbs. (0.70–1.20 Nm). It must not fluctuate more than 2.6 inch lbs. (0.30 Nm).
8. If necessary, loosen the adjusting screw until the pinion rotating torque is within specification. Hold the adjusting nut in this position and torque the locknut to 29–43 ft. lbs. (39–58 Nm). If this will not correct the rotating torque, it will be necessary to replace the retaining spring.

1991–96 Sentra

1. Set the gears in the neutral position and loosen the locknut.
2. Torque the adjusting screw 2 times to 26 inch lbs. (2.9 Nm).
3. Loosen the adjusting screw and retorque to 1.7 inch lbs. (0.2 Nm).
4. Rotate the pinion to move the rack back and forth 2 times. Return to the neutral position.
5. Slowly rotate the pinion and measure the rotating torque in a 180° range. Find the position where the rotating torque is maximum.
6. Loosen the adjusting screw at that position and torque the adjusting screw to 26 inch lbs. (2.9 Nm), then back it off 50–70°.
7. Prevent the adjusting nut from turning and torque the locknut to 29–43 ft. lbs. (39–59 Nm).
8. Check the steering gear does not bind.

OVERHAUL

Overhaul of the manual steering gear is recommended to be performed by qualified steering gear rebuilders. The cost for specific components may not be as cost effective as purchasing a rebuilt unit.

Power Steering Gear

REMOVAL & INSTALLATION

1982–86 Vehicles

1. Raise and support the car on jackstands.
2. Disconnect the hose clamp and hose at the steering gear. Disconnect the flare nut and the tube at the steering gear, then drain the fluid from the gear.
3. Using the Ball Joint Remover tool HT72520000, remove the tie rod from the knuckle.
4. Place a floor jack under the transaxle and support it.
5. Remove the exhaust tube and the rear engine mount.
6. Remove the steering column lower joint.
7. Unbolt and remove the steering gear unit and the linkage.
  To install:
8. Install the power steering gear assembly to the vehicle. Torque the tie rod-to-steering knuckle nut to 26–36 ft. lbs. (35–49 Nm), the steering gear-to-frame clamp bolts to 43–58 ft. lbs. (58–79 Nm), the lower joint-to-pinion gear bolt to 22–29 ft. lbs. (29–39 Nm), the lower joint-to-steering column bolt to 22–29 ft. lbs. (29–39 Nm), the low pressure hose clip bolt to 9–17 inch lbs. (1.02–1.92 Nm) and the high pressure hose-to-gear to 11–18 ft. lbs. (15–25 Nm).
9. Bleed the power steering system and check the wheel alignment.

→When installing the lower steering joint to the steering gear, make sure that the wheels are aligned with the vehicle and the steering joint slot is aligned with the steering gear cap or spacer mark.

1987–96 Vehicles

♦ See Figure 61

1. Raise and support the vehicle safely, then remove the wheels.
2. Disconnect the power steering hose from the power steering gear and plug all hoses to prevent leakage.
3. Disconnect the side rod studs from the steering knuckles.
4. Support the transaxle with a suitable transmission jack and remove the exhaust pipe and rear engine mounts.
5. Remove the lower joint assembly from the steering gear pinion. Before disconnecting the lower ball joint set the steering gear assembly in neutral by making the wheels straight. Loosen the bolt and disconnect the lower joint. Matchmark the pinion shaft to the pinion housing to record the neutral gear position.
6. Remove the steering gear and linkage assembly from the vehicle.
   To install:
7. Installation is the reverse of the removal procedure observing the following:
   a. Make sure the pinion shaft and pinion housing are aligned properly.
   b. Torque the high pressure hydraulic line fitting to 11–18 ft. lbs. (15–25 Nm) and lower pressure fitting to 20–29 ft. lbs. (27–39 Nm).
   c. When attaching the lower joint, set the left and right dust boots to equal deflection.
   d. Torque the gear housing mounting bracket bolts to 54–72 ft. lbs. (73–97 Nm).

→When installing the lower steering joint to the steering gear, make sure that the wheels are aligned with the vehicle and the steering joint slot is aligned with the steering gear cap or spacer mark.

8. Refill the power steering pump, start the engine and bleed the system. Refill the power steering pump, start the engine and bleed the system.

→On most vehicles, the O-ring in the lower pressure hydraulic line fitting is larger than the O-ring in the high pressure line. Make sure the O-rings are installed in the proper fittings. Observe the torque specification given for the hydraulic line fittings. Over-tightening will cause damage to the fitting threads and O-rings.

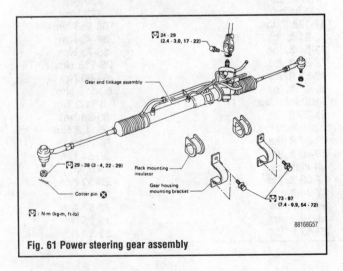

Fig. 61 Power steering gear assembly

ADJUSTMENTS

1987–90 Vehicles

♦ See Figure 62

Adjustment is usually performed only after over haul and replacement of major parts. A special socket wrench KV48100700, or equivalent, must be used with an inch lbs. torque wrench in performing this work.

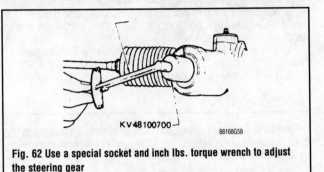

Fig. 62 Use a special socket and inch lbs. torque wrench to adjust the steering gear

1. Disconnect the unit and remove it from the car as previously outlined.
2. Rotate the pinion shaft from lock-to-lock, counting the turns. Then, divide the number of turns in half, and turn the shaft that distance from either lock to center it.
3. Loosen the locknut and loosen the adjusting screw. Then, torque it to 43 inch lbs. (4.87 Nm). Loosen it and torque it again to that figure.
4. Loosen the adjusting screw and torque it to 0.43–1.74 inch lbs. (0.048–0.197 Nm). Loosen the locknut and apply locking sealer to the lower threads of the adjusting screw as well as the retainer cover surrounding it. Then, tighten the locknut to 29–43 ft. lbs. (39–58 Nm).
5. Move the rack through its entire stroke several times. Then, install the torque wrench and special socket and measure the rotating torque of the pinion 100° either side of the neutral position. The torque should be 6.9–11.3 inch lbs. (0.78–1.28 Nm) with a maximum of 16 inch lbs. (1.8 Nm).
6. If the torque is incorrect, readjust the screw appropriately. When the rotating torque is correct, reapply sealer and retorque the locknut as necessary.

1991–96 Sentra

♦ See Figure 63

1. Set the rack to the neutral position without fluid in the gear.
2. Coat the adjusting screw with locking sealer and screw it in.
3. Lightly tighten the locknut.
4. Torque the adjusting screw to 43–52 inch lbs. (4.9–5.9 Nm).
5. Loosen the adjusting screw and retorque to 1.7 inch lbs. (0.2 Nm).
6. Rotate the pinion to move the rack back and forth 2 times. Return to the neutral position.
7. Slowly rotate the pinion and measure the rotating torque in a 180° range. Find the position where the rotating torque is maximum.
8. Loosen the adjusting screw at that position and torque the adjusting screw to 43 inch lbs. (4.9 Nm). Back it off of the adjusting screw 40–60°.
9. Prevent the adjusting nut from turning and torque the locknut to 29–43 ft. lbs. (39–59 Nm).

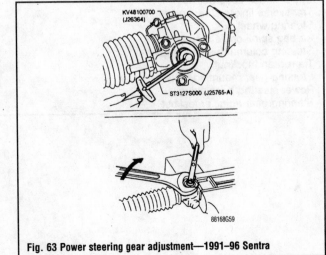

Fig. 63 Power steering gear adjustment—1991–96 Sentra

10. Measure the pinion rotating torque with an inch lbs. torque wrench. The normal torque should be 6.9–11.3 inch lbs. (0.8–1.3 Nm) and the maximum deviation is 3.5 inch lbs. (0.4 Nm).

11. If the rotating torque is not within specifications, readjust the rotating torque.

12. Check the steering gear does not bind.

OVERHAUL

Overhaul of the power steering gear is recommended to be performed by qualified steering gear rebuilders. The cost for specific components may not be as cost effective as purchasing a rebuilt unit.

Power Steering Pump

REMOVAL & INSTALLATION

1982–90 Vehicles

1. Remove the hoses at the pump and plug and openings shut to prevent contamination. Position the disconnected lines in a raised attitude to prevent leakage.

2. Loosen the power steering pump drive belt adjuster and the drive belt.

3. Loosen the retaining bolts, then remove the braces and the pump from the vehicle.

4. To install, reverse the removal procedures. Adjust the belt tension and bleed the power steering system. Refer to Section 1 for belt routing.

1991–96 Sentra

1. Remove the air cleaner duct and air cleaner.

2. Loosen the idler pulley locknut and turn the adjusting nut counterclockwise, in order to remove the power steering belt. Refer to Section 1 for belt routing.

3. Remove the drive belt on the air conditioning compressor, if so equipped.

4. Loosen the power steering hoses at the pump and remove the bolts holding the power steering pump to the bracket.

5. Disconnect and plug the power steering hoses and remove the pump from the vehicle.

6. Installation is the reverse of the removal procedure. Fill and bleed the power steering system.

BELT ADJUSTMENT

1. Loosen the tension adjustment and mounting bolts.

2. Move the pump toward or away from the engine so the belt deflects ¼–½ in. (6–13mm) midway between the idler pulley and the pump pulley under moderate thumb pressure.

3. Tighten the bolts and recheck the tension adjustment.

BLEEDING THE POWER STEERING SYSTEM

1. Fill the pump reservoir and allow to remain undisturbed for a few minutes.

2. Raise the car until the front wheels are clear of the ground.

3. With the engine off, quickly turn the wheels right and left several times, lightly contacting the stops.

4. Add fluid if necessary.

5. Start the engine and let it idle until it reaches operating temperatures.

6. Repeat Steps 3 and 4 with the engine idling.

➡**Do not allow the steering linkage to contact the stops for any longer than 15 seconds, with the engine running.**

7. Stop the engine, lower the car until the wheels just touch the ground. Start the engine, allow it to idle and turn the wheels back and forth several times. Check the fluid level and refill if necessary.

TORQUE SPECIFICATIONS

Component	U.S.	Metric
Wheel lug nuts		
steel wheels	100 ft. lbs.	136 Nm
aluminum wheels	90 ft. lbs.	122 Nm
Sealed hub bearing nut	137-188 ft. lbs.	186-255 Nm
MacPherson strut-to-body bolt	23-31 ft. lbs.	32-42 Nm
Piston rod locknut	43-54 ft. lbs.	58-73 Nm
Strut-to-knuckle bolts	72-87 ft. lbs.	98-118 Nm
Ball joint-to-lower control arm	40-51 ft. lbs.	54-69 Nm
Gusset-to-body bolts	65-87 ft. lbs.	88-118 Nm
Stabilizer-to-control arm	80-100 inch lbs.	9.0-11.3 Nm
Lower shock absorber bolt	51-65 ft. lbs.	69-88 Nm
Upper shock absorber nut	78-104 inch lbs.	8.8-11.8 Nm
Transverse link-to-steering knuckle	72-87 ft. lbs.	98-118 Nm
Steering wheel nut	29-40 ft. lbs.	39-54 Nm
Air bag spiral cable screw	24 inch lbs.	4.0 Nm
Steering column-to-steering gear	17-22 ft. lbs.	23-30 Nm
Tie rod end locknut	27-34 ft. lbs.	37-46 Nm
Steering gear mounting bolts	54-72 ft. lbs.	73-97 Nm
Power steering hose fitting	11-18 ft. lbs.	15-25 Nm
Steering gear adjuster locknut	29-43 ft. lbs.	39-59 Nm

88168C03

9

BRAKES

BRAKE OPERATING SYSTEM

Basic Operating Principles

Hydraulic systems are used to actuate the brakes of all modern automobiles. The system transports the power required to force the frictional surfaces of the braking system together from the pedal to the individual brake units at each wheel. A hydraulic system is used for two reasons.

First, fluid under pressure can be carried to all parts of an automobile by small pipes and flexible hoses without taking up a significant amount of room or posing routing problems.

Second, a great mechanical advantage can be given to the brake pedal end of the system, and the foot pressure required to actuate the brakes can be reduced by making the surface area of the master cylinder pistons smaller than that of any of the pistons in the wheel cylinders or calipers.

The master cylinder consists of a fluid reservoir along with a double cylinder and piston assembly. Double type master cylinders are designed to separate the front and rear braking systems hydraulically in case of a leak. The master cylinder coverts mechanical motion from the pedal into hydraulic pressure within the lines. This pressure is translated back into mechanical motion at the wheels by either the wheel cylinder (drum brakes) or the caliper (disc brakes).

Steel lines carry the brake fluid to a point on the vehicle's frame near each of the vehicle's wheels. The fluid is then carried to the calipers and wheel cylinders by flexible tubes in order to allow for suspension and steering movements.

In drum brake systems, each wheel cylinder contains two pistons, one at either end, which push outward in opposite directions and force the brake shoe into contact with the drum.

In disc brake systems, the cylinders are part of the calipers. At least one cylinder in each caliper is used to force the brake pads against the disc.

All pistons employ some type of seal, usually made of rubber, to minimize fluid leakage. A rubber dust boot seals the outer end of the cylinder against dust and dirt. The boot fits around the outer end of the piston on disc brake calipers, and around the brake actuating rod on wheel cylinders.

The hydraulic system operates as follows: When at rest, the entire system, from the piston(s) in the master cylinder to those in the wheel cylinders or calipers, is full of brake fluid. Upon application of the brake pedal, fluid trapped in front of the master cylinder piston(s) is forced through the lines to the wheel cylinders. Here, it forces the pistons outward, in the case of drum brakes, and inward toward the disc, in the case of disc brakes. The motion of the pistons is opposed by return springs mounted outside the cylinders in drum brakes, and by spring seals, in disc brakes.

Upon release of the brake pedal, a spring located inside the master cylinder immediately returns the master cylinder pistons to the normal position. The pistons contain check valves and the master cylinder has compensating ports drilled in it. These are uncovered as the pistons reach their normal position. The piston check valves allow fluid to flow toward the wheel cylinders or calipers as the pistons withdraw. Then, as the return springs force the brake pads or shoes into the released position, the excess fluid reservoir through the compensating ports. It is during the time the pedal is in the released position that any fluid that has leaked out of the system will be replaced through the compensating ports.

Dual circuit master cylinders employ two pistons, located one behind the other, in the same cylinder. The primary piston is actuated directly by mechanical linkage from the brake pedal through the power booster. The secondary piston is actuated by fluid trapped between the two pistons. If a leak develops in front of the secondary piston, it moves forward until it bottoms against the front of the master cylinder, and the fluid trapped between the pistons will operate the rear brakes. If the rear brakes develop a leak, the primary piston will move forward until direct contact with the secondary piston takes place, and it will force the secondary piston to actuate the front brakes. In either case, the brake pedal moves farther when the brakes are applied, and less braking power is available.

All dual circuit systems use a switch to warn the driver when only half of the brake system is operational. This switch is usually located in a valve body which is mounted on the firewall or the frame below the master cylinder. A hydraulic piston receives pressure from both circuits, each circuit's pressure being applied to one end of the piston. When the pressures are in balance, the piston remains stationary. When one circuit has a leak, however, the greater pressure in that circuit during application of the brakes will push the piston to one side, closing the switch and activating the brake warning light.

In disc brake systems, this valve body also contains a metering valve and, in some cases, a proportioning valve. The metering valve keeps pressure from traveling to the disc brakes on the front wheels until the brake shoes on the rear wheels have contacted the drums, ensuring that the front brakes will never be used alone. The proportioning valve controls the pressure to the rear brakes to lessen the chance of rear wheel lock-up during very hard braking.

Warning lights may be tested by depressing the brake pedal and holding it while opening one of the wheel cylinder bleeder screws. If this does not cause the light to go on, substitute a new lamp, make continuity checks, and, finally, replace the switch as necessary.

The hydraulic system may be checked for leaks by applying pressure to the pedal gradually and steadily. If the pedal sinks very slowly to the floor, the system has a leak. This is not to be confused with a springy or spongy feel due to the compression of air within the lines. If the system leaks, there will be a gradual change in the position of the pedal with a constant pressure.

Check for leaks along all lines and at wheel cylinders. If no external leaks are apparent, the problem is inside the master cylinder.

DISC BRAKES

Instead of the traditional expanding brakes that press outward against a circular drum, disc brake systems utilize a disc (rotor) with brake pads positioned on either side of it. An easily-seen analogy is the hand brake arrangement on a bicycle. The pads squeeze onto the rim of the bike wheel, slowing its motion. Automobile disc brakes use the identical principle but apply the braking effort to a separate disc instead of the wheel.

The disc (rotor) is a casting, usually equipped with cooling fins between the two braking surfaces. This enables air to circulate between the braking surfaces making them less sensitive to heat buildup and more resistant to fade. Dirt and water do not drastically affect braking action since contaminants are thrown off by the centrifugal action of the rotor or scraped off the by the pads. Also, the equal clamping action of the two brake pads tends to ensure uniform, straight line stops. Disc brakes are inherently self-adjusting. There are three general types of disc brake:

1. A fixed caliper.
2. A floating caliper.
3. A sliding caliper.

The fixed caliper design uses two pistons mounted on either side of the rotor (in each side of the caliper). The caliper is mounted rigidly and does not move.

The sliding and floating designs are quite similar. In fact, these two types are often lumped together. In both designs, the pad on the inside of the rotor is moved into contact with the rotor by hydraulic force. The caliper, which is not held in a fixed position, moves slightly, bringing the outside pad into contact with the rotor. There are various methods of attaching floating calipers. Some pivot at the bottom or top, and some slide on mounting bolts. In any event, the end result is the same.

DRUM BRAKES

Drum brakes employ two brake shoes mounted on a stationary backing plate. These shoes are positioned inside a circular drum which rotates with the wheel assembly. The shoes are held in place by springs. This allows them to slide toward the drums (when they are applied) while keeping the linings and drums in alignment. The shoes are actuated by a wheel cylinder which is mounted at the top of the backing plate. When the brakes are applied, hydraulic pressure forces the wheel cylinder's actuating links outward. Since these links bear directly against the top of the brake shoes, the tops of the shoes are then forced against the inner side of the drum. This action forces the bottoms of the two shoes to contact the brake drum by rotating the entire assembly slightly (known as servo action). When pressure within the wheel cylinder is relaxed, return springs pull the shoes back away from the drum.

Most modern drum brakes are designed to self-adjust themselves during application when the vehicle is moving in reverse. This motion causes both shoes to rotate very slightly with the drum, rocking an adjusting lever, thereby causing rotation of the adjusting screw. Some drum brake systems are designed to self-adjust during application whenever the brakes are applied. This on-board adjustment system reduces the need for maintenance adjustments and keeps both the brake function and pedal feel satisfactory.

Adjustments

DRUM BRAKES

▶ See Figure 1

1. Raise and support the rear of the vehicle on jackstands.
2. Remove the rubber cover from the backing plate.
3. Insert a brake adjusting tool through the hole in the brake backing plate. Turn the toothed adjusting nut to spread the brake shoes, making contact with the brake drum.

➡ **When adjusting the brake shoes, turn the wheel until considerable drag is felt. If necessary, hit the brake drum with a rubber hammer to align the shoes with the drum.**

4. When considerable drag is felt, back off the adjusting nut a few notches, so that the correct clearance is maintained between the brake drum and the brake shoes. Make sure that the wheel rotates freely.

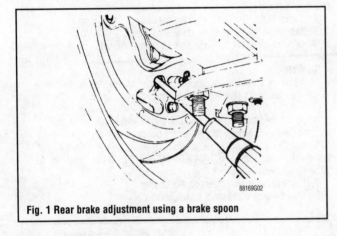

Fig. 1 Rear brake adjustment using a brake spoon

BRAKE PEDAL HEIGHT ADJUSTMENT

▶ See Figure 2

Before adjusting the pedal, make sure that the wheel brakes are correctly adjusted. Pedal free height adjustment can then be made using the brake booster input rod.

1. Loosen the lock nut on the brake booster input rod.

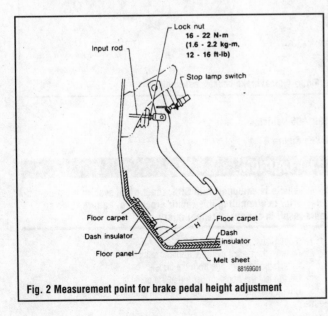

Fig. 2 Measurement point for brake pedal height adjustment

2. Adjust the pedal height by rotating the input rod, until the proper pedal height is obtained. The pedal height (floorboard to pedal pad) should be as follows:
- 1982–86 vehicles—MTX–7.64–8.03 in. (194–204mm)
- 1982–86 vehicles—ATX–7.76–8.15 in. (197–207mm)
- 1987–90 vehicles—MTX–6.30–6.61 in. (160–168mm)
- 1987–90 vehicles—ATX–6.46–6.85 in. (164–174mm)
- 1991–96 Sentra—MTX–5.83–6.22 in. (148–158mm)
- 1991–96 Sentra—ATX–6.18–6.57 in. (157–167mm)

3. Once the proper height measurement has been obtained, tighten the locknut and verify proper brake light operation.

Brake Light Switch

REMOVAL & INSTALLATION

1. Disconnect the negative battery cable.
2. Disconnect the wiring connector at the switch.
3. Remove the switch lock nut.
4. Remove the switch.
5. Install the switch and adjust it so the brake lights are not on unless the brake pedal is depressed.

ADJUSTMENT

Adjust the clearance between the brake pedal and the stop lamp switch or the ASCD switch, by loosening the locknut and adjusting the switch. The clearance should be as follows:
- 0–1.0mm for 1982–84 vehicles
- 0.3–1.00mm for 1985–90 vehicles
- 0.1–0.3mm for 1991–94 vehicles
- 0.3–1.00mm for 1995–96 vehicles

Once the proper clearance has been obtained, tighten the locknut and verify proper brake light operation.

Master Cylinder

✳✳ WARNING

Clean, high quality brake fluid is essential to the safe and proper operation of the brake system. You should always buy the highest quality brake fluid that is available. If the brake fluid becomes contaminated, drain and flush the system and fill the master cylinder with new fluid. Never reuse any brake fluid. Any brake fluid that is removed from the system should be discarded.

REMOVAL & INSTALLATION

1982–90 Vehicles

▶ See Figures 3 and 4

1. Clean the outside of the master cylinder thoroughly, particularly around the cap and fluid lines.
2. If equipped with a fluid level sensor, disconnect the wiring harness from the master cylinder.
3. Disconnect the brake fluid tubes, then plug the openings to prevent dirt from entering the system.
4. Remove the mounting bolts at the firewall or the brake booster (if equipped) and remove the master cylinder from the vehicle.
To install:
5. Bench bleed the master cylinder by using old brake pipes. Bend the brake pipes around into the reservoir. Place the master cylinder in a vise and fill the reservoir with DOT 3 brake fluid. Pump the piston using a pushrod until all the air bubbles are gone.
6. Install the master cylinder to the vehicle. Connect all brake lines and fluid level sensor wiring is so equipped. Refill the reservoir with brake fluid and bleed the system.

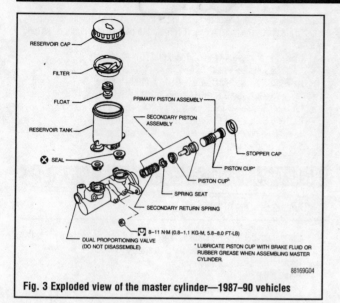

Fig. 3 Exploded view of the master cylinder—1987–90 vehicles

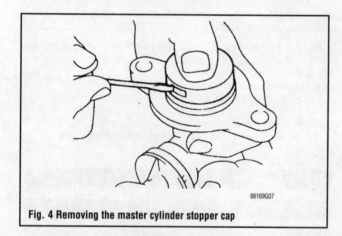

Fig. 4 Removing the master cylinder stopper cap

7. Torque the master cylinder nuts to 72–96 inch lbs. (8–11 Nm) and the brake pipe fittings to 12–14 ft. lbs. (17–20 Nm).

➡ Use DOT 3 brake fluid in the brake systems.

1991–96 Vehicles

1. Clean the outside of the master cylinder thoroughly, particularly around the cap and fluid lines.
2. Using a ball type suction device (similar to a turkey baster), remove as much brake fluid from the fluid reservoir as possible.
3. Disconnect the brake fluid tubes, then plug the openings to prevent dirt from entering the system.
4. Remove the nuts securing the master cylinder to the brake booster.
5. Remove the master cylinder from the vehicle.

⁂ WARNING

When removing the master cylinder from the vehicle, use extreme care not to get any brake any brake fluid onto painted surfaces

To install:
6. Install the master cylinder onto the booster mounting studs. Secure the master cylinder to the booster with the retaining nuts and tighten the nuts as follows:
- 1991–94 vehicles—72–96 lbs. (8–11 Nm)
- 1995–96 vehicles—9–13 ft. lbs. (15–18 Nm)
7. Refill the reservoir using DOT 3 approved brake fluid.
8. Bleed the master cylinder as follows:
   a. Using your fingers, plug both line ports. Cover your hand and the exit ports with a rag to prevent fluid from spraying.

b. Have a helper **slowly** depress the brake pedal.
   c. Before releasing the brake pedal tightly seal both ports using your fingers.
   d. Repeat this procedure until air can no longer be heard exiting the ports and only fluid is being released.
9. Once the master cylinder has been properly bled, connect both brake lines. Tighten the flare nuts to 11–13 ft. lbs. (15–18 Nm).
10. Bleed the remainder of the brake system following the procedures outlined in the Bleeding Brake System portion of this section.

Power Brake Booster

REMOVAL & INSTALLATION

▶ See Figure 5

1982–90 Vehicles

1. Disconnect the master cylinder brake pipes. Remove the master cylinder mounting nuts and pull the master cylinder assembly away from the power booster.
2. Detach the vacuum lines from the booster.
3. Detach the booster pushrod at the pedal clevis.
4. Unbolt the booster from under the dash and lift it out of the engine compartment.

   To install:
5. Install the brake booster. Torque the master cylinder-to-booster nuts to 72–96 inch lbs. (8–11 Nm), and the booster-to-firewall nuts to 72–96 inch lbs. (8–11 Nm).
6. Adjust the length of the pushrod so that the distance between the pushrod clevis hole and the rear face of the booster is 5.9 in. (150mm) for 1982–86 vehicles. The output rod length from the end of the rod to the front face of the booster should be 0.4045–0.4144 in. (10.275–10.525mm) for the 1987–90 vehicles.
7. Connect the vacuum lines to brake booster.
8. Start the engine and check brake operation.

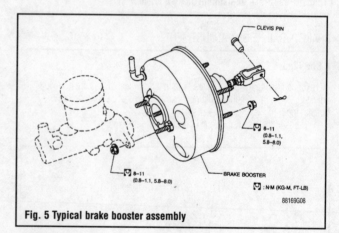

Fig. 5 Typical brake booster assembly

1991–96 Vehicles

▶ See Figure 6

⁂ CAUTION

If the vehicle is equipped with SRS, the air bag system must be disabled prior to attempting this repair procedure. Failure to do so could result in serious personal injury.

1. If applicable, disarm the SRS system.
2. Remove the master cylinder from the vehicle.
3. Detach the vacuum line from the booster.
4. Disconnect the booster pushrod at the pedal clevis.
5. Unbolt the booster from under the dash and lift it out of the engine compartment.

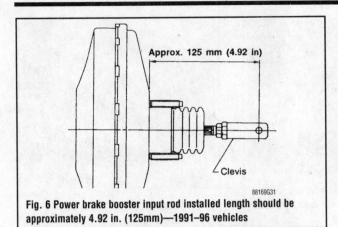

Fig. 6 Power brake booster input rod installed length should be approximately 4.92 in. (125mm)—1991–96 vehicles

To install:

6. On vehicles without ABS, before installing the brake booster, adjust the length of the pushrod so that the distance between the pushrod clevis hole and the rear face of the booster is 4.92 in. (125mm).

7. Install the brake booster to the vehicle and secure with retaining nuts from inside the vehicle. Tighten the retaining nuts to 9–12 ft. lbs. (13–16 Nm).

8. Install the master cylinder assembly.

9. Connect the vacuum lines to brake booster.

10. Start the engine and check brake operation.

Brake Proportioning Valve

1982–86 vehicles are equipped with brake proportioning valves of several different types. The valves all do the same job, which is to separate the front and rear brake lines, allowing them to function independently and preventing the rear brakes from locking before the front brakes. Damage, such as brake line leakage, in either the front or the rear brake system will not affect the normal operation of the unaffected system. If, in the event of a panic stop, the rear brakes lock up before the front brakes, it could mean the proportioning valve is defective. In that case, replace the entire proportioning valve.

REMOVAL & INSTALLATION

1982–86 Vehicles

▶ See Figure 7

1. Remove the brake line tubes from the proportioning valve, then plug the openings to prevent dirt from entering the system.

2. Remove the mounting bolt(s) and the valve from the vehicle.

3. To install, reverse the removal procedures. Refill the master cylinder reservoir and bleed the brake system. Torque the brake pipe fittings to 12–14 ft. lbs. (17–20 Nm).

1991–96 Vehicles

▶ See Figure 8

These vehicles use two different type proportioning valves; an integral type which is incorporated into the master cylinder, and a separate type mounted on the firewall. The integral type is serviced with the master cylinder as an assembly. The procedure below is for the separate type.

1. Drain the fluid from the brake system as follows:

a. Connect a rubber hose to each brake bleeder valve.

b. Open each bleeder valve, while a helper slowly depresses the brake pedal.

c. Repeat this procedure until the brake system is empty.

2. Using a line wrench, disconnect the four brake lines from the valve.

3. Loosen the mounting bolt and remove the valve from the vehicle.

To install:

4. Position the valve assembly in the vehicle.

5. Connect the four brake lines to the valve assembly, but do not fully tighten.

6. Install the mounting bolt and tighten to 11–13 ft. lbs. (15–18 Nm).

7. Refill the brake system with new DOT 3 brake fluid.

8. Following proper procedures, bleed the entire brake system.

Brake Hoses And Lines

Metal lines and rubber brake hoses should be checked frequently for leaks and external damage. Metal lines are particularly prone to crushing and kinking under the vehicle. Any such deformation can restrict the proper flow of fluid and therefore impair braking at the wheels. Rubber hoses should be checked for cracking or scraping; such damage can create a weak spot in the hose and it could fail under pressure.

Any time the lines are removed or disconnected, extreme cleanliness must be observed. Clean all joints and connections before disassembly (use a stiff bristle brush and clean brake fluid); be sure to plug the lines and ports as soon as they are opened. New lines and hoses should be flushed clean with brake fluid before installation to remove any contamination.

REMOVAL & INSTALLATION

▶ See Figures 9, 10, 11 and 12

1. Disconnect the negative battery cable.

2. Raise and safely support the vehicle on jackstands.

3. Remove any wheel and tire assemblies necessary for access to the particular line you are removing.

4. Thoroughly clean the surrounding area at the joints to be disconnected.

5. Place a suitable catch pan under the joint to be disconnected.

6. Using two wrenches (one to hold the joint and one to turn the fitting), disconnect the hose or line to be replaced.

7. Disconnect the other end of the line or hose, moving the drain pan if necessary. Always use a back-up wrench to avoid damaging the fitting.

8. Disconnect any retaining clips or brackets holding the line and remove the line from the vehicle.

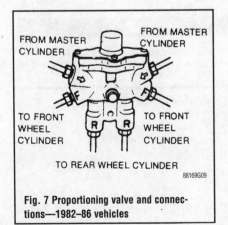

Fig. 7 Proportioning valve and connections—1982–86 vehicles

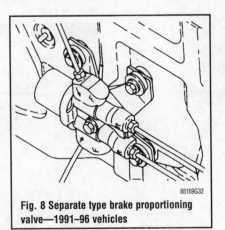

Fig. 8 Separate type brake proportioning valve—1991–96 vehicles

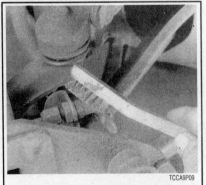

Fig. 9 Use a brush to clean the fittings of any debris

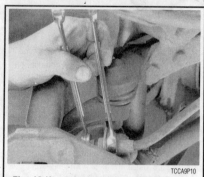

Fig. 10 Use two wrenches to loosen the fitting. If available, use flare nut type wrenches

TCCA9P10

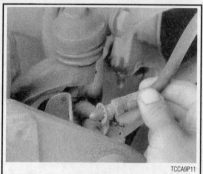

Fig. 11 Any gaskets/crush washers should be replaced with new ones during installation

TCCA9P11

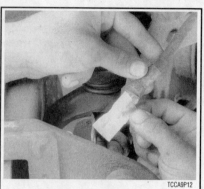

Fig. 12 Tape or plug the line to prevent contamination

TCCA9P12

➡If the brake system is to remain open for more time than it takes to swap lines, tape or plug each remaining clip and port to keep contaminants out and fluid in.

To install:

9. Install the new line or hose, starting with the end farthest from the master cylinder. Connect the other end, then confirm that both fittings are correctly threaded and turn smoothly using finger pressure. Make sure the new line will not rub against any other part. Brake lines must be at least 1/2 in. (13mm) from the steering column and other moving parts. Any protective shielding or insulators must be reinstalled in the original location.

⁜ WARNING

Make sure the hose is NOT kinked or touching any part of the frame or suspension after installation. These conditions may cause the hose to fail prematurely.

10. Using two wrenches as before, tighten each fitting.
11. Install any retaining clips or brackets on the lines.
12. If removed, install the wheel and tire assemblies, then carefully lower the vehicle to the ground.
13. Refill the brake master cylinder reservoir with clean, fresh brake fluid, meeting DOT 3 specifications. Properly bleed the brake system.
14. Connect the negative battery cable.

System Bleeding

▶ See Figure 13

System bleeding is required whenever air in the hydraulic fluid causes a spongy feeling pedal and sluggish response. This is almost always the case after some part of the hydraulic system has been repaired or replaced. **Use DOT 3 brake fluid in all systems.**

1. On vehicles equipped with anti-lock brake (ABS) systems, turn the ignition switch to the **OFF** position and disconnect the negative battery cable. All other steps apply to both ABS and conventional brake systems.
2. Fill the master cylinder reservoir with DOT 3 brake fluid.
3. On 1982–93 vehicles, the bleeding sequence is as follows:
- Left rear
- Right front
- Right rear
- Left front
4. On 1994–96 vehicles, the bleeding sequence is as follows:
- Right rear
- Left front

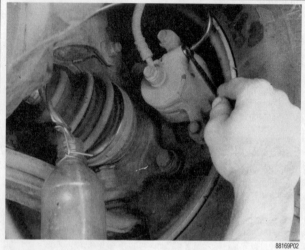

Fig. 13 Connect a hose and clear bottle filled with brake fluid to the bleeder screw as shown

88169P02

- Left rear
- Right front
5. Starting with the first point in the bleeding sequence, connect a clear hose over the bleeder screw. Submerge the other end of the hole in clean brake fluid in a clear glass container. Make sure the clear hose in below the brake fluid level.
6. Open the bleeder valve, while a helper slowly pumps the brake pedal. Pump the pedal several times (in long strokes) until fluid free of bubbles is discharged.
7. On the last pumping stroke, hold the pedal down and tighten the bleeder screw. Check the fluid level periodically during the bleeding operation.
8. Repeat this procedure for the remainder of the system, following the proper sequence.

⁜ WARNING

Do not allow the reservoir to run dry during the bleeding procedure. To prevent damage to the master cylinder, it is best not to exceed ⅔ pedal travel.

9. Check that the brake pedal is now firm with the engine not running. If not, repeat the bleeding operation.

FRONT DISC BRAKES

Brake Pads

▶ See Figures 14, 15 and 16

REMOVAL & INSTALLATION

▶ See Figures 17 thru 23

1. Remove the reservoir cap from the master cylinder.

➡When the caliper pistons are retracted into the caliper the brake fluid level will rise. Therefore, it may be necessary to remove some brake fluid from the master cylinder reservoir.

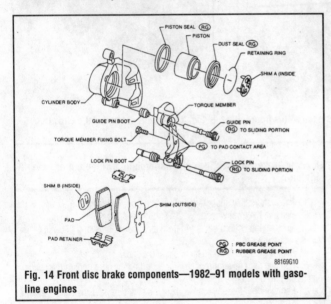

Fig. 14 Front disc brake components—1982–91 models with gasoline engines

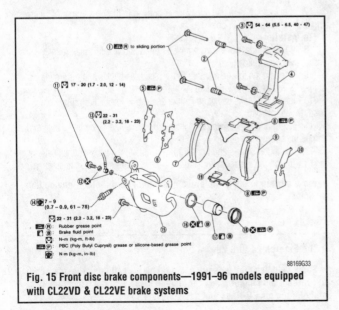

Fig. 15 Front disc brake components—1991–96 models equipped with CL22VD & CL22VE brake systems

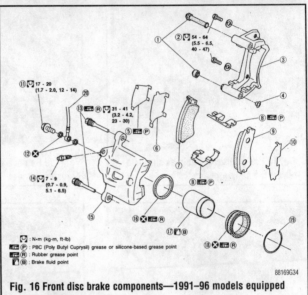

Fig. 16 Front disc brake components—1991–96 models equipped with AD18VE brake systems

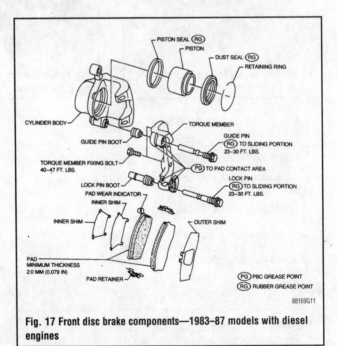

Fig. 17 Front disc brake components—1983–87 models with diesel engines

2. Check the level of fluid in the master cylinder. If the fluid is near the maximum level, use a clean syringe to remove fluid until the level is down well below the lip of the reservoir.

3. Raise and support the front of the vehicle on jackstands, then remove the wheels.

4. Using a large C-clamp, push the caliper piston into the caliper bore.

5. Remove the bottom guide pin from the caliper and swing the caliper cylinder body upward and hang by a wire.

6. Remove the brake pad retainers and the pads.

To install:

7. Inspect the following items for signs of wear or deterioration. Repair or replace any problem items, before continuing.

Fig. 18 Use a large C-clamp as shown to retract the caliper piston

Fig. 19 Remove excess fluid from the master cylinder reservoir using a syringe

Fig. 20 With the lower caliper mounting bolt removed, swing the caliper upward to access the brake pads

Fig. 21 Remove the brake pads from the caliper holder

Fig. 22 Remove the brake pad shims from the old brake pads

Fig. 23 Remove the anti-rattle clips from the caliper holder

- All brake hardware (mounting pins, shims, clips, etc.)
- Brake rotor
- Brake caliper

8. Clean and lubricate caliper slide pins and brake pad mounting surfaces.

➥Wheel bearing grease or an anti-seize compound can be used to lubricate contact points.

9. Install the brake pads and caliper assembly. Torque the guide pin to 23 ft. lbs. (31 Nm).
10. Install the wheels and lower the vehicle to the ground.
11. Apply the brakes a few times to seat the pads.
12. Check the master cylinder and add fluid if necessary. Bleed the brakes, if necessary.

INSPECTION

You should be able to check the pad lining thickness without removing the pads. Check the Brake Specifications chart at the end of this section to find the manufacturer's pad wear limit. However, this measurement may disagree with your state inspection laws. When replacing pads, always check the surface of the rotors for scoring, hard spots (black discoloration's), and/or wear. Also check that the rotors are within specifications for thickness, parallelism and run-out. If any problems exist with the brake rotor the rotor must be resurfaced or discarded.

Brake Calipers

REMOVAL & INSTALLATION

✳✳ CAUTION

Brake pads may contain asbestos, which has been determined to be a cancer causing agent. Never clean the brake surfaces with compressed air! Avoid inhaling any dust from any brake surface! When cleaning brake surfaces, use a commercially available brake cleaning fluid.

1. Raise and safely support vehicle.
2. Remove the front wheels.
3. Remove the bottom guide pin from the caliper and swing the caliper cylinder body upward as hang by a wire.
4. Remove the brake pad retainers and the pads.
5. Remove the brake fluid hose connector bolt; be sure to plug the openings to prevent dirt from entering the system.
6. Remove both torque member fixing bolts and remove the caliper assembly from the vehicle.
7. If necessary, separate the cylinder body from torque member by removing both upper guide pin bolt.

To install:

8. If the cylinder body was removed from the torque member, loosely install the upper guide pin bolt.
9. Connect the torque member to the steering knuckle and torque the caliper-to-torque member bolts to 47 ft. lbs. (64 Nm).
10. Install the brake pads and caliper assembly. Torque both guide pin bolts to 23 ft. lbs. (31 Nm).
11. Using new copper washers, install the brake line to the brake caliper and torque the connecting bolt to 12–14 ft. lbs. (17–20 Nm).
12. Install the wheels and tighten the lug nuts to the proper specification.
13. Top off the master cylinder and bleed the brake system as necessary.

➥Make certain to pump the brake pedal until hard, before moving the vehicle!

OVERHAUL

▶ **See Figures 24 thru 29**

➥Some vehicles may be equipped dual piston calipers. The procedure to overhaul the caliper is essentially the same with the exception of multiple pistons, O-rings and dust boots.

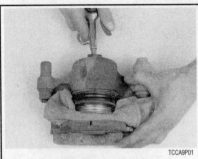

Fig. 24 For some types of calipers, use compressed air to drive the piston out of the caliper, but make sure to keep your fingers clear

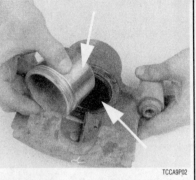

Fig. 25 Withdraw the piston from the caliper bore

Fig. 26 Use a prytool to carefully pry around the edge of the boot . . .

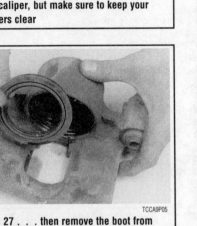

Fig. 27 . . . then remove the boot from the caliper housing, taking care not to score or damage the bore

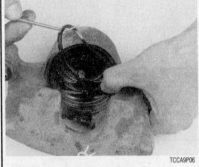

Fig. 28 Use extreme caution when removing the piston seal; DO NOT scratch the caliper bore

Fig. 29 Use the proper size driving tool and a mallet to properly seal the boots in the caliper housing

1. Remove the caliper from the vehicle and place on a clean workbench.

✷✷ CAUTION

NEVER place your fingers in front of the pistons in an attempt to catch or protect the pistons when applying compressed air. This could result in personal injury!

➡Depending upon the vehicle, there are two different ways to remove the piston from the caliper. Refer to the brake pad replacement procedure to make sure you have the correct procedure for your vehicle.

2. The first method is as follows:
   a. Stuff a shop towel or a block of wood into the caliper to catch the piston.
   b. Remove the caliper piston using compressed air applied into the caliper inlet hole. Inspect the piston for scoring, nicks, corrosion and/or worn or damaged chrome plating. The piston must be replaced if any of these conditions are found.
3. For the second method, you must rotate the piston to retract it from the caliper.
4. If equipped, remove the anti-rattle clip.
5. Use a prytool to remove the caliper boot, being careful not to scratch the housing bore.
6. Remove the piston seals from the groove in the caliper bore.
7. Carefully loosen the brake bleeder valve cap and valve from the caliper housing.
8. Inspect the caliper bores, pistons and mounting threads for scoring or excessive wear.
9. Use crocus cloth to polish out light corrosion from the piston and bore.
10. Clean all parts with denatured alcohol and dry with compressed air.

To assemble:
11. Lubricate and install the bleeder valve and cap.
12. Install the new seals into the caliper bore grooves, making sure they are not twisted.
13. Lubricate the piston bore.
14. Install the pistons and boots into the bores of the calipers and push to the bottom of the bores.
15. Use a suitable driving tool to seat the boots in the housing.
16. Install the caliper in the vehicle.
17. Install the wheel and tire assembly, then carefully lower the vehicle.
18. Properly bleed the brake system.

Brake Disc (Rotor)

♦ **See Figures 30 and 31**

REMOVAL & INSTALLATION

✷✷ CAUTION

Brake pads may contain asbestos, which has been determined to be a cancer causing agent. Never clean the brake surfaces with compressed air! Avoid inhaling any dust from any brake surface! When cleaning brake surfaces, use a commercially available brake cleaning fluid.

1982–86 Vehicles

1. Refer to the Caliper removal and installation procedures in this section, and remove the caliper and the torque member from the steering knuckle.

→Do NOT disconnect the brake tube (if possible), support the assembly on a wire.

2. Remove the grease cap, the cotter pin, the adjusting cap, the wheel bearing locknut and the thrust washer from the drive shaft.

3. Using Wheel Hub Remover tool KV40101000 and ST36230000, press the wheel hub/disc assembly from the steering knuckle.

4. Remove the disc-to-wheel hub bolts and separate the disc from the wheel hub (1982–86).

5. Install wheel hub/disc assembly to the vehicle. Torque the disc-to-wheel hub bolts to 18–25 ft. lbs. (25–34 Nm). Refer to wheel bearing adjustment in Section 8.

6. Install the caliper assembly and any other components to the vehicle.

7. Bleed brake system if necessary.

1987–96 Vehicles

♦ **See Figure 32**

→On 1987 and later vehicles, the brake disc can be removed from the hub without removing halfshaft nut and bearings.

1. Raise the front of the vehicle and support it on jackstands.
2. Remove the front wheels.
3. Refer to the Caliper removal and installation procedures in this section, and remove the caliper and the torque member from the steering knuckle.

→Do NOT disconnect the brake tube (if possible); support the assembly using a wire.

4. Insert two bolts (size M8 x 1.25) into the threaded holes in the brake rotor.

5. Gradually and evenly, tighten the bolts to remove the drum from hub.

To install:

6. Remove the two bolts from the threaded holes.
7. Install the rotor onto the hub assembly.
8. Install the caliper assembly to the vehicle.
9. Install the front wheels and properly torque the lug nuts.
10. Lower the vehicle to the ground and check brake operation.

INSPECTION

♦ **See Figures 33 and 34**

Visually inspect the surface of the rotors for scoring, hard spots (black discoloration's), and/or wear. Scoring or other surface imperfections, can be corrected by machining the brake rotor surface, providing there is enough available material to machine. Hard spots are caused by excessive heating of the rotor surface and usually can not be removed by resurfacing the rotor. Perform the following inspection procedures to determine if the rotor is okay, and if not, whether to resurface or discard the brake rotor.

1. Using a micrometer, check the thickness of the disc. Compare the reading to the brake specification chart in this section. If the rotor is below minimum thickness it must be discarded.

2. Using a dial indicator, check the run-out of the disc. Compare the reading to the brake specification chart in this section. If the measurement is greater than the maximum, resurface or replace the disc.

3. Check the parallelism of the disc, using a micrometer and measuring at four equally spaced points around the rotor. Compare the reading to the brake specification chart in this section. If the measurement is greater than the maximum, resurface or replace the disc.

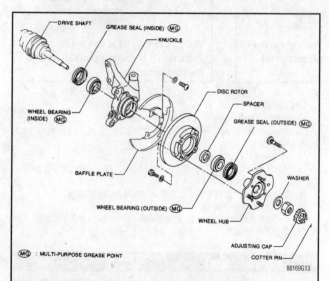

Fig. 30 Front disc and hub assembly—1982–86 vehicles

Fig. 31 Remove the caliper assembly and suspend it with a piece of wire

Fig. 32 Proper method of removing the brake rotor from the hub assembly—1987–96 vehicles

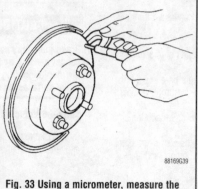

Fig. 33 Using a micrometer, measure the rotor thickness and parallelism

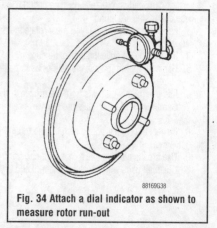

Fig. 34 Attach a dial indicator as shown to measure rotor run-out

REAR DRUM BRAKES

☀ CAUTION

Brake shoes may contain asbestos, which has been determined to be a cancer causing agent. Never clean brake surfaces with compressed air! Avoid inhaling any dust from any brake surfaces! When cleaning brake surfaces, use a commercially available brake cleaning fluid.

Brake Drum

REMOVAL & INSTALLATION

☀ CAUTION

Brake shoes may contain asbestos, which has been determined to be a cancer causing agent. Never clean the brake surfaces with compressed air! Avoid inhaling any dust from any brake surface! When cleaning brake surfaces, use a commercially available brake cleaning fluid.

1982–90 Vehicles

➡ **For rear wheel bearing procedures, refer to Section 8 1982–90).**

1. Raise the rear of the vehicle and support it on jackstands.
2. Remove the wheels.
3. Release the parking brake.
4. Remove the grease cap, the cotter pin and the wheel bearing nut (1982–90). Remove the drum without removing wheel bearing nut (1991–92 Sentra).
5. Pull off the drum, taking care not to drop the tapered bearing.

To install:

6. Install the drum assembly to the vehicle. Adjust the wheel bearing and adjust as outlined in section 8.
7. Install the wheels.

1991–96 Vehicles

▶ **See Figures 35 and 36**

1. Raise the rear of the vehicle and support it on jackstands.
2. Release the parking brake.
3. Remove the rear wheels.
4. Insert two bolts (size M8 x 1.25) into the threaded holes in the brake drum.
5. Gradually and evenly, tighten the bolts to remove the drum from hub.

➡ **It may be necessary to back off the brake shoe adjustment, if the shoes interfere with removal.**

To install:

6. Remove the two bolts from the threaded holes.
7. Install the drum onto the hub assembly.
8. Install the rear wheels.
9. Adjust the rear brake shoes, if necessary.
10. Lower the vehicle to the ground and check brake operation.

INSPECTION

After removing the brake drum, wipe out the accumulated dust with a damp cloth.

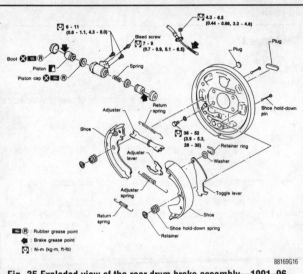

Fig. 35 Exploded view of the rear drum brake assembly—1991–96 Sentra, others similar

Fig. 36 Tighten the bolts to press the brake drum from the hub assembly

☀ CAUTION

DO NOT blow the brake dust out of the drums with compressed air or lung power. Brake linings contain asbestos, a known cancer causing substance. Dispose of the cloth after use.

Inspect the drum for cracks, deep grooves, roughness, scoring or out-of-roundness. Replace any brake drum which is cracked.

Smooth any slight scores by polishing the friction surface with the fine emery cloth. Heavy or extensive scoring will cause excessive brake lining wear and should be removed from the brake drum through resurfacing.

Brake Shoes

INSPECTION

♦ **See Figure 37**

1. Remove the brake drum.
2. Using a ruler, or similar tool, measure the shoe lining thickness as follows:
   • On bonded type linings—measure the minimum height the lining extends above the steel shoe.
   • On riveted type linings—measure the minimum height the lining extends above the rivet head.
3. Compare the readings to the specification found in the Brake Specifications chart at the end of this section.

➡ **This measurement may disagree with your state inspection laws.**

4. When replacing brake shoes, always check the surface of the brake drums for scoring or wear. The brake drums should resurfaced or machined if badly scored.

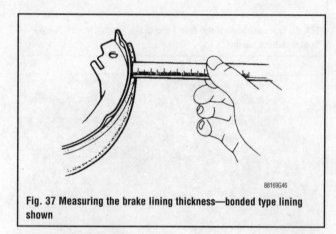

Fig. 37 Measuring the brake lining thickness—bonded type lining shown

REMOVAL & INSTALLATION

✻✻ CAUTION

Brake shoes may contain asbestos, which has been determined to be a cancer causing agent. Never clean the brake surfaces with compressed air! Avoid inhaling any dust from any brake surface! When cleaning brake surfaces, use a commercially available brake cleaning fluid.

1982–90 Vehicles

1. Refer to the Brake Drum removal and installation procedures in this section, and remove the brake drum.
2. Clean all brake hardware, using an approved brake cleaner and catch the run off with a pan.

➡ **It is a good practice to clean the dust from the from the brake components prior to disassembly. This will prevent excessive contact with the brake dust.**

3. Service one side at a time. Use the other as an example for installation. Release the parking brake lever, then remove the anti-rattle spring and the pin from the brake shoes.

➡ **To remove the anti-rattle spring and pin, push the spring/pin assembly into the brake shoe, turn it 90° and release it; the retainer cap, spring, washer and pin will separate.**

4. Supporting the brake shoe assembly, remove the return springs and brake shoes.

➡ **If the brake shoes are difficult to remove, loosen the brake adjusters. Place a heavy rubber band around the cylinder to prevent the piston from coming out.**

To install:

5. Clean the backing plate and check the wheel cylinder for leaks.
6. Lubricate the backing plate pads and the screw adjusters with lithium base grease.
7. Install the brake shoes and springs.
8. Install the drum assembly.
9. Adjust brakes and bleed system if necessary.

1991–96 Vehicles

♦ **See Figures 38, 39, 40 and 41**

➡ **If you are not familiar with the procedures involved in brake replacement, disassemble and assemble one side at a time, leaving the other wheel intact, as a reference. This will reduce the risk of assembling brakes incorrectly. Special brake tools are available to make this repair easier.**

1. Raise and support the vehicle safely.
2. Remove the rear wheels.
3. Release the parking brake and remove the brake drum.
4. Clean all brake hardware, using an approved brake cleaner and catch the run off with a pan.

➡ **It is a good practice to clean the dust from the from the brake components prior to disassembly. This will prevent excessive contact with the brake dust.**

5. Place a heavy rubber band or clamp around the wheel cylinder to prevent the piston from coming out.
6. Remove the return springs, adjuster assembly, hold-down springs, and the brake shoes.

Fig. 38 Prior to disassembly, use a spray type brake cleaner to remove dust from the brake hardware

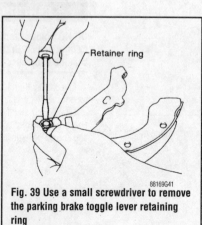

Fig. 39 Use a small screwdriver to remove the parking brake toggle lever retaining ring

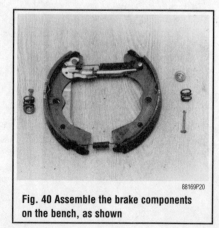

Fig. 40 Assemble the brake components on the bench, as shown

Fig. 41 If the hub is in the way, use needlenose pliers to remove and install the adjuster spring

7. Disconnect the parking brake cable from the toggle lever.
8. Remove the retainer ring and the toggle lever from the brake shoe.
To install:
9. Clean the backing plate and check the wheel cylinder for leaks.
10. The brake drums must be machined if scored or out of round.
11. Install the toggle lever to the proper brake shoe and secure with the retainer ring.
12. Connect the parking brake cable to the toggle lever.
13. Hook the return springs into the new shoes. The return spring ends should be between the shoes and the backing plate. The longer return spring must be adjacent to the wheel cylinder. A very thin film of lithium grease may be applied to the pivot points at the ends of the brake shoes. Also, grease the shoe locating buttons on the backing plate.

➡Be careful not to get grease on the linings or drums.

14. Install the adjuster assembly (rotate nut until adjuster rod is at its shortest point) between brake shoes. Place one shoe in the adjuster and piston slots and pry the other shoe into position.

REAR DISC BRAKES

❊❊ CAUTION

Brake pads may contain asbestos, which has been determined to be a cancer causing agent. Never clean brake surfaces with compressed air! Avoid inhaling any dust from any brake surfaces! When cleaning brake surfaces, use a commercially available brake cleaning fluid.

Brake Pads

REMOVAL & INSTALLATION

1991–96 Sentra

▶ See Figures 42, 43, 44 and 45

❊❊ WARNING

The Sentra rear brake system incorporates the parking brake mechanism into the rear brake caliper; therefore, do NOT attempt to press the piston into the bore (as performed on the front disc brakes), or the caliper assembly will be damaged.

1. Check the level of fluid in the master cylinder. If the fluid is near the maximum level, use a clean syringe to remove fluid until the level is down well below the lip of the reservoir.

➡When the caliper pistons are retracted into the caliper the brake fluid level will rise. Therefore, it may be necessary to remove some brake fluid from the master cylinder reservoir.

15. Position the brake shoes on the backing plate and secure in place using the hold-down springs.

➡Before installing the brake drum, inspect the assembled brake components. Verify that all components are properly positioned and secured in place.

16. Install the drums and wheels.
17. Adjust the brakes and bleed the hydraulic system, if necessary.
18. Lower the vehicle and road test it for proper brake system operation.

Wheel Cylinders

REMOVAL & INSTALLATION

❊❊ CAUTION

Brake shoes may contain asbestos, which has been determined to be a cancer causing agent. Never clean the brake surfaces with compressed air! Avoid inhaling any dust from any brake surface! When cleaning brake surfaces, use a commercially available brake cleaning fluid.

1. Remove the Brake Drum & Brake shoes following the procedures outlined in this section.
2. Disconnect the flare nut and the brake tube from the wheel cylinder, then plug the line to prevent dirt from entering the system.
3. Remove the wheel cylinder-to-backing plate bolts and the wheel cylinders.

➡If the wheel cylinder is difficult to remove, tap it with a soft hammer to release it from the backing plate.

To install:
4. Install the wheel cylinder assembly to the backing plate.
5. Connect all brake lines and torque retaining bolts to 60–96 inch lbs. (6–11 Nm) and pipe fitting to 12–14 ft. lbs. (17–22 Nm). Install the brake drum.
6. Bleed the brake system as outlined in this section.

2. Raise and support the vehicle safely.
3. Remove the rear wheels.
4. Release the parking brake and remove the cable mounting bracket bolt. Remove the bracket and the lock spring.
5. Remove the lower slide pin bolt and pivot the caliper body upward.
6. Remove the pad springs, pad shims and the brake pads.
To install:
7. Clean the piston end of the caliper body and the area around the pin holes.
8. Using a suitable pair of needle nose pliers, carefully turn the piston clockwise, while pushing the piston into the caliper body. Use care not to damage the piston boot.

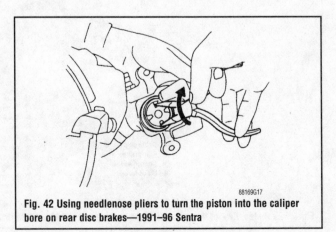

Fig. 42 Using needlenose pliers to turn the piston into the caliper bore on rear disc brakes—1991–96 Sentra

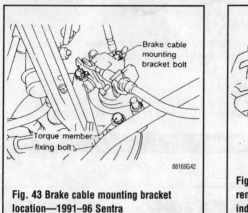

Fig. 43 Brake cable mounting bracket location—1991–96 Sentra

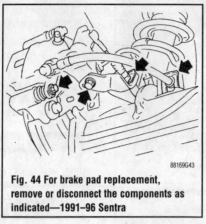

Fig. 44 For brake pad replacement, remove or disconnect the components as indicated—1991–96 Sentra

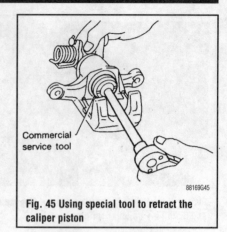

Fig. 45 Using special tool to retract the caliper piston

➡**A variety of special tools are available aid in retracting the rear caliper piston**

9. Coat the pad contact area on the mounting support with a silicone based grease.

10. Install the pads, shims and the pad springs. Always use new shims.

11. Position the caliper body in the mounting support and tighten the pin bolt to 28–38 ft. lbs. (38–52 Nm).

12. Operate the parking brake several times to properly seat the brake pads.

13. Install the wheels and lower the vehicle.

14. Verify proper brake operation before attempting to move the vehicle.

INSPECTION

You should be able to check the pad lining thickness without removing the pads. Check the Brake Specifications chart at the end of this section to find the manufacturer's pad wear limit. However, this measurement may disagree with your state inspection laws. When replacing pads, always check the surface of the rotors for scoring, hard spots (black discoloration's), and/or wear. Also check that the rotors are within specifications for thickness, parallelism and run-out. If any problems exist with the brake rotor the rotor must be resurfaced or discarded.

Brake Caliper

REMOVAL & INSTALLATION

◆ **See Figure 46**

1. Raise and support the vehicle safely.
2. Remove the rear wheels.

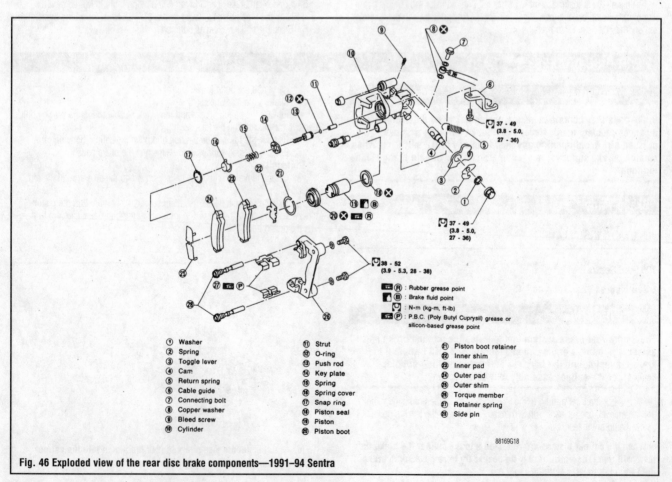

① Washer
② Spring
③ Toggle lever
④ Cam
⑤ Return spring
⑥ Cable guide
⑦ Connecting bolt
⑧ Copper washer
⑨ Bleed screw
⑩ Cylinder
⑪ Strut
⑫ O-ring
⑬ Push rod
⑭ Key plate
⑮ Spring
⑯ Spring cover
⑰ Snap ring
⑱ Piston seal
⑲ Piston
⑳ Piston boot
㉑ Piston boot retainer
㉒ Inner shim
㉓ Inner pad
㉔ Outer pad
㉕ Outer shim
㉖ Torque member
㉗ Retainer spring
㉘ Side pin

🔧 R : Rubber grease point
🔧 B : Brake fluid point
🔧 : N·m (kg-m, ft-lb)
🔧 P : P.B.C. (Poly Butyl Cuprysil) grease or silicon-based grease point

37 - 49 (3.8 - 5.0, 27 - 36)
37 - 49 (3.8 - 5.0, 27 - 36)
38 - 52 (3.9 - 5.3, 28 - 38)

Fig. 46 Exploded view of the rear disc brake components—1991–94 Sentra

3. Release the parking brake.

4. Remove the cable guide bracket bolt and lock spring.

5. Disconnect the parking brake cable from the toggle lever.

6. Disconnect the brake hose from the caliper and plug.

7. Remove the slide pin bolts and lift off the caliper body.

To install:

8. Clean the piston end of the caliper body and the area around the pin holes.

9. Using the proper tool, carefully turn the piston clockwise back into the caliper body. Take care not to damage the piston boot.

10. Coat the pad contact area on the mounting support with a silicone based grease.

11. Install the pads, shims and the pad springs. Always use new shims.

12. Position the caliper body in the mounting support and tighten the pin bolts to 28–38 ft. lbs. (38–52 Nm).

13. Connect the brake hose and tighten the connecting bolt to 12–14 ft. lbs. (17–20 Nm).

14. Connect the parking brake cable to the toggle lever.

15. Install the cable guide bracket bolt and lock spring.

16. Operate the parking brake several times to properly seat the brake pads.

17. Properly bleed the brake system.

18. Install the wheels and lower the vehicle.

19. Verify proper brake operation before attempting to move the vehicle.

OVERHAUL

1991–94 Vehicles

♦ See Figures 47, 48, 49 and 50

1. Following proper procedures, remove the brake caliper from the vehicle.

2. Remove the caliper piston by turning counterclockwise with a suitable tool.

3. Remove the piston boot retainer using a suitable prybar.

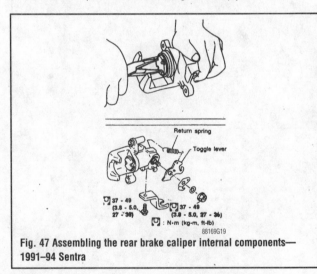

Fig. 47 Assembling the rear brake caliper internal components—1991–94 Sentra

4. Using a suitable pair of pliers, pry off the snapring and remove the spring cover, spring, key plate, pushrod and strut.

5. Using care not to damage the cylinder body, remove the piston seal

6. Remove the return spring and toggle lever.

To assemble:

7. Inspect all components for damage, rust, corrosion or cracks.

❈❈ WARNING

Do NOT attempt to polish the piston or cylinder body bore. These surfaces are plated and will be damaged.

8. Clean all components in denatured alcohol and dry with compressed air.

9. Lubricate external moving parts with special brake system grease and internal components with brake assembly lubricant.

10. Insert the cam with the depression facing towards the open end of cylinder.

11. Apply special rubber grease to the strut and pushrod. Install the strut and pushrod.

12. Match the depressions in the cylinder bottom with the key plate protrusions and install the key plate.

13. Install the spring, spring cover. Using snapring pliers and the snapring, secure the components in place.

14. Lubricate and install the piston seal.

15. Install the piston by turning it clockwise with a suitable turning tool.

16. Install the toggle lever and return spring. Torque the lever nut to 27–36 ft. lbs. (37–49 Nm).

17. Reinstall the caliper to the vehicle.

1995–96 Vehicles

♦ See Figures 51, 52, 53, 54 and 55

1. Following proper procedures, remove the brake caliper from the vehicle.

2. Remove the caliper piston by turning counterclockwise using a suitable tool.

3. Remove the piston boot retainer using a suitable prybar.

4. Disassemble the caliper piston as follows:

   a. Remove the snapring from the back of the piston.

   b. Remove the adjusting nut.

5. Using a suitable pair of pliers, remove the snapring from the caliper bore.

6. Remove the spring cover, spring, spring seat, key plate, pushrod and strut from the caliper bore.

7. Using care not to damage the cylinder body, remove the piston seal

8. Remove the return spring, toggle lever and cable guide from the caliper body.

To assemble:

9. Inspect all components for damage, rust, corrosion or cracks.

❈❈ WARNING

Do NOT attempt to polish the piston or cylinder body bore. These surfaces are plated and will be damaged.

10. Clean all components in denatured alcohol and dry with compressed air.

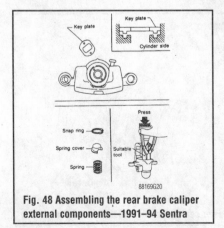

Fig. 48 Assembling the rear brake caliper external components—1991–94 Sentra

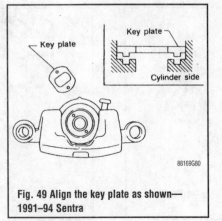

Fig. 49 Align the key plate as shown—1991–94 Sentra

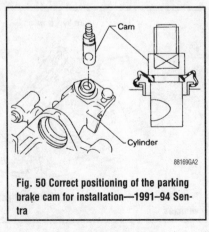

Fig. 50 Correct positioning of the parking brake cam for installation—1991–94 Sentra

11. Lubricate external moving parts with special brake system grease and internal components with brake assembly lubricant.

12. Insert the cam with the depression facing towards the open end of cylinder.

13. Apply special rubber grease to the strut and pushrod. Install the strut and pushrod.

14. Match the depressions in the cylinder bottom with the key plate protrusions. With the key plate properly positioned, secure it in place using the snapring.

15. Install the spring seat, spring and spring cover. Using the snapring, secure the components in place.

16. Assemble the piston adjuster components and install in the piston.

➡**Make certain that the adjuster is correctly positioned in the piston and facing the proper direction.**

17. Lubricate and install the piston seal.

18. Fit the piston boot to the piston and position the piston in the caliper bore.

19. Install the piston by turning it clockwise with a suitable tool.

20. Install the toggle lever, return spring and cable guide. Torque the lever nut to 18–22 ft. lbs. (25–29 Nm) and the cable guide bolt to 20–27 ft. lbs. (26–36 Nm).

21. Reinstall the caliper.

Brake Disc (Rotor)

REMOVAL & INSTALLATION

1991–96 Sentra

1. Raise the vehicle and support safely.
2. Remove the rear wheel.
3. Remove the brake caliper as outlined in this section.

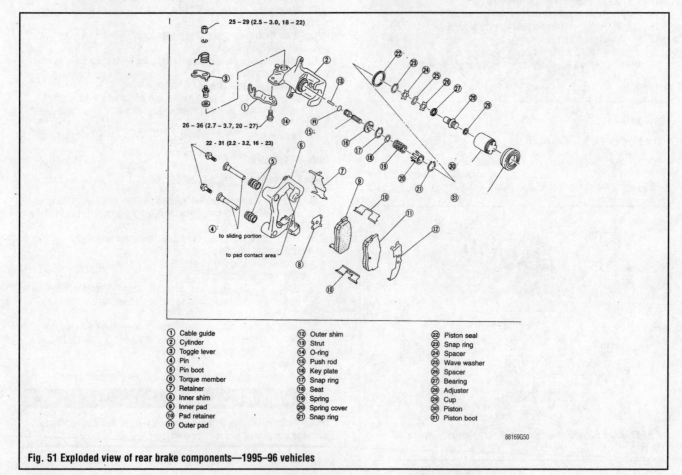

① Cable guide	⑫ Outer shim	㉒ Piston seal
② Cylinder	⑬ Strut	㉓ Snap ring
③ Toggle lever	⑭ O-ring	㉔ Spacer
④ Pin	⑮ Push rod	㉕ Wave washer
⑤ Pin boot	⑯ Key plate	㉖ Spacer
⑥ Torque member	⑰ Snap ring	㉗ Bearing
⑦ Retainer	⑱ Seat	㉘ Adjuster
⑧ Inner shim	⑲ Spring	㉙ Cup
⑨ Inner pad	⑳ Spring cover	㉚ Piston
⑩ Pad retainer	㉑ Snap ring	㉛ Piston boot
⑪ Outer pad		

Fig. 51 Exploded view of rear brake components—1995–96 vehicles

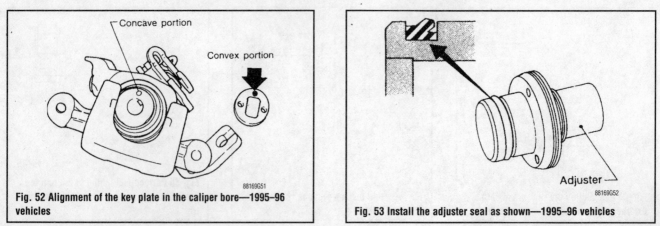

Fig. 52 Alignment of the key plate in the caliper bore—1995–96 vehicles

Fig. 53 Install the adjuster seal as shown—1995–96 vehicles

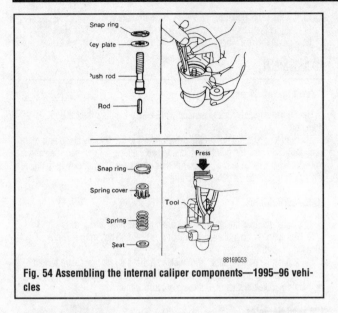

Fig. 54 Assembling the internal caliper components—1995–96 vehicles

Fig. 55 Assembling the caliper piston assembly—1995–96 vehicles

INSPECTION

♦ **See Figures 33 and 34**

Visually inspect the surface of the rotors for scoring, hard spots (black discoloration's), and/or wear. Scoring or other surface imperfections, can be corrected by machining the brake rotor surface, providing there is enough available material to machine. Hard spots are caused by excessive heating of the rotor surface and usually can not be removed by resurfacing the rotor. Perform the following inspection procedures to determine if the rotor is okay, and if not, whether to resurface or discard the brake rotor.

1. Using a micrometer, check the thickness of the disc. Compare the reading to the Brake Specification chart in this section. If the rotor is below minimum thickness it must be discarded.

2. Using a dial indicator, check the run-out of the disc. Compare the reading to the Brake Specification chart in this section. If the measurement is greater than the maximum, resurface or replace the disc.

3. Check the parallelism of the disc, using a micrometer and measuring at four equally spaced points around the rotor. Compare the reading to the brake specification chart in this section. If the measurement is greater than the maximum, resurface or replace the disc.

➠Do NOT allow the caliper to hang from the brake hose. Hang the caliper by a wire.

4. Remove the brake caliper torque member.
5. Remove the rotor retaining screw and rotor.

To install:

6. Install the rotor and retaining screw.
7. Install the torque member, brake pads and caliper as outlined in this section. Torque the member bolts to 28–38 ft. lbs. (38–52 Nm).
8. Install the rear wheel and lower the vehicle.
9. Pump the brakes a few times before driving.

PARKING BRAKE

Cables

REMOVAL & INSTALLATION

1982–86 Vehicles

♦ **See Figure 56**

FRONT CABLE

1. Raise and support the rear of the vehicle on jackstands.
2. Place the parking brake lever in the released position.
3. Separate the front cable from the rear cable at the equalizer.
4. Remove the center console.
5. Disconnect the parking brake lamp switch harness connector, then remove the seat belt anchor bolts.
6. Remove the control lever mounting bolts and the front cable bracket mounting screws.
7. If necessary, separate the front cable from the parking brake control lever by breaking the pin.

➠If the pin must be broken to separate the front cable from the control lever, be sure to use a new pin in the installation procedures.

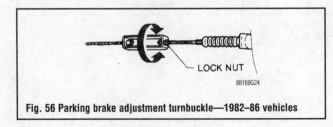

Fig. 56 Parking brake adjustment turnbuckle—1982–86 vehicles

To install:

8. Install the control lever/front cable assembly in through the driver's compartment with a new pin if necessary.
9. Connect the parking brake lamp switch harness connector and the seat belt anchor bolts.
10. Install the center console.
11. Connect the rear end of brake cable to the attaching point.
12. Adjust the parking brake cable.

REAR CABLE

1. Refer to the Brake Drum or Disc removal and installation procedures in this section, and remove the brake drum or disc.
2. At the cable adjuster, loosen the adjusting nut, then separate the rear cable from the adjuster.
3. Remove the brake shoes from the backing plate, then separate the rear cable from the toggle lever (rear drum brakes). Remove the cable retainer and cable end from the toggle lever (rear disc brakes).
4. Pull the cable through the backing plate and remove it from the vehicle.

To install:

5. Install the brake cable through the backing plate (drum brakes).
6. Install the brake shoes with cable attached and drum (drum brakes). Connect the cable to the toggle lever and torque the cable retainer to 36–60 inch lbs. (5–6 Nm) (disc brakes).
7. Connect the brake cable at the adjuster.
8. Adjust the parking brake cable.

1987–96 Vehicles

FRONT CABLE

1. Remove the center console assembly.
2. Loosen and remove the parking brake cable adjusting nut at the base of the parking brake lever.

3. From under the vehicle, disconnect the parking brake cables at the equalizer.

4. Unbolt the parking brake lever from the center console.

5. Unbolt and remove the front parking brake cable from the vehicle.

To install:

6. Install the front parking brake cable into the parking brake lever and start the adjusting nut on the front cable.

7. Install the lever and cable assembly. Tighten the mounting bolts.

8. From under the vehicle, connect the parking brake cables at the equalizer.

9. Install the center console assembly.

10. Adjust the parking brake cable.

REAR CABLE—DRUM BRAKES

1. Raise and properly support the vehicle

2. Remove the rear wheel.

3. At the cable adjuster, loosen the adjusting nut, then separate the rear cable from the equalizer.

4. Remove the rear brake drum.

5. Remove the brake shoes from the backing plate

6. Separate the rear cable from the toggle lever.

7. Remove the bolts and nuts that secure the cable to the under body.

8. Pull the cable through the backing plate and remove it from the vehicle.

To install:

9. Install the brake cable through the backing plate.

10. Install the brake shoes, with cable attached, to the toggle lever.

11. Install the brake drum.

12. Install the bolts that secure the cable to the under body.

13. At the cable equalizer, connect the parking brake cable.

14. Adjust the parking brake cable.

15. Install the rear wheels and lower the vehicle.

REAR CABLE—DISC BRAKES

1. Raise and properly support the vehicle

2. At the cable adjuster, loosen the adjusting nut, then separate the rear cable from the equalizer.

3. Remove the cable guide bracket bolt and lock spring.

4. Disconnect the parking brake cable from the toggle lever.

5. Remove the bolts and nuts that secure the cable to the vehicle under body.

6. Remove the cable from the vehicle.

To install:

7. Connect the cable to the toggle lever.

8. Install the cable guide bracket bolt and lock spring.

9. Install the bolts that secure the cable to the under body.

10. At the cable equalizer, connect the parking brake cable.

11. Adjust the parking brake cable.

12. Install the rear wheels and lower the vehicle.

ADJUSTMENT

▶ **See Figures 57 and 58**

Handbrake adjustments are generally not needed, unless the cables have stretched.

There is an adjusting nut on the cable under the car, usually at the end of the front cable and near the point at which the two cables from the rear wheels come together (the equalizer). Some models also have a turnbuckle in the rear cable to compensate for cable stretching.

1982–86 Vehicles

1. Adjust the rear brakes with the parking brake fully released.

2. Apply the hand brake lever so that it is 6–7 notches from its fully released position.

3. Adjust the parking brake turnbuckle so that the rear brakes are locked.

4. Release the parking brake. The wheels should turn freely. If not, loosen the parking brake adjuster until the wheels turn with no drag.

1987–96 Vehicles

▶ **See Figure 59**

➡ **Make sure the rear brakes are properly adjusted prior to making any adjustments to the parking brake.**

1. Make sure that the rear brakes are in good condition.

2. Carefully remove the dust boot from around the parking brake lever.

3. The adjustment is made by determining the amount of force needed to pull up on the lever. A force of 44 lbs. (195 N) should be needed to raise the lever 7–8 notches for drum brake vehicles or 8–9 notches for disc brake vehicles.

4. To adjust the pull, raise and support the vehicle safely on jackstands. There is an adjusting nut on the hand brake clevis rod. Loosen the locknut and turn the adjusting nut to establish the correct pull.

5. Tighten the adjuster locknut.

6. With the parking brake released, the rear wheels should turn freely. When the parking brake lever is pulled up 6–8 notches, the rear wheels should not turn.

7. Bend the parking brake warning lamp switch plate so that the warning lamp illuminates when the parking brake lever is raised 1 notch. The warning lamp should extinguish after the parking brake lever is completely released.

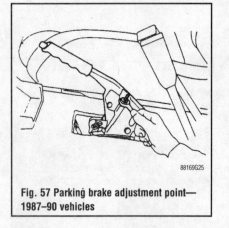

88169G25

Fig. 57 Parking brake adjustment point—1987–90 vehicles

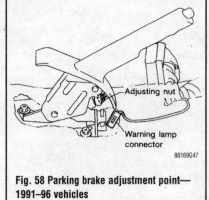

88169G47

Fig. 58 Parking brake adjustment point—1991–96 vehicles

88169P16

Fig. 59 Remove the center console and use a 10mm wrench to adjust the brake cable tension

ANTI-LOCK BRAKE (ABS) SYSTEM

Description and Operation

Anti-lock braking systems (ABS) are designed to prevent locked-wheel skidding during hard braking or during braking on slippery surfaces. The front wheels of a vehicle cannot apply steering force if they are locked and sliding; the vehicle will continued in its previous direction of travel. The four wheel anti-lock brake systems found on Nissan vehicles hold the wheels just below the point of locking, thereby allowing some steering response and preventing the rear of the vehicle from sliding sideways under braking.

There are conditions for which the ABS system provides no benefit. Hydroplaning is possible when the tires ride on a film of water, losing contact with the paved surface. This renders the vehicle totally uncontrollable until road contact is regained. Extreme steering maneuvers at high speed or cornering beyond the limits of tire adhesion can result in skidding which is independent of vehicle braking. For this reason, the system is named anti-lock rather than anti-skid.

Under normal braking conditions, the ABS system functions in the same manner as a standard brake system. The system is a combination of electrical and hydraulic components, working together to control the flow of brake fluid to the wheels when necessary.

The anti-lock brake system Electronic Control Unit (ECU) is the electronic brain of the system, receiving and interpreting speed signals from the speed sensors. The ECU will enter anti-lock mode when it senses impending wheel lock at any wheel and immediately controls the brake line pressure(s) to the affected wheel(s). The actuator assembly is separate from the master cylinder and booster. It contains the wheel circuit valves used to control the brake fluid pressure to each wheel circuit.

System Operation

When the ECU receives signals showing one or more wheels about to lock, it sends an electrical signal to the solenoid valve(s) within the actuator to release the brake pressure in the line. The solenoid moves to a position which allows some pressurized brake fluid to flow out of the brake line into a holding reservoir. As the wheel unlocks or rolls faster, the ECU senses the increase and signals the solenoid to re-apply hydraulic pressure. Additionally, the ECU can signal the solenoid to hold present line pressure, allowing neither increase nor decrease if the situation requires it.

This cycling occurs several times per second when ABS is engaged. In this fashion, the wheels are kept just below the point of lock-up and control is maintained. When the hard braking ends, the ECU resets the solenoids to its normal or build mode. Brake line fluid pressures are then increased or modulated directly by pressure on the brake pedal. Fluid released to the ABS reservoirs is returned to the master cylinder by the pump and motor within the actuator.

On most systems, the front wheels are controlled individually, although the Sentra and NX Coupe's system links control with the opposite rear wheel. Depending on the model, the rear wheel solenoid circuits may receive the same electrical signal or be under individual control.

The operator may hear a popping or clicking sound as the pump and/or control valves cycle ON and OFF during normal ABS operation. The sounds are due to normal operation and are not indicative of a system problem. Under most conditions, the sounds are only faintly audible. If ABS is engaged, the operator may notice some pulsation in the body of the vehicle during a hard stop; this is generally due to suspension shudder as the brake pressures are altered rapidly and the forces transfer to the vehicle.

Although the ABS system prevents wheel lock-up under hard braking, as brake pressure increases wheel slip is allowed to increase as well. This slip will result in some tire chirp during ABS operation. The sound should not be interpreted as lock-up but rather as an indication of the system holding the wheel(s) just outside the point of lock-up. Additionally, the final few feet of an ABS-engaged stop may be completed with the wheels locked; the electronic controls do not operate below approximately 6 mph.

SERVICE PRECAUTIONS

- If the vehicle is equipped with air bag or Supplemental Restraint Systems (SRS), always properly disable the system before working on or around system components.
- Always use a digital, high-impedance volt-ohmmeter (DVOM) for testing unless otherwise specified. Minimum impedance should be 10 megohms.
- Certain components within the ABS system are not intended to be repaired individually. Only those components with disassembly procedures should be serviced.
- Do not use rubber hoses or other parts not specifically specified for the ABS system. When using repair kits, replace all parts included in the kit. Partial or incorrect repair may lead to functional problems and require the replacement of components.
- Lubricate rubber parts with clean, fresh brake fluid to ease assembly. Do not use lubricated shop air to clean parts; damage to rubber components may result.
- Use only DOT 3 brake fluid from an unopened container. Do not reuse drained fluid.
- If any hydraulic component or line is removed or replaced, it may be necessary to bleed the entire system.
- A clean repair area is essential. Always clean the reservoir and cap thoroughly before removing the cap. The slightest amount of dirt in the fluid may plug an orifice and impair the system function. Perform repairs after components have been thoroughly cleaned. Do not allow ABS components to come into contact with any substance containing mineral oil; this includes used shop rags.
- The anti-lock brake controller is a microprocessor similar to other computer units in the vehicle. Ensure the ignition switch is OFF before removing or installing controller harnesses. Avoid static electricity discharge at or near the controller.
- If any arc welding is to be done on the vehicle, the ABS controller should be disconnected before welding operations begin.
- If the vehicle is to be baked after paint repairs, disconnect and remove the ABS ECU from the vehicle.
- Never disconnect any electrical connection with the ignition switch ON unless instructed to do so in a test.
- Avoid touching module connector pins.
- Leave new components and modules in the shipping package until ready to install them.
- Always touch a vehicle ground after sliding across a vehicle seat or walking across vinyl or carpeted floors to avoid static charge damage.
- Never allow welding cables to lie on, near or across any vehicle electrical wiring.
- Avoid allowing extension cords for power tools or drop lamps to lie on, near or across any vehicle electrical wiring.

DEPRESSURIZING THE SYSTEM

This is a low pressure system, No special system depressurization is necessary. Follow normal service procedure for bleeding, filling and repairs to the system.

SYSTEM REFILL

The brake fluid reservoir is located on top of the master cylinder. While no special procedures are needed to fill the fluid, the reservoir cap and surrounding area must be wiped clean of all dirt and debris before removing the cap. The slightest dirt in the fluid can cause a system malfunction. Use only DOT 3 fluid from an unopened container. Use of old, polluted or non-approved fluid can seriously impair the function of the system.

SYSTEM BLEEDING

On vehicles equipped with anti-lock brake (ABS) systems, turn the ignition switch to the **OFF** position and disconnect the negative battery cable. All other steps apply to both ABS and conventional brake systems.

For the specific procedure, refer to bleeding of the conventional brake system as outlined in this section.

Self-Diagnosis and Diagnostic Codes

READING CODES

1991–94 Vehicles

♦ **See Figures 60 and 61**

When the ECU detects a fault, the ABS warning light on the dash will light. The ECU will perform a self-diagnosis to identify the problem area. When the vehicle is presented with an apparent ABS problem, it must be test driven above 19 mph (30 km/h) for at least 1 minute; this allows the ECU time to satisfactorily test the system and store a diagnostic trouble code.

➡ **The ECU does not have the ability to store codes. When a problem occurs, the ignition switch must remain in the ON position, in order to retrieve the fault code(s).**

The trouble code will be displayed by the flashing of the LED on the ECU. The display begins when the vehicle comes to a full stop after the self-diagnosis process. The engine must be running for the code to display. The stored code will repeat after a 5–10 second pause.

After repairs have been made, the vehicle should be driven above 19 mph (30 km/h) for at least 1 minute to verify the problem has been corrected.

1995–96 Vehicles

♦ **See Figures 62, 63 and 64**

Trouble codes can be viewed by activating the ABS warning lamp. The lamp will flash a series of pulses. The first set of ON/OFF pulses will indicate the tens digits. They will be followed by a 1.6 second break and then the units digits will be displayed.

1. Drive the vehicle for at least one minute above 20 mph (32 km/h).
2. Turn the ignition switch to the off position.
3. Locate the Date Link Connector (DLC) near the fuse box and ground terminal **L** of the connector.
4. Observe the ABS warning lamp. The lamp will flash any stored trouble codes, beginning with Code 12.

CLEARING CODES

1991–94 Vehicles

Turn the ignition switch **OFF**, then restart the vehicle and drive above 19 mph (30 km/h) for at least one minute. If the system is functioning properly and there are no malfunctions the light should remain **OFF**.

1995–96 Vehicles

1. Locate the Date Link Connector (DLC) near the fuse box and ground terminal **L** of the connector.
2. Turn the ignition switch to the **ON** position.
3. Within a 12 second time period, disconnect and reconnect the ground connection at terminal **L** three times.

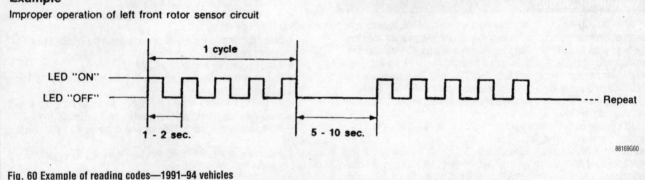

Example

Improper operation of left front rotor sensor circuit

Fig. 60 Example of reading codes—1991–94 vehicles

No. of LED flashes	Malfunctioning parts or circuit
1	Left front actuator solenoid circuit
2	Right front actuator solenoid circuit
3	Both actuator solenoid circuits
5	Left front wheel sensor circuit
6	Right front wheel sensor circuit
7	Right rear wheel sensor circuit
8	Left rear wheel sensor circuit
9	Motor and motor relay
10	Solenoid valve relay
15	Sensor rotor
*16	Solenoid valve relay or control unit
Warning activates and LED "OFF"	Power supply and ground circuit

Fig. 61 Diagnostic trouble code chart—1991–94 vehicles

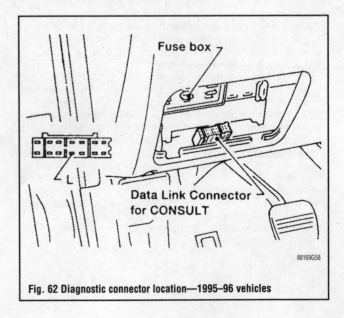

Fig. 62 Diagnostic connector location—1995–96 vehicles

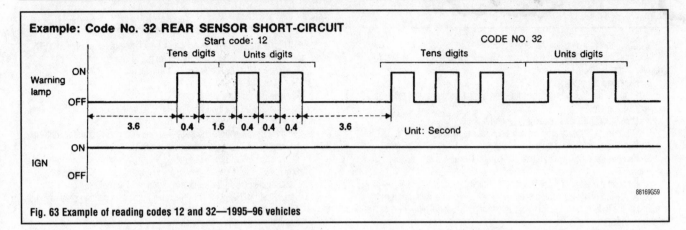

Fig. 63 Example of reading codes 12 and 32—1995–96 vehicles

Code No. (No. of LED flashes)	Malfunctioning part
45	Actuator front left outlet solenoid valve
46	Actuator front left inlet solenoid valve
41	Actuator front right outlet solenoid valve
42	Actuator front right inlet solenoid valve
51	Actuator rear right outlet solenoid valve
52	Actuator rear right inlet solenoid valve
55	Actuator rear left outlet solenoid valve
56	Actuator rear left inlet solenoid valve
25	Front left sensor (open-circuit)
26	Front left sensor (short-circuit)
21	Front right sensor (open-circuit)
22	Front right sensor (short-circuit)
35	Rear left sensor (open-circuit)
36	Rear left sensor (short-circuit)
31	Rear right sensor (open-circuit)
32	Rear right sensor (short-circuit)
18	Sensor rotor
61	Actuator motor or motor relay
63	Solenoid valve relay
57	Power supply (Low voltage)
71	Control unit
Warning lamp stays on when ignition switch is turned on	Control unit power supply circuit Warning lamp bulb circuit Control unit or control unit connector Solenoid valve relay stuck Power supply for solenoid valve relay coil
Warning lamp stays on, during self-diagnosis	Control unit
Warning lamp does not come on when ignition switch is turned on	Fuse, warning lamp bulb or warning lamp circuit Control unit
Warning lamp does not come on during self-diagnosis	Control unit

Fig. 64 Diagnostic trouble code chart—1995–96 vehicles

➡The ground connection must remain grounded for at least a one second duration.

4. When the codes have been successfully erased, the warning lamp will extinguish.

INITIAL CHECKS

Visual Inspection

Before diagnosing an apparent ABS problem, make absolutely certain that the normal braking system is in correct working order. Many common brake problems (dragging parking brake, seepage, etc.) will affect the ABS system. A visual check of specific system components may reveal problems creating an apparent ABS malfunction. Performing this inspection may reveal a simple failure, thus eliminating extended diagnostic time.

1. Inspect the tire pressures; they must be approximately equal for the system to operate correctly.
2. Inspect the brake fluid level in the reservoir.
3. Inspect brake lines, hoses, master cylinder assembly and brake calipers for leakage.
4. Visually check brake lines and hoses for excessive wear, heat damage, punctures, contact with other parts, missing clips or holders, blockage or crimping.
5. Check the calipers for rust or corrosion. Check for proper sliding action if applicable.
6. Check the caliper pistons for freedom of motion during application and release.
7. Inspect the wheel speed sensors for proper mounting and connections.
8. Inspect the sensor wheels for broken teeth or poor mounting.
9. Inspect the wheels and tires on the vehicle. They must be of the same size and type to generate accurate speed signals.
10. Confirm the fault occurrence with the operator. Certain driver induced faults, such as not-releasing the parking brake fully, will set a fault code and trigger the dash warning light. Excessive wheel spin on low-traction surfaces may set an ABS fault code. High speed acceleration or riding the brake pedal may also set fault codes and trigger a warning lamp. These induced faults are not system failures but examples of vehicle performance outside the parameters of the control unit.
11. Many system shut-downs are due to loss of sensor signals to or from the controller. The most common cause is not a failed sensor but a loose, corroded or dirty connector. Incorrect adjustment of the wheel speed sensor will cause a loss of wheel speed signal. Check harness and component connectors carefully.

Hydraulic Actuator

DESCRIPTION

The actuator is located in the engine compartment. The actuator contains the solenoid control valves, pump(s) to return fluid to the brake master cylinder, reservoirs for temporary collection of brake fluid released from the lines as well as check and relief valves.

The relays and solenoids are controlled by the ECU. Under normal braking conditions, the solenoids are in the open or pressure-build position, allowing brake fluid to pass proportional to pedal pressure. During anti-lock function, the solenoids are commanded into positions to either hold or release brake fluid line pressures as required. When anti-lock function is no longer needed, the solenoids reset to the normal position. Additionally, if the ECU detects a system fault, the solenoids are immediately released to the normal or default position.

The control relays for the pump motor and solenoid valves are located externally on/or near the actuator. The relays are controlled by the ECU and are the only actuator components that can be serviced separately. Any other failure associated with the actuator requires the entire unit to be replaced.

REMOVAL & INSTALLATION

1. Disconnect the negative battery cable.
2. Drain the brake fluid from the system. Use a syringe or similar tool to drain the fluid reservoir.
3. Drain the power steering fluid.
4. Properly discharge the air conditioning system using correct refrigerant recovery equipment.
5. Disconnect the power steering line and hose.
6. Disconnect all connectors from the actuator relay bracket.
7. Remove the mounting nut for the relay bracket.
8. Remove the bolt holding the relay bracket. The bolt is located just below the relays.
9. Remove the actuator relay box with its bracket.
10. At the top of the actuator, disconnect the 2 brake lines running from the actuator to the master cylinder. It is not necessary to disconnect the lines at the master cylinder.
11. Completely remove the 2 lines running from the actuator to the dual proportioning valve.
12. Remove or loosen the mounting nuts holding the actuator to the bracket.
13. Remove the actuator grounding bolt.
14. Carefully lift the actuator forward and out of the vehicle.
To install:
15. Install the actuator into the vehicle.
16. Install the grounding bolt.
17. Install and tighten the nuts holding the actuator to its bracket.
18. Connect the brake lines between the actuator and the proportioning valve. Tighten the fittings to 13 ft. lbs. (17 Nm).
19. Connect the 2 brake lines to the top of the actuator, tightening them to 13 ft. lbs. (17 Nm).
20. Install the remaining components in the reverse order of removal.
21. Refill the power steering fluid.
22. Refill the brake fluid and bleed the system thoroughly.
23. Connect the negative battery cable.
24. Recharge the air conditioning system.

ABS Electronic Control Unit (ECU)

DESCRIPTION

The solid-state control unit computes the rotating speed of the wheels by the signal current sent from each sensor. When impending lock-up is detected, the ECU signals the actuator solenoids to move to predetermined positions to control brake fluid pressure to the wheels. The ECU also controls the ON/OFF operation of the solenoid valve relay and the pump relay.

The ECU constantly monitors the function of components within the system. If any electrically detectable fault occurs, the control unit will illuminate the dashboard warning light to alert the operator. When the dash warning lamp is lit, the ABS system is disabled. The vehicle retains its normal braking capabilities without the benefit of anti-lock.

If an electrical fault is found, the ECU will assign and store a diagnostic or fault code. The code may be read and used for system diagnosis. The later model vehicles have the capability of storing up to 3 codes. If more than one fault occurs on any other vehicles, the system will only store one code and the vehicle must be road tested after repairs to allow any remaining fault to be identified.

TESTING

The are no provisions for testing the ECU in the field. Proper diagnosis of a problem with the ECU, requires testing of all associated components within the suspected circuit. By ruling out potential components and wiring circuits, the ECU can be determined to be the cause of a suspected problem.

➡**It is important to follow all proper troubleshooting procedures before suspecting a faulty ECU.**

REMOVAL & INSTALLATION

The ECU is located behind the right kick panel. Remove the panel and ECU. Make sure the multi-connector is tight before going any further.
1. Turn the ignition switch to the **OFF** position.
2. Disconnect the negative battery cable.
3. Remove the right front kick panel.
4. Remove the nut and bolt holding the ECU to the body. Note the ground lug on the bolt.
5. Lift the ECU away from the body. Release any retainers on the multi-pin connector and separate the connector from the ECU.
6. Remove the ECU from the vehicle.
To install:
7. Position the ECU in the vehicle and connect the multi-pin connector.
8. Secure the ECU in place with the retaining nut. Attach the ground lug to the bolt before installing the retaining bolt.
9. Install the right side kick panel.
10. Connect the negative battery cable.
11. Check ABS light operation and verify proper operation.

Actuator Motor Relay

DESCRIPTION

The actuator motor relay is located externally on/or near the actuator. The relay supplies power to the actuator motor and is controlled by the ECU. Power is supplied to the relay from the battery, through a pair of fusible links.

TESTING

1991–94 Vehicles

▶ **See Figure 65**

1. Disconnect the negative battery cable.
2. Disconnect the motor (4 terminal) relay located on the right front strut tower.
3. Connect an ohmmeter between terminals 3 and 4 of the relay.
4. Verify the resistance is greater than 10 kilo-ohms.
5. Connect a 12 volt source to terminals 1 and 2.
6. Verify there is continuity between terminals 3 and 4.
7. If not as specified, replace the relay.

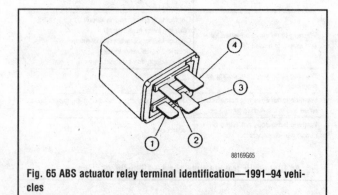

88169G65

Fig. 65 ABS actuator relay terminal identification—1991–94 vehicles

1995–96 Vehicles

▶ **See Figures 66 and 67**

1. Disconnect the negative battery cable.
2. Disconnect the motor (4 terminal) relay located at the actuator.
3. Connect an ohmmeter between terminals 30 and 87 of the relay. Continuity should NOT exist.
4. Connect a 12 volt source to terminals 85 and 86.
5. Verify there is continuity between terminals 30 and 87.
6. If not as specified, replace the relay.

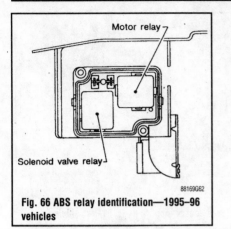

Fig. 66 ABS relay identification—1995–96 vehicles

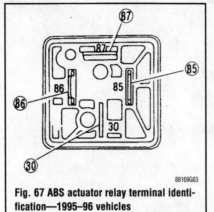

Fig. 67 ABS actuator relay terminal identification—1995–96 vehicles

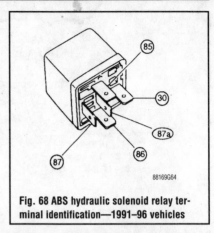

Fig. 68 ABS hydraulic solenoid relay terminal identification—1991–96 vehicles

REMOVAL & INSTALLATION

1. Disconnect the negative battery cable.
2. Locate the relay box and remove the cover.
3. Identify the proper relay and pull the relay from the box.
To install:
4. Align the relay terminals with the sockets in the relay box and firmly press the relay into position.
5. Install the relay cover.
6. Connect the negative battery cable.

Hydraulic Solenoid Relay

DESCRIPTION

▶ **See Figure 68**

The hydraulic solenoid relay is located externally on/or near the actuator. The relay supplies power to the actuator control solenoids and is controlled by the ECU. Power is supplied to the relay from the battery, through a fuse on 1991–94 vehicles, or a fusible link on 1995–96 vehicles.

TESTING

1. Disconnect the negative battery cable.
2. Disconnect the hydraulic solenoid (5 terminal) relay located at or near the actuator.
3. Connect an ohmmeter between terminals 30 and 87A of the relay and verify there is continuity.
4. Connect an ohmmeter between terminals 30 and 87 of the relay and verify there is no continuity.
5. Connect a 12 volt source to terminals 85 and 86.
6. Verify there is no continuity between terminals 30 and 87A.
7. Next with the 12 volt source still connected to terminal 85 and 86, connect the ohmmeter between terminals 30 and 87 of the relay.
8. Verify there is continuity between terminals 30 and 87.
9. If not as specified, replace the relay.

REMOVAL & INSTALLATION

1. Disconnect the negative battery cable.
2. Locate the relay box and remove the cover.
3. Identify the proper relay and pull the relay from the box.
To install:
4. Align the relay terminals with the sockets in the relay box and firmly press the relay into position.
5. Install the relay cover.
6. Connect the negative battery cable.

Speed Sensor

DESCRIPTION

The speed of the front and rear wheels is monitored by the speed sensors. A toothed wheel rotates in front of the sensor generating a small AC voltage which is transmitted to the ABS ECU. The ECU compares the signals and reacts to rapid loss of wheel speed at a particular wheel by engaging the ABS system. Each speed sensor is individually removable. In most cases, the toothed wheels may be replaced if damaged, but disassembly of other components such as hub and knuckle, constant velocity joints, axles or the final drive unit may be required.

TESTING

1. Disconnect the negative battery cable.
2. Raise and safely support the vehicle.
3. Disconnect the sensor wire connector.
4. Connect a meter set to the 5 volt AC scale between the terminals of the sensor connector.
5. Spin the wheel at approximately 1 revolution per second (60 rpm).
6. Verify the sensor produces a voltage of 0.25–3.00 volts AC.
7. Set the meter to the ohms scale and measure the resistance across the speed sensor.
8. Verify the resistance is as follows:
• 1993–94 Vehicles—0.8–1.30 kilo-ohms
• 1995–96 Vehicles—0.8–1.20 kilo-ohms
9. Next, verify the sensor is not grounded by connecting one lead of the ohmmeter to the sensor and the other lead to a ground. Then check the other pin on the sensor connector.
10. Verify there is NO continuity between either pin and ground at the sensor. If not as specified, replace the wheel speed sensor.

➡ **If the sensor fails the A/C voltage test, inspect the axle and bearing assembly for vibration, the toothed sensor wheel for cracks or missing teeth.**

11. Lower the vehicle and connect the negative battery cable. Reconnect the wheel speed sensor.

REMOVAL & INSTALLATION

Front Wheel Speed Sensor

▶ **See Figures 69 and 70**

1. Raise and safely support the front of the vehicle.
2. Remove the tire and wheel.
3. On some models, it may be necessary to remove the inner fender liner.

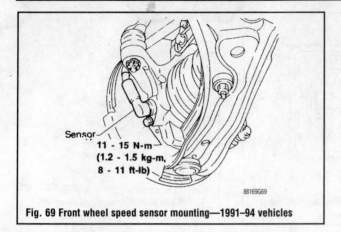

Fig. 69 Front wheel speed sensor mounting—1991–94 vehicles

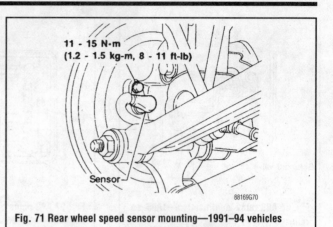

Fig. 71 Rear wheel speed sensor mounting—1991–94 vehicles

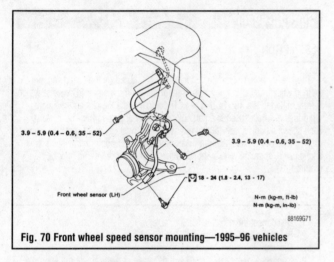

Fig. 70 Front wheel speed sensor mounting—1995–96 vehicles

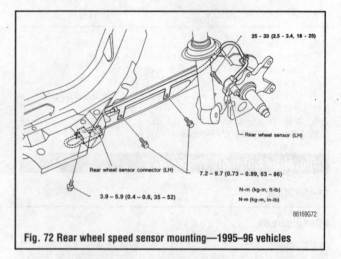

Fig. 72 Rear wheel speed sensor mounting—1995–96 vehicles

4. With the ignition switch **OFF**, disconnect the wheel speed sensor lead from the ABS harness. Remove any retaining bolts or clips holding the harness in place.

➡ Clips and retainers must be reinstalled in their exact original location. Take careful note of the position of each retainer and of the correct harness routing during removal.

5. Remove the bolt(s) holding the speed sensor.
6. Carefully remove the sensor straight out of its mount. Do not subject the sensor to shock or vibration; protect the tip of the sensor at all times.
To install:
7. Fit the sensor into position. Make certain the sensor sits flush against the mounting surface, it must not be crooked.
8. Install the retaining bolt(s). Torque the mounting bolts as follows:
• 1991–94 vehicles—96–132 inch lbs. (11–15 Nm)
• 1995–96 vehicles—13–17 ft. lbs. (18–24 Nm)
9. Route the sensor cable correctly and install the harness clips and retainers. The cable must be in its original position and completely clear of moving components. Tighten the clip retaining bolts to 15 ft. lbs. (20 Nm).
10. Connect the sensor cable to the ABS harness.
11. Install the inner fender liner if it was removed.
12. Install the wheel and tire.
13. Lower the vehicle to the ground.

Rear Wheel Speed Sensor

♦ See Figures 71 and 72

1. Raise and safely support the rear of the vehicle.
2. Remove the tire and wheel.
3. With the ignition switch **OFF**, disconnect the wheel speed sensor lead from the ABS harness. Remove any retaining bolts or clips holding the harness in place.

➡ Clips and retainers must be reinstalled in their exact original location. Take careful note of the position of each retainer and of the correct harness routing during removal.

4. Remove the single bolt holding the speed sensor.
5. Carefully remove the sensor straight out of its mount. Do not subject the sensor to shock or vibration; protect the tip of the sensor at all times.
To install:
6. Fit the sensor into position. Make certain the sensor sits flush against the mounting surface; it must not be crooked.
7. Install the retaining bolt(s). Torque the mounting bolts as follows:
• 1991–94 vehicles—96–132 inch lbs. (11–15 Nm)
• 1995–96 vehicles—18–25 ft. lbs. (25–33 Nm)
8. Route the sensor cable correctly and install the harness clips and retainers. The cable must be in its original position and completely clear of moving components. Tighten the clip retaining bolts to 15 ft. lbs. (20 Nm).
9. Connect the sensor cable to the ABS harness.
10. Install the inner fender liner if it was removed.
11. Install the wheel and tire.
12. Lower the vehicle to the ground.

Wheel Sensor Ring

DESCRIPTION

The wheel sensor ring is used to trigger the wheel speed sensor. The sensor ring is mounted to either the front CV-joint or the rear wheel bearing/hub assembly.

The ring gear teeth provide a method of accurately changing the air gap between the sensor and ring gear. As the ring gear rotates, the changing air gap directly affects the sensor's magnetic field; this causes the voltage signal to vary between a high and a low output. The ECU detects the rate of this change and thus, calculates the wheel speed.

TESTING

Testing of the wheel sensor ring is limited to a visual inspection of the ring. Inspect the ring for cracks, damaged or missing teeth. If the ring shows any signs of damage, replace the ring and recheck the wheel speed sensor operation.

REMOVAL & INSTALLATION

Front Sensor Ring

▶ **See Figures 73 and 74**

1. Raise and properly support the vehicle.
2. Remove the front halfshaft as outlined in Section 8.
3. Use a suitable puller to press the sensor ring from the CV-joint.

To install:

➡ **Always install a new sensor ring. Do NOT attempt to reuse the old sensor ring.**

4. Properly support the CV-joint in a vise or a similar holding fixture.
5. Place the NEW sensor ring around the CV-joint.

6. Use a hammer and a block of wood to install the sensor ring. Make certain the ring is completely seated around the CV-joint.
7. Following proper procedures, reinstall the halfshaft.
8. Lower the vehicle and verify proper ABS operation.

Rear Sensor Ring

▶ **See Figures 75 and 76**

1. Raise and properly support the vehicle.
2. Remove the rear hub and bearing assembly as outlined in Section 8.
3. Use a suitable puller to press the sensor ring from the wheel hub.

To install:

➡ **Always install a new sensor ring. Do NOT attempt to reuse the old sensor ring.**

4. Place the NEW sensor ring around the wheel hub.
5. Use a shop press and the proper size bearing plate, to install the sensor ring. Make certain the ring is completely seated around the wheel hub.
6. Following proper procedures, reinstall the hub and bearing assembly.
7. Lower the vehicle and verify proper ABS operation.

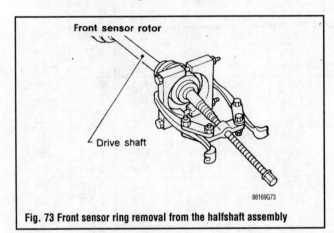

Fig. 73 Front sensor ring removal from the halfshaft assembly

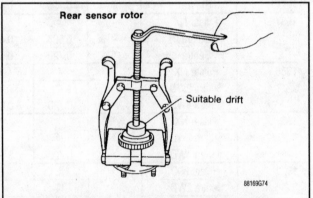

Fig. 75 Rear sensor ring removal from the halfshaft assembly

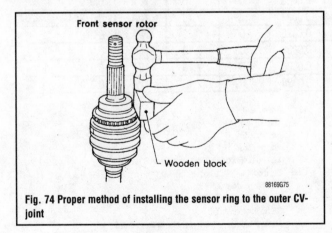

Fig. 74 Proper method of installing the sensor ring to the outer CV-joint

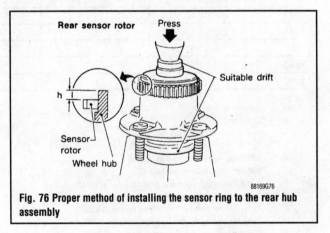

Fig. 76 Proper method of installing the sensor ring to the rear hub assembly

BRAKE SPECIFICATIONS
All measurements in inches unless noted

Year	Model		Master Cylinder Bore	Brake Disc			Brake Drum Diameter			Minimum Lining Thickness	
				Original Thickness	Minimum Thickness	Maximum Run-out	Original Inside Diameter	Max. Wear Limit	Maximum Machine Diameter	Front	Rear
1982	Sentra		0.750	0.523	0.433	0.0047	7.09	7.13	N/A	0.079	0.059
1983	Pulsar NX		3	0.484	0.394	0.0028	7.09	7.13	N/A	0.079	0.059
	Sentra	1	3	0.484	0.394	0.0028	7.09	7.13	N/A	0.079	0.059
	Sentra	2	4	0.720	0.630	0.0028	8.00	8.05	N/A	0.079	0.059
1984	Pulsar NX		5	0.484	0.394	0.0028	7.09	7.13	N/A	0.079	0.059
	Sentra	1	3	0.484	0.394	0.0028	7.09	7.13	N/A	0.079	0.059
	Sentra	2	4	0.720	0.630	0.0028	8.00	8.05	N/A	0.079	0.059
1985	Pulsar NX		3	0.484	0.394	0.0028	8.00	8.05	N/A	0.079	0.059
	Sentra	1	3	0.484	0.394	0.0028	8.00	8.05	N/A	0.079	0.059
	Sentra	2	4	0.720	0.630	0.0028	8.00	8.05	N/A	0.079	0.059
1986	Pulsar NX		3	0.523	0.433	0.0028	8.00	8.05	N/A	0.079	0.059
	Sentra	1	3	0.523	0.433	0.0028	8.00	8.05	N/A	0.079	0.059
	Sentra	2	6	0.720	0.630	0.0028	8.00	8.05	N/A	0.079	0.059
1987	Pulsar NX		7	8	9	0.0028	8.00	8.05	N/A	0.079	0.059
	Sentra	1	3	0.523	0.433	0.0028	8.00	8.05	N/A	0.079	0.059
	Sentra	2	6	0.720	0.630	0.0028	8.00	8.05	N/A	0.079	0.059
1988	Pulsar NX		7	8	9	0.0028	8.00	8.05	N/A	0.079	0.059
	Sentra 2WD		3	10	11	0.0028	8.00	8.05	N/A	0.079	0.059
	Sentra 4WD		4	0.720	0.630	0.0028	9.00	9.05	N/A	0.079	0.059
1989	Pulsar NX		7	8	9	0.0028	8.00	8.05	N/A	0.079	0.059
	Sentra 2WD		4	10	11	0.0028	8.00	8.05	N/A	0.079	0.059
	Sentra 4WD		4	0.720	0.630	0.0028	9.00	9.05	N/A	0.079	0.059
1990	Pulsar NX		3	8	9	0.0028	8.00	8.05	N/A	0.079	0.059
	Sentra 2WD		4	10	11	0.0028	8.00	8.05	N/A	0.079	0.059
	Sentra 4WD		4	0.720	0.630	0.0028	9.00	9.05	N/A	0.079	0.059
1991	Sentra NX		12	13	14	0.0028	7.09	7.13	N/A	0.079	15
1992	Sentra NX		12	13	14	0.0028	7.09	7.13	N/A	0.079	15
1993	Sentra NX		12	13	14	0.0028	7.09	7.13	N/A	0.079	15
1994	Sentra		12	13	14	0.0028	7.09	7.13	N/A	0.079	15
1995	Sentra		16	17	18	0.0028	7.09	7.13	N/A	0.079	15
1996	Sentra		16	17	18	0.0028	7.09	7.13	N/A	0.079	15

1 Gasoline engines
2 Diesel engines
3 With small bore master cylinder: 0.750
  With large bore master cylinder: 0.9375
4 With small bore master cylinder: 0.8125
  With large bore master cylinder: 1.000
5 Non-turbocharged model with small bore master cylinder: 0.7500
  Non-turbocharged model with large bore master cylinder: 0.9375
  Turbocharged model with small bore cylinder: 0.8125
  Turbocharged model with large bore cylinder: 1.0000
6 Diesel model with small bore master cylinder: 0.8125
  Diesel model with large bore master cylinder: 1.0000
7 Single camshaft engine with small bore master cylinder: 0.7500
  Single camshaft engine with large bore master cylinder: 0.9375
  Dual camshaft engine with small bore master cylinder: 0.8125
  Dual camshaft engine with large bore master cylinder: 1.0000
8 All except SE models: 0.484
  SE models: 0.720
9 All except SE models: 0.394
  SE models: 0.630

10 Sedan: 0.484
   Wagon: 0.720
11 Sedan: 0.394
   Wagon: 0.630
12 XE and GXE models with 1.6L engine: 8.125
   Std model with 1.6L engine: 0.7500
   All other models: 0.8750
13 All front rotors except SE models: 0.720
   SE front rotors: 1.035
   All models equipped with rear disc brakes: 0.326
14 All front rotors except SE models: 0.630
   SE front rotors: 0.935
   All models equipped with rear disc brakes: 0.236
15 With rear drum brakes: 0.059
   With rear disc brakes: 0.079
16 Without ABS: 0.8125
   With ABS: 0.8750
17 All front disc brakes: 0.720
   All with rear disc brakes: 0.326
18 All front disc brakes: 0.630
   All with rear disc brakes: 0.236

88169C11

10

BODY AND TRIM

EXTERIOR

Doors

ADJUSTMENT

Front and Rear

▶ **See Figures 1 and 2**

Proper door alignment can be obtained by adjusting the door hinge and door lock striker. The door hinge and striker can be moved up-and-down fore-and-aft in enlarged holes by loosening the attaching bolts.

➡**The door should be adjusted for an even and parallel fit for the door opening and surrounding body panels.**

Hood

REMOVAL & INSTALLATION

▶ **See Figures 3 and 4**

1. Open the hood and protect the body with covers to protect the painted surfaces.
2. Mark the hood hinge locations on the hood for proper reinstallation.
3. With the help of an assistant, hold both sides of the hood while unscrewing the bolts securing the hinges to the hood. Carefully remove the hood.

To install:

4. Install the hood with the help of an assistant. Align the hinges to the bolt holes and install the bolts. Position the hood and hinges to their original positions and tighten.

5. Slowly close the hood, making sure it does not contact the painted surfaces. Adjust as necessary and torque the bolts to 12–14 ft. lbs. (16–19 Nm).

ALIGNMENT

▶ **See Figures 5 and 6**

The hood can be adjusted with bolts attaching the hood to the hood hinges, hood lock mechanism and hood bumpers. Adjust the hood for an even fit between the front fenders.

1. Adjust the hood fore and aft by loosening the bolts attaching the hood to the hinge and repositioning hood.
2. Loosen the hood bumper locknuts and lower (turn) the bumpers until they do not contact the front of the hood when the hood is closed.
3. Set the striker at the center of the hood lock, and tighten the hood lock securing bolts temporarily.
4. Raise the 2 hood bumpers until the hood is flush with the fenders. Tighten the bumper locknuts.
5. Tighten the hood lock securing bolts after the proper adjustment has been obtained.

Trunk Lid

REMOVAL & INSTALLATION

▶ **See Figures 7 and 8**

1. Open the trunk lid and position a cloth or cushion to protect the painted areas.
2. Mark the trunk lid hinge locations or trunk lid for proper reinstallation.

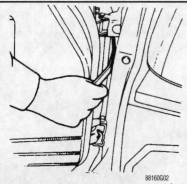

Fig. 1 After loosening the retaining bolts, use a prytool to adjust the door hinge

Fig. 2 The door lock striker can be adjusted in 4 directions

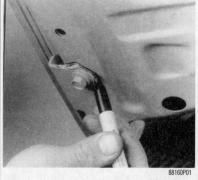

Fig. 3 A felt tip marker can be used to outline the hood hinge mounting locations

Fig. 4 Use a socket wrench to unfasten the retaining bolts

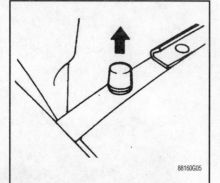

Fig. 5 Hood height can be adjusted by raising or lowering the bumper rubber

Fig. 6 After adjusting the hood, properly position the hood lock and tighten its mounting bolts

Fig. 7 Trace an outline around the trunk lid hinge before removal

Fig. 8 Use a large screwdriver or wrench to unfasten the hex head bolts

3. With the help of an assistant, support the trunk lid on both sides while removing the bolts attaching the trunk lid to the hinge. Carefully remove the trunk lid.

To install:

4. Install the trunk lid with the help of an assistant. Align the hinges to the bolt holes and install the bolts. Position the trunk lid and hinges to their original positions and tighten.

5. Slowly close the trunk lid, making sure it does not contact the painted surfaces. Adjust as necessary and torque the bolts to 12–14 ft. lbs. (16–19 Nm).

ALIGNMENT

♦ **See Figures 9 and 10**

1. Loosen the trunk lid hinge attaching bolts until they are just loose enough to move the trunk lid.

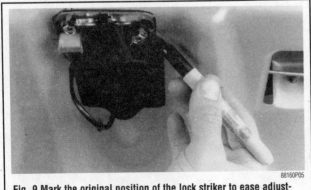

Fig. 9 Mark the original position of the lock striker to ease adjustment

2. Move the trunk lid fore and aft to obtain a flush fit between the trunk lid and the rear fender.

3. To obtain a snug fit between the trunk lid and weatherstrip, loosen the trunk lid lock striker attaching bolts enough to move the lid, working the striker up and down and from side to side as required.

4. After the adjustment is made tighten the striker bolts securely.

Hatchback or Tailgate Lid

REMOVAL & INSTALLATION

1. Open the lid and disconnect the rear defogger harness, if equipped.
2. Mark the hinge locations on the lid for proper relocation.
3. Position rags between the roof and the upper end of the lid to prevent scratching the paint.
4. Support the lid and remove the through-bolts for the gas shocks, if equipped.
5. Support the lid and remove the support bolts for the hinge retaining bolts, then remove the lid.

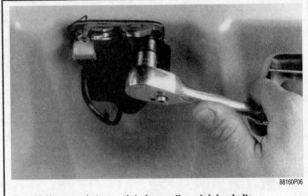

Fig. 10 Use a socket wrench to loosen the retaining bolts

To install:

6. Install the lid with the help of an assistant. Align the hinges to the bolt holes and install the bolts. Position the lid and hinges to their original position and tighten.

7. Slowly close the lid, making sure it does not contact the painted surfaces. Adjust as necessary and torque the bolts to 12–14 ft. lbs. (16–19 Nm).

➡ **Be careful not to scratch the lift support rods. A scratched rod may cause oil or gas leakage.**

ALIGNMENT

♦ **See Figures 11, 12, 13 and 14**

1. Open the hatchback lid.
2. Loosen the lid hinge to body attaching bolts until they are just loose enough to move the lid.
3. Move the lid up and down to obtain a flush fit between the lid and the roof.
4. After adjustment, tighten the hinge attaching bolts securely.

Grille

REMOVAL & INSTALLATION

♦ **See Figures 15 and 16**

1. Remove radiator grille bracket bolts.

➡ **Early models use clips to hold the radiator grille assembly to the vehicle.**

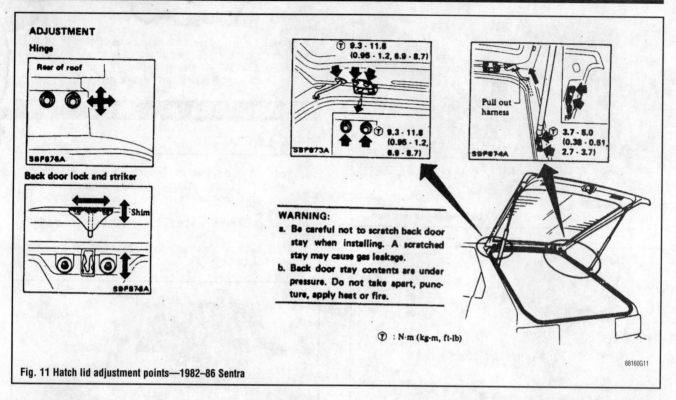

ADJUSTMENT

Hinge

Rear of roof

SBF875A

Back door lock and striker

Shim

SBF876A

T 9.3 - 11.8
(0.95 - 1.2, 6.9 - 8.7)

T 9.3 - 11.8
(0.95 - 1.2, 6.9 - 8.7)

SBF873A

Pull out harness

T 3.7 - 5.0
(0.38 - 0.51, 2.7 - 3.7)

SBF874A

WARNING:
a. Be careful not to scratch back door stay when installing. A scratched stay may cause gas leakage.
b. Back door stay contents are under pressure. Do not take apart, puncture, apply heat or fire.

T : N·m (kg-m, ft-lb)

88160G11

Fig. 11 Hatch lid adjustment points—1982–86 Sentra

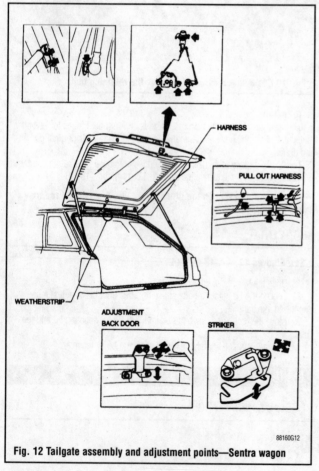

HARNESS

PULL OUT HARNESS

WEATHERSTRIP

ADJUSTMENT
BACK DOOR

STRIKER

88160G12

Fig. 12 Tailgate assembly and adjustment points—Sentra wagon

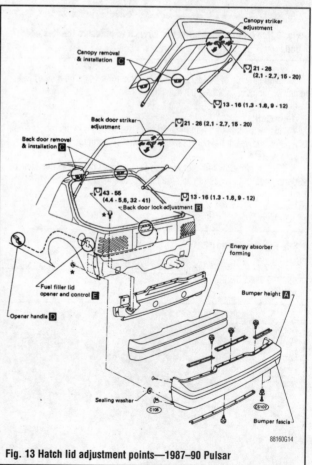

Canopy striker adjustment

Canopy removal & installation [C]

21 - 26 (2.1 - 2.7, 15 - 20)

13 - 16 (1.3 - 1.6, 9 - 12)

Back door striker adjustment

21 - 26 (2.1 - 2.7, 15 - 20)

Back door removal & installation [C]

13 - 16 (1.3 - 1.6, 9 - 12)

43 - 55 (4.4 - 5.6, 32 - 41)

Back door lock adjustment [B]

Energy absorber forming

Fuel filler lid opener and control [E]

Opener handle [D]

Bumper height [A]

Sealing washer

C106

C$107

Bumper fascia

88160G14

Fig. 13 Hatch lid adjustment points—1987–90 Pulsar

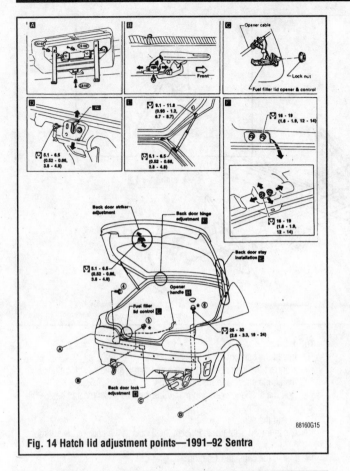

Fig. 14 Hatch lid adjustment points—1991–92 Sentra

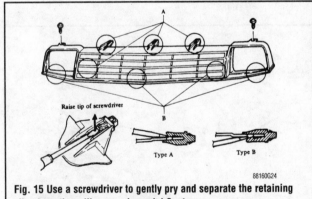

Fig. 15 Use a screwdriver to gently pry and separate the retaining clips from the grille on early model Sentras

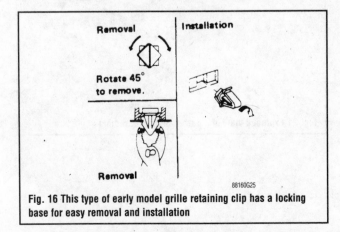

Fig. 16 This type of early model grille retaining clip has a locking base for easy removal and installation

2. Remove radiator grille from the vehicle.
3. To install reverse the removal procedures.

➥The radiator grille assembly is made of plastic; never use excessive force to remove it.

Outside Mirrors

REMOVAL & INSTALLATION

◆ See Figures 17, 18, 19 and 20

Manual

1. Remove control knob handle.
2. Remove door corner finisher panel.

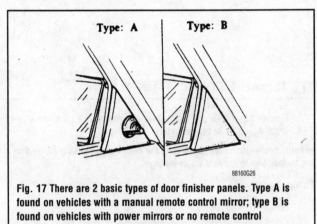

Fig. 17 There are 2 basic types of door finisher panels. Type A is found on vehicles with a manual remote control mirror; type B is found on vehicles with power mirrors or no remote control

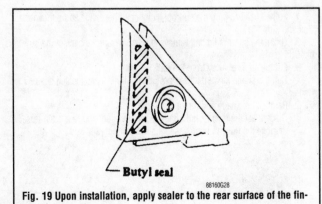

Fig. 18 There are typically 3 fasteners securing the mirror to the door

Fig. 19 Upon installation, apply sealer to the rear surface of the finisher panel

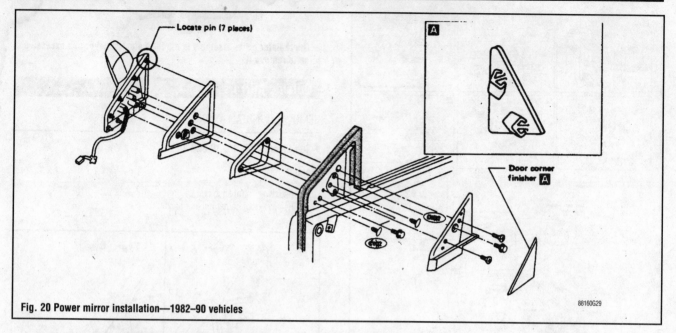

Fig. 20 Power mirror installation—1982–90 vehicles

88160G29

3. Remove mirror body attaching screws, and then remove mirror body.
4. Installation is in the reverse order of removal.

➡ **Apply sealer to the rear surface of the door corner finisher panel during installation to prevent water leakage.**

Power

1. Remove door corner finisher panel.
2. Remove mirror body attaching screws, and then remove mirror body.
3. Disconnect the electrical connection.

➡ **It may be necessary to remove the door trim panel to gain access to the electrical connection.**

4. Installation is in the reverse order of removal.

Antenna

REMOVAL & INSTALLATION

Refer to the "Radio" and related component procedures in Section 6.

Power Sunroof

REMOVAL & INSTALLATION

◆ See Figure 21

1. Fully close or tilt up the sunroof. Fully open the shade and remove the clips and side trim.
2. Close the sunroof lid and remove the 6 nuts from the back of the sunroof lid.
3. Lift the sunroof away from the roof.
4. Pull the shade forward and remove the 4 shade locks located beside the shade.
5. Remove the shade and motor assembly.
6. Disconnect the interior light harness and the front and rear drain hoses.
7. Remove the nuts and bolts securing the sunroof rails and remove.

To install:

8. Install the sunroof rails, nuts and bolts.
9. Connect the interior light harness and the front and rear drain hoses.
10. Install the shade and motor assembly.
11. Pull the shade forward and install the 4 shade locks located beside the shade.
12. Install the sunroof into the roof.
13. Close the sunroof lid and install the 6 nuts to the back of the sunroof lid.
14. Install the clips and side trim.

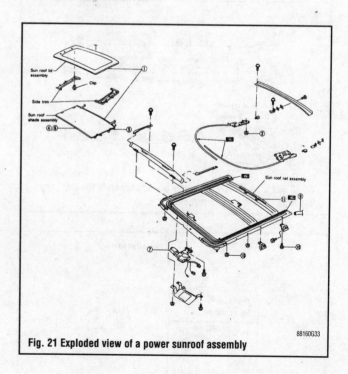

Fig. 21 Exploded view of a power sunroof assembly

88160G33

INTERIOR

Instrument Panel and Pad

REMOVAL & INSTALLATION

1982–86 Vehicles

1. Disconnect the negative battery cable. Set "TEMP" lever to maximum "HOT" position and drain the engine coolant.

❊❊ CAUTION

When draining the coolant, keep in mind that cats and dogs are attracted by ethylene glycol antifreeze, and are quite likely to drink any that is left in an uncovered container or in puddles on the ground. This will prove fatal in sufficient quantity. Always drain the coolant into a sealable container. Coolant should be reused unless it is contaminated or several years old.

2. Disconnect the heater hoses at the engine compartment.
3. Disconnect the choke control cable, harness connectors, hood latch control cable, speedometer cable, and radio aerial cable.
4. Remove the 2 screws from the lower side of the instrument hood and remove it.
5. Remove the 2 screws from the top of the instrument cluster, pull it out to disconnect the electrical connectors, and remove it.
6. Slide the ashtray out and then unscrew and remove the ashtray slider bracket.
7. Remove the radio knobs and bezel. Disconnect the antenna and power cable, remove the attaching bolts, and remove the radio.
8. Remove the heater control bezel. Disconnect the heater cables and electrical connector and remove the heater control from the dash.
9. Remove the instrument panel section located just above the glovebox drawer by removing the attaching bolt on the right and then unclipping the panel section. Tilt the glove box drawer downward, work the hinge pins out of the dash at top and bottom and remove it.
10. Remove the small panels out of the top left and top right of the dash by prying them very gently. Remove the 2 small screw covers from either side of the center of the dash at the top.
11. Remove the 4 bolts from the bottom of the instrument panel assembly (one at each corner and 2 below the radio). Then, support the assembly (perhaps with the help of an assistant). Remove the 4 bolts (one under each cover) that support the assembly at the top and remove it from the car.

To install:

12. With a helper, put the instrument panel into position and hold it there. Then, install the 4 bolts that fasten the unit at the top.
13. Install the 4 bolts that fasten the unit at the bottom. Install the bolt covers on the top of the panel.
14. Install the glovebox and adjacent instrument panel section by reversing the removal procedure.
15. Install the heater control, connect the cables, and adjust them. Connect the electrical connector.
16. Install the radio by reversing the removal procedure.
17. Install the ashtray slider and the ashtray.
18. Install the instrument cluster in reverse of the removal procedure. Install the instrument hood.
19. Connect the choke control cable, harness connectors, hood latch control cable, speedometer cable, and radio aerial cable.
20. Refill the engine with coolant. Reconnect the battery. Start the engine and check for leaks. Refill the cooling system after the engine has reached operating temperature and has then been allowed to cool.

1987–90 Vehicles

▶ See Figure 22

➡ **This is a very lengthy procedure, requiring complete removal of the instrument panel.**

1. Disconnect the negative battery cable. Remove the upper defroster grilles by gently pulling them upward to free the 8 clips fastening each of them in place.
2. Slide a thin, flat instrument in to release the clips by depressing the tangs on top and on the bottom of the center and right side air discharge grilles. Then, slide them out of the instrument panel.
3. Remove the 4 bolts from the top of the instrument panel cover (these are accessible at either end of the slots for the defroster grilles, removed earlier).
4. Remove the 2 screws from underneath the cluster bezel and the 2 from the underside of the cluster hood. Then, use a thin, flat object to depress the locking pawl in the fastener located at the top left of the cluster bezel; then, slide this fastener out of the dash. Now, slide the cluster bezel out of the dash.
5. Remove the instrument panel cover from the instrument panel by pulling it straight back so as to disengage the mounting pawls from the panel underneath, and remove it.
6. Remove the mounting screws from the underside and front of the instrument cluster and then pull it out of the dash panel far enough for you to gain

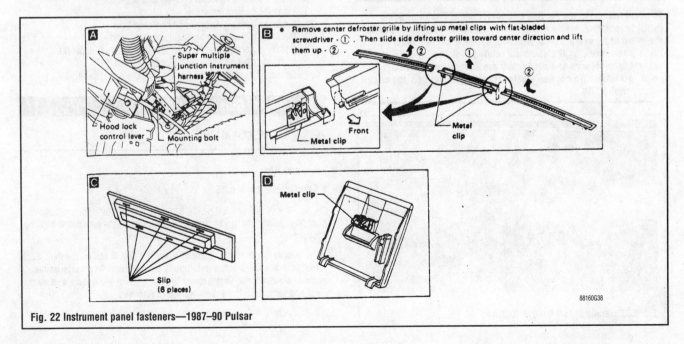

Fig. 22 Instrument panel fasteners—1987–90 Pulsar

access to the electrical connectors. Disconnect these connectors and then remove the cluster by sliding it out of the dash.

7. Remove the large screw cover from the rear part of the rear console. Remove the console mounting screw located underneath it. Remove the small screw cover from the front of the console and remove the screw underneath that. Remove the rear console.

8. Remove the screw from either side of the front console. Remove the gearshift knob by unscrewing it. Then, remove the forward section of the console.

9. Slide out the ashtray drawer, depress the lock, and then remove it. Remove the 2 mounting screws (accessible from underneath) and then remove the ashtray slider.

10. Remove the 2 mounting screws and then remove the radio/heater control bezel. Disconnect the electrical connector for the heater control. Disconnect the air door cables the control actuates.

11. Then, remove the 2 mounting screws and pull the radio out for access to the electrical connector and antenna cable connector. Disconnect these and remove the radio.

12. Remove its mounting bolt and then disconnect the Super Multiple Junction connector from under the dash.

13. Remove the 2 mounting screws and remove the fuse block.

14. Remove the hood latch release.

15. Remove the left and right side instrument panel mounting screws, accessible from underneath and located near the corners of the unit. Then, pull the unit outward and remove it from the vehicle.

To install:

16. Put the instrument panel into position so the mounting pawls line it up and install the right and left side mounting screws.

17. Install the hood release and fuse block. Connect the Super Multiple Junction connector and install its mounting bolt.

18. Install the radio and the heater control.

19. Install the ashtray slider and ashtray.

20. Install the front console and then the rear console. Install the gearshift knob.

21. Put the instrument cluster into position, connect all the electrical connectors and install it.

22. Install the instrument cluster bezel.

23. Install the instrument panel cover.

24. Install the center and right air discharge grilles.

25. Install the upper defroster grilles. Reconnect the battery and refill the cooling system.

1991–96 Sentra

♦ See Figures 23 and 24

✲✲ CAUTION

To avoid rendering the Air Bag or Supplemental Restraint System (SRS) inoperative, which could lead to personal injury or death in the event of a severe frontal collision, extreme caution must be taken when servicing the electrical related systems. All SRS electrical wiring harnesses and connectors are covered with YELLOW outer insulation. Do not use electrical test equipment on any circuit related to the SRS.

Fig. 23 Carefully pry off the trim buttons . . .

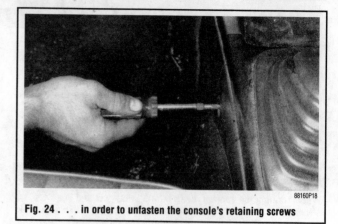

88160P18

Fig. 24 . . . in order to unfasten the console's retaining screws

1. Turn the ignition switch to the **OFF** position, then disconnect the negative battery cable. Wait at least 10 minutes before proceeding to effectively disarm the Supplemental Restraint System (air bag). For further information on the SRS, refer to Section 6 of this manual.

2. Remove the steering wheel as outlined in Section 8.

3. Remove the steering column cover and lower instrument panel trim. Refer to illustration **D**.

4. Remove the glove compartment lid and box. Refer to illustration **E**.

5. Remove the transaxle finisher and shift lever boot. Refer to illustration **G**.

6. Remove the console assembly. Refer to illustration **H**.

7. Remove the center ventilator control cable at the unit side. Refer to illustration **I**.

8. Remove the instrument cluster lid and cluster. Refer to illustration **F**. Disconnect the speedometer cable and electrical connectors.

9. Remove the deck pocket and radio as outlined in Section 6.

10. Remove the A/C and heater control assembly.

11. Remove the center lower instrument panel.

12. Remove the instrument panel and pads from the vehicle. Refer to illustration **A** and **B**.

To install:

13. Install the instrument panel and pads into the vehicle with the help of an assistant.

14. Install the center lower instrument panel.

15. Install the A/C and heater control assembly.

16. Install the deck pocket and radio as outlined in Section 6.

17. Install the instrument cluster lid and cluster.

18. Install the center ventilator control cable at the unit side.

19. Install the console assembly.

20. Install the transaxle finisher and shift lever boot.

21. Install the glove compartment lid and box.

22. Install the steering column cover and lower instrument panel trim.

23. Install the steering wheel as outlined in Section 8.

24. Connect the negative battery cable, then check the operation.

Door Panel, Glass and Regulator

REMOVAL & INSTALLATION

Front and Rear

♦ See Figures 25 thru 36

1. Remove the regulator handle by pushing the set pin spring clip from the shaft, then pulling the handle straight off. Also remove the escutcheon from the door panel.

➡To remove the regulator handle, a special tool is recommended. Such a tool is available in many automotive parts stores. As an alternative, you can place a cotton rag around the shaft under the handle and work it back and forth until the set pin spring is removed.

2. Unfasten and remove the armrest (if detachable from the panel) and the

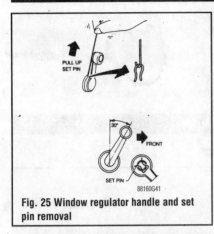

Fig. 25 Window regulator handle and set pin removal

Fig. 26 A special tool simplifies window regulator handle removal

Fig. 27 With the set pin clip retracted, pull the regulator handle from the shaft . . .

Fig. 28 . . . and remove the escutcheon from the door panel

Fig. 29 Remove the inside door handle's escutcheon

Fig. 30 Some fasteners are concealed behind trim buttons, which must be carefully pried off

Fig. 31 Unfasten the screws which retain the armrest or built-in armrest portion of the panel

Fig. 32 Remove the trim button, if equipped . . .

Fig. 33 . . . then unfasten the screws retaining the front edge of the door panel

Fig. 34 Also remove the screws retaining the rear edge of the door panel

Fig. 35 After removing all fasteners and carefully prying the panel free, lift it from the door

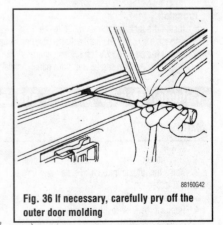

Fig. 36 If necessary, carefully pry off the outer door molding

inside door handle escutcheon. If equipped, unscrew the pop-up door lock knob.

3. Remove the door panel with a special removing tool. Do not damage the cardboard finish panel by forcing. Use 2 prybars rapped with electrical tape if a door finish panel removing tool is not available. Remove the sealing screen.

4. On some models, it may be necessary to remove the outer door molding.

5. Lower the door glass with the regulator handle until the regulator-to-glass attaching bolts appear at the access holes in the door inside panel.

6. Raise the door glass and draw it upwards.

7. Remove the regulator attaching bolts and remove the regulator assembly through the large access hole in the door panel.

To install:

8. Lubricate the regulator with all-purpose grease. Install the window regulator assembly in the door.

9. Connect all mounting bolts and check for proper operation.

10. Adjust the window if necessary, then install the door sealing screen and finish panel.

11. Install the armrest (if applicable) and other attachable components to the door panel.

12. Install the window regulator handle.

Door Locks

REMOVAL & INSTALLATION

▶ **See Figure 37**

1. Remove the door panel and sealing screen.

2. Remove the rod from the lock cylinder by turning the resin clip.

3. Loosen the nuts attaching the outside door handle and remove the outside door handle.

4. Remove the screws retaining the inside door handle and lock, then remove the door lock assembly from the hole in the inside of the door.

5. Remove the lock cylinder by removing the retaining clip.

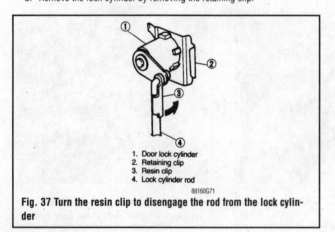

1. Door lock cylinder
2. Retaining clip
3. Resin clip
4. Lock cylinder rod

88160G71

Fig. 37 Turn the resin clip to disengage the rod from the lock cylinder

To install:

6. Install the lock cylinder and clip to the door.

7. Engage the rod to the lock cylinder, then position the resin clip.

8. Install the door lock assembly and handles.

9. Install the sealing screen and door panel, as well as all attaching parts.

Tailgate/Hatch/Liftgate Lock and Latch

REMOVAL & INSTALLATION

1. Disconnect the negative battery cable.

2. Raise the liftgate and remove the inner trim panel. Refer to door trim panel in this section.

3. Disconnect the control rods from the lock and latch assembly.

4. Remove the lock-to-liftgate retainer.

5. Remove the latch retaining bolts and remove the entire assembly from the gate.

To install:

6. Install the latch and lock to the liftgate. Torque the retaining bolts to 10 ft. lbs. (14 Nm).

7. Connect the control rods and install the trim panel.

8. Connect the negative battery cable and check operation.

Electric Window Motor

REMOVAL & INSTALLATION

▶ **See Figure 38**

1. Remove the door trim panel and sealing screen as outlined in this section.

➡ **It may be necessary to remove the window regulator from the door assembly. If so, refer to the procedures in this section.**

2. Remove the power widow motor and regulator mounting bolts.

3. Remove all electrical connections and cable connection.

4. Remove the power window motor from the vehicle.

5. Installation is in the reverse order of removal.

Inside Rear View Mirror

REMOVAL & INSTALLATION

1. Remove the rear view mirror mounting bolt cover.

2. Unfasten the rear view mirror mounting bolts.

3. Remove the mirror.

4. Installation is in the reverse order of removal.

Windshield and Fixed Glass

REMOVAL & INSTALLATION

If your windshield, or other fixed window, is cracked or chipped, you may decide to replace it with a new one yourself. However, there are two main reasons why replacement windshields and other window glass should be installed only by a professional automotive glass technician: safety and cost.

The most important reason a professional should install automotive glass is for safety. The glass in the vehicle, especially the windshield, is designed with safety in mind in case of a collision. The windshield is specially manufactured from two panes of specially-tempered glass with a thin layer of transparent plastic between them. This construction allows the glass to "give" in the event that a part of your body hits the windshield during the collision, and prevents the glass from shattering, which could cause lacerations, blinding and other harm to passengers of the vehicle. The other fixed windows are designed to be tempered so that if they break during a collision, they shatter in such a way that there are no large pointed glass pieces. The professional automotive glass technician knows how to install the glass in a vehicle so that it will function optimally during a collision. Without the proper experience, knowledge and tools, installing a piece of automotive glass yourself could lead to additional harm if an accident should ever occur.

Cost is also a factor when deciding to install automotive glass yourself. Performing this could cost you much more than a professional may charge for the same job. Since the windshield is designed to break under stress, an often life saving characteristic, windshields tend to break VERY easily when an inexperienced person attempts to install one. Do-it-yourselfers buying two, three or even four windshields from a salvage yard because they have broken them during installation are common stories. Also, since the automotive glass is designed to prevent the outside elements from entering your vehicle, improper installation can lead to water and air leaks. Annoying whining noises at highway speeds from air leaks or inside body panel rusting from water leaks can add to your stress level and subtract from your wallet. After buying two or three windshields, installing them and ending up with a leak that produces a noise while driving and water damage during rainstorms, the cost of having a professional

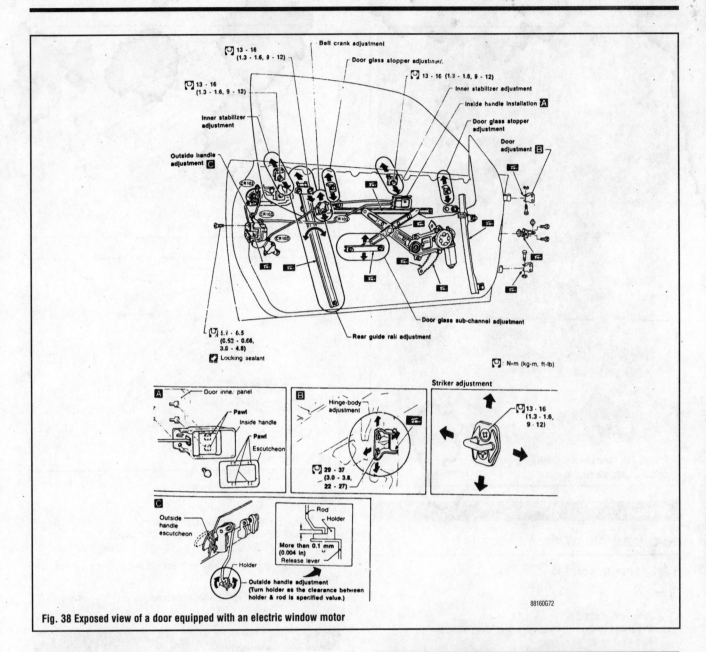

Fig. 38 Exposed view of a door equipped with an electric window motor

do it correctly the first time may be much more alluring. We here at Chilton, therefore, advise that you have a professional automotive glass technician service any broken glass on your vehicle.

WINDSHIELD CHIP REPAIR

▶ **See Figures 39 and 40**

➥**Check with your state and local authorities on the laws for state safety inspection. Some states or municipalities may not allow chip repair as a viable option for correcting stone damage to your windshield.**

Although severely cracked or damaged windshields must be replaced, there is something that you can do to prolong or even prevent the need for replacement of a chipped windshield. There are many companies which offer windshield chip repair products, such as Loctite's® Bullseye™ windshield repair kit. These kits usually consist of a syringe, pedestal and a sealing adhesive. The syringe is mounted on the pedestal and is used to create a vacuum which pulls the plastic layer against the glass. This helps make the chip transparent. The adhesive is then injected which seals the chip and helps to prevent further stress cracks from developing

➥**Always follow the specific manufacturer's instructions.**

Fig. 39 Small chips on your windshield can be fixed with an aftermarket repair kit, such as the one from Loctite®

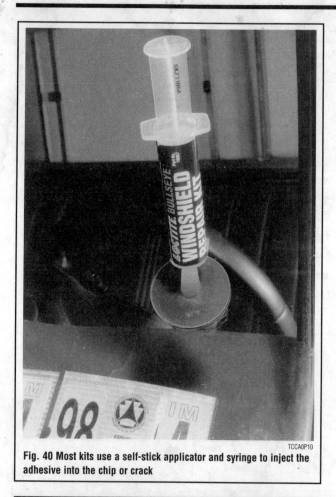

Fig. 40 Most kits use a self-stick applicator and syringe to inject the adhesive into the chip or crack

Seats

REMOVAL & INSTALLATION

▶ See Figures 41, 42 and 43

Front

1. Remove front seat bolt trim cover and mounting bolts.
2. Disconnect the seat electrical connectors from underneath.
3. Remove front seat assembly.
4. Installation is in the reverse order of removal. Torque the mounting bolts to 32–41 ft. lbs. (43–56 Nm).

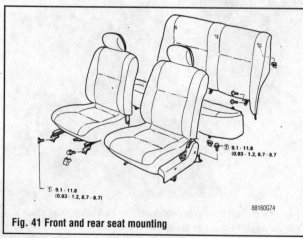

Fig. 41 Front and rear seat mounting

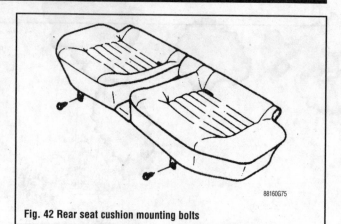

Fig. 42 Rear seat cushion mounting bolts

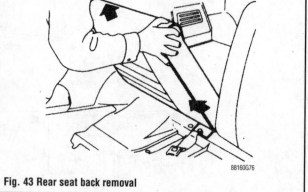

Fig. 43 Rear seat back removal

Rear

1. Remove the rear seat cushion mounting bolts.
2. Remove the screw attaching the luggage floor carpet.
3. Remove the rear seat back by tilting forward and pulling straight up.

➡ On hatchback models, the rear seat back is removed in a similar manner.

4. Install the seat back and torque the retaining bolts to 12–14 ft. lbs. (16–20 Nm).

Power Seat Motor

REMOVAL & INSTALLATION

▶ See Figure 44

1. Disconnect the negative battery cable.
2. Remove the seat from the vehicle as outlined in this section.
3. Disconnect the control cables and electrical connectors from the seat bottom.
4. Remove the power motor retaining bolts and motor.
   To install:
5. Lubricate all components with multi-purpose grease before installation.
6. Install the motor and torque the bolts to 12–14 ft. lbs. (16–19 Nm).
7. Connect the cables and electrical connectors.
8. Install the seat into the vehicle.
9. Connect the battery cable and check operation.

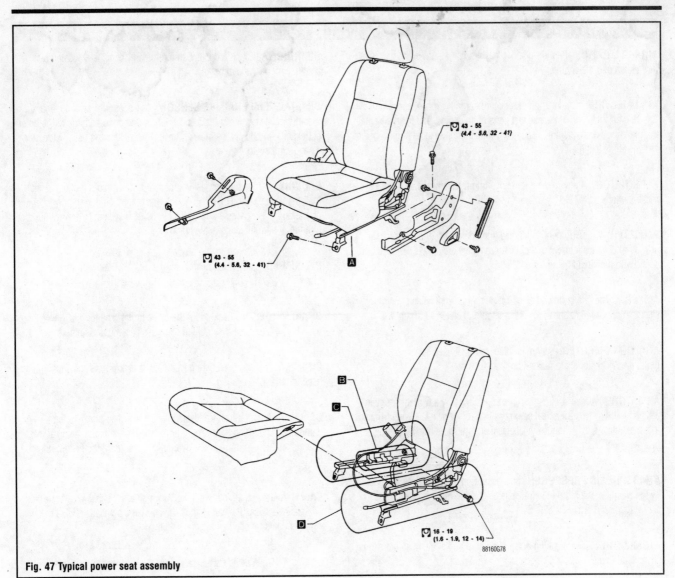

Fig. 47 Typical power seat assembly

TORQUE SPECIFICATIONS

Component	U.S.	Metric
Door hinge bolts	15-20 ft. lbs.	21-29 Nm
Hood and trunk bolts	12-14 ft. lbs.	16-19 Nm
Bumper shock absorber bolts	25 ft. lbs.	34 Nm
Bumper cover bolts	10 ft. lbs.	14 Nm
Fender bolts	12-14 ft. lbs.	16-20 Nm
Liftgate lock bolts	10-14 ft. lbs.	14-18 Nm
Front seat mounting bolts	32-41 ft. lbs.	43-56 Nm
Rear seat mounting bolts	12-14 ft. lbs.	16-20 Nm
Seat belt retaining bolts	25-30 ft. lbs.	34-41 Nm
Power seat belt bolts	32-41 ft. lbs.	43-55 Nm
Power seat belt upper buckle bolts	4-5 ft. lbs.	5-7 Nm
Power seat motor bolts	12-14 ft. lbs.	16-19 Nm

88160C01

GLOSSARY

AIR/FUEL RATIO: The ratio of air-to-gasoline by weight in the fuel mixture drawn into the engine.

AIR INJECTION: One method of reducing harmful exhaust emissions by injecting air into each of the exhaust ports of an engine. The fresh air entering the hot exhaust manifold causes any remaining fuel to be burned before it can exit the tailpipe.

ALTERNATOR: A device used for converting mechanical energy into electrical energy.

AMMETER: An instrument, calibrated in amperes, used to measure the flow of an electrical current in a circuit. Ammeters are always connected in series with the circuit being tested.

AMPERE: The rate of flow of electrical current present when one volt of electrical pressure is applied against one ohm of electrical resistance.

ANALOG COMPUTER: Any microprocessor that uses similar (analogous) electrical signals to make its calculations.

ARMATURE: A laminated, soft iron core wrapped by a wire that converts electrical energy to mechanical energy as in a motor or relay. When rotated in a magnetic field, it changes mechanical energy into electrical energy as in a generator.

ATMOSPHERIC PRESSURE: The pressure on the Earth's surface caused by the weight of the air in the atmosphere. At sea level, this pressure is 14.7 psi at 32°F (101 kPa at 0°C).

ATOMIZATION: The breaking down of a liquid into a fine mist that can be suspended in air.

AXIAL PLAY: Movement parallel to a shaft or bearing bore.

BACKFIRE: The sudden combustion of gases in the intake or exhaust system that results in a loud explosion.

BACKLASH: The clearance or play between two parts, such as meshed gears.

BACKPRESSURE: Restrictions in the exhaust system that slow the exit of exhaust gases from the combustion chamber.

BAKELITE: A heat resistant, plastic insulator material commonly used in printed circuit boards and transistorized components.

BALL BEARING: A bearing made up of hardened inner and outer races between which hardened steel balls roll.

BALLAST RESISTOR: A resistor in the primary ignition circuit that lowers voltage after the engine is started to reduce wear on ignition components.

BEARING: A friction reducing, supportive device usually located between a stationary part and a moving part.

BIMETAL TEMPERATURE SENSOR: Any sensor or switch made of two dissimilar types of metal that bend when heated or cooled due to the different expansion rates of the alloys. These types of sensors usually function as an on/off switch.

BLOWBY: Combustion gases, composed of water vapor and unburned fuel, that leak past the piston rings into the crankcase during normal engine operation. These gases are removed by the PCV system to prevent the buildup of harmful acids in the crankcase.

BRAKE PAD: A brake shoe and lining assembly used with disc brakes.

BRAKE SHOE: The backing for the brake lining. The term is, however, usually applied to the assembly of the brake backing and lining.

BUSHING: A liner, usually removable, for a bearing; an anti-friction liner used in place of a bearing.

CALIPER: A hydraulically activated device in a disc brake system, which is mounted straddling the brake rotor (disc). The caliper contains at least one piston and two brake pads. Hydraulic pressure on the piston(s) forces the pads against the rotor.

CAMSHAFT: A shaft in the engine on which are the lobes (cams) which operate the valves. The camshaft is driven by the crankshaft, via a belt, chain or gears, at one half the crankshaft speed.

CAPACITOR: A device which stores an electrical charge.

CARBON MONOXIDE (CO): A colorless, odorless gas given off as a normal byproduct of combustion. It is poisonous and extremely dangerous in confined areas, building up slowly to toxic levels without warning if adequate ventilation is not available.

CARBURETOR: A device, usually mounted on the intake manifold of an engine, which mixes the air and fuel in the proper proportion to allow even combustion.

CATALYTIC CONVERTER: A device installed in the exhaust system, like a muffler, that converts harmful byproducts of combustion into carbon dioxide and water vapor by means of a heat-producing chemical reaction.

CENTRIFUGAL ADVANCE: A mechanical method of advancing the spark timing by using flyweights in the distributor that react to centrifugal force generated by the distributor shaft rotation.

CHECK VALVE: Any one-way valve installed to permit the flow of air, fuel or vacuum in one direction only.

CHOKE: A device, usually a moveable valve, placed in the intake path of a carburetor to restrict the flow of air.

CIRCUIT: Any unbroken path through which an electrical current can flow. Also used to describe fuel flow in some instances.

CIRCUIT BREAKER: A switch which protects an electrical circuit from overload by opening the circuit when the current flow exceeds a predetermined level. Some circuit breakers must be reset manually, while most reset automatically.

COIL (IGNITION): A transformer in the ignition circuit which steps up the voltage provided to the spark plugs.

COMBINATION MANIFOLD: An assembly which includes both the intake and exhaust manifolds in one casting.

COMBINATION VALVE: A device used in some fuel systems that routes fuel vapors to a charcoal storage canister instead of venting them into the atmosphere. The valve relieves fuel tank pressure and allows fresh air into the tank as the fuel level drops to prevent a vapor lock situation.

COMPRESSION RATIO: The comparison of the total volume of the cylinder and combustion chamber with the piston at BDC and the piston at TDC.

CONDENSER: 1. An electrical device which acts to store an electrical charge, preventing voltage surges. 2. A radiator-like device in the air conditioning system in which refrigerant gas condenses into a liquid, giving off heat.

CONDUCTOR: Any material through which an electrical current can be transmitted easily.

CONTINUITY: Continuous or complete circuit. Can be checked with an ohmmeter.

COUNTERSHAFT: An intermediate shaft which is rotated by a mainshaft and transmits, in turn, that rotation to a working part.

CRANKCASE: The lower part of an engine in which the crankshaft and related parts operate.

CRANKSHAFT: The main driving shaft of an engine which receives reciprocating motion from the pistons and converts it to rotary motion.

CYLINDER: In an engine, the round hole in the engine block in which the piston(s) ride.

CYLINDER BLOCK: The main structural member of an engine in which is found the cylinders, crankshaft and other principal parts.

CYLINDER HEAD: The detachable portion of the engine, usually fastened to the top of the cylinder block and containing all or most of the combustion chambers. On overhead valve engines, it contains the valves and their operating parts. On overhead cam engines, it contains the camshaft as well.

DEAD CENTER: The extreme top or bottom of the piston stroke.

DETONATION: An unwanted explosion of the air/fuel mixture in the combustion chamber caused by excess heat and compression, advanced timing, or an overly lean mixture. Also referred to as "ping".

DIAPHRAGM: A thin, flexible wall separating two cavities, such as in a vacuum advance unit.

DIESELING: A condition in which hot spots in the combustion chamber cause the engine to run on after the key is turned off.

DIFFERENTIAL: A geared assembly which allows the transmission of motion between drive axles, giving one axle the ability to turn faster than the other.

DIODE: An electrical device that will allow current to flow in one direction only.

DISC BRAKE: A hydraulic braking assembly consisting of a brake disc, or rotor, mounted on an axle, and a caliper assembly containing, usually two brake pads which are activated by hydraulic pressure. The pads are forced against the sides of the disc, creating friction which slows the vehicle.

DISTRIBUTOR: A mechanically driven device on an engine which is responsible for electrically firing the spark plug at a predetermined point of the piston stroke.

DOWEL PIN: A pin, inserted in mating holes in two different parts allowing those parts to maintain a fixed relationship.

DRUM BRAKE: A braking system which consists of two brake shoes and one or two wheel cylinders, mounted on a fixed backing plate, and a brake drum, mounted on an axle, which revolves around the assembly.

DWELL: The rate, measured in degrees of shaft rotation, at which an electrical circuit cycles on and off.

ELECTRONIC CONTROL UNIT (ECU): Ignition module, module, amplifier or igniter. See Module for definition.

ELECTRONIC IGNITION: A system in which the timing and firing of the spark plugs is controlled by an electronic control unit, usually called a module. These systems have no points or condenser.

END-PLAY: The measured amount of axial movement in a shaft.

ENGINE: A device that converts heat into mechanical energy.

EXHAUST MANIFOLD: A set of cast passages or pipes which conduct exhaust gases from the engine.

FEELER GAUGE: A blade, usually metal, or precisely predetermined thickness, used to measure the clearance between two parts.

TURBOCHARGER: An exhaust driven pump which compresses intake air and forces it into the combustion chambers at higher than atmospheric pressures. The increased air pressure allows more fuel to be burned and results in increased horsepower being produced.

VACUUM ADVANCE: A device which advances the ignition timing in response to increased engine vacuum.

VACUUM GAUGE: An instrument used to measure the presence of vacuum in a chamber.

VALVE: A device which control the pressure, direction of flow or rate of flow of a liquid or gas.

VALVE CLEARANCE: The measured gap between the end of the valve stem and the rocker arm, cam lobe or follower that activates the valve.

VISCOSITY: The rating of a liquid's internal resistance to flow.

VOLTMETER: An instrument used for measuring electrical force in units called volts. Voltmeters are always connected parallel with the circuit being tested.

WHEEL CYLINDER: Found in the automotive drum brake assembly, it is a device, actuated by hydraulic pressure, which, through internal pistons, pushes the brake shoes outward against the drums.

MASTER INDEX